ROUTLEDGE LIBRARY EDITIONS:
PUBLIC ENTERPRISE AND PRIVATIZATION

Volume 13

THE ECONOMICS OF PUBLIC ENTERPRISE

THE ECONOMICS OF PUBLIC ENTERPRISE

V.V. RAMANADHAM

Routledge
Taylor & Francis Group
LONDON AND NEW YORK

First published in 1991 by Routledge

This edition first published in 2019
by Routledge
2 Park Square, Milton Park, Abingdon, Oxon OX14 4RN

and by Routledge
52 Vanderbilt Avenue, New York, NY 10017

Routledge is an imprint of the Taylor & Francis Group, an informa business

British Library Cataloguing in Publication Data
A catalogue record for this book is available from the British Library

ISBN: 978-0-367-14233-9 (Set)
ISBN: 978-0-429-25929-6 (Set) (ebk)
ISBN: 978-0-367-19045-3 (Volume 13) (hbk)
ISBN: 978-0-429-20008-3 (Volume 13) (ebk)

Publisher's Note
The publisher has gone to great lengths to ensure the quality of this reprint but points out that some imperfections in the original copies may be apparent.

Disclaimer
The publisher has made every effort to trace copyright holders and would welcome correspondence from those they have been unable to trace.

The economics of public enterprise

Public enterprises have played a central part in the development of all mixed economies in the post-war period, but they are now in a crisis phase. Privatisation has pushed back the level of public enterprise almost throughout the world. Where public enterprises remain, they are being brought under significant reforms.

This book presents a comprehensive critique of public enterprise, analysing why its performance has fallen far short of expectations. Part one is concerned with the establishment of public enterprises: the case for them, the circumstances in which they emerged, the extra enterprise objectives attached to them, and the decisions on their investment feasibility and capital structure.

Part two looks at the working of public enterprises: the state of their financial performance, the peculiarities of pricing, the determination of targets which they should meet, the continuous monitoring and evaluation of their operations.

Macro concerns are the focus of Part three. Among the issues addressed are the level of indirect taxation and subsidisation implicit in the pricing structures of public enterprises, the links between public enterprise and the public exchequer and the implications of their operations for distributional equity. In Part four the extent to which privatisation can solve the problems of public enterprise is discussed. The book ends with some broad conclusions on the future of public enterprise. Throughout, the approach is analytical, but the arguments are supported by extensive examples from both developed and developing economies.

The author

V. V. Ramanadham has spent a lifetime working in the field of public enterprise. Sometime a visiting fellow at Templeton College, Oxford, he is currently co-ordinator of the United Nations Development Programme Interregional Network on Privatisation. His previous publications for Routledge include *Privatisation in the UK, Public Enterprise and Income Distribution* and *Privatisation in Developing Countries*.

The economics of public enterprise

V. V. Ramanadham

ROUTLEDGE

London and New York

To my parents
V. Seshayya Sastry
and
V. Janakamma

First published 1991
by Routledge
11 New Fetter Lane, London EC4P 4EE

Simultaneously published in the USA and Canada
by Routledge
a division of Routledge, Chapman and Hall, Inc.
29 West 35th Street, New York, NY 10001

Typeset by J&L Composition, Filey, North Yorkshire
Printed in Great Britain

British Library Cataloguing in Publication Data
Ramanadham, V. V., *1920–*
The economics of public enterprise.
1. Public bodies
I. Title
350
ISBN 0–415–04332–8

Library of Congress Cataloging in Publication Data
Ramanadham, V. V. (Venkata Vemuri), 1920–
The economics of public enterprise/V. V. Ramanadham.
p. cm.
Includes bibliographical references.
1. Government business enterprises. 2. Privatization.
3. Economic history – 1945– I. Title.
HD3850.R342 1990
338.9--dc20

90–8313
CIP

Contents

List of Figures

List of Tables

Preface

The aim of this study is to present a comprehensive critique of public enterprise, bringing together economic, administrative, and managerial considerations. It draws attention to the inadequately appreciated fact that public enterprise is an aspect of public finance, to the overemphasis it has received from the angle of public administration, and to the formal rather than substantive approach that governments have, on the whole, adopted in dealing with it. It proceeds on the hypothesis that public enterprise is a means to an end, the end being national well-being, and not an end in itself.

The approach of the study is essentially analytical; but illustrative references have been drawn from country situations while building up to a point or argument. Though in a few chapters they are in the form of brief empirical sections, they have generally been placed as appendices. There is a large number of appendices, aimed at providing illustrative material from the experience of different countries, especially where it is of a distinctive nature. They contain extensive, useful, factual material or statistical computations, which, however, have been isolated from the text so as not to disturb the flow of an argument.

The study constantly distinguishes between the circumstances of the developed and the developing countries. The differences are more than those of degree. The nature of a problem and the ways in which it is sought to be resolved are not always the same in the two cases. The developing countries themselves cannot all be bundled together – either in seeking an explanation for a problem or in devising a solution; and this is also kept in mind.

The study brings out the point that problems and poor solutions have not been the monopoly of developing countries, though the economic and political circumstances of developed countries have given them a high degree of sustaining capability in the face of public enterprise impacts on the national economy.

The study is divided into four parts. Part I is concerned with considerations related to the establishment of public enterprises: the case for them, the circumstances in which they emerged, the extra-enterprise objectives attached to them, and the decisions on their investment feasibility and capital structure.

Part II looks at the working of public enterprises: the state of their financial performance, the peculiarities of pricing, the determination of targets which they should meet, the continuous monitoring of their operations, and the evaluation of their performance as well as their contribution to national well-being.

Part III is devoted to macro concerns such as the elements of indirect taxation and subsidisation implicit in the price structures of public enterprises, the precise links between public enterprise and the public exchequer, the implications of their operations for distributional equity, and the full range of the government's interface with them.

Part IV examines in detail how far privatisation is an answer to the many problems experienced in the establishment (or expansion) and working of public enterprises, and in the area of government relationships with them. It ends with certain broad conclusions on the future of public enterprise.

I submit a word of prudence. The circumstances of public enterprise including the government's relationships with it have been under constant change in every country, particularly under the impact of privatisation since the mid-eighties. Thus here and there an illustrative reference may not exactly represent the current situation in that country. The purpose of the reference does not suffer, however.

I have made the country references as widespread as possible, subject to constraints on data availability. In a few chapters, for example, on targets, and privatisation, the unique experience of the UK has called for particular mention in proceeding with the analysis and the argument.

This study has been in progress for a long time and is based on my researches and practical experience with public enterprises and governments over nearly fifty years. My long association with the Andhra and Osmania Universities and the Institute of Public Enterprise in India, and the several years I spent at the London School of Economics, London Business School, and Templeton College, Oxford, have helped me formulate the analytical structure of my study. And my assignments in the United Nations – Department of Technical Co-operation for Development, and United Nations Development Programme – over twenty years in the field of public enterprise have given me plentiful opportunities of understanding the way it works in different countries – developed and developing – in all regions of the world, and the way governments act *vis-à-vis* public enterprise.

I have constantly had the benefit of discussions with a large number of academics and practitioners and of observing the patterns of thinking of experts assembled at national, regional, and international seminars. Of the many who helped improve my analysis of the problems of public enterprise

I would mention two names, Professor Sir Arnold Plant and Professor Ronald H. Coase, my teachers at the London School of Economics, who grilled me for two years during my doctoral research.

V. V. Ramanadham
Associate Fellow
Templeton College
Oxford

Part I

The Genesis

1 The concept and rationale of public enterprise

It is useful to commence a study of public enterprise with an enquiry into what public enterprise signifies, and why it has assumed prominence in many countries. The former question is covered in the first section of this chapter. The second section considers the other question in terms of theory. The third briefly touches on the political dimension relevant to the establishment of public enterprise, and the last draws on governmental perceptions responsible for the prominence of public enterprise.

A prefatory observation, which applies not only to this chapter but to most others, is that generalisations are difficult in view of, not only global diversities of experience, but periodic changes in the organisations and working conditions in a given country, and, on occasion, could be faulty. It is necessary, further, to draw a distinction between developed and developing countries at several points of the analysis. Not all the developing countries themselves can be bundled together, either, though some broad similarities among them are traceable in the rationale and working of public enterprise.

THE CONCEPT OF PUBLIC ENTERPRISE

The concept of public enterprise, briefly, is that it refers to an organisation which combines in itself elements of 'publicness' and 'enterprise'.[1]

The elements of publicness may be set out under three heads:

(a) The entrepreneurial and major operational decisions are made by non-private agencies and the essential criterion of the decisions is not limited to the financial returns that accrue to the investors. The source of decisions may be understood in two senses: (i) the agencies which take the decisions, and (ii) the criteria on which decisions are taken. The latter are the more important. Where an agency takes a decision, what is important is not that it takes it out of its power but that the decision rests on criteria that have a public purport. Several chapters, for example, 1, 3 and 13, go into this question in detail.

(b) The net benefits of operations accrue, not to private parties, but to the public. The reason is that the equity capital belongs to the government or some other public agency. In the case of a public enterprise which has no equity capital, there can be different ways of profit utilisation, but there is no investor in the sense of equity holder to whom it goes.

(c) The enterprise is expected to be accountable to society. This follows directly from the element of public decision implicit in the concept of public enterprise. What is implied is not simply that the managers are accountable to those that decide, but that the enterprise as a whole, including the governmental agencies that take the decisions, should be accountable to society. In formal terms the accountability may be to parliament, 'the ultimate guardian',[2] but it is essentially to the public, including consumers, through a proper system of evaluation (see Chapter 9).

The enterprise characteristics of the organisation may be understood in the following terms:

(a) It is expected to be financially viable, by intention and in the long run. In this way it can hope to be under market disciplines, right from the procurement of capital, if necessary.

(b) The prices it charges should be based on related costs. This requirement goes beyond the overall coverage of costs by price proceeds. It is possible that an identified segment of operations is relieved of the requirement of cost-based prices for extra-enterprise reasons. That segment would be in the nature of a non-enterprise.

Viability and cost–price relationships are the elements that distinguish a public enterprise from several public activities, for example, those in the field of education, justice, and environment.

The term 'public enterprise' signifies that the organisation should represent a synthesis of the characteristics of 'publicness' with those of 'enterprise'. This is the essential problem that public enterprise presents. The synthesis is made particularly difficult because, on the whole, there is greater clarity on the enterprise characteristics than there can be on publicness, and the decisional forces, however, tend towards publicness rather than the enterprise requirements in many cases.[3]

While the concept of public enterprise, as described above, is of fundamental importance, a definition is necessary when the government intends to apply a law or a directive to public enterprises, or when public enterprise data have to be included in statistical computations, for example, while making arrangements for audit say, by the Comptroller and Auditor-General in India, or by the Audit Corporation in Tanzania, or while compiling national statistics in the UK.[4] In several cases where a definition is not attempted rigorously, a schedule is included in the law listing the enterprises that come within its purview.

Most definitions go by the ownership criterion. One hundred per cent ownership by the government, and other public agencies together, is a clear case. Majority ownership (that is, above 50 per cent) gives the government ample powers of public decision since it can influence board decisions. Minority ownership is assumed to be a condition under which the government does not enjoy significant decisional powers. The assumption may be wrong in practice, since the government directors tend to have a disproportionately significant opportunity of influencing board decisions, or if the articles of association of the enterprise are so framed as to make certain areas of operations specifically subject to government control.

Control potential, besides ownership, is an important aspect of the definition, though it is difficult to operationalise it in statistical terms, unlike ownership.

A public enterprise may be understood to be an organisation in which the majority ownership and/or control is non-private, and which is intended to be viable through sales activity on the basis of price–cost relationships.[5] This is, of course, a conceptual statement, but it marks out enterprises from non-enterprises in the public sector; it applies to all forms of enterprises – departmental organisations, public corporations and government companies – and it is fairly neutral to how significant the autonomy of the managers is in a given case.

THE RATIONALE OF PUBLIC ENTERPRISE: IN THEORY

At the outset one has to distinguish public enterprise that owes essentially to ideology or the interests of a person or group possessing powers of decision, from that evolved on a 'pragmatic' basis, for want of a better term. It is to the latter that most part of the argument in this chapter relates. The two categories of forces coexist in some proportion in many cases, and it is not always easy to draw a neat distinction between the political and the pragmatic origins of public enterprise.

The emergence of public enterprise in developed economies has, by and large, been linked with post-development problems. For instance, the needs of rationalisation, restructuring, or rehabilitation of industries already well developed were prominent in the UK nationalisations during 1945–51. The bulk of the 1946–7 nationalisations in Austria were owed to the need of 'profound reorganisation and comprehensive planning . . . to overcome their fatal propensity to a crisis and breakdown'.[6] To cite another example – Italy, a major motivation behind the inception of Istituto per la Recostruzione Industriale (IRI) was the rehabilitation of many depressed enterprises.[7]

Most public enterprises in developing countries have, on the other hand, come into being in their early stages of development. A somewhat common thematic argument is, therefore, possible in their case, namely, that public enterprise has essentially been a product of the development strategy adopted by them. They did not leave investment and growth entirely to the market forces, for the latter were too ineffective to steer development on lines that the government, through conscious planning, preferred. The preferences expressed themselves in terms of aggregate investment, sectors of activity, location of activity, and the pace of investment over the time-scale. In most countries private entrepreneurship and investment were found to be inadequate to satisfy public preferences in the areas of growth and distributional equity.

The growth aspects

The growth argument may be developed as follows. There is a preferred aggregate figure of investment during a plan period; its sectoral and regional disaggregations and timing are so formulated that all complementarities necessary for achieving the overall rate of growth can be ensured. Further, all this is really intended to be in deliberate consistency with the investment strategies expected to be adopted in the succeeding plan periods. (Such perspective planning is illustrated in Figure 1.1 where C represents the growth rates, say, over a fifteen-year period – low at first but buoyant progressively; while C_1 represents one of the inferior possibilities, which private entrepreneurs ordinarily prefer.)[8]

Figure 1.1 Growth rates

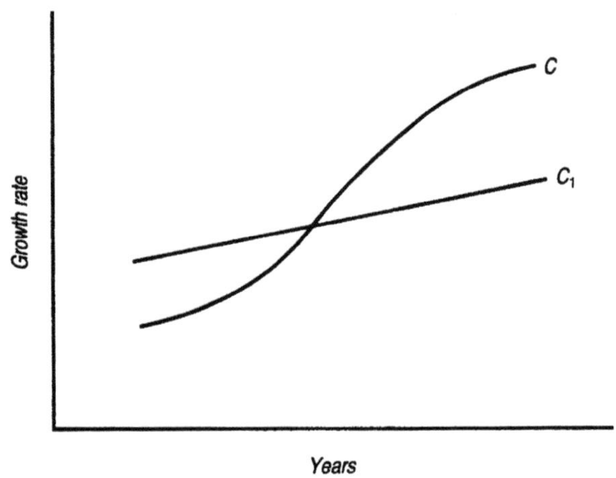

Let us see how public enterprise becomes relevant under this argument. We are not debating the plan assumptions. Taking them as given, we come across three problems:

(i) The investment planned is larger than can be undertaken by domestic private capital. Hence the need for deficit financing, or foreign capital which, on balance, the government wishes to borrow and invest or attract in partnership with it in an approved activity.

(ii) Private investors in developing countries have an obvious preference, in the early years, for trading and light manufacturing activities, as against the industrial activities, including new technologies, which the plan strategy emphasises. The government has, therefore, to bring about some diversion of the funds available with private investors into the preferred directions, through public borrowings followed by public investment.

(iii) When large proportions of private savings have to be diverted from consumption to investment, the government has to step in through taxation and public borrowings, likely to be followed by public investment.

The next step in the argument concerns the financial rate of return likely to be realised from the cross-section of investments. It would be low for a long while for three reasons: (i) gestation, owing to heavy capital intensities and the establishment of large capacities (for example, of steel, heavy engineering, and chemical plants); (ii) the decision to provide developmental incentives to related sectors of activity; and (iii) distributional objectives realisable through input and output policies.

The rates of return are illustrated in Figure 1.2 by curve R_1 under assumption (i), R_2 under assumptions (i) and (ii), and R_3 under assumptions (i), (ii) and (iii); whereas the private investors' expectations of rate of return take the shape of R_4. Thus the need for public enterprise presents itself, as long as R_1, R_2, or R_3 is below R_4. It is not inevitable, in theory, for the government can persuade private entrepreneurs to invest by guaranteeing them the R_4 rates of return through subsidies in one form or another. (The Indian Government adopted this method to a limited extent while inducing private investments in railways in the early years.) But this technique proves cumbersome when applied to a substantial proportion of the plan investments.

The way in which investments divide themselves between public and private enterprises may be explained as follows. Where a given investment during a given time span has the prospect of a far lower rate than is acceptable to private investors – because it cannot, or is not, allowed to earn higher – public enterprise comes in. Where the rate is marginally lower, the government may encourage private investment and decide to subsidise it. Where it is high enough for private investors, private investment takes place.

Figure 1.3 shows on the *X*-axis the possible rates of return from an investment during a given period and on the *Y*-axis the rates permitted by the government. Assume that *PQ* or *QR* represents the rate below which private investors are unwilling to undertake investment. None of the investments falling in the *PQRO* area would interest private investors.

Figure 1.2 Financial rates of return

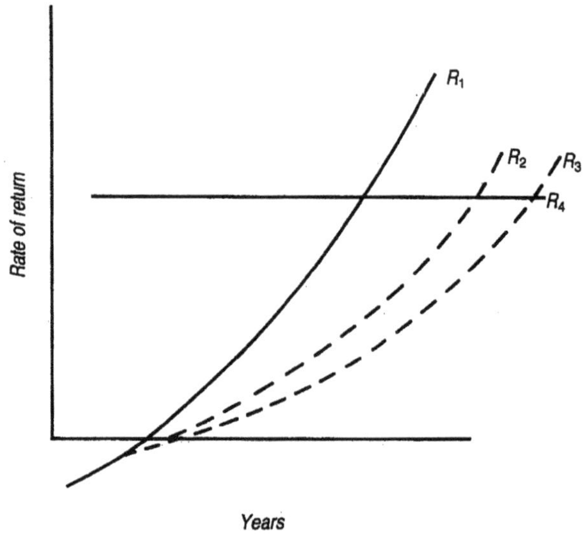

Investments represented by points *A, B,* and *C* have to be in the public sector; those represented by *D, E,* and *F* have also to be in the public sector; investments represented by *G, H,* and *I* can be induced in the private sector through governmental subsidies; and private investors flock to projects with returns of *J, K,* and *L,* though the government may also consider undertaking them.

Over time the relative segments of investment in the public and private sectors are influenced by changes in (i) the possible rates of return, (ii) the permissible rates of return, and (iii) the rates of return acceptable to private investors. For example, certain changes in plan strategy in terms of capital-output or capital–labour ratios, progressive utilisation of capacities, increasing yields of social overhead capital raise the possible rates. Reduced market imperfections and declining emphasis on certain social returns and extra-enterprise objectives raise the permitted rates of return. Reduced risks of investment can affect the rates of return acceptable to investors; at the same time increasing average rates of return on investments in the economy tend to push their expectations upward.

The exact proportion of public investments is, therefore, specific to the country and its plan strategy. Hence differences exist in the relative extent of public enterprise among countries.

Several pieces of statistical data support this view. For example, according to UNIDO studies, the share of the public sector varied among nine countries (Democratic Yemen, Egypt, India, Iraq, Mexico, Somalia, Sri Lanka, Turkey, and Tanzania) between 7.8 per cent and 85.0 per cent of the total manufacturing output in different years during 1969–76; and

Figure 1.3 Returns on investment

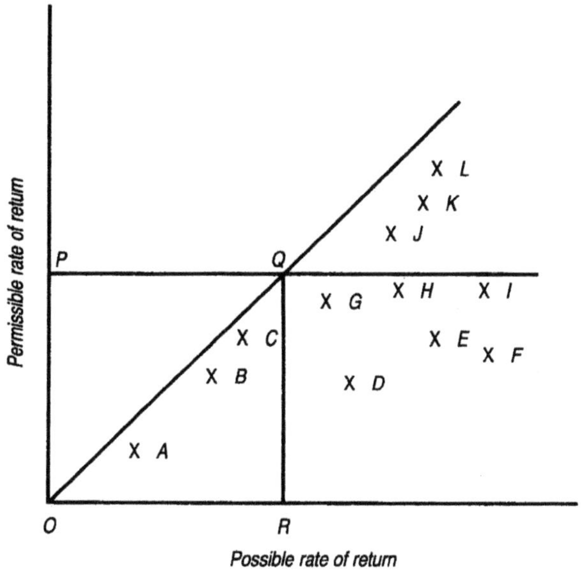

public investments varied between 10.0 per cent and 97.9 per cent of the total investments in manufacturing among twenty countries in a similar period. (The highest figures, it is true, related to 'socialist' economies like Egypt (89.6), Iraq (97.9), Somalia (79.9), and Yemen (76.2); but even among them significant differences exist.)[9]

Let us look at what happens to the funds in private hands, which are not attracted into the channels of investment preferred by the government. There are four possibilities:

(i) They go into channels that the investment plan of the government leaves open, for example, housing, trade, speculation, and small-scale consumer goods.
(ii) They get diverted into consumption.
(iii) They reach the government through its tax and borrowings policies, the more surely if the lenders assume that the interest they receive is likely to be higher or steadier than the returns that an alternative channel offers.
(iv) They flee abroad. This is unlikely under the foreign exchange restrictions, except illegally.

Governments have tried to counter the first two contingencies as far as possible, through laws that make speculative investments difficult or unattractive, by creating conditions that discourage (conspicuous) consumption, or by tax measures under which the utilisation of funds as per (i) and (ii) above turns out to be expensive.

The scope for private investment can expand even in a sector or enterprise such as steel or chemicals characterised by a relatively low rate of return under a given plan strategy. Certain parts of it, especially the downstream operations, are capable of making profits that can attract private investments. These can be 'disintegrated' from the 'whole', and private enterprise let in.

But there are two qualifications. First, the disintegrations may appear (or prove) to be cumbersome to attempt, under the technical conditions and constraints of co-ordination characteristic of developing countries in the early stages of development. Second, such disintegrations will result in lowering the rates of return on the investment which remains in the public sector, and the public exchequer will face the problem of raising revenues equal to the profits lost under the disaggregations.

In brief, the argument so far has been that public enterprise arose out of the investment strategies usually adopted in developing countries, and was treated as a tool in realising higher rates of growth than the market forces by themselves might achieve over a long time span.

Some global evidence may be introduced at this point.

Data, presented in a recent IMF study, on the percentage share of public enterprise investments in gross fixed capital formation for seventy–two countries, for the latest year during 1974–82 for which data were available, indicate that (i) the share was the lowest in developed countries – 11 per cent on an average for eighteen countries; (ii) that it was the highest in many African countries – 32 per cent on an average for seventeen countries; (iii) that it was somewhat lower in the Asian countries – 27 per cent on an average for eleven countries; and (iv) that it was the lowest among developing countries in Latin America – 23 per cent on an average for twenty-three countries. The highest percentages were associated, no doubt, with countries characterised by ideological adherence to public enterprise, like Burma, Algeria, Egypt and Pakistan (after 1972).[10]

Data for the mid-1960s and early 1970s, as processed by the United Nations, also reveal similar tendencies. In seven out of twenty four African countries, the share of public investment in gross fixed capital formation was 50 per cent and above; it was so only in two out of sixteen Asian countries, and two out of nineteen Latin American countries. These figures evidence the relevance of the development status for the size of public investment.[11] Further, there was relative dominance of the infra-structural sectors in the investment strategy. The share of transport and communications was above 30 per cent of all public investments in nine countries, and 10 to 30 per cent in twenty-two; and that in power and other utilities was above 40 per cent in one country and 10 to 30 per cent in eighteen.[12] The figures would be far higher if services and agriculture were excluded from the calculation; and if data for the pre-1970 plans, representing stages of lesser development, were analysed.

Let us look at the argument that certain factors can make an investment decision in public enterprise more economical than a similar one in the private sector.

First, it can result in the setting up of a capacity that meets, not merely the current demands, but the foreseeable increases in demand with the passage of time. An optimum-sized enterprise can be planned with the eventual prospect of reaching the lowest unit costs possible. Such is the case with the decreasing-cost industries, to which category many of the public utilities belong. (In Figure 1.4 this is represented by curve AC_1 which has the lowest costs in the long run as against the alternative possibilities of AC_2 representing a private investment looking at the current demand, or $AC3$, AC_4 . . ., which represent piece-meal expansions from AC_2 as demand grows.)

Figure 1.4 Economics of large size

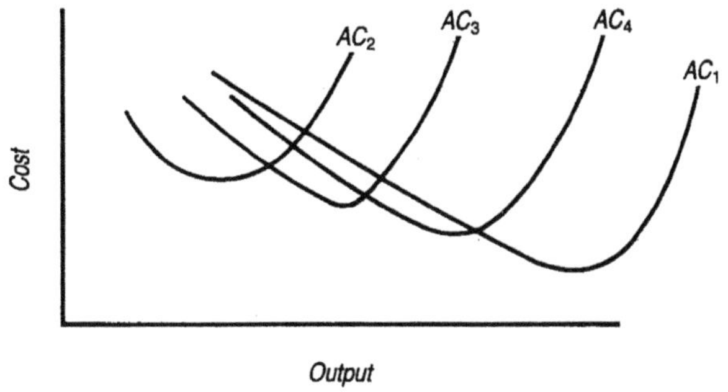

Second, an investment decision in the public sector has the chance of being a part of a package of investment decisions that represent the necessary backward and forward complementarities which contribute to the utmost economy of the package, independently of its own direct financial returns.

Third, most public enterprises in developing countries proceed on the basis of absorbing, and/or developing, a new technology.[13] This is expensive, to start with. A private investor, on the other hand, does not mind adopting the cheaper alternative of importing the required inputs and technology. The long run will prove the economy of the public enterprise strategy. Even in the short run, shadow pricing of foreign exchange used by the imports in the latter case suggests a similar conclusion.

The distributional aspects

There is a connection between the origins of public enterprise and the theme of distributional justice, particularly in developing countries:

Monopoly

In sectors where the domestic markets for a given product are small, there may not be room for more than one unit;[14] even that may not be optimal, technically, though it is the smallest possible. It tends to be a monopoly. Tendencies of duopoly and oligopoly are also likely to prevail in several sectors for similar reasons. The situation presents two options of public policy: either to let private monopolies develop and control them effectively, or to establish public enterprises. The smaller the technical capacity of the government to exercise monopoly control, the stronger the choice of public enterprise. The choice is strengthened by the fact that some monopoly units remain under-utilised and, therefore, ungainful, within the possible price structures; or that they have exclusive opportunities of making profits without the threat of competition and tests of market discipline. Governments rated these as compelling reasons to step in with direct investment initiative, even if in terms of a joint venture.

Another aspect of monopoly operations which has induced governments to keep them in the public sector is that a public monopoly could come in handy in implementing price differentials according to public preferences.

Public enterprise structures have generally reflected the predominance of monopolies. To cite some illustrative figures, 100 per cent of the public enterprises in mining, electricity, and services in Sri Lanka were monopolies in 1974; 90 per cent in transport; 40 per cent in manufacturing; and about a third in trade and construction.[15] About the same time in Nepal 47 per cent of the value added in the public enterprise sector came from monopolies, 23 per cent from duopolies and 18 per cent from oligopolies.[16] The UK, among developed economies, also illustrated a high proportion of monopolies among public enterprises.

Concentration

There is heavy skewness in the distribution of wealth and income in most developing countries. (The 1968–9 estimates for Bangladesh showed that 5 per cent of the people received 20.4 per cent of the total income, while 80 per cent of the people lived below the poverty line.)[17] About 40 per cent of the population is below the poverty line in India and Nepal.

A few wealthy persons would be the most certain to take prompt advantage of the growth opportunities, for (i) they have the resource base to start with, can offer it as collateral for borrowings and attract foreign financial collaboration; and (ii) they can command the scarce managerial skills available in the country. Their entrepreneurial risks would be small in view of the government's efforts in providing infrastructural facilities and a variety of investment incentives and tax reliefs. Further, being the first entrants in an industrial sector, and perhaps enjoying monopolistic powers, they have ample opportunities of intensifying their degree of ownership and control over the economy through gradual diversification of entrepreneurial interests. (The few wealthy Karachi-based families of Pakistan illustrate the point.)[18]

Public enterprise, in theory, can curb this process by promoting the forces of deconcentration. As a high proportion of fresh investments in the economy occurs in the public sector, a relative decline occurs in concentration in private hands. Where nationalisations take place, as in Pakistan after 1972,there would be an absolute decline in the concentration as well. Portugal also illustrates how the elimination of the power of the 'forty-families' oligarchy' constituted a 'popular motive' for large-scale 'nationalisation of the family-owned commercial banks and insurance companies' and the 'commanding heights' of the economy.[19]

Even where the government nationalises an enterprise, the owners, no doubt, forfeit the profit opportunities from that enterprise. But if they receive a cash compensation for the property taken over, they can use it for investment in some other direction and gain profit incomes, as in Ghana, where some compensations that could not be repatriated due to foreign exchange difficulties were reinvested in other permitted channels, for example, agricultural enterprise, the dividends from which enjoyed special concessions of repatriation.[20]

Where the government offers bonds, not cash, as compensation, the incomes of the past owners will be limited to interest, which is likely to be lower than the probable profits; and their wealth and income concentration begins to weaken. (Capital appreciations also accrue to the government.)

If such unique measures as the offer of compensation from future profits, if and when they occur, are implemented, concentration in private hands is further weakened.

Of course expropriation without compensation totally eradicates the problem of ownership concentration in so far as it relates to the properties taken over.

At the same time there is an opposite force at work. A substantial part of the capital expenditures of public enterprises (or elsewhere in the public sector) relates to construction work or to inputs other than those imported. These, along with contracts even for the supply of large teams of labour, end up in the lap of the already established owners of capital. In fact these activities carry with them very little uncertainty as to profits, unlike the investments in the projects. In this way there can be an acceleration of the trends of economic concentration; and this has happened in several developing countries.

This disadvantage has been realised from experience in countries like India where gradually public enterprises have been established to undertake the construction and technology components of project capital expenditures, for example, Hindustan Steelworks Construction Ltd, Indian Road Construction Corporation Ltd, National Building Construction Ltd, and National Projects Construction Corporation Ltd; but these do not adequately meet the problem. Many developing countries still depend largely on private contractors, domestic or domestic-cum-foreign for the completion of public enterprise projects. Correspondingly, the argument that public enterprise weakens concentration is weakened.

There is a unique aspect of deconcentration which some developing countries, particularly the African countries and Malaysia, actively pursued, namely, the indigenisation of economic activity. What is implied is a restructuring of industrial and commercial activity in such a way that the indigenous nationals substantially improve their share in the public economy, in comparison with the non-indigenous nationals. Public enterprise can be employed as an instrument in this process.

First, the indigenous people may require preferential treatment in entry into business and industry through easy credit on soft terms of interest, low rents for industrial sheds, and offer of assured markets at preferential prices. All these can only be provided by appropriate public enterprises (such as Kenya Industrial Estates Ltd, which offers loans at subsidised rates of interest, and the National Construction Corporation (in Kenya) which gives building contracts almost exclusively to black Kenyans).

Second, the government may initially acquire shares relating to indigenised properties for eventual transfer to private investors. The Permodalan Nasional Berhad of Malaysia is a good example of public enterprises set up for such a purpose.[21]

Third, large-scale indigenisations undertaken suddenly may land many enterprises in the hands of the government (as illustrated by the sudden expulsion of Asians from Uganda in the early 1970s), for there might be no local investors capable of stepping in to take them over.

On the whole, the involvement of the government in financial intermediation stretches itself over a long time. Besides, there will be need for effective public supervision to ensure that the financial incentives poured on the beneficiaries are not misplaced.

There is enough documentation on the fact that an improved pattern of income distribution has been a plan target in many developing countries, and also that it was often believed that public enterprise would go some way in achieving that goal. (The processes, as well as the results, are discussed in chapters 6 and 12.)

Foreign capital

The dominance of foreign capital in the national economy has been a significant factor in giving a stimulus to public enterprise in many developing countries. Julius K. Nyerere's observation that 'the pragmatist in Africa . . . will find that the choice is between foreign private ownership on the one hand and collective ownership on the other', applies to most developing countries which have been highly resentful of foreign capital control over the economy. Having just emerged out of colonial status, they

from. In Figure 1.5 curve *R* indicates the combinations with reference to an enterprise in a given period. Assume that the combination *A* represented by social returns SR_1, and the consequent financial returns FR_1 is preferred (by the government). The first question to examine is whether a private enterprise can offer a superior combination of returns, for example, *B* – FR_1 and SR_2, or *C* – FR_2 and SR_1, or *D* – Fr_2 and Sr_2. It is doubtful if a private enterprise sacrifices financial returns for the sake of social returns, as defined in chapter 3. If social returns at the level of SR_1 are a must under the government's plan strategy, and if the corresponding FR_1 is below the financial rate of return acceptable to a private enterprise, say FR_p, the comparative advantage is obviously in favour of public enterprise.

Figure 1.5 Comparative advantage of public enterprise

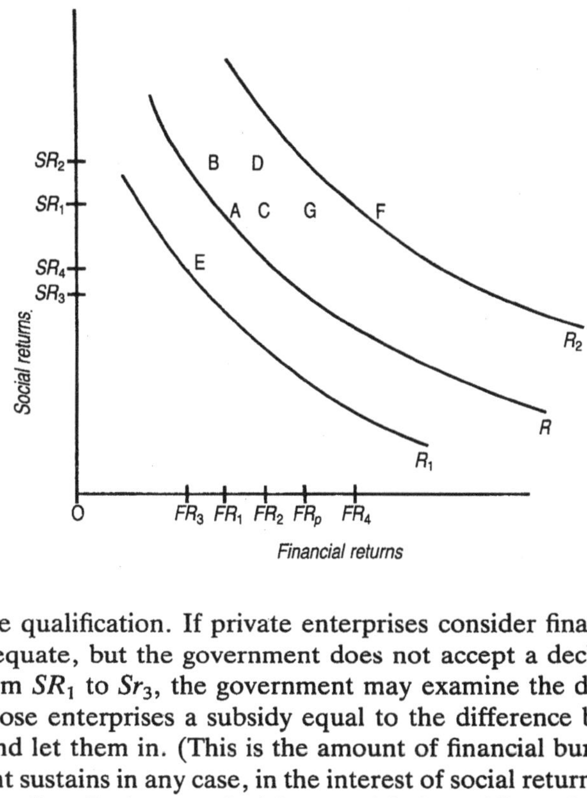

With one qualification. If private enterprises consider financial returns FR_p as adequate, but the government does not accept a decline in social returns from SR_1 to Sr_3, the government may examine the desirability of offering those enterprises a subsidy equal to the difference between FR_p and FR_1 and let them in. (This is the amount of financial burden that the government sustains in any case, in the interest of social returns SR_1.) Such a measure ordinarily does not find favour with the public exchequer, unless there is clear prospect that private enterprise operations will be more economical than corresponding public enterprise operations and can be induced into the field on receipt of a subsidy even smaller than the difference between FR_p and FR_1. When the measure works, the comparative advantage is not necessarily in favour of public enterprise. However, the Third World scenario in the early stages of development did not give much hope for this prospect.

Basically, the comparative advantage of public enterprise is likely to be positive:[28]

(i) where the activity is prone to be a monopoly or has to be maintained as a monopoly for some governmentally approved reason, and control over it, if in the private sector, is unlikely to be effective;
(ii) where viability is (or is kept) low for any reason that the enterprise management cannot surmount;
(iii) where technology is only importable and prompts governmental intervention of a regulatory or control nature so as to avoid or minimise foreign managerial control over the enterprise;
(iv) where capital resources are only importable and the government seeks to avoid or minimise managerial control over the enterprise by the foreign supplier of funds;
(v) where the potentiality of the enterprise to add to the concentration of wealth and income in the community is high and therefore prompts policy intervention by the government;
(vi) where the government's social policy preferences so touch the enterprise as to affect its surplus position adversely; and
(vii) where the organisation of the enterprise in the public sector does not expose it to any costs additional to those it would sustain by being organised in the private sector.

The last condition is a crucial one and can be negative and substantially reduce the comparative advantage of public enterprise in practice, as the next chapter will show, in spite of its relative merits on grounds of scale economies and investment packages, as argued in the previous section. The actual financial returns realised in practice might, therefore, be FR_3, rather than the expected FR_1; the actual social returns realised might be SR_4, as against the expected SR_1; and the actual combination of financial and social returns realised might be $E - FR_3$–SR_4, which is inferior to the expected FR_1–SR_1 combination (A). If such a deviation of actuality from expectation holds good right through, curve R is lowered to R_1.

There can be opposite reasons which make an upward movement of the curve possible. As markets become less imperfect over time and the economies of externalities and investment packages unfold themselves, the curve R might move towards R_2. That is, every SR can be realised along with a higher FR than before, for example, SR_1 and FR_4 (combination F).

At the same time private entrepreneurs themselves would enter the sector from the combination of G(FR_p and SR_1) onwards. If the government's expectations of social returns do not exceed the level of SR_1, G is the point beyond which public enterprise has no comparative advantage.

If the government's insistence on social returns drops, as time passes, below SR_1, the scope for the entry of private enterprise is enlarged; it can get higher financial returns than FR_4, without jeopardising the preferred social returns. The latter do not jeopardise its acceptable rate of financial returns, either.

Another reason why the curve R might rise to R_2 may be noted. A given financial return can result from high prices and low output, or low prices and large output in certain cases. The latter is often considered to be a superior method barring situations of acute resource or input constraints, for more markets are served than under the other method. If it is considered that social returns are higher this way, for every level of financial returns there are higher social returns than are assumed in the curve R.

The social–financial returns combinations would be dissimilar among different enterprises or sectors and the elasticities of the curves (such as R) would also be dissimilar in different ranges of financial or social returns. Changes over time also produce curves (such as R_1) in dissimilar patterns. Hence the concept of comparative advantage has to be addressed in an enterprise-specific and time-specific manner.

Let us turn to the issue of operationalising the concept. To start with, there is the problem of computing financial and social returns. Let us assume that estimates of financial results, uninfluenced by considerations of extra-financial objectives, exist. (This is the assumption in all investment feasibility studies.) What remains is to determine various possible levels of social returns so as to select, in the knowledge of corresponding values of financial returns, the most preferred combination, a point like A in the graph.

There is an obvious difficulty. Different social returns – for example regional development and income redistribution – are in heterogenous units; and a single point on the Y-axis is not easy. Two steps are, therefore, necessary. First, each identified social return has to be give a cost tag. Second, weights have to be attached to the different items of social returns, so that we end up with a single value in terms of money, to be used in selecting the best combination of social and financial returns.

The computation becomes easier if the government chooses to proceed in terms of the fewest necessary items of social returns. For example, in the case of a public enterprise designed essentially to prevent a massive lay-off of workers, that alone could be treated as the desired social returns – The National Textile Corporation Ltd of India is a typical example; and even a single physical unit (man hours) could be plotted on the Y-axis.

The financial worth of a social return may be estimated in two ways. Where it is expressible in terms of a cost addition in the accounts of the enterprise, that figure may be estimated. Where it is expressible in terms of a revenue reduction in the accounts of the enterprise, that figure may be the needed estimate. Regional development (through an uncommercial investment), employment promotion, and technology development are examples of the former kind; while price reductions, price discriminations, and uneconomical product mix are examples of the latter. (Some items overlap: regional development, for example, which has implications of both cost addition and revenue reduction.)

For each composition of social returns in terms of the items and of the level under each head, an aggregate value can then be estimated. This, along with the financial returns that the desired social returns make possible, will be one possible combination of overall returns. Several such combinations can be computed to form a curve such as *R*, and the most preferred among them, assumed to be *A* here, chosen in a given case.

It is with reference to the realisation of such a preferred combination of social and financial returns that the comparative advantage of a public enterprise has to be evaluated.

Let us turn, finally, to the application of the concept of comparative advantage. How easy is it in practice?

Where a sector of activity is new to the country (for example heavy engineering in the 1950s in India), the costs of development as well as the anticipated social returns are likely to be so heavy that it is difficult to find a private enterprise (interested in profit) willing to undertake the project. The comparative advantage is wholly on the side of public enterprise, unless the government is prepared extensively to subsidise an enterprise set up in the private sector. Many of the arguments for public enterprise listed in the following section on governmental perception come under this category.

Where a public enterprise operates as a monopoly in a given sector of activity, there is no private enterprise with which to compare its operations. One has to make assumptions on the possibilities of cost reduction and marketing improvements under a possible private enterprise; and the resulting estimates of its financial results have to be evaluated along with the social returns that are desired to be realised from the activity. If the latter do not interest a private enterprise at all or cannot be guaranteed under mutually agreeable rules of governmental subsidisation, public enterprise retains its comparative advantage.

It is where both public and private enterprises operate in a given line of business that comparison is somewhat easy. Even here it would be necessary to undertake several adjustments to cost and revenue figures so as to make the compared enterprises sufficiently comparable. In particular, any cost reliefs or market protections enjoyed by public enterprises have to be allowed for (see chapters 3 and 5). There is another caveat: if public enterprises can easily improve their position through organisational or operational reforms, and if the latter are practicable, it is their level of results consistent with such reforms that ought to be brought into the comparison. (In many cases the fact or threat of comparison itself prompts the reforms.)

With reference to sectors in which no private enterprise operates alongside public enterprise(s) it is possible to make international comparisons, particularly in terms of percentage returns on investments and, more importantly, of physical indices of productivity and performance such as man hours per steel ingot or consumption of energy per ton of output. But these do not represent the likely achievements of private enterprise in the local situation. Allowance has to be made by applying what is known as the 'efficiency factor' (in the context of preparing project documents) reflecting the probable lower levels of productivity achievable in developing countries than are recorded in the advanced economies. Further, the impacts of the 'learning curve' in the local situation have to be fully noted in the course of the exercise.

To conclude – the idea underlying the concept of comparative advantage is simple, namely, that in a mixed economy public enterprise is to be preferred when it has advantage over private enterprise in a given sector and situation. But less simple are the substance in terms of which the advantage is to be understood and the technique of evaluating the comparative advantage, as the following chapters (2 and 3) confirm. Nevertheless, it would be purposeful to keep the concept in mind and proceed in the direction of constantly evaluating the comparative advantage of an enterprise (being) organised in the public sector.

A basic point in the context of comparative advantage is that the comparison is with a local private enterprise and not with a foreign-owned enterprise or a multinational branch operating in the country, unless the government has a long-term policy of permitting it to operate unfettered in the sectors concerned. To prevent the effects of foreign ownership of investment is, in fact, an important component of the social returns aimed at in many cases.

THE POLITICAL DIMENSION

Political factors have been of no small significance in strengthening the bias for public enterprise even in mixed economies. It would be unrealistic to overlook this. In fact, the reason why curve R generally lowers itself to the position of R_1 in Figure 1.5 is related to the consequences of political considerations.

For instance, the view is widely held that in the UK the reasons for the post-1945 nationalisations were not primarily economic, though some economic rationale was introduced in explaining the decisions.[29] Industrial relations and lagging investments apart, steel nationalisation has been considered by some as 'a purely political effort . . . in no way relevant to the economic needs of Britain in 1967.[30] The all-pervasive measures of nationalisation attempted in France on the assumption of power by the Mitterand government provide another illustration from the developed world, as also do the opposite measures of denationalisation which have begun to be pursued since 1982 consequent on a change in the composition of the government.

Some of the clearest evidence of political bias for public enterprise comes from Pakistan and Sri Lanka. In Pakistan large-scale nationalisations took place during 1972–5 when the People's Party took the reigns of government. On its overthrow in 1977, the government's policy slid towards a preference for assigning a dominant role to private enterprise.[31]

The political impacts on the nature of enterprise in Sri Lanka are amenable to temporal classification on the following lines:

1946–54: pro-public; *1954–6*: pro-private (under the United National Party); *1956–65*: pro-public (under the People's United front); *1965–70*: slight tilt towards private enterprise; *1970–7*: pro-public (under the United Left Front);[32] *since 1977*: pro-private under the United National Party.

History is replete with several other examples. Nationalisation was part of the political platform in Bangladesh.[33] Public enterprise grew at an extraordinary pace in Peru in the twelve years after 1968 under the military regime.[34] Nationalisations were the order of the day in Chile under Allende, just as privatisations have been since his removal. 'Sweeping nationalisations' – of 244 private enterprises – took place in Portugal during 1975–6 under the political ideology of the MFA leadership after the collapse of the old regime.[35] Jamaica under the People's National Party during 1974–80 witnessed 'an extraordinary collection of enterprises' in the state sector; while both before and after that regime the fervour for public enterprise was low.[36] Nicaragua's public enterprise sector experienced a sudden boost on the downfall of the Somoza dictatorship, followed by the confiscation of the vast agricultural, industrial, and commercial empire of his family. And in Algeria, the building of a socialist state, the major preoccupation of the revolution, was pursued through state control of all the key sectors of the economy.[37]

To conclude – it is sometimes difficult to categorise the origins of public enterprise as pragmatic or political. Both forces often operate concurrently. However, the overlapping impact of political ideology shows itself in some countries (for example, Syria, Egypt, Somalia, Ethiopia, and Sudan) under 'socialist' constitutions proclaiming the paramountcy of public enterprise as a national strategy, and during certain regimes of government in others, including the UK.

THE RATIONALE OF PUBLIC ENTERPRISE BY GOVERNMENTAL PERCEPTION

This section contains an inferential account of the reasons for public enterprise as perceived by governments at the time of investment decision. The material, selectively gathered from an extensive range of official and other documents, is in excerpts (in full sentences or clauses or phrases) under appropriate captions, and provides empirical support to the foregoing arguments.

The documents surveyed go as far back as the 1950s. This is by design, for inferring a profile of decision-making in the early stages of development planning and public enterprise. Even the more recent documents have been supportive of the initial thinking, though comments on experience have been ubiquitous.

For economy in footnoting, the large number of seminars referred to are listed in Appendix 1.1 and serially numbered; and the parenthesis attaching to a citation in the text includes, first, the number of the seminar from which it is picked, the year of the seminar, and any further references to the title of the paper quoted, if different from the report of the seminar.

Plan strategy and social gain

The need for public enterprise depended on 'the speed of the growth and the kind of growth that the government envisages'. 'Much will depend upon the relative emphasis placed at a particular stage of economic development on infra-structural, agricultural and industrial enterprises.' (Extracted from 3, 1966, p. 1)

'To achieve, within a given period, the targets laid down in the plans.' (6, 1969, Société d'Economie et de Mathématique appliquées, Paris, p. 4)

With reference to Africa

'National economic development involves extensive public investments in all sectors of the economy aimed at fostering balanced and rapid growth.' (3, 1966, p. 19)

'To realise economic targets which cannot be realised by the private sector' in African countries. (11, 1972, Michael N'gangbet, 'Control of Government Enterprise in African Countries', p. 3)

'The newly independent African States felt the need to resort to public enterprises to satisfy their immediate requirements, organise or re-organise their economy, secure integrated development and lay the foundations for economic independence ... The establishment of public enterprises satisfied a practical need of developing countries.' (5, 1969, pp. 37–8)

Senegal

To promote a balance between productive and social sectors; to reduce the pronounced regional disparities; government's direct involvement in sectors of 'high social benefit'. (*Cinquième plan quadriennial de la développement économique et sociale 1977–81*)

Phillipines

To provide 'the necessary social overhead capital and other services for accelerated economic growth and development'. (*Four-Year Development Plan 1974–77*, p. 202)

Iran

'Priority to investment in capital-intensive heavy industry particularly through public sector'. (*Fifth Development Plan 1973–78, Revised: A Summary*, p. 10)

Sierra Leone

Public enterprise is 'visualised as the principal institutional instrument for achieving important Plan objectives such as rapid industrial development'. (*National Development Plan 1974/75 – 1978/79*, p. 39)

Jamaica

'For (a) the achievement of the targeted rate of industrial investment; (b) the promotion of a desirable pattern of industrial location'. (15, 1979, p. 7)

Swaziland

'The implementation of the development plan will ... involve public investments.' Also, 'to fill certain gaps left by the private sector'. (*Post-Independence Development Plan 1969/70 – 1973/74*, p. 17)

Somalia

'More as a training ground for future industrial workers than as an investment which will make immediate returns.' (*Five-Year Development Programme 1974–78*, p. 163)

Thailand

'The Government is prepared even to operate, particularly public activities, at a loss where it benefits the public.' (*National Economic Development Plan 1961–1966, Phase II, 1964–66*, p. 154)

Trinidad and Tobago

'The public sector must be expected to play the role of the prime mover in the economy.' (*White Paper on Public Participation in Industrial and Commercial Activities*, Port-of-Spain, 1972, p. 7)

Asia

'Public enterprise rested, on the whole, on the concept and hope of social gains in the process of development, even "at a loss" over a considerable period.' (2, 1959, p. 3)

Africa

The need to diversify the mono-product economies. (3, 1966; 5, 1969, p. 4)

Botswana

Diversification needed in the economy that is disproportionately dependent on livestock and minerals. (*National Development Plan 1976–81*, p. 21)

India

'To promote critical development in terms of social gain or strategic value rather than on considerations of profits.' (15, 1979, p. 6)

Arab countries

In some Arab countries 'it was the surplus rather than a shortage of available revenue that led to the expansion of the public sector', because of oil revenues which were 'too large for the private sector to absorb' (*Public Enterprises and Development in the Arab Countries*, New York, 1978, p. 1)

Status of private entrepreneurship

Public enterprise was found necessary since private investors did not come forward sufficiently. Even in Japan 'state ownership was the first step to its industrialisation'. (Yoshitake, K. (1973) *An Introduction to Public Enterprise in Japan*, London, p. 65)

Asia

'The lumpy nature of economic development frequently requires that an enterprise should adapt itself not only to existing demand but to a future, planned demand, in a way that the ordinary profit-minded entrepreneur would regard as commercially hazardous – and rightly so.' (2, 1959, p. 3)

On a global scale

Many governments have been 'sceptical of the ability of private investors'. 'The more complex, the more capital-intensive and the more slow-yielding an enterprise is, the greater the likelihood' of its being in the public rather than in the private sector. (3, 1966; extract cited in 5, 1969, pp. 1–2)

Mauritius

Mauritius is 'singularly unfortunate' in attracting external investment. 'There currently appears no alternative to the Government of Mauritius to plan an increasing role in the promotion of commercial ventures.' (5, 1969, Brown, J. C. 'The Role of Public Enterprises in Mauritius', p. 2)

Sudan

'Lack of interest, or rather hesitation so far on the part of the private sector ... Prohibitive amount of capital required ... Such projects do not yield quick and attractive returns for investors.' (11, 1972, Saeed, O. H. 'Industrial Development Strategy in the Sudan', pp. 10–15)

Brazil

Some areas 'beyond the organisational and financial resources of Brazilian private companies'. (15, 1979, p. 4)

India

Basic industries which the 'private sector had shunned for long'. (15, 1979, p. 6)

Pakistan

With large-scale nationalisations, private capital further 'shied away' from industry rather than commerce. 'The vacuum had to be filled by public enterprise.' (16, 1981, Beg, H. U. 'Project Cost Overruns, Nature and Impact of Delays in Project Implementation', p. 3)

Ghana

'Most of Ghana's present entrepreneurs are farmers and small traders ... Manufacturing and similar enterprises ... would clearly lie beyond their entrepreneurial horizon ... The State itself is pre-eminently suited for this role.' (*Seven-Year Development Plan 1963/64 to 1969/70*, Accra, 1964, pp. 19–20)

Singapore

Government participation in joint ventures resulted from private capital having been 'sluggish' first. Li, Lee Sheng (1976) 'Public Enterprise and Economic Development in Singapore', *Malayan Economic Review*, vol. XXI, no. 2, p. 51)

Niger

'It is worth mentioning that there is not much interest on the part of the nationals in industrial development . . . Local preference for trading rather than industrial development.' (UNIDO (1977) *Industrialisation of the Least Developed Countries*, ID/WG 234/13, p. 33)

Aid to private enterprise

In many countries public enterprise stepped in with the aim of developing private enterprise, by leading the way, by providing investor confidence, and by sharing risks through joint ventures. The most common direction has been the provision of finance through public financial institutions, variously termed as development banks, industrial development corporations, or finance corporations. Where they offer finance through equity rather than loans, elements of public ownership of the beneficiary enterprises also prevail.

Development corporations of various kinds have been a common phenomenon in most countries, including the UK with its National Enterprise Board. In large countries with federal structures, such as India and Nigeria, the corporations exist both at the central government level and at the state government level. Financial public enterprises are so important and distinctive in nature that they are accorded a separate listing in the IMF's annual volumes of *Government Financial Statistics*. The aid-to-private-enterprise perception clearly indicates that public enterprise has often been intended as a means to development and not as an end in itself.

Botswana

Active intervention by the government 'not to stifle private initiative but create favourable conditions'. (*National Development Plan 1976–81*, p. 15)

The National Development Bank was set up to fill a gap in the credit structure of the country, 'by providing credit facilities to those people who . . . cannot have recourse to the commercial lending institutions'. (*National Development Plan 1969–73*, p. 125)

Jordan

'The purpose' of the government's participation is to 'pave the way for the private sector to enlarge its participation and contribution to development'. (*Five-Year Plan 1976–80*, p. 41)

Nigeria

To develop the infrastructure whose absence 'increases both the initial and operational costs of projects thereby compromising the commercial feasibility of economically desirable projects'. (*Third National Development Plan 1975–80*, vol. I)

Ghana

The Industrial Development Corporation concentrates 'on those industries which would not come into existence without government participation'. (*Second Development Plan 1959–64*, Accra, 1959, p. 19)

Korea

Korea Development Finance Corporation: to promote private enterprise.

Japan

'Though the government was not active in the public ownership in the industrial field, it was active in the other field: financing private industries . . . Through these financial corporations the state was controlling at least one-third of the nation's investment spending during the boom of the 1950s.' (Yoshitake, K. (1973) *An Introduction to Public Enterprise in Japan,* London).

Arab countries

In the Arab countries, government participation in banks, trade and insurance was 'to encourage rather than discourage private enterprise'. It 'means confidence for the average private would-be investor' in an 'under-developed culture with respect to shareholding companies in general'. (*Public Enterprises and Development in the Arab Countries*, New York, 1978, p. 16)

Control over the economy

Public enterprise was favoured on the ground that it would enable the government to control the economy, by gaining control, as in India, of 'the commanding heights of the economy'. (15, 1979, p. 41)

This term refers, as per a World Bank study, to 'the natural resource and capital intensive sectors of the manufacturing industries'. (*State Intervention in the Industrialisation of Developing Countries: Selected Issues*, 1979, p. iv)

Zaire

Main goal: 'to have the key sectors of the nation's economy under state control'. (Sauliniers, A. H. (1976) *The Growth of the Zairean Public Sector since Independence*, Austin, Texas, p. 7)

Belize

'To own and control the "commanding heights" of the economy, i.e., activities which have a major importance in the economy.' (Seminar on the Role and Management of Public Enterprises, Fuller, R. A. (1976) 'Public Enterprises in Belize', p. 3)

Africa

'Large-scale investment by a foreign company would have detrimental political implications.' (5, 1969, p. 5).

'Most of the countries which recently achieved national sovereignty, anxious to be free from the constraints of foreign capital on their policy, nationalised the private enterprises completely or partially.' (11, 1972, Michael N'gangbet, 'Control of Government Enterprises in African Countries', p. 3)

'The trend . . . is strongly towards joint ventures in which the Government . . . becomes the majority shareholder and the foreign private business the minority investor.' (UNIDO, 1979 *Industrial Development Survey*, vol. III, p. 138)

Egypt

To ensure that the 'national economy remains in the hands of the nation'. (11, 1972, Basada, R. S. 'Methods of Creation and Development of Public Sector in Egypt', p. 17)

Trinidad and Tobago

'The need for greater national control of the economy.' (15, 1979, p. 8)

Brazil

For the 'absorption of foreign capital'. (3, 1966, Filito, A. V. 'Organisation and Administration of Public Enterprises in Brazil', p. 1)

Senegal

In 1960 all means of production were dominated by foreign enterprises and socio-economic development was abandoned to the free play of market forces. (*Cinquième plan quadriennal de la développement économique et sociale 1977–81*)

Latin America

The relevance of a joint venture agreement to foreign capital is emphasised by the cases studied by Sidney Weintraub: 'In each case it seems clear that the venture would not have come to fruition had not the host government been given some share of the equity.' (*The Government–Private Joint Venture as a Confidence Builder in Non-fuel Mineral Investment*, Austin, Texas, 1979 p. 3)

Arab countries

'Most Arab joint ventures have a clear governmental character.' (*Public Enterprises and Development in the Arab Countries*, New York, 1978, p. 184)

Nepal

Foreign aid 'has played a key role in the establishment of some public enterprises'; even low-priority industries were set up. (*Performance of Public Enterprises in Nepal (Macro Study)*, Kathmandu, 1977, p. 50)

Swaziland

Swaziland's economy is 'dominated by foreign interests'. (*Second National Development Plan: 1973–77*, p. 9) 'Since independence national influence over the domestic economy has also been progressively strengthened through the expansion of direct participation of central government or the Swazi Nation in commerce, industry and mining.' (*Post-Independence Development Plan, 1969/70 – 1973/74*, p. 22). Also, minority investments in major enterprises, 'to ensure that a greater proportion of profits from the manufacturing sector remains in Swaziland'. (p. 44)

Kenya

'Greater Kenyan participation in the economy would be advanced by increasing the contribution of the public sector to total production.' (*Development Plan 1970–1974*, p. 34)

Deconcentration

Public enterprise was intended to accelerate deconcentration in the ownership of industry. This idea may be presented under different heads.

Anti-monopoly

France

'To combat monopolies or impose sanctions', for example Renault. (6, 1969, p. 4)

Ghana

The government will 'seek some measure of participation' whenever 'an enterprise operates under monopoly conditions', or in a 'one-factory industry'. (*Second Plan 1959–64*, p. 104)

Zambia

'In our industrial development we have no choice but to make use of monopolies . . . In relation to some products it simply cannot sustain more than one factory' (Kaunda, K. D., 1968, *Zambia's Economic Revolution*, pp. 22, 65). Enterprises enjoying monopoly or near-monopoly 'must give Government a controlling interest so that their affairs are closely watched and their policies are adopted to run in line with the national interest'. (Kaunda, K. D. (1970) *Take up the Challenge*, Lusaka, p. 61)

Uganda

'The inherently monopolistic character of many important economic undertakings, in a small country like Uganda, also requires more intimate government involvement in these undertakings in order, particularly, to protect the interests of consumers.' (*Uganda's Plan III, 1971/2–1975/6*, p. 20)

Ownership and social restructuring

Here the emphasis has been not only on deconcentration in general, but on indigenisation of ownership. Oftentimes the idea of restructuring the society was also prominent.

Pakistan

'An unstated objective' of Pakistan Industrial Development Corporation was 'to diversify the ownership of industrial capital from a few Karachi-based families'. (16, 1981, Burki, S. J. 'The Role of Public Enterprises in the Economies of Developing Countries', p. 9)
Greater intervention for the benefit of small investors, and broadening the ownership of industry. (*Fourth Five-Year Plan 1970–75*, pp. 15–17)

Indonesia

The government will support the economically weak groups in the matter of capital, marketing and improving skills. (*Second Five-Year Plan 1974/75 - 1978/79*, p. 151)

Malaysia

The major objective is 'to enable public enterprises to expand their activities in support of greater involvement of the Malays and other indigenous people in commerce and industry'. (*Third Malaysia Plan 1976–80*, pp. 232–3)

To establish industrial activities in 'selected growth areas' and to create 'a Malay commercial and industrial community', (*Second Malaysia Plan 1971–75*, p. 7)

'Foreign interests accounted for as much as 61 per cent of the total share capital invested in the corporate sector ... Chinese ownership accounted for about 22 per cent ... The ownership of share capital of Malays and Malay interests, on the other and, is a mere 2 per cent of the overall total.' (*Mid-Term Review of the Second Malaysia Plan 1971–75*, Kuala Lumpur, 1973, p. 81)

Bangladesh

Non-Bengalis controlled 47 per cent of the fixed assets and 72 per cent of private industrial assets. In particular, West Pakistan's '43 families' controlled 45.1 per cent of the total assets of privately-controlled firms in the Eastern Wing (which became Bangladesh) (*Public Enterprise in an Intermediate Regime: A Study in the Political Economy of Bangladesh*, Dacca, 1980, pp. 57, 59)

Thailand

Third National Economic and Social Development Plan (1972–76) conceives of public enterprises 'to prevent private monopolies'. (p. 19)

Spain, Israel, and Iran

In Spain, Israel, and Iran some public enterprises were established 'with the specific purpose of introducing competition into an area hitherto monopolised by undynamic private undertakings'. (3, 1966, p. 9)

Mozambique

'Empresa des Lojas de Poro was established in 1976 to combat speculation, to further price reduction and stabilization'. (*The Role of the Public Sector in Promoting the Economic Development of Developing Countries* (Report of the Secretary-General, United Nations, New York, 1977, p. 17)

Egypt

'The inherited feudal system and the system of ownership in agriculture or industry had to be changed in order successfully to introduce measures of radical social change'. (11, 1972, Mettwally, A. O. 'Scope and Organisation of the Egyptian Public Sector', p. 2)
'Strong feudal class of large land owners whose interests were identified with those of foreign powers' had to be dealt with. (4, 1969, El-Said, M. M. 'On the Many Problems Arising from the Control and Management of Public Enterprises Being Established in African Countries', p. 3)

Tanzania

Arusha Declaration: 'To prevent the accumulation of wealth to the extent that is inconsistent with the existence of a classless society.' (15, 1979, p. 8)

Asia

'To redress social imbalance found ... between different sectors of the population.' (13, 1976, p. 3)

Africa

Marketing Boards were established 'mainly to eliminate the expatriate middlemen'. (8, 1969, Udoji, J. O. 'Reforming the Public Enterprises in Africa', p. 5)

Uganda

'To shift the commercial and industrial activities from the hands of non-citizens with full participation ... by its citizens.' (4, 1969, Ogwal, B. E. 'The Management of Public Enterprises in Uganda', p. 1)

Austria

'Nationalisation excluded from Austrian politics a traditionally very conservative, even fascist-minded sector of the property classes.' (Lancine, F. (1977) *The Development of the Austrian Public Sector since World War II*, Austin, Texas, p. 24.

Distributional justice

Public enterprise was expected to assist in improving the structure of income and wealth distribution.

On a global scale

To deal with 'a grossly unequal distribution of income which is the inescapable accompaniment of an economic development in which private enterprise is playing the major role'. (3, 1968, p. 20)

Egypt

'Large public sector is necessary to prevent exploitation of the working population by a limited number of private owners of big enterprises.' (11, 1972, Besada, R. S. 'Methods of Creation and Development of Public Sector in Egypt', p. 21)

Pakistan

'The role of the public sector was explicitly recognised to include reduction in inequalities in the distribution of income, wealth and economic power.' (*Third Five-Year Plan 1965–70*, p. 29)
'A more aggressive social policy is needed even at the cost of a slower growth rate than [to] tolerate a further growth in inequalities in income distribution.' (*Fourth Five-Year Plan 1970–75*, pp. 12–13)

Morocco

'Moroccanisation should not be for the sole benefit of the wealthiest but an instrument of equitable redistribution of income.' (*Plan de Développement Economique et Sociale 1973–77*)

India

An improvement of wage share is to be brought about at the expense of the consumption of owners of property. (*Draft Fifth Five-Year Plan 1974–79*, p. 23)

Uganda

'It will be the government policy to make all basic social services available to those in the lowest income brackets free of charge or at greatly subsidised rates of charges.' (*Development Plan 1971–76*, p. 23)

Tanzania

'The private sector cannot be relied upon . . . to achieve economic justice by controlling the principal means of production.' (*Second Five-Year Plan for Economic and Social Development*, vol. I, Dar es Salaam, 1969, pp. xiv, 3, 6)

Savings for investment

Public enterprises were expected to raise surpluses and assist in promoting savings for investment.

Nigeria and Ghana

Marketing Boards were 'substantial sources of capital for development'. (8, 1969, Udoji, J. O. 'Reforming the Public Enterprises in Africa', p. 5)

Sri Lanka

'A socialist economy must rely heavily on the surpluses or profits generated by public enterprises for the savings necessary for further investment.' (*Five-Year Plan 1972-76*, p. 132)

Ghana

'Such enterprises will be expected to make a contribution to the public revenues within a reasonable time.' (*Seven-Year Development Plan 1963/64 – 1969/70*)

Tanzania

A number of public enterprises are 'important savings institutions'. (*Development Plan 1969–74*, p. 224)

Nepal

The public enterprises already established should make sizeable contributions to the government revenue. (*Fifth Plan 1975–80*)

UNIDO's study entitled *Profitability and Effective Measures of Public Enterprises: Brief Summary of Country Experiences*, showed that 'many of the participating countries reported that their manufacturing public enterprises are not required to show a profit on their operations' (p. 1). In this respect 'a distinction' exists 'between the developed "mixed" economy countries and the less developed ones' (p. 2).

'Through "the joint fund method" all public enterprise surpluses can be centralised for national use' (4, 1969, p. 44).

Special considerations

Public enterprise has been necessary for the sake of meeting the ravages of serious occurrences like war and closure of borders.

Jordan

'Public investment was dictated by the problems which Jordan faced following the events of 1948.' (*Five-Year Plan 1976–80*, p. 5)

Austria

After the world war 'a set of ownerless enterprises' none untarnished by a Nazi past to take over. (Lauterbach, A. (1978) *The Austrian Public Sector in International Perspective: A Socio-historical Evaluation*, Austin, Texas, p. 1)

Agency of development

There was a general feeling in many countries that public enterprise, on the whole, constituted a major instrument in the hands of the government to promote development.

Tanzania

Public enterprise was considered as the 'principal agency of economic expansion'. (11, 1972, Chacha, T. M. 'The Case of the NDC', p. 1)

Asian countries

In Asian countries 'public enterprises are more and more chosen as vehicles of development ... because of the inadequacy of the existing tools'. (13, 1976, p. 1)

Italy

IRI, ENI, EFIM, and so on, operate partly as 'an instrument of public policy'. (6, 1969, and Marsan, V. A. 'Financing of Manufacturing Companies in a State Holding System')

Syria

'The public industrial sector is regarded as the spearhead of the country's development efforts.' (12, 1973, 'Review and Appraisal of the Process of Decision Making and Management in the Public Industrial Enterprise Sector in Syria', p. 6)

Ghana

'The government will rely primarily on parastatal organisations to carry out its responsibilities in productive enterprises.' (*Third Development Plan 1971/72 – 1975/6*, p. 21)

To conclude: the purpose of the above citations has been to grasp the elements of pragmatism in favour of public enterprise, by and large. The conclusion applies to developed countries as well, for example, Canada, 'where virtually every level of government . . . has made extensive use of public enterprise',[38] and the US with its Tennessee Valley Authority in the 1930s, which provided an inspiration to many countries in the establishment of public corporations.

How the pragmatism worked in practice will be the subject matter of the following chapter.

CONCLUSION

There is a case for public enterprise wherever its comparative advantage over private enterprise is established in financial-cum-social terms. In most developing countries the government has conceived of it as an instrument of development strategy and resorted to it wherever private investments would not adequately help in accomplishing that strategy.

The multiple objectives of development plans have also applied to public enterprises. These, besides political considerations, have complicated their purpose, in practice.

APPENDIX 1.1

Seminars whose documents have been used or referred to in Chapter 1

UN seminars

1. Seminar on the Organisation and Administration of Public Enterprises in the Industrial Field (United Nations, Rangoon, 1954).
2. Seminar on Public Industrial Management in Asia and the Far East (UN Economic Commission for Asia and the Far East, New Delhi, 1959).
3. Seminar on Organisation and Administration of Public Enterprises (United Nations, Geneva, September–October 1966).
4. Seminar on the Management of Public Enterprises (UN Economic Commission for Africa, Bizerte, December 1968).

5. Seminar on the Role of Public Enterprises in Planning and Plan Implementation (UN Economic Commission for Africa, Mauritius, September 1969).
6. Interregional Seminar on Financial Aspects of Manufacturing Enterprises in the Public Sector (UN Industrial Development Organisation, Rome, 1969).
7. Interregional Seminar on Government Accounting and Financial Management (United Nations, Beirut, 1969).
8. Expert Working Group on Measures for Improving Performance of Public Enterprises in Developing Countries (United Nations, Hercegnovi, 1969).
9. Meeting of Experts on the Administration of Public Enterprises in Latin America and the Caribbean (Santiago, November, 1969).
10. Reports of the Sub-Committees of the Inter-American Committee on the Alliance for Progress (Washington 1970).
11. Seminar on the Role of the Public Sector in the Economic Development of Africa (UN African Institute for Economic Development and Planning, Cairo, May–June 1972).
12. Expert Group Meeting on Review and Appraisal of Progress in the Implementation of the International Development Strategy for the Second Development Decade (UN Economic and Social Office in Beirut, Beirut 1973).
13. Conference on Asian Development Strategies and the Role of Public Enterprise (Eastern Regional Organisation for Public Administration (EROPA), Tehran, October 1976).
14. Regional Joint Consultation on Management of Public Industrial Enterprises in Africa (UN Industrial Development Organisation, Dakar 1978).
15. Expert Group Meeting on the Role of the Public Sector in the Industrialisation of the Developing Countries (UN Industrial Development Organisation, Vienna, May 1979).
16. International Symposium on Economic Performance of Public Enterprises (UN and Government of Pakistan, Islamabad, November 1981).
17. Studies by the Regional and Country Studies Branch, Division for Industrial Studies (UN Industrial Development Organisation, Vienna, 1983).
18. Seminar on Evaluation of Public Enterprises and Social Responsibilities of Public Enterprises (Islamabad, Pakistan, November 1983).

Commonwealth secretariat seminars

19. Seminar on the Role and Management of Public Enterprises (Kingston, October 1976).

20. Seminar on Performance Evaluation of Public Enterprises (Gaborne, Botswana, April 1978).
21. Seminar on National Policies and Programmes for Public Enterprise Management Training (London, November 1979).
22. Seminar on Relationships between Parliament and Public Enterprises (Colombo, 1979).
23. Seminar on Government Executive and Supervisory Control over Public Enterprises (New Delhi, 1982).

2 The emergence of public enterprise

The previous chapter considered the rationale of public enterprise in theory and by governmental perception. This chapter focuses on certain aspects of how it emerged, which have an impact on its performance: the genesis of public enterprise, the nature of public entrepreneurship, the organisational structure, and the application of the concept of comparative advantage in practice. The chapter aims at examining whether the cross-section of public enterprises emerged in perfect consonance with its theoretical justification.

NATIONALISATION AND SPONSORING

There is a broad distinction n the way public enterprise came into being in developed and developing countries. In the former, it resulted mainly, though not exclusively, from the nationalisation of industries or enterprises that existed, for example, in the UK, France, and Austria. This was accompanied by several advantages: the structural framework of the industry was already set; and the needed technological know-how and managerial skills were already available. What was needed was a remedy for noticed deficiencies such as poor industrial relations and arrears of investment, some technological rationalisation – as in British coal, electricity, and railways, or a cautious injection of social preferences in the operations.

Most public enterprises in developing countries have, generally, though not exclusively, been the product of governmental sponsoring[1] or creation for the first time. They represented the very beginnings of activity in many sectors. Nationalisation has been of secondary importance, except in ideological situations referred to in the previous chapter, and for the expropriation of foreign capital. For example, major banks, life insurance, coal, oil, electricity, and rail and air transport were the few important cases of nationalisation, as against hundreds of enterprises sponsored afresh by the central and state governments, in India. Except for some foreign capital take-overs, Tanzania, Kenya, and several other African countries had too little to nationalise but much to initiate. To cite another example, in Sri Lanka the number of public enterprises owing to nationalisation was

20 as against 567 that were newly sponsored, by 1974.[2] In terms of capital the proportion of the sponsored segment in the aggregate public enterprise sector is far higher; for it relates generally to capital-intensive activities. Creating almost the first units in many new sectors entailed serious problems of investment decision, technology, marketing, and organisation.

The nationalisations themselves were, in many countries, 'vigorous rather than orderly',[3] for example, in Egypt in 1961 under Laws nos 117, 118 and 119, and in 1963 under Laws nos 72 and 65, in Sudan under the Acquisition Act of 1970 and the Companies Act of 1970, in Iraq in 1964, in Pakistan in the early 1970s, and in 1970 in Uganda. In Bangladesh the Abandoned Properties Ordinance of 1972 vested 725 enterprises in the government overnight,[4] reflecting the 'government's lack of preparedness "for a large public sector", created at one stroke'.[5] In the case of nationalisation of foreign-owned enterprises, there was a sudden departure of the former managers, literally creating a managerial vacuum, for example, in Madagascar and Mozambique.

Two major factors weighed heavily on the establishment of enterprises by the government. First, several items of national development costs, inevitable in the early stages of development, found their way into the accounts of those enterprises. For instance:

(i) Techniques of feasibility analysis prior to investment decision were not only imperfect but frequently complicated by foreign collaborating interests.
(ii) The choice of right technology proved difficult and expensive. It did not necessarily guarantee high net social benefits. Several empirical studies provide evidence.[6]
(iii) The assumptions of inter-industry relationships did not often prove correct; and capacity imbalances in related sectors became common.
(iv) Foreign collaboration acquired on a turnkey basis kept domestic technical skills slow in developing.
(v) Civil servants had to fill the gaps in managerial talent. The result was not in the interest of efficiency, as evidenced by the comments of the Ndegwa Committee on public enterprises in Kenya in 1979. These comments can apply to many other countries as well.

The other factor, which impinged heavily on public enterprises, concerned errors in development planning itself. For example:

(i) The temporal perspective of planning implied the choice of capital – and intermediate – goods investments, slow-yielding projects and excess capacities on grounds of eventual economy. The concept of scale economies was overworked.
(ii) Social preferences in the location of industrial activity and employment led to the emergence of public enterprises whose capacity for commercial efficiency was low.

(iii) Concepts of social welfare and equity in the spread of benefits of development widely resulted in large uncommercial investments.
(iv) Resource constraints experienced in the course of plan implementation affected the funds available for the capital expenditures of public enterprises, and disturbed their economical sequencing. Several imbalances developed in capital input structures.[7] Many cost overruns occurred, with permanent consequences for the cost structures of the enterprises.

Apart from these exogenous considerations, public entrepreneurship has some inherent characteristics. First, it has a bias towards physical rather than financial orientation and places emphasis on the ability to produce a given output, the more certainly the newer the technology. Marketing considerations take a secondary place and, correspondingly, financial criteria are subordinated to the aims of commissioning the plant and keeping it working. The search for the least-cost production function and the most favourable input–output ratio tends to be far from vigorous.

Second, there develops a tendency towards overcapitalisation, in the sense of higher capital intensity than is strictly necessary, given an output goal. This results from various considerations:

(i) Excessive capacities are set up, partly on grounds of eventual economies of scale and partly not to err on the side of underproduction.
(ii) Capital outlays increase because of frequent changes in design, uneconomical sequences in expenditure, and imbalances in the creation of capacity.
(iii) Extravagance in capital expenditure is probable, because of the relative ease of securing funds from the government.
(iv) When foreign collaboration is involved, it is not improbable that the collaborator already protects his financial interest through inflated prices for the construction, equipment, and technology inputs, thanks to the technical inexpertise of the host government to detect and prevent such practices.

Third, public entrepreneurship is influenced by a multi-enterprise approach, transcending the requirements specific to a given enterprise. While defensible on grounds of an investment package, this might often upset the commercial viability of certain enterprises.

Fourth, the enterprise is hardly under fear of bankruptcy. It is insulated from 'uncertainty' in capital markets. For, in most cases, the government is the source of equity as well as loan capital (directly or under guarantee), and ultimately bails out an enterprise in hard times.

Finally, entrepreneurial decisions in public enterprises are liable to be politicised in two ways – through the intrusion of political considerations in implementing an 'approved' social interest such as the development of a backward region, and through the subtle impact of the personal interests of those in authority.

It is possible that the quality of public entrepreneurship improves where an established public enterprise undertakes expansions, rather than the government, as in the UK or Italy. In developing countries the initiative generally comes from the government even when it is a public enterprise that, technically, undertakes a new project; for the outlays are very large and have serious implications of foreign exchange and domestic resource mobilisation. Experience shows that entrepreneurship by a public enterprise is more competent when it is an activity-specific enterprise (like the British Steel Corporation) or a sectoral holding company (like the National Fertiliser Corportion of Pakistan Ltd) than when it is a heterogeneous multisectoral corporation (like the Industrial and Commercial Development Corporation Ltd of Kenya). When a finance corporation takes the entrepreneurial initiative, the quality of entrepreneurship is likely to improve if there is significant participation by private investors in a given venture.[8]

To conclude, the deficiencies in governmental entrepreneurship are the combined effect of developmental compulsions and implementational shortcomings. Even when the former are treated as given constraints, there ought to be ways of minimising the latter, without affecting the goals of plan strategy. In analysing the problem, the first, though difficult, step would be to isolate the two categories of effects, without exaggerating the impacts of plan strategy.

ORGANISATIONAL UNIFICATION

One of the basic features of the evolution of public enterprise has been the unification of a wide range of operations within a single enterprise. The techniques and extent of the unification substantially differ from the broadly market-orientated trends in the private sector. To the extent that transactions are unified within a firm so that it represents no larger than the size necessary to be economical, the position would be similar in both sectors. In many cases, however, the unification goes beyond that point and has a deleterious effect on the economics of the enterprise.

The term, organisational unification, is conceptually different from centralisation, in government, of enterprise decisions, though the two can go together. Even unitary structures can be accompanied by high decisional concentration in government, as in Portugal, Nigeria, and India; while unified structures, generally conducive to such centralisation, are not necessarily so in every case, as Sweden and Austria illustrate.[9] It is the way in which the relationships between the government and an enterprise are formulated and followed that determines the nature and extent of centralisation.[10]

Autonomous enterprises, which came out of departmental origins, represent a special case of managerial centralisation in government, as illustrated by the Electricity Boards in India and the Post Office in the UK.[11]

Typology of unification

The organisational unification can be classified under three heads: (a) at the enterprise level; (b) at the sectoral level; and (c) at the overall level. (a) and (b) can go together where a single public enterprise occupies a whole sector, for example, the National Coal Board of the UK – recently renamed as the British Coal Corporation – and Nigerian Airways.

At the enterprise level

This represents large-scale unification of operations or transactions within an enterprise. The repertoire of public enterprises is full of such instances. The preference for large units is best illustrated by Hungary, where about two-thirds of all industrial employment was in enterprises exceeding the 2,000 worker level in 1979, representing a far higher dominance of large, multiplant enterprises than in Western Europe. Concentration in the largest three enterprises was about 75 per cent in twenty-four out of sixty-one sectors of activity; it was 100 per cent in seventeen.[12] (The government has since discouraged growth in largeness; and there has been 'break-up of some existing large companies into smaller units'.[13] Emphasis on breaking large units into smaller ones is also illustrated by Österreichische Industrieverwaltungs AG (OIAG), the umbrella apex of Austria's public enterprises.

There are two kinds of unification under this head: (i) where it refers to a broadly similar activity, for example, the Kenya Meat Commission, and (ii) where it is composed of diverse operations or serves quite different product markets, for example, the Hindustan Machine Tools Ltd (in India), which produces machine tools and wrist-watches, whose technological interrelationships are at best nominal; ANCAP (Administration National de Combustibles, Alcohol y Portland) in Uruguay, producing combustibles, alcohol, cement and chemicals; and the Port Authority of New York and New Jersey, managing tunnels and bridges, three major airports (John F. Kennedy, La Guardia and Newark), bus facilities, PATH railway, marine terminals (New York and New Jersey) and the World Trade Center. Ghana Industrial Holding Corporation, till 1986, was a single gigantic multisectoral enterprise. It has become a holding complex since.

At the sectoral level

Here the unification of operations has a sectoral context and can be of three kinds:

A monolithic enterprise covering the entire public sector activity in a given line:

For example, the British Steel Corporation, Electricité de France, and Bharat Heavy Electricals Ltd in India into which even the far earlier Heavy Electricals Ltd was merged.

A sectoral holding company:

This differs from the above in that the operations are organised primarily in legally distinctive companies but are tied together into a holding structure, for example, the Kenya Tourist Development Corporation, and Comision Nacional de la Industria Azucarera (in Mexico).

Two subdivisions are possible under this head, on the criterion of coverage: a holding company that does not cover the entire public sector activity in a given line, for example, the Fertilizer Corporation of India, and one that does, for example, the Mineral Development Corporation of Zambia (recently renamed as Zambia Consolidated Copper Mines Ltd). The latter category seems to be the more common or preferred category, towards which the former generally moves over time, as illustrated by the Steel Authority of India Ltd, into which Hindustan Steel Ltd and Bokaro Steel Ltd were amalgamated in 1973.

Also two subdivisions are possible on grounds of activity: a holding company that has no operations of its own and one that has. For instance, the Kenya Tea Development Authority not only holds equity in some forty tea manufacturing companies, but undertakes leaf buying, and marketing; whereas the National Fertiliser Corporation of Pakistan has only 'holding' functions.

Yet another distinction is possible as between a holding company that is wholly confined to a given sector, as in the examples cited above, and one that is predominantly so. For example, Ente Nazionale Idocarbuni of Italy is essentially an energy enterprise but it has some textile companies in its complex; Salzgitter AG of West Germany, mainly a steel complex, has some energy and trade units too; and Renault of France, mainly an automobile company, has some real estate, machine tools, and agricultural machinery subsidiaries (see Appendix 2.1A). Holding apexes that are not identified with a single major sector come under the following category.

A multisectoral holding company:

A common phenomenon, this is broadly divisible into two categories: a financing institution which, by virtue of its functions, happens to hold shares in a variety of companies and has no particular reason to hold on to any of them; and an apex which holds equity in companies otherwise than as a financial institution. National Finaciera of Mexico (whose origins of equity holding lay in the conversion of loans not recovered into shares),[14] the National Enterprise Board in the UK and the Industrial Development Bank of Kenya, belong to the former kind, while Istituto per la Ricostruzione Industriale (IRI) of Italy (see Appendix 2.1B), the National Development Corporation (in Tanzania), Instituto Nacional de Industria (INI) of Spain, Pertamina of Indonesia, Industrial Development Corporation of Zambia, and Pernas of Malaysia belong to the latter kind.

At the overall level

Though strictly similar to the previous category, an organisational unification that covers almost the entire public enterprise in the country merits being noted as a distinctive category. For instance, Zambia has ZIMCO (Zambia Industrial and Mineral Corporation) which is the pyramidical apex for all the public enterprises, including large subholding companies like the Industrial Development Corporation, Zambia Consolidated Copper Mines Ltd, and the National Import and Export Corporation Ltd. Similarly overall is the coverage of OIAG of Austria, with almost all public enterprises – iron and steel, coal, engineering, oil and natural gas, chemicals, non-ferrous metals, and other industries – coming under it. Guyana covers most of its public enterprise under two holding companies, GUYSTAC (diversely multisectoral) and BIDCO (mineral). Malawi's Industrial Development Corporation and the Seychelles National Development Corporation are near examples. The recently revived Corporacion Nacional de Empresas Publicas of Argentina also merits mention under this category. The Administrative Reforms Committee in Sri Lanka recommended in 1988 the formation of a Public Investment Corporation as a holding complex for all non-departmental, non-infrastructural enterprises in the public sector. In fact there will be 'no parent ministry' 'for a public commercial enterprise' (Report no. 10, Colombo, p. 25).

It is not possible to associate a country with any exclusive pattern of unification, except for such somewhat obvious cases as Zambia and Austria, Guyana and the Seychelles. However, there can be some generalisation on the broad approach of the government in most cases. The unitary approach, that is, the non-holding complex type, is, by and large, characteristic of the UK, France, Sri Lanka, India, Fiji, Jamaica, Barbados, Somalia, Thailand, Nepal, Nigeria, and so on, though several enterprises are over-large and monolithic. Sectoral holding companies have been popular in Iraq, Syria, Guinea, Sudan, Egypt, Bangladesh, Pakistan, Tanzania, and Italy; and overall holding companies in Uganda, Sweden, and Malawi. Within such general biases there are some significant exceptions. For example, the UK had some holding company elements in the National Bus Company, National Freight Corporation, and National Enterprise Board; and some major monolithic public enterprises have a few 'inherited' subsidiaries, or have formed subsidiaries for 'non-mainstream' businesses (for example, the British Steel Corporation)[15] or for activities conducted in foreign countries, or in respect of functions likely to be privatised in the first instance, for example, British Rail. India, despite a unitary approach, has some large sectoral holding complexes: the Steel Authority of India Ltd, Industrial Development Bank for medium- and long-term financing, and National Textile Corporation Ltd. Unlike in coal and steel, the oil enterprises remain separate entities, for example, the Oil Corporation of India Ltd, Hindustan Petroleum Corporation Ltd, Bharat

Petroleum Co. Ltd, and Madras Refineries Ltd; and the nationalised banks remain as separate entities too. Spain, despite the large holding company bias reflected in INI, has several largely unitary enterprises like the Telephone Co., Tobacco Co., and Petro Liber, directly looked after by the Direccio General del Patrimonio in the Ministry of Finance[16] (see Appendix 2.2A). France, with generally unitary enterprises, has an extremely large Institute for Industrial Development. Canada's large public enterprise sector has several islands of holding companies, some very large indeed, like Canadian National Railways with many sub-subsidiaries, some of which have their own subsidiaries, with sub-subsidiaries in some cases, for example, Canadian National Transport Corporation. The crown corporation structure of Canada is interesting, as shown in Appendix 2.2B.

Three conclusions emerge:

(a) Most countries present a variety of unification patterns, ranging between the unitary and the multisectoral types (see Appendix 2.3 for public enterprise structures in Pakistan, Tanzania, and Kenya.)
(b) Public enterprises have been very large, in broad comparison with private enterprises; and there has been an unmistakable trend towards organisational unification of some kind, more deliberately than in the private sector.
(c) Bias for the holding company pattern has been ubiquitous in all regions. The Italian IRI has been a stimulant of the bias. Proposals have been aired in the UK in favour of holding company structures,[17] in Portugal (under Decree Law 279/82), Trinidad and Tobago,[18] India,[19] and so on. New holding structures are being created in some countries; while existing holding structures are being dismantled or rationalised in some others like Bangladesh and Sudan.

There was a proposal by the Labour Party Study Group in the early 1970s in favour of establishing a State Holding Company to be entitled the National Enterprise Board:

> The NEB would 'hold' all existing government shares in joint public-private firms, for example, in British Petroleum, Short Brothers, and in companies which are wholly government-owned, such as Rolls Royce. It would be provided with an industrial base at its creation by the take-over of a controlling interest in firms in the growth sectors of industry. It would hold all shares which are acquired in future in return for government financial assistance to individual firms and industries. It is already the policy of the Party that wherever the state puts public money into private industry, it shall take shares in return. If the public sector is to play its full part in overall planning for investment, pricing, and full employment, it is essential that wherever the NEB takes over a company by acquiring shares in it, those shares must be either a total holding, or at least a controlling interest.

(Opposition Green Paper (197?) *The National Enterprise Board: Labour's State Holding Company*, London, p. 12)

Reasons for unification

The reasons why many public enterprises are very large may be examined under two heads: economies of scale, and extra-enterprise objectives.

Economies of scale

The basic purpose of organisation is that the enterprise is as large as is necessary for reaping economies of scale. (Reference may be made to the early works of E.A.G. Robinson, R.H. Coase and Sargant Florence.)[20] When the government organises an activity in the public sector or nationalises an activity, it can create large enough units to be optimal, for example, Electricity Area Boards in the UK removing the diseconomies of hundreds of small distribution units,[21] and Coal India Ltd which would put an end to the unscientific methods of exploitation of 11 railway collieries, 214 coking mines, and 711 non-coking mines.[22] The small business units unified under the State Economic Development Corporations in Malaysia are further examples of economies being reaped in marketing, management, and finance.

While technical economies in production are an incontrovertible justification for unifications, certain other benefits can be claimed as well. Research and development can be organised on an economical scale; a total view of supply and demand in a given activity can be taken; and operations can be most appropriately distributed among the constituent units on the criterion of costs at the margin. The costs of expansions can be minimised through the availability of the managerial and financial resources and entrepreneurial skills which the large/apex unit commands.

These claims call for close circumspection. Beyond the scale economies at the technical level, claims of economy really emanate from the substitution of apex decisions for market forces, and are valid only where the market forces are too weak or undependable. Further, the lower the homogeneity of the products produced, the weaker the scale economies. The precise sources of technical economies have to be identified[23] and sizes beyond which expansion is not necessary for realising them have to be established. The urge to do so had been weak in the generality of public enterprises, either because of the lack of competition, the ultimate corrective, or because of extra-enterprise considerations deemed to be compelling. Where a unitary structure becomes clearly supra-optimal, and is not to be broken into separate units, a holding company structure, within which it is broken into subsidiaries, may offer some relief. This, however, is also a potential source of diseconomies, as the next section shows.

Technical economies are a doubtful explanation in the case of many large monolithic structures. Left to themselves, individual enterprises expand or contract on criteria of optimality, as far as possible, under conditions of competition. On the other hand a unification often lets infra- or supra-optimal units remain, by sheltering them from competition, and brings about allocational inefficiency in the use of resources. There can be an exceptional circumstance. If competition is higly imperfect and does not lead to the evolution of optimal or most economical units, the unification can function as a surrogate for competition and bring about an economical structure of enterprises in the sector concerned – as in the earlier cited examples of British Electricity or Coal India Ltd. But the enterprises ought to be put back into independent status once the required conditions of economical structure are established in the sector of activity. Experience shows that this hardly ever happens; instead, an empire begins to build up, as in the case of Bharat Heavy Electricals Ltd or Hindustan Machine Tools Ltd of India; and not even economical inter-unit reorganisations within the apex take place, as evidenced by the National Textile Corporation Ltd of India.

As regards the benefit of a 'financial blanket' that a large unit or apex provides to the constituent segments of operations, the question arises: is it justifiable to shelter operations that cannot stand on their own feet? There is national advantage in scaling them down or in closing them; but the largeness of the enterprise stands in the way of such a desirable measure.

In brief, scale economies are at a maximum in the case of fairly homogeneous operations in certain sectors, less so in the case of a sectoral holding complex composed of already economical units, and at a minimum in the case of a multisectoral apex or a merely financing complex.

Extra-enterprise considerations

These have constituted an important reason for the evolution of large monolithic or holding complexes, sectoral or multisectoral. The arguments usually advanced in their favour are as follows.

First, that they make possible co-ordination among the operations unified under the apex and can plan the activities in accordance with government policies.[24] This argument is of value in the case of operations whose economical co-ordination is not otherwise likely because of acute market imperfections, as mentioned above. But when it refers to co-ordination in the investment, employment and technology policies of the constituent units, the rationale as well as the criteria of action ought to come from the government and not from the apex, for example, that raising coking coal should be no higher than at a specified rate, or contraction in employment in a unit should not be higher than at a specified rate. In fact, such guidelines ought to be all-industry in nature, inclusive of private enterprises as well, and the government should promote appropriate advisory councils, if necessary, in formulating them.

Second, that the apex board healthily distances the operating units from the government: the ideal in respect of government control should be that it is minimal, consistent with the autonomy that the operating units deserve to have, and not that an intermediate tier should be built up to which to delegate it. At the worst the latter can assume the minister's role to some extent, which parliament would not appreciate, and compound the problems for the operating units flowing from above. (The observations of the UK Select Committee on Nationalised Industries are relevant in this context.)[25]

A peculiar twist to the argument was given in India under a short-lived experiment of making the chairman of the gigantic holding company, Steel Authority of India, ex-officio secretary of the minstry concerned in 1973. Only in a few cases, such as the IRI of Italy and OIAG of Austria, did the government, on the whole, stand away from extending direct control contacts to the subsidiaries, and the latter are allowed to operate almost as if they were private enterprises. Besides the government's extra-enterprise preferences have been laid down in Italy, under the Planning Report of state-holding enterprises for 1987, adding, however, that the operating conditions of a public enterprise must not differ from those of an enterprise operating under market conditions.[26]

The argument that the government finds it easier to control the public enterprise sector through a few large apex points has no intrinsic virtue, for it refers to the machinery of control network, whereas the basic point is that the criteria of control should be postulated, so that the convenience that a few apex units offer becomes a matter of secondary interest. For example, under the pyramidical ZIMCO structure in Zambia under the chairmanship of the president of the country for a long time, a unique form of centralised control evolved itself (see Appendix 2.4).

Third, that large unifications have a strategic national role to play in developing economies: they can minimise the consequences of transnationals' threats to close down certain operations or withdraw certain facilities (of access to inputs or markets) unless over-liberal concessions are conceded to them. Large public enterprises can meet such challenges out of their strength; the costs may be high, but they are likely to be the minimum necessary national costs of development. Experience shows that 'balanced' solutions have been reached in most countries through the formation of joint ventures between a large or apex public enterprise in the host country, like the Industrial Development Corporation Ltd of Zambia, and foreign capital.

On close examination this argument relates to the strength of a developmental corporation in promoting new enterprises, rather than to the holding of such creations under its umbrella for all time. The National Development Corporation of Tanzania is a good example in this context. It promoted enterprises but hived them off from time to time (see Appendix 2.5).

Fourth, that large organisations can, through strength, explore export markets, implement price reductions, and bear losses on export and foreign exchange losses more easily than small individual units can. This is not a conclusive argument. The services involved can be organised through a specialist export organisation (probably sectoral) that might offer higher benefits due to its scale economies, and can be acquired by any enterprise – even a private enterprise – as needed and across the market.

Finally, that scarce managerial resources can be most economically used under the pattern of large units: the economy of managerial overheads would be positive if it is not countervailed by the many sources of diseconomy associated with large units, outlined in the next section. Instances of small, multisectoral units being unified into holding companies, for example, the State Economic Development Corporations of Malaysia, are on the border line. The main value of the apex in such cases lies in its functions which managers of small units may not be able to fulfil with economy and efficiency. But the subsidiaries should be hived off soon enough. It is also claimed, with some justification, that a large apex can avoid the situation of wasteful bids by operating units for managers and equipment, which are in short supply.

There is a 'managerial' reason why public enterprises (like the Co-operative Wholesale Establishment in Sri Lanka and several in the Philippines) are tempted to set up subsidiaries. The latter are not vulnerable to the cumbersome control measures that the parent is under. For good or for bad, the managers can enjoy autonomy denied to them in respect of operations, when conducted by the subsidiaries.

Costs of unification

Large sizes in the public enterprise sector have entailed costs in the following ways:

(a) In several cases technical economies of largeness have been nominal and countered by managerial diseconomies characteristic of over-centralisation of the decisional process, for example, in Iraq,[27] and overstandardisation of operating and managerial procedures.
(b) Large sizes have stifled managerial growth and limited the cost and revenue benefits of managerial initiative. For example, at the firm level little autonomy is retained under the system of enterprise unions in Syria; and the 'group aproach' of the Ghana Industrial Holding Company (GIHOC) in Ghana has not succeeded, as hoped, in offering employees greater opportunities of development and for sharing experiences.
(c) Powerful all-enterprise unions affect desirable developments in promoting productivity-linked wage systems at the plant level and in introducing employee emoluments on local or operating-plant criteria.

Instead, overall agreements tend to be arrived at to the disadvantage of the enterprise and the consumer, as illustrated by the Post Office strike in the UK in 1988, which sought to blanketise the wage additions deemed necessary by management in a few centres for attracting the required number of workers.[28]

There is evidence to suggest that the managers in charge of the sub-units of an overlarge enterprise are generally aggrieved when compelled to exceed their budgets because of 'an expensive centrally determined wage deal which had been imposed on them'.[29] Further, there is a perceptible 'strike proneness' in large plants (as per studies in the UK),[30] as well as a trend towards adversarial relationships between management and labour.[31]

(d) Errors of decision are possible with a pattern of organisation that provides no alternative to the 'administered' decisional process in large units. Further, the apex level develops a bureaucratic interest in disfavouring changes in a line of thinking; and new errors are often likely to cover up, or follow, earlier decisions which yielded poor results.

(e) Every large enterprise may not, for that reason alone, be a monopoly. Where it is, through its total control or dominant share of the market, disadvantages of cross-subsidisation emerge.[32] Later chapters will discuss the implications of monopoly in public enterprise.

There are many huge conglomerates in the private sector, for example, British American Tobacco Industries (whose multisectoral spread is shown in Appendix 2.6). But there are important differences. First, the essential reason for their largeness is financial, with 'little industry logic', and the subsidiaries are 'put together more by size than by purpose'; the hope of high profit, whatever the means of industrial organisation, is basic. Second, their accountability is to the shareholders for whom increased profit is the goal. Third, the top executives have high personal gains through enlarged size and periodic take-over bids. These considerations are of little significance in the case of public enterprise, where the government is expected to take ownership initiative and size decisions on clear social cost-benefit considerations. Even the aim of profit should be consistent with, and not independent of, the cost structures of the enterprises.

Some of the costs of unification have, in the absence of corrective organisational changes, assumed the character of intrinsic costs of public enterprise.

Conclusion

Large units, particularly holding complexes, have been common in the public sector – in both developed and developing countries – for a variety of reasons, for example:

(i) The idea that an entire industry brought into or set up in the public sector should be under one apex – as in the UK where the Transport Commission under the 1947 Transport Act was perhaps the most curious amalgam, heading the Docks and Inland Waterways Executive, Road Transport Executive, The London Transport Executive, the Hotels Executive, and the Railway Executive.
(ii) Governmental unpreparedness for a sudden measure of large-scale nationalisations, for example, in Pakistan, Bangladesh, Sudan, and Egypt.
(iii) The intention to set up a promotional agency, technically distanced from the ministries, for example, in Tanzania, Uganda, and Kenya; also in the UK which set up the National Enterprise Board.
(iv) The need to establish an umbrella for a large number of 'sick' units bailed out through nationalisation – possibly for an orderly reversion to the private sector, for example, IRI of Italy, the National Textile Corporation Ltd. in India, and GIHOC of Ghana.
(v) Hopes of economy in operations and an undefined or ill-defined 'convenience' as an organisation.

The last is a residuary cause, relevant to several monolithic and holding company structures, the newly-emerging ones in particular.

COMPARATIVE ADVANTAGE IN REALITY

Though the concept of the comparative advantage of public enterprise is traceable in official policy enunciations in some countries,[33] it did not receive effective attention in practice, with the result that even the enterprises credited with comparative advantage at the stage of investment decision, did not enjoy it when they came into being.

There are three categories of reasons:

(a) Certain intrinsic costs of public enterprise were overlooked at the point of decision to set up a public enterprise.
(b) The social returns realised from public enterprise were far lower than were originally estimated.
(c) The 'learning curve' proved to be far longer than anticipated in many cases.

Intrinsic costs of public enterprise

During the earliest decisions on public enterprise it was not realised that it intrinsically entailed certain costs, the kind to which private enterprise was not exposed. As experience revealed them, sporadic attempts were made, with limited or no success, to deal with the causes. The costs may be analysed under five heads: (i) costs of government involvement in creating a public enterprise and thereafter; (ii) costs of excessive unification; (iii) costs of political and parliamentary scrutiny; (iv) costs of public audit; and (v) costs of public managerial behaviour.

Costs of government involvement

The government involves itself in the decision to establish a public enterprise – almost exclusively as an entrepreneur in the case of a new establishment, and significantly as owner-cum-entrepreneur in the case of an expansion on the part of an existing enterprise or of a contraction or liquidation of an existing capacity. The characteristics of public entrepreneurship presented in the first section of this chapter suggest that there are costs which flow from the defectiveness of an investment decision and the dilatory and non-professional processing of investment approval (see chapter 4). Governments have generally been concerned more with 'the form' of an investment proposal than with its 'content'.[34] The capital–output ratio exceeds the estimated level, there is serious lock-up of capital due to time overruns, and heavy overruns occur in project costs. Appendix 2.7 illustrates the alarming cost implications of entrepreneurial decision and implementation in the public sector in India, with reference to 290 major projects and brings out the 'capital waste' that has occurred.

Turning to post-investment matters, the government involves itself in the decisional/managerial behaviour of a public enterprise in two ways: as owner and as government. Involvement on grounds of ownership is an ownership prerogative; but it manifests itself in a manner that proves relatively costly.[35] Government approval of the management's proposals and issuance of operational guidelines can be a 'painfully slow' process[36] and uncoordinated in intragovernment parlance. All this implies an element of cost in the way the legitimate ownership interest manifests itself in public enterprise.

The managerial involvement of the government as government ought to be common, in theory, in both public and private sectors, but it is confined in the latter case to the written word of the law, whereas it transcends it in many ways in public enterprise (as chapter 13 elaborates). In brief, government interventions tend to get internalised into, and (mis)taken for, managerial behaviour. Aimed as a remedy for 'market failure', they have introduced costs of 'government failure'.

Costs of excessive unification

The nature and origins of these costs were set out in the previous section.

Costs of political and parliamentary scrutiny

Public enterprise operations come within the constraints of parliamentary accountability, for constitutional reasons. Their finances are a matter of interest to parliament, so are their physical operations, especially those containing 'public' elements, and labour matters. The impact on the enterprises is a function of how extensively parliament wields its control channels such as the question hour, debate, motions, bills, special committees, and direct contacts with, and visits to, the enterprise.[37] Parliamentary interface with public enterprise can 'unnerve' the managers – to quote Herbert Morrison – and 'tend to develop in them a rather red-tapeish, unadventurous and conventionally civil service frame of mind',[38] the more so in developing countries. Public enterprises sustain costs of suppressed managerial initiative and risk-taking, particularly when parliament assumes a 'monitoring' role.

In addition to the constitutionally valid concerns of parliament with public enterprise, there often occur politicised interventions of an unstructured nature. These could be costly to public enterprise, as the Inquiry Commissions on Nigerial railway, airway, port, and electricity enterprises vividly brought out in the 1960s (see chapter 13).

Further, there are cases of open political scrutiny of public enterprise operations. In Tanzania, for example, the ruling Party, Chama Cha Mapundizi (CCM), is empowered to assume some role in the scrutiny of public enterprise activities; and in Kenya the single party, Kenya African National Union (KANU), has recently been declared as superior to the country's parliament.

Costs of public audit

Barring a few countries like the UK, public enterprises come within the audit purview of the Auditor-General (AG). He usually extends his 'regularity' audit to 'propriety' audit. The Comptroller and Auditor-General (CAG) has 'test audit' powers in India in the case of enterprises he does not wholly audit. The Financial Administration Act of Canada envisages the AG as the auditor or joint auditor of each parent crown corporation from 1989, unless he waives the appointment. Even in the UK, a private member's Parliamentary Control of Expenditure (Reform) Bill in 1983 aimed to give the CAG 'inspection rights to carry out the economy, efficiency and effectiveness examinations of the use of resources by nationalised industries'. It was not passed; but the view exists in some quarters that the CAG would be an appropriate agency for efficiency audit.[39]

The AG's audit is not merely an external audit but one loaded with potential for direct parliamentary notice, often through the Public Accounts Committee or any Select Committee on Public Enterprises. Two dangers exist. There develops an uneasy interface between public enterprise managers and their political masters; and there obtains an undue focus on mistakes or risks that failed, while risks that succeeded are not adequately considered for the sake of a comprehensive perspective. The managers, therefore, act constantly under a fear complex, begin to place value on not being positive lest they commit a mistake and invite criticism, and on acting in conformity with political pressures. Successful business does not exclude a risk that fails but consists of more successful risks than unsuccessful risks. This principle would soon be forgotten. Further, there will be an attempt to involve as many governmental agencies as possible in decision-making, so that the managers cannot be singled out for a faulty decision. On the whole, managerial initiative tends to be dampened. Herein lies an implicit intrinsic cost.

Costs of public managerial behaviour

Though non-departmental forms of public enterprise have been brought into existence on the ground that they would be free from Civil Service rules and departmental procedures, history is replete with instances of progressive application of departmental routines to their managerial processes. The enterprises have also been shackled by excessive standardisation in respect of input acquisition and hiring and firing, often in the name of fairness in public-sector transactions.

In effect, public enterprise managers lack the autonomy that their counterparts in the private sector possess. It is sometimes argued that there is little difference between the government's managerial impacts on public enterprise managers and those of a large private sector apex board on the managers within its complex. There is an asymmetry. In the latter case the goals are clearly laid down and are generally financial in nature; both control and evaluation are goal-orientated and not politically motivated; appropriateness of means in a given situation has a premium over standardisation and precedent; and conditions are created for the availability of all resources needed for attaining the goal. In all these respects public enterprise managers are at a disadvantage; and improvements in the situation have generally been marginal in effect. No wonder, it is for this reason that, though the most efficient professional managers are in the public sector, in countries like Nepal, public enterprise operations do not reflect their efficiency.[40]

The institutional constraints on managerial behaviour were not dispassionately evaluated at the time public enterprises came into being. These have been simplified sometimes into poor accounting skills or technical ability, though these, no doubt, persisted and aggravated the problem in the least developed countries.

Attempts to reduce the unseen costs of inhibited managerial behaviour have not attained enough success in the cross-section of developing countries.

Social returns actually realised

The second reason why the comparative advantage of many public enterprises has been lower in practice than was assumed at the time of their establishment is that the social returns actually realised fell far short of the anticipated levels. Assuming that the original decision in their favour was justified, their continued operations would not be, in this circumstance. For example, not only have many Zambian public enterprises huge accumulated losses, but in 'social terms the picture is not different'.[41] In Kenya, the National Construction Corporation, marked by heavy losses, did not develop a strong local contracting class either, as intended;[42] and some other public enterprises led to 'some de-Kenyanisation of the economy, which was not the original intent'.[43] In India, one of the objectives of Bharat Heavy Plate and Vessels Ltd is to develop export markets with a view to earning foreign exchange. 'Precious little has been done in this field.'[44] It is said of the Food Production Corporation in Ghana that 'all in all the operations have made no impact on the economy of the country'.[45]

An interesting illustration may be cited from the UK. The low net revenue target of 3 per cent on assets of the Forestry Commission is sought to be justified by arguments of social returns which 'appear increasingly dated'.[46] Thus a low financial return is earned along with uncertain social returns, contrary to original expectations.

Another version of the disadvantage is that whatever social returns are realised, are realised at higher costs, and therefore with lower financial returns than were considered acceptable when the enterprise was set up. And attempts are usually made to explain away the low financial results by eulogising the social returns, the more easily the less precise the latter. The Harnai Woollen Mills established in the underdeveloped region of Baluchistan and the Lakarna Sugar Mills set up in a region which provides too little sugar cane for crushing are examples from Pakistan;[47] the large sports stadium at Volta[48] and the glass factory at Aboso, from Ghana;[49] and the classic Bura Irrigation Project, from Kenya.

This explanation may be illustrated by referring to Figure 1.5 in Chapter 1. The actual combination of financial and social returns might turn out to be E, rather than A, which was originally expected.

The learning curve

Assuming that the estimate of social and financial returns was reasonably correct at the point of establishing a public enterprise, and that their desired combination was consciously determined, developing countries have faced the problem of the learning curve having been far longer than expected. The reasons were outlined in the section dealing with public entrepreneurship. The problem was partly the result of over-ambitious plan targets in many cases.[50] There was a 'crowding-out' effect in developmental activity. It is important to note that the financial consequences devolved disproportionately on public enterprises, since the more difficult of the industrial projects had to be in the public sector. These enterprises began to carry in their books certain costs of national gestation in development, for which adequate provision had not been conceived of at the time of project decision.

The reference here is not to the expected costs of initiating a development, which implicitly go into the estimates of social and financial returns (for example, curve *R*, in Figure 1.5), but to unanticipated increases in them.

To sum up the argument: governments, in general, have not evaluated the comparative advantage of a public enterprise properly and from time to time. While in theory many enterprises had justification for being in the public sector to start with, not all of them retained it even as they came into being, and some may have lost it over time. The concept has not been upheld in the dynamic sense.

At this point it is relevant to comment on the sectoral demarcations between public and private enterprises announced by several governments, first by India in 1948 (revised in 1956), and in due course by Trinidad and Tobago, Ghana, Uganda, Pakistan, and so on (see Appendix 2.8). They broadly implied that investments in certain sectors of activity were reserved for the government, for example, railways or heavy chemicals; some were open to both public and private investment, and some were nearly the preserve of private enterprise. These were acclaimed as a source of clarity on government policy. But how far were they justified on grounds of comparative advantage?

There are three problems. First, the sectoral demarcations may have appeared to agree with the circumstances of the investment and product markets at the time they were announced. Over time these must have altered, so much so that unless the demarcations were constantly revised they would have the disadvantage of being too static.[51]

Second, it is not necessarily in terms of a whole sector of activity that the comparative advantage of public enterprise is to be, or can be, established. It can vary from high to low, from region to region, scale to scale, period to period, and in terms of technology, even within a given sector.

Third, if strictly followed, the demarcations discourage managerial motivation for certain backward and forward integrations of an intersectoral nature, with corresponding losses of potential economies of industrial organisation.

A survey of the sectoral composition of public enterprise in many countries suggests that it is wide of the original lines of demarcation. (There is practically no sector of activity which public enterprise has not entered in India, for example, or in Pakistan or Kenya.) There must have been justifying reasons in some cases, for example, market differentiation in which private investors are not interested, the bailing out of a 'sick' unit, regulation of the output and price policies of private enterprises, or the achievement of some desired social returns. When these are the reasons, they constitute one version of the concept of comparative advantage in favour of the enterprises concerned, and not necessarily whole sectors of activity, provided that the combination of social and financial returns in each case is calculated to be superior to what an alternative form of enterprise might produce.

A concluding observation. In this section social returns as a criterion were taken as 'given'. Questions were not raised as to whether and how far a social return should be pursued through a public enterprise and as to whether and how far a social return had intrinsic justification in the situation of the national economy. The former question will be considered in the next chapter, while the latter is strictly outside the purview of this book, except for limited references at certain points of discussion. Another version of the latter question is whether an investment which no private enterprise would touch at all, and for that reason at once falls within the comparative-advantage range of public enterprise, is at all worth undertaking, taking into account the opportunity costs of the funds involved for the national economy as a whole. There will be some reference to this in chapter 4.

CONCLUSION

Chapters 1 and 2 suggest the following conclusions:

(a) On grounds of pragmatic choice, there is a clear case for public enterprise in specific situations,[52] but its potential as a means to maximise national well-being needs to be evaluated from time to time in an enterprise-specific manner. This is rarely done; and the idea that a public enterprise was a means to the end of national well-being slipped in practice in most countries, if for no other reason than governmental inertia or an undeclared ideological stance.

(b) The theoretical advantages of many public enterprises have been seriously affected by the way in which they were conceived of and organised. Yet governments have not succeeded in taking sufficient action to reverse the effects for nearly four post-war decades.

Later chapters consider in detail the factors that have affected the rationale of many a public enterprise, and the ineffectiveness of techniques employed by governments to deal with them.

APPENDIX 2.1A

Figure 2.1 The structure of Renault (France) (as on 31 December 1978)

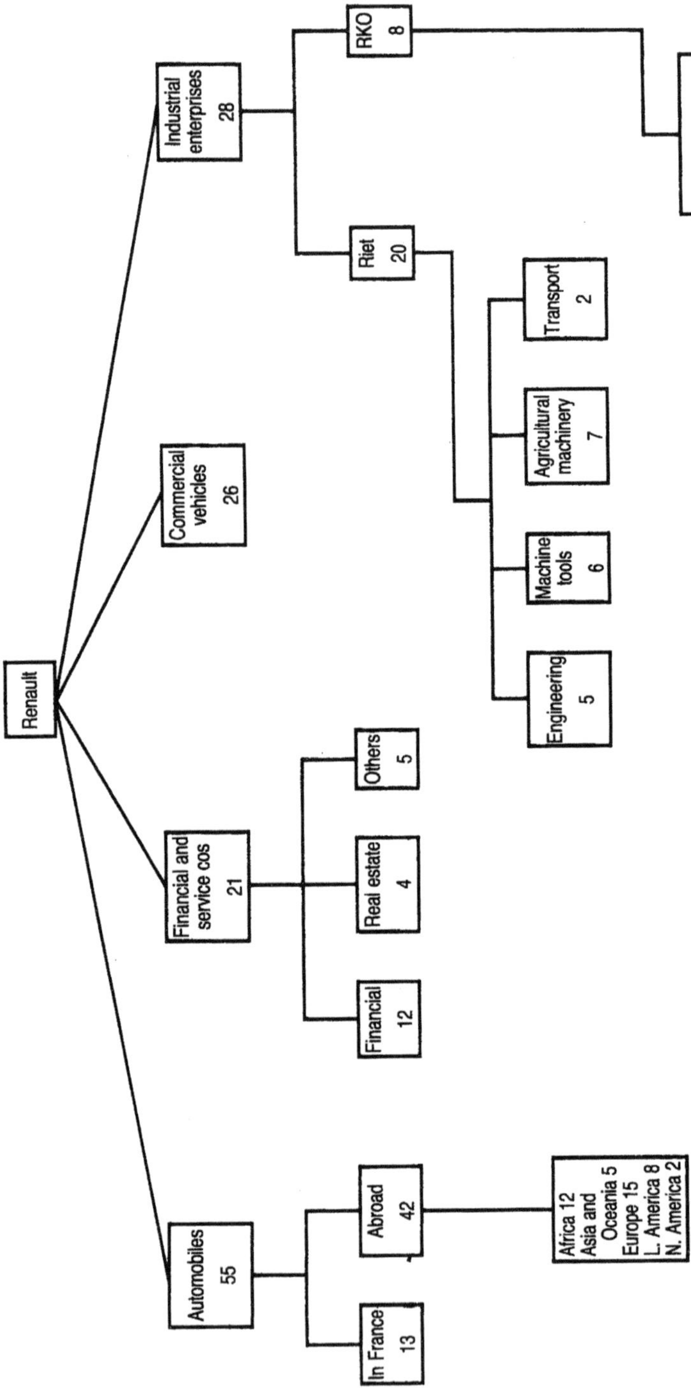

Note: The numbers indicate the number of subsidiary companies.

APPENDIX 2.1B

Table 2.1 The IRI holding complex (1987)

Sub-holding company	*IRI's equity (%)*	*No. of subsidiaries (held by IRI group)*			
		100% equity	*50–100%**	*Less than 50%*	*Total*
1. Banca Commerciale Italiana	59	2	5	4	11
2. Credito Italiana	67	1	3	6	10
3. Banco de Roma	77	2	1	5	8
4. Banco di Santa Spirito	86	1	–	–	1
5. COFIRI	90**	–	1	–	1
6. SIFA	60	–	–	–	–
7. FINSIDER	99.82	26	9	–	35
8. FINMECCANICA	99.99	15	1	–	16
9. STET	79	26	6	1	33
10. FINMARE	99.98	15	1	–	16
11. ITALSTAT	99.99	23	17	–	40
12. SME	64	8	2	–	10
13. SOFIN	100	11	7	4	22
14. FINSIEL	83	5	5	2	12
15. SPI	95***	–	2	2	4
16. FINCANTIERI	99.99	4	5	–	9
17. ALITALIA	56	3	4	–	7
18. RAI	99.55	4	1	–	5
19. Training		1	1	–	2
20. Others		3	1	–	4
		150	72	24	246

Source: Istituto per la Recostruzione Industriale (IRI), *1987 Annual Report*, Rome.

* Mostly 90 to 99.99%.
** By IRI family.
*** SOFIN 5 %.

APPENDIX 2.2A

Table 2.2 The structure of public enterprise in Spain

Three holding complexes:	
National Institute for Industry (INI)	189 subsidiaries
National Hydrocarbons Institute (INH)	28
Directorate of State Property	81
Unitary enterprises reporting directly to a ministry	114
Total	412

Source: CEEP (1984) *Public Enterprise in the European Economic Community.*

APPENDIX 2.2B Non-departmental Crown Corporations in Canada (1983)

There were thirty-eight unitary enterprises and fourteen holding complexes. The latter together held 100 per cent interest in 125 companies, 50 to 99 per cent in 33 companies, and less than 50 per cent in 141 companies.

For example, Petro Canada family included 57 fully-owned companies, 678 with significant holdings (near or above 50 per cent), and 19 with less than 5 per cent holding. On the whole the complex covered 144 companies.

Canadian National Railway Company had five subholding companies of which three subsidiaries had their own subsidiaries. On the whole the complex covered sixty-five companies.

Source: Volume III, The President of the Treasury Board (1988) *Annual Report to Parliament on Crown Corporations and Other Canadian Government Interests of Canada,* Ottawa, pp. 347–54.

APPENDIX 2.3 Some public enterprise structures in Pakistan, Tanzania, and Kenya

Table 2.3 Public enterprise in Pakistan (1986–7)

Public enterprise in the manufacturing sector was composed of holding companies as follows, in 1986–7:

Holding company	*No. of subsidiaries*
Federal Chemical and Ceramics Corporation Ltd	14
National Fertilizer Corporation Ltd	6
Pakistan Automobile Corporation Ltd	12
Pakistan Industrial Development Corporation Ltd	9
State Cement Corporation Ltd	13
State Engineering Corporation Ltd	11
State Petroleum Refining and Petrochemical Corporation Ltd	3

Source: Annual Report 1986–87, vol. I, *Public Sector Industries*, Ministry of Production, Experts Advisory Cell, Islamabad, 1988.

Most of the non-manufacturing public enterprises were unitary enterprises. Among them was the huge monolithic, Water and Power Development Authority.

Table 2.4 The organisational structure of public enterprise in Tanzania (1985)

Sector	*Unitary enterprises*	*Holding companies*	*No. of subsidiaries*
Finance	Central Bank of Tanzania	National Bank of Commerce	1
	The Rural Dev. Bank	The Investment Bank	1
		The Housing Bank	1
		National Ins. Corp.	1

Sector	*Unitary enterprises*	*Holding companies*	*No. of subsidiaries*
Trade	Board of External Trade	Board of Internal Trade	28
	National Shipping Agency	State Motor Corp.	
Industries	The Cigarette Co. Ltd	National Dev. Corp.	18
	The Industries Studies & Counselling Organisation	National Textile Corp.	14
		National Chemical Industries Ltd	10
	The Industrial Research & Dev. Organisation	The Savings Corp.	11
		The Leather Associated Industries Ltd	6
		The Breweries Ltd	1
		Small Industries Dev. Organisation	1
		The Karatasi Associated Industries Ltd	6
Lands		National Housing Corp.	1
National Resources & Tourism	The Fisheries Corp.	The Wood Industry Corp.	13
	Ngorongoro Conservation Authority	The Tourist Corporation	7
	The National Parks Company		
	The Wildlife Corp.		
Minerals		State Mining Corporation	7
Water and Energy	The Electric Supplies Company	The Petroleum Dev. Corporation	5
	Rufiji Basin Dev. Authority		
	Urban Water Dev. Authority		
Livestock		The Livestock Dev. Authority	6
Agriculture	The Pyrethrum Board	The Tea Authority	2
	Central Agricultural Products Export Corp.	The Sisal Authority	8
	The Cotton Authority	Cotton Authority of Tanzania	3
	Multipurpose Oilseed Processing Co. Ltd	Cashewnut Authority of Tanzania	2
	Uyole Agricultural Corporation	National Milling Corp.	3
		The Tobacco Authority	1
		Sugar Development Authority	4
		National Agriculture & Food Corp.	20
Works	Mwananchi Engineering & Construction Co.		
	National Estate & Designing Co. Ltd		
Communications & Transport	The Railway Corp.	National Transport Co.	11
	Air Tanzania Corp.		
	The Harbours Authority		
	Posts & Telecommunications		

Figure 2.2 Some holding company unifications in Kenya (1987)

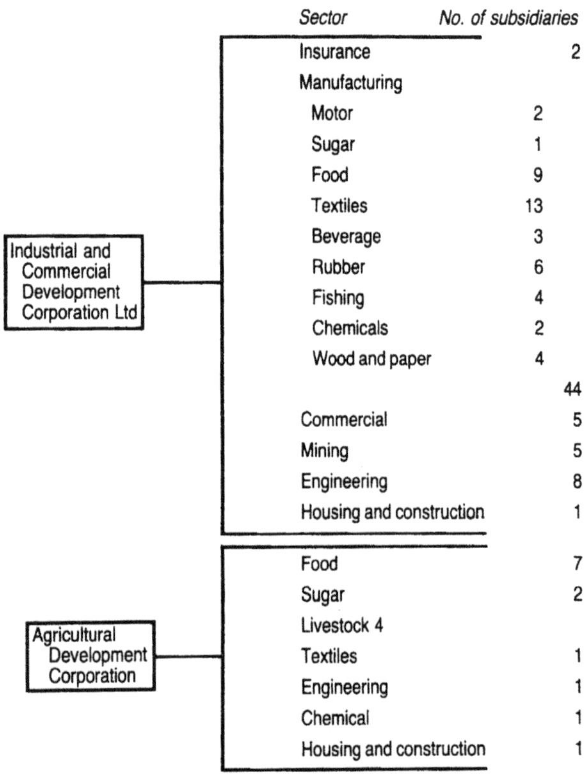

APPENDIX 2.4 ZIMCO (Zambia Industrial and Mining Corporation)

Table 2.5 The structure of ZIMCO

1. *Major holding companies*	*No. of subsidiaries*
INDECO	24
Zambia Consolidated Copper Mines	18
National Import & Export Corporation	9
Nitrogen & Chemicals of Zambia	17

2. *Total number of enterprises under ZIMCO*		
First level	36	
Total number of subsidiaries and associated companies	92	
		128
Fully-owned by government		
First level	27	
Second level	59	
Less than fully-owned		
First level	9	
Second level	33	
		128

Source: ZIMCO, *Annual Report 1988*, Lusaka.

The 1988 structure provides a contrast to what prevailed in the mid-1970s. There has been considerable rationalisation, in favour of unitary companies hived out of large subholding complexes, most importantly from INDECO.
The earlier structure is indicated in Figure 2.3.

APPENDIX 2.5 National Development Corporation (of Tanzania): a case of periodic hive-off

The National Development Corporation (of Tanzania) (NDC) was set up in 1965. It took over certain government assets and investments (and loans) in companies. As a developmental agency it had an investment portfolio spread widely over almost all sectors (except transport) in the early years, as illustrated in Figure 2.4.

However, NDC's function was, strictly, to 'develop' and not to hold on to shares in subsidiaries permanently, unlike the Industrial and Commercial Development Corporation (of Kenya). It was required by government directive to transfer certain 'developed' operating subsidiaries to other parastatals from time to time, for example:

In 1973

National Cashew Co. Ltd; Tanit Co. Ltd; Mtwara Cashew Co. Ltd; Tanzania Cashew Machines Ltd; Tanganyika Meerschaum Corp. Ltd; Nyanza Salt Mines (T) Ltd; Tanzania Diamond Cutting Co. Ltd; and Williamson Diamonds Ltd.

In 1974

East African Industries Ltd; Blanket Manufacturers Ltd; Mwanza Textile Mills Ltd; Kilimanjaro Textile Mills Ltd; National Textile Industries Corp. Ltd; Tanzania Bag Corp. Ltd; and Tanganyika Extract Co. Ltd.

Figure 2.3 The structure of Zambia Mining and Industrial Corporation Ltd (ZIMCO) in the mid-1970s

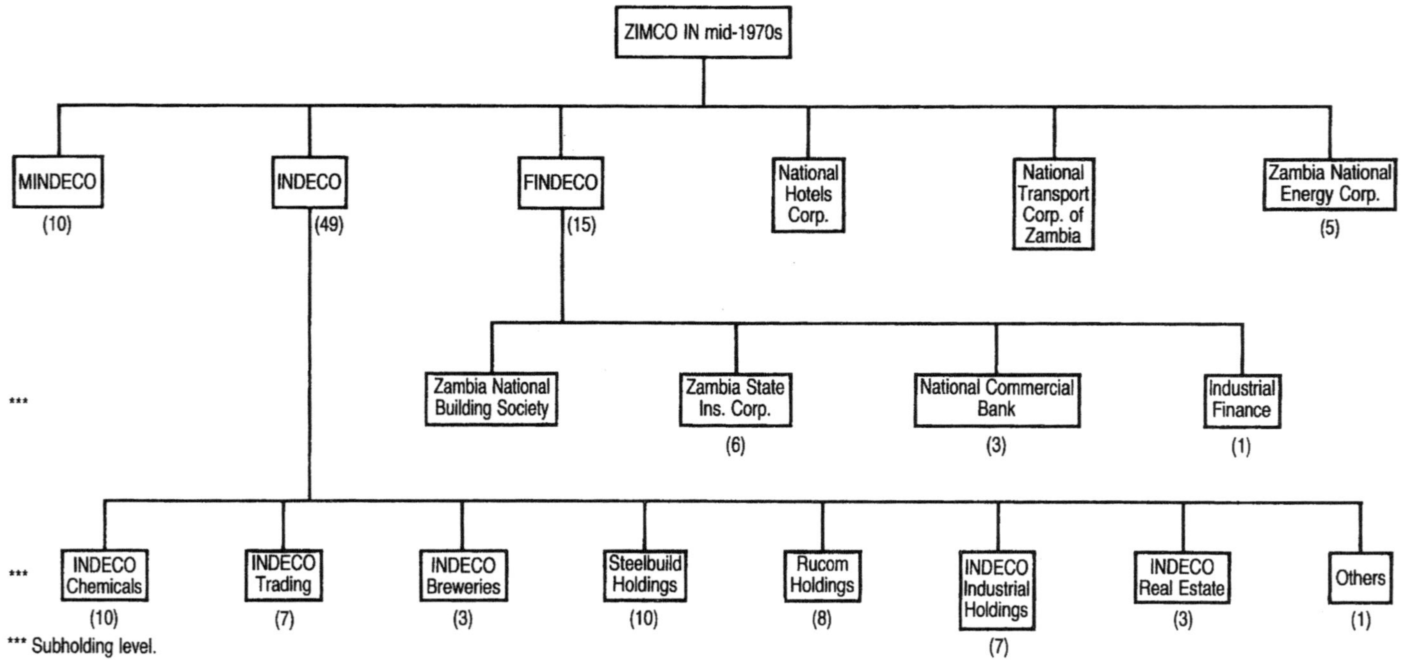

Note The bracketed numbers represent the subsidiary companies under each head.

Figure 2.4 The NDC group investments and commitments (1968–9)

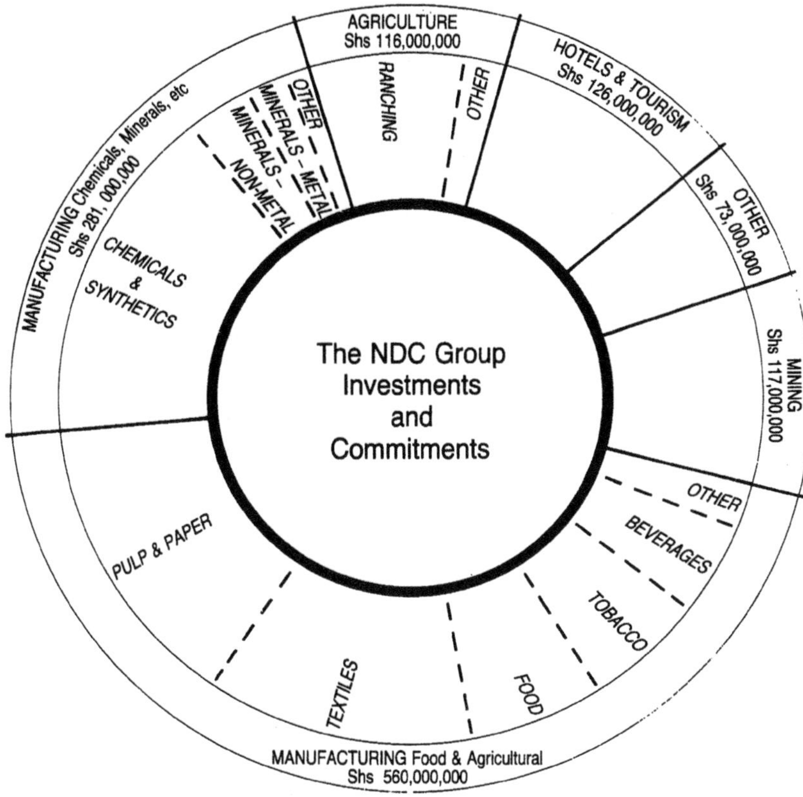

Source: National Development Corporation, *Annual Report and Accounts 1968/69*.

In 1979

Printpak Tanzania Ltd; National Printing Co.; Tanzania Publishing House; Kibo Paper Industries; East African Publication; Tanzania Hides and Skins; Tanzania Tanneries; Mwanza Tanneries; Morogoro Tanneries; Tanzania Shoe Co.; Morogoro Shoe Co.; Morogoro Canvas Mill; Morogoro Leather Goods; Morogoro Industrial Total; Tanzania Breweries; Tanzania Distilleries; Tanganyika Instant Coffee; Tanzania Cigarette Co.; Mwanza Brewery; Malting Project; Ceramics; Sheet Glass; and Glass Containers.

These transfers were accompanied by the formation of new corporations and by certain companies becoming autonomous, for example, Tanzania Karatasi Associated Industries; Tanzania Leather Associated Industries; Tanzania Saruji Corp.; Tanzania Breweries Ltd.; Tanzania Cigarette Ltd.; and Tanganyika Instant Coffee joined the Tanzania Coffee Authority.

The periodic hive-offs were substantial. For example, from a total investment portfolio of Tsh 763 million, by 1975 Tsh 351 million was hived off. Similarly, in 1979 the after-hive-off sales revenue was Tsh 1,378 million, as against the pre-hive-off figure of Tsh 2,488 million.

1980

1980 witnessed another major hive-off, this time the companies and projects belonging to the chemical sector in the main: General Tyre (E. A.) Ltd; Tanganyika Tegry Plastics; Rubber Industries; Pharmaceuticals; Sabuni Industries; Polysacks; Gypsum Recovery; Power Alcohol Pesticides; Tanzania Automobile Manufacturing Co.; MTAVA; Valmet Tractor Assembly; Motorcycle and Trailers and Low Loaders.

The after-hive-off sales revenue was estimated in 1980 at Tsh 1,060 million, as compared with the pre-hive-off figure of Tsh 1,836 million.

A few interesting comments may be made on NDC's experience:

First, it lives up to its developmental character, and projects and subsidiaries that grow of age are hived off, either into autonomous enterprises or into (new) sectoral corporations. This keeps NDC from growing into a monster without purpose. It is less a financial holding complex than an industrial development agency, unlike ICDC of Kenya, which has gradually taken the character of a financial apex.

Second, from every hive-off NDC suffers a decline in its relatively profit-established operations and revenues, while simultaneously it shoulders responsibilities for developing new projects that naturally take time to come to fruition. Thus NDC remains almost continuously a public enterprise in gestation.

Third, NDC has borne, significantly, costs of national gestation in industrial development. These pass through its books.

No wonder its capital composition, exclusive of reserves, reflect this position. For instance, in 1979 grants were 95 per cent of all non-reserve capital.

Table 2.6 Grants in Tanzania in 1979

Government	(Tsh)
Shares	5.7 million
Grants	309.8
Grants from other parties	0.6
TAMCO-funds (Commissions)	1.9
	318.0
Loans	7.5
Non-govt loans	1.6
	327.1

Source: National Development Corporation, Annual Reports (from the first to the fifteenth, 1979), Dar es Salaam.

APPENDIX 2.6 The structure of British American Tobacco (BAT) Industries

BAT Industries is one of the UK's largest companies. Turnover in 1988 amounted to £17.7bn with pre-tax profits struck at £1.6bn. BAT Industries employs some 32,000 in the UK – representing 10 per cent of the world-wide work-force.

Eagle Star and Allied Dunbar represent a major force in the UK insurance industry. The recent £2.9bn acquisition of Farmers Group in the US turned BAT Industries into the UK's largest insurance group.

Argos, with a nationwide network of catalogue showrooms, is one of the country's fastest-growing retail operations.

Wiggins Teape is the leading European manufacturer of carbonless papers and one of the largest paper merchants in Europe, with six paper mills and five factories in the UK.

BAT's UK tobacco manufacturing operations export to some 160 markets world-wide. Leading brands include Benson & Hedges, John Player Special, and State Express 555.

Turnover 1988
£17.6bn (+3 per cent)
Pre-tax profit
£1.6bn (+18 per cent)
Attributable profit
£949m (+21 per cent)
Earnings per share
20.10p (+19 per cent)
Dividends per share
20.10p (+19 per cent)
Source BAT's annual report

Estimated breakup values are listed as follows:

	£m
Eagle Star	1,900
Allied Dunbar	1,500
Farmers	3,200
Wiggins Teape	1,100
Argos	680
BATUS (all US)	5,400
BATCO (UK tobacco)	2,180
BATIG (WG)	630
Other tobacco	2,580
Share stakes	1,935
Total	21,105

	£m
Less est. net debt	3,000
Total valuation	18,105
Valuation per share	1,191p

BATUS includes Brown & Williamson (tobacco), Saks Fifth Avenue, Marshall Field's and Appleton Papers.
Source: Observer, 16 July 1989 (London).

APPENDIX 2.7

Table 2.7 Cost inflations of public enterprise projects (India)

Some data of projects under implementation with cost exceeding Rs 20 crores (as on 31 March 1987)		
1.	No. of projects with original approved cost of over Rs 20 crores	290
2.	Total original cost of these projects (Rs crores)	46,444.03
3.	Anticipated cost (Rs crores)	69,649.05
4.	No. of projects having cost overrun	186
5.	Range of cost overrun	0–961%
6.	No. of projects having time overrun	162
7.	Range of time overrun	0–204%
8.	Total expenditure up to 3/86 (Rs crores)	26,064.05
9.	Expenditure during the year 3/86 to 3/87 (Rs crores)	7,980.20
10.	Cost-weighted original time for construction (without railways)[a]	68.31 months
11.	Cost-weighted anticipated time for construction (without railways)[b]	97.86 months
12.	Cost-weighted time overrun (11/10)	29.55 months
13.	Weighted time overrun (12/10)	43.3%

Source: Morris, S. and Raman, G. V. G. (1988) *The Process of Investment Decisions in the Public Sector: A Study of the Delays and Cost Overruns*, Institute of Public Enterprise, Hyderabad.

Note: In respect of 133 projects, the 'capital waste' factor was computed at 195.03 per cent.

(a) Original time for completion project-wise averaged with the original approved costs as weights over all projects excluding the railways, since for very many railway projects the date or anticipated date of completion are not available. There was an error in the official computations arising out of the numerical machines assuming the anticipated dates as zero since the data was not available, for railway projects. There is still another error in government's aggregate reporting. Further, while the sectoral weighted time for completion is correctly given (except for railway projects mentioned above), the aggregate is given as a simple sum over the sectors! We have recomputed the correct values.

(b) Anticipated time for completion of projects averaged, with the anticipated cost as weighted over all projects excluding railways.

APPENDIX 2.8 Sectoral Demarcations

Ghana – three categories:

1. 'Industries reserved entirely to the government.'
2. 'Those in which government participation is mandatory.'
3. 'Those open freely to private enterprise' (in which government participation is not precluded).

Source: Second Development Plan 1959–74, p. 17.

Nepal – three categories:

1. Those directly undertaken by the government, for example, public utilities.
2. Those set aside in the private sector with economic assistance from the government, for example, agricultural development and fertilisers.
3. Those left to the private sector.

Source: The Second Three Year Plan 1962–65, Kathmandu, p. 36.

Sri Lanka – in 1957 three schedules were drawn up:

1. 'Wholly owned and controlled by State' (monopolies and basic industries).
2. 'Joint list' for secondary-level industries.
3. Consumer and intermediate goods (exclusively for the private sector).

Source: Lakshman, W. D. (ed.) (1979) *Public Enterprises in the Economic Development of Sri Lanka*, Colombo.

3 Extra-enterprise objectives

This chapter commences with a discussion of the concept of extra-enterprise objectives of public enterprises. A fairly comprehensive range of such objectives ordinarily assigned to them is reviewed next, and the nature of their impacts on the finances of the enterprise is analysed. An appendix (3.1) is included on the results of an empirical survey conducted in Pakistan in 1983.

THE CONCEPT

The popular title for the subject matter of this chapter is 'social objectives' or 'non-commercial objectives'. But it would be more accurate to designate them as 'extra-enterprise' objectives. For these are not derived from criteria internal to the enterprise, and they would connote a non-emotive term. Usually they are external in origin. They entail a reduction in its net revenue; hence the enterprise, by itself, does not choose to undertake them.

The financial adversity flows from:

(i) a loss from the activity undertaken in response to those objectives;
(ii) a lower margin in that activity than could be gained from activities undertaken on enterprise criteria; or
(iii) a loss or reduction in the profit sustained in realising the enterprise objectives, because of the diversion of certain inputs to extra-enterprise objectives.[1]

There are two exceptions to the net revenue reduction element in the definition of an extra-enterprise objective. The first is where it only shifts an output from one market to another or shifts the employment of inputs from one region to another, but is net-revenue neutral. (Here the assumption is that the enterprise does not have resources to serve both markets or regions; or else, it would by itself choose to serve both markets on enterprise criteria.) For example, if the government, on wider 'social' considerations, wants an electricity enterprise to supply electricity in one region rather than another, it is possible that it can so plan its operations as to satisfy that objective without any effect on its net revenue position. Another illustration is where the government sets the objective of exportation, at a certain level, as against domestic sales, both being equally profitable to the enterprise.

The other exception is where an enterprise enjoys the benefit of the 'cost-plus' formula in pricing its output. An extra-enterprise objective that raises its costs will have no adverse effect on its net revenue. For example, an electricity generating enterprise, if allowed to sell on a cost-plus basis, can shift its full cost burden to the electricity distribution enterprises and any other customers. It is the latter that suffer from 'inherited' extra-enterprise objectives; their accounts reflect the financial consequences.

An extra-enterprise objective causes financial adversity to an enterprise in two ways. It forces the enterprise managers to go in for inputs on criteria unrelated to productivity and efficiency. Or, it forces them to make output (and price) decisions that deviate from the cost basis and from the criteria of a maximising price structure. In either case, they move away from market-orientated 'enterprise' behaviour and become an agency for a 'public' preference, in terms of the argument in the opening section of chapter 1.

Let us look at certain familiar observations on objectives. First, that certain 'social' objectives are of commercial value to the enterprise itself;[2] and the examples cited include research and development, and being a model employer. To the extent that such inputs are of commercial value to the enterprise over a foreseeable long term, they are really enterprise objectives. That the decisions regarding them may have come from outside the enterprise does not necessarily make them extra-enterprise objectives; the management may have been too slow or unintelligent to initiate the decisions. On the other hand, if the scale on which the expenditures are incurred, for example, for training or welfare – far exceeds the long-term needs of the enterprise (and is far larger than what comparable private enterprises implement), there is an element of extra-enterprise objectives.

Second, that setting up a large capacity, in spite of the losses or low profits in the early years, is a social objective that is financially beneficial to the enterprise in the long run. This is in fact an enterprise objective, similar to the one above, and concerns the economies of scale.

Third, that certain 'services provided mainly for social reasons', convey significant social benefits, that is, benefits to other than their direct users, and are yet profitable.[3] These, being profitable, really represent enterprise objectives, though it is true that others, besides the enterprise's direct consumers, also benefit. All operations of enterprises contain social benefits, in varying degrees. Our concern here is with objectives which have an 'extra-enterprise' dimension in the sense that they have an unfavourable effect on the finances of the enterprise.

At this point it may be noted that not every extra-enterprise objective necessarily originates 'externally', though usually it does, and that not every 'externally' originating decision contains an extra-enterprise objective (as defined here), though usually it does. Sometimes extra-enterprise objectives are internalised in the decision process. That is, the board of directors may take the decision – under overt or covert pressures – or may itself assume the worthwhileness of an extra-enterprise objective. Likewise, an external decision may, in fact, contain elements of viability; its external origin may be due to the bureaucratic peculiarities of decision-making in the public sector, or to the fact that the government is in a better position to take a view on the national economies of scale in respect of a given activity or a package of activities, or to the inadequacies of managerial initiative at the enterprise level.

A broad conclusion on the interrelationship between an external decision and an extra-enterprise objective is that the latter usually emerges from the former.

There is no suggestion here that extra-enterprise objectives are not desirable. In fact they represent the 'public' part of the concept of public enterprise. Our analysis relates to their implications and to the limits of the suitability of a public enterprise in realising them.

There are two prefatory points. First, if a public enterprise treats certain objectives as 'extra-enterprise' in nature, there is no implication that the management is anti-social in outlook. Second, every extra-enterprise objective assigned to a public enterprise is not necessarily in the social interest on deep analysis.

Figure 3.1 is useful in annotating some of the points made in this section. Objectives may originate in the enterprise or externally (I or II in the figure). Many of the former (IA) are commercial in criteria but some may end up as being antisocial (IAii), while the others[4] may rest on non-commercial criteria (IB), though some of them turn out to be antisocial (IIBii). IAii, IBii and IIB should attract serious attention from policy-makers. It is not the origin of a decision or objective but its substance in point of criteria and effects that should be our main concern. (The term 'antisocial' is used here to signify a result that seems to go against the patterns of economic or social well-being explicitly or implicitly derived from government white papers, budget statements or development plans.)

EXTRA-ENTERPRISE OBJECTIVES

Figure 3.2 presents a fairly comprehensive, though not exhaustive, range of extra-enterprise objectives, under the broad heads of 'macroeconomic' and 'non-economic' objectives. (II2 and II3 can be placed under category I as well.)

Figure 3.1 Public enterprise objectives

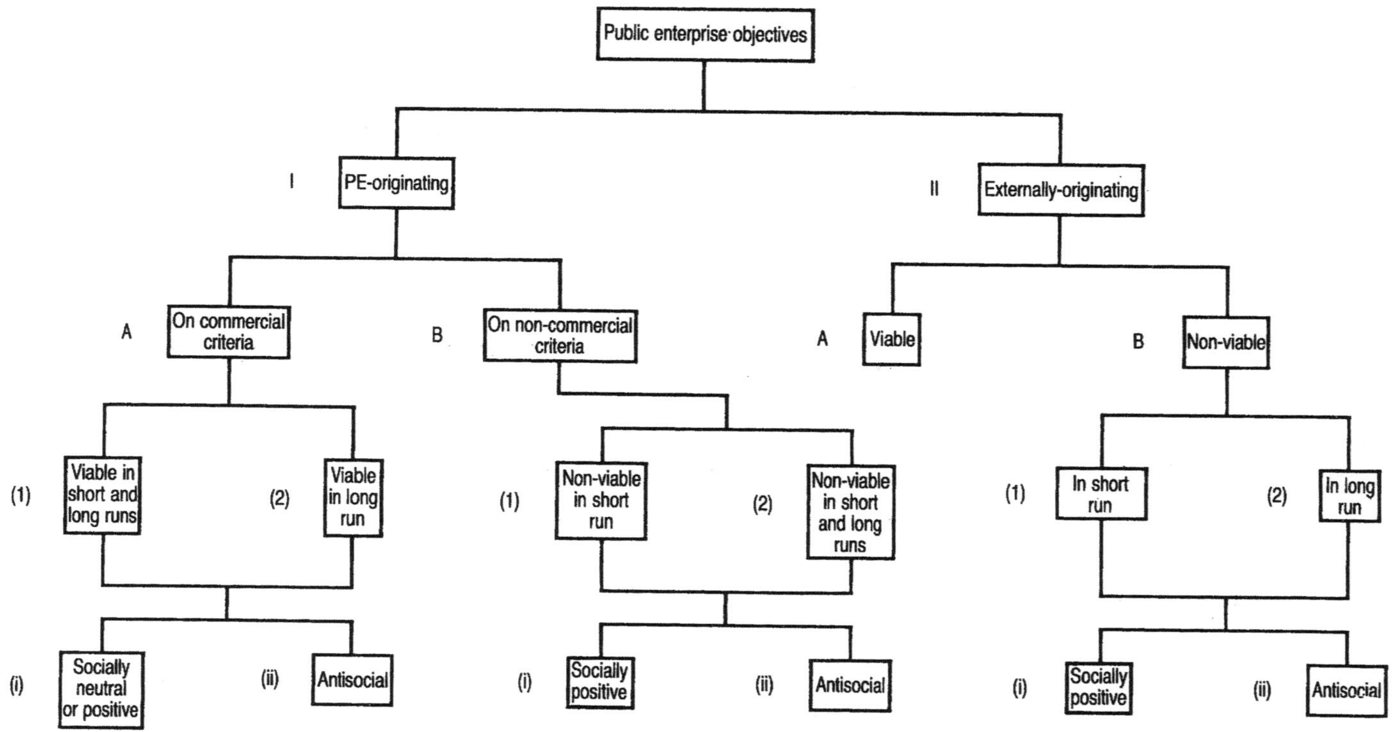

Figure 3.2 Extra-enterprise objectives

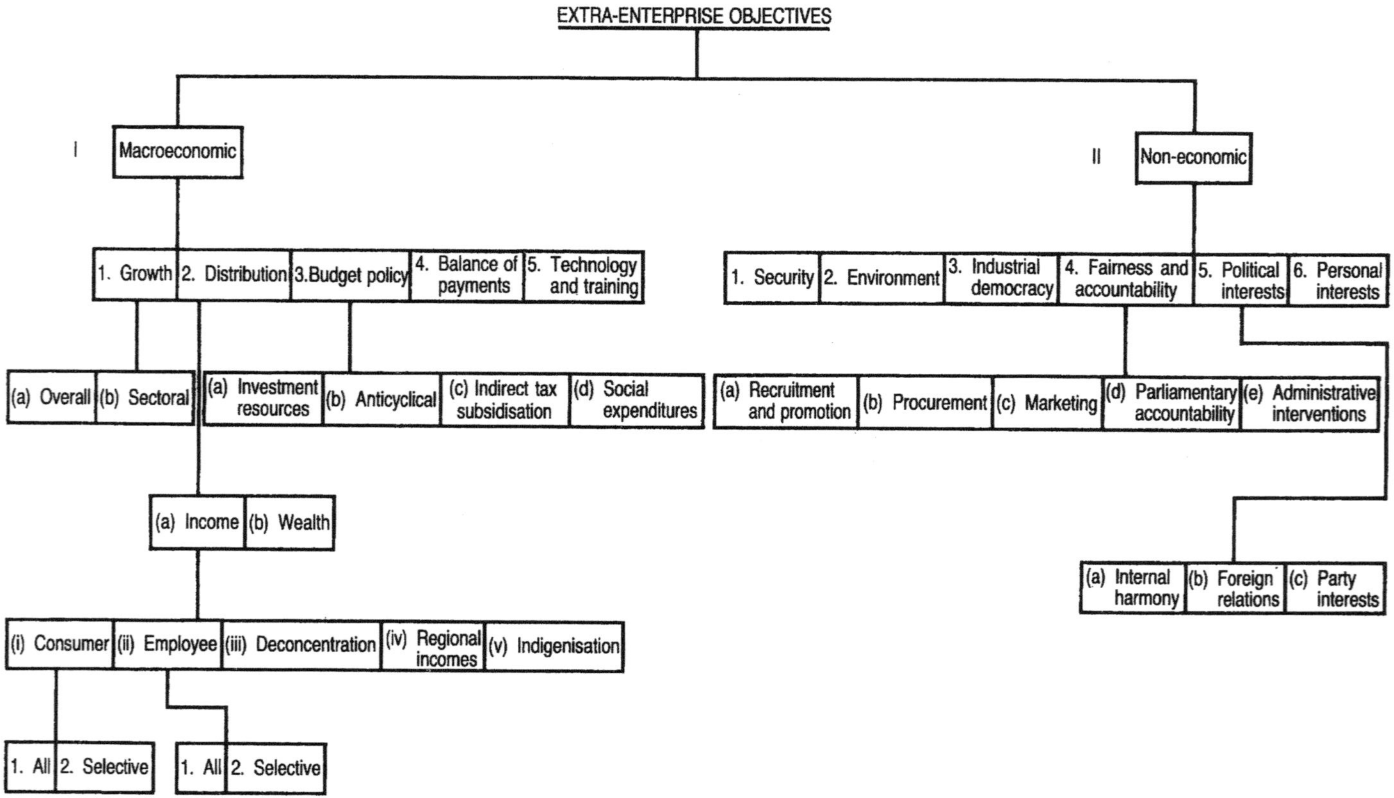

Macroeconomic objectives

Growth (I1)

Three aspects of the growth objective may be highlighted:

(i) The prices may be promotional all along, for example, the Development Bank Section of the Commonwealth Banking Corporation's loan policies in Australia; Japanese National Railway's lowered prices due to 'the burden of social obligations';[5] Irish Transport Authority (CIE)'s unprofitable services '. . . as a necessary part of social and economic infrastructure in Ireland'; and the Rural Development Corporation's 'commercially unviable projects in order to implement the Government policy for agricultural expansion' in Zambia.[6]
(ii) A project may be marked by an accelerated rate of growth that represents 'haste'.[7]
(iii) Some projects in the public sector as well as the sequence of capital expenditure depend, essentially, on the rate of flow of foreign aid.[8]

Distribution (I2)

Investments channelled into backward areas through deliberate external decision or pressure tend to raise incomes in such areas, though at the expense of the net revenues of the enterprise concerned. Price and output policies favouring given groups of consumers affect the gross revenues of the enterprise. Employee benefits, which owe to extra-enterprise criteria, raise the costs of the enterprise, and other things being equal, it suffers a reduction in net revenue. When public disfavour of 'big' suppliers and sales agencies induces the enterprise to spread its orders uneconomically over several suppliers of inputs, for example, over small-sized ancillaries, as in India – and its product distribution over several marketing agencies, its costs of production/selling increase and its net revenue falls, given a price level that cannot be raised.

Decisions on localising or indigenising the ownership and, more particularly, the management of enterprises, may have foreign exchange gains as well as freedom from foreign control of the economy; but if introduced prematurely or in an unplanned manner, such objectives can affect their financial results either in the short run or over a fairly long run.

Two instances of distributional policies touching on wealth may be mentioned here. An enterprise whose outputs such as electricity and water have a tendency to improve property values in the area served, may be persuaded to offer them in certain socially preferred areas. Here the impact on the enterprise may be neutral, if the cost and demand conditions in the preferred areas are similar to those elsewhere; it will be unfavourable if those conditions are worse in the preferred areas. In any case property owners in those areas benefit. Concessional credits by a financial institution for small loanees are another example of extra-enterprise preferences for deconcentration in wealth, though at financial cost to the enterprise.

The other instance concerns the ownership of shares of the enterprise. If a major proportion of the share capital not held by the government is required to be allotted to workers or others holding small lots, there is a desired deconcentration result. Such an objective can be neutral to the financial results of the enterprise, unless the highly dispersed voting rights introduce problems of managerial accountability and directoral efficiency.

Budget policy (I3)

Certain budget policies can present financial disadvantage to a public enterprise. For example, it may be persuaded to undertake a capital expenditure far in advance of need, as in the UK, where the Central Electricity Generating Board had to complete the Drax Power Station,[9] 'to provide business for the British heavy electrical engineering industry and to provide additional long-life coal-fired generating capacity'.[10] A slightly different version of the problem commonly arises in many developing countries; an enterprise goes ahead with capital expenditures while certain necessary complementary investment decisions in related areas do not fructify because of budget problems, or while its major consumer enterprises are not ready to buy its outputs. For example, the Central Government budget permits investments in heavy electrical plants, while the state government budgets, for their own reasons, may not provide enough money for the expansion of State Electricity Boards, the customers of those plants, in India.

Two familiar areas of extra-enterprise decisions with anti-cyclical objectives are price controls and capital expenditure controls, which touch public enterprises more rigidly than they affect private enterprises. The UK experience in the 1970s bears out the severe financial impacts of such objectives, despite the compensations received from the government (see Appendix 3.2). Extra-enterprise pressures in favour of prices containing elements of indirect taxation or subsidisation are common in many countries. High welfare expenditures are characteristic of public enterprises on the ground that they are expected to be 'model' employers. To the extent that these are not relevant to raising productivity, they constitute an extra-enterprise objective.

Balance of payments (I4)

National objectives in this area, no doubt, affect both the public and private sectors, though in practice the impacts are weightier on public enterprises. The impacts can be as follows:

(i) 'Buy national' pressures that may raise costs.[11]
(ii) Imports from certain countries rather than others, the latter implying harder currencies though supplying better goods or offering effectively lower prices.
(iii) A ban on certain imports leading to underutilisation of capacity or imbalance in the use of capacity.
(iv) Export of certain outputs, though at low margins, and at no contribution to overheads at all if export prices are below marginal costs.
(v) Alteration in the product mix to suit export markets, though at an increased cost for the enterprise at the margin.
(vi) Cuts in the availability of foreign exchange resources for capital expenditures or major maintenance or rehabilitation: the more serious, the more crucial the imported equipment. Many African countries, for example, Tanzania in the context of its airways and road passenger services, illustrate this phenomenon.[12]

Technology and training (I5)

Here the objectives are apparently internal to the enterprise; but they can have elements of externality in the following circumstances:

(i) The nature, quantum and timing of R & D programmes and expenditures, as well as training (abroad, in particular), are usually subject to government approval and can turn out to be different from what the enterprise itself may consider to be in its own interest, taking its long-term requirements into account. From the country's point of view there may be economies in a given enterprise undertaking them, irrespective of its own needs.
(ii) The enterprise may be induced to go in for an inferior production function in the name of intermediate technology, or for utilising certain low quality inputs (like lignite instead of coal) available locally.

Though these factors seem to apply to all enterprises in the country, public enterprises tend to be particularly affected; for in the early stages of industrialisation it is generally public enterprises that undertake expenditures on technology development in developing countries.

The importance attached by the government to research and technology development may be inferred from the fact that several nationalisation Acts in the UK laid down that the enterprise should, from time to time, settle with the minister a general programme of research and 'technological development'.[13] The technology objectives can have diverse impacts on the enterprise: its capital expenditure can rise, partly through the capitalisation of large-sized R & D expenditures, of which some may have been infructuous; the recurring expenses go up; and write-offs of experimental expenditures can occur from time to time.

Non-economic objectives

Security (II1)

Considerations of national security apply to all enterprises. Yet, occupying the relatively basic sectors of activity, public enterprises experience constraints under this head in heavy measure, for example, by having to develop a local output, such as aircraft, as against an import, whatever the cost, or by having to line up with the defence equipments of certain friendly countries.

Environment (II2)

The impacts of environmental concerns are similar. These are becoming progressively effective and apply to private enterprises too.[14] The latter, however, do not go beyond the legal requirements. Where the environment-oriented costs to be borne are too heavy, private enterprise might not even enter the sectors concerned, assuming that they have other investment options.

Industrial democracy (II3)

In the sense of worker membership on boards, this may be considered as a step in improving worker motivation and productivity and as a desirable feature of enterprise management. Sweden, France, and Germany[15] have pursued it for a long time and the UK rather experimentally.[16] There is a potential in this objective for non-homogeneity of the board and a constant pressure for employee benefits, with severe cost impacts.[17]

Fairness and accountability (II4)

It is inherent in the concept of a public enterprise that it has to be, and appear to be, fair and accountable in its behaviour. This is one of the points of commonality between public enterprise and public administration. (Chapter 13 refers to this issue from another angle.) Though efforts have been in progress in interpreting this principle so as not to affect enterprise efficiency, unfavourable impacts, such as the following, are in abundant evidence:

(a) Recruitment, promotion, and salary structures:

The less autonomous the enterprise in this regard, the less efficient its human resource deployment. The Statutory Corporations Service Board in Nigeria (abolished after 1974), the empanelling of managers by the Bureau of Public Enterprises in India, the salary classifications imposed by the Standing Committee on Parastatal Organisations in Tanzania, and difficulties in getting government approvals for creating a new (desirable) post – are all examples of constraints on enterprise behaviour.

(b) Procurement:

The requirement that decisions on input acquisition should pass through elaborate tender procedures, if not through the government's own machinery for purchases, can prove costly to the enterprise. The input may come in late, it may be of poor quality, and the source may not be the best in the long run.

(c) Marketing:

Extra-enterprise biases in favour of the 'small' man and of deconcentration may force the enterprise to design a marketing system that is composed of many small agencies – an arrangement not necessarily economical to it. Further, if the enterprise is prevented from entering downstream activities, for example, retail distribution, it is effectively denied certain highly profitable avenues of profit.

(d) Parliamentary accountability and administrative interventions:

These are necessary in theory but manifest themselves in such a way as to become sources of intrinsic cost to public enterprises, as may be seen from chapters 2 and 13.

Political interests (II5)

These generally influence the macroeconomic extra-enterprise objectives, though sometimes they are probably pursued in a covert manner, and may run counter to stated macroeconomic goals. They can represent the short-term interests of political groups and tend to convert enterprises into pockets of political patronage. R. C. Pozen's study on Ghana cites many illustrations.[18] Contributions to political funds (for example, in Korea)[19] and price policies being 'influenced by the interests of party politics' in Japan[20] are further examples. Foreign aid agreements with certain countries may be a political expedient for the ruling party; and projects aided by 'friendly countries' may be located in places without economic justification.

Personal interests of powerful individuals (II6)[21]

These get transmitted to public enterprise in informal ways – even through the process of board appointments.

The extra-enterprise objectives (II5) and (II6) have been so strong in some cases as to deserve being categorised as 'unstated objectives'.[22]

PUBLIC POLICY

Assuming that the government decides to realise an objective which turns out to be in the nature of an extra-enterprise objective with reference to a public enterprise, it has two options of policy: to assign it to the enterprise or to pursue it through its own budgetary and regulatory instruments. If it adopts the former option, it has

(a) to specify the extra-enterprise objective in managerially clear terms;
(b) to quantify its financial impacts on the enterprise:
(c) to formulate the most appropriate modalities of financing the impacts; and
(d) to preserve the institutional character of the enterprise as an autonomous form of organisation.

The specification

The need to specify the extra-enterprise objectives to be pursued by a public enterprise arises from the following considerations:

(i) Since a public enterprise, by definition, has a 'public' purpose to achieve, apart from behaving as a mere 'enterprise', it is necessary to inform the managers of the extra-enterprise goals to be accomplished by it.
(ii) If financial targets are set for an enterprise, there is particular need to clarify to the managers the extra-enterprise objectives in relation to which the targets have been set, and which are also expected of them, consistently with the financial targets (see chapter 7 for further comments).

The objectives have to be specified in close consultation with the enterprise managers, so as to ensure that the enterprise will be capable of accomplishing the goals (for instance, is an export goal realistic, considering the market conditions?). The managers can offer useful clues as to how certain of the objectives can be refined in respect of scale, location, and time span.

Several options exist as regards the modality of specification of the objectives. The problem is similar to the case of targets and is fully discussed in chapter 7. The Act governing an enterprise can (and ought to) indicate clearly the direction of extra-enterprise goals; but the specifics have to come, from time to time, through directives. A recent UK practice has been to indicate them through letters to the chairman of the enterprise.[23] Government companies – a growing number in many countries – have no specific Acts governing them; and the Memorandum and Articles of Association do not take care of the objectives with which we are dealing. (This does not seem to be realised by ministries in some countries.)[24]

Another point about the specification is that it has to be transparent, so that, in some way, Parliament notices the extra-enterprise objectives enjoined on an enterprise and the public have some knowledge of why an enterprise pursues certain policies that are not justified by commercial motivation, for example, pricing that has no basis in related costs.

The quantification

The quantification of the financial impacts of an extra-enterprise objective on an enterprise presupposes that the precise nature and extent of the objective have been established in the first place, instead of keeping it open-ended, for example, regional development. This not only rules out vague claims of consequences by management but reveals to the government the exact extent of non-viable operations enjoined on the enterprise.

We may examine the impacts under three heads: capital expenditures, costs, and revenues:

Capital expenditures

These are increased by objectives which:

(i) involve an uneconomic location of activity, entailing expensive construction and acquisition of inputs, for example, the cotton mills in Baluchistan (Pakistan) and the heavy electricals plant in Hardwar (India);
(ii) involve the choice of poor technology, for example, the surgical plant of Indian Drugs and Pharmaceuticals Ltd and Hindustan Photo Films Ltd (in India);
(iii) involve the establishment of excess capacity, that is, capacity over and above what the enterprise, on commercial criteria, considers as reasonable and economical over the long run, for example, Heavy Engineering Corporation Ltd (India); and/or
(iv) involve excessive construction costs in the interest of local suppliers of equipment and technical skills.

Three financial consequences follow: the enterprise is overcapitalised; the annual related costs (through interest charges, depreciation, and maintenance) increase; and the cash requirements for debt-servicing increase. Thus both viability and liquidity problems arise.

It would be necessary to establish the extent of increase in capital expenditure occasioned by extra-enterprise objectives, so that the most appropriate techniques of providing compensation can be designed.

Techniques of investment feasibility studies under different assumptions of such objectives can help in indicating it, though one can never be definitive; and care should be taken not to inflate, deliberately, the cost excesses attributable to such objectives. The annual costs flowing from the excess in capital expenditure can then be calculated. However, factors such as (ii) above reveal their impacts only as the project comes into being and struggles to come into production; and on factor (iii) a difference of view is likely between the government and the enterprise managers on the estimates of future demand from which the extent of excess capacity is to be deduced. Thus the establishment of the 'excess' in capital expenditures attributable to extra-enterprise objectives will be a continuing and imprecise exercise.

Average costs

First we shall look at the impacts of extra-enterprise objectives on the cost per unit produced. The items of cost affected have to be identified and the extent of adverse financial consequence quantified. The nature of the objective imposed on an enterprise gives a clue to these facts. For example, surplus labour, which is not permitted to be eliminated, is an obvious element of excess cost. So are the high costs of ancillary-supplied inputs as compared with open market prices. In the case of uneconomic location, the excess costs of acquiring the inputs and marketing the outputs may be calculated. Costs of poor technology, which cannot be set right for extra-enterprise reasons, may also be traceable. These identifications and quantifications would be in the nature of a continuing exercise. (The cost impacts change (probably decline) over time.)

Where an extra-enterprise objective imposes a slowing down of planned capital expenditures, the enterprise may be compelled to go in for high revenue expenditures to realise some of the good effects of the foregone capital expenditures – for example, expensive maintenance of old vehicles whose replacement is rendered impossible.[25] There are two sources of cost excess here: first, the additional maintenance charges; and second, the high interest charges on short-run borrowings.

Revenues

The following are the major versions of the revenue impacts:

(i) Prices are so controlled that the enterprise has to sell below what it could get in the market or below 'related' costs (that is, costs attributable to the output concerned).

(ii) The enterprise is prevented from applying techniques of price discrimination with the aim of improving its net revenues. This may result, indirectly, from controls or guidelines on the output mix, which have the effect of curtailing the more profitable outputs and expanding the less profitable or unprofitable outputs. (The 'standard cloth' which National Textile Corporation Ltd of India is required to produce up to a specified level illustrates this.) Relatively fast expansions in the supply of rural electricity or in the opening of village branch offices of banks or post offices belong to this category. (For example, National Telecommunications Corporation of Nepal faces the problem of rural–urban product mix.)

(iii) The enterprise is under overt or covert pressures not to be strict in the collection of dues from 'poor' customers. Agricultural development corporations and small industry development or industrial estates corporations usually experience such pressures. As a result, the effective income per unit sold declines below the nominal price charged.

(iv) Constraints on marketing arrangements reduce the revenue per unit sold. These may rest on the objective of deconcentration.

In conclusion, the quantification of financial impacts can be attempted only in cases of transparent communication of extra-enterprise objectives to the enterprise, but not in 'covert' cases.

Financing the impacts

The government should compensate for the financial impacts of extra-enterprise objectives. Or else, (a) the enterprise may adopt discriminatory price structures, involving cross-subsidisations, so as to keep its net revenue satisfactory; (b) where it cannot do so, it records deficits, which the government has eventually to wipe out in some way; (c) the deficits demoralise the managers and, for that reason, tend to be aggravated further; and (d) the policy of offering compensations forces the government, often through parliamentary processes, to look rigorously at the (continuing) propriety of a given extra-enterprise objective and the scale on which it is sought to be realised. For instance, the Statutory Corporations (Financial Provisions) Act passed in the UK in 1974, visualised limits to 'the aggregate amount of payments' from the Treasury to the nationalised industries whose revenue accounts reflected deficits due to 'their compliance with the national policy relating to limitation of prices' (sections 1 and 2).

Further, the government would be impelled to minimise the compensation burdens by exploring the least costly modalities of realising a given objective: for example, should it be realised through a public enterprise, or through a system of competitive bids, public and private, wherever possible, or directly through ministerial operations? A point may also be reached in some cases where the decision is that an extra-enterprise objective is not commensurate with the cost burden it entails.

There are several ways in which the compensation may be offered. It can be linked with the capital structure of the enterprise or with its operations, according to the nature of impact in a given case.

Where the impact is clearly to inflate the capital outlay, the compensation may be aimed at minimising its financial consequences in the following ways:

(i) Capital grants, including free land, may be offered. This method will not give rise to financial costs year after year. Or an 'endowment fund' may be created.
(ii) A sizeable equity can be provided. This does not involve any obligatory cost to the enterprise, unlike interest on loan capital.
(iii) Loans may be converted into equity from time to time, thereby reducing the obligatory capital costs.
(iv) Loans may be offered at no interest or at low rates of interest. They may be deemed 'irredeemable' in some cases.
(v) Moratoria may be conceded in respect of interest payments and/or loan repayments.
(vi) Capital reductions may be undertaken periodically, having the effect of reducing the capital costs.

The main issue is whether the method results in a compensation which approximates to the financial impact of a given extra-enterprise objective. In practice all the above devices have been used in such a way that it is difficult to distinguish when they represented devices of compensation as against being general remedies for financial ills. The best approach would be to offer as a grant (or an endowment fund without interest or dividend responsibility) an appropriate part of the capital expenditure, which is clearly non-commercial in intent and result; and in all the other cases to prefer the open method of an annual compensation linked to the financial impacts. The others – (ii) to (v) – are no doubt purposeful, but not as compensations for extra-enterprise objectives (see chapters 4 and 5 for further comments).

There is another method, which clearly specifies the extra-enterprise nature of the objective implicit in some operations. The government may establish with an enterprise an 'earmarked' fund which totally finances the operations concerned. The revenues and costs are booked to that account and the net results accrue to the government. Losses sustained in the course of those operations are automatically borne by the government. These may also be termed an 'on-behalf-of' government activity undertaken by the enterprise. For instance, several earmarked funds exist in the case of Nacional Financiera of Mexico, meant for the promotion of mineral and small industries, and so on.

Where the impacts are on recurrent costs and revenues, corresponding recurrent measures are necessary. These imply a compensation for a cost excess or a revenue reduction which results from an extra-enterprise objective.

Several problems arise. First, should the aim of the compensation be to compensate the enterprise for the full impact of the cost excess or revenue reduction sustained by the enterprise, or to offer a payment only if the enterprise has an overall deficit? Strictly the former is the right approach, for it maintains the distinction between its 'enterprise' operations and the 'extra-enterprise' operations. The latter course may, however, be preferred by the government;[26] for it makes a compensation unnecessary when the enterprise does not make a loss on the whole. Cross-subsidisations take place. Some markets end up financing the extra-enterprise objectives.

Second, when a revenue reduction is sought to be compensated, should it be arrived at in terms of total cost or marginal cost? The latter would be the less expensive course from the government's point of view, in the case of enterprises working within capacity and under decreasing costs. It has justification where the enterprise has unused capacity which it can put to use in producing the outputs required, even if under an extra-enterprise objective. Where the enterprise has opportunities of using the unused capacity to produce outputs that offer it a higher price than that implicit in the extra-enterprise objective, the compensation should equal the difference between the two prices. Where the additional capacity has to be created or existing capacity is overworked, the compensation should cover the total new costs.

Where compensation under the head of capital has already been provided, no recurring compensation under the head of capital costs would be necessary as long as the operations under extra-enterprise objectives fall within the capacity to which the 'capital compensation' was originally related. If, however, the required prices fall below the marginal costs, additional compensation would be justified.

Third, where an enterprise can sell its outputs in a given market at a high price but is required, under extra-enterprise objectives, to offer a lower but profitable price, is it entitled to a compensation? It is, assuming that the high price is such as would not be censured by any monopoly commission as affecting the public interest. Implicit here is the question: how high can the price be? Chapter 6 looks at it.

Annual or recurrent measures of compensation can, broadly, be of two kinds: those designed directly to represent the financial impacts of an extra-enterprise objective, and those that are not. (The compensations implemented in the UK in the 1970s belonged to the former category. Price controls exerted as an instrument of anti-inflation policies were a major example; and 'social costs grants' and payments for 'promotion of sales of coal to electricity' have been common with the National Coal Board.)[27] The former method has been emphasised in official reports and pronouncements in many countries,[28] for example, in respect of the purchasing activities of the Kenya Meat Commission, and the purchasing of maize through buying centres by the National Cereals and Produce Board in Kenya. But it has not been adopted on anywhere near the necessary scale. The reasons are (i) that there is no formal documentation on the transmission of an extra-enterprise objective from the government to the enterprise; (ii) that the techniques of establishing the compensation amounts are poor; and (iii) that the sectoral ministries concerned do not succeed in securing from the Ministry of Finance or the budget agency an allocation towards the compensations.

The category of *ad hoc* measures of compensation, not directly related to a declared extra-enterprise objective, is the more common method employed by governments in many countries. They include:

(i) exemption of an enterprise from certain taxes, most importantly excise duties, stamp duties, import duties and other duties;[29]
(ii) waiver of interest due on government loans;
(iii) non-insistence on loan repayments to the government;
(iv) certain enterprise costs being incurred through government departments;
(v) an *ex post* subsidy to cover the losses of the enterprise rather than the impacts of specified extra-enterprise obligations; and
(vi) periodic write-off of capital.

The autonomous character of the enterprise

The advantages claimed for the autonomous form of a public enterprise would be at a maximum:

(i) when its extra-enterprise objectives are determined by mutual consent *ex ante*, communicated to the managers in clear terms, and duly compensated for, promptly;
(ii) when the extra-enterprise objectives are expressed in a structured manner, for example, through an Act or governmental direction, and not in an informal or covert manner; and
(iii) when it is reasonably possible to distinguish and measure the operations traceable to extra-enterprise objectives from the rest.

PUBLIC ENTERPRISE AS A MEDIUM OF EXTRA-ENTERPRISE OBJECTIVES

How far is it desirable to make a public enterprise the medium of extra-enterprise objectives?

First, certain objectives are more or less enterprise-specific; and the government may have little choice except to realise them through a given enterprise. The opening up of a new area through railway extensions, improving the commercial potential of a region by doubling the railway track, or converting the metre gauge to broad gauge, and the extension of electricity supplies to rural areas on the periphery of existing urban systems, illustrate the point.

Second, certain objectives can be realised otherwise than through a given enterprise, but considerations of economy and efficiency make it the most preferable medium. (The above point may even be considered as an extreme version of this one.) Thus crop purchase may be entrusted to an existing agricultural corporation, the production of coarse cloth to a textile enterprise, and specialised technical training to a 'high-tech' enterprise already conducting it on its own scale of requirements.

Third, where the technical interrelationship between the operations of an enterprise and those related to an extra-enterprise objective is marginal, or an apparent interrelationship can be ignored, without loss of efficiency or economy, the government has the option of exploring alternative modalities. For instance, an agency may be set up to undertake the objectives concerned, for example, housing and training activities or export promotion. Such an agency can commonly work for several enterprises, yielding economies of scale in the realisation of the objective. The government can offer the necessary compensation to that single agency. This might prove to be lower than the aggregate of compensations paid to different enterprises undertaking the same objective in bits and pieces.

Fourth, every extra-enterprise objective needs to be analysed rigorously so as to establish at what it precisely aims and then the question should be addressed as to whether it is to be pursued most advantageously through a given public enterprise. For instance, if helping the farmer is the objective, it has to be broken down into the alternative channels of help, for example, loans, fertiliser, seed, and price support, and the best channel has to be identified. The approach should be not to consider how a given enterprise can be made to undertake an extra-enterprise objective, but how best the end results of the objective can be achieved through one channel or another, the enterprise being one of the channels.

Fifth, an extra-enterprise objective – or a 'social objective', to use the more popular term – can be undertaken by a department of the government, rather than by an enterprise in some cases. Such an arrangement eliminates the government-enterprise problems relating to quantifications and compensations, and ensures automatic parliamentary scrutiny of governmental decisions. It can have the disadvantage, often serious, of being more expensive than the enterprise option.

'SOCIAL RESPONSIBILITIES' OF PRIVATE ENTERPRISE

Private enterprises have progressively undertaken actions that reflect their growing awareness of 'social responsibilities'. There is, however, an asymmetry between the private and public sectors in this respect. Fundamentally we should keep in mind the definition of an extra-enterprise objective used in this chapter: it is one that has an unfavourable impact on the net revenue of the enterprise.[30]

A large proportion of the social expenditures incurred by private enterprises are strictly meant to improve their market position. Donations to research institutions can have the effect of promoting fundamental research that benefits their own technology in the long run. In fact, that might be the most economical way of deriving research results of a basic nature. Several contributions, for example, to an arts museum, raise their goodwill, which is of no small significance in improving their market position in the long run.

Basically their 'social' expenditure commitments are an appropriation of profits realised but rarely, if ever, undertaken with the sure effect of a reduction in net revenue, unlike public enterprise commitments towards surplus labour, regional development and price preference to select groups. This is the most important difference to note.

In most cases a substantial part of their social-responsibility expenditures is what otherwise might have gone as taxes.

Finally the 'social' expenditure decisions of private enterprises are those taken internally, unlike those of public enterprises, which, in most cases, are 'external' in origin. This difference raises many problems as delineated in this chapter.

CONCLUSION

Experience suggests that in both developing and developed countries the problem of extra-enterprise objectives has been approached in a haphazard manner. (Appendix 3.4 shows the confusion which prevailed in the UK in this regard.) *Ex ante* decisions and quantifications have been an exception, rather than the rule, partly because governments have been diffident in owning such objectives and seeking parliamentary votes for funds, and partly because the technical skills needed to deal with the intricacies of the problem have not been available in most countries.

Extra-enterprise objectives have been pursued, however, by public enterprises. But neither their financial implications nor the opportunity costs of the net revenue reductions involved have been evaluated.

The problem has been addressed, sometimes 'residually', through periodic and *ad hoc* capital write-offs or governmental injection of cash to improve the liquidity of the enterprises concerned. Even this *fait accompli* method has not been employed in every deserving case.

The lack of a method in pursuing extra-enterprise objectives has had an unfortunate consequence, namely, uncertainty and frustration in managerial behaviour in public enterprise.

APPENDIX 3.1

Table 3.1 A survey of extra-enterprise objectives in Pakistan

What are social objectives? (1)	*How are social objectives determined?* (2)	*Impact on net revenue* (3)	*Remarks* (4)
Pakistan Steel Corp. Ltd			
Training for other public enterprises as well, in the metallurgical field. Exploitation of mineral resources in underdeveloped regions. Free technical assistance and guidance to consumers. Subsidised fresh vegetables and fruits from P. Steel farms. Subsidised canteens, housing schemes on easy instalments. Recruitment from Baluchistan, the most underdeveloped province.	No formal directive or communication by the government; only shared consensus between the government and the corporation.	Separate accounting for all activities will be introduced. Heavy impact of landed cost parity pricing policy.	PE can be a vehicle for social policies. But allowance is needed in monitoring. Conflicts between financial and social criteria is sometimes not resolved. Below-market prices lead to hoarding, black-marketing and unintended shortages.
House Building Finance Corp.			
Objectives of Corp. is itself 'social' in nature: to provide a house for every household. House finance in underdeveloped regions like NWFP and Baluchistan. To rehabilitate refugees from India and Bangladesh. To create employment in housing activities directly or indirectly.		Government loans to Corp. at 2% below bank rate.	

Table 3.1 Continued

What are social objectives? (1)	*How are social objectives determined?* (2)	*Impact on net revenue* (3)	*Remarks* (4)
Karachi Electric Supply Corporation Ltd			
Top priority for power connections in less developed urban areas. Social objectives 'inseparable' from its own objectives.	Social objectives are not fixed by the government or by any other institution.	Impact of spares and fuel should be subsidised. Best way to provide for social objectives is to have a strong financial base.	
State Cement Corporation of Pakistan Ltd			
Highly capital intensive technology limits employment generation and the application of socially oriented objectives. To develop adequate manpower cushion for the up-coming private sector projects. To distribute scarce energy products optimally among manufacturing, services, and among regions. To distribute cement in rural and remote areas. To set up plants in backward regions like NWFP and Southern Punjab.	Broad policies are communicated by the government – e.g. on labour policies and training.	Social objectives reduce revenues. Labour strength which cannot be maintained on strictly economic criteria.	

Ghee Corporation of Pakistan Ltd			
Uninterrupted availability of vegetable ghee in the remotest part of the country. Development of less developed areas.		Social objectives are not quantified.	
Pakistan Automobile Corporation Ltd			
Distribution priorities are set by government. Price mark-up is lowest on tractors, next on buses etc. Two units located in Baluchistan.	Only partially indicated by the government through policy statements, administrative letters, and directives. Board decisions are taken in conformity with them. Basic minimum guidelines from government are necessary.	Quantification and laying down of target data for specific objectives necessary. Allocation of merit factor to various objectives necessary.	With more private units in the sector, there may be hope for freedom of action.
Pakistan Television Corporation Ltd			
Some commercially non-viable projects in backward areas.			

Note
These are excerpts from the views of top managers of public enterprise, conducted in a survey by the author during 1983 in the course of his workshops at Karachi, Lahore, and Islamabad.

Appendix 3.2

Table 3.2 Periods of government price restraint on nationalised industries in the UK

Industry	*Period*	*Nature of specific intervention*
Gas	1965/66	Proposed increase deferred for 3 months on National Board of Prices and Incomes (NBPI) recommendations.
	1966/67	General price restraint and price freeze meant industry could not increase prices.
	1967/68	Gas Boards were not allowed to implement a surcharge on tariffs initially and the case was referred to NBPI who eventually granted an increase in unit revenue after a substantial loss had been incurred.
	1969/70 and 1970/71	A tariff increase was delayed for a year pending an inquiry by the National Board for Prices and Incomes.
	1971/72	CBI initiative required that the Gas Council was forced to pare down a 7.5% proposed price increase to 5%. The restraint was used to defer the implementation of the increase for six months. No changes in the structure of domestic tariffs were allowed.
	1972/73	Gas prices were frozen because of general restraint imposed in Autumn 1972 by the government's counter-inflation programme.
	1973/74	Gas Corporation not allowed to increase prices to domestic consumers until January 1974. No changes in the structure of domestic tariffs were allowed.
British Rail	1966	Increase not allowed under period of severe price restraint seriously affected the Board's finances. A price increase approved by the Transport Tribunal had still not been implemented by the end of 1967 because the NBPI had not reported.
	1967	A general increase in ordinary fares and season ticket rates was rejected.
	1971/72	Because of CBI initiative prices were restrained.
	1971–1973	Because of counter-inflation policy only small price increases were allowed that were inadequate to cover cost increases.
	1973	Restriction of freight and parcels price increase below application.
	1974	Two-month delay in getting the Price Commission to accept a price rise.

Industry	*Period*	*Nature of specific intervention*	
Steel	1969	December 1968 price increases were sought but they were referred to NBPI and not implemented until June 1969 and not in full until November 1969.	
	1970	Government delayed a requested price increase for 3 months.	
	1971	Price increase averaging 14% was proposed but the government advised the BSC to restrict the increase to half the amount.	
	1971/72	Under the CBI initiative the Corporation was only allowed to increase prices by 4.6% and the increase was deferred until April 1972.	
	1973	Since January 1973 price restraints on Treaty of Paris products (two-thirds of output) have been removed.	
Electricity	1965/66	NBPI deferred a London Electricity Board price increase for a short time.	
	1967/68	NBPI recommended that CEGB Bulk Supply Tariff be fixed at a lower level than that sought by the Electricity Board.	
	1970/71	Direct government action to hold prices down but not within any overall policy.	
	1971/72	CBI initiative and Electricity Boards only allowed to increase price by 5%.	
	Nov 1971	Counter Inflation Act	Increases under price restraint less than desired
	1973	Counter Inflation Act restraint less than desired.	
	1973	Counter Inflation Order	
	Feb 1975	Increases allowed were slightly below those sought by the Electricity Council.	
Coal		No real evidence of price restraint.	
Post Office	1968/69	A small loss of revenue was incurred because of a delay, caused by referral to the NBPI, in a price increase.	
	1970/71	Price increases not allowed in full.	
	1971/72	Price rises kept down to 3% because of CBI initiative.	
	1972/73	Post Office price rises curbed because of official restraint.	
	1973/74	Severe restraint under Stage II of the Counter Inflation Act.	

Source : National Economic Development Office (1977) *A Study of UK Nationalised Industries: their role in the economy and control in the future*, Background paper 5: *Price Behaviour*, London, pp. 17–18.

APPENDIX 3.3

Government assistance to National Coal Board under the Coal Industry Act, 1973

The Coal Industry Act, 1973, made the following main provisions for assistance:

(a) Reducing the book value of the Board's assets and writing-off of accumulated deficits, which would give the Board continuing benefit of about £40m a year in the form of reduced depreciation and capital charges.
(b) Government grants for 'social' costs arising from colliery closures and mineworkers' pensions up to total limits of £85m over the three years to March 1976 (which may be extended by Order to March 1978, with a limit of £140m for the five years).
(c) Extension of the Redundant Mineworkers Payments scheme to March 1976 (or by Order to March 1978) with a limit of £60m on the aggregate of the payments under it (£100m if the period is extended).
(d) Government grants to the Board to meet the cost of extra coal burned at power stations, to a limit of £50m over the three years to March 1976 (which may be increased by Order to not more than £100m).
(e) Government grants of up to £210m over the three years to March 1976, to help the Board moderate contraction of the industry, bearing in mind the heavy concentration of coal-mining in assisted areas.
(f) Government grants to cover coking coal production and costs of stocking coal and coke above a certain level up to total limits of £85m over the three years to March 1976 (which may be extended by Order to March 1978, with a limit of £145m for the five years).

With the exception of (a), these provisions did not come into effect until 1 April 1973. The government grants quoted as being available are maxima and do not automatically accrue to the Board; the actual sums paid will either depend upon the actual levels of expenditure incurred or be the subject of prior annual agreement with the Secretary of State.

Source: National Coal Board, *Annual Report and Accounts, 1972–73*, pp. 3–4.

APPENDIX 3.4

Comments on the extra-enterprise objectives of public enterprises in the UK

The nature of this problem is demonstrated in the following cases:

(a) The Post Office Act, 1969, provides little specific guidance on the definition and extent of public service obligations. The board sets its own business aims and objectives. Ministers and civil servants in the Department of Industry have not wished to contribute to this process but are not necessarily in agreement with the consequences of the board's interpretation of its role. The recent appointment of a Post Office Review Committee,† with wide ranging terms of reference, seems in part to reflect this uncertainty.

(b) The role of the British Rail board is particularly unclear. The board's expectation that the Railways Act 1974 would give adequate guidance has not been fulfilled, and the functions of the Department of the Environment‡ in relation to the board are overlapping and confused. What each expects of the other is ambiguous or unrealistic.

(c) The Electricity industry is concerned about the extent to which it is supposed to perform social service functions and is worried about an apparent lack of consistency in government policies towards the industry and the absence of a coherent policy towards the energy sector as a whole.

(d) The publication of BSC's long-term development plan** has been followed by a sequence of events which reveal a major and continuing disagreement between the board and government on the relative priorities to be attached to commercial and social obligations.

(e) The National Bus Company is unsure of the extent of its social service role. Consistent guidance is not obtainable in a situation where it is dependent on revenue support from approximately 50 separate authorities.

† Established in November 1975, under the chairmanship of Mr C. F. Carter.

‡ In September 1976 a separate Department of Transport was created, to which these sponsor functions have been transferred.

** *British Steel Corporation: Ten year development strategy,* Cmnd 5226, 1973.

Source: National Economic Development Office (1976) *A Study of UK Nationalised Industries: their role in the economy and control in the future*, London, p. 24.

4 Investment and capital structure

This chapter starts with a review of investment decision and implementation. Then follow sections devoted to an analysis of the way in which a public enterprise procures capital and to questions of composition of capital. Finally we shall examine restructuring, a problem commonly encountered by public enterprise in many countries.

THE INVESTMENT

This may be considered in three stages: (a) conceptual aspects, (b) feasibility analysis, and (c) implementation. Under each head public enterprise presents certain unique features.

Conceptual aspects

The reasons why the government intends to invest by itself in a given sector at a given place at a given unit of time are presented in chapters 1 and 3. Here we shall limit ourselves to the conceptual questions that arise while proceeding with investment action.

If we assume that the government has a development plan or a firm idea of how the economy should be evolved through some degree of intervention on its part, the first requirement of an investment decision is that it should agree with, flow from, and help realise, the national goals. Where it does, the products produced, the temporal sequence of the activity, and the locational and personal accrual of benefits, would all contribute towards the maximisation of social well-being, as conceived in the plan. A public investment decision would then be superior to a private investment decision in the sense that it 'satisfactorily' addresses the questions of externalities in respect of costs and benefits, maximisation of long-term growth, and distributional reform. It is hard to say how satisfactorily it does, because of two fundamental problems.

First, the national parameters have to be clear, in so far as they govern public investment. The most difficult of them are in the nature of value judgements. For example, the social rate of discount has to be set, which determines whether, in the eye of society or the government, the investment is justified through a comparison of today's value of benefits with that in the future. Despite technical competence, the social rate of discount is ultimately a judgemental decision. The lower this rate, the more probable the investment decision. The way in which the flow of costs and revenues are estimated for the future periods significantly influences the decision.

Another major judgemental factor concerns income distribution. The question to be addressed here approximates to the following: precisely how valuable is it to add a dollar of income to certain income brackets rather than others, or to a certain region as against the others?[1] Depending on the answer, weights have to be attached to the benefits, so that the cost-benefit analysis reflects national preferences in the area of income distribution; and financial returns lost in the course of the investment are deemed worth losing, since they are outweighted by the distributional gains.

The process, on the whole, calls for shadow pricing of various inputs, since the market prices do not reflect their real or scarcity value in a developing economy. In particular, a shadow price has to be attached to foreign exchange – and many public enterprises have absorbed a high proportion of it in the country's development process – other inputs which have scarcity value, and labour, which raises unique difficulties from the political standpoint. The cost-benefit analysis which incorporates the above ideas may be undertaken in five stages (as outlined in the UNIDO *Guidelines*, 1978):[2]

1. Calculation of financial profitability at market rates.
2. Shadow pricing of resources to obtain the net benefit at economic (efficiency) prices.
3. Adjustment for the project's impact on savings and investment.
4. Adjustment for the project's impact on income distribution.
5. Adjustment for the project's production or use of goods such as luxury consumer goods and basic needs whose social values are less than or greater than their economic values.

A separate adjustment under 2, 3, 4, or 5 can show the implications of cost-benefit analysis with reference to a given factor, while cumulative adjustments from 2 to 5 reflect the final picture that results from the application of all relevant national parameters to the investment proposal.

To conclude: The value of cost-benefit analysis depends on (i) how clear the government is as regards the extra-enterprise implications of a proposed investment, (ii) how technically competent the exercise for adjustments such as shadow pricing and the fixing of weights is, and (iii) how non-political the enumeration of social costs and benefits happens to be.

Many public enterprise investments give room for doubting whether these conditions are adequately satisfied. John Weiss's conclusion from a detailed analysis regarding the Larkana Sugar Mill in Pakistan applies to many other cases: 'The project appears to be an undesirable means of committing government resources.' The 'three main claims' made in favour of the project are not justified, namely, (a) the project would save foreign exchange, (b) it would stimulate a domestic equipment industry and (c) it would raise income levels in the locality of the project.[3]

Feasibility analysis

Feasibility analysis refers to processed documentation which incorporates all the relevant data on the proposed investment, duly adjusted at appropriate stages for social cost-benefit purposes. It helps the government to decide whether to undertake the investment or reject it. In this section we shall look at the problems which arise in the public enterprise sector and render decisions on feasibility studies difficult and often defective.

The data included in the feasibility study or project document are only estimates. Once the investment decision is taken on the basis of a positive project document, the following deviations begin to take place, and some of them may be quite large, as experience shows:

1. The actual output size or product mix varies from what was included in the feasibility study.
2. The production function varies from the feasibility assumptions.
3. The intake of labour and the wage rates (usually) jump up beyond the assumed levels.
4. The time sequence of construction and commissioning of the project differ.
5. Items of capital expenditure, for which provision was not made originally, come in.
6. The feasibility assumptions on the availability of raw materials and their sources as well as on the existence of markets, especially export potentialities, turn out to be understatements costwise and overstatements revenuewise.
7. The 'learning curve' in respect of technology absorption is far longer than assumed.
8. The quantities of imported inputs exceed the assumptions of import substitution originally made.

This is not a hypothetical list of shortcomings. A review of projects in many countries shows that they are real and occur in multiple combination.

To some extent these may be attributed to technical inadequacy in preparing a feasibility study. But there are two factors which ought to be considered as deliberate. First, there is an overambitious statement of the revenue potentialities – in respect of both markets and price prospects. Second, there is a desire on the part of the governmental agency concerned to secure approval for the project from the highest approving level. After the project is commenced, additional expenditures are proposed and, even under criticism from parliamentary committees, have to be

Figure 4.1 Assumed and actual costs and revenues

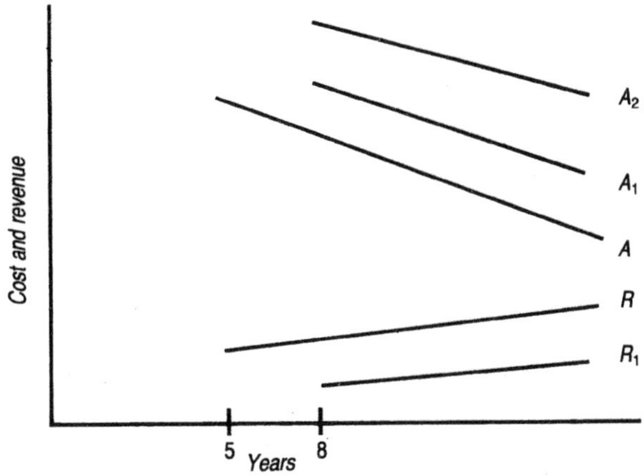

approved. The longer such approval takes, the more uneconomical the project becomes.

The diseconomy of the investment is represented in Figure 4.1.

Curve A represents the average cost per unit as per the assumptions contained in the feasibility study regarding the technology, commissioning at the end of the fifth year, and improved rates of utilisation from then on; and R represents the net revenue prospects, based on the assumptions of demand and price potential. If, in actual practice the commissioning is delayed up to the end of the eighth year, the cost curve rises to A_1; and the disadvantage would be a permanent one.

If, in addition, the degree of utilisation of capacity stays far below the feasibility assumption, the cost curve rises to A_2. (This disadvantage can be removed over time if utilisation improves.) If the conditions of demand are far poorer than those assumed, the net revenue takes the shape of R_1. This disadvantage remains serious, though utilisation improves, if demands prove to be less strong than those hoped for.

This figure is of value in that it brings out three of the common and serious features of investments in public enterprise, namely, delays and cost overruns,[4] underutilisation (often because of excess capacity being set up), and overstatement of revenue prospects. Shadow pricing of inputs raises the costs further, though generous social-benefit assumptions (for example, the value attached to income distribution) may make the net revenue position appear better than in the above figure. It may be recalled that quantifications in all these respects are value judgements, and in any case the causes of A_1 and A_2, as against the assumed A, are not necessarily related to social benefit or social cost parameters.

There is one aspect of national goals to which specific reference seems to be necessary in the light of experience. There has been a relatively high proportion of 'social expenditures' in the total capital outlay, covering housing and other amenities. They have the effect of inflating the costs in the early years relative to the outputs. The Bura irrigation scheme in Kenya illustrates the point (along with several other aspects of non-economic project decision). It has given rise to the criticism that 'development of social infrastructure should not be ahead of that of production'.[5] (The original estimate – in the mid-1970s – of 13 per cent return was scaled down to 6.75 per cent 'over 5 years if half the infrastructure costs are discounted'.)

Before we proceed to discuss the implementation aspects, let us look at the question of ensuring that an investment decision is the best decision from the macro angle. This implies that it is not enough that feasibility analysis establishes the worthwhileness of a project proposal. It is necessary to ensure that it is better than all the alternatives that can reasonably be conceived. When an electricity enterprise proposes a project, investment decision should go beyond an analysis of its feasibility. If the objective is to increase energy supply and could be achieved also by gas, coal, or oil, comparable alternatives in the energy sector as a whole have to be considered; and the social cost-benefit analysis should take into account the impacts of investment in one part of the sector over the others. Where the objective is reducible to providing electricity only, alternative proposals have to be investigated in the area of electricity. For example, should it be based on nuclear fission or on traditional technology? Further, we need to consider the size and cost questions from the long run perspective. Where locational alternatives exist, without loss of cost efficiency, social cost benefit analysis has yet another specific dimension.

A major problem in project decision in public enterprise concerns selection from alternatives. In the first place there should be adequate scope for the alternatives to come up before the decisional bodies. It is in this respect that the monopoly structure of a public enterprise in a given sector or subsector causes problems. It may not sufficiently throw up alternatives. Equally vital is the capability of government departments to scout for intrasectoral, or even intersectoral, alternatives which can be compared before an investment decision is taken.

All this may appear to be complex. But where major investments are involved and the projects concerned have long spans, it is useful to go through the scenario of investments before funds are committed. The institutional set-up within the government, and as between the government and the public enterprises concerned, is of great relevance in this connection. Further, the more the investment decision is delegated to an enterprise, the less the prospect of a genuine comparison of possible alternatives. Attempts to delegate investment powers to the chief executives of enterprises in the name of autonomy have to be evaluated from this angle. If the tasks of reviewing feasibility analysis and comparing alternatives are decentralised to public, non-departmental agencies, there is a good prospect of realising the objectives of an investment decision in the public enterprise sector.

Implementation

Several problems of implementation qualify the assumed goodness of an investment decision:

1. The time lag between the submission of a project document to the government and approval by the government is inordinately long in many cases, so much so that, even as the capital expenditures commence, the situation is one of cost escalations on grounds of price changes.
2. As capital expenditures commence there is no guarantee that funds will be released by the government in precise regard for the time frame envisaged in the project document. This has been the most important cause of diseconomy at the implementation stage in many countries. The consequences include an imbalance in the project components, which affects the prospect of early production activity, the wasteful capitalisation of interest on capital which is not put to use or whose use in production is bound to be delayed, depreciation (before use) of assets already created, and obsolescence in some cases.[6] Add to these the probable surplus of manpower at all levels, recruited in accordance with the time frame of the project document even if the need is smaller under delayed construction work.

All these factors have a permanent impact on the cost structure of the enterprise, as Figure 4.2 illustrates.

Assume that A represents the capital expenditures over eight years, visualised in the project document, and that some production activity is expected at the end of the fourth year, and that C represents the cost per unit estimated over a 12-year period. If the actual capital expenditures are

Figure 4.2 Capital expenditures and annual costs

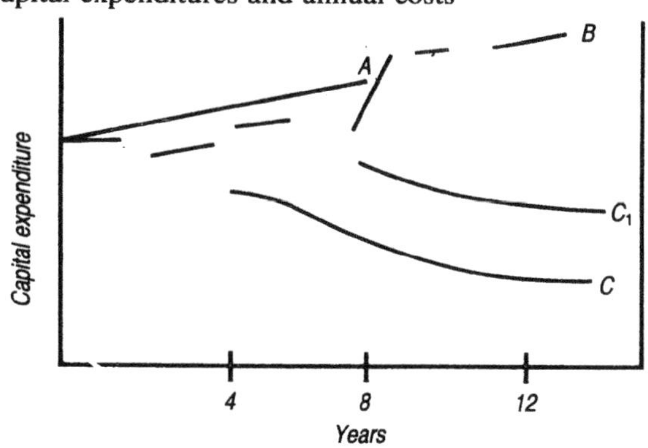

indicated by *B* with breaks in some years and deviations from *A*, there may be no production, say, until the eighth year, and the cost curve may take the shape of C_1. (Incidentally, there will be no revenue up to the eighth year.)

Assuming that the government has no funds to release during certain years – probably because it spreads its resources thinly over too wide an area of investment, it is worth examining if the enterprise concerned can be allowed to go to the market for funds, with government guarantee, if necessary. The fact that the interest costs may be high is not conclusive in terms of economic cost. Even from the narrow standpoint of the enterprise accounts, that disadvantage is probably offset by the permanent cost handicaps suggested by the above figure.

An alternative measure of policy exists. The purpose of Figure 4.2 is to emphasise the loss in net benefits from a given investment. The government should examine the desirability of postponing the commencement of capital expenditure in new projects during the years when its financial stringency makes anticipated releases to a project in progress difficult. If the net loss in benefit through such postponements is less than the benefits lost in the case of the project in progress, such a step would be justified on a social cost-benefit basis which takes into account the interrelationships among all investments of the government. There is a major hurdle, though. Different ministries may be involved, and those likely to be affected have to be convinced or appeased, but they may be politically too powerful.

Third, changes are often introduced in the output structure and size after the project construction is commenced. These generally fail to undergo the same rigorous tests of cost-benefit analysis as the original project proposal did. Often they are treated on an emergency basis, the more so if they originate in political interests.

In concrete terms, certain additional capital expenditures are incurred at a higher cost per unit of output than if the output modifications formed part of the original project proposal, and/or certain capital expenditures incurred already might prove to be infructions and need to be superseded by fresh outlays. As a consequence, the cost structure to which the project will eventually be exposed will be inferior to what it could have been had the modifications been a part of the original project proposal itself.

THE SOURCES OF CAPITAL

This section refers to the long-term capital of a public enterprise, other than internal resources. There can be three sources: the government, the market, and a public sector holding company. Financial public enterprises intended to assist both public and private borrowers are considered as a part of the market.

The government has been the major supplier of capital in the form of grants, equity, and loans. The latter two are the more important segments.

This section concerns loan capital, since the extent of equity that the government supplies is a matter of ownership policy, which is considered in chapter 14 on privatisation.

Let us examine the arguments in favour of the government being the exclusive or predominant supplier of loans.

First, there can be co-ordination between the borrowing policies of the government and those of public enterprises. The view has some significance if it refers to macro policies of encouraging investments in the economy or discouraging them in accordance with the government's policy towards recession or inflation. Even then a more desirable way would be for the government to agree possible levels of investment with the enterprises, without necessarily tying them to it as lender. The timing of borrowings on the part of public enterprise can have some effect on the absorbing capacity of the markets in respect of government's own borrowings and on the interest rates on the borrowings. Where such consequences appear to be material, an appropriate time schedule of public enterprise borrowings can be agreed. Where the borrowings are unpostponable, the effects have to be sustained.

Another version of the argument is that, if a public enterprise has to borrow from the government only, the government would be in a position to exercise control over it. Here again the basic point is that control by criteria has to be independent of the borrowing arrangement; it is when control is *ad hoc* that the borrowing arrangement assumes importance for the government.

Second, that the government can ensure against the 'crowding out' effects of public enterprise borrowings in the capital markets. As argued elsewhere in this study, the basic issue relates to the justification for given investments rather than the fact that the borrowings are made by public enterprises.

Third, that there is an economy in the costs of borrowing, since the government can borrow at lower rates of interest than the enterprises. This has been a major argument in the UK.[7] The economic cost of capital used remains the same, irrespective of this factor. However, there is a distributional effect, namely, that lenders secure less through interest incomes.

Fourth, that government loans have two features which loans from private parties do not have, namely, they can be converted into equity at the discretion of the government, and they can be written off when the need arises.

Finally, that several public enterprises are unable to borrow from the market, either because their profit record is too poor or because the projects to be financed by the borrowings are not attractive to the suppliers of funds except at very high rates of interest or under government guarantee of interest and repayment. There has been a tendency in recent years for some profit-making public enterprises to raise funds through public deposits; in most cases these enjoy government guarantee.

Borrowing from the government – through the National Loans Fund – has been the feature of the nationalised industries in the UK,[8] except for foreign borrowings in a few cases. The French nationalised industries have begun to borrow in the open market in their own names since 1964. Sixty-five per cent of the loan capital of central government enterprises in India comes from the government itself (1985); it neared 90 per cent in such sectors as coal, power, transportation equipment, and textiles. The situation is similar in most other developing countries.

An intermediate mechanism between the government and the market has been in vogue in some countries. A holding company borrows funds on the strength of its total creditworthiness and lends funds to its subsidiaries. The latter by themselves would not be able to attract funds at comparable rates of interest. Here again the economic cost of the capital would be independent of this 'subsidiary' arrangement. IRI of Italy is an example in this connection.

An obvious disadvantage of exclusive lending by the government has been the overextension of public enterprise in many countries, mainly because the financing of their projects has depended more on the easy and cheap money that this method made possible than on valid criteria of investment and reliable feasibility analysis. If the criteria and analyses are rigorous, the dangers of this method would be subdued.

To conclude – the arrangement under which public enterprises should exclusively borrow from the government is, on the whole, questionable. If they are encouraged to borrow from the market, whenever they can, the government would conserve its scarce investible resources for use in directions in which the capital markets, looking for satisfactory financial returns, would not be interested.

Where a public enterprise is expected to look to the market for funds, the government should help in improving its creditworthiness by introducing reasonable additions of equity capital and by ensuring that it builds up reserves. Lenders' confidence would improve under these conditions.

THE CAPITAL STRUCTURE

The proportions of equity and loan capital which the government provides a public enterprise have significance in some ways but not precisely in the way they have in the private sector. There is an asymmetry between the two cases.

A sizeable proportion of equity capital promotes confidence on the part of the lenders; and the enterprise would be able to raise loans on favourable terms. This argument has limited validity in the case of public enterprise where most or all of its loan capital is derived from the government itself or from other sources under government guarantee.

An enterprise, whose profit prospects are high, wishes to keep a sizeable proportion of capital in the form of loans. The cost of loan capital being limited to interest, it has the opportunity of saving a large part of the profit for dividends. Further loan repayments in the course of time would reduce the interest costs and help it build up reserves or issue bonus shares. There is an incidental advantage. Its share prices go up; so does its goodwill. In the case of public enterprise fully owned by the government these advantages are not of material significance, for the entire net revenue eventually belongs to the government, in whichever way it is termed. The question of share values may not arise in most cases since the shares are not quoted on the stock exchange.

There is a tax-oriented argument in the context of the equity–loan ratio. The enterprise can take off interest on loans from the net revenue before its assessable income is computed. If it has only equity capital, the entire net revenue is liable to corporation taxation. This argument has limited relevance to a public enterprise, where the interest, dividend, and taxes all go to the government. (Chapter 11 contains some comments on this problem from the standpoint of the exchequer–public enterprise link.)

However, there are certain considerations which lend weight to the concept of the equity–loan proportion in the case of public enterprise.

First, where an enterprise has to contract, whatever the reason, a reduction in capital is easier to effect through loan repayments than through a reduction in equity capital. The latter is not impossible but depends on compliance with several legal requirements under the company law or the specific statute governing the enterprise.

Second, equity gives the government the opportunity of selling shares to the public, if it applies the policy of privatisation to a given enterprise. In order to gain such convenience, among other reasons, the government had to convert the public corporations into joint stock companies in the UK, with share capital, in preparation for privatisation.

Third, where an enterprise operates in a highly competitive market and private enterprises in the sector have equity capital, it would be purposeful to create a comparable proportion of equity in the capital structure. It gains in justification where the sector concerned is particularly exposed to severe fluctuations. During hard times the enterprise is relieved of the obligations in interest charges, to the extent of its equity capital. The public dividend capital introduced in some nationalised industries in the UK (like the British Steel Corporation and British Airways) illustrates this argument.[9]

The validity of the argument depends on how far the assumptions are satisfied in practice. The enterprise has to be profitable in the long run, so that, while it has a cost relief during unfavourable times, it makes up for it during good times. On an average, the dividends should be satisfactory. In this way equity is a device of cash convenience in the sense that an enterprise which faces the liquidity problem on occasion is not compelled to raise funds for meeting the cost of capital, at least to the extent of its equity capital. But this ought not to be a disguised device to exempt it from the cost of capital or to show that it is not in the red.

In many cases the equity device has been employed with the purpose of giving the enterprise a cost relief because it was unable to raise a net revenue, or because it accumulated heavy loss. The conversion of loans into equity is a familiar practice. These are question-begging practices. It would be preferable to design open remedies in appropriate cases, as argued in chapter 3; even a major financial restructuring involving some write-off of capital is a commendable step. Equity ought not to be used as a device for condoning non-viability or window-dressing the real financial state of the enterprise.

Several enterprises, in both developing and developed countries, have made a plea for equity because loan capital involved high interest charges which could not be met and had led to further borrowings. For example, the National Bus Company (in the UK) presented this view for many years,[10] and so did the British Coal Corporation: 'The interest charges ... are a formidable burden forces to bear and bring out existing financial structure into question ... The Corporation has no equity capital.'[11]

Fourth, the relative amounts of equity and loan capital have some significance in connection with the bonus systems which entitle the employees to a share of the net profit. If the net profit is defined as the profit that remains after the interest on loans is deducted, the less the loan capital, the better for the employees. To the extent that they can influence decisions, they would raise their voice in favour of a relatively low loan component.

It is interesting to note that all the above arguments do not lead to a bias in a single direction. For instance, the tax argument favours a high loan proportion from the angle of the enterprise, while the bonus argument favours a high equity proportion from the angle of the workers.

There is a serious implication of equity during the construction stage of an enterprise. Loan capital attracts interest which is capitalised, since it is a cost which cannot be met from current revenues. But equity is apparently costless; and to the extent of its economic cost, not paid, capitalisation does not take place. In fact this is claimed to be an advantage of the equity device. In real fact it is not, from the community's standpoint. It understates the capital outlay and harbours underpricing, with all the macro disadvantages indicated in chapter 6.

Three conclusions may be outlined:

(a) There is no single sovereign ratio suited to all enterprises. It should depend on its market circumstances and, in any case, should not be a device for anything more than a cash convenience during difficult periods of operations.
(b) Where the government holds to a policy of 100 per cent ownership of an enterprise, that is, all equity is (to be) held by it and the enterprise is in need of additional capital which the government is unable to supply, the government may let it borrow in the capital markets. In

this way the loan proportion in the capital rises, without choice on the part of the enterprise. If the government and the enterprise resent this effect, the only option would be for the enterprise to forfeit the prospect of capital additions.

(c) Where the enterprise is a joint venture with private participation, the equity–loan ratio has to bear some relationship to private sector practices. In particular, the interest of the private shareholders in deriving high dividend incomes has to be respected. Further the government should favour the conversion of accumulating profits into bonus shares to some extent from time to time. Even otherwise, the private shareholders have a claim to the reserves, but they do not derive direct dividend benefits therefrom. If the shares are not quoted in the market or if there are restrictions on share transfers, they do not gain from appreciation in share values either.

RESTRUCTURING

As the title of this section suggests, it refers to an enterprise in operation. There are, however, aspects of restructuring which have relevance in some way to investment decisions. Those are covered here.

Financial restructuring

The most frequent factor that occasions the financial restructuring of an enterprise is accumulated losses (considered in detail in chapter 5). This usually leads to a decision to write-off capital to the extent warranted by the losses. Several nationalised enterprises in the UK – for example, the British Steel Corporation, National Coal Board, and British Railway Board – underwent capital reconstruction through a write-off from time to time. Such a step is overdue in many developing countries in respect of a large number of enterprises. The write-off may refer to government loans, if that suffices, or to equity, as well, if necessary; and where the amount to be written off is too large, the government has to inject cash for the repayment of the debts contracted by the enterprise for financing the losses.

An effective write-off is one which not only gives the enterprise a clean balance sheet but ensures its future viability; or else, the need for a write-off repeats itself in no time. It is for this reason that an adequate cash injection is necessary is some cases, over and above the bare need to satisfy the creditors.

In practice, governments have not generally followed adequate policies of financial reconstruction for various reasons:

(i) A write-off may be considered as an open admission of failure on the part of the enterprise. This might be politically embarrassing to the government.

(ii) The government takes an unrealistic position by arguing that the enterprise will turn around in the future.
(iii) The government does not have enough resources to introduce fresh capital in the enterprise.

The need for the write-off is a *fait accompli*. The longer it is delayed, the more uneconomic the situation becomes. Yet many governments have been taking haphazard measures; they introduce some cash, often too little and too late (Kenya Meat Commission is an example); they encourage bank credit to ailing enterprises; they let cross-debts be of some help; and/or they refrain from taking any fundamental measures by going through the motions of discussion and committee studies for a long time.

Apart from timely financial restructuring in individual cases, the government should undertake a dispassionate aggregation of such needs in the public enterprise sector. They should be classified under different heads, first, in terms of magnitudes: for example, cases which only require the write-off of loans, cases which (also) require the write-off of equity, and cases where cash has to be injected. (Elaborate legal procedures might be involved in some cases.) Next they should also be classified in terms of urgency, from an overall angle. This prevents *ad hoc* attention to individual enterprises, often influenced by, and reflecting, personal inclinations or political pressures. In other words, it is desirable to formulate an overall strategy of financial restructuring. This is all the more imperative when the government has limited funds for the purpose. Where cash resources are to be introduced it might be economical, on balance, for the government to borrow the required funds and employ them as the restructuring strategy commends. If the government refrains from such a step, investments already made, assets already created, and technological and other developments already achieved, will remain infructions in many cases.

There is a bottom line. Not every enterprise in heavy accumulated deficits should automatically be eligible to generous measures of financial restructuring. Where their future viability is in doubt, for whatever reason, contraction or liquidation would be a preferable policy.

Physical restructuring

Not all restructuring meant to improve the allocational efficiency of an investment is exclusively financial in nature. There are three other areas in which major restructuring may be necessary:

(i) The original investments may have resulted, despite careful cost-benefit analysis, in unviable projects, in the sense that the capacities set up have proved excessive or alternatively infra-optimal, the location turns out to be uneconomical (beyond original assumptions, if any), the technology is deficient by current standards, and the product structure originally envisaged is unrealistic when compared with the demands met in the course of time. Suitable adjustments should be made in all these respects, involving some rectifying investments.

(ii) The organisational structure of the enterprise may be affecting the viability of the investment which is otherwise viable. Chapter 2 deals with this question in detail. While overlarge enterprises (like the British Transport Commission of 1947) need to be broken, enterprises which are too small to be optimal should be brought together, either through appropriate amalgamations, or through the disintegration of certain functions (like marketing, purchasing, or major maintenance), into a common unit capable of scale economies. For example, many public enterprises at the state level in India, Malaysia, and Nigeria belong to the latter category.

There is another dimension to organisational restructuring. The objectives of the enterprise should be homogeneous as far as possible, so that economies of scale as well as of specialisation are possible. And production in areas where the enterprise has no economies of scale at all in a competitive market should be given up.

(iii) In some cases rehabilitation or modernisation of the plant may be necessary, if it is run down. If competitors are better placed, the disadvantage of not doing so would be very material.

To conclude this section – first, restructuring involves more than financial restructuring in most cases, since the eventual objective is to place the enterprise on an assured road to viability. Second, governments spread resources too thinly over a large number of enterprises warranting financial restructuring. Third, they generally show more interest in setting up new projects than in fully capitalising the existing areas. Further, many enterprises are provided with too little working capital, with the result that moneys meant for capital expenditures are sometimes diverted to current purposes – a measure that deviates from the project feasibility proposal. Finally, timely and adequate restructuring is a corollary of proper investment, since it moves the project towards the accomplishment of the investment criteria.

CONCLUSION

Investment decision has been one of the weakest factors in the field of public enterprise. Cost-benefit analysis is an approach whose success depends on the soundness of the implicit value judgements. Market conditions have, in many cases, differed substantially from the estimates contained in the feasibility study. The discounted cash flow technique is again as good as the discount rate adopted, and more fundamentally, it is neutral to the estimates of costs and revenues.

A public enterprise that substantially fails to come up to the intended standards of investment efficiency is in need of restructuring – the earlier the better, on both micro and macro grounds. Restructuring is not an exclusively financial exercise; attention should be focused on the apparently non-financial elements which impact on investment efficiently.

The question of equity–loan ratio has limited significance in fully-owned public enterprise. In any case equity should not operate as a disguised source of subsidy.

Many governments have begun to attach serious concern to the poor returns the investments in public enterprise have been producing. They should dispassionately examine whether any social returns of a compensatory nature are really accruing. Where the answer is doubtful or negative, the situation must be deemed unfavourable even on the basis of social cost-benefit analysis.

APPENDIX 4.1

Table 4.1 The feasibility study

Project background and history
- State:
  - Name and address of project promoter
  - Project orientation: market or raw material oriented
  - Market orientation: domestic or export
  - Economic and industrial policies supporting the project
  - Project background

Market and plant capacity
- List annual data on:
  - Demand
  - Projected sales
  - Production programme
  - Plant capacity

Materials and inputs
- Describe general availability of:
  - Raw materials
  - Auxiliary materials
  - Factory supplies
  - Utilities
- List annual supply requirements of material inputs

Location and site
- Describe location and state plant site

Project engineering
- Describe layout and scope of the project
- State technology finally selected
- Summarise equipment selected
- Describe required civil engineering works

Plant organisation and overhead costs

Manpower
State selected type and size of labour force
State selected type and size of staff

Implementation scheduling
Duration of plant erection and installation
Duration of production start-up and running-in period

Financial and economic evaluation
Total investment costs
List major investment data in local and foreign exchange, as needed, for:
Land and site preparation
\+ civil.engineering works
\+ technology and equipment
\+ pre-production capital csots
\+ working capital

= total investment costs

Project financing (assumed)
Sources of financing
Impact of cost of financing and debt servicing on project proposals
Public policy and regulations on financing
Financing institutions
Required financial statements
Financial ratios
Total production or manufacturing costs (at feasible normal capacity)
List annual data for:
Factory costs
\+ administrative overheads
\+ sales and distribution costs

= operating costs
\+ financial costs
= depreciation

= total production or manufacturing costs

Financial evaluation
Net present value
Internal rate of return

Pay-back period
Simple rate of return
Break-even analysis
Sensitivity analysis

National economic evaluation
Appraise the project proposal from the national economic point of view

Conclusions
Major advantages of project
Major drawbacks of project
Chances of implementing the project

Source: *Manual for the Preparation of Industrial Feasibility Studies*, New York: UNIDO, 1978, pp. 31–3, 151–2.

Table 4.2 Financial and economic evaluation

National economic evaluation

Preliminary tests
- Project exchange rate
- Effective rate of protection

Cost-benefit analysis. When applying the UNIDO method of economic project evaluation, estimate:
- Direct benefits to aggregate consumption
- Direct costs to aggregate consumption
- Indirect benefits and costs to aggregate consumption
- Redistribution of income

To apply the UNIDO method, calculate:
- Shadow price of labour
- Shadow price of foreign exchange
- Shadow price of investment

Estimate social rate of discount

Financial evaluation

Compute commercial profitability criteria
- Net present value
- Internal rate of return
- Pay-back period
- Simple rate of return
- Break-even analysis
- Sensitivity analysis

Source: *Manual for the Preparation of Industrial Feasibility Studies*, New York: UNIDO, 1978, pp. 31–3, 151–2.

Part II

The working

5 Financial performance

This chapter commences with a cross-sectional reference to the financial performance of public enterprises in different regions over the last four decades. Our main interest is analytical, in reviewing the accuracy of the accounting facts and exploring the factors underlying the state of performance. The accounting adjustments needed in interpreting them will also be indicated.

Three aspects of performance will be considered: continuing losses, accumulated losses, and self-financing/reserves. Policy measures needed to deal with the situation will be indicated under each head.

Illustrative empirical material will be shifted to the appendices, except for the introductory references to some country situations in the first section.

Two prefatory observations are necessary. This chapter does not intend to suggest that non-financial returns are unimportant; and the question of whether a public enterprise must make a profit or a high profit will be reserved until the next chapter.

THE STATE OF FINANCIAL PERFORMANCE

In general the financial performance of public enterprises has been unsatisfactory in most countries, developed and developing, in all regions. Annual returns have been low, there are large accumulated losses, and capital write-offs have been frequent. This section provides illustrative references to the situation.

The UK

The 1961 White Paper observed that the financial performance of nationalised industries 'has generally fallen short of . . . hopes'.[1] Until the early 1980s they were characterised by relatively low rates of return. Appendix 5.1 gives comparative data on public and private enterprises.

Austria

OIGA, the public enterprise apex, made a deficit of more than ASch 12 billion in 1986 (*The Financial Times*, London, 3 December 1987).

Pakistan

Dividend payments in 1984–5 amounted to 2.41 per cent of the investment, and interest on loans from the Federal Government was paid at about 6 per cent.[2]

Malaysia

About 186 out of 736 public enterprises made losses in 1986 and 255 earned returns below 4 per cent.[3]

Nepal

The gross profit was 1.4 per cent on capital employed in 1985–6 and 3.5 per cent in 1986–7.[4]

Korea

'In 1982 the rate of returns of operating capital was estimated to be only 3.7 per cent for the Government Invested Enterprises, as against a 10.1 per cent for industry as a whole.'[12]

Philippines

The financial rate of return for non-financial corporations (before government transfers) varied between −25.3 per cent in 1975 and 0.1 per cent in 1983, and that of financial corporations, between 1.6 per cent and 1.4 per cent.[13]

Trinidad and Tobago

The non-petroleum public enterprises recorded 'negative savings' of $688 million in 1985.[14]

Peru

The net profit of public enterprises was negative in 1987 in most sectors of activity.[15]

Sri Lanka

'The subsidised corporations have failed to break even with the government grant, and the entities that are required to earn profits are operating at recurring losses . . . Some corporations in effect are insolvent, if not for government backing.' (Eighth Report from the Committee on Public Enterprises, Parliamentary Series no. 77, Colombo, 1985, pp. 26–7.)

Kenya

Many public enterprises 'expected to be viable' 'have not been profitable'.[5] Several, including some big units have never made a profit since inception.[6] 'Performance in this sector as a whole remains disappointing' (Budget speech for 1982–3, Nairobi, 1982, p. 5).

Nigeria

The government's investments in public enterprise are over 23 billion, but the annual returns are below half a billion Naira.[7]

Ghana

The performance of public enterprises has been 'abysmal'; their 'low profitability' has been a concern to the government.[8]

Zambia

The financial performance of public enterprises has been 'quite mediocre', and the holding complex ZIMCO 'had no after-tax profits' after 1980.[9]

Zaire

The financial performance of public enterprises has been 'extremely poor'. The mining firm GECAMINES excepted, they had an average return of 0.9 per cent of equity capital between 1983 and 1985.[10]

Some other African countries:[11]

Niger

In 1983 net deficits of the 'studied' public enterprises equalled 40 per cent of its 1982 GDP.

Tanzania

Between 1976 and 1979 a third of all public enterprises ran at losses.

Mali

The losses of public enterprises were 6 per cent of GDP at the end of the 1980s.

Togo

Eight public enterprises alone had losses equal to 4 per cent of GDP in 1980.

The foregoing evidence[16] is sufficiently strong to suggest that the financial performance of public enterprises has, on the whole, been unfavourable. This is the end result of a variety of factors as shown in the fifth section of this chapter.

SOME CONCEPTUAL ISSUES

Let us pursue some points of conceptual interest.

The returns profile

The first concerns generalisations on the aggregate performance of the public enterprise sector. This is, indeed, of relevance to the public exchequer, as chapter 11 shows. Otherwise it would be more purposeful to look at the disaggregated profile of financial returns, so as to gain a precise idea of the seriousness of the problem. One or a few highly profitable or losing enterprises may influence the overall result of percentage of return on capital. This hardly tells the full story. To illustrate from Indian data: the 214 public enterprises of the central government, covered by the Bureau of Public Enterprises report, earned 12.5 per cent of gross profit on capital outlay in 1986–7 – an apparently impressive figure. The most profitable enterprise, the Oil and Natural Gas Commission, had a pre-tax profit of Rs 21,050 million which represented a little less than half of the total profit earned by all profit-making enterprises, exceeded the combined loss of all the loss-making enterprises, and accounted for two-thirds of the aggregate net profit of the 214.[17]

The facts that the aggregate figure does not disclose are that 100 out of the 214 made losses, and that the capital outlay associated with losses or very low profits was quite significant. These details come out of a returns profile. That is one way of dealing with the limitations of aggregates and averages. In fact, it is desirable to know, additionally, the numbers of enterprises marked by different ranges of returns. Appendix 5.2 gives such information for Malaysia and shows both the numbers and the capital outlay involved in the case of Peru, Pakistan, and India. More than half the total number in Malaysia had losses or very low returns (below 4 per cent in 1986); about half in number and three-fourths in capital outlay were marked by losses or returns below 6 per cent in Pakistan in 1981–2; and the situation in Peru was similar.

Another useful version of the returns profile consists of a statement of returns by sector of activity. While still being subject to limitations of aggregates within sectors, it can indicate which sectors lag in profitability; and this can be meaningful in unfolding the 'public' purpose of government ownership in certain sectors like public utilities and heavy engineering. However, 'manufacturing or consumers goods' categories might be too heterogeneous in composition to be of much use in drawing inferences. One might expect these to be profitable, but the Indian data, shown in chapter 10, do not confirm that impression (Table 5.10 in Appendix 5.2 also shows a typical sector profile – for Nepal).

The net revenue figures

How acurate, conceptually, is the net revenue figure, in terms of which the foregoing inferences were drawn? There are many reasons that prompt this question. The net revenue figure is the difference between revenues and costs as recorded in the accounts. It is doubtful if the costs recorded represent 'economic costs'[18] on the definition that the value of an input is its opportunity cost, or for practical purposes, what someone else would pay for it. A close review of the accounting and financial practices relating to public enterprises in both developed and developing countries suggests that the costs, on the basis of which the net revenue figure is derived, are not economic costs, and that the real net revenues are, therefore, lower than even the low recorded figures. This conclusion helps us emphasise the unnoticed losses sustained by the economy as a whole through the undervaluation of several resources used by public enterprises.

The single largest source of cost understatement relates to the capital employed. The rule should be to enumerate all capital injections, fix an economic price for each of them, compute the cost for use of each item of the capital employed, and aggregate all such costs. Laws do not require this procedure, nor do governments in practice. In fact, confusion at the level of policy has encouraged governments and enterprises to pursue financial practices which clearly fall short of the conceptual requirements of costing. (Chapter 3 hints at some of the practices.) Let us enumerate the factors causing deviations from economic costing:

(a) An enterprise may receive a grant from the government initially or from time to time to enable it to undertake certain capital expenditures.[19] The grant is not accompanied by an annual servicing obligation. Hence, there is no cost entry in the accounts.

(b) An enterprise receives equity from the government, on which the servicing obligation in the form of dividend is contingent on profit being available and the directors declaring a dividend. Accounts do not treat it as a cost. (Chapter 4 brings out the details of this issue.)

(c) An enterprise receives loans from the government – free for some years or all along, or at low rates of interest. In the last case interest enters the financial accounts as a cost but at less than the market rate.

(d) Reserves or retained earnings do not warrant any cost entry in the accounts because no payment (interest or dividend or a share in profit) is obligatory for the use of this resource.

(e) Interest not paid on government capital – not an unusual occurrence – may be provided for in the profit and loss account, but shown as a liability in the balance sheet.[20] In the following years it is not treated as an interest-eligible liability; in this way a cost understatement occurs.

(f) Depreciation policies are a major element of cost distortion. An enterprise may provide it on historical cost basis or on current cost basis. The former entails a lower cost debit than the use of assets currently employed warrants.

(g) An enterprise may decide to capitalise certain expenditures which commercial procedure justifies being treated as deferred revenue expenditures; but they are not promptly written down.

(h) An asset may remain uncapitalised, though brought into use. It remains as work-in-progress and no depreciation is provided in respect of it.

(i) An enterprise may make lower provisions for bad debts than circumstances warrant. The debtors continue on the balance sheet as an over-aged asset.

(j) The valuation of stock may be defective, for example, on production cost basis, as against the market-price basis where the latter is lower; or large unsaleable inventories are carried on in the balance sheet.

(k) An enterprise may treat the sale of an asset as regular sales, inflating the gross revenue. The higher the overstatement, the higher the sale value is in comparison with the book value of the asset.

(l) An enterprise may not make full provision for obsolescence in respect of its stocks or equipment.

(m) An enterprise may overlook making full provisions for claims against it from customers, or creditors, or workers (for example, for gratuities), or tax authorities, or other parties.

(n) An enterprise may not fully provide for shortages discovered in the course of physical verification of stocks or properties.

(o) Some costs which belong to the enterprise operations may be borne by the government. They do not enter the accounts of the enterprise.[21]

Appendix 5.3 contains a wealth of illustrative material on the ways in which costs get understated either deliberately or through wrong accounting policies adopted by Indian public enterprises, as disclosed by the Comptroller and Auditor-General (CAG) in his report for 1984.[22]

The most serious understatement occurs in respect of the cost of using capital resources. This does not figure in audit reports, including the CAG's, for the simple reason that the law does not require provision for the economic cost of capital. The reference is to items (a), (b), (c), and (d) cited above. Historical cost depreciation is another serious cause of net revenue overstatement.

It is necessary to insist that every public enterprise should provide notional statements that disclose its real status of profitability after allowing for these deficiencies. The first is a notional statement of cost of capital and recomputed net revenue as shown in Table 5.1.

Table 5.1 Recomputed net revenue (I)

1.	*Capital employed*	
	Equity	*a*
	Long-term loans	*b*
	Reserves	*c*
	Total (*a* + *b* + *c*)	*d*
2.	*Notional cost of capital* (at, say, 12 per cent)	*e*
3.	*Net revenue before interest* (as recorded in the accounts)	*f*
4.	*Real net revenue* (*f* – *e*)	*g*
5.	*Real net revenue* (as per cent of capital employed) (*g* as % of *d*)	*h*

An example is worked out in Appendix 5.4 (Table 5.11) showing that the recomputed loss of the Heavy Engineering Corporation Ltd (of India) was Rs 7,100 million in 1981–82 as against the figure of Rs 2,300 million shown in the accounts. In the case of the British Steel Corporation, the recomputed figure of loss was £357 million in 1987–88 as against the accounting profit of £41 million; and the accumulated loss by 1987–88, with 1981–82 as the starting point was £4,864 million as against the accounting figure of minus £642 million (see Table 5.12.)

There is need for another qualification. The components of capital employed in Table 5.1 are historical figures. It might be better to use, instead, the current value figure of net assets on which the notional cost may be worked out. This would take the place of '*d*' in the above computation. Item 5 would also be worked out in terms of that net asset value.

As regards depreciation also, information should be required as shown in Table 5.2, wherever the current cost method is not already adopted.

Table 5.2 Recomputed net revenue (II)

1.	Net revenue before interest (as recorded in the accounts)	*a*
2.	Depreciation on current cost basis	*b*
3.	Depreciation on historical cost basis	*c*
4.	Additional provision for depreciation $(b - c)$	*d*
5.	Recomputed net revenue $(a - d)$	*e*

Such information is required of the nationalised industries in the UK. Their annual reports contain supplementary statements which clearly reveal the substantial difference in net revenue under the two methods. (Appendix 5.5 contains a condensed version relating to the British Airports Authority for 1975–85.)

As regards the other causes of over- or under-statement in net revenue, effective audit would be the best source of information, particularly where the CAG has direct responsibility for the audit or has powers of issuing directives to private auditors. A brief statement (of the causes and figures) may be produced and appended to the annual report of the enterprise, bringing out the net effect of errors in accounting policy or practice on the final figure of net revenue. Table 5.3 is an illustrative format.

Table 5.3 Recomputed net revenue (III)

1.	Net revenue as recorded in the accounts	*a*
2.	Overstatement of net revenue through the following errors or practices	*b*
3.	Understatement of net revenue through the following errors or practices	*c*
4.	Recomputed net revenue $(a - b + c)$	*d*

The purpose of this section is to suggest that the total real cost of operations of a public enterprise has to be established and that its net revenue figure needs to be recomputed on grounds of economic costing. There is no suggestion of any aspersion on the managers.

ACCUMULATED DEFICITS

Deficits accumulated over a series of years are another serious aspect of the financial performance of several public enterprises in almost every country.

The obvious reason is that deficits are incurred year after year and policy measures are not promptly taken to deal with the situation.

Some selective evidence is provided in Appendix 5.6 to suggest that a sizeable proportion of the total number of public enterprises is marked by accumulated deficits, and that the size of such deficits is relatively precarious in most cases. For example, a little more than half the total number of enterprises had accumulated deficits in India by 1985–86; and these amounted to about a third of their total equity plus long-term loan capital (see Table 5.14). Cumulative losses in some enterprises in Sri Lanka (by 1986) were as high as three and four times the value of the fixed assets (see Table 5.16). Thirty per cent of the government's share capital in Nepal's public enterprises was eroded by accumulated deficits by 1986 (see Table 5.17). Twenty Peruvian public enterprises in the non-financial sector had accumulated losses which eroded net worth by more than 50 per cent (in several cases by more than 100 per cent) between 1983 and 1986 (see Table 5.18).

Accumulated losses are an acute source of cash problems. They are financed by bank loans. The loans are ordinarily short term in nature and at high rates of interest. The interest paid on the loans necessitated by accumulated losses is a substantial figure and, in several cases, can make a difference between loss and profit in the annual financial record. Appendix 5.7 (Table 5.19) contains a detailed illustration with reference to the 112 enterprises (of the central government) with accumulated deficits in India for the year 1985–86. The interest on the deficits at the rate of 14 per cent (which represented the average rate on loans) exceeded the recorded figure of loss before interest in all but 24 cases. In other words, the annual record of most of the enterprises was *not* one of loss arising out of the year's operations, though the accounts suggest that all of them made losses in the year. The most remarkable instance is the Heavy Engineering Corporation Ltd, the notorious loser, whose accumulated losses were so high that the financial charges related to them were about four times its loss before interest in 1985–86.

The figures of accumulated deficits are likely to continue in the books of many public enterprises for a long time. Hence, for the sake of conceptual clarity on the real status of profitability year after year, it is desirable to ask for a supplementary statement such as is shown in Table 5.4 in the annual report.

Table 5.4 Financial impact of accumulated deficits

1.	Accumulated deficits	*a*
2.	Interest at x% on (1)	*b*
3.	Year's profit or loss before interest	*c*
4.	Year's profit or loss before interest, after deducting the interest on accumulated losses $(c - b)$	*d*
5.	Item (3) as per cent of capital employed	*e*
6.	Item (4) as per cent of capital employed	*f*

SELF-FINANCING

The accounts of some public enterprises indicate that they have accumulated sizeable reserves and have been able to self-finance expansions. But how correct, conceptually, is the figure?

The term 'self-financing' or 'reserves' is uncontroversial when the profits or net resources are retained after all costs, on the basis of economic costing, are met in the first place. Earlier analyses raise doubts on whether the reserves satisfy this definition. When current cost depreciation is not adopted, the figure of profit retained is fictitious. More importantly, the full costs of capital may not have been met before the figure of retained profits is shown in the accounts. No cost obligation is met in the case of grants; low or no obligation is met in the case of government loans; low or no dividends are paid on equity capital; and no profit transfer to the government takes place for the use of reserve capital. Appendix 5.8 contains detailed evidence on the non-payment of dividends on government equity in India.

The conceptual inaccuracy mentioned here applies to developed countries also. For instance, British Airways added to its reserves a total amount of £693 million during 1983–7. But it did not pay dividends in any of those years. Assuming a notional dividend of 10 per cent on the public dividend capital of about £180 million, the 'escaped' dividend payment would amount to about £72 million. The real additions to reserves were therefore £693 million minus £72 million.[23] (In fact we have to make another (downward) adjustment for the notional payments, not made, for the use of the reserve capital itself.)

The so-called reserves are not really net of proper payments for the use of equity (and other) capital. The first impression that an enterprise has been able to achieve large self-financing needs to be suitably revised.

In establishing the real level of reserves, it is difficult to decide how far back to go; ideally, one has to start from the inception of the enterprise. But it might be more realistic to expect the auditors, in particular the CAG, to bring it out by making the necessary adjustments for a period of, say, five years back. Thereafter, annual adjustments can be applied to that figure.

The initial recomputation may be as shown in Table 5.5.

Every year later on the adjustment '$f - (b + c + d)$' should be applied to h to establish the real level of reserves. This would generally be less than h.

This methodology also helps compare the reserve accumulation or self-financing accomplishments of different public enterprises, or of a public enterprise with those of private enterprises in a similar line of business.

For illustrative purposes, a detailed recomputation is made in the case of the National Development Corporation of Tanzania for a fifteen-year period and presented in Appendix 5.9. Once the 'escaped' costs of capital are taken into account, the book value of TSh 113 million of reserves

Table 5.5 Recomputed reserves

1.	Reserves as per the accounts	*a*
2.	Dividends paid over the past 5 years	*b*
3.	Interest paid on long-term loans over the past 5 years	*c*
4.	Profits transferred to the government over the past 5 years	*d*
5.	Total capital employed over the past 5 years (aggregate of each year's total of equity, long-term loans and reserves)	*e*
6.	Notional payments due for use of capital at . . . per cent on (5)	*f*
7.	Difference between notional payments due and actual payments $(f - (b + c + d))$	*g*
8.	Real level of reserves $(a - g)$	*h*

(in 1979) becomes a negative figure of TSh 338.2 million on a notional interest rate of 10 per cent on all capital employed (or – TSh 230.2 million on a notional interest rate of 8 per cent).

THE RATIONALE OF DEFICITS

Why are deficits so common in public enterprise? Figure 5.1 tries to classify the reasons.

Two points of clarification regarding the construction of the figure are necessary. First, while the factors *A* to *E* are broadly distinguishable from one another, they are not completely exclusive of one another. Second, extra-enterprise objectives listed under investment factors (*A*1) concern the capital cost and any continuing impacts of investment decisions motivated by such objectives. Those objectives might or might not be held as valid today. Extra-enterprise objectives listed under government interventions (*D*10) refer to current objectives; and *D*11 refers to other interventions by the government in its capacity as owner-cum-entrepreneur.

The figure makes possible some important conclusions, both for a proper understanding of the problem of deficits and for the formulation of appropriate remedial policies:

(a) The inefficiency of the managers constitutes barely a fraction of the problem. (In some developing countries like India and Nepal the more competent professional managers are reputed to be in the public sector, in fact.) The arrows from *D* and *C*6 towards *E* suggest that managerial inefficiency at any unit of time is partly the product of government interventions and organisational structures.

(b) Some factors impacting on the financial performance of a public enterprise are 'historical'. For instance, *A*1, *A*2, *A*3, and *C*7 are past facts with a continuing legacy. (Appendix 5.10 illustrates the 'inherited' cost difficulties of the British Steel Corporation.)

(c) Another factor which has an impact similar to that of accumulated

Figure 5.1 Causes of public enterprise deficits

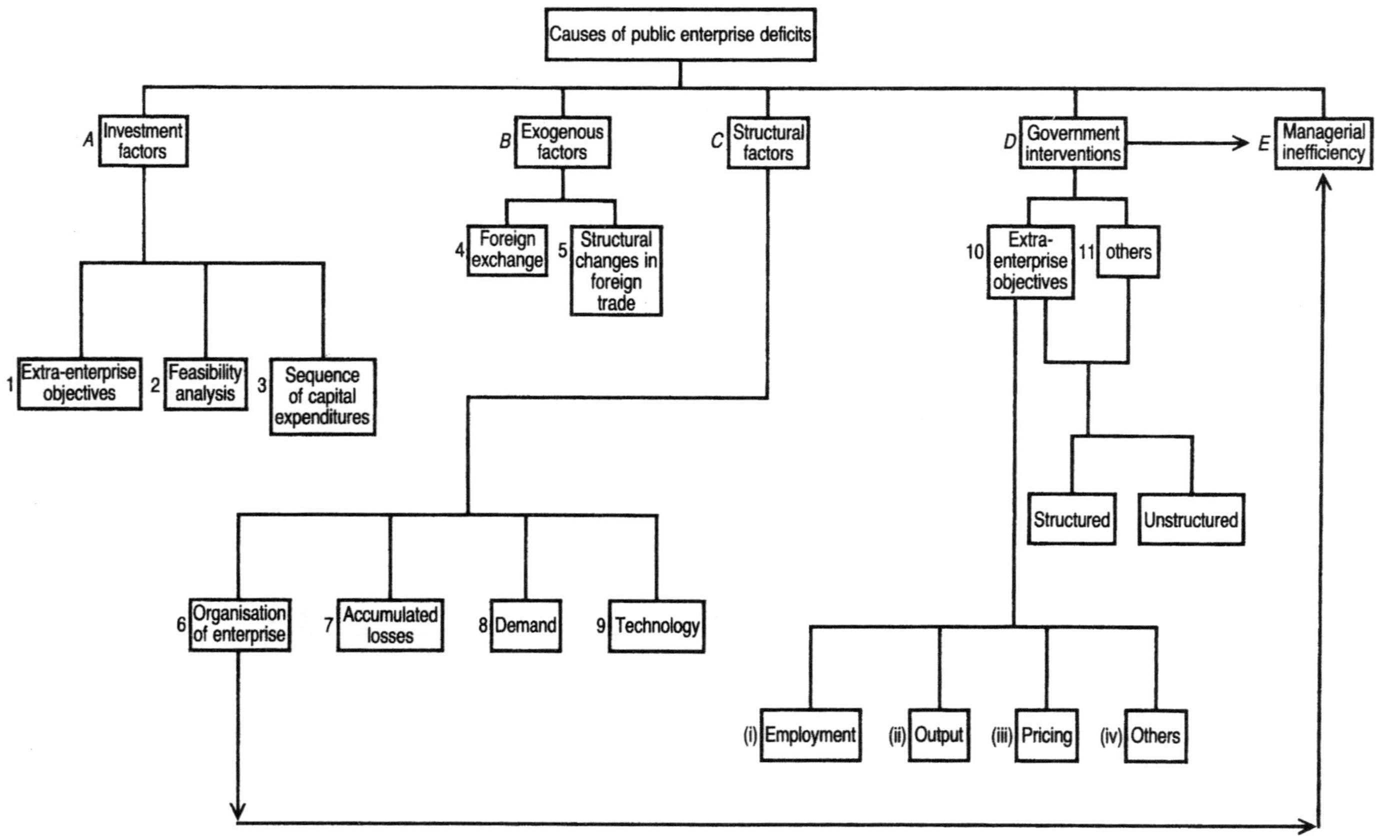

losses consists of overaged government arrears, as in Portugal, in lieu of which an enterprise has to find funds elsewhere, incurring financing charges not meant for its current operations.

(d) Some factors originate in the government's strategy of development, for example, *D*10 (i), (ii), (iii) and (iv) and *C*6 (which refers to those structural aspects of the organisation like a holding company or monolithic form which the enterprise managers by themselves cannot alter).

(e) Certain factors are exogenous, even beyond the government's control, immediately, or at all, for example, *B*4 and *B*5 and *C*8 and *C*9. Talented managers can respond somewhat through structural changes in size, product mix, and technology, provided factor *D* permits.

The analysis suggests that our understanding of the financial performance of a public enterprise improves from the computation of the probable consequences of the factors *A* to *D*, as far as possible. The exercise is bound to be difficult and full agreement between the government and the managers is unlikely to ensue. Yet an attempt is logical and will be fruitful.

Briefly, under the head of investment factors (*A*), the aim should be to establish a figure representing that part of the capital outlay which corresponds to excess capacity, uncommercial motivations and infructuous or 'dead' investment.[24] The annual costs of servicing it, and of the permanent handicaps of location and technology it imposes, may then be calculated. Under factor *B* clear calculation is possible in such cases as currency depreciation causing foreign exchange losses. As regards factor *C*, it is easy to calculate the cost of accumulated losses, but as regards *C*8 and *C*9 a rough estimate is necessary of the costs incurred in the absence of desirable changes in the production function and the product mix, which it has not been possible to introduce for reasons other than managerial incompetence. Factor *D*10 has to be treated as suggested in chapter 3 and the uncompensated financial impacts quantified. Estimates of the financial impacts of government interventions (*D*11) – especially the structured ones – are possible where they have quantifiable implications such as a price freeze, disapproval of a lay-off, closure of a plant, or a compulsive input acquisition. These are not unimportant in practice. Yet several consequences of interventions will remain unquantifiable, for example, frequent changes of the chief executive.

All these estimates should be aggregated and shown as a deduction from the year's costs or as an addition to the net revenue figure. The adjusted figure of financial returns would be nearer the truth when one seeks to know the performance potential of the enterprise during the year. That would also be nearer the state of performance for which the managers might be held responsible.

The exercise suggested in this section is of utmost significance in the context of evaluation of a public enterprise and also of privatisation, as chapters 9 and 14 show respectively. The managers, the government, and the agencies of evaluation should co-ordinate their efforts in producing the necessary supplementary statements of adjustments to the accounting figure of financial returns. Some of the adjustments, like those suggested in this section, tend to increase that figure, while those suggested in the fourth section tend to reduce it.

CONCLUSION

The ways in which the financial performance of public enterprises can be improved should systematically follow the trail of Figure 5.1. (Other chapters discuss the details of how this may be attempted.) The efforts would no doubt be subject to serious technical and political limitations, though pressures from international agencies have been giving a stimulus to needed reforms. But the answers should be eventually found internally.

Poor financial results are a disquieting feature of public enterprises but, on the whole, are due to the managers in small part. Their performance has to be, and can be, improved, no doubt, through (i) training, particularly in the least developed countries; (ii) autonomy which stimulates initiative; (iii) managerial compensations linked with performance; and (iv) the introduction of market disciplines in the enterprise operations. These means rest on the initiative of the government in most countries.

The non-managerial causes of poor performance are of two kinds: those whose impact can be rationalised or eliminated through appropriate policy measures involving government initiative, and those that cannot easily be removed, given the conditions of development planning adopted by the government.

A basic requirement in the context of financial returns of a public enterprise is to attempt supplementary statements of adjustment as argued in this chapter. At the minimum, they provide the means for an accurate perspective of facts; hopefully they can trigger right remedial policies which would otherwise be less likely or accurate.

APPENDIX 5.1

Figure 5.2 Rates of return in public and private enterprises in the UK

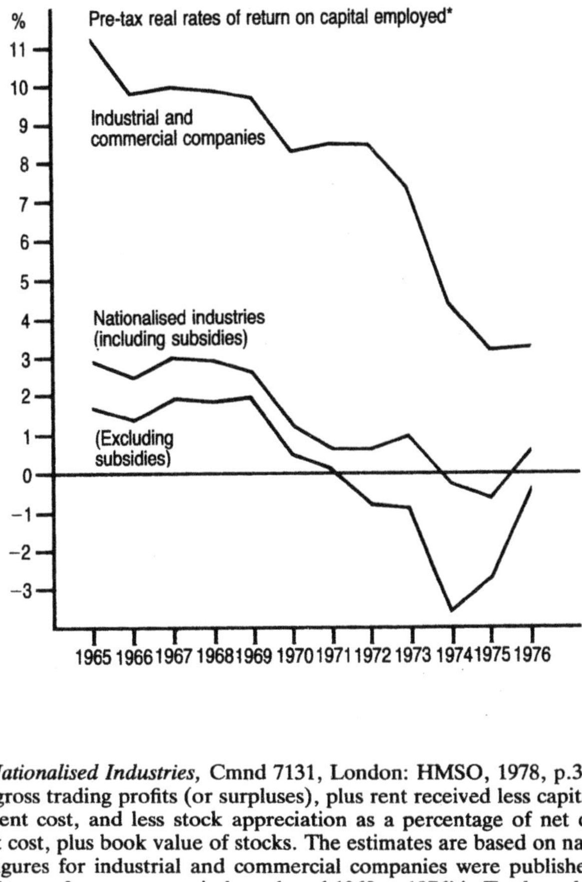

Source: The Nationalised Industries, Cmnd 7131, London: HMSO, 1978, p.36.

* Defined as gross trading profits (or surpluses), plus rent received less capital consumption at replacement cost, and less stock appreciation as a percentage of net capital stock at replacement cost, plus book value of stocks. The estimates are based on national accounts data. The figures for industrial and commercial companies were published in an article 'Companies' rate of return on capital employed 1960 to 1976' in Trade and Industry for 16 September 1977.

APPENDIX 5.2 Returns profiles of public enterprises

Table 5.6 Return on capital employed in public enterprises in Malaysia (1986)

Percentage return	*No. of enterprises*
Negative	186
0 – 4	255
5 – 9	70
10 – 14	59
15 – 19	40
20 and above	126
Total	736

Source: Ministry of Public Enterprises (1989) 'Privatisation in Malaysia', in Ramanadham, V. V. (ed.) *Privatisation in Developing Countries*, London.

Table 5.7 Net profit–net worth ratios in public enterprises in Peru (1985)

Percentage	*No. of enterprises*	*% of net worth*
Negative	23	50
0 – 4	7	20
5 – 9	6	5
10 – 14	6	4
15 – 19	1	0.2
20	13	10
N.A.	10	12

Source: Felipe Ortiz de Zevallos, M. (1989)'Privatisation in Peru', in Ramanadham, V. V. (ed.) *Privatisation in Developing Countries*, London.

Table 5.8 Returns on public enterprise investments in Pakistan (1981–82)

Percentage	*No. of enterprises*	*Capital employed (mill. Rs)*
Negative	26	3,871
0 – 6	21	38,639
6 – 10	9	4,219
10 and above	44	8,240
Total	100	54,969

Source: *Annual Report 1982–83*, vol. II (Statistical Appendices) *Public Sector Industries* (Experts Advisory Cell) in so far as manufacturing enterprises are concerned; and *Government-sponsored Corporations 1981–82* for the others.

Table 5.9 Public enterprises in India – gross profit* as percentage of capital employed (1986–87)

Percentage	*No. of enterprises*	*% of total no.*
Less than 0	60	30
0 – 4	17	8.5
4 – 9	22	11
10 – 14	37	18.5
15 – 19	28	14
20 – 29	19	9.5
30 and above	17	8.5
Total	200	100

Source: Bureau of Public Enterprises (1988) *Public Enterprises Survey 1986–87*, vol. 1, New Delhi, pp. 42–64.
*Before interest and profit.

Table 5.10 Sectoral profile of returns in Nepal (1970/71 to 1986/87)

	Gross profits as % of capital employed					
	1970/71	*1980/81*	*1983/84*	*1984/85*	*1985/86*	*1986/87*
Manufacturing	8.6	3.0	3.4	5.2	3.5	3.9
Public utilities & others	–0.8	2.4	10.7	–2.7	2.1	–0.1
Trade	65.5	–	–	–830.8	24.2	14.5
Total (non-financial)	7.1	–15.6	3.3	–3.9	1.3	2.5
Financial	3.3	3.3	2.6	0.7	1.8	6.9
Total (all sectors)	5.8	–4.7	2.9	–2.6	1.4	3.5

Source: Ministry of Finance, Corporation Coordination Division, Kathmandu.

APPENDIX 5.3 Errors and misrepresentations in public enterprise accounts

The purpose of this appendix is to illustrate, from the authoritative comments of the Comptroller and Auditor-General of India on the accounts of many public enterprises for 1982–3, the inaccurate impressions that the published figures can produce regarding the real nature of results and the amount of profit. The comments relate to various aspects of accounting policy, practice, and presentation, for example, the revenue and capital expenditure decisions, the capitalisation of revenue expenditures and the incorrect treatment of certain expenditures as deferred revenue expenditures or vice versa, practices of asset valuation, the treatment of subsidies received from the government, decisions on depreciation, non-provision for certain costs (for example through 'cash' rather than 'accrual' basis), incorrect treatment of special incomes and expenditures, inaccuracies in computing payments due to the government, for example, interest and 'surplus payable to government', and so on.

It may be noted that these illustrations represent the simpler of the accounting problems discussed in the chapter, originating, essentially, in 'incorrect' omissions or commissions of accounting, which watchful audit can reveal. They do not reflect the 'macro' elements of accounting practices and presentations brought out in the chapter, suggesting the need for adjustments of 'notionality'. With these, ordinarily, the auditors, under the laws, are not very concerned, nor is the Auditor-General, on the whole.

Bharat Aluminium Corporation Ltd

The company had not been able to determine the actual cost of each product.

Bharat Coking Coal Limited

(a) Profit was overstated due to:

  (i) Overstatement of closing stock by Rs 25.67 lakhs resulting from inclusion of rejected coal, shale and coal loaded into a wagon which was missing even before weighment.
  (ii) Overvaluation of closing stock of coal by Rs 316.63 lakhs by inclusion of element of expenses on handling and loading yet to be incurred in future.
  (iii) Non-provision for obsolete and unserviceable stores and spares (Rs 26.47 lakhs).

(b) Capital stores worth Rs 19.94 lakhs issued to collieries in earlier years continued to be shown as stock in transit.

Bharat Earth Movers Limited

The fact that change in the method of valuation of work-in-progress had the effect of decrease in profit by Rs 78.50 lakhs was not disclosed.

Bharat Gold Mines Limited

Loss was overstated by Rs 5.78 lakhs and understated by Rs 2.79 lakhs due to:

(a) Excess provision for gratuity and treatment of capital expenditure as revenue expenditure.
(b) Treatment of capital profit on sale of assets as miscellaneous income and understatement of consumption of raw materials, stores, and spares.

Bharat Heavy Electricals Ltd

Fixed overheads having been absorbed on the base of production actually achieved, which was much less than the rated capacity of the plant, the product cost per unit was very high.

Bharat Petroleum Corporation Limited

Profit was overstated by Rs 54.55 lakhs due to:

(a) Under provision of depreciation amounting to Rs 47.45 lakhs.
(b) Accounting of Rs 7.10 lakhs as income on scrap material which was actually held in stocks as on 31-3-1983.

Bharat Heavy Plate and Vessels Limited

Profit was overstated due to:

(a) Inclusion of fabrication charges in the value of work-in-progress at 97.5 per cent of proportionate realisable value (which was higher than cost) instead of lower of the proportionate realisable value or cost (Rs 36.00 lakhs).
(b) Inclusion of an item valued Rs 3.40 lakhs both in work-in-progress and finished stock.
(c) Non/under – provision for doubtful debts (Rs 4.26 lakhs).
(d) Overstatement of despatches to customers (Rs 1.27 lakhs).
(e) Taking credit for income in excess and non-admissible claims (Rs 0.96 lakhs).
(f) Non-provision for liabilities in respect of royalty and value of returnable scrap (Rs 1.18 lakhs).

Braithwaite and Company Limited

The effect of the change in the accounting policy towards evaluation of project cost which resulted in reduction in loss by Rs 12.62 lakhs was not disclosed.

Bridge and Roof Company (India) Limited

Provision for contingencies had been made at 10 per cent of profits instead of the usual one-third of profits.

Central Coalfields Limited

Immovable assets of closed mines which could not be used in other mines, were not written off (Rs 2.73 lakhs).

Central Inland Water Transport Corporation Limited

Subsidy amounting to Rs 1.50 lakhs received from the Government of India for procurement of certain capital equipment had been shown under paid-up capital.

Coal India Limited

The impact of the National Coal Wage Agreement III for the period from 1 January 1983 to 31 March 1983 was not quantified and provided for.

Dredging Corporation of India Ltd

Cost of installation of fixed assets, wherever departmentally done, had not been capitalised.

Eastern Coalfields Limited

Loss was understated due to:	(Rs in lakhs)
(a) Taking excess credit for claims for subsidy from Coal Price Regulation Account for Retention Price	260.76
(b) Short provision for depreciation	13.91
(c) Underprovision of liabilities in respect of stores consumed, overtime payable, other revenue expenditure, etc.	3.54
(d) Overstatement of closing inventories	2.47
(e) Non-provision of liability for gratuity	7.09
(f) Underprovision for bad debts	2.20

Electronics Corporation of India Limited

(a) Liability for excise duty in respect of goods lying in the factory was not provided for.
(b) Demands aggregating Rs 31.29 lakhs raised against the company by sales tax authorities were not accounted for.

Heavy Engineering Corporation Limited

(a) Inventory of semi-finished products was overvalued by Rs 13.55 lakhs due to:
  (i) double adjustments, and
  (ii) adoption of higher rates.
(b) Inventory was overvalued/overstated as no provision was made on:
  (i) castings/forgings (Rs 20 lakhs) declared surplus/scrap on account of cancellation/suspension of orders but valued at current rates.

(ii) Refractory bricks/patterns (Rs. 35.69 lakhs) which had become unfit for operational use or deteriorated.

Heavy Engineering Corporation Ltd

Uniform policy for valuation of goods, closing stock of finished as well as semi-finished goods, was not followed in different divisions of the company.

Hindustan Antibiotics Limited

(a) Revenue expenditure of Rs 62.90 lakhs incurred on certain plants during the year on trial operations, beyond normal allowable commissioning period of six months from the date of completion, was treated as capital expenditure.
(b) Change in the basis of providing depreciation resulted in less charge for depreciation amounting to Rs 86.99 lakhs.

Hindustan Aeronautics Limited

(a) Profit was overstated by Rs 208.73 lakhs due to:

   (i) Inclusion of prior period sales in current year's sales (Rs 11.77 lakhs).
   (ii) Overvaluation of sales by Rs 109.65 lakhs due to taking the sales at the latest fixed cost quotation, instead of at the Raw Material Service (RMS) order rates.
   (iii) Inclusion of miscellaneous income of Rs 72.08 lakhs relating to the previous years in current year's income.
   (iv) Reduction of miscellaneous income relating to previous year from expenditure of current year (Rs 2.50 lakhs).
   (v) Treating miscellaneous expenditure (Rs 12.73 lakhs) for the year as prior period expenses.

(b) Profit was understated by Rs 53.71 lakhs due to:

   (i) Treating deferred revenue expenditure of Rs 31.93 lakhs as revenue expenditure.
   (ii) Inclusion of consumption/miscellaneous expenditure relating to previous years as that of current year (Rs 21.78 lakhs).

Hindustan Copper Limited

Profit (Rs 1.46 lakhs) on sale of fixed assets had been treated as revenue, instead of transferring the same to capital reserve.

Hindustan Fertilizer Corporation Limited

Revenue expenditure of Rs 95.27 lakhs during trial operations beyond the normal period up to six months from the date of completion of Haldia Plant was treated as capital expenditure.

Hindustan Insecticides Limited

Revenue expenditure of Rs 184.72 lakhs incurred during trial operations beyond the normal period of 6 months from the date of completion of DDT (Technical) plant was treated as capital expenditure instead of deferred revenue expenditure.

Hindustan Shipyard Limited

Customs and countervailing duties were short-provided to the extent of Rs 10.50 lakhs.

Man-days required for completion of vessels and guaranteed repair costs had not been taken into account in determining the realisable value, with the result that work-in-progress was overvalued by Rs 34.32 lakhs.

Work-in-progress was overvalued by Rs 46.50 lakhs by inclusion of value of steel cut-pieces lying on the shop-floor.

Indian Dairy Corporation

During the year, the company had changed the method of accounting of interest on loans given for dairy projects with moratorium on payment of interest from accrual basis to actual receipt basis, and as a result of this the interest income had been understated to the extent of Rs 893.31 lakhs. The accounting of the interest on loan on cash basis is not only contrary to the accepted principles of commercial accounting but also against the provisions of the Companies Act, 1956.

Indian Drugs & Pharmaceuticals Limited

Loss was understated on account of:

(a) Capitalisation of expenditure on replacements (Rs 19.58 lakhs) which should have been charged to revenue.
(b) Overcapitalisation of depreciation (Rs 8.20 lakhs).
(c) Inventories were overstated due to adoption of rates higher than realisable value/actual cost, inclusion of obsolete packing material and life-expired medicines.
(d) Short provision of depreciation by Rs 98.26 lakhs on account of adopting lower rates.
(e) Non-capitalisation of plant and machinery (valued at Rs 18.94 lakhs)

already installed/commissioned, thereby resulting in undercharge of depreciation to the extent of Rs 2.84 lakhs.

(f) Non-provision for expected loss of Rs 2.69 lakhs on sale of surplus material.

(g) Sales for the year included prior period transactions to the extent of Rs 10.13 lakhs.

Indian Iron & Steel Company Limited

(a) No provision/underprovision was made on account of the following:	(Rs in lakhs)
(i) Interest on arrears of Steel Development Fund contribution payable to J.P.C.	563.81
(ii) Doubtful advances	39.45
(iii) Depreciation	45.28
(iv) Employer's contribution to Provident Fund, unserviceable/obsolete spares, etc., sole selling agency commission, rebate payable to SSIC units	65.16
(b) Sales were overstated as a result of:	
(i) inclusion of goods rejected by the customer	20.17
(ii) double accountal of the same transaction	15.67

IISCO Stanton Pipe & Foundry Company Limited

Loss on disposal of components of an abandoned project was underprovided by Rs 20.27 lakhs due to assessment of realisable value of the components at their original cost instead of at scrap value.

Indian Oil Corporation Limited

Fixed assets had been overstated by Rs 29.13 lakhs due to capitalisation of base rent and amortisation charges which should have been charged off to the profit and loss account.

Mogul Line Limited

The difference between depreciation calculated on the revalued cost and that on the original cost of assets was charged to Capital Reserve for Revaluation of Assets instead of to the profit and loss account.

National Fertilizers Limited

Cost adopted for valuation of closing stock included Rs 727.71 lakhs on account of elements of general administrative and financial expenses and loss of Rs 30.61 lakhs incurred on the sale of sulphur.

National Textile Corporation (Andhra Pradesh, Karnataka, Kerala and Mahe) Limited

(a) Loss was understated due to:

 (i) Treatment of modernisation expenditure of revenue nature (Rs 7.74 lakhs) as deferred revenue expenditure.
 (ii) Inclusion of subsidy (Rs 12.59 lakhs) relating to earlier years in the current year's income.

(b) The fact that the holding company had waived (subject to formal sanction) recovery of interest outstanding up to 31 March 1982 amounting to Rs 7,97,16,874 and Rs 2,18,97,301 for the year was not disclosed.

Punjab Maize Products Limited

Depreciation amounting to Rs 14.11 lakhs on the Starch and Effluent Treatment Plants commissioned in November 1982 and February 1982 respectively was not provided, nor the fact of non-provision disclosed.

Rashtriya Chemicals & Fertilizers Limited

Profit was overstated by Rs 3.61 crores due to capitalisation of revenue expenditure.

Steel Authority of India Limited

Fixed Assets included condemned locomotives/machinery valued at Rs 19.89 lakhs (written-down value).

The Fertilizer Corporation of India Limited

(a) Revenue expenditure during trial operations beyond the allowable period of six months from the date of completion of the Ramagundam and Talcher Plants was treated as capital expenditure instead of deferred revenue expenditure, resulting in understatement of loss by Rs 2890.85 lakhs.

(b) Expenditure of Rs 233.74 lakhs (mostly on account of pay and allowances) incurred on the Korba Project from 1 April 1975 to 31 March 1983, the construction on which had not been done since December 1974, was included in capital works-in-progress instead of treating it as deferred revenue expenditure.

(c) Loss was understated by Rs 191.00 lakhs because shortages of urea noticed during physical verification were not provided for.

The North-Eastern Regional Agricultural Marketing Corporation Ltd

Cost accounts were not maintained by the company.

The State Trading Corporation of India Limited

While working out the surplus payable to government in respect of edible oils, overheads to the extent of Rs 128.81 lakhs and Rs 34.62 lakhs were overcharged in 1980–81 and 1981–82, resulting in understatement of 'Surplus Payable to Government', and overstatement of profit by Rs 183.43 lakhs; this had not been adjusted in the current year.

Western Coalfields Ltd

Additions to fixed assets did not include installation/erection expenses incurred departmentally in some areas. There were cases of negative balances of fixed assets.

Plant and machinery had been capitalised at the time of issue from central stores even if they were lying either in stores or lying uninstalled in the colliery sub-stores.

In some mines under development, there had been negative capitalisation which was adjusted against expenditure on other development mines.

In many cases, buildings and plant and machinery had been capitalised on an *ad hoc* basis or estimated value, and so on, as complete details were not available.

Source: Report of the Comptroller and Auditor-General of India: Union Government (Commercial) 1984 Part II, New Delhi, 1985, pp. 1–81, 85–95.

APPENDIX 5.4

Table 5.11 Recomputed net revenues – Heavy Engineering Corporation Ltd (1981/82 to 1986/87) (in crores of Rs)

	1979–80	*1980–81*	*1981–82*	*1984–85*	*1985–86*	*1986–87*
I (a) Paid-up capital	162	162	164	168	173	177
(b) Long-term loans:						
Government	132	147	164	305	314	341
Others	23	23	24	28	30	31
(c) Internal resources	100	109	119	137	143	149
Total capital employed	417	441	471	638	660	698
(d) Profit (loss) before interest	−15	−27	−14	−32	−20	−3
(e) Interest paid:						
on govt. loans	12	15	0.1	11	40	51

Table 5.11 Continued

	1979–80	1980–81	1981–82	1984–85	1985–86	1986–87
On other loans	8	9	8.5	11	11	14
(f) Net profit (loss) as per accounts	−35	−51	−23	−54	−70	−68

Source: Bureau of Public Enterprises, *Public Enterprises Survey 1981–82*, vol. 3, New Delhi, pp. 190–1, and 1986–87, vol. 3, pp. 238–9.

II (a) Notional cost of capital at 12% on total capital employed	50	53	57	77	79	84
(b) Actual interest charges on long-term loans	20	24	8.6	22	51	65
(c) Escaped costs of capital (II (a) – II(b))	30	29	48.4	65	28	19
(d) Net revenue (loss) after cost of capital (I(f) – II(c))	−65	−80	−71.4	−119	−98	−87

Source: Section II is computed by the author.

Table 5.12 British Steel Corporation: recomputed losses (1981–88) (£ m)

		As per accounts		*Recomputed data*		
Year	*Public dividend capital (PDC)*	*Profit (loss)*	*Accumulated loss*	*Cost of PDC*	*Profit (loss)*	*Accumulated loss*
1981–82	2,618	−504	−799	262	−766	−1,565
1982–83	2,361	−869	−665	236	−1,105	−2,670
1983–84	2,757	−256	−921	276	−532	−3,302
1984–85	3,424	−383	−1,161	342	−725	−3,927
1985–86	3,980	38	−1,126	398	−360	−4,287
1986–87	3,980	178	−1,023	398	−220	−4,507
1987–88	3,980	41	−642	398	−357	−4,864

Sources: *For 1981–86 data*:
Monopolies and Mergers Commission (1988) *British Steel Corporation*, p. 191.
For 1986–88 data:
British Steel Corporation, *Annual Reports*.
Last 3 columns: calculated by the author.

APPENDIX 5.5 Supplementary statement of depreciation and net revenue

Table 5.13 British Airports Authority – Ten-year summary of accounts (1975/76 to 1984/85)(in £m)

	1975/76	*1976/77*	*1977/78*	*1978/79*	*1979/80*	*1980/81*	*1981/82*	*1982/83*	*1983/84*	*1984/85*
Total passengers	31.8	34.9	35.6	40.7	44.0	43.3	43.7	44.1	46.5	51.4
Total aircraft movements	695,368	698,182	679,491	736,303	800,723	763,316	737,908	754,691	781,683	819,277
Cargo and mail (tonnes)	580,778	626,231	677,245	729,060	737,966	706,659	699,626	685,233	745,799	835,954
	Historic cost accounts					*Current cost accounts*				
	£m	*£m*	*£m*	*£m*	*£m*	*£m*	*£m*	*£m*	*£m*	*£m*
Income	77.6	103.2	125.1	162.2	191.3	254.0	277.4	283.7	316.2	361.6
Expenditure †	50.3	60.6	74.4	108.0	131.5	165.5	181.7	185.5	199.3	216.3
Depreciation, obsolescence, etc.	10.6	21.8	21.2	23.6	24.8	50.6	56.0	63.2	65.3	73.3
Trading profit	16.7	20.8	29.5	30.6	35.0	37.9	39.7	35.0	51.6	72.0
Interest, etc.	(3.5)	(3.2)	(5.2)	(1.2)	0.5	1.4	1.0	(5.8)	(5.3)	(7.9)
Profit before tax	13.2	17.6	24.3	29.4	35.5	–	–	–	–	–
Current cost operating profit	–	–	–	–	–	36.3	38.6	30.2	49.5	69.5
Taxation	7.1	15.7	8.9	13.8	12.5	21.0	16.0	7.0	28.4	39.0
Allocation to reserves	5.1	1.9	15.4	15.6	23.0	18.3	22.4	21.0	17.6	24.9
Net assets at 31 March	123.3	317.9	332.9	347.9	370.1	820.2	851.7	935.0	990.7	1,094.7
Capital expenditure in year	42.2	42.4	36.8	33.3	54.2	78.4	83.6	98.3	132.4	161.3
Reserves	37.8	218.3	269.4	285.1	307.9	762.9	794.1	877.9	808.1	881.1
Financing of capital expenditure from internal sources	66.5%	100%	100%	100%	100%	100%	100%	93.1%	86.5%	94.0%
Return on average net assets	15.0%	7.0%	8.7%	9.8%	11.0%	5.9%	5.6%	3.9%	5.4%	6.9%

Source: British Airports Authority (1986) *Annual Report and Accounts 1984/85*, London, p. 57.
†*Before depreciation on tangible fixed assets.*

APPENDIX 5.6 Data on accumulated deficits

Table 5.14 India: Central Government enterprises with accumulated deficits (1985–86) (Rs lakhs)

Sector	*No. of enterprises*
1. Steel	4
2. Minerals and metals	7
3. Coal	4
4. Chemicals, fertilisers, and pharmaceuticals	17
5. Heavy engineering	11
6. Medium and light engineering	9
7. Transportation equipment	9
8. Consumer goods	12
9. Agro-based industries	3
10. Textiles	14
11. Trading and marketing services	8
12. Transport services	3
13. Contracts and consultancy services	3
14. Industrial development and technical consultancy	4
15. Development of small-scale industry	1
16. Tourist services	1
17. Section – 25 companies	2
Total	112

Total equity plus long-term loan capital: Rs 27,940 mill.
Accumulated losses: Rs 8,430 mill.

Source: Bureau of Public Enterprises (1988) *Public Enterprises Survey 1986–87*, New Delhi.

Table 5.15 India: State of Karnataka: accumulated losses (1986)

Sector (1)	*Total no. of enterprises* (2)	*No. of enterprises with accumulated losses* (3)	*Total share capital in the sector (Rs mill.)* (4)	*Total accumulated losses in the sector (Rs mill.)* (5)	*(5) as % of (4)* (6)
1. Sectoral development corporations	15	12	663	79	12
2. Weaker section development enterprises	2	2	170	15	9
3. Service enterprises	7	4	118	210	178
4. Marketing enterprises	4	–	59	–	–
5. Production enterprises	22	12	2,286	2,656	116
6. Organisations under special statute	4	2	1,622	1,174	72
7. Deemed government companies	3	2	78	138	177
Total	57	34	4,996	4,272	86

Source: Bureau of Public Enterprises, *State of Karnataka*, Bangalore, India.

Table 5.16 Sri Lanka: cumulative losses of public enterprises (1986)

Enterprises to be converted into public limited companies	*Cumulative losses as % of fixed assets*
Ceylon Plywoods Corp.	17.9
Ceylon State Hardware Corp.	391.2
National Paper Corp.	19.0
British Ceylon Corp.	242.2
British Ceylon Milling Corp.	282.4
Ceylon Extraction Co. Ltd.	483.4
Colombo Commercial Co.	39.7
National Textiles Corp.:	
Mattagama Mill	9.9
Pagoda Mill	3.9
Thulhiriya Mill	21.1
Veyangoda Mill	429.5

Source: Public Enterprise Division, Government of Sri Lanka.

Table 5.17 Nepal: cumulative deficits of public enterprises

At end of 1985–6	Rs 1.35 bn
As percentage of the government's investments in share capital	30

Source: Economic Survey 1986–87 (1988) Kathmandu, p. 35.

Table 5.18 Peru: accumulated losses in productive state-owned enterprises (SOEs) (expressed as the reduction in net worth between years)

Net worth reduction (%)	*86/83 SOEs*
100	4
50–100	5
25–50	5
0–25	6
SOEs with accumulated losses	20

Source: Felipe Ortiz de Zavallos, M. (1989) in Ramanadham, V. V. (ed.) *Privatisation in Developing Countries*, London.

APPENDIX 5.7

Table 5.19 Financial costs of accumulated losses of Indian public enterprises (1985–86) (Rs lakhs)

(1) Enterprise	(2) Accumulated loss	(3) Interest on the deficits at rate of 14% (14% of (2))	(4) Recorded figure of loss before interest	(5) Profit or loss after adjustment ((3)–(4))
Steel				
1 The Indian Iron & Steel Co. Ltd	39,680	5,555	4,908	647
2 Mishra Dhatu Nigam Ltd	3,186	446	409	37
3 Sponge Iron India Ltd	45	6	0	6
4 Steel Authority of India Ltd	16,510	2,311	0	2,311
Minerals & Metals				
5 Bharat Aluminium Co. Ltd	29,008	4,061	4,453	−392
6 Bharat Gold Mines	2,773	388	93	295
7 Bharat Refractories Ltd	4,251	595	0	595
8 Hindustan Copper Ltd	14,377	2,013	2,104	−91
9 India Firebricks & Insulation Ltd	1,364	191	154	37
10 Kudremukh Iron Ore Co. Ltd	19,890	2,785	2,073	712
11 Manganese Ore (India) Ltd	10	1	0	1
Coal				
12 Bharat Coking Coal Ltd	76,873	10,762	7,883	2,879
13 Coal India Ltd	10,387	1,454	0	1,454
14 Eastern Coalfields Ltd	71,958	10,074	2,572	7,502
15 Western Coalfields Ltd	10,454	1,464	3,312	−1,848
Chemicals, Fertilizers & Phar.				
16 Bengal Immunity Co. Ltd	421	59	205	−146
17 Bengal Chemicals & Phar. Ltd	2,254	316	370	−54
18 The Fertilizers & Chemicals (Travancore) Ltd	4,128	578	0	578
19 The Fertilizers Corp. of India Ltd	73,380	10,273	8,744	1,529
20 Goa Antibiotics & Phar. Ltd	90	13	0	13
21 Hindustan Antibiotics Ltd	3,679	515	4	511
22 Hindustan Fertilizers Corp.	43,247	6,055	3,237	2,818
23 Hindustan Insecticides Ltd	459	64	183	119
24 Hindustan Salts Ltd	72	10	0	10
25 Indian Drugs & Phar. Ltd	14,563	2,039	1,341	698
26 Indian Medicines Phar. Corp.	25	4	0	4
27 Maharastra Antibiotics & Phar.	276	39	0	39
28 Orissa Drugs & Chem. Ltd	51	7	0	7
29 Punjab Maize Products Ltd	771	108	88	20
30 Rajasthan Drugs & Chem. Ltd	77	11	0	11
31 Sambhay Salts Ltd	104	15	0	15
32 Smith Stanistreet Phar. Ltd	252	35	63	−28
Heavy Engineering				
33 Bharat Process & Mechanical Engineering Ltd	1,113	156	134	22

Table 5.19 Continued

(1) Enterprise	(2) Accumulated loss	(3) *Interest on the deficits at rate of 14% (14% of (2))*	(4) *Recorded figure of loss before interest*	(5) *Profit or loss after adjustment ((3)–(4))*
34 Bharat Wagon & Engineering Co. Ltd	51	7	0	7
35 Braithwaite & Co. Ltd	5,500	770	377	393
36 Bridge & Roof Co. (India) Ltd	8	1	0	1
37 Burn Standard Co. Ltd	4,821	675	0	675
38 Heavy Engineering Corp. Ltd	50,195	7,027	1,857	5,170
39 Jessop & Co. Ltd	6,780	949	0	949
40 Mining & Allied Machinery Corp.	15,575	2,181	344	1,837
41 Triveni Structurals Ltd	1,841	258	0	258
42 Tungabhadra Steel Products Ltd	250	35	0	35
43 Weighbird India Ltd	279	39	56	−17
Medium & Light Engineering				
44 Bharat Brakes & Valves Ltd	849	119	137	−18
45 Bharat Dynamics Ltd	445	62	0	62
46 Bharat Pumps & Compressors	1,370	192	0	192
47 Biecco Lawrie Ltd	1,986	278	117	161
48 Central Electronics Ltd	390	55	0	55
49 H.M.T. Bearings Ltd	166	23	0	23
50 National Instruments Ltd	2,159	302	113	189
51 Richardson & Cruddas (1972) Ltd	2,424	339	193	146
52 Semi Conductors Complex Ltd	1,165	163	200	−37
Transportation Equipment				
53 Central Inland Water Transport Corp.	11,972	1,676	359	1,317
54 Cochin Shipyard Ltd	5,498	770	8	762
55 Cycle Corp. of India Ltd	2,741	384	518	−134
56 Garden Reach Shipbuilding & Engineering	8,535	1,195	0	1,195
57 Hindustan Shipyard Ltd	6,842	958	1,964	−1,006
58 Hooghly Dock & Port Engineering Ltd	4	0.56	27	−26
59 Mazagon Dock Ltd	3,514	492	0	492
60 National Bicycle Corp. (I) Ltd	1,711	240	302	−62
61 Scooters India Ltd	8,191	1,147	523	624
Consumer Goods				
62 Bharat Ophthalmic Glass Ltd	2,768	388	188	200
63 Hindustan Newsprint Ltd	1,899	266	0	266
64 Hindustan Paper Corp. Ltd	2,850	399	1,317	−918
65 Hooghly Printing Co Ltd	31	4	12	−8
66 Hindustan Vegetable Oil Corp.	568	80	0	80
67 The Mandya National Paper Mills	2,098	294	235	59

Table 5.19 Continued

(1) Enterprise	(2) Accumulated loss	(3) Interest on the deficits at rate of 14% (14% of (2))	(4) Recorded figure of loss before interest	(5) Profit or loss after adjustment ((3)-(4))
68 Nagaland Pulp & Paper Co Ltd	6,931	970	1,418	−448
69 National Jute Mfg. Corp. Ltd	1,083	152	3,467	−3,315
70 National Newsprint & Paper Mills	13	2	0	2
71 Rehabilitation Industries Corp.	4,332	606	376	230
72 Tannery & Footwear Corp. of India	5,167	723	327	396
73 Tyre Corp. of India Ltd	1,484	208	576	−368
Agro. Based Enterprises				
74 The Mim Tea Co. Ltd	53	7	0	7
75 N.E. Regional Agr. Marketing Corp.	8	1	12	−11
76 State Farms Corp. of (I) Ltd	744	104	0	104
Textiles				
77 The British India Corp. Ltd	5,650	791	0	791
78 Cawnpore Textiles Ltd	323	45	44	1
79 Elgin Mills Ltd	3,839	538	365	173
80 National Handloom Dev. Corp. Ltd	13	2	0	2
81 N.T.C. (Holding Co.) Ltd	853	119	0	119
82 N.T.C. (A.P.K. Kerala) Ltd	7,454	1,044	491	553
83 N.T.C. (Delhi) Ltd	5,875	823	660	163
84 N.T.C. (Gujarat) Ltd	5,119	717	1,278	−561
85 N.T.C. (M.P) Ltd	10,196	1,427	458	969
86 N.T.C. (Maharastra North) Ltd	10,153	1,421	1,013	408
87 N.T.C. (South Maharastra) Ltd	8,246	1,154	162	992
88 N.T.C. (Tamilnadu) Ltd	759	106	0	106
89 N.T.C. (U.P.) Ltd	7,472	1.046	1,011	35
90 N.T.C. (W.B. Bihar) Ltd	16,672	2,334	2,282	52
Rendering Services				
Trading & Marketing Services				
91 Bharat Leather Corp. Ltd	198	28	11	17
92 The Cardamom Trading Corp.	4	0.56	4	-3
93 Central Cottage Industries Corp. (I)	64	9	0	9
94 The Cotton Corp. of India Ltd	10,022	1,403	0	1,403
95 The Handicrafts & Handloom Corp.	39	5	0	5
96 The Jute Corp. of India Ltd	5,326	746	48	698
97 N.E. Handicrafts & Handlooms Dev.	115	16	28	−12

Table 5.19 Continued

(1) Enterprise	(2) Accumulated loss	(3) Interest on the deficits at rate of 14% (14% of (2))	(4) Recorded figure of loss before interest	(5) Profit or loss after adjustment ((3)–(4))
98 Tea Trading Corp. of India Ltd	1,530	214	0	214
Transport Services				
99 Helicopter Corp. of India Ltd	4	0.56	4	−3
100 The Mogul Line Ltd	10,183	1,426	1,002	424
101 Delhi Transport Corp. Ltd	69,951	9,793	8,836	957
Contracts & Construction Services				
102 Hindustan Prefab Ltd	589	82	38	44
103 Hindustan Steelworks Constr. Ltd	6,502	910	0	910
104 Indian Road Constr. Corp. Ltd	3,021	423	447	−24
Industrial Dev. & Tech. Consultancy				
105 Educational Consultancy India	16	2	0	2
106 Engineering Projects (I) Ltd	14,280	1,999	1,030	969
107 The National Industrial Dev. Corp.	21	3	0	3
108 Projects & Dev. India Ltd	1,515	212	0	212
Development of Small Industries				
109 The National Small Industries	539	75	0	75
Tourist Services				
110 Hotel Corp. of India Ltd	668	94	59	35
Section 25 Companies				
111 Artificial Limbs Mfg. Co (I) Ltd	1,168	164	111	53
112 Trade Fair Authority of India	325	46	0	46

Source: Bureau of Public Enterprises (1988) *Public Enterprises Survey 1986–87*, New Delhi.

APPENDIX 5.8 Dividend payments by Indian public enterprises with profits after tax (1986–87)

Number of public enterprises with net profit after tax: 100

Number which did not pay dividend: 46

Total paid-up capital of the 46 enterprises Rs 112,358.5 million

Notional dividend at 10 per cent would be Rs 11,236.3 million

Total net profit, after tax, of public enterprises which did not pay dividends: Rs 7,563.3 million

All this was added to reserves.

If dividend was paid, the reserves would have been less by Rs 11,236 million minus 7,563 million or Rs 3,673 million during 1986–87.

Let us next look at the 14 public enterprises that declared dividends but at less than 10 per cent on capital:

Dividends at 10 per cent of paid-up capital would amount to Rs 439.5 million.

Dividends paid amounted to Rs 209.5 million.

Having paid this amount, the 14 enterprises added to reserves Rs 792.8 million. But the real addition, 'net' of full cost of equity, was only Rs 792.8 million −Rs 230 million (that is, Rs 439.5−Rs 209.5 million), that is, Rs 562.8 million.

It is possible to infer that most part of the reserves of public enterprises as of today are the result of escaped dividend payments. They are not 'net' of equity-capital costs.

Source: Computed from Bureau of Public Enterprises (1988) *Public Enterprises Survey 1986–87*, vol. 1, New Delhi, pp. 55–7, 64–5, 124–7.

APPENDIX 5.9 Reserve funds of the National Development Corporation (of Tanzania)

In Table 5.20 the figures of capital fund, reserves, loans, and total are taken from the published annual reports of the National Development Corporation of Tanzania. (In respect of 1969–71, for which the reports were missing, rough estimates are included in the tabulation.) The capital fund is comprised of shares and grants. The latter are the far more important segment, for example, TSh 318 million in 1979, as against TSh 5.7 million of shares held by the government. The financial charges cited in column (6) represent the interest provided on loans. Columns (7) and (8) show the notional opportunity cost of total capital employed, on the two bases of 8 and 10 per cent rates of interest. Columns (9) and (10) are the costs of capital escaped, respectively on the bases of 8 and 10 per cent, and are arrived at by deducting the amounts in column (6) from those in columns (7) and (8).

The reserves or internally generated funds of column (3) – TSh 113 million by 1979 – are fictitious.

Table 5.20 Reserve funds of the National Development Corporation (of Tanzania) (TSh mill.)

Year	Capital fund	Capital and revenue reserves	Loans	Total	Financial charges	Cost of capital		Capital costs not provided for	
						at 8%	at 10%	at 8%	at 10%
(1)	(2)	(3)	(4)	(5)	(6)	(7)	(8)	(9)	(10)
1965	95	19	9	123	0.6	9.8	12.3	9.2	11.70
1966	95	27	7	129	0.14	10.3	12.9	10.16	12.76
1967	97	68	79	244	3.8	19.5	24.4	15.6	20.5
1968	125	94	109	328	5.8	26.2	32.8	20.4	27.0
1969*									
1970*				350	24.0	84.0	105.0	60.0	81.0
1971*									
1972	174	115	172	461	11.2	36.9	46.1	25.8	35.0
1973	150	99	136	385	9.4	30.8	38.5	21.3	29.0
1974	92	54	130	276	8.3	22.1	27.6	13.8	19.3
1975	184	62	138	384	9.7	30.7	38.4	21.0	28.7
1976	231	82	130	443	9.6	35.4	44.3	25.8	34.6
1977	295	158	56	509	3.7	40.7	50.9	37.0	47.2
1978	371	121	62	554	4.1	44.3	55.4	40.3	51.4
1979	318	113	81	512	0.2	41.0	51.2	40.8	51.0
Total					90.4	431.7	539.7	341.2	449.2

Source: National Development Corporation.
Annual Reports, Dar es Salaam.

Note
* Rough estimates only.

Taking into account the escaped costs of capital, the figure comes down to minus TSh 227.2 million (or minus TSh 336.2 million) on the basis of 8 per cent notional cost of capital (or 10 per cent).

This computation clearly illustrates the inaccuracy of the 'reserves' figure appearing in the books of many public enterprises.

APPENDIX 5.10 The British Steel Corporation's inheritance

OPERATING AND STRUCTURAL WEAKNESSES

The Steel Corporation's present difficulties, culminating in the operating loss of £45 million in 1971–2, are largely explained by the condition of the industry when it was brought into public ownership. It had, and still has, a number of grave weaknesses, the most important of which are as follows:

1. The great bulk of the steelmaking capacity which BSC inherited was obsolete. In 1967 high-cost processes (open-hearth, Kaldo, and other non-LD convertors) accounted for two-thirds of all production.[1] The proportion of first-rate plant was so low because for a variety of reasons the British steel industry had not to any appreciable extent switched over to the new low-cost process of LD. In 1969, which was after BSC had taken charge, but before it had had a chance to remedy the situation, only 28 per cent of British steel was produced by LD or other pure oxygen methods. In the other OECD countries the proportion was nearly half and France was the only place where the switch to oxygen-steelmaking had been slower than it had in Britain.[2]
2. Not only was most of our steel-making capacity obsolete but nearly all our steelworks were too small for full efficiency. The Benson Committee, which the industry set up just before it was nationalised, concluded that an up-to-date steelworks required a capacity of between 3.5 and 5 million ingot tons.[3] In 1965 only about a third of bulk steelmaking capacity was at works able to produce more than 1.3 million tons and as late as 1969 Port Talbot was the only British plant with a capacity of over 2 million tons. Yet Japan had thirteen, Germany had eight, and Canada, Italy, and France had three each.[4]
3. Partly due to the failure to secure economies of scale, the British steel industry's productivity was relatively low. The Iron & Steel Board estimated that between 1955 and 1965 output per man hour increased by around 150 per cent in Italy and Japan; by about two-thirds in France, Holland, Canada, and Belgium; and by 58 per cent in Germany. But in Britain it only rose 39 per cent and in the USA 25 per cent.[5] The Board calculated that by the end of the period the *level* of output per man hour was about a quarter higher in the European Coal and Steel

Community than it was here. Moreover, it is apparent from a UN study that in 1964 Poland and Czechoslovakia were level or ahead, that in Sweden and Russia output per man hour was around 50 per cent greater, and that in the USA it was well over twice as high.[6]

4. The utilisation of plant and equipment was very poor, which again helps to explain why British output per man was so low. When BSC took over, the productivity of its blast furnaces was only 43 per cent of the full capacity level. In 1969 the highest rating achieved anywhere was only 69 per cent (at Llanwern), whereas in some other countries the best furnaces were operating at 110–130 per cent.[7] The position was similar at the steelmaking stage where even the industry's new LD furnaces had a poor utilisation.[8] However, it was probably at the finishing end that the utilisation of equipment was at its worst. It is impossible to quote any summary statistic, but it is evident that at a considerable number of works (including Llanwern, Ravenscraig, Shelton, and Jarrow), mills operated at well below their potential capacity.[9]
5. The last major weakness of the steel industry when it was taken over was the poor location of many works and their lack of access to deep water. In 1967 only one of the ports through which iron ore was imported was able to take vessels of more than about 20,000 tons, whereas most European and Japanese ports were able to handle 80,000 tonners. As a result the British steel industry was at a serious cost disadvantage which was compounded by the fact that four major works which depended on imported ore (Ebbw Vale, Shotton, Consett, and Ravenscraig) were on average about 20 miles from the ports which served them.[10]

There is no point now that the industry has been finally nationalised in trying to decide how far its old owners were to blame for this sad state of affairs but what is relevant, and beyond dispute, is that BSC inherited little but problems.

FINANCIAL DIFFICULTIES

These problems had become so acute that the industry's profitability had already collapsed. Between 1957 and 1961 the companies which were to be nationalised had consistently had an operating profit of over £100 million, that is, after depreciation, but before tax and interest. By 1965–6 the figure was less than £50 million and in 1966–7 it was down to only about £24 million.[11] But the companies' financial position was even weaker than this suggests.

(a) Due to rising prices and technical change insufficient depreciation was being provided. BSC set aside an extra £17 million in 1967–8, having cut its basic depreciation period to a more realistic fifteen years.[12]

(b) Maintenance was being neglected, as the Corporation subsequently discovered when it had to make good the backlog and ran into costly operating difficulties.[13]

(c) The industry's central ore importing organisation was trading at a loss of about £3 million during 1967.[14]

When these factors are allowed for, the Corporation's private predecessors can have done little more than break even during 1966–7.

The industry's perilous financial position helps to explain why its capital expenditure fell to such a low ebb during the mid–1960s. This is often attributed to the threat of nationalisation, but the Iron & Steel Board, which was in an excellent position to judge, declared in its final report that 'There is . . . no evidence that the prospect of nationalisation led companies to hold back development schemes which they considered desirable on commercial grounds and could afford to finance. Indeed, several substantial schemes have been submitted for the Board's consent since the beginning of 1967.'[15]

Note

This article is reproduced – without the footnotes – from Richard Pryke's Memorandum to the Select Committee on Nationalised Industries, Session 1972–73 (1973) *British Steel Corporation*, London: HMSO, 141, pp. 312–14.

6 Pricing

This chapter aims at an analysis of the problems of pricing in so far as they are specific to public enterprise. Several matters of close relevance to it are considered in different contexts and in some detail in chapters 4, 5, 7, and 11; hence references to them will be very brief here. Questions that apply equally to public and private enterprises, like monopoly, will only be considered with a focus on the qualifying factors in the case of public enterprise.

THE ROLE OF PRICES

The role of public enterprise prices in the national economy is basically similar to that of private enterprise prices, but they have, or tend to be assigned, certain additional obligations:[1]

(a) Prices should bring about an efficient allocation of resources. They would lead to over-extensions of investment in some directions, in which they are 'too low'. If they are very heterogeneously above or below costs without admissible reason in different sectors, they would lead to distortion in the investment patterns in the economy. There can also be a situation where 'artificially low' prices might coincide with under-investment if additions to capital investment are ceiled, for any reason, and the prices do not provide for internal resources for expansions. Non-expansions in such a situation bring about distortions in the patterns of development in customer-industries.

(b) Prices should not cause shifts of benefit among consumers by being quite diversely related to costs in different markets in a given sector or in different sectors.

(c) Prices should not be a material source of shifts of benefit as between customers on the one hand and employers and investors on the other.

However, prices of public enterprises can be a tool of extra-enterprise objectives:

(i) Prices may, with due qualifications, be a vehicle of income redistribution among consumers, regions, or sectors of activity.

(ii) Prices, in certain sectors, may be a preferred means of government policies, for example, against inflation or for preventing price hikes in the private sector; or in promoting the development of indigenous technological capability in a given sector.
(iii) Prices may be employed as a means of indirect taxation and of mobilising resources for the exchequer.[2]

PRICING AND THE INVESTMENT DECISION

There is a close relationship between pricing and the original investment decision. The latter is based on a feasibility study, of which estimates of 'future' prices are an integral part. In one sense, therefore, the intended prices in respect of a project or enterprise are 'given', and if other actuals – relating to costs and markets, for example – compare well with those contained in the feasibility study, the level of prices can be or has to be similar to that postulated in it. One may expect that the problem that remains would be marginal.

In the real world the problem is not so neat, for several reasons:

(a) A public enterprise may belong to the 'inherited' kind; and feasibility data concerning the original investments in it are not available or are so intermeshed in different projects as to be of little use in offering guidance on pricing.
(b) Many public enterprise investment decisions have been based on too inadequate or inaccurate data and provide little guidance to pricing.[3]
(c) Most importantly, what matters is the current situation of markets – input and output – whatever may have been the feasibility estimates; and pricing has to address them.
(d) Whatever the original price expectations at the time the project was decided upon, the government may have later developed consumer biases which it wants to be implemented through the prices of the enterprise.
(e) Add to these factors the situation of exchequer liquidity, which may impact on the government's pressures on certain public enterprise prices from time to time, either upwards or downwards.

However, the decision on investment and capitalisation has a two-fold relevance to pricing. For one thing, it contains a statement of the social returns or externalities credited to a project. Where these are substantial, pricing has to be such as enables society to realise them. For another, if the capital structure in a given case was so designed as to compensate for the financial impacts of preferred externalities – for example, through a large dose of capital grants – the cost basis of pricing has to be computed with due regard to the intentions implicit in the capital structure. In other words, the implications of economic costing for price fixing have to be reviewed correspondingly.

THE PRICE LEVEL

This section refers mainly to a public enterprise which has monopoly in all its markets. (The case of monopoly in some markets will be discussed in the next section.) It is in the position of a price-maker and, in theory, can charge as high as the consumer can bear, consistent with its aim of profit maximisation. In practice, there are three possibilities:

1. It can adopt the principle of profit maximisation and charge high prices.
2. It can charge profit-raising prices, but without any set reference to costs in individual cases or to a set quantum of profit.
3. It can charge prices that result in losses.

The first is hardly the case except possibly with fiscal monopolies. (Perhaps the cross-section of private enterprises themselves do not adopt this method rigorously.) The second is a common case, where targets of profit are either not set or so set as to make possible an indefinite profit accrual. The third, paradoxically, is true in several cases, where, for some reason, valid or otherwise, a public enterprise monopoly makes losses, for example, the state electricity boards in India.

There is a common undercurrent in the three cases, namely, that the managers behave on their own volition in fixing the price level, even if through internal guidelines on profit. As argued in chapter 7, this is not the most correct position in public enterprise; there is need for governmental involvement directly or indirectly, in a structured manner.

The price should be cost-related, so that its role in the national economy, outlined in the first, can be satisfactorily accomplished. Apparently a simple principle, this has not been satisfied by the public enterprise sector in developed as well as developing countries. (In the UK, for example, the White Paper (Cmnd 3437) of 1967 contained a major theme, namely, that 'nationalised industries should price to cover their long run marginal costs', but as pointed out by the NEDO report in 1976, this principle was not followed 'for the most part'.)[4]

There are two sets of problems in implementing the principle that public enterprise prices should be cost-based or cost-related: technical, and judgemental.

Technical problems

The first relates to the very definition of 'cost' to which the price is to be related, even in the case of an enterprise producing a fairly homogeneous product. Average cost is the simplest base from the angle of calculation; but economic logic suggests the desirability of using the marginal cost basis instead.[5]

Two difficulties arise here:

1. We need to have a definition of 'marginal cost'. In the case of an

enterprise marked by heavy underutilisation, a price that recovers the marginal cost and makes a contribution towards the fixed costs is welcome. Here the price-base is the short-run marginal cost, which improves the utilisation of an existing capacity. It has allocational justification in that it permits consumption at a price that (more than) covers immediate cost. The justification is great where the enterprise has a sunk investment whose alternative use is limited.

There are two important qualifications:

(a) The so-called marginal costs may refer to inputs which have a scarcity value, for example, coal or electricity in an energy-short economy. Hence their uses foregone in other directions have to be evaluated.

(b) Promoting consumption through the low rates might lead to wasteful consumption.[6] This might be a special version of the earlier point in some cases.

The long-run marginal cost improves the principle in certain ways. It takes into account the opportunity cost of the investment over the long run. Further it reduces the difficulty of identifying marginal costs in the short run. For instance, should wages be included or not? In most cases they tend to be an inescapable cost under union and political pressures. Are certain expenditures on major repairs to be included? There also remains the problem of estimating the cost of technological change and obsolescence over the long run.

The longer the period with reference to which the marginal cost is conceived, the nearer it comes to the average cost, subject to the qualifications outlined later in this section.

2. The difference between the average cost and the marginal-cost-based price represents a loss, except where the latter is the higher figure (as in the case of an enterprise dependent on exhaustible resources or input sources likely to be progressively expensive to tap, like a coal-mine). Electricity is a well-known example of a decreasing cost industry where marginal-cost pricing has considerable justification but leads to losses. The losses have to be met by the exchequer.[7] The state of widespread underutilisation in the public enterprise sector aggravates this problem in developing countries. Whether it is realistic to expect the government to feed such losses is a serious question, but only part of the question. Equally serious is the question as to whether distributional effects follow, which are less desirable than the allocational effects of marginal-cost prices (see chapter 12, fourth section).

   Second, the costs which constitute the basis of prices should be 'economic' costs, as discussed elsewhere in the book, for example, in chapter 5. Or else the rate base would be artificially low in real fact, and even if prices apparently cover it, allocational disadvantages remain.

   Third, where an enterprise has clearly an excess capacity – not the same as underutilisation at a given unit of time – the cost-base has to be adjusted downward for the elements of excess, and the consumer should be charged no higher than a price related to the adjusted cost-base. This is not to be mistaken for marginal-cost pricing. There is, no doubt, a cost to the exchequer resulting from such an adjustment. But that would be a cost of faulty investment decision; it is not to be treated as a loss from marginal-cost pricing.

Fourth, the cost structure of the enterprise cannot be taken as an automatic price base without enquiring into the efficiency of the enterprise. As shown elsewhere (for example, chapters 5 and 13 (Appendix 13.1)), reasons apart, efficiency is low – in some cases extremely low – in the public enterprise sector of developing countries. Hence prices related to costs unadjusted for inefficiency would be disadvantageous to the consumer. They would be in the nature of a subsidy for inefficiency. (It may be noted that the terms of reference remitted to the Monopolies and Mergers Commission in the UK include, significantly, a review of the cost structure of the enterprise concerned and of the potential for its improvement (see Appendix 9.1).

Fifth, costs clearly traceable to extra-enterprise objectives have to be isolated, and the rest should form the basis of pricing. Not to do so would defeat the economic logic of the government's intention to realise certain externalities and implement distributional preferences through the medium of a public enterprise.

There is a fundamental issue relating to the concept of average cost. This has meaning where the enterprise produces a homogeneous product. Where it does not, or where the product can be differentiated into submarkets, even if it appears to be the same physically, the 'average cost' would have significance in terms of each product market. Or else we would be ignoring the cost differentials among the submarkets. The disadvantage might be less where marginal cost is the basis of pricing, if it is assumed that it refers to the costs directly identified as relatable to a given product or submarket.

Judgemental problems

A major issue in public enterprise pricing concerns the extent to which the prices ought to contain elements of profit. The profit element, while being a function of the monopoly opportunities of the enterprise, has to reflect its extra-enterprise obligations (see chapter 3) and – a somewhat overlapping consideration – its budget-link (see chapter 11). In this way even the average figure of profit earned by private enterprises in the sector(s) concerned or by all enterprises in the economy would only have the value of an initial guideline as to what profit levels are admissible at a given unit of time, on the whole. But that would be an important guideline. The real problem starts at that point. For, the exact element of profit that an individual public enterprise should be allowed to earn has to be deduced from a judgement of what its 'publicness' signifies and how it impacts on its profit potential. To express the idea in another way, how high should profit retention or self-financing be?[8]

The need for judgement is equally great when the government expects an enterprise to make a heavy compromise with the possible profit it earns. It would be ideal to make a judgement on how the profit of an individual enterprise should be realised. The simplest way would be for the enterprise to raise its prices.[9] While in some cases the enterprise may have no choice but to raise prices, there must be adequate provision for an external scrutiny, from time to time, of the potential for other measures directed at the profit aim.

The cost-plus method, adopted in some cases, appears to connote that the government has decided on the extent of addition to costs, which is permissible towards the profit element. Assuming that the 'plus' figure is uncontroversial, we have to make sure that this method does not operate as a virtual guarantee to the enterprise that its costs would be treated as an unquestioned base to which the 'plus' applies. Regulatory arrangements should be set up for enquiring into its cost structure and no higher than an admissible cost-base should be employed in determining the price level, with a 'plus' inclusion. This requirement would be particularly strong when the plus is expressed in terms of a percentage of 'cost'. Public utility regulation is expected to go into this question thoroughly. However, in the case of public enterprises the investigation could be superficial, since the government has to bear the shortfall in incomes not recovered through prices. Chapter 14 contains further comments on price control through the *RPI* minus *X* technique.

Experience suggests that government action in providing individual public enterprises with guidelines, if not more positive stipulations as regards the profit element to be aimed at while pricing, has been unsatisfactory. Part of the reason consists of indecisiveness on the part of the government itself, generally for political reasons. Pressures from international agencies like the IMF and the World Bank are inducing some change in their approach; but price enhancements – which would be a necessary decision in most cases – have to be weighed against the civil riots they might provoke – as in Jordan, Venezuela, and Zambia in recent years.

In concluding the discussion on the cost basis of prices, we may refer to inter-enterprise pricing in the public sector. In general, this is conducted on an *ad hoc* basis permitting quite diverse price-cost relationships at the various stages of sale, for example, coal to electricity, electricity to steel, and steel to shipyards, and it distorts the cost structures of the buying enterprises and complicates the evaluation of the allocational soundness of investments in different enterprises. Instead, a clear policy of cost-related pricing, with, if necessary, a subsidy at the consuming end, is preferable.

THE PRICE STRUCTURES

Many public enterprises formulate a structure of prices which contains variations between products, regions, times of consumption, or groups of consumers. In other words they subdivide the market into several segments and maintain price differences among them. These often harbour cross-subsidisations.

Every price difference does not signify cross-subsidisation. In many cases there are differences in the costs of supplying the product in different markets. Price differences attributable to cost differences cannot be considered as cross-subsidisations. Peak and off-peak markets in transport and electricity are an example. In fact, not to offer low prices, that is, prices below total cost but above the marginal cost in the off-peak periods, amounts to uncommercial behaviour. Such low prices add to sales without adding to the costs or prices of the other consumers. This argument applies to public and private enterprises equally.

On the other hand, uniform prices, which give the impression of non-discriminatory pricing, contain cross-subsidisations if the costs of supply in the different markets are different (see chapter 10 for further discussion).

Electricity tariffs for domestic, commercial, and industrial consumers are a common example of cross-subsidisations in many countries; farm tariffs are a special instance. Appendix 6.1 gives data on agricultural power tariffs in India in 1987–8. The average tariff varied between 9.6 per cent and 65.8 per cent of the total average rate per kW of power sold, among the different states; and as a percentage of total operating cost per kW sold it varied between 8.5 and 46.4. Not only cross-subsidies in favour of agriculture are obvious, but there are wide variations from state to state, on no stated or publicly-accepted principle.

Even when changes are effected in the price structures, elements of cross-subsidy often remain undisturbed. Indonesia provides an illustration. Within an average 25 per cent increase announced in electricity tariffs in March 1989, small-scale social institutions faced increases of only 13.8 per cent, as against large hotels (40.3 per cent), and businesses.[10]

Differential rates of interest charged on house loans or small industry loans are similar in nature. Kenya provides an example of low domestic prices of tea as against the far higher export prices. Such cross-subsidisations occur in developed countries too. The NEDO study referred to the 'losses or low contributions on particular services (e.g., call offices and telegrams)' being covered by 'pricing trunk calls at well above cost', and to cross-subsidies 'between customers in different areas within the four price zones . . . in operation'.[11]

There are three reasons for cross-subsidisations. First, where a public enterprise faces competition in certain of its markets, it may offer relatively low prices so as to attract customers from competitors. This is objectionable on two grounds: the high-priced markets yield a benefit to the low-priced markets for no other reason that that the enterprise faces competition in the latter; and the pricing practices present conditions of unfair competition with the private sector, traceable to the organisational advantage conferred on the public enterprise. (The appliances trade of the British Gas Corporation is a case in point.)

Second, the attribution of costs to a market is not an easy task; hence cross-subsidisations can occur without positive intention on the part of the managers. Here we face a fundamental question: how far do we go in subdividing the enterprise into different markets for establishing cross-subsidies? Broadly, the answer depends on the technological or market interrelationships among two or more products. The less they are, the more justified that there should be distinctive costing and revenue enumerations. Stipulations requiring separate financial statements for different products are based on this principle. For example, different airports or seaports organised under an apex body, machine tools and wrist-watches produced by a monolithic enterprise, passenger, parcel and goods services provided by a railway, rural and other supplies of electricity, are all examples of separable markets, among which cross-subsidisations can and ought to be established.

Further down the line attempts to discover them might involve too many assumptions in respect of either revenue or cost allocations to be of much use, for example, route-wise cross-subsidies in a road transport enterprise or an airline. Yet if conditions of competition exist – or can exist, under cost-based pricing, in particular routes, the elements of cross-subsidy need to be established. Even where competition does not exist, it is reasonable to establish the price-cost relationships on different routes in order to identify, if not prevent, cross-subsidies. In many cases they can be established (see Appendix 10.1 relating to the Indian Airlines Corporation which operated, on an average, 145 services during 1984–7, of which only 51 met total operating costs, and 46 did not meet direct operating costs. Thirty-six of the latter category did not meet even 'cash costs'.[12] The burden of loss is met by the passengers on the paying routes).

Third, certain markets are sought to be favoured as a sequel to public policy, for example, agricultural consumption of electricity or journalists' travel by a transport agency. In fact public enterprise derives one of its justifications from its adaptability to public preferences in price determination.[13]

As argued elsewhere in this book, public policy should disfavour prices which contain cross-subsidies; and where an extra-enterprise objective exists, it is preferable, in general, to pursue it through government budget policies rather than by imposing the burdens involved on the strong markets.

DISTRIBUTIONAL PRICES

The term 'distributional price' may be understood to signify a price that has a distributional implication, for example, to benefit certain consumers. It may be low in two senses:

(a) It may be lower than a corresponding price in the private sector. This presupposes that conditions of enforceable dual pricing exist in a given sector and that the public enterprise price is available to select groups of consumers only.
(b) It may be lower than the related cost. Where the enterprise produces different products or caters to different submarkets, the prices in the preferred cases may be kept lower than the related costs, or may exceed the related costs by a lower proportion than the prices in the other markets. Many public enterprises are large and multiproduct in nature; hence these are real possibilities.

Low prices with distributional motivations may be discovered under two heads, prices for final consumers, and prices for intermediate consumers.

Prices for final consumers

The enterprise managers face two difficulties in this case. First, they have to identify precisely those among their total clientele who deserve distributionally low prices. They cannot be certain as regards the criteria such as personal income, family income, family size, family expenditure, physical characteristics and handicaps, occupational characteristics, and age. Nor are they, as managers, entitled or competent to make judgements on such factors. Where they do on their own volition, they transgress the bounds of accountability implicit in the concept of autonomous public enterprise.[14] The target group has, therefore, to be identified for them by the government. Second, it is not easy to enforce the low prices in such a way that they reach only the intended consumers and that there are no leakages of benefit to other (richer) consumers, as in the case of CONAPSU of Mexico,[15] or the state stores in Ethiopia, where 'poor women' buy 'scarce essentials' at low prices, 'not for themselves but for the merchants who resell the items ... at higher prices at their private stores' (*New York Times*, 7 September 1989, p. 7).

The chances of enforceability are high where the output can only be supplied through a technical device which can be identified with a consumer, for example, a gas or electrical meter. Even here it is not certain that a poor consumer is behind the meter. A usual way in which such price concessions are intended to reach the target group is by providing them with identity cards, for example, students travelling by rail or bus. This can be effective when the consumption takes place at the point where the identity of the consumer is verified. (Entry to a park or zoo is one such instance.) When a ration card is used, it is not certain that the benefit does not leak to unintended consumer groups, except where the card refers to a minimum consumption requirement of the target consumer group – this is not certain even in the case of rice and sugar in certain developing countries. An incidental requirement is that the government has to determine the size of output that is alone eligible to the low price.

Electricity enterprises provide the most common illustration of pricing structures which have distributional implications.[16] Though residential consumption in low sizes is relatively expensive, it is offered low prices. A small-sized consumption of electricity is presumed to signify that the consumer deserves a low price on distributional grounds. The presumption may not be true in every case. Nor is large consumption invariably associated with wealthy consumers in every case.

The following tariff structures referring to electricity consumption by residential customers illustrate distributional motivation:

Domestic tariffs (Nepal, 1983)

0 – 25 units	44 paise per unit
26 – 100	66 paise per unit
101 – 300	80 paise per unit
Above 300	90 paise per unit

Residential tariffs: Both Water and Power Development Authority (WAPDA) and Karachi Electricity Supply Company (KESC) (Pakistan, 1987)

0 – 50 units	34 paise per unit
51 – 250	40 paise per unit
251 – 600	50 paise per unit
601 and above	70 paise per unit

For agricultural tube wells:

Energy charges:

16 paise per kWh in Baluchistan and NWF (underdeveloped regions)

23 paise elsewhere

Fixed charges:

Rs 17 per kW in Baluchistan and NWF

Rs 19 elsewhere

A practical problem with distributional prices is that in the course of time it can become difficult to distinguish the low prices defensible on distributional grounds from other low prices which the managers may deliberately or unwittingly charge. As a result, conditions of random preference develop.

In conclusion – it would be ideal for the government to formulate policy on the following lines: first, to determine whether the objective is to help a targeted income group *per se* or to provide it with price relief with reference to a given product; second, if the latter is the case, to inform the enterprise about the target group, the size of output eligible to low price, and the extent of price concession preferred; third, to offer an open subsidy to meet the financial disadvantage that this causes the enterprise; and fourth, to disfavour cross-subsidisations within the enterprise, which might enable it to make up such financial disadvantages. If these steps are scrupulously followed, the goverment would be induced to be very selective in effecting distributional transfers through public enterprise prices. (To refer to the earlier cited case of the Indian Airlines Corporation, none of these steps has been followed, in spite of the comments and recommendations of the Committee on Public Undertakings.)

Prices of intermediate goods

It is often assumed in developing countries that public enterprises supplying intermediate goods should sell them at relatively low prices so that they yield distributional benefits at the level of the buying enterprises. If the latter are labour intensive their employees benefit: further, if they sell outputs to final consumers who deserve low prices on distributional grounds, those consumers derive benefit in the process.

There are two issues to be considered in this context. First, are the benefits of low prices derived by the buying enterprises passed on to their consumers or workers, assuming that they are the eligible target groups? If they are not, but are mopped up as profits and go to the investors who belong to higher income brackets, the distributional value of the low prices is meagre.

Second, there may be several stages of production activity before products reach the final consumer; or at each successive stage in the production process a part of the output might be reaching the final consumer, for example, domestic consumers of electricity, while the rest is sold as an intermediate good, for example, industrial power. The income effects have to be traced, stage by stage, and this would be a difficult task.

As mentioned in the previous section, the broad approach should be to price the product on the cost basis and provide for a subsidy at the consuming level, if adjudged as necessary.

A basic issue here concerns the conflict between growth and distributional objectives. Where an intermediate good is sold at a relatively low price on grounds of growth, there are accompanying effects on grounds of distribution. The two must be compared, compositely as between the selling and buying enterprises, before low prices are allowed for intermediate goods.

PRICES IN COMPETITIVE MARKETS

Though a public enterprise operating in a sector along with private enterprises is assumed to be a price taker, there are certain situations in which its pricing presents special features.

Where private enterprises begin to raise prices in a sector by controlling supplies or otherwise operating as an informal cartel, the government may employ a public enterprise as a device to control that process by requiring it to sell the product at lower prices. The other enterprises would then be forced to reduce their prices and the consumer benefits. The Utility Stores Corporation of Pakistan provides an example. It offers essential consumer goods at low prices with the object, among others, of acting 'as a moderator and a deterrent to profiteering, hoarding, etc.'.[17] If the public enterprise is able to maintain its low prices without making losses, there will be no disadvantage to the exchequer; but if it makes losses, a compensation from the government would be necessary. That might be considered as a due cost of controlling monopolies in certain 'essential' sectors. To take another example, the Nepal Food Corporation has a price monitoring role, providing supplies in time, and distributing food materials in remote areas. In the land-locked situation of Nepal, where private enterprises can easily profiteer, the pricing role of this corporation is distinctive.

The effectiveness of such 'regulatory pricing' depends on whether the public enterprise concerned is in a position to expand, if necessary, so as to answer a major part, if not the whole, of the demand. Otherwise, dual markets develop, in which some fortunate or identified consumers derive the product at the public enterprise prices and the rest have to look to the other suppliers for their requirements. There is another danger, unless appropriate preventive measures are introduced. The low-priced products sold by the public enterprises might be cornered by the other sellers and the entire supply might be sold at higher prices. The marketing imperfections of developing countries might help in that process. To cite an example from India, 'the users of coal are paying Rs 1,000 but the public enterprises are not allowed to charge more than Rs 100 per tonne', with the result that 'the difference is siphoned off ... The benefit goes to black marketeers'.[18]

Where the government fixes prices for a product which is produced by both public and private enterprises, one possibility is that the prices are kept at a level that enables the public enterprise to meet its costs or make an intended profit. If, through its inefficiency, or any other reason, its costs are higher than those of the competing enterprises, the latter begin to enjoy excessive profits. In fact they might consider it an advantage to have public enterprise(s) in the sector with low efficiency.

Another possibility is that the price is determined by the government at a level consistent with the total costs and total demand in the sector concerned. But since different enterprises have difficult cost levels, those with costs that are below the price pay the difference into a pool or a 'price equalisation fund' which finances those whose cost exceeds the price. This method has two merits. First, it provides against private enterprises deriving a windfall profit, unlike under the previous method, and second, it implies that the public enterprise does not end up with a loss which has to be met eventually by the exchequer.

However, this technique of pricing has the serious disadvantage of dampening the incentive of the efficient enterprises to strive for cost economics; for the difference between whatever cost they achieve and the price goes into the pool, substantially, if not wholly. The public enterprise is likewise under no impulse to effect cost economies, since the pool finances the difference between the price fixed and its cost.

This defect can be removed by supplementing the pricing technique with the condition that, where an enterprise achieves a cost reduction, it will be entitled to keep a share of it for itself and an agreed part of it can be passed on as bonus to the employees. It will represent a reward for efficiency. A logical corollary is to follow, namely, that, where an enterprise fails to achieve, over time, cost economies in 'controllable' areas, it will be penalised by receiving less than the difference between the price and its cost under a specified formula. In practice this corollary may be of limited value, because the loss that thereby accrues to the public enterprise has eventually to be met by the government. Measures that compel the employees to improve efficiency have to be devised – both the carrot and, sparingly, the stick.

There is a more important dimension to this technique. In the short run, when the demand can only be met by both the high-cost and low-cost enterprises continuing to produce, there ought to be a reasonable prospect for the contraction of the high cost unit as time goes on, unless they improve their cost structures. That would make price reductions possible. Or else this technique implies a permanent subsidy to inefficiency.

In practice, it is doubtful if contraction or exit on the part of a public enterprise is possible on the scale necessary. This cannot happen in what the government considers as a 'core' area in the economy, or in an area where the protection of employment in the enterprises concerned is deemed to be of paramount importance.

Before we conclude this section, let us refer to a common situation of competitive prices on a global scale. A serious problem arises when the international price is much lower than the cost of production on the part of a domestic public enterprise. Banning the import or taxing it so heavily that the domestic product becomes saleable, is one method. When this is not contemplated, and where efforts at cost reduction are far from helpful, the government would be compelled to introduce a pricing formula that incorporates sizeable subsidies, so that the consumer is not affected and production continues to take place. The bottom line, of course, is that it is implicit in the country's development strategy that the production should continue to exist, irrespective of high cost and of international non-competitiveness. A typical example is provided by the 'international parity price' (IPP) principle followed in the case of ships produced by the Cochin Shipyard Ltd in India. International prices are extremely low, in comparison with local costs (and are even alleged to be 'dumped' prices – Rs 35 crores in the case of a tanker, recently, as against the local cost of Rs 69 crores). A complicated IPP method has been formulated under which the government pays the shipyard a direct subsidy of 20 per cent of the IPP, the buyer pays 10 per cent over and above the IPP 'towards partial cost of import substitution', and he will also pay 'escalation charges' in respect of the statutory rise in prices of controlled duties on imported items and increases in wages under wage awards – within 7 per cent of IPP on the whole.

All these do not meet the problem of local costs, inclusive of cost of capital, being higher than the price proceeds. Hence several other devices are also contemplated, such as a moratorium on loan repayments and interest holiday (from 1982 to 1987), conversion of all loans or at least 75 per cent of loans into equity, and offers of concessions meant for industries declared as having 'deemed export status'.

With exit being considered out of the question in a case like this, the issues are simply the following:

(a) There should be effective pressures (or incentives to employees) to reduce costs.
(b) A government judgement is needed on the extent to which the consumer should be made to bear the cost burden of local production. This is linked with the import impediments that the government is prepared to impose, as an alternative approach, subject to any international or common market restrictions.
(c) The entire subsidy needed should be offered by the government in an open manner, instead of disguising it (and dissipating it) in different cost reliefs or artificial cost circumstances, which do not apply to all industries in the country.

An interesting illustration may be added at this point. The Oil and National Gas Commission (of India) alleged that the prices it has to pay for indigenous supplies of equipment (mostly public enterprises) are 'more than 100 per cent' higher than international prices. The Committee on Public Undertakings suggested the creation of a 'national subsidy fund' to help indigenous producers.[19] This can be a transparent method, applicable to all relevant cases, while individual public enterprises can be freed from random burdens of high input costs traceable to the national strategy of promoting domestic production.

PRICE CONTROL

In the light of the foregoing discussion on the role of prices in the public enterprise sector, the government has to address three important questions while intervening in the price-fixing autonomy of the enterprise managers.

First, do they follow, reasonably satisfactorily, cost-related pricing?

Second, do they give effect to agreed non-commercial objectives, if any? And are the implicit deviations from cost-related pricing no more than are necessary for achieving the agreed results?

Third, are price enhancements effected to a greater degree than might be necessary to achieve agreed surplus results? And how strong are the pressures for improving productivity and attaining cost economies?

Each of these questions has special relevance to public enterprise, as discussions elsewhere in the book show.

Apparently the managers' autonomy is inversely proportional to the external interventions in pricing. In reality, the autonomy that should logically be preserved is preserved if:

(a) as regards the first question, cost is laid down as the basis of a price;
(b) as regards the second question, agreed arrangements are made *ex ante*, within which the managers are free to act; and,
(c) as regards the third question, periodic reviews are initiated on the mechanics of surplus accomplishment.

The autonomy of management would be less affected if these questions were entrusted to an independent agency than if the government departments themselves determine them. The sixth section of chapter 13 looks at this aspect in detail.

Price controls have, in general, not taken care of the issues raised in this section in a methodical way. They have been *ad hoc* in most cases, and neither their impacts on enterprise finances have been carefully worked out, nor has it been established that the expected results of the controls were ensured in every case. Two consequences followed. Broadly, the enterprise managers find their autonomy in pricing heavily restricted, and serious underpricing prevails in large segments of the public enterprise sector.

CONCLUSION

The pricing problems of public enterprises are serious because in the first place many of them are monopolies, large in size, and monolithic (or holding-company) in structure; and where they seem to be competing with private enterprises the competition is often under unfair conditions in their favour. The problems are aggravated because of the lack of clarity on the cost to which to relate a price, on the financial objectives, and on the managerial incentives for improved performance. In short, the role of prices in the case of a given public enterprise tends to remain indefinite.

It is to this issue that the government has to address itself, in the interest of the enterprises as well as the national development strategy. Or else, periodic interventions in price fixing turn out to be *ad hoc* in nature and inconsistent among different enterprises and consumer groups.

APPENDIX 6.1

Table 6.1 Low rates on agricultural power (1987–88)

State	*Agricultural average rate as % of*	
	total average per kW sold	*total operating cost per kW sold*
(1)	(2)	(3)
Andhra Pradesh	9.6	8.5
Assam	50.8	24.1
Bihar	13.18	7.2
Gujerat	47.8	43.3
Haryana	44.2	23.4
Himachal Pradesh	35.7	17.5
Karnataka	18.3	14.4
Kerala	65.8	46.4
Madhya Pradesh	34.0	31.5
Maharashtra	11.4	11.6
Meghalaya	46.1	28.6
Orissa	33.9	28.5
Punjab	20.6	9.9
Rajasthan	40.0	29.7
Tamil Nadu	17.7	12.5
Uttar Pradesh	37.5	28.7
West Bengal	40.1	33.4
All Boards	25.8	20.1

Source: Andhra Pradesh State Electricity Board, *Statistics at a Glance (1987–88)*, Hyderabad, India, p. 130.

7 Targets

This chapter deals with various aspects of targets which may be set for a public enterprise. It commences with a discussion of the concept of targets, and the reasons why it is desirable to set them. After a discussion, next, of the net revenue target, the need for determining additional targets will be explored and some of them will be considered in detail. Then follows a critique of the system of targeting as a whole. (This chapter contains an extensive reference to the UK which has the longest experience in target setting.)

THE CONCEPT

Obligations, objectives,[1] targets, and performance aims are used, at random, as substitutable terms in the literature on public enterprise. The underlying purpose is about the same in all cases. Yet at the risk of being considered a semantic exercise, some distinction among the terms seems to be desirable. Objectives (and obligations) may be understood to refer to reasonably indicative and enterprise-specific enunciations, even if unquantified, of what an enterprise is expected to accomplish. The 'duties' laid down in public enterprise Acts hardly satisfy this concept, as may be seen, for instance, from the UK's Coal Industry Nationalisation Act 1946 and Kenya's Industrial Development Ordinance 1955. The former charges the enterprise (The National Coal Board) with

> making supplies of coal available, of such qualities and sizes, in such quantities and at such prices as may seem to them best calculated to further the public interest in all respects, including the avoidance of any undue or unreasonable preference or advantage. (Section 1(1))[2]

The Industrial and Commercial Development Corporation (of Kenya)

> shall have regard . . . in particular, to the desirability of ensuring that any such undertaking or enterprise . . . will be of long-term value in relation to the development of Kenya, whether or not it is likely to prove

self-supporting or to furnish direct profits either immediately or in the future. (Section 3(2))

It is difficult to imagine a wider blank cheque. Even the apparently detailed objectives, developed by certain enterprises (for example, by the British Transport Docks Board cited in Appendix 7.1) were only 'generalised statements of intent'.[3] Objectives should be more enterprise-specific than the Acts lay down or could lay down.

A commendable development has been in progress in recent years in the UK in postulating guidelines that come near to the connotation of objectives. Let us refer to the National Coal Board again. The Chancellor of the Exchequer refined its objectives, for example, to ensure 'a satisfactory return on capital while competing in the market place', to 'aim at that share of the market which they can profitably sustain in competition with other fuels', and not to 'plan on any continuing tranche of sales which will not be profitable'.[4] Another attempt in the direction of somewhat specific objectives is available with reference to the UK's Central Electricity Generating Board: 'to explore and exploit the full potential of nuclear power to contribute to the cheap, effective and safe production of electricity', and to 'set prices so as to reflect the costs at the margin of meeting demands on a continuing basis'.[5]

In the area of financial behaviour of enterprises legislation has, at best, had an indicative purport. The UK Acts commonly speak of securing revenues that are 'not less than sufficient ... for meeting all charges properly chargeable to revenue, taking one year with another'.[6] Their broad purport has been to require financial viability at least in break-even terms. But none of the Acts answers such questions as the following:

(a) How high can the net return of a given enterprise be?
(b) How long is the long run for the purpose of taking one year with another?
(c) Is the financial duty of the enterprise to be understood in overall terms only?

Two developments have gradually taken place. First, the 'not-less-than' clause specifically covered, besides costs properly chargeable to the revenue account, allocations to reserves considered 'adequate' by the enterprise and as per any directions of the Secretary of State.[7] Here is an attempt towards answering the first question.

Second, some recent Acts, instead of repeating the 'not-less-than' financial obligation, described the financial duties of the enterprise as those that 'may from time to time be determined by the Secretary of State with the approval of the Treasury and after consultation with the Corporation'.[8]

The approach of the British Acts has been followed by some countries and the legendary 'not-less-than' clause occurs in a few of their Acts. But the majority are silent in this respect, and so are the governing documents of government companies as a cros-section.

It would be useful to distinguish targets from objectives. First, objectives contain elements of political or social preferences, explicit or implicit; they originate from the government[9] (or a public agency to which the task is delegated by the government), and they need to be quantified into targets.

Second, objectives have a longer-term perspective than targets. The latter constantly call for attention to the conditions of the factor and output markets encountered, whereas the direction of the objectives remains.

Third, most objectives are indicative, whereas targets have to be firm and quantitatively specific.[10] Chapter 3 argues for this in the context of extra-enterprise objectives.

Fourth, when an enterprise is created, there would be no enterprise management with which to agree objectives, whereas targets referring to a going concern have to be agreed with its management.

A brief word on 'performance aims' – it seems to be appropriate to bracket them together with targets. But it would not be correct to argue

(a) that targets are set by the government and agreed with the enterprise, whereas performance aims are set by the management itself;[11] and
(b) that targets refer to net revenue while performance aims concern other aspects of enterprise operations.[12]

On the whole, performance aims have gained distinction from net revenue targets,[13] and have been considered as an important qualification to a bare net revenue target, in the UK.

In the context of our analysis, targets connote those agreed between the enterprise and the government, and not the many internal targets set by the enterprise as managerial tools. (Chapter 8 elaborates the latter category.)

THE NET REVENUE TARGET

Basically the need for governmental determination of targets arises from the very concept of public enterprise, as chapters 1 and 3 show. The 'public' and 'enterprise' characteristics have to be synthesised. Three particular reasons may be highlighted with reference to the net revenue target.

There is a vague notion that the managers of public enterprises, as a cross-section, do not have the same degree of profit motivation as their counterparts in private enterprise.[14] Also alleged are 'financial mismanagement, waste and malpractices in many parastatals',[15] and the managers' concern 'for their own financial benefits rather than the overall success' of the enterprise.[16]

Here is a sad comment on public enterprise managers of Nigeria in the early 1970s:

> The staff of these enterprises ... grossly undercharge their friends and

> relatives . . . One would be shocked to know that several million Naira are lost daily from this act alone in many of these organisations in Nigeria, notably the Airways, Ports Authority, Railways, National Shipping Line, National Electricity Power Authority, Telecommunications, to name only a few . . . Unscrupulous staff members have diverted assets of these bodies to their private use without being found out.[17]

At least in theory, net revenue targets obligate public enterprise managers to strive to reach them, the more so when they are not threatened by competition.[18]

Public enterprise boards are unpredictable in their financial impacts. The special interests and pressures of directors can affect the financial well-being of an enterprise, for example, workers' representatives keen on raising wages, and farmers' representatives on inflating input prices earned by them.[19] There can be some check on their representational excesses, if the board is obliged to meet a government-set target of net revenue.[20]

Equally important is the check that a net revenue target places on interventions by the government and other public agencies, once definitive targets of net revenue exist.[21] Even the Monopolies and Mergers Commission (in the UK) is prevented from considering 'any question relating to the appropriateness of any financial obligations or guidance as to financial objectives (however expressed) imposed . . . or given . . . by or under any enactment, or otherwise by a Minister'.[22]

A strong case in practice arises from the poor financial returns of the cross-section of public enterprises. (Chapter 5 gives details.) Governments have begun to think in terms of setting targets.

Analytically the 'external' determination of net revenue targets for a public enterprise is necessary, not only to improve the allocative efficiency of investments, but to enunciate the limits to its profit 'maximisation' efforts. The macro objective ought to be 'to secure the maximum social return on the capital invested', while the concern of the enterprise is 'properly with the financial return'.[23]

Using the familiar enterprise diagram, the enterprise aims, in theory, at a net revenue of *PQRS*, the maximum it can achieve. This, let us say, works out at 15 per cent on capital. The government may wish that the net profit should be lower, say $P_1 Q_1 R_1 S_1$, which works out at 10 per cent on capital. This may be set as a target, with an eye on the resultant social returns (see Figure 7.1).

Three aspects of the net revenue target call for analysis: the level of the target, the form of the target, and the degree of disaggregation of the target in relation to a given enterprise.

The level

The factors that influence the determination of the exact level are as follows:

Figure 7.1 Preferred net revenue

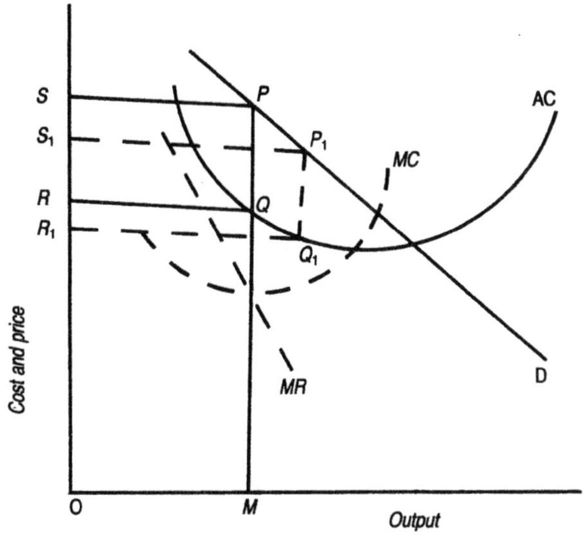

(a) The target, to start with, should bear 'close relationship'[24] to the cost of capital. In theory the latter connotes the opportunity cost of capital – that 'elusive beast'[25] – difficult to quantify precisely but essential to uphold as a macro back-drop. In the UK this was represented by the 'required rate of return' (RRR).[26]

It is necessary to link the target with the current value of the capital used and not its historic value.

(b) The investment needs of the enterprise influence the target.[27] But the higher the figure, the higher the burden on the present consumer through high prices for the sake of the future consumer.

Where a public enterprise enjoys monopoly power, and its profit retention practices escape challenge by any monopolies commission, unrestrained self-financing should not be a major determinant of the target. In the UK, however, it has been an 'obvious' purpose of financial targets 'to increase the extent to which the industries were able to finance their investments and to decrease their direct dependence on the Exchequer and the capital market'.[28]

(c) The net revenue target can be devised as an instrument of indirect taxation affecting a given product or market.

(d) If, on the other hand, an enterprise is expected to offer substantial social returns, the net revenue target may be set relatively low.[29] Where such operations constitute a small proportion of its total operations, a preferable approach would be to compensate the enterprise for specific obligations and proceed with target determination without being inhibited by this consideration. But where the entire activity or a major part of it, such as afforestation, irrigation or postal service in a developing country, is credited with considerable social returns, the government might favour determining a relatively low target level.

(e) A practical determinant of the target consists of 'what could reasonably be expected' from the enterprise.[30]

This is a function of such factors as:

(i) the cost and demand conditions of the enterprise;
(ii) the nature of fluctuations anticipated in the business concerned; and
(iii) the degree of managerial flexibility in influencing costs and revenues (see Appendix 5.10 for many 'inherited' causes of high cost).

(f) The target has to take realistic note of the capital structure of the enterprise, especially where it has heavy accumulated losses. It would be preferable to restructure the enterprise before determining the target.

(g) The extent of gestation in the outlays of the enterprise should influence the level at which the target is set. Interesting provisos can be devised. For example, the target may apply to the capital or assets 'in commission', as in the case of British electricity, where the 'net assets' are explicitly stated as 'excluding work in progress'.[31] The point may be broadened to suggest that 'excess capacity' should also have a lowering impact on target setting.

The net revenue target is not the same as the test discount rate which may be employed in the context of project evaluation. Nor is it exactly the RRR in the UK parlance, which signifies the return expected on 'new investments as a whole'.[32] This would be common to all public enterprises, whereas the net revenue target varies among them and applies to the total capital outlay or total net assets, subject to any disaggregations (see section below).

The composition of capital in terms of equity, loans, and reserves is, strictly, irrelevant to the concept of the net revenue target. The latter relates to the total figure of outlay or net assets.

While the net revenue target can vary among enterprises, its arithmetical determinants, namely, the revenue and cost components of the calculation, should be uniformly defined and exceptions should be highlighted.

The form

The net revenue target can be expressed in several forms:

(a) *An absolute figure*: This method, adopted in the UK in certain years for the British Steel Corporation, the British Railways Board's inter-city services, and the British Shipbuilders,[33] implies the specification of the amount of net revenue in absolute terms. There are two problems. First, it does not automatically take care of changes (usually increases) in the assets base or in operations from year to year, unless every year the target is altered. Second, it does not allow of easy comparisons among different enterprises or among different years in respect of the same enterprise.

The absolute form has value for the public exchequer, especially where it is negative and involves a governmental subsidy or where profits are expected to be transferred wholly or partly to the exchequer. It helps the budget authority in making a precise estimate of the cash flow between the exchequer and the enterprise.

Besides, it may also be convenient in a situation where the capitalisation of an enterprise is fictitious and schemes of restructuring, including write-offs, are overdue, for example, the British Steel Corporation in the early 1980s.

(b) *A percentage of capital outlay or net assets employed*: This is the most usual form, for example, an average 6 per cent return on net assets (during 1980–3).[34] It would be logical to express it in terms of current costs. This method has been adopted in the UK (see Appendix 7.2). There is a complication – in certain enterprises capital reductions may have been effected, so much so that the base on which to set the target would turn out to be lower than in cases where, with similar earning potentialities, a capital reconstruction has not been undertaken.

(c) *Break even*: The connotation of break even corresponds to the 'not-less-than' provision to some extent, though the latter, strictly permits of higher than break-even returns. This form has an attraction in the case of enterprises which have chronically been loss-making, for example, the British Steel Corporation for which the target was 'to reach break-even before interest in 1984–5'.[35]

Unlike the above case, the National Coal Board (in the UK) was set a break-even target 'after interest and special grants from 1983–84'.[36] The formula should be clear on the treatment of interest charges and government grants and compensations. Disguised within such a treatment, a 'break-even' target may be synonymous with a negative percentage net return target.

(d) *A percentage on turnover*: This can be of value in the case of enterprises which have a relatively small capital base and an extremely low capital–output ratio. A good illustration is provided by the (UK) Post Office which had a net revenue target of 2 per cent on turnover (after historic and supplementary depreciation, *and after interest*) for the years 1980–3;[37] and 3.25 per cent on turnover before interest, in 1986–7.

It automatically takes care of changing price levels and turnover volumes. Where profits through a trading enterprise – like a marketing board – are the aim, this target form is particularly appropriate: the more so if the government wants to use it as a means of indirect taxation.

(e) *Self-financing percentage*: The emphasis in this case is on the proportion of capital expenditures to be met from the internal resources of the enterprise. There are two differences from the preceding target forms. First, this refers to the net revenue retention *after* interest and dividend payments. Second, the figure is linked with the capital expenditure programmes of the enterprise.

This target form can signify exchequer interest in limiting the impacts of the enterprise on capital markets or on the government budget for financing its expansion programmes.

By itself the self-financing target does not permit of an inter-enterprise comparison in profitability. For two enterprises with similar targets may in fact be earning quite dissimilar amounts of net revenue in terms of capital or assets or turnover. These targets are under the influence of the forward capital programmes, which can be quite different in the two cases.

Disaggregation

We shall examine whether the net revenue target should apply to the enterprise as a whole or whether it should be disaggregated suitably for different parts. The question assumes significance with:

(a) enterprises producing outputs that are separable into major product lines or 'profit centres' (as illustrated by the British Steel Corporation, Water and Power Development Authority (of Pakistan), and all railway enterprises);
(b) enterprises spread over a wide region – over the entire nation in several cases (as illustrated by the British Airports Authority, Nigerian Electricity Corporation, CONASUPO of Mexico, FELDA of Malaysia, and Lesotho National Bus Corporation); and
(c) enterprises with a distinctive mix of commercial and non-commercial outputs (as illustrated by the National Small Industries Development Corporation (in India), Agricultural Development Corporation (in Kenya), and Tourist Development Corporation of Malaysia).

The case for subsidiary intra-enterprise targets of net revenue is strong on the following grounds:

(i) They can regulate cross-subsidisations among separable lines of business by permitting the managers to pursue different net revenue targets in different markets.
(ii) They can reflect extra-enterprise motivations, if any, in certain categories of operations, for example, the 'public service obligation'

payments by the government to the British Railways Board in respect of certain passenger service.

(iii) If the government contemplates privatisation, the subsidiary targets prove helpful in disclosing the financial potential of different parts of the enterprise operations, so that appropriate decisions may be taken on what to sell, when to sell, and for how much.

Few governments have determined targets; and far fewer have disaggregated them. Even in the UK where financial targets have a long history, the trend towards disaggregated targets has been recent and selective, for example, in British Rail and the Post Office.

ADDITIONAL TARGETS

The usefulness of a net revenue target is subject to several qualifications.

First, it is not necessarily met out of efficiency. Where the enterprise has monopoly power, the prices may be manipulated so as to achieve the target[38] – either through a general rise in the price level or through price discriminations.

Second, the managers may resort to cost manipulations (or window-dressing) so as to reach the net revenue target easily, but at the expense of the long-run interest of the enterprise. For example, the provisions for depreciation and bad debts may be kept low; maintenance expenditures may be minimised; certain revenue expenditures may be capitalised; and so on.

Third, the net revenue target would have little meaning without reference to the quality of the product.[39] It might even induce the enterprise to lower the quality if that helps it meet the target easily.

Fourth, meeting the net revenue target may become such an obsession with the managers that they feel discouraged to undertake growth strategies that contain elements of risk and long gestation (unless the latter are fully provided for while determining the net revenue targets).

Finally, assume that a net revenue target is fixed rather low on grounds of social returns. There is no guarantee that, while it is realised, the expected social returns have materialised. There ought to be some targets for the latter.

For these reasons it seems logical to formulate some additional targets as well, as shown in Figure 7.2. But several points need attention regarding the targets package.

First, it is extremely wide-ranging, and no country has adopted even a fraction of it. The interest in a few countries like Senegal, India, Gambia, and Pakistan to develop some kind of a memorandum of understanding or performance contract, during the mid-1980s, reflects appreciation of the basic need for a package of targets, in whatever shape.

Figure 7.2 The spectrum of targets

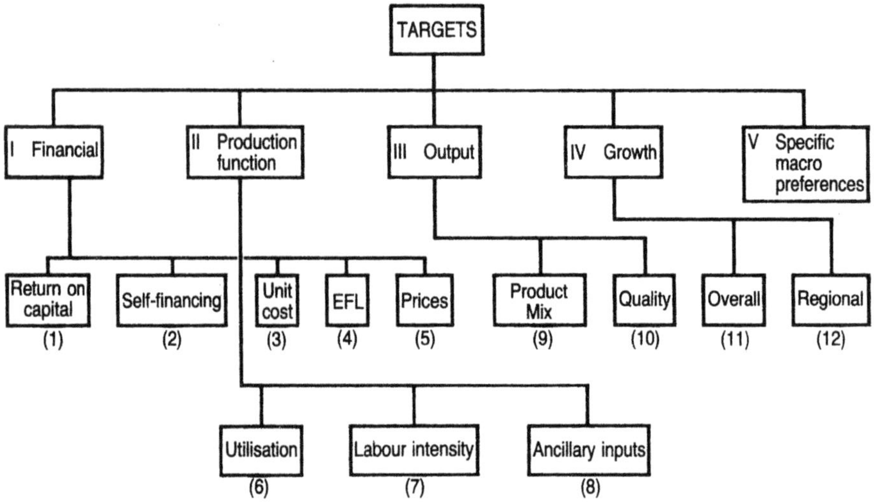

Second, the targets are not mutually exclusive. Almost every one of the five target heads has some impact on everyone else. Take, for example, an export earnings target under V. It affects I if exports are less remunerative than domestic sales; it affects II if a relatively expensive production technique is necessitated by the exportation standards. Its effect can be similar on III (output mix and quality) with corresponding consequences for I (in particular for (1) and (2)). IV is influenced to the extent that investment and location decisions have to suit export-output requirements. The conclusion is that if several targets are set, they must be mutually consistent or else some may be reached while some others are not.

Third, the interrelationships among net revenue targets, pricing guidelines, and investment criteria merit specific analysis. If a public enterprise is expected to work at socially preferred prices and produce socially preferred outputs it is these that have to be targeted. If these are fed into the investment criteria, the net financial results just follow. The net returns are thus 'the residuum';[40] and a net revenue target should be the result, not the cause, of pricing and investment policies.[41]

The argument is sound, in theory. However, it has been found necessary, in practice, to express 'in a simple way the sort of performance which an efficient undertaking should achieve over a period of years while pursuing sound investment and pricing policies'.[42] While there is 'an element of play in the three factors' – net revenue objectives, pricing, and investment criteria – 'it would be a mistake', as argued by the Head of the Government Economic Service (in the UK), 'to regard any two of them as sufficient'.[43]

It is interesting to note that the UK chronology has been from targets to pricing rules and investment criteria – theoretically, the wrong sequence in a perfect world. But the less perfect the world is, the greater the need for such compromise techniques of targeting. The fact that investment criteria have been far from definitive and pricing rules rarely enunciated, makes net revenue targets a necessary means of expressing the government's (or society's) expectations from a public enterprise in practice. Where pricing or output guidelines, on occasion, emerge from the government, after net revenue targets are determined, the interrelationships have to be analysed and quantified; and a compensation may be found necessary for any financial consequences on the enterprise. Or else, one of the targets or guidelines needs to be modified.

In the early years of public enterprise, as chapter 1 argues, investment, output, and pricing preferences were under heavy 'social' influence and net revenues just followed. Today they are considered by governments as alarmingly low and their attitude has become pro-net-revenue. It should not be overlooked that the emphasis on net revenue targets is bound to make investment and/or pricing targets 'residuary'. There is plentiful evidence on the paramountcy of net revenue targets in practice.[44]

Fourth, while a multiple package of targets is attractive in theory, it is so wide as to create room for interventions from the government in the name of setting, monitoring, and periodically altering a great variety of financial and physical targets. An essential virtue of targets, namely, reasonable definiteness, is likely to be lost. Besides, several agencies other than finance and parent ministries would be drawn into the exercise. This might or might not be an advantage.[45]

Experience suggests that there have been few multi-target determinations agreed between the government and individual public enterprises. However, one can deduce an implicit appreciation of the need for attention to be paid to targets other than an exclusive net-revenue target, from the attempts made in France[46] and more recently in India,[47] Pakistan[48] and Senegal,[49] in reforming government relationships with public enterprises.

Let us discuss some of the more important targets other than the net revenue and self-financing targets.

Cost targets

Cost targets are intrinsically good in themselves. They exert a pressure for cost reductions and help in minimising resource use for a given output. They would be meaningful when they refer to segments of costs which managers can control.

In stipulating cost targets one has to look into their relationship with net revenue targets. At least three situations can be distinguished. The first is where, with a given scale of output and product mix within a given capacity, the enterprise achieves cost economies; that is, the cost

Figure 7.3 Cost economies

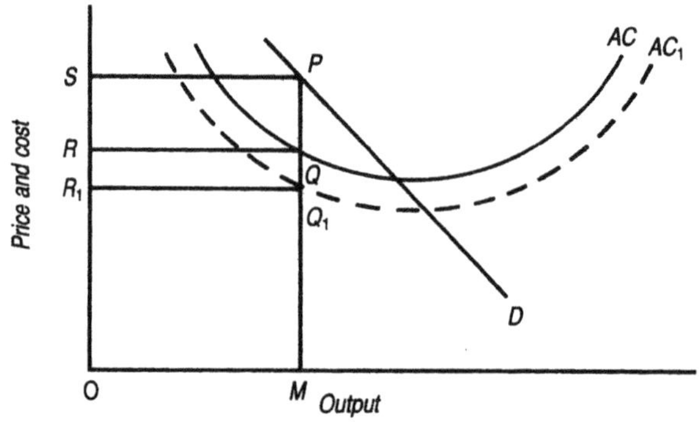

curve is lowered. This has implications for prices, outputs and net revenues.

In Figure 7.3, if the net revenue target corresponds to *PQRS*, the lowered costs (AC_1) make possible a higher net revenue PQ_1R_1S if the price and output remain constant. It is also possible, through internal decisions and external pressures, that the output is increased or the price reduced, so that either the same net revenue as targeted is realised or some variation of it above the target, but under conditions of different output and price. This situation corresponds to Michael Posner's proposition of increasing output subject to a profit constraint, cited in note 44.

The second case of cost reduction is what results from an increase in output when the enterprise works under increasing returns. This may result from new managerial initiatives or simply from an increase in demand for some sudden reason. Here the cost reduction is basically traceable to the existence of unused capacity and to a consequent spread of fixed costs over a larger output than before. The target of net revenue may even be lowered, if necessary, particularly if the government prefers the new scale of output and prices.

The third situation of cost reduction is one where the product mix changes. Outputs which can be supplied at relatively low costs may be increased, and those which cost relatively high amounts, decreased. Assuming no countervailing price changes, the net revenue increases.

Thus cost and net revenue targets have to be conceived together. There is an important point of asymmetry between them. Intra-enterprise disaggregation of net revenue targets cannot be so extensive as that of cost targets, just as an enterprise cannot be disaggregated into so many profit centres as it can into cost centres. Where a share of the total revenue cannot easily be attributed to a cost centre, a cost target can be devised for it, but not a net revenue target.

Cost targets relating to the most important inputs or set of costs (for example, total marginal costs) would be purposeful. A target relating to labour would be meaningful, for example, where the activity is highly labour intensive.

External financing limit (EFL)

This may be defined as 'the limit on the amount of finance an industry can raise from external sources (that is, excluding internally generated sources of finance such as profits and depreciation) in any one financial year'. The external sources include 'government grants and subsidies to sustain non-commercial activities'. This target represents a post-1976 development in the UK and is intended as a 'short-term operating control' on the enterprise, 'in contrast to financial targets which are a medium term method of control'.[50]

While in most countries the government has an influence on public enterprise borrowings, even if in an *ad hoc* or unstructured manner, it has been enshrined in the UK in EFLs so formally that it has earned the epithet of a financial target/objective.[51] Its impact as a target is so real, severe, and controversial that it merits an in-depth analysis.

The major reasons for strict EFLs are that public enterprises are expected to take their share of the limitations implicit in the Public Sector Borrowing Requirements and that their borrowings do not 'crowd out' the capital markets. The basic issue, however, ought to be whether a proposed investment is justified on its own merits and passes whatever tests of investment criteria are upheld. To starve an investment irrespective of this consideration can hurt projects that are intrinsically worth launching. On this there is substantial evidence from the UK scene. Several nationalised industries claimed that 'major profitable earning projects' were delayed. The EFL is admittedly a short run – if not, annual – target, based on cash-control considerations, and can be illogically restrictive of investment decisions that have long 'lead times'.[53]

Moreover, it forces an enterprise to increase internal resources so as to be able to maximise its capital expenditures. That is, the burdens of expansion are excessively imposed on the present consumers.[54]

The EFL is a blunt instrument for controlling capital expenditures by a public enterprise. An easier device consists of the government openly disapproving of them if and where it decides that the projects concerned are not worth investing in (either for commercial or for social reasons). The projects do not improve in their investment justification if the funds come, not from external borrowings, but from internal resources.

The principle of the EFL target can be salvaged if it is restricted to the revenue or recurring cash flows as between the government and a public enterprise. Then it boils down to setting an *ex ante* limit on the subsidy that it may expect from the government; and it may be redesignated as the Annual Subsidy Limit (ASL). There is great need for such a formalised definition of the public exchequer-enterprise cash flows. Incidentally, this device pays regard to the logic of distinguishing current transactions from capital transactions. Where the government decides that certain enterprises should transfer to the public exchequer a part of their net revenues, a 'negative' ASL can be determined – in the same way as negative EFLs have been devised, in some cases in the UK – for example, British Airways.[55]

In relation to investment needs, an EFL would be immaterial if the enterprise is allowed to borrow in the capital market, so that a feasible project which the government cannot finance may nevertheless have the prospect of coming into being. However, a socially justifiable project for which the enterprise would not be able to borrow funds other than through the government can be in danger of exclusion.

It is claimed that the EFL prompts an enterprise to explore cost economies. True, but it is a crude instrument, oftentimes the cost reductions are not genuine; they result from cutting back expenditures that, in the long-run interest of the enterprise, ought not to be cut.[56] It encourages short-run savings but increases long-run costs.[57] The EFL being an annual target, even window-dressing can take place on occasion as the enterprise may just postpone an expenditure by a few days so that the current year's EFL is not prejudiced.

The major emphasis of the EFL is on the cash flow of the enterprise. There is danger of its adopting policies that satisfy this criterion in the short run but affect net revenues in the long run, for example, price reductions so as to increase cash sales, and the offer of discounts so as to induce debtors to pay dues before due dates.[58]

It is interesting to record the following estimates, by the Treasury, of the relative importance of the different measures adopted by the nationalised industries of the UK in 1980–1 in order to keep within their EFLs.[59]

Of the total EFL measures of £1,580 million:[60]

deferred payments accounted for –	28%
earlier or larger price increases for –	25%
reductions in current spending for –	24%
cuts in capital expenditures for –	13%
higher asset disposals for –	2%
and miscellaneous measures for –	9%

These data prompt the question – is the EFL target an end in itself, irrespective of the ways in which it is met?

In using the EFL target, intra-enterprise disaggregations are necessary to avoid gainful segments of business subsidising the less gainful or losing ones.[61] Further, there ought to be different EFLs for current and capital transactions.

In conclusion, the EFL target may prove to be incompatible with the net revenue target if it creates cash stringency which forces an enterprise to undertake price enhancements and investment cuts that affect its realisation of the net revenue target over the medium term. This result is most likely if, where conflict arises between the two targets, the EFL takes precedence over the net revenue target.[62]

Guidelines on pricing

The need for governmental attention to pricing was indicated in the discussion on net revenue targets and in chapter 6. If 'absolute' price controls or price ceilings are introduced on macroeconomic grounds, their impact on the net revenue target has to be evaluated and dealt with properly. As for the prices autonomously determined by an enterprise, pricing guidelines should be given by the government or a public agency empowered to do so. The object should be to prevent price discriminations and cross-subsidisations that reflect an abuse of monopoly power, and to show the nature and relevance of the cost basis of prices in a situation where, due to lack of effective competition, it is in danger of being ignored.

Non-financial targets

There can be a broad range of non-financial targets, as shown in Figure 7.2. But there is need for selectivity, in resorting to them. At a given unit of time a certain non-financial target may seem to be important, for example, total output.[63] This has to be mentioned, and its impact, if any, on the net revenue or other financial targets, such as unit cost, has to be evaluated.

On the whole it would be wise to go in for the minimum number of 'agreed' non-financial targets, and leave it to the enterprise to formulate subtargets for internal use in respect of a large number of targetable aims. No wonder very few non-financial targets have been set in the UK, for example, 'terminal passengers per pay roll hour' in the case of British Airports Authority (even this was termed a 'performance aim').[64]

There is a difference between developed and developing countries in target determination. Public enterprises in the former, by and large, are considered as essentially commercial enterprises,[65] whereas in developing countries their extra-enterprise objectives are important. Hence there is need to lay down targets at least in the major areas of such objectives, for example, the extent of investments in backward regions, the proportion of merit goods in the output plan, and the rate of employment expansion or contraction. It is common to find a bundle of financial and non-financial obligations mentioned, but none of them is quantified into a target.[66]

Another difference between developed and developing countries in the context of target setting is that, on the whole, the governments in the latter countries are more sensitive to the idea of contracting their avenues of intervention which a system of targets implies. There is extensive evidence on the interventions.

Some illustrations may be drawn from Ghana and Nigeria.

The Minister and MP from Tema, 'without informing the Board', sent orders to reduce rent on the lowest income housing at Tema Development Corporation (TDC) by almost 50 per cent and eliminated the Corporation's system of recovering rents directly from the wages of locally employed tenants. He 'imposed substantial losses on TDC to court favour with the Tema electorate'. Also, one goal 'at odds with profit maximisation' in the case of the State Distilleries 'concerned a convert scheme by some politicians to obtain payoffs' (R. C. Pozen (1976) *Legal Choices for State Enterprises in the Third World*, New York, pp. 120, 144).

'We found that the Board tended to pay more attention to their political interest rather than to the real interest of the Authority' (*Report of the Tribunal of Inquiry into the Affairs of the Nigerian Ports Authority*, Lagos, 1967, p. 194).

'The ascending of the politician, as a politician, in organisations like the Nigerian Railways Corporation, inevitably obscured the aims and objects of these institutions' (*Report of the Tribunal of Inquiry into the Affairs of the Nigerian Railway Corporation*, Lagos, 1967, p. 154).

'Some Board Members ... were more concerned with their own financial benefits rather than the overall success of the Railway undertaking' (ibid., p. 277).

'A witness told us that a one-time Chairman of the Board of Directors did not know the difference between the offices of the Nigerian Airways and those of the N.C.C. political party' (*Report of the Tribunal into the Affairs of W.A.C.C. (Nigeria) Ltd.*, Lagos, 1968, p. 20).

THE TARGET SYSTEM

There are four overall considerations concerning targets as a system. First, a decision has to be taken on whether a target should be set in definitive numbers, say, '*x*' or '*x* per cent', or in terms of a minimum, say, not less than '*x*' or '*x* per cent', or in terms of a maximum, say, not more than '*x*' or '*x* per cent', or in terms of a range say, between '*x*' and '*y*'. The first gets interpreted in practice in the sense of the second, but differs from the latter in that it does not convey an open-ended determination. 'More or less', '*x*' is what is intended; 'over three or five years', or 'taking one year with another' over a specified period, is a formula that conveys that determination. On the other hand, the 'not-less-than' determination leaves it open to the enterprise to go sky-high.[67] It represents indifference to the use of monopoly power or inexpert, gross undertargeting. The third method is the converse of the second and signifies the undesirability of an over-achievement. The fourth has the value of indicating the minimum that is expected as well as the upper point beyond which the enterprise is not expected to go; for, exceeding that point is considered, on whatever ground, as monopoly or antisocial behaviour. The choice of the method varies with the substantive coverage of the target. The first is the most generally used (for example, in the UK) with reference to net returns, though the third method seems to be superior and can operate as a check on monopoly profits and extremely high self-financing. Cost reduction or output targets may be brought under the second method; similarly, any other productivity targets. The third may be applied to retrenchments or closures of operations; and the last, again, to net revenues and to the components of the product mix. These illustrations are intended to suggest that target specificity should not be such as converts targeting into a rigid control.

Second, what is the incentive for the enterprise managers to reach a target, even if an agreed one? Losing the job is hardly a realistic answer in most socio-economic systems. It would be helpful to work out a system of incentives which makes it worthwhile for the managers, in terms of money and other benefits, to reach the targets and, wherever desirable, to exceed them. The obverse would be to make them feel the pinch of not realising the targets, gently to start with.

Third, even the most expertly evolved and agreed targets may fail to be reached on occasion. One has to review the situation so as to locate the cause under one or more of three heads: the managers, the government, and exogenous factors. Managers may have been responsible for the underrealisation because of 'inefficiency', including inability to respond to business fluctuations; the government may have contributed to the situation either by making less resources available to the enterprise than are necessary for reaching the targets, or by adopting an unproductive or efficiency-inhibiting interface with the enterprise; and/or circumstances beyond the control of the enterprise may have brought about the problem, for example, a shift away of export demands or a structural change in technology. How to deal with the exogenous factors is not the issue here. The credibility of targeting must be reasserted by tackling the first two factors. If experience shows that they cannot be tackled, targets may have to be altered (lowered). Or else, gradually they will not be taken seriously by either side to the agreement.

Finally, targets, once set, ought not to stay static all the time. Attempts should be made to revise them upwards or downwards, according to market conditions and shifts in extra-enterprise preferences. Reasons cited in the foregoing paragraph are also relevant in this context. The need for discerning revision would be great in developing countries in the early years of target setting.

'CONTRACTS'

There are many countries where targets are not set yet. In some they exist for some, not all, public enterprises, for medium-term in some cases, and for a year only in others. Where targets exist they are usually net revenue-oriented; other financial and non-financial targets are very exceptional.

The French system of contracts, which really aims at covering some of the qualifications to net revenue targets, has not been consistently followed in France over time; many enterprises did not have contracts in several years. During conflicts between the short-term aims of the government and the longer-term aims of a public enterprise, the contract could become a 'dead letter'.[68] The original contracts were replaced in the late 1970s by 'contract plans' which were somewhat less elaborate and more short term in nature.

The contract method has spread to a few countries, for example, in French West Africa, India, and Sri Lanka. In Senegal, in particular, a 'contract plan' is designed in the case of public utilities and industrial enterprises; and a 'statement of objectives' in the case of certain predominantly developmental agencies. In India the document is termed a memorandum of understanding. The term suggests that it is not a 'contract', which it would be unrealistic to enforce against the government (or even the enterprise) in a court of law. Eleven such documents were signed in 1988–9.[69] A brief note with specific reference to the content of the various memoranda is appended, aimed only at bringing out points of general interest from the technical angle. In Sri Lanka the attempt is towards a 'performance contract'.

Appendices 7.3 and 7.4 indicate the highlights of contracts in France and The Gambia; and Appendix 7.5 provides a note on the memorandum of understanding in vogue in India.

The contract or memorandum technique has the best chance of success:

(a) if the terms or targets are arrived at after considering several options of technology, product mix, prices and rates of enterprise expansions, and are related to a medium term rather than one year;
(b) if the government refrains from interventions in enterprise affairs beyond what the memorandum says and offers the managers the necessary financial and other resources (for example, import licences, electricity, and water) and autonomy in pricing, input policies and productivity improvement, except for any limitations transparently conceived in the memorandum;
(c) if the delegation of investment and managerial powers from the government to the enterprise managers, visualised as requisite in the memorandum, is scrupulously followed in practice;
(d) if the memorandum is suitably disaggregated among the major constituent units of the enterprise, particularly in the case of a large monolithic or holding company;

(e) if the extra-enterprise objectives are enunciated and properly dealt with, as argued in chapter 3; and
(f) if the structural handicaps of the enterprise, if any, are duly corrected or allowed for in drafting the memorandum.

Clearly these are not easy conditions to fulfil, but effort should be made to approximate to them as nearly as possible. Different departments or levels of government (for example, federal, state, and local) may act disparately to the disadvantage of the memorandum, not out of deliberate intention. Where their actions cannot be improved in favour of the memorandum, the impacts have to be fed into it as constraint. Likewise, where holding company structures limit maximal managerial behaviour within the enterprise, the estimated impacts have to be fed into it as constraint.

CONCLUSION

Governments which have no experience of setting targets should realise that the 'contract' method is more complex. Adequate technical work is a prerequisite for the success of either method. Corporate planning can help in the exercise. Chapter 13 has some comments on it.

The essential merit of a system of targets or a contract is that it exists. It signifies a dialogue between the government and the enterprise. It concretises the concept of government accountability, besides the managers'. If well formulated, it can create some balance between the long-term interests of the enterprise and the shorter-term interests of the government.

The technique succeeds more from internal motivation within the country than from external pressure such as a conditionality laid down by an international lending agency.

APPENDIX 7.1 The specific objectives of the British Transport Docks Board (as defined by the Board)

(a) *National*: to conduct its affairs in a way that is consistent with the national interest and in this regard to recognise the important role that the docks industry plays in the economic well-being of this country. Within this overall national interest to be alert to the needs, interests and welfare of the individual communities in whose areas the ports are situated.
(b) *Productivity*: to make the most efficient use of the resources within its control by the employment of the best management methods and techniques available and continually to improve the productivity of its

resources by challenging present methods and by creating an environment that stimulates beneficial change and improvement.

(c) *Financial*: to employ its financial resources in a way that will ensure the long-term financial viability of each of the ports and of the Board as a whole and to establish and meet return on investment goals for each of the ports. In so doing to have regard to the financial obligations of the Transport Acts, 1962 and 1968, and to the Financial and Economic Objectives of the Nationalised Industries (Cmnd 1337 and Cmnd 3437).

(d) *Commercial*: to occupy the leading position in a port industry by providing the highest quality of service at a competitive cost. To ensure continual growth by vigorously promoting the use of the ports to the benefit of all concerned.

(e) *Personnel*: to create a secure but challenging environment for its employees by providing safe and agreeable working conditions, making full use of each individual's capabilities, offering opportunity for personal achievement and development, ensuring fair and equal treatment for all, and providing remuneration and benefits based on merit and contribution within the framework of a sound and consistent structure of wages, salaries and pensions.

(f) *Technological*: to employ the best economic techniques in the maintenance of its assets and ensure the most efficient forms of construction for investment projects. To contribute to the technological growth of the port industry by actively identifying future needs and requirements of port users and by supporting and undertaking applied research designed to fulfil such needs.

Source: First Report from the Select Committee on Nationalised Industries, Session 1971–72 (1972) *British Transport Docks Board*, London: HMSO, 312, p. x.

APPENDIX 7.2 Financial targets in the UK

Early 1980s

NATIONAL COAL BOARD
Break even on profit and loss account after interest and special grants from 1983–84.

ELECTRICITY (ENGLAND AND WALES)
Average annual rate of return after current cost depreciation but before interest and tax of 1.8 per cent on net assets valued (excluding work in progress) at current cost over the period 1980–81 to 1982–83.

BRITISH GAS
Average annual rate of return (related to current cost operating profit after depreciation but before interest and tax) of 3½ per cent on net assets valued at current cost over period April 1980 to March 1983.

BRITISH STEEL
Reduce loss before interest to £225 million in 1981–82 and to achieve break even in 1982–83.

BRITISH TELECOMMUNICATIONS
Five per cent return on average net assets revalued to replacement cost (before interest, but after historic and supplementary depreciation) for each of the three years from 1979–80 to 1981–82 (as indicated in Cmnd 8175, revision of the target for the remaining year of the period is being considered).

POSTS
Two per cent return on turnover (after historic and supplementary depreciation, and after interest) for each of the three years 1980–81 to 1982–83.

GIRO
Average annual return of 13 per cent before interest on net assets over 1979–80 to 1981–82, plus £5 million over the three years towards reducing the accumulated deficit.

BRITISH AIRWAYS
Average rate of return of 6 per cent before interest but after supplementary depreciation on mean net assets revalued at current cost, over the three financial years 1979–80 to 1981–82.

BRITISH AIRPORTS AUTHORITY
Average rate of return of 6 per cent per annum on net assets revalued to current cost over the three financial years 1980–81 to 1982–83.

BRITISH RAIL
The industry as a whole is required to break even after receipt of grant at a predetermined level. The objective of individual businesses is to earn a current cost operating profit sufficient to achieve the required rate of return on investment after providing for all direct and appropriate indirect costs. In addition, interim targets have been set for the individual businesses as follows:

SEALINK
Five per cent rate of return on net assets valued at current cost (after current cost depreciation) by 1982.

INTER-CITY
By 1982 should achieve £28 million improvement (at 1979 prices) in 1978

level of contribution to total indirect costs of the railway after charging all direct costs, provision for full current cost depreciation and amortisation of the assets, interest and the net cost of train catering.

FREIGHT
By 1982 should aim to cover two-thirds of current cost depreciation and amortisation as opposed to 30 per cent in 1978.

SCOTTISH TRANSPORT GROUP
Current cost operating profit equivalent to 4½ per cent per annum of net fixed assets at current cost over the period to 31 December 1983.

BRITISH SHIPBUILDERS
1981–82 maximum trading loss of £75 million before crediting intervention fund assistance.

Nationalised industries performance aims

BRITISH GAS CORPORATION	*5 per cent reduction in real unit costs by 1982–83 on 1980–81 base*
POST OFFICE	*Constant real unit costs 1978–79 to 1982–83*
BRITISH TELECOM	*Reduction in real unit costs of 5 per cent per year 1978–79 to 1982–83*
BRITISH AIRPORTS AUTHORITY	*3 per cent increase in passengers per employee; 2½ per cent reduction in expenditure per passenger, on average in 1980–81, 1981–82 and 1982–83*
SCOTTISH TRANSPORT GROUP	*Hold constant or reduce in real terms operating costs per vehicle mile.*

Source: Eighth Report from the Treasury and Civil Service Committee, Session 1980–81 (1981) *Financing of the Nationalised Industries*, vol. II, London: HMSO, 348–II, pp. 47–9.

Table 7.1 Financial targets in the UK in the mid-1980s

Industry	*Previous target*	*Achievement against previous target*	*Current target*
BRITISH COAL	Break even after interest and social grants set for 1988–9	Break even yet to be achieved	Break even after social grants by 1988–9. In 1986–7 made a £286 million Historic Cost Loss
ELECTRICITY (ENGLAND AND WALES)	1.4% return on current cost net asets in 1983–4 to 1984–5	−0.4%	2.75% return on current cost net assets between 1984–5 and 1987–8. Achieved 2.65% in 1985–6 and 3.12% in 1986–7. But planned to drop to 2.45% in 1987–8
NORTH OF SCOTLAND HYDRO-ELECTRIC BOARD	1.75% current cost return on net assets employed of per cent over 3 years to March 1986	Achieved 2.23% return	2.7% current cost return on net assets employed for 4 years to 1986–7
SOUTH OF SCOTLAND ELECTRICITY BOARD		Achieved 2.8%	
BRITISH STEEL CORPORATION	1986–7, 5% return on capital employed (including S/T borrowing) before interest and exceptional items	1986–7 Achieved 7%	Current financial and performance targets including EFL, are still under review

Table 7.1 Continued

Industry	*Previous target*	*Achievement against previous target*	*Current target*
POST OFFICE	Mails and Counters: 4.5% current cost profit on turnover in 1985–6	Mails: 4.6% return Counters: 5.3% return	3.25% current cost profit before interest on turnover in 1986–7. Also set are subordinate targets on same basis for letters, parcels and counters. In 1986–7 these were 3%, 6%, 1.3% respectively; and in 1987–8 2.8%, 6.7%, 1.2%. Achieved 1986–7 for posts overall 3.1%, letters 3.3%, parcels 6.3%, counters 1.5%
NATIONAL GIROBANK	Average 19% return on historic cost assets between 1982–3 and 1984–5	Achieved 33.1% in 1982–3; 25% in 1983–4; 26.4% in 1984–5; 23.7% in 1985–6; 24.6% in 1986–7	Average 22% return on historic cost assets between 1985–6 and 1987–8
BRITISH RAIL	Public Sector Obligation (PSO) grant to be reduced to £736 million by 1986. Inter-city and rail freight to achieve CCA profit of 5% in 1988	PSO grant in 1986 was £712 million	Public Sector Obligation grant to be reduced to £555 million by 1989–90. Inter-city to be ineligible for grant after 1987–8. Rail freight freightliner, parcels, Travellers Fare, Inter-city taken together should earn a 2.7% current cost return on net assets before interest by 1989–90

Table 7.1 Continued

BRITISH WATERWAYS BOARD	Break even, taking one year with another	Break even achieved	Break even
NATIONAL BUS COMPANY			None set in the light of privatisation
SCOTTISH TRANSPORT GROUP	(i) SBG: 4.5% return before interest on net current cost fixed assets (ii) Calmac; Break even after grant (iii) Other: £0.2 million	In 1985 (i) 4.7% return achieved (ii) £0.7 million profit (iii) £0.9 million profit	SBG: 4% return on average net current cost fixed assets between 1986 and 1990. New target to be set for other businesses
BRITISH SHIPBUILDERS	None determined since 1982–3 when trading loss was to be limited to £10 million (out-turn was a loss of £148 million in 1986–7)		
CIVIL AVIATION AUTHORITY	7% return before interest on average net current cost assets between 1983–4 and 1986–7 (did not cover all services)	1983–4 – 6.5% 1984–5 – 17.9% 1985–6 – 11.9% 1986–7 – 13.3%	7% return before interest on average net current cost assets between 1985–6 and 1987–8 (does not cover all services)
WATER (ENGLAND AND WALES)	1.45% return on average current cost assets in 1985–6 1.6% return on average net current cost assets in 1986–7	1.56% achieved in 1985–6	1.9% return on average net current cost assets in 1987–8
LONDON REGIONAL TRANSPORT	For 1984–5 to 1987–8 to reduce revenue support to £75 million by 1987–8	£93m revenue support forecast out-turn for 1986–7	Targets for 1988–9 and future years to be announced

Note: BWB have different targets for each business sector, however, their main target is their statutory duty to break even.

Table 7.1 Continued

Pre-privatisation targets	
BRITISH TELECOM	Return on current cost capital employed: 1983: 5.5%; 1984: 6.5% Reduction in unit cost: 1983: 2.7%; 1984: 5.8%
BRITISH AIRWAYS	Real rate of return on net assets for 1982–3 and 1983–4: Average of 5.75%
BRITISH GAS	Average annual return of 4.0% of current cost operating profit on average net assets at current cost: for 1983–4 to 1986–7

APPENDIX 7.3 Example of a 'contrat de programme' in France

The 'contrat de programme' between the government and the Société Nationale des Chemins de Fer Français (SNCF) is comprised in the letters of 16 and 25 July 1969 passing between the Ministry of Transport and the SNCF and the letters of 22 and 30 November 1971 passing between the Ministries of Transport and Economy and Finance and the SNCF, supplementing the first exchange of letters.

These exchanges cover the years 1969 to 1973. The contract was extended to cover 1974 and 1975 by a document dated 30 March 1974 signed jointly by the Ministers concerned and the president of the SNCF. The contract and its extension are fairly detailed. The letter of 16 July 1969 consists of twelve large pages of typescript; the supplementary agreement of 30 March 1974, which maintains in force all previous understandings except in so far as they are modified by the supplementary agreement, comprises eight pages and a page of signatures.

The contract has the following rubrics:

(a) reforms affecting the activities and structure of the SNCF. In the supplementary agreement this becomes simply 'activities and structure of the SNCF';
(b) modification of the legal and financial relationships between the state and the SNCF. In the supplementary agreement this becomes 'the SNCF's means of action towards the re-establishment of financial equilibrium';
(c) government measures in the field of general transport policy;
(d) application of foregoing commitments. In the supplementary agreement this becomes 'general provisions'.

ACTIVITIES AND STRUCTURE

The original agreement had under this head provisions covering:

(a) the passenger stopping-train services – the principal provision being agreement by the state to the closure or transfer to the roads of 10,000 kilometres of services in the years 1969 to 1972;
(b) the reorganisation of other SNCF services and facilities. Some of the provisions appear relatively minor but the principal ones endorse the closure of 5,000 kilometres of merchandise services and the withdrawal of underutilised express passenger services to the extent of 5 million train-kilometres before 1973;
(c) the introduction of an incentive scheme for employees;
(d) the number of employees – to be reduced to 270,000 by December 1973 on the basis of the then existing hours of work.

The original agreement contained no express provision in regard to productivity. This was remedied in the 1971 exchange of letters which provided for the achievement of an average annual rate of increase of 'productivité globale' of at least 4.25% during the 5 years 1969 to 1973.

The supplementary agreement:

(e) deferred the completion of the reduction of passenger stopping-train services until 30 June 1975 (it seems it has since been deferred *sine die*) and provided for the extension of state compensation payments;
(f) modified the provisions for reorganisation of services and introduced numerous new provisions;
(g) extended the productivity provision to apply for a further two years.

FINANCIAL RELATIONSHIPS AND PROVISIONS

The original agreement had under this head provisions covering:

(a) tariff policy – consisting in a rather vague undertaking by the state not to oppose moderate average increases necessary to balance the revenue account by 1973/74 at the latest;
(b) managerial autonomy – the SNCF being accorded freedom to undertake the 'reforms and reorganisation necessary to achieve financial equilibrium';
(c) investment – but the essential arrangements were contained in the 1971 exchange of letters which fixed the level of investments in 1972 and 1973 and the means of financing them, as well as stipulating a real return of 13% as the minimum for investments undertaken to reduce costs;
(d) adjustments for special burdens – being various subventions from the state to cover costs, such as disproportionate pension charges borne by the railways, that distorted competition with other forms of transport.

The supplementary agreement contained very specific provisions about price increases in 1974 and 1975, about the level of investments in those years and the means of financing them; and it also provided a contingency provision of 100 million francs per annum for the revenue account.

GOVERNMENT TRANSPORT POLICY

The original agreement had under this head provisions covering:

(a) long distance road transport – being principally a state undertaking by means of the licensing arrangements to keep competition between rail and road at the then existing level;
(b) equalisation of infrastructure costs – being principally various state subventions aimed at equalising the burdens of the SNCF with those of competitive forms of transport;
(c) equalisation of the rate-fixing powers of the railways with those of competitive forms of transport.

The supplementary agreement showed the state as adhering generally, but rather more loosely, to the preceding engagements.

APPLICATION OF THE CONTRACT

The original agreement included a reservation for 'evolution of economic conditions' and for consultations in the event of unexpected developments. The supplementary agreement renewed these provisions.

Source: Prepared by Maurice R. Garner for the National Economic Developments Office Background Paper no. 2, *Relationships of Government and Public Enterprises in France, West Germany and Sweden*, London, 1976, pp. 61–3.

APPENDIX 7.4 Format of a performance contract in The Gambia

1. **Statement of mission**
   - Clear statement of enterprise's mandate in terms of rationale, strategic objectives, and major activities.
2. **Objectives**
   - Statement of medium-term objectives by major activity.
   - Should separate commercial and non-commercial activities.
   - Quantified where possible.
3. **Performance targets**
   - Quantified medium-term performance targets (financial, economic, operating) by major activity and on a consolidated basis.
   - Major assumptions and constraints behind performance targets with respect to external and internal factors (for example, prices of major inputs, wage levels, and so on), including government policies affecting enterprise operations.
4. **Responsibilities and commitments**

   (a) *Government*
   - Financial support in terms of operating subsidies for non-commercial activities, loans and equity infusions, authorisations for borrowings or loan guarantees, debt forgiveness and clearance of arrears.
   - Statement of tariff approvals, or a clear process for review/approval of tariff requests.
   - Degree of managerial autonomy with respect to personnel management (recruitment, layoffs, promotions, salary levels) and procurement.
   - Policy measures to be implemented.

(b) *Enterprise*
- Dividends to be paid.
- Investment levels.
- Service, production and/or employment levels.
- Reporting to government.

Source: Material made available at a CAFRAD–Commonwealth Secretariat Workshop held at Accra, Ghana, in May 1988.

APPENDIX 7.5 A note on the 'memorandum of understanding' method of India

This note seeks to highlight points of general technical interest, in a close study of the eleven memoranda formulated for 1988–9.

1. Generally the memoranda are for one year, though some limited projections for the following year(s) are found in five cases.
2. The financial (and physical) details are more like budget estimates taken from the books of the enterprise than a few strategic targets towards which the budgets should be projected: for example, 'incidental revenue' and 'non-operating revenue' in the case of the Indian Airlines Corporation.
3. A common omission concerns the crucial question of extra-enterprise objectives and the arrangements for compensations. Further, there are no clauses relating to cross-subsidisations – for example, in the State Trading Corporation of India Ltd, and the Indian Airlines Corporation.
4. Another common feature is that the memoranda refer to the apex level of the enterprise. All the eleven enterprises are monolithic or large holding companies, with significant elements of monopoly power in different (or all) markets. There are no 'agreed' targets by major products or regions, that is, targets agreed between the government and the enterprise. The apex, no doubt introduces them for internal managerial purposes, but these do not signify deliberated government attention to possible cross-subsidisations.
5. In several cases like the Indian Airlines Corporation, the major problem impacting on efficiency is the organisational structure. There is no mention of the need to rationalise it, for example, by an effective subdivision of the total activity, so as to improve the cost structure and raise net revenues.
6. A fairly common omission refers to consumer standards. Air India and the Indian Airlines Corporation illustrate the point in particular.
7. Many paragraphs read like pious wishes. For example, the State Trading Corporation of India Ltd 'will promote Indian exports through counter trade and generate additionality by export of identified engineering and

chemical items and projects in new markets' (p. 54). The question to be addressed is – at what cost?

8. There is no attempt at financial restructuring. Without this, target fixing would appear to be an unconvincing exercise for an enterprise like the Heavy Engineering Corporation.
9. The aim of evaluating the enterprises in the light of the memoranda is subject to heavy limitations derived from the above considerations. Further, the evaluation is proposed to be conducted by a committee full of officials, except for one expert. Basically it refers to evaluation at the A level and, with some luck, at the B level (see Chapter 9).

(Refer to *Memorandum of Understanding between Public Sector Undertakings and Government of India for 1988–89*, New Delhi, 1989.)

8 Monitoring

This chapter commences with conceptualising monitoring in the context of public enterprise. Two levels of monitoring will be distinguished: the enterprise-level and the all-public enterprise level. Several aspects of indicators as a means of monitoring an enterprise will be discussed next. Finally, certain issues in all-public enterprise monitoring will be dealt with. The somewhat unique experiences of the UK and Kenya in monitoring will be presented in the form of brief appendices.

THE CONCEPT OF MONITORING

The term monitoring conveys different meanings to different people. For the purpose of our analysis it may be understood as a running appraisal of enterprise operations in a comprehensive manner by using indicators which encapsulate the processes and substance of the operations. It is to be distinguished from 'control'. In fact, a good monitoring system can yield the benefit of abridging governmental control while enriching its quality. For control would then be based on a continuous grasp of the enterprise situation through a regularised inflow of desired data in a predetermined pattern.

Monitoring has to be distinguished from evaluation, too. It helps the latter, but does not serve as a substitute for it, as the next chapter shows. A well-designed set of monitoring indicators can help the government in fixing targets which are an essential prerequisite of evaluation.

Monitoring has also to be distinguished from an aimless influx of information into government offices, which helps neither evaluaton nor control in a logical manner.

MONITORING AT THE ENTERPRISE LEVEL

A good monitoring system should bifurcate the area which is best left to the chief executive (or the board) of the enterprise and that which the government has to monitor. Not that the indicators relating to the former area must not be provided to the government, but the government's

Figure 8.1 Monitoring indicators

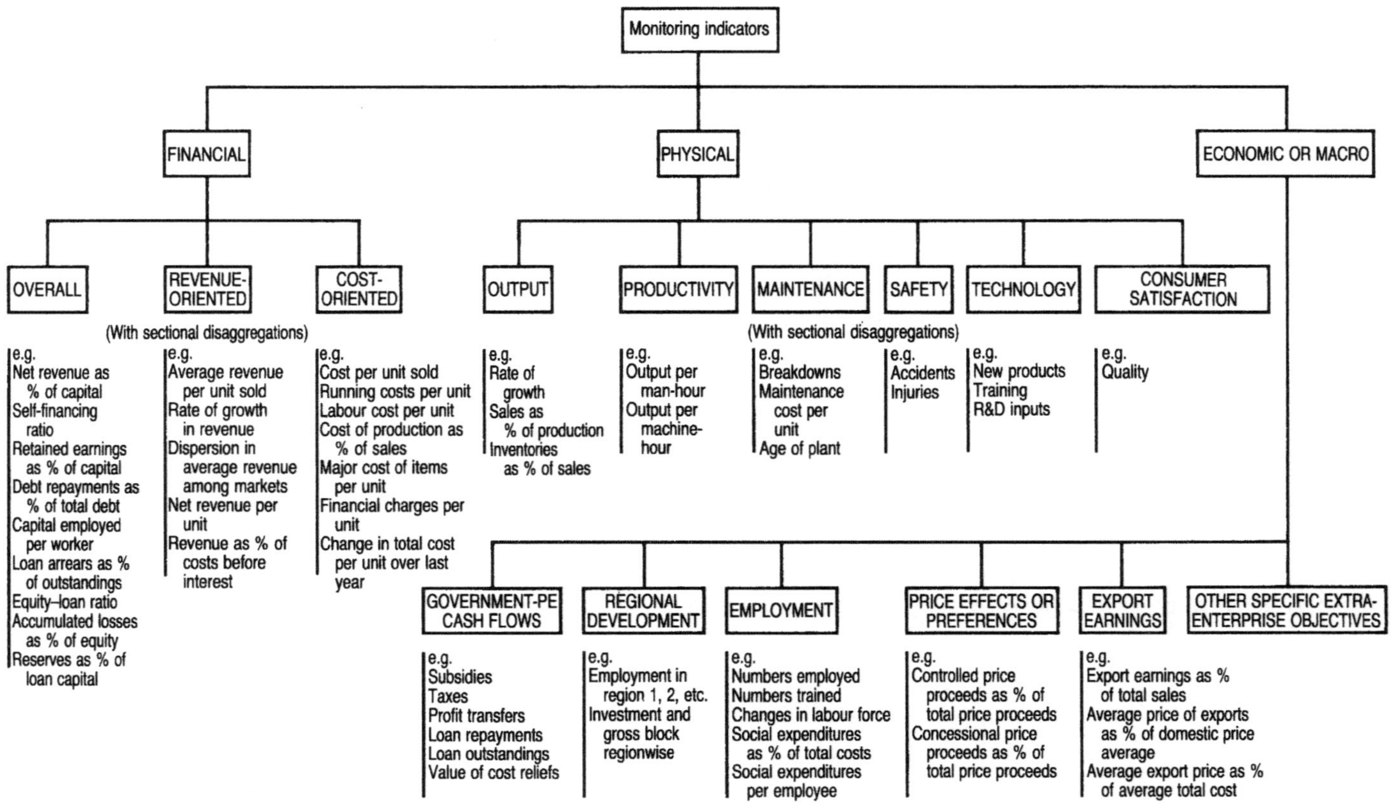

attention is best focused on the indicators relating to the latter area, that is, indicators of overall interest, with direct relevance to macro considerations. Experience suggests that in most countries (a) a 'system' of monitoring is not designed; (b) monitoring indicators are not carefully formulated; (c) the respective areas of monitoring by the enterprise and by the government are not marked out; and (d) the motions of information flow within the enterprise and to the government are maintained without adequate utility.

A well-designed monitoring system yields three benefits. First, it enables top management to gain a full understanding of the way in which the operations are taking place and of their financial, physical, and organisational dimensions. If properly disaggregated, it alerts all junior managers and supervisory staff to aim at the expected results. Second, it indicates if the operations are wide of any budgeted targets, provides an early warning, and prompts the necessary mid-course corrections in operations. Third, it serves as a solid base for enterprise–government dialogue on a continuous basis.

The formulation of indicators in an enterprise-specific manner is the most crucial part of the monitoring system. These are divisible into three categories: financial, physical, and economic or macro. Figure 8.1 shows a breakdown, along with some illustrative indicators under each head.

The macro indicators are distinct to public enterprises; and some of them cover extra-enterprise objectives. They represent an attempt to operationalise such objectives so that not only the results that the government wants to achieve through the medium of public enterprise are expressed in quantified terms in some detail, but their impacts on the costs or revenues of the enterprise are also sought to be measured. As far as possible the indicators should aim to show not only the accomplishments in absolute terms, but the nature and quantum of costs implicit in achieving the extra-enterprise objectives through the medium of the enterprise. The indicators cited under the head of export earnings illustrate the point; they must show not only the value of exports, but whether the exports have been possible because the enterprise offered concessional prices and what the revenue disadvantage has been in that process. Incidentally this information minimises subsequent differences between the government and the enterprise on questions of compensation.

There are two points meriting particular notice regarding the physical indicators. While the emphasis of private enterprises on the use of inputs in physical terms is subordinate to the raising of a high profit, public enterprises are expected to work towards the conservation of physical resources, using certain resources which are in plentiful supply rather than certain others which are scarce, as far as is technically feasible. In an extreme case the profit consideration becomes secondary. In other words, there are subtle elements of extra-enterprise objectives in some of the physical indices themselves: for example, output per man-hour under conditions of deliberately controlled capital intensity and technological sophistication. Besides, many public enterprises have borne the responsibility for establishing capability in the production of a new or high-tech product. This might have been at a relatively high cost and under conditions of relatively low productivity. The latter would be reflected in such indicators as output per man-hour or machine-hour. Likewise the indicators under the head of technology might be initially – or for a long time – unfavourable; yet they are to be accurately compiled.

As regards the financial indicators, there is great similarity with those in the private sector, though greater emphasis should be placed on intra-enterprise disaggregations, since public enterprises are comparatively large and since their operations tend to harbour cross-subsidisations characteristic of monopoly power.

The task of monitoring the financial indicators may be substantially left to the chief executive of the enterprise or its board of directors, except for the 'overall' category referring to such items as net revenue, debt servicing, self-financing, and accumulated losses. Many of the physical indicators can also be entrusted to the enterprise, except for such items as technology and safety. The macro indicators have to be monitored by the government.

In this way the monitoring load of the government can be reduced without disadvantage. However, the responsibility rests with the government to make sure that the board and the chief executive of the enterprise are competent to conduct monitoring effectively and actually do so. Where this is in doubt in the case of a given enterprise, either the government has to extend its area of monitoring, or take the assistance of management consultants to help the enterprise in developing monitoring efficiency.

To conclude: the indicators should be meaningful from the angles of (i) net revenue, (ii) cost efficiency, (iii) use of resources, (iv) growth, (v) exchequer interest, (vi) consumer satisfaction, and (vii) extra-enterprise preferences. The relative importance of these segments varies from enterprise to enterprise. For example, in the case of monopolies, segments (ii) and (vi) would be of particular interest; in the case of revenue monopolies segment (v) would be; in the case of enterprises using exhaustible resources, segment (iii); and so on. The designing of indicators improves if relevant consumer agencies participate in the task, in respect of quality of output and supply conditions. The mechanics of such participation has to be carefully worked out, so that the enterprise managers and the consumers do not develop adversarial attitudes.

CLASSIFICATIONS OF INDICATORS

The indicators are broadly divisible into 'absolute indicators' and 'derivatives' or 'relative' indicators. The former represent the sizes of variables which have a meaning in themselves, both for the enterprise and for the national economy. Examples include output, capacity, numbers employed, capital invested, foreign exchange earned, current expansions, and capital issues. In many cases these have relevance for the development goals and targets, if any, of the country: for example, the output of a specified tonnage of coal.

The 'relative' indicators show the relationships between two numbers and are, in a sense, of greater importance because they bring out the way in which the absolutes have been achieved. For instance, it is important to know at what cost an output has been achieved, or an export has been realised; how the production and selling activity relates to the consumers' needs; and how the enterprise operations look from the angle of the public exchequer.

The 'relative' indicators can be classified, broadly, under four heads: (i) efficiency-oriented, (ii) consumer-oriented, (iii) exchequer-oriented, and (iv) oriented to extra-enterprise objectives. There is no suggestion that the indicators under one head have no relevance to another. They are all interrelated, but the focus is distinctive under each head.

Efficiency-oriented indicators

These can be either financial or physical. Examples are provided in Figure 8.2. The financial indicators, such as returns on turnover or capital employed, administrative expenses per unit of sales, or gross revenue and internal resources as a proportion of capital expenditures, show the efficiency with which certain absolutes, for example, turnover, gross revenues, or capital expenditures have materialised. With necessary qualifications, too severe in some cases, such indicators can help in interenterprise comparison.

The 'relative' indicators in the physical category reflect the efficiency of achievement by relating a physical input to an achievement. This would be free from the price factor. For example, energy used for a unit of output or wastage per unit of output is better indicated in physical than in financial terms, free from the changing price levels of the product, energy, and materials. Another interesting example is share in the market. It is often desirable to supplement the indicator on sales showing an increase or decrease, with one showing the share of the enterprise in the market. A similar comment applies to 'expansion' by the enterprise. A better perspective in this area comes from an indicator relating its expansion to the aggregate expansion in the sector concerned.

Consumer-oriented indicators

These are of particular relevance to public utilities and activities in areas such as milk, meat, and pharmaceuticals. Indicators relating to intervals between bus services, telephone calls not connected, frequency of cuts in electricity supply, and adulteration in milk are of significance, the more so

Figure 8.2 Indicators (by orientation)

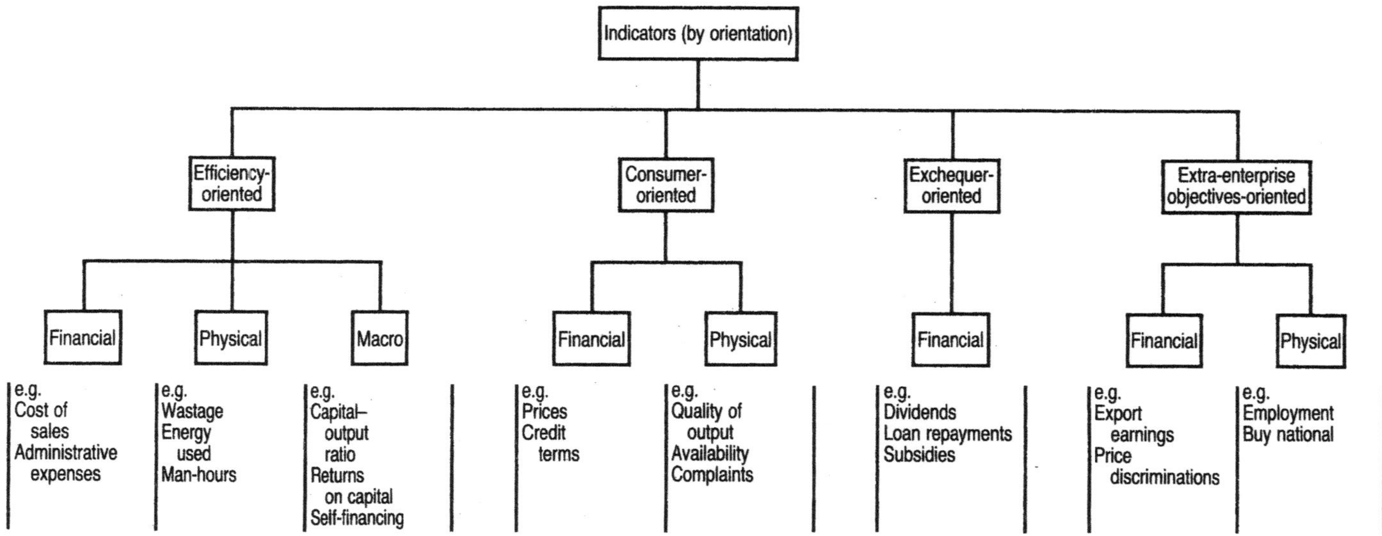

when the public enterprise concerned is a monopoly. Prices in relation to cost (marginal/total) and the retail price index would also be useful indicators from the consumers' angle. Appropriate indicators should be designed to reflect demands not met. In fact these call for intensive market surveys.

Exchequer-oriented indicators

These are financial in nature and have relevance to the flows of funds between the enterprise and the government. (Chapter 11 goes into the substantive aspects in this area.) Mention may be made, specially, of indicators that bring out certain macro implications of the financial situation of the enterprise: average interest on government loans as a percentage of that on non-government loans, dividends declared as a percentage of the year's profits, and government contributions of capital as a percentage of total capital funds acquired by the enterprise in a year. Such indicators are of value in informing the public of the extent of market discipline to which the enterprise is exposed.

Indicators oriented to extra-enterprise objectives

We find very few of these, on the whole, though the 'publicness' of a public enterprise calls for them. (The figure contains illustrations.) Here again it would be useful, in certain areas, to aim at indicators that compare the figures of the enterprise with comparable figures in the sector of activity concerned: for example, average wage as a percentage of the sectoral average, if the latter were meaningful; social expenditures per employee as per cent of the corresponding figure for the sector as a whole or in some other major enterprises in the sector.

THE UTILITY OF INDICATORS

An indicator is useful if it is conceived meaningfully and reflects an aspect of the operations which is worth watching. It is purposeless to build up an innumerable series for its own sake.

An enterprise may be keen on formulating indicators that turn out to be favourable, while others – for example, those in the consumer-oriented category – might not attract its attention, except under government pressure.

While interpreting the financial indicators through a comparison with a previous period's figures, or moving averages or targets, if any, we have to allow for price changes in certain cases, for example, average revenue or cost per unit of output sold; in certain others, like dividends paid as a percentage of profits earned, or internal resources as a percentage of capital expenditures, such adjustments for price changes are not necessary.

The rate of return on capital employed or the profit (after tax) as a percentage of equity raises a complication in interpretation. The returns or profits are a 'current' value under the influence of changes in the value of money, whereas the capital figure is a historic value. On the other hand, if the indicator is in terms of net assets valued at current cost, interpretation would be straightforward.

While interpreting an indicator, its integral relationship with certain others has to be noted. For example, 'cost of maintenance of trucks per unit of transport work done' has to be considered along with the 'age of trucks' and the 'rate of replacement of trucks'. 'Tea leaf bought at a buying centre' should be reviewed in conjunction with the 'number of buying centres' and the total leaf bought. The former may have declined for no other reason than that the number of buying centres increased for some internal or extra-enterprise reason, but the total buying has not. To take another example, 'output per man-hour' should be interpreted along with 'capital employed per unit of output', for it may have increased for no other reason than that there has been increased mechanisation.

Due attention should be paid to the circumstances beyond the control of the personnel apparently responsible for an indicator. 'Raw material wastage' is heavily influenced by the nature of the raw material and technology available. If the latter are not of good quality, perhaps basically because of scarcity of foreign exchange, and the consequential use of inferior raw material, the indicator turns out to be unfavourable.

It would be useful to annotate the factors that impact on an indicator, so that not only the level achieved can be properly understood but channels of improving it suggest themselves. At this point illustrative reference may be made to the specific mention of the 'major factors affecting the indicators' in the annual report of the British Airports Authority for 1980–1, namely, (i) acquisition of airports, (ii) revaluation of assets for the historic cost purposes, (iii) security measures, and (iv) adoption of current cost accounts. These have to be kept in mind while interpreting some of the indicators provided in the report.

Though the large number of indicators referred to in the foregoing paragraphs are useful in monitoring the operations of an enterprise, it does not follow that they should all be published in its annual report. In many countries a large number of public enterprises do not include any indicators in their annual reports. The nationalised industries in the UK provide some performance indicators, but the practice varies widely from enterprise to enterprise.

Some, like the British Steel Corporation, give only physical indicators.[1] The Electricity Council publishes some 'financial indicators', some 'manpower indicators', and some 'technical indicators'.[2] The British Airports Authority published 'service indicators', mostly consumer-focused, for example, 'complaints per 100,000 passengers', and 'percentage availability of mechanical equipment'.[3] The British Railways Board publishes extensive statistical data ranging over productivity and unit costs, passenger trends and freight trends, and then gives, under the caption of 'performance indicators', figures for four years in respect of forty-one items for 'rail business', thirty-six for 'passenger business' and eighteen for 'other activities'[4] (see Appendix 8.2 for details on the UK practices).

MONITORING THE TOTALITY OF PUBLIC ENTERPRISE

In a mixed economy, with an extensive public enterprise sector, it is necessary for the government to monitor its total performance. This differs from monitoring every enterprise and brings out several aggregate aspects which do not come out of it.

First, a variety of interenterprise transactions needs monitoring, with the objeci, broadly, of how far they deviate from market disciplines:

(a) Interenterprise pricing is a major area meriting monitoring. Experience suggests that it does not follow any clear or uniform economic principle. For instance, coal may be supplied to railways at a relatively low price – with reference to related costs – and fertilisers to an agricultural development corporation; financial institutions may price loans low to a small industry corporation or housing corporation, and so on. The disguised price subsidies may not be available uniformly to all public enterprises (or to any private enterprise). The efficiency structure of the public enterprise sector gets distorted in a random manner.
(b) Where more than one enterprise operates in a sector, for example, fertilisers or cement, do the units compete? Or do they develop complacency and operate as a covert cartel? The extent to which market disciplines guide their production and marketing activities needs monitoring.
(c) Cross-debts among public enterprises are a serious problem in many countries (see Appendix 8.1 with reference to Ghana). These raise several complications. The working capital problems of some enterprises are aggravated; in some cases interest may not be charged on the debts, so that the larger and the more aged the debt the greater the disadvantage to the creditor enterprise. Some debtor enterprises might be using a debt 'within the family' as a substitute for raising working capital in the natural banking channels; and there are administrative costs on the part of all the creditor enterprises in chasing recoveries.

Second, the impacts of the public enterprise sector on private enterprises need watching. Of utmost importance in this regard are wage settlements. Overgenerous offers of wages and incentive payments unconnected with productivity, which are common in developing countries, prompt corresponding demands in the private sector, sooner or later.

Third, it is worth monitoring whether the public enterprise sector presents unfair competition to private enterprises. It may enjoy access to low-cost capital; it may receive preferential allotments of foreign exchange; it may be exempt from certain taxes or import duties; and lapses under the company law may be overlooked. Unfortunately these are the gift of the government itself. Yet the government should watch the effects and try to phase them out, barring exceptional cases.

Fourth, the managerial culture prevailing in the public enterprise sector should be monitored, so that (a) it comes near the requirements of economy and efficiency, for example, through organisational decentralisation and performance incentives, (b) it imbibes the spirit of market disciplines, for example, oversecurity of job or play-safe attitude must be minimised, and (c) an excessive flight of managerial personnel to the private sector should be noted with an eye on removing the causes.

Fifth, there is the notion that the aggregate demands of public enterprise for capital must be monitored to see if they have a 'crowding-out' effect on the private sector. This is valid only in two circumstances: when it borrows with government guarantee, so that it can borrow more funds than it might otherwise be able to borrow at equally low rates; and when the government borrows funds at low rates of interest for the sake of its capital contributions to public enterprise. In both these circumstances a 'crowding-out' effect can be presumed to exist, which is traceable to the public sector status of the enterprise. Public enterprise borowings in other cases reflect the market valuation of the investment feasibility of the enterprises in their own right.

The bank credit that public enterprise absorbs for financing its accumulating losses has to be considered a diversion of funds whose alternative opportunity cost is high. The larger the aggregate of accumulated losses, the greater the disadvantage to private enterprise in securing credit for its own purposes. Such abuse of bank credit merits being monitored.

Finally, let us look at an important area of all-public enterprise monitoring, namely, its fulfilment of desired extra-enterprise obligations. Governments, in general, have made little progress in this area. For instance, the Bureau of Public Enterprises in India presents some indicators in its annual surveys on public enterprise.[5] But there are several limitations. For instance, regional development through public enterprise has been indicated through 'absolutes' of gross block and employment, state by state. More illuminating would be some 'relative' indicators, for example, gross block of public enterprise as per cent of total gross block in the organised sector in the regions concerned; public enterprise employment as percentage of total employment in the organised sector in the regions concerned; and employment per unit of gross block in public enterprise as percentage of employment per unit of gross block in private enterprise in the regions concerned. Further, the 'regions' into which the data are broken down should be smaller than the 'states'. It would be desirable, in fact, to present the indicators in terms of the 'backward' areas, as contrasted with those for the other areas. (Official criteria of a 'backward' region do exist in India.) Another example relates to the changes in the average annual per capita emoluments of the employees in public enterprise. They convey less meaning by themselves than when they are accompanied by figures of the retail price index or cost-of-living index. Further, they need to be supplemented with indicators of average annual per capita emoluments in the organised private sector. (All these data do exist in India.)

Monitoring of public enterprise as a whole has not been attempted in effective terms in any country so far. In fact few governments produce any all-public enterprise report at all annually; and several realise that they do not have a full census of public enterprise facts in a systematic manner. Limited interest is shown in the UK in monitoring self-financing and borrowings, particularly as a sequel to the external financing limits technique[6] (see chapter 7).

Finally, all-public enterprise has to be undertaken jointly by the Ministry of Finance and the sectoral Ministries concerned, in the same way as monitoring at the enterprise level has to be, the finance ministry taking the lead in the exercise.

MONITORING INDICATORS AND PERFORMANCE INDICATORS

Before we conclude, reference may be made to the overlap between the two terms 'monitoring indicators' and 'performance indicators'. They are similar in nature, but the latter are generally understood to relate to certain results of enterprise operations which are highlighted to the public and are probably agreed with government. Appendix 8.2 brings out this idea with reference to the UK where performance aims have gradually been agreed and performance indicators, corresponding to them but not limited to them, are included in the annual report. Monitoring indicators are more disaggregated, in general; most of them are a part of internal managerial logistics; and not many of them are to be published in the annual report, sometimes for reasons of either being too detailed or of being confidential in nature. For example, material waste in process *X* in factory *Y* in place *Z* during the night shift, or 'prices by agreement' with major customers.

The strategy of bifurcating the monitoring function as between the government and the enterprise takes care of the subtle distinction between monitoring and performance indicators to a large extent. Indicators falling in the court of the government – perhaps some of them at least – are eligible to be shown as performance indicators in the annual report; while the rest remain essentially the preserve of managerial logistics.

The highly disaggregated monitoring indicators can form an excellent base for decisions on what performance indicators would be most relevant to governmental attention and/or public notice (through the annual reports) and for formulating them in a technically acceptable manner.

CONCLUSION

The success of monitoring depends, first, on its being conceived other than in terms of control and evaluation, and second, on the appropriateness of the indicators, given the nature of functions of the enterprise. It can be counter-productive if the government takes upon itself the entire range of monitoring.

Monitoring of the totality of public enterprise, as distinct from a mere concern for the exchequer interest, is important, especially in economies where it has been in existence for some decades now.

Every public enterprise should be required to include in its annual report selective indicators reflecting the major aspects or implications of its working. The enterprise should agree their nature, number, and definitions with the government and/or relevant technical and consumer agencies. Figures for a few years should be provided, so as to make conclusions on trends possible.

Finally, indicators are but statistical numbers. They help in monitoring, but monitoring would be useful if it went beyond the figures with emphasis on a proper perspective of the substance they were designed to represent.

Appendix 8.2 is about performance indicators in public enterprise in the UK, where there has been a governmentally stimulated effort on the part of the nationalised industries in evolving the right indicators, and Appendix 8.3 shows public enterprise monitoring in Kenya, where the government and certain major public enterprises have endeavoured to design a 'system' of monitoring, with technical assistance from the United Nations. The inadequacy of monitoring both at the enterprise level and the government level, characteristic of many countries, is illustrated by Appendix 8.4, referring to the Indian Airlines Corporation.

APPENDIX 8.1 Cross-debts of public enterprises in Ghana

The seriousness of cross-debts of public enterprises in Ghana is brought out by studies by the State Enterprises Commission, relating to eighteen state-owned enterprises (see table below).

Table 8.1 Cross-debts of public enterprises in Ghana

(1) Amount owing between the 18 SOEs is 5.23 billion cedis for goods sold and services rendered.

(2) Indebtedness of the 18 SOEs to the Government of Ghana, as at 30 June 1986 is 40.216 billion cedis, broken down as follows:

Table 8.1 Continued

	¢	
(a) Taxes and duties	5.965 billion	
(b) Unpaid dividend	85.0 million	
(c) Loans:		
(1) Domestic (direct)	2.358 billion	
(Guaranteed)	374.8 million	
	2.733 billion	(1)
(2) External (direct)	16.115 billion	
(on-lent)	15.316 billion	
	31.431 billion	
TOTAL	40.216 billion	(2)
(3) Indebtedness of 18 SOEs to others amounts to 14.322 billion cedis as categorised below:		
	¢	
(d) To other SOEs outside the 18	568.38 million	
(b) To other creditors (non-SOEs)	1.349 billion	
(c) To domestic banks (short-term)	342.150 million	
(long-term)	12.06 billion	
TOTAL	14.322 billion	(3)

Source: 'The Study of Indebtedness between 18 selected SOEs as at 30 June 1986' Accra, September 1987, pp. 10–11.

APPENDIX 8.2 Performance indicators in public enterprise in the UK

Concerted action on performance indicators in the UK owes its origins to the White Paper of 1978 on the *Nationalised Industries* and seems to have come as a sequel to the financial targets that the government had been fixing for several years before then. The government observed that the 'published financial targets should be supplemented by publication of performance indicators'.[1] By implication the exercise entailed discussions between the enterprises and the respective sponsor-ministries.[2]

The indicators published in the annual reports are overall in nature. Disaggregations below the apex level of the enterprise are, by and large, kept for use within the enterprise,[3] except for such broad distinctions as posts and Giro in the case of the Post Office, and railways, freight liner, ships, hovercraft, harbours, and hotels in the case of the British Railways Board.

The indicators are presented in most reports under the head of performance indicators, though in a few cases other terms are used, for example, 'service statistics' (London Transport), 'quality of telephone, growth of business' (British Telecom, which gives separately thirty-one financial indicators under the title of 'Ten-year financial summary'). Table 8.2 is a rough classification of the indicators into financial and non-financial categories (the references are to pre-privatisation enterprises).

Table 8.2 Performance indicators

Enterprise	*Financial*	*Non-financial*	*Total*	*Report referred to*
British Gas Corporation	18	12	30	1980–81
Electricity Council (for the electricity supply industry as a whole)	10	8	18	1981–82
Central Electricity Generating Board	2	3	5	1978–79
British Railways Board*	5	7	12	1978
London Transport**	5	11	16	1980
National Freight Corporation	4	–	4	1978
The Post Office	3	9	12	1982–83
British Telecom	31	20	51	1981–82
British Airports Authority	11	5	16	1980–81
British Steel Corporation	3	9	12	1982–83
Associated British Ports Holding PLC	–	–	–	1982
National Bus Company	6	7	13	1981–82
National Coal Board***	–	8	8	1982
British Airways****	16	26	42	1983–84

* For railways only.
** For buses only.
*** Besides, there are many financial statistics elsewhere in the report that qualify for being termed performance indicators.
**** The earlier distinct caption 'key indicators' (for example, in 1978) did not continue.

Greater interest attaches to the broad subdivisions of each category. A few illustrations are helpful. The British Gas Corporation had the subtitles 'financial performance ratios', 'ratios based on therms sold', 'ratios based on employees', and 'ratios based on domestic tariffs'. The Electricity Council adopted the titles 'financial indicators', 'manpower indicators', and 'technical indicators'. The National Freight Corporation had only 'financial performance indicators', any other kind being added in the case of its groups and companies. British Telecom subdivided the non-financial indicators into 'quality of telephone service' and 'growth of business'.

Though there is no uniform system in the computation and presentation of the indicators yet, the composition of the indicators suggests, on a detailed study, that, financial indicators of the standard variety apart, there has been an emphasis on three areas, by and large:

(i) *Manpower: utilisation and productivity*: for example, ratios based on manpower (British Gas Corporation); mails man-hour productivity, and postman turnover (The Post Office); employees per 1,000 customers, employees per MW of declared net capability, employees per GWL sold (Electricity Council); and passengers per employee and value added per employee (British Airports Authority).

(ii) *Unit cost*: for example, added costs per customer (Electricity Council); Public Service Obligation (PSO) 'contract' payments per passenger mile (British Railways Board); average cost per passenger mile (London Transport); expenditure per passenger, and passengers per unit asset (British Airports Authority).

(iii) *Consumer interest*: for example, passenger trains arriving on time or less than 5 minutes late as percentage of total passenger trains (British Railways Board); calls that fail due to British Telecom, calls which obtain 'engaged' or 'no reply', yearly fault reports per telephone, fault reports cleared by end of the next working day, and calls answered within 15 seconds (British Telecom); and complaint analysis (per 100,000 terminal passengers) – general, catering, baggage and other facilities, airport-wise (British Airports Authority).

Comparisons with the retail price index

This occurs, in most cases, in order that the degree of parallelism between that and the enterprise prices can be scrutinised.

There have been ten-year comparison statements in most cases (for example, the British Airports Authority and the British Gas Corporation), so that the trends of the indicators can be noticed.

There is another area in which a limited number of indicators have been designed – international comparisons. The Central Electricity Generating Board rightly called attention to 'uncertainties surrounding any comparison between countries' and gave but one indicator, plant capacity (GW) percentage plant capacity. British Railways Board likewise referred to the importance of establishing 'the effects of the physical and statutory environment on the performance of the railway business' before valid international comparisons are made.[4] The main thrust of the indicators in this area has been on the 'support from public funds as a proportion of GDP'. (This has been shown to be the lowest in the UK on the European scene.) The Post Office introduced two indicators – the cost of an inland letter, and the number of post offices per 20,000 of population.[5]

In the European scenario of competition, and with the European Economic Community's directives against non-transparent public subsidies, such international comparisons are quite purposeful. But inferences are subject to qualifications.

It is obvious that the purposefulness of an indicator must be clear both to the management that computes it and the public who see it published in some form.

The British Airports Authority is the only enterprise that annotated its indicators vividly in its report for 1980–81:

Total passengers/movements/employees: These portray 'the size of the business in real terms'.

Income/expenditure/trading profit per passenger: These show 'the overall growth of the business in unit terms, the passenger being the prime unit indicator'.

Landing and packing fees per passenger: This shows 'in real terms what is happening to the landing/packing charges as they are perceived by the airline customer'.

Passenger/income/value added per employee: value added divided by staff costs: These measure 'employee performance at the level of the total business'.

Capital expenditure per passenger: 'In a capital-intensive business it is important to show whether the rate of investment is being maintained in real terms.'

Passenger/income per unit asset: These 'indicate a higher throughput rate per £1 of assets if they were increasing, i.e., an increase in the productivity of capital'.

Net assets per employee: 'An increase in the ratio indicates greater capital intensity, and a reduction of greater labour intensity.'

Here are a few comments on the UK experience. First, the exercise on indicators has not yet reached the status of a system across the board. Both in quality and in quantity the indicators present wide differences: Associated British Ports (British Tansport Docks Board) and the British Steel Corporation come at the minimal end.

Second, the perfomance indicators do not cover as much as can be hoped for from the angle of the consumer. Apart from a comprehensive range of 'quality-of-output' indicators, there ought to be evolved, in due course, indicators that reflect the cost-basis of prices and cross-subsidisations among consumers. For instance, they ought to help in pursuing questions like the following: which group of travellers or region benefits from the low fare structures of British Rail; what inter-product differentials exist in Post Office pricing, unsupported by cost differences; how do airports or seaports help one another financially; are workers in certain coal-pits subsidised by those in others; and do some groups of customers derive relatively high benefits from gas tariffs, as against others? Whatever one's attitude to the social justification in such cases may be, the basic facts should come out from the indicators.

Third, the indicators that respond to macro concerns are not adequate on the whole – particularly in the areas of investment, regional well-being, foreign exchange contributions, employment impacts, growth strategies, and income distribution.

We do find a few (very interesting) indicators, no doubt, for example, the Central Electricity Board's index of average earnings of employees in the UK divided by the retail price index; the British Gas Corporation's gas costs as a proportion of single person's pension, of couples' earnings; the British Railways Board's Public Sector Obligation (PSO) 'contract' payments per passenger mile, and as a percentage of gross domestic product; the British Airport Authority's value added divided by staff cost; the National Coal Board's social costs, less grants; the National Bus Company's local authority revenue support as a percentage of turnover; and the British Steel Corporation's employment costs as a percentage of value added. Such indicators should be more numerous and common with all the enterprises.

Fourth, it is only in one case reviewed, namely, the Post Office, that a comparison is made between four indicators and 'targets'. Two of these are 'externally' set: profit target and external financing limit; the other two are probably 'internally' set: quality of service – first class letters and second class letters. No doubt targets in respect of the first two items would be easy for every enterprise to present and compare performance indicators with; but a larger number of less overall and physical targets including quality of output and manpower utilisation should also be brought in and performance indicators compared with them.

Here is an interesting postscript on performance indicators in the post-privatisation era. In some cases they do not appear at all in the annual reports, for example, in 1988 – British Telecom and British Gas; and in the case of British Airways, the two pages of statistical and 'derivative' indicators of the 1983–4 report were abridged into one page, with fewer details in the 1988 report.

NOTES

1 (1978) *The Nationalised Industries*, Cmnd 7131, London: HMSO: London, p. 27.
2 British Railways Board, *Annual Report and Accounts 1978*, London, p. 16; the White Paper on *Nationalised Industries: A Review of Economic and Financial Objectives*, Cmnd 3437, London, 1967, p. 12: 'The Government Departments . . . will continue to develop, in consultation with industries, indicators of performance'.
3 Central Electricity Generating Board, *Annual Accounts and Reports, 1978–79*, p. 8: 'The Board uses a number of indicators to measure its performance, and some of the more important ones' are shown in the report.
4 British Railways Board, *Annual Report and Accounts 1978*, London, p. 17.
5 The Post-Office, *Report and Accounts 1982–83*, London.

APPENDIX 8.3 Public enterprise monitoring in Kenya

This note presents the monitoring system developed in Kenya since 1984, with technical assistance from the United Nations. It is likely to be of interest to many developing countries, from the angle of logistics.

The Government Investments Division (GID) of the Ministry of Finance has the 'responsibility ... for continuous monitoring of Government enterprises'.[1] The monitoring exercise is tailored to two levels: monitoring by the enterprise itself and monitoring by GID. The strategy has been to decentralise the monitoring activity as far as possible, consistent with efficiency. Thus only a limited number of monitoring indicators are specifically marked out for scrutiny by GID. These are the ones that concern overall aspects, for example, net return on capital outlay, costs of social-policy operations, rate of growth, and debt-servicing. As regards the rest, which constitutes the major part, some intra-enterprise decentralisation, hierarchical, product-wise or regionwise, is planned, though at the beginning it is to be implemented cautiously, because of the uncertain competence of the levels below senior management in several cases.

In respect of the monitoring shouldered by the enterprise, GID has to assure itself, in some way, that the enterprise has been effective in the task. The range of indicators, which GID currently considers it proper to monitor, should contract as the managements of individual parastatals achieve demonstrable efficiency in management and monitoring.

Monitoring by GID does not represent all-government monitoring. Yet it is a necessary first step, since parent ministries are not sufficiently active *vis-à-vis* public enterprises yet.

The monitoring indicators are financial, physical, and economic. The last category, representing macro concerns, naturally occupies varying proportions of the total monitoring matrix of the enterprises. It is noteworthy that the macro concerns or social preferences have, for the first time, been identified, by no means exhaustively, and exposed to quantification, by no means conclusively. This does not imply that the entire exercise of dealing with the subject of extra-enterprise objectives, as outlined in chapter 3, has been undertaken. However, the indicators come in handy in effectuating the Ndegwa recommendation that the losses incurred by public enterprises, because of 'public policies', should be 'explicitly subsidized by the Government'.[2]

The financial and physical indicators have been so formulated that they help the enterprise managements, almost for the first time, to achieve some precision in quantification in important areas of decision-making. Among the foremost of such areas is the linking of wages and incentives with productivity,[3] which the President of Kenya has recently emphasised. Another refers to the disaggregation of costs and revenues by major product or region covered by the enterprise.

The monitoring matrix is designed in the following format:

Current indicator (1)	Previous period (2)	Same period in the previous year (3)	Target if any (4)	Comments (5)

The purpose of columns (2), (3) and (4) is to compare the value of an indicator for a given period (month, quarter or half-year) with certain previous values or with targets, if any.

As the technique of comparison becomes familiar, the management may extend it to cover moving averages over three or five years.

Monitoring manuals have been prepared for several enterprises in an enterprise-specific manner. The indicators are not just a standard set. They are the result of discussions between an enterprise and GID. Gradually the parent ministries are expected to join in. The monitoring exercise is devised to suit the precise organisational structures of individual parastatals, as illustrated below, and the necessary patterns of disaggregation have been worked out:

(i) *The unitary type*, for example, the Chemilil Sugar Factory, Uplands Bacon Factory, and Mt Kenya Textile Mills.

(ii) *The regionally spread-out type*, for example, the Kenya Power and Lighting Co. Ltd and the Kenya Industrial Estate Ltd.

(iii) *The multi-product type*, for example, the Kenya Meat Commission, Kenya Posts and Telecommunications Corporation, and Kenya Railways Corporation.

(iv) *Holding-company type, focused on a single sector*, for example, the Kenya Tourist Development Corporation.

(v) *Holding-company type, with a multisectoral spread*, for example, the Industrial and Commercial Development Corporation of Kenya.

(vi) *Holding-company type, with 'own' operations as well*, for example, the Agricultural Development Corporation and Kenya Tea Development Authority Corporation.

The monitoring role of the government needs to be refined in the course of time in the case of joint ventures, with majority or minority public ownership, and of the subsidiaries of holding companies under public ownership.

In the case of widely spread-out enterprises such as the Kenya Industrial Estates Limited, with its twenty-eight centres of operation, and the Agricultural Development Corporation with its twenty-nine farms, it was decided that, while the matrix to be filled in at the headquarters level could be confined to the overall and broad regional disaggregations, detailed indicators for the various parts of the enterprise should be incorporated in a 'secondary matrix', which attracts headquarters interest on the principle of 'exception'. And there would be corresponding decentralisation of monitoring within the hierarchy of the enterprise.

Though simple as a concept, the exercise required extensive preparation. First, monitoring indicators were formulated in consultation with the enterprise; and the top management were orientated to them. The next step consisted of an intensive training programme for the senior levels of management, which helped refine the indicators, as well. These two stages had the benefit of impressing the finance and non-finance departments with the interfunctional mutualities implicit in the monitoring exercise, especially at the stage of inference. A third step was also taken in the case of some large and spread-out enterprises. The middle and junior levels in the regions were exposed to the basics of the exercise, so as to create a full understanding of the purpose, meaning, and value of monitoring; in particular, they should not mistake it as a disguised form of additional control.

There is an important step yet to be taken for the maximum success of the monitoring exercise, namely, that the parent ministries ought to spearhead it, from the government side.

NOTES

1 (1984) *Development Plan 1984–88*, Nairobi, p. 119.
2 (1982) *Working Party on Government Expenditures*, Nairobi, p. 44.
3 'President Moi said yesterday that salaries in parastatal organizations ought to be commensurate with the performance and productivity of the workers. He said it was unreasonable for a worker in a parastatal which never made profit to continue earning a handsome salary ... Salaries in such institutions should be reorganized to reflect their individual efficiency.'
(*Daily Nation*, Nairobi, 14 August 1985)

APPENDIX 8.4 An instance of poor monitoring: the Indian Airlines Corporation

The following excerpts from the Report of the Comptroller and Auditor-General of India on the Indian Airlines, 1987, suggest that inadequate attention was paid by the enterprise – nor was there effective persuasive monitoring by the government – to establish the right tools and indicators of monitoring in several areas of operations, earning revenues and controlling expenditure:

'1.6 A review of uneconomic routes carried out during 1983–84 revealed that 38 of these had sustained losses consecutively for 5 years (1979–84). 22 of these routes did not cover even the direct operating cost. The Committee on Public Undertakings had expressed in their Forty-Second Report (1981–82) that there was no case for operating any route without recovering even the direct cost except for a brief period as a promotional venture, unless Government, in public interest, direct the Airlines otherwise. No specific directions from Government, in this regard were, however, available with IA. IA also did not conduct a review of its uneconomic routes after 1983–84 as desired by the Committee on Public Undertakings.' (para 3.7)

'1.8 The Engineering bases at Delhi, Calcutta and Hyderabad had spent more time on various jobs connected with the maintenance and overhaul of aircraft (Boeing-737, F-27 and HS-748) as compared to norms. The additional expenditure on extra technical man-hours alone worked out to Rs 3.07 crores during 1981–82 to 1985–86. Though some norms have been laid down for the maintenance and overhaul of these aircraft the capacity of the workshop for each types of these jobs has not been determined so far . . . (March, 1987). Admittedly there is idle capacity in Dart Engine shop at Safdarjung. There is excess capacity in Hyderabad also as it was planned for maintenance of HS-748 aircraft operating for 25,000 hours per annum which has come down to 23,239 hours in 1985–86.' (paras 4.2.1, 4.3 and 4.4)

'1.9 The idle hours in the workshops at Calcutta were as much as 14.58 per cent of the available capacity in 1984–85 and 10.78 per cent in 1985–86. The cost of idle hours in all the workshops worked out to Rs 2.06 crores during 1981–82 to 1985–86. This does not include Southern Region where idle hours were not booked separately during 1982–83 to 1985–86.'

'1.12 Despite the fact that Airbus had been in active service for over ten years, no detailed norms had been fixed for various checks/jobs till 18th June, 1987.' (para 4.6)

'1.14 There was no system in IA to arrive at the total available cargo capacity. Some exercise done for 3 months (August–October, 1981) for five sectors of Airbus operation (Delhi–Bombay, Delhi–Madras, Delhi–Calcutta, Delhi–Hyderabad and Delhi–Bangalore) revealed considerable cargo capacity remaining unutilised.' (para 5.6)

'1.15 IA offered discounts/concessions on fares to 28 categories of travellers. The revenue foregone on this account is, however, not being ascertained. The Committee on Public Undertakings had suggested in their Forty-Second Report (1981–82) that discounts should be regulated in accordance with certain set criteria to be laid down by Government. Government informed the Committee that the Government was reviewing the matter in order to formulate guidelines for implementation by Corporation. No such guidelines have, however, been laid down so far (May, 1987)' (paras 5.10 and 5.11)

'1.18 There was excess inventory holding of aircraft spares. The value of non-moving and slow-moving stores was Rs 1345.12 lakhs and that of surplus stores was Rs 148.91 lakhs as on 31st March, 1986.' (paras 7.2 and 7.3)

'1.19 Fuel is the largest single item of operating cost of IA. Despite detailed studies made and economy measures recommended, there was no significant reduction in average hourly fuel consumption by various types of aircraft. In the case of Airbus and Boeing the fuel consumption was always higher than the standard consumption prescribed by the manufacturers of these aircraft.' (para 9.1)

'The reply of the management indicated contradictory positions in as much as while norms were admittedly necessary for assessment and control of manpower and shop performance, monitoring of such norms and quantification for purposes of management information was not being done.' (p. 13)

Source: Report of the Comptroller and Auditor-General of India, Union Government (Commercial) 1987, Part II, *Indian Airlines*, New Delhi, pp. 1–3, 13.

9 Evaluation

A simple definition of evaluation in the context of public enterprise is that it is an attempt to establish how far an enterprise has achieved what it is intended to achieve; how far it has achieved the best results possible; and how acceptable its role is *vis-à-vis* the national economy. This is a heavily loaded definition. The first part of it presumes that we know what an enterprise is intended to achieve, the second refers to its degree of efficiency and economy in the use of its resources, and the third goes beyond the mere capability of the enterprise managers.

Historically, 'evaluation' has not been among the basic public concerns in the early stages of public enterprise, say in the 1940s and 1950s, for various reasons:

(a) In most countries, the concept of long-term, perspective planning developed a bias for public enterprise investments in many sectors, marked by relatively long gestation. This subdued the keenness of governments to initiate evaluation.
(b) In many countries several national costs of development as well as extra-enterprise objectives were so enmeshed in the financial results of public enterprises that there was no great enthusiasm for evaluation.
(c) The general emphasis in developing countries was disproportionately on the physical aspects of growth, for example, ability to produce certain outputs and achieve technological progress, rather than on financial results, including cost structures. The situation lent little rigour to the idea of evaluation.
(d) One may suspect that most governments in both developed and developing countries were too defensive of public enterprise to undertake strict evaluation.
(e) For many years public thinking was concerned with the issue of 'accountability' versus 'autonomy' and emphasis was laid on whom public enterprises should be accountable to rather than by what criteria they should be evaluated.[1]

Gradually the substantive content of evaluaton began to occupy everyone's attention. The reason, to no small extent, has been the poor performance of most public enterprises.

The problem of evaluation of public enterprise is different from, and more difficult than, in the private sector. First, it is complicated by the mix of enterprise and extra-enterprise objectives. Second, it calls for special attention to economic costing in view of the many price distortions by which it is characterised (as argued in chapter 5). Third, there is need to introduce certain macro criteria into the evaluation, as illustrated by the *C* and *D* levels mentioned in the next section. Fourth, little assistance, in general, is available to evaluation from the stock exchange, for the majority of public enterprises are not listed there, or are not marked by active share transfers.

In this chapter we shall first examine the concept of evaluation with reference to public enterprise, and proceed to discuss its substance, adopting a typological approach. The requisites of proper evaluation will be considered next. Then follows a review of the agencies of evaluation. The salient features of evaluation practices in some countries are highlighted. The chapter concludes with an indication of the data base needed for meaningful evaluation. An appendix is provided, giving tabular details of the suggested data base.

THE CONCEPT OF EVALUATION

Evaluation may be conceived at four levels: *A* – evaluation of the performance of the managers; *B* – evaluation of the performance of the enterprise; *C* – evaluation of the outcomes of the enterprise operations for society; and *D* – evaluation of the comparative advantage possessed by the enterprise. The analogy of concentricity may be employed here, though the levels are neither strictly transitive from *A* to *D*, nor are they mutually exclusive in substance (see Figure 9.1).

A is the most commonly emphasised level. For example, NEDO (in the UK) referred to the need for 'reassurance to Government and Parliament about the effectiveness of management organisation and procedures within the industry'.[2] The *A* level can refer not only to financial magnitudes but to intended physical and extra-enterprise obligations.

One has to go further to the *B* level, which brings into evaluation all the actors concerned, of whom the government is a material component, as shown in chapters 2 and 13.[3] The *B* level, which is gaining progressive recognition,[4] should distinguish, as far as possible, between structured interventions (*B*I) and unstructured interventions (*B*II). The former include board composition and the issuing of directives, which have the sanction of some law or subordinate legislation, whereas the latter are informal, *ad hoc* and political – difficult, but important enough, to establish.[5]

A word on the overlap between the *A* and *B* levels. The actual results recorded in the books of the enterprise are a product of managerial behaviour and external impacts. While on *A*, we should try to isolate the

Figure 9.1 Four levels of evaluation

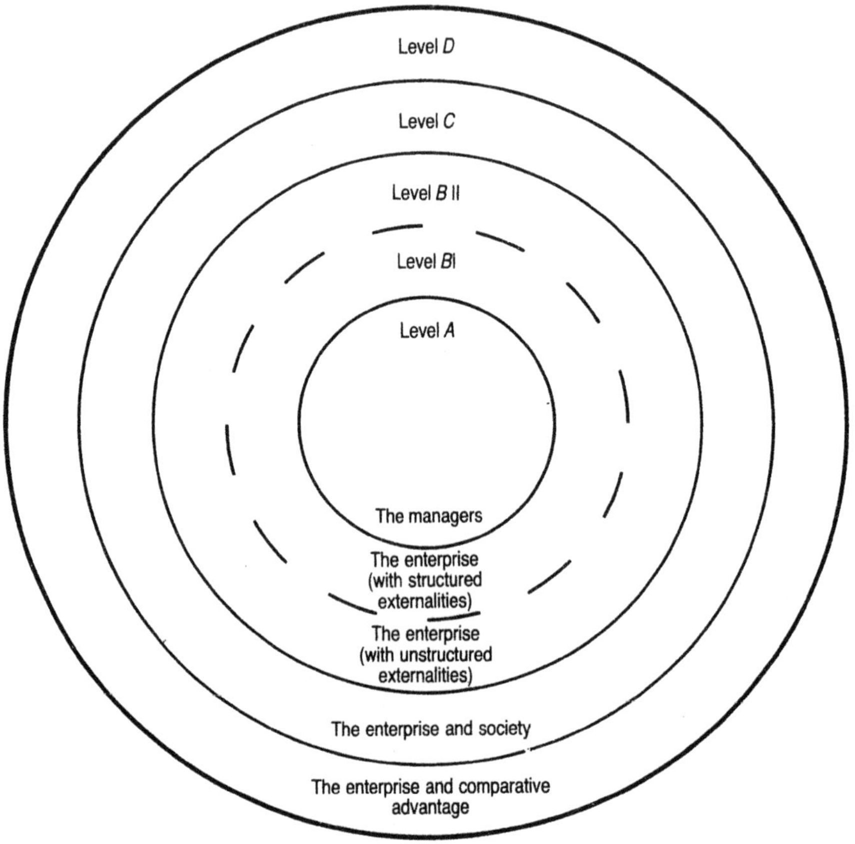

latter, so that their substantive propriety and net impacts on the enterprise may be evaluated at the *B* level. The *A* and *B* level evaluations together can help us address the accountability of the government agencies or officials for their interventions, for their actions and inactions.

At the *C* level the focus shifts from the actors (the managers and the sources of external intervention) to how society reacts to the net outcomes of the working of the enterprise. Here we go beyond the question of whether an achievement met a target, or the managers and the enterprise did well or poorly. Our focus is on how society values the outcomes, even if differently from an earlier date; the more essentially, when it is so. A few examples help reveal the significance of the *C* level. An enterprise (for example, IRI of Italy) may have been required to invest in certain (backward) regions, and it may have fulfilled the requirement. We need to evaluate how society reacts to the results as they unfold themselves. Or, an enterprise (for example, in India) may have been asked to encourage or depend on ancillaries in certain ways and it has done so. We need to evaluate how the economy as a whole treats the results. Or, an enterprise, for example, the Kenya Tea Development Authority, exports its output so as to earn foreign exchange, as desired by certain government agencies. We need to evaluate whether this national benefit is outweighed by any national disadvantages of foreign exchange losses through food imports occasioned by limitations on hectarage available for food production in the course of expanding tea farming.

The question whether a given extra-enterprise objective is intrinsically good for the economy was described, in chapter 3, as of peripheral interest to the enterprise concerned. Level *C* evaluation goes into that question. It is of immense macro interest in a country where many a public enterprise is used as a medium of extra-enterprise objectives. The evaluation would be on the basis of realised outcomes, as against hypothetical forecasts upheld at the time when such an objective was formulated; and it could prompt desirable changes in the very formulation of such an objective.

The final stage – the *D* level – consists of an evaluation of the comparative advantage that a public enterprise possesses as against an alternative kind of unit in the conduct of given operations. Chapters 1, 2 and 14 contain many details of this aspect.

There are substantive overlaps among the different levels of evaluation. Levels *A* and *B* are obviously close to each other, but the distinction is purposeful from the angle of 'accountability'. The *D* level is not totally independent of *A* and *B*. In some cases where the *D* level evaluation is against an enterprise, the *A* and *B* levels may establish that the reasons are remediable and that the *D* level results can be different when the reasons are remedied.

The concept of levels of evaluation has systemic validity and the *C* and *D* levels are to be considered as an integral part of the development strategy, particularly in developing countries. Let us briefly annotate what evaluation implies at each level.

At level *A* it would be necessary to establish the results traceable to managerial behaviour, after allowing for external causes as far as possible. The latter include exogenous factors, extra-enterprise objectives, and governmental interventions. Further adjustments should be made to costs and revenues for the factors delineated in chapter 5 and for inflation. Then we evaluate if the results measure up to any set targets or, when targets are not set, if the results are the best that could be attained.

Level *B* differs from *A* in that it concerns the totality of the results of the enterprise. The efficacy of interventions from outside is examined; for example, are they the right ones for achieving any targets set; or, if no targets are set, how conducive are they to maximal behaviour on the part of the managers? A specific aspect of the evaluation at this level consists of whether the government agencies concerned exercised their statutory powers adequately for the good performance of an enterprise.[6]

The substance of the *C* level borders on macro judgements on the net outcomes of enterprise operations. For example, is the profit earned too high? Does society today prefer a different pattern of trade-offs between financial and non-financial returns than the ones originally conceived and realised? Are certain benefits which flow from the output and price policies of the enterprise, which may be correct on grounds of cost and demand, justified on social criteria? Are expansions proposed on grounds of high profitability justified on grounds of national investment strategy?

The relevance of the *D* level is considerably enhanced by the current trends of thinking on privatisation.

Chapter 1 showed how public enterprise had a case when it came into being. *C* and *D* level evaluations show whether and how far it is valid today, enterprise by enterprise.

THE SUBSTANCE OF EVALUATION: A TYPOLOGICAL APPROACH

Different public enterprises present varying degrees of complexity in evaluation. An illustrative typology of their relevant characteristics is tabulated in Table 9.1. Column 2 indicates, through italics, the more difficult among the characteristics.

Table 9.1 Typology of public enterprise characteristics

Characteristic (1)	*Some annotation* (2)
1. Organisation structure	*Holding complex*/unitary/joint venture/ sectoral/multi-sectoral/*integration*
2. Size	*Large*/small
3. Product mix	Single/*multi-product*
4. Capital-output/labour ratio	*High*/low
5. R & D	*Sophisticated*/simple
6. Location	Single/*dispersed*/*backward-region*
7. Monopoly	*High*/low
8. Market composition	*Public-sector oriented*/not so
9. Externalities	*Significant*/low infra-structural/public-utility
10. Financial viability	High/bare/*negative*
11. Special factors	*Significant*/nominal

Organisational structure

Certain crucial aspects under this head are: (a) the holding complex; (b) backward and forward integrations; (c) monolithic structure; (d) extent of ownership; and (e) development planning strategy. In particular, (a) and (c) call for reviews of overcentralisation and cross-subsidisations; (b), of transfer pricing and economies of integration; (d), of joint venture complications; and (e), of rates of growth in investment and output.

Size

Of special relevance here are the economies of scale, the existence of excess capacity, and cross-subsidisations.

These two considerations warrant a meticulous examination since many public enterprises are overlarge units, in general.

Product mix

This raises questions of diversification in the interest of surplus maximisation and cross-subsidisations among different product markets. And it is necessary to examine whether it will be appropriate to determine more than a single (overall) target (of net revenue, and so on).

Capital-output/labour ratio

The need to economise the use of capital, a scarce resource, and to maximise the share of labour in the production function, has to be emphasised in developing countries, in particular.

R & D

This is crucial for technological self-reliance in the long run and can economise demands on scarce foreign exchange. Particular interest attaches to this issue in the evaluation of a joint venture involving a foreign partner, for there could be several traps for foreign exchange slippage.

Location

Several public enterprises are located wrongly from the cost angle, though social benefits are claimed. Evaluation has to unfold the diseconomies of locational inheritance and provide a factual basis for the *C* level evaluation of macro trade-offs. Where an enterprise has dispersed plants, we have to evaluate how cost-efficient decisions at the margin are, as outputs are expanded or curtailed.

Monopoly

This is a common characteristic of many public enterprises. It calls for rigorous evaluation of cost efficiency, cross-subsidisations, wastefulness in the use of resources, exploitation of the consumer, and income distribution in favour of employees. The terms of reference usually remitted to the Monopolies and Mergers Commission in the UK illustrate the point.[7]

Of particular significance in a monopoly situation is evaluation of the pricing basis – the long run marginal cost, for example, the more so if, as in the UK, it is specifically commended by the government.

Market composition

Apart from the element of monopoly, three aspects merit a close look: (a) the relative dominance of sales to government and public enterprise; (b) breakdown of sales into domestic and foreign markets; and (c) practices of unfair competition with actual or potential competitors.

Externalities

Here is a unique concern for public enterprise evaluation: to establish (a) how far set extra-enterprise objectives have been realised and how economically; (b) whether the managers unilaterally practised such objectives; (c) whether the compensations built into the capital and revenue accounts have been adequate or overgenerous; and (d) whether changes in the techniques of compensation are desirable. Considerations (a), (c), and (d) would be of particular relevance to *C* level evaluation.

Financial viability

This is an obvious consideration, subject to the factor above.

Special factors

Evaluation has to cover any unique considerations underlying the genesis of a public enterprise, for example, poor industrial relations, mismanagement, or chronic sickness. Where an enterprise represents a 'bailing-out' take-over, improvements in the original circumstances have to be watched for.

The foregoing analysis suggests that the difficulties of evaluation vary with the enterprises. An illustration is provided in Table 9.2 on an *A* to *C* scale of complexity in the case of certain public enterprises in the UK, India, Pakistan, and Kenya.

In conclusion, the typology approach emphasises that merely 'measuring up' to a set target or an improvement over the previous year's performance is not all that evaluation has to look for; it must be concerned with evaluating the implications of the characteristics of enterprises cited in this section.

THE PREREQUISITES OF EVALUATION

The prerequisites of evaluation may be presented under three heads: prior determination of objectives, performance indicators, and appropriate accounting.

Table 9.2 Evaluation complexity of select enterprises

	UK		*India*		*Kenya*		*Pakistan*	
Characteristic	*British Steel Corp.*	*British Railways Board*	*State Electricity Boards*	*Modern Bakeries Ltd*	*Industrial & Commercial Development Corporation*	*Mumias Sugar Co.*	*Pakistan Industrial Development Corporation*	*Karachi Electricity Supply Company*
1. Organisational structure	*A*	*A*	*A*	*A*	*A*	*C*	*A*	*C*
2. Size	*A*	*A*	*A*	*B*	*A*	*B*	*A*	*C*
3. Product mix	*C*	*A*	*B*	*C*	*A*	*C*	*A*	*C*
4. Capital-output/labour ratio	*A*	*A*	*A*	*C*	*A*	*C*	*A*	*A/B*
5. R & D	*A*	*A*	*B*	*C*	*A*	*C*	*A*	*C*
6. Location	*A*	*A*	*A*	*A*	*A*	*C*	*A*	*C*
7. Monopoly	*C*	*C*	*A*	*C*	*A*	*C*	*A–C*	*A*
8. Market composition	*C*	*C*	*C*	*C*	*B*	*C*	*B*	*C*
9. Externalities	*B*	*A*	*A*	*C*	*A*	*B*	*A*	*A*
10. Financial viability	*A*	*A*	*A/B*	*C*	*A*	*A*	*A*	*C*
11. Special factors	*C*	*C*	*C*	*C*	*C*	*C*	*B*	*C*

Note: *A* connotes the highest complexity and *C* the lowest.

Prior determination of objectives

Enterprise objectives set *ex ante* are helpful in the process of evaluation,[8] for they provide a benchmark for evaluation. (The annual reports of public enterprises in the UK contain statements of financial and other criteria and of achievements against them.)

First, apart from financial objectives or targets, the social returns or extra-enterprise obligations, which may be expressible in non-financial terms, should be indicated *ex ante*.

Second, apart from the quantified target numbers, there must be a way of bringing the substantive characteristics of an enterprise, as shown in Table 9.1, into the evaluation, for example, managerial overcentralisation, cross-subsidisations, production function and technology. Here evaluation may be judgemental to some extent, and not merely statistical.

Third, the utility of predetermined objectives or targets is limited to the *A* and *B* levels of evaluation, where one can conclude that 'so-and-so' result was expected and 'so-and-so' result was realised. At the *C* level the emphasis is not on this but on how society today reacts to whatever the results are. Similarly, targets are of little purpose at the *D* level, except to reinforce conclusions where even a targeted result is not achieved.

In reality, objectives or targets are not set *ex ante* in most countries and for most enterprises. Hence the best approach would be on the following lines: (a) Subject to all known constraints, could the managers have done better than they did? This is a question-begging proposition – for 'better' in what terms, financial or non-financial? And what is the trade-off between the recorded financial returns and any claimed social returns? (b) How necessary have governmental interventions been, and how efficient from the angle of enterprise performance and of the national economy?

Where objectives or targets are not predetermined, the corporate plan can serve as a proxy, if one exists, and is agreed with the government. Where it is incomprehensive or not agreed with the government, its utility as a point of reference in evaluation is limited, especially with reference to any extra-enterprise objectives unilaterally incorporated in it by the managers.

Performance indicators

If satisfactory performance indicators, as discussed in chapter 8, are established, they help in evaluation by indicating some areas (of performance) where recorded values can be deemed to be significant. There are three qualifications. First, they may not be the only ones for evaluation to go by. For example, an indicator showing price changes would have full meaning if the evaluator looked at import prices also, so that the competitiveness of the enterprise may be analysed. (Maybe the import prices represent dumping, but this is worth establishing.) Second, though an improvement over a previous year (or period) is commendable, the very computational basis of an indicator needs review. Sometimes it may not tell the full story. A declining unit cost, for example, calls for a look in terms of output produced as well as output sold, and also in terms of major disaggregations of the product mix. Third, where closely-related indicators suggest a conflicting picture of performance, evaluation has to rest on a 'balanced' view of them. For example, where a target is met for the volume of output, say, maize seed, output indicators per hectare, per man-day, and per unit of fertiliser employed, should also be evaluated for the degree of economy underlying the achievement of the output target. Where these indicators are unfavourable, an overall judgement is necessary, though weighting can be a useful statistical aid; but questions like how much of output increase is a good trade-off for how much of unit cost rise remain judgemental issues in the end.

A package of indicators is of value in evaluation. If, for example, the real unit cost indicator of an agricultural enterprise moves up while the net revenue target is reached, an analysis has to be made as to whether any implicit price measures have been justified, for example, by the need to raise outputs by going to marginal lands under conditions of water scarcity or low soil fertility, or because investments necessary for attaining cost economies were not possible.

Where targets are not set, performance indicators, if properly monitored over a few years, pave the way for proper targets being worked out in the course of time.

Appropriate accounting

Appropriate accounting is a systemic requisite of evaluation. It should be based on economic costing, as discussed in chapter 5, and the maximum possible disaggregations of costs and revenues among parts of the enterprise are necessary. For evaluation by 'average' cost or revenue data is inappropriate, especially in the case of large enterprises and monopolies.[9] Cross-subsidisations, which are among the important areas for evaluation, cannot be adjudged in the absence of reliable accounting disaggregations. Whether the agency of evaluation adopts a view on the merits of cross-subsidisations or not, the facts have to be established. Thereby the managers can be persuaded to adopt cost-based pricing to the extent possible or desirable, and take proper decisions on the product mix and on output expansions or contractions.

Finally, evaluation calls for accounting imputations, as far as possible, to operations conducted on extra-enterprise criteria. Whether compensations follow or not, is a different matter. The factual base has to be set so that in the course of evaluation, such policy questions come up for proper solution. It would be of particular value at the *C* level of evaluation. The need for thoroughness in cost imputations may be illustrated with reference to a small industry development enterprise which is required to offer loans to small and new entrepreneurs at relatively low rates of interest. The actual subsidy enjoyed by them is not limited to what those rates suggest. There is another element of public cost which has to be identified, namely, the relatively high level of overheads per dollar of loan sustained in providing loans of 'small' sizes in 'remote' areas, involving assiduous chasing and marked by 'high' risks of recovery. The systemic relevance of proper accounting is considerable when evaluation aims at a comparison of several enterprises operating in a given sector.

In conclusion, there are two qualities that a good system of evaluation must possess. The first is that it ought to ensure for the managers an incentive to do well or to do better. Incentive-linked techniques of emoluments are purposeful from this angle. At the minimum the processes of evaluation ought not to act as a disincentive to the managers. Second, there ought to be adequate provision for the evaluation of the evaluation system itself from time to time; or else, it has the danger of degenerating into a bureaucracy or an institutionalised vested interest.

THE AGENCIES OF EVALUATION

This section deals with the question of who evaluates, on the assumption that what is to be evaluated is determined and that the prerequisites of evaluation are in place. Our concern here is not with partial enquiries prompted by some scandal[10] or related to particular aspects of enterprise operations,[11] nor with agencies that an enterprise may itself set up in the normal course of organisational logistics, for example, an efficiency wing or an audit board.

Our focus is on external agencies charged with the function of evaluation in fairly comprehensive terms. They can be classified broadly under governmental and non-governmental agencies. The former may be either departmental or non-departmental. There can be three categories of departmental agencies: (i) parent ministry, (ii) the finance ministry; and (iii) an inter-ministerial body or a cabinet office agency. In theory the approach of the first is sectoral; that of the second is financial; and the third can take an overall governmental view of the enterprise. Subject to these differences, they all have certain common limitations. They cannot even conduct a thorough evaluation at the *A* level, for the constraints on managerial behaviour from government interferences have to be dispassionately identified and their impacts duly quantified. Strictly what they can hope to achieve is monitoring, as suggested in the previous chapter. When we think of the *B* level, the suitability of these agencies is more in question, for they have to evaluate themselves, bringing out how far their actions or inactions have proved economical or otherwise to the enterprise, and how far their interventions have been the structured or unstructured ones. Besides, the direction of evaluation tends to gain a 'control' twist, examining how far an enterprise has obeyed government circulars. This can be an absorbing pastime in a country where there is a plethora of such circulars.[12] Further, departmental agencies are under the subtle influence of ministers whose short-term political interests affect the evaluation.

In several countries the government has an ideological bias for public enterprise even though it apparently favours the concept of a mixed economy. It would be difficult for it to undertake evaluation with expertise and impartiality – especially at the *C* and *D* level.

The Comptroller and Auditor-General (CAG) can be a non-departmental agency of evaluation. He has constitutional responsibility for making sure that government funds are properly spent. In most countries his reviews have initially been limited to somewhat legalistic audit, and often accused – to quote from the Multisectoral Commission of State Enterprises of Peru – as 'asphyxiating, immobilising and crushing state-owned enterprises'.[13] Improvements have, no doubt, been made in some countries, as the next section shows, in broadening the CAG's remit to cover 'propriety' audit. Yet this institution has certain intrinsic handicaps as an evaluation agency, even if it acquires technical expertise through consultants. It cannot go sufficiently into the merits of any policy objectives or decisions of the enterprise. Except for an *A* level evaluation where the basic targets are predetermined, it has limited capability to go into judgements on government interventions (relevant to the *B* level), and perhaps little authority or special competence to proceed to the *C* and *D* levels. If the CAG begins to transgress into all levels of evaluation, he becomes controversial and the credibility of his august office may be jeopardised.[14]

Parliamentary committees are a non-executive institution conducting enqiiries into the working of public enterprises in some countries. The Committee on Public Undertakings in India, for example, has the function 'to examine, in the context of autonomy and efficiency of the public undertakings, whether the affairs of the public undertakings are being managed in accordance with sound business principles and prudent commercial practices'.[15]

These committees have many strong points in their favour. They have high political authority; they can call for evidence, almost as they wish; they can try to establish the interventions of government departments and ministries in the operations of an enterprise; they can present views on non-commercial or extra-enterprise implications of enterprise operations; and they can expect the government to respond to their recommendations. Their views on matters pertaining to the *C* level of evaluation can be meaningful, the more so when they persuade the government to outline a policy response.

On the other hand, parliamentary committees can have severe shortcomings. Their reviews are subject to political considerations; and the composition of the committee is of material significance.[16] Their technical competence is limited, and it is not certain that they decide to benefit effectively from expert assistance from outside. Their utterances have a forceful, often inhibiting, impact on managerial behaviour in public enterprises, even where the government does not accept their criticism.

Turning to the non-government agencies, we can distinguish between two categories. First, there are price commissions, pay commissions, and monopoly commissions, whose functions cover both private and public enterprises. Their focus is on specific all-economy issues such as prices or incomes or monopoly practices; and public enterprises may come in for review from that angle only. This can, by no means, represent evaluation as understood in this chapter.

The other category consists of agencies specially established for the evaluation of public enterprises. These may be subdivided into two groups. The first is that of enquiry commissions concerning specific enterprises, set up on an *ad hoc* basis, for example, the Serpell Committee on the Review of Railway Finances (in the UK), appointed by the Secretary of State for Transport in 1982:

> to examine the finances of the railway and associated operations, in the light of all relevant considerations, and to report on options for alternative policies, and their related objectives, designed to secure improved financial results in an efficiently run railway in Great Britain over the next 20 years.

Other examples include commissions on various enterprises in Ghana (for example, on the Cocoa Purchasing Company, and on the State Distilleries), inquiry commissions on railways, electricity, ports, and airways in Nigeria (in the 1960s), and the Life Insurance Corporation Enquiry Committee in India (1959). Such agencies generally deal with specified aspects of the enterprise operations and function on an *ad hoc* basis, without developing institutional memory or continuity. We do not have the advantage of consistency in the methodology of evaluation; nor are all enterprises covered as a matter of course. Generally those with some scandal or in a crisis attract a review commission, for example, the Presidential Commission of Inquiry into the Affairs of Air Lanka Limited in 1987.

The other group refers to agencies intended to undertake evaluation of public enterprises on a continuous basis. Evaluation gets institutionalised in this case. The ideal would be a Public Enterprise Commission (PEC) (whatever its precise name) set up outside the government with evaluation functions in the main. It may undertake commercial or businesslike appraisals, establish the impacts of governmental interventions, identify the net consequences of extra-enterprise objectives, offer an adequate factual base for delineating the role of the enterprise in the national economy as of now, and analyse its comparative advantage as against a private, co-operative, or departmental organisation. The functions may touch some allied areas as well, for example, to assist in target setting, but must exclude activities that contain elements of control (for example, of operations, investment, and pricing) or fault-finding.

The commission has to be provided with adequate resources to command the necessary technical skills in house, and from outside on occasion, and with statutory powers to obtain information from the enterprises. It would be good to keep it small in size, composed of an economist, an engineer, and a chairman with experience in business affairs. An accountant and a management (personnel) expert may be added eithe at the top level or just below it. Importantly, none of these should have, or be suspected to have, a political background or a trade union background; and none of these appointments should be considered as a berth for a civil servant, active or retiring or encountering difficulties of proper placement within the bureaucracy. The members should be appointed for a period of three to five years; and not all should retire at the same time.

The commission may be recommendatory in nature. Required action arising out of its findings is to be taken by the ministries concerned; and final determinations on questions pertaining to extra-enterprise objectives and operations and to the role of an enterprise in the national economy should be the prerogative of the government, with the necessary degree of parliamentary involvement.

The commission does not have to replace some of the existing agencies such as the CAG, the Parliamentary Committees and any price or monopoly commissions, which have their own useful and constitutional purpose. It only functions as the focal point for all appraisals that are, in so far as public enterprises are concerned, relevant to the evaluation process benefiting from the findings of such other agencies.

There are few agencies yet that approximate to this concept. The Corporacion Nacional de Desarrollo (CONADE), set up in Peru in 1981 under D.L.206, has partial semblance, especially with reference to the *D* level evaluation. Apart from this, its main function is 'to direct and orient state intervention in entrepreneurial activities'[17] and it has a 'long-term approach for establishing a general framework for improving overall efficiency'.

The Sindicatura General de Empresas Publicas (SIGEP), recently established in Argentina as a decentralised institution, apparently resembles the PEC idea, but there are two material differences – its board is wholly governmental in composition with the Minister of Economics as President and its functions include not only 'to centralise, homogenise and evaluate information relating to the enterprises', but 'to exercise external control of the public enterprises'.[18]

The Experts Advisory Cell of Pakistan is yet another with some resemblance to the PEC idea. There are differences, however: (i) though predominantly meant to oversee and evaluate the performance of each holding corporation, company, and unit, its functions include 'monitoring' and 'processing' of project schemes and expansions, and so on, which can convert it into a multi-purpose body discharging certain departmental functions of monitoring and control; (ii) its coverage extends to the enterprises within the jurisdiction of the Ministry of Production only; and (iii) its Board of Governors includes officials, with the Minister of Production as chairman. Subject to these limitations, it functions fruitfully in target-setting and evaluation at the *A* and, to a limited extent, the *B* levels. In particular, it takes care of providing incentives to the managers to realise or exceed the targets.

The ingredients of the PEC concept are that:

(a) it should be located outside the government and be non-governmental in composition;
(b) it should not be loaded with functions of control or continuous monitoring;
(c) it should cover nearly the entire public enterprise sector in the country;
(d) the major targets of net revenue, and so on, should be agreed between the enterprise and the government (or with the PEC as a delegatee of the government); and
(e) it should be given guidelines by the government or parliament on the non-commercial or extra-enterprise preferences sought to be implemented through the medium of a given public enterprise.

EVALUATION IN SELECTED COUNTRIES

This section seeks to highlight the distinctive aspects of the system of evaluation of public enterprises in some countries – the UK, Pakistan, India, Korea, and Argentina.

The UK

(a) Adequate attention has been paid gradually to the systemic requisites of evaluation. Objectives, targets, and performance aims have been refined over the years. Performance indicators have been evolved, as illustrated in the previous chapter. Corporate plans have been improved, though these are still criticised as a 'banal activity'.[19] Statements of current cost accounting figures are insisted upon.
(b) The public enterprise sector in the UK is considered essentially as a commercial sector, and for the limited exceptions on grounds of extra-enterprise objectives, compensations are provided in some way, though not adequately.
(c) The emphasis has been on the *A* level of evaluation, on the whole, though some enquiries – for example, by the Monopolies and Mergers Commission (MMC) – deal with 'the public interest' impacts of the monopoly operations of enterprises.
(d) The *D* level of evaluation relating to comparative advantage hardly exists, though privatisation has been in progress under a policy decision of the Conservative Government since 1978.

(e) The Comptroller and Auditor-General (CAG) does not audit the accounts of nationalised industries. However, the sponsor ministries have welcomed reports by him on the effectiveness of the monitoring done by them. These can help in *B* level evaluations, though on the CAG's own admission, the reports do not set out 'to examine the efficiency of the industries themselves'.[20]
(f) The National Board for Prices and Incomes touched public enterprises from the exclusive angles of prices and incomes.
(g) The Select Committee on Nationalised Industries (until 1983) and the Departmental Committees (since then) enquire into certain aspects or all aspects of an enterprise's operations. But these are not intended to be evaluations in specific terms. The MMC has emerged as the main instrument for enquiries which significantly cover the substance of evaluation as delineated in the second section of this chapter. (The terms of reference to the MMC in the case of some public enterprises are cited in Appendix 9.1.)
(h) A fully-fledged Efficiency Audit Commission, exclusively for public enterprises, has not been set up.[21]
(i) Consumers' councils are another typically British institution, with a statutory basis, which has some role in expressing views and complaints on output standards and allied matters. They have not been very effective, though.

On the whole, the problem of evaluation is less complex in the UK than in many developing countries for various reasons. Most of the nationalised industries belong to the category of public utilities; their operations are treated essentially as commercial; interference from the government is relatively restrained; several preconditions for the success of evaluation exist; there is a strong tradition of monopoly control; and compulsions of national development strategy are minimal in so far as public enterprise operations are concerned.

Pakistan

The unique point of interest about the system of evaluation is the Experts Advisory Cell (EAC), more or less a governmental agency attached to the Ministry of Production (which looks after many, but not all, of the public enterprises). It lays down performance criteria for individual enterprises, assigns weights to the criteria, and compiles a composite performance indicator (see Appendices 9.2 and 9.3). It fixes a target for the subsequent year as against each criterion over a scale abbreviated into five grades; and finally a weighted grade of achievement is computed for the enterprise. This is used in determining the bonus to the staff. This method has the merit of providing an incentive to managers to improve performance.

EAC also computes 'public profit' by making adjustments to the accounting figures. 'Social adjustments' in respect of non-commercial objectives are expected to be undertaken gradually. As of now, statements entitled 'economic overview' appear to be too general and defensive of the enterprises.[22]

The EAC technique represents an attempt, even if incomplete, at treating evaluation as a system. Its utility is high in respect of the *A* level evaluation, leading to managerial compensations. As it proceeds towards *B*, *C* and *D* levels, its limitations of location, constitution and incomplete jurisdiction are likely to affect its efficacy as an evaluation agency.

A special unit was set up in the office of the Auditor-General (AG) in 1979 for evaluating public enterprise performance on a continuing basis. The methodology has essentially been one of financial analysis, equally applicable to a private enterprise, and overlaps to some extent with EAC's work.

India

(a) Efforts have been in progress for more than a decade to enunciate the objectives of individual public enterprises. The Committee on Public Undertakings (CPU) has been bringing pressure on the government in this respect. In the early 1980s certain short-term targets of profit, output, and capacity utilisation were fixed by the Bureau of Public Enterprises (BPE). The memorandum of understanding (MOU) method followed since the mid-1980s stipulates the objectives to be achieved by the enterprise as well as the obligations on the side of the government. This can be a step in evaluation but does not represent full-fledged evaluation, for all the necessary prerequisites are not in place – the *C* and *D* levels are outside its scope, the distinctive issue of the extra-enterprise objectives is not addressed, nor are the substantive aspects of evaluation, varying with the enterprise, and outlined in the second section of this chapter, taken care of. No non-governmental agency exists for evaluation (see Appendix 9.4).

(b) The CAG, who has substantial responsibility for auditing public enterprises, has gradually improved the tone of his function with the establishment of the Audit Board device (in 1969). An Audit Board, composed of a chairman and two whole-time members belonging to the Audit service, and two part-time members with special expertise appointed by the government with the CAG's concurrence, is set up for an enterprise to be audited. This system broad-bases the audit beyond the regularity and narrowly-financial orientation. The examination brings out rich factual material which can be used in a full-fledged evaluation by a non-governmental agency. However, it does not address questions of governmental interventions and accountability, extra-enterprise objectives, and the *C* and *D* levels of evaluation.

(c) The Bureau of Public Enterprises, a multi-purpose governmental agency (see Appendix 13.7) has at best been a data base, has done some monitoring, and has acted as a medium of control with indefinite rigour. Its annual reports are claimed to be evaluatory documents for the use of parliament. In fact they fall short of being useful in that way.[23]

(d) The Monopolies and Restrictive Practices Commission (MRCP), unlike the MMC of the UK, does not have jurisdiction over public enterprises. Thus a major instrument of evaluatory review has remained unused. The disadvantage is all the greater, since many public enterprises are overlarge, present problems of cross-subsidisation, and warrant monopoly reviews.

(e) A basic handicap to managerial efficiency as well as the environment for evaluation, described in the following terms, needs effective correction, or else evaluation would be an unconvincing exercise in so far as the enterprise managers are concerned.

> The prevalent atmosphere of public undertakings of late has been one of vigilance, unwarranted suspicion, uninformed criticism by all and sundry including senior representatives of the Government, and the apportioning of the entire blame for failure on the management. The critics do not take into account the non-availability of funds in time, or unwarranted interference by the Government.[24]

In a country with a large public enterprise sector, the absence of an evaluation 'system' is a serious gap in developmental strategy.

Korea[25]

A system of evaluation has been developed under the Government-Invested Enterprise (GIE) Management Act of 1983. It addresses the performance of the managers, not that of the enterprise, and is limited to the variables within their control. A major basis of evaluation is 'public profitability', not private profitability, as far as possible. The key indicators relevant to an enterprise are set out and weights attached to them. Quantitative indicators account for 70 per cent of the aggregate and qualitative indicators – such as R & D, long-term planning, Management Information System (MIS) and internal control, and service quality – for 30 per cent. Scores are determined as: outstanding (95 to 100 per cent), excellent (90 to 94), good (85–89), satisfactory (80–84) and poor (75–79); and the managers receive an 'extra bonus' in money at 3 months' salary/wages, 2½ months', 2 months', 1½ months', and 1 month's respectively.

It is claimed that GIE performance has improved beyond expectation.

Apart from the problem of designing the most relevant and non-duplicative indicators, the system merits the following basic comments:

(a) In a sense it is an exercise in measurement, appropriate for providing incentive payments to managers and could be applied even to private enterprise. (The resulting improvement in performance is intrinsically welcome.)

(b) It does not address sufficiently or at all the factors that distinctively complicate the working of public enterprises, for example, governmental interventions, extra-enterprise objectives, and exogenous events which affect public enterprises far more heavily than private enterprises.

(c) The evaluating agency is institutionalised essentially within the government, with a GIE Management Evaluation Council at the top composed of the Minister of Economic Planning as chairman, eleven other ministers including the Minister of Finance, and three 'temporary commissioners' from the private sector. The rest of the institutional framework is overweighed by the apex.

(d) Presidential support to the system and spectacular reduction in sectoral ministry interventions are claimed as some of the factors responsible for its successful implementation. It is doubtful how far such conditions of success can prevail under different political systems in larger countries, encountering diverse interests of regional development and income distribution.

(e) The system, as designed, can present a serious problem of developmental strategy. Where the latter implies investments, technologies, and operations that interfere with the high score of an enterprise, adversarial relationships can develop between the government and the managers, unless the results are readjusted for these factors. The system needs to be improved for the incorporation of such extra-enterprise objectives (whose implications are discussed in chapter 3).

Argentina

Sindicatura General de Empresas Publicas (SIGEP) conducts evaluation in three steps: x1 relating to the national environment (for example, balance of payments, the government's budgetary situation, and trends in GDP); x2 relating to the sectoral situation relevant to the enterprise; and x0 concerning the enterprise. At the x0 level it produces a comprehensive technical, economic, and financial profile covering planning, control and information systems, marketing operations, economic situation, financial situation, investment plans, human resources, quality of service, and goal fulfilment.[26]

The x2 – x1 – x0 approach respects the linkages between the enterprise and external influences, though it does not, by itself, provide any guidelines on the internalising of external preferences. Another qualification to the efficacy of SIGEP is that it is not just an evaluation agency; it is heavily geared to the mechanics of control. For instance, it has three divisions: Legality, Auditing, and Performance Control. It is in the last, in fact, that evaluation figures. This is a serious limitation. It can well lead to an unproductive conflict of interests on the part of SIGEP; and it would be tempting for it to lean more towards control than evaluation.

THE DATA BASE FOR EVALUATION

The evaluation of a public enterprise would be facilitated if the evaluating agency had access to a comprehensive set of data concerning its operations, apart from the monitoring indicators and the targets. The data needed are set out in full tabular format in Appendix 9.5.

CONCLUSION

Evaluation has gradually been realised as an imperative need, if for no other reason than the poor financial returns of public enterprise. But a comprehensive system has not emerged yet. The emphasis of whatever methods are adopted has essentially been on producing an overall index of improvement in results over the preceding year; and this has been linked in most cases to managerial eligibility to an incentive or bonus income.

The implications of the 'public' characteristic of the enterprises are not addressed by the evaluation processes designed so far. Consequently, the problem of evaluating the way in which the public and enterprise characteristics are synthesised in a given case is left untouched.

Apart from evaluating managerial performance and the impacts of governmental involvements, it is necessary to evaluate the results of a public enterprise on the criterion of how they agree with the socio-economic needs today, and whether they signify a loss in its comparative advantage. These (*C* and *D* levels of evaluation) are of immense relevance to the thinking on privatisation.

The most important condition for the success of evaluation of public enterprises is that the government ought not to feel obliged to take an over-defensive role in their favour. This condition is most likely to be satisfied if the evaluation agency is non-governmental in nature.

From all points of view, a Public Enterprise Commission, as suggested in this chapter, would be the most fruitful agency of evaluation.

APPENDIX 9.1 Illustrative terms of reference remitted to the Monopolies and Mergers Commission (UK)

The terms (A) concerning the British Gas Corporation refer specifically to the 'monopoly situation'; (B) refers to 'efficiency and costs' in the case of the North of Scotland Hydro-Electric Board – the usual pattern of the terms; (C) refers to the Central Electricity Generating Board and indicates an elaboration of the aspects of efficiency to be looked into; and (D), referring to the Welsh Water Authority is similar to (C), except for the additional reference to the 'agreed' objectives and to the 'comparative performance of water authorities'.

These excerpts suggest that MMC has been playing the *de facto* role of an evaluation agency, subject to the minister's powers of reference and definition of terms of reference.

A. *British Gas Corporation*

On 1 December 1977 the Director General of Fair Trading sent the following reference to the Commission:

FAIR TRADING ACT 1973
MONOPOLY REFERENCE
SUPPLY OF CERTAIN DOMESTIC GAS APPLIANCES

The Director General of Fair Trading in exercise of his powers under Sections 47 (1), 49 (1) and 50 (1) of the Fair Trading Act 1973 hereby refers to the Monopolies and Mergers Commission the matter of the existence or possible existence of a monopoly situation in relation to the supply in the United Kingdom of each of the following descriptions of goods, being appliances designed for domestic use and for burning gas supplied through a main (whether or not adaptable to burn gas not so supplied), namely,

(i) cookers;
(ii) space heaters; and
(iii) instantaneous water heaters.

The Commission shall upon this reference investigate and report on the questions whether a monopoly situation exists in relation to the supply in the United Kingdom of each of the aforementioned descriptions of goods and, if so:

(*a*) by virtue of which provisions of section 6 of that Act that monopoly situation is to be taken to exist;
(*b*) in favour of what persons that monopoly situation exists;
(*c*) whether any steps (by way of uncompetitive practices or otherwise) are being taken by that person or those persons for the purpose of exploiting or maintaining the monopoly situation and, if so, by what uncompetitive practices or in what other way;
(*d*) whether any action or omission on the part of that person or those persons is attributable to the existence of a monopoly situation and, if so, what action or omission and in what way it is so attributable; and
(*e*) whether any facts found by the Commission in pursuance of their investigations under the preceding provisions of this paragraph operate, or may be expected to operate, against the public interest.

For the purposes of this reference:

'cookers' includes ovens, grills, hotplates and spits whether or not supplied separately;
'space heaters' does not include boilers or other heaters for central heating systems or gas fires to which boilers are attached; and
'instantaneous water heaters' means appliances in which water is immediately heated as it flows to the point of delivery.

The Commission shall report on this reference within a period of two years.

B. *North of Scotland Hydro-Electric Board*

1. On 28 February 1985 the Department of Trade and Industry sent to the Commission the following reference:

The Secretary of State, in exercise of his powers under Section 11(1)(a) of the Competition Act 1980, hereby refers to the Monopolies and Mergers Commission ('the Commission') the questions set out below relating to the efficiency and costs of the North of Scotland Hydro-Electric Board ('the Board') in discharging its functions.
The Commission shall upon this reference investigate and report on the following questions:

(i) whether in discharging its functions the Board could improve its efficiency and thereby reduce its costs, with particular reference to:
  (*a*) the Board's procedures for planning, appraising and supervising capital investment projects and major current expenditure projects and for evaluating the actual results of such projects in the light of the relevant plans or forecasts;
  (*b*) the efficiency and effectiveness of the Board's management and financial information systems and management communication systems and the relationship of those systems to the Board's structure and organisation;
  (*c*) the performance aims which affect the Board; and
(ii) whether, in relation to any matter falling within question (i) above, the Board is pursuing a course of conduct which operates against the public interest.

The Commission shall report upon this reference within a period of six months beginning on the date hereof.

C. *Central Electricity Generating Board*

1.1 On 29 September 1986 the Department of Trade and Industry sent to the Commission the following reference:

The Secretary of State, in exercise of his powers under Section 11(1)(a) of the Competition Act 1980, hereby refers to the Monopolies and Mergers

Commission ('the Commission') the questions set out below relating to the efficiency and costs of the Central Electricity Generating Board ('the Board') in discharging its functions for the transmission of electricity in bulk, except in so far as any of those questions relate to, or may involve consideration of, the Board's arrangements for recovering those costs through tariffs.

The Commission shall upon this reference investigate and report on the following questions:

(1) whether the Board could improve its efficiency and thereby reduce its costs in the planning, development, maintenance and operation of its electricity transmission system, bearing in mind the national importance of the integrated supply grid and the Board's statutory obligations with regard to electricity supply, with particular reference to:
  (*a*) the efficiency and effectiveness of the Board's management of its electricity transmission system and its financial and management information systems;
  (*b*) the Board's procedures for evaluating and determining the need for and the appropriate rate of investment in projects for the extension, strengthening, repair, maintenance, replacement and refurbishment of assets employed on the electricity transmission system, and considering particularly investment standards and appraisal methods, standards of security of supply, and the achievement of a satisfactory return on expenditure;
  (*c*) the arrangements for co-ordinating planning of, and investment in the Board's electricity transmission system with the planning of, and investment in the Area Boards' distribution systems;
  (*d*) its operation of the electricity transmission system, including the appropriateness of operational standards of security of supply;
  (*e*) the arrangements for encouraging and taking account of technological development in the specification, design, construction and operation of plant and equipment for the electricity transmission system (including communication, monitoring and control systems);
  (*f*) the programming of investment in the electricity transmission system and its implications for the efficiency of the procurement of plant and equipment used in that system; and

(2) whether in relation to any matter falling within the question set out in (1) above, the Board is pursuing a course of conduct which operates against the public interest.

The Commission shall report on this reference within a period of six months beginning with the date hereof.

D. *Welsh Water Authority*

1.1 On 7 September 1987 the Department of Trade and Industry sent to the Commission the following reference:

The Secretary of State, in exercise of his powers under Section 11(1)(a) and (b) of the Competition Act 1980, hereby refers to the Monopolies and Mergers Commission (the 'Commission') the questions set out below relating to the efficiency and costs of, and the service provided by, the Welsh Water Authority (the 'Authority'), except in so far as those questions relate to, or may involve consideration of:

(i) the Authority's charging policy, or
(ii) the discharge of any of its water supply duties through the Chester Waterworks Company and the Wrexham and East Denbighshire Water Company.

The Commission shall upon this reference investigate and report on the following questions:

(1) Whether and, if so, to what extent there is scope for the Authority by the end of the Authority's financial year 1989–90 to put in hand or achieve net cost savings with particular reference to items (*a*)–(*g*) below. In so doing, the Commission shall so far as practicable quantify any such scope and shall indicate the scale of gross cost reductions and gross additions to expenditure which might be involved.
  (*a*) its management structure and the effectiveness of its management and control of manual and non-manual staff;
  (*b*) its industrial relations, working practices and the effectiveness of any bonus schemes;
  (*c*) the capital investment programme with particular regard to the scope for cost saving investment;
  (*d*) its management information and control systems including the use of performance management;
  (*e*) its method of identifying tasks and setting standards for its arrangements for carrying out repair, maintenance and day-to-day operations and the cost effectiveness of these arrangements;
  (*f*) the scope for making greater use of external resources by contracting out;
  (*g*) the costs of compliance with requirements under the laws of the United Kingdom and the European Economic Community and of maintaining or improving standards of service to customers with particular regard to the extent to which such costs are necessarily incurred.
(2) whether, in relation to any matter falling within question (1) above, the Authority is pursuing a course of conduct which operates against the public interest.

In making their recommendations, the Commission should have regard to:

(*a*) the objectives for the Authority agreed between the Secretary of State for Wales and the Authority and in particular:

(i) the need to offer a quality of service that is acceptable having regard to costs and to effects on the environment and to remedy recognised deficiencies over a reasonable period, and
(ii) the need to achieve the service objectives at the least costs and with steadily improving efficiency.

(*b*) available material on the comparative performance of water authorities.

The Commission shall report on this reference within a period of six months beginning with the date hereof.

APPENDIX 9.2 Performance evaluation in Pakistan: a format (1987–88)

UNIT

After discussion the following targets are mutually agreed for the year 1987–88:

	Wts	*A*	*B*	*C*	*D*	*E*
1. Profitability						
2. Physical production						
3. Physical energy consumption						
4. Others						

It is agreed that pre-tax profit shall not be less than Rs . . . million. In addition, any increase in the targets for following costs ratios shall proportionately affect the final grades:

	Unit of measurement
I. Raw material consumption:	
(i)	
(ii)	
(iii)	
(iv)	
II. Total labour cost	

III. Energy consumption:
- (i) Electricity
- (ii) Natural gas
- (iii) Furnace oil

IV. Financial expenses

$$\text{Profitability} = \frac{\text{Profit before tax}}{\text{Total assets}} \times 100.$$

(Profit before tax reflecting actual performance of year under review only.)

NOTE: 1. Targets can be adjusted according to the impact of the National Budget.
2. Targets can be reviewed by the EAC after the unit's budget is approved by the Board and the Corporation.
3. The percentage improvement from one grade to another is not uniform from one enterprise to another.

APPENDIX 9.3 Functions of the Experts Advisory Cell (EAC)

1. Formulation of proposals for financial restructuring and reorganisation of the companies and units.
2. Review of the annual budgets in respect of production, sale and profit of the companies and units.
3. Oversee and evaluate the performance of each holding corporation, company and unit.
4. Preparation of monthly, quarterly and annual performance reports.
5. Special management and proprietory audit of corporations, companies and units as and when required.
6. Determination and co-ordination of annual plan targets for production and investment, ensuring that these targets are achieved.
7. Processing of schemes for the balancing, modernisation and expansion of existing units and companies and setting up of new projects.
8. The monitoring of the implementation of ongoing projects. Identification of bottle-necks in the completion of projects on time and within the sanctioned costs.
9. Collection and collation of data of the operating companies and new projects for other Federal Ministries and Organisations.

APPENDIX 9.4 The Indian technique of the memorandum of understanding

The objective of the memorandum of understanding between an enterprise and the government is mentioned as developing a relationship between them, conferring on the enterprise the freedom needed for its long-term objectives, while conforming to the government's policy goals and ensuring parliamentary accountability.

The long-term objectives generally refer to capacity utilisation, techno-economic performance, quality of output, economic and financial viability, requirements of modernisation and expansion, and consumer satisfaction.

Several powers are delegated to the enterprise in the areas of capital expenditure and replacement expenditures incentive schemes within specified limits, and raising resources through borrowings.

Detailed statements are prepared of results to be achieved, plant-wise (and quarter-wise in most cases), in respect of production, gross margin, net profit and internal resource generation, subject to changes in prices, taxes, freights and wage settlements.

The government will allow for constraints in the availability of basic inputs such as energy, while evaluating their performance, expeditiously approve of investment proposals, and make foreign exchange available as planned.

A few brief comments:

(a) In the background of government-enterprise relationships, several enterprise managers suspect that the memorandum might end up as an agreement between 'unequal' parties.
(b) It is not clear how far the memorandum technique encourages adequate decentralised autonomy within many of the extremely large-sized public enterprises.
(c) The required degree of clarity does not exist on the precise nature and extent of government goals *vis-à-vis* individual public enterprises; nor does clarity exist on the connotation of parliamentary accountability. There could be problems for certain enterprises from time to time on both these grounds.
(d) The memorandum of understanding addresses the issue of managerial performance only, that is, the *A* level of evaluation as per the argument of chapter 9, but does not do justice to the evaluation of extra-enterprise interventions and impacts (the *B* level), or to the *C* and *D* levels. When these are contemplated, there is need for a non-governmental agency for evaluation.

APPENDIX 9.5 The data base for evaluation

Table 9.3 Objectives of public enterprises: as on – year

Enterprise (1)	*Objectives* (2)	*Financial and other duties (as per the objectives governing legislation or directives)* (3)

Note Column (2) may be filled from the Act governing the enterprise or from its memorandum of association or from any specific directives given by the government from time to time. Column (3) may have very meagre information in most cases. Any targets set would figure here.

Table 9.4 Holding company structure: as on – year

Enterprise	*No. of subsidiaries*			*Sectoral spread (no. of subsidiaries)*		
	100% of equity	*50–100% of equity*	*Less than 50% of equity*	*One sector*	*Two sectors*	*Three or more sectors*
(1)	(2)	(3)	(4)	(5)	(6)	(7)

Note The ownership and control interests of the enterprise, as well as their sectoral spread are of significance in the context of evaluation. The connotation of the term 'sector' has to be consistent among all enterprise entries. For example, is a sugar factory in the agricultural sector or in the manufacturing sector?

Table 9.5 Board of directors: as at – year

		Representation from government						
Enterprise	*Total no.*	*Finance*	*Parent ministry*	*Other agencies*	*From public enterprises*	*Functional directors*	*Sitting members of Parliament*	*Is chairman the managing director?*
(1)	(2)	(3)	(4)	(5)	(6)	(7)	(8)	(9)

Note The Board composition is relevant to the directoral style in many ways. Column (9) throws light on the status of the chief executive and on the likelihood of dualism at the apex level.

Table 9.6 Capital–output ratio: during – year

Enterprise	*Total capital outlay*	*Value of output*	*(3) as % of (2)*	*Rate of change in (4) over five years past*
(1)	(2)	(3)	(4)	(5)

Note Total capital outlay, as elsewhere, is composed of grants, equity, loans, and reserves. The money values of columns (2) and (3) are not easily comparable but there is no easy way out, except by some price-indexing of columns (2) and (3) with a base year some five years back. Once this is done, column (5) will have full meaning.

Table 9.7 Labour–output ratio: during – year

Enterprise	*Value of output*	*Man-hours*	*Output per man-hour*	*Rate of change in (4) over five years*
(1)	(2)	(3)	(4)	(5)

Note Here again column (2) is in need of price-indexing with five-year-back base; then the figures of rate of change in column (5) will have full meaning.

Table 9.8 Current finances: during – year

	Revenue				Gross				Net
Enterprise	Sales	Other	Total (2)+(3)	Cost of Sales	margin (4)–(5)	Overhead costs	Net margin	Finance costs	profit (8)–(9)
(1)	(2)	(3)	(4)	(5)	(6)	(7)	(8)	(9)	(10)

Note Column (6) reveals the cases where even the 'direct costs' are not met by revenues; and column (8), in conjunction with column (10), reflects the realistic position of the figure of capital as it stands in the books. Repeated minuses in column (10) and, more certainly, even in column (8), are reminders of the urgency of capital restructuring.

Table 9.9 Return on capital: from year – to year –

	Return on capital outlay %					
Enterprise	Year	Year	Year	Year	Current year	Average %
(1)	(2)	(3)	(4)	(5)	(6)	(7)

Note Columns (2) to (6) show the trend over the past five years, and along with (7) can have a lesson for target fixing.

Table 9.10 Value added: during – year

Enterprise	Value added	Total wage bill	(3) as % of (2)	Turnover	(2) as % of (5)	Capital outlay	(2) as % of (7)
(1)	(2)	(3)	(4)	(5)	(6)	(7)	(8)

Note Columns (4), (6), and (8) show certain relationships without which the absolutes in column (2) will have little meaning. Column (4) in particular reflects the wage benefits offered by an enterprise, in relative terms; and inter-enterprise differences can be checked with the corresponding capital–output figures of Table 9.6

Table 9.11 Welfare expenditures: during – year

Enterprise (1)	*Housing* (2)	*Transport* (3)	*Education and health* (4)	*Others* (5)	*Total* (6)	*Per employee* (7)	*Average wage income* (8)

Note Columns (2) to (6) refer to the excess of expenditure incurred over any revenue received by the enterprise from the employees or others. Inter-enterprise differences in column (7) will be revealing in many ways, the more so when studied along with column (8) showing the average wage income of the employees.

Table 9.12 Foreign exchange earnings: during – year

Enterprise (1)	*Earnings* (2)	*Payments* (3)	*Net amount* (4)	*Estimated import substitution* (5)

Note Column (3) refers to all payments involving foreign exchange – salaries, raw materials, spares, royalities, maintenance, profit or interest repatriations, training expenditures, and so on. The value of import substitutions entered in column (5) is likely to be an approximation. In principle it is twofold: the foreign exchange savings that are realised by the country because local production makes certain imports unnecessary; and the savings realised because of technological accomplishments that make unnecessary certain imports (of equipment, consultancy, royalties, and so on).

Table 9.13 Employment: during the – year

	Managerial staff				*Workers*			
Enterprise	*Senior*	*Middle level*	*Junior*	*Total*	*Skilled*	*Semi-skilled*	*Casual*	*Total*
(1)	(2)	(3)	(4)	(5)	(6)	(7)	(8)	(9)

Note The classifications of managerial staff and workers are to be effected on criteria consistently applied to all enterprises. Column (8) should contain 'casual' numbers in year-units, so that column (9) would have meaning.

Table 9.14 Inputs from ancillaries and small units: during – year

	Raw materials			*Semi-finished inputs*		
Enterprise	*Total*	*From ancillaries or small units*	*(3) as % of (2)*	*Total*	*From ancillaries or small units*	*(6) as % of (5)*
(1)	(2)	(3)	(4)	(5)	(6)	(7)

Note The terms 'ancillary' and 'small' units should be defined consistently for all the enterprises. Columns (5) and (6) should cover maintenance work also, that is, a service, as against tangible inputs only, for example, spares and parts. Inter-enterprise differences in columns (4) and (7) show up the extra-enterprise benefits that different enterprises yield in the area of 'small' entrepreneurial incomes, not that they can be high in every case.

Table 9.15 Plant utilisation: during – year

	Degree of utilisation (%)			*Rate of change in utilisation over past five years (%)*		
Enterprise	*Product* A	*Product* B	*Product* C	*Product* A	*Product* B	*Product* C
(1)	(2)	(3)	(4)	(5)	(6)	(7)

Note Products *A*, *B*, and *C* are indicative of the major product lines with which a part of the plant can be linked. Columns (2), (3), and (4) call for a definition of rated capacity on a basis consistent among all enterprises – particularly in respect of shifts, reserve capacity, and necessary down-time for maintenance. Low figures in columns (5), (6), and (7), if coupled with low figures in corresponding columns (2), (3), and (4), reflect excess capacity, in the extreme.

Table 9.16 Rate of growth (over past 5 years): from year – to year – (percentages)

Enterprise	*Output*	*Employment*	*Investment*	*Internal resources*
(1)	(2)	(3)	(4)	(5)

Note The output values in column (2) are highly susceptible to the price factor, and call for indexing with a suitable back-year base. To a small extent column (5) is also affected by the degree of change in output prices, though tempered by some corresponding changes in direct costs. Column 4 also calls for a close look for price changes on capital goods and technology.

Table 9.17 Medium-term plan (for 3 to 5 years): year – to year –

	Output		*Capital outlay*		*Internal resources*		*Employment*	
Enterprise	*Current year*	*% change*	*Current year*	*% change*	*Current year*	*% change*	*Current year*	*% change*
(1)	(2)	(3)	(4)	(5)	(6)	(7)	(8)	(9)

Note Column (3) can be meaningful only when adjustments are made for the price changes anticipated. To a lesser extent, columns (5) and (7) also merit some attention to the price factor. The table, on the whole, summarises the major parameters of the corporate plan of each enterprise. If any others, not indicated, are worth recording, the table can be suitably elaborated. Divestments, incidentally, are covered by column (5).

Table 9.18 Extent of monopoly power during – year

			Product A			
Enterprise	*Output*	*Total domestic production*	*Imports*	*Total available output (3)+(4)*	*(2) as % of (3)*	*(2) as % of (5)*
(1)	(2)	(3)	(4)	(5)	(6)	(7)

Note These data indicate the relative position of the enterprise in the market for product A. Similar tabulations are necessary for other major products of the enterprise also.

Part III

The macro aspects

10 Tax and subsidy elements in public enterprise prices

This chapter is in the nature of a bridge between Part II, especially chapters 5 and 6, and this part, chapters 11 (in particular) and 12. It builds up on several analyses contained in the former chapters and looks at prices from the macro angle of public finance.

The first section deals with the concept of tax and subsidy elements in the prices of public enterprises. The nature of 'related cost' which constitutes the analytical basis of such elements will be examined next. Then follows a review of the policy implications of the tax and subsidy elements. An illustration will be provided from the UK scene, along with a longer empirical study relating to Indian public enterprises.

THE CONCEPT OF TAX AND SUBSIDY ELEMENTS

The basic assumption underlying the analysis is that the consumer is entitled to expect that the price bears a close relationship to the costs incurred in the supply of the output. These may be termed 'related costs', signifying the costs related or attributable to the output which he takes by paying a price.

Where the price exceeds the related cost of supply of a product, the price may be deemed to contain elements of taxation; and where the price falls short of the related cost of the product supplied, it may be considered to contain elements of subsidy. The consumer bears a tax burden in the former case and enjoys a subsidy benefit in the latter. The former resembles indirect taxation and the latter resembles disguised subsidisation; for they are not derived directly from the government budget.

The tax and subsidy elements analysed in this chapter do not necessarily represent distributional motivations.

Let us apply the concept to different situations.

The simplest case is that of a single-product enterprise. Where the product is sold at a price that exceeds the related cost – the aggregate cost in this case – the enterprise raises a surplus which reflects tax elements. If the price proceeds fall below the related costs, it incurs a loss which reflects subsidy elements. If the prices just equal the related costs, that is, if the situation is one of break even, there is neither a tax element nor a subsidy element.

An enterprise may subdivide its markets and apply different prices to the different markets. It is assumed that the product is not transferable from one market to another, at the discretion of the consumer. Apart from the overall situation of surplus, loss, or break even, the main point of interest here is that the enterprise operates varying price–cost differentials in the different markets. Several situations of discriminatory pricing can be distinguished.

Market *A* is charged a higher price than market *B*; *B* has no demand for the product at any higher price; production for *B* is within the existing capacity of the enterprise; and supplying *B* does not raise the average cost, and in fact may reduce it. Under these conditions serving market *A* alone raises the cost recoverable from it. Market *B* really gives *A* some relief in respect of the fixed costs of the enterprise. While *B* enjoys an element of subsidy in its price in the sense that its price is lower than the average total cost, *A* does not subsidise *B*. This conclusion depends on certain assumptions. First, that there is no alternative source of supply for *A*, which is cheaper. That is, the enterprise has monopoly in so far as *A*'s demand is concerned. Second, that the capacity set up by the enterprise to satisfy *A*'s demand represents the most economical possible size. That is, a smaller capacity tailored to suit *A*'s demand is not possible to set up on technical grounds, or, if set up, it turns out to be more costly to operate.

The conclusion on tax and subsidy elements changes as we relax the assumptions. For instance, assume that *B* can pay a higher price than the one charged. Either the enterprise does not make an effective market analysis which shows that *B*'s price can be raised without affecting that market, or the enterprise is under external pressures not to raise *B*'s price. (Electricity prices for agriculture are a typical example.) *B*'s contribution towards the fixed costs of the enterprise could have been higher and could have helped lower *A*'s prices, other things being equal. Thus the subsidy enjoyed by *B* is, to that extent, at the expense of *A*.

Assume next that *B*'s price is below the marginal cost of supplying the product in that market – an exceptional but not improbable circumstance in the public sector (see Appendix 10.1). Here not only *B* receives a subsidy but *A*'s prices bear the impact of it, if it is assumed that the enterprise achieves an overall break even at least. The tax elements in *A*'s prices approximate at least to the shortfall of *B*'s price below marginal cost. If *B* were not supplied, *A* would have been spared the burden of the shortfall. If, instead of achieving a break even, the enterprise makes a loss to the extent of that shortfall, the subsidy enjoyed by *B* gets shifted to the public exchequer. If the enterprise makes a surplus despite the non-recovery of a part of the marginal costs of supply to *B*, *A* is under a double disadvantage of tax burdens. It bears the brunt of *B*'s partial non-payment of marginal cost and also, independently of this, the impact of the enterprise raising an overall surplus.

Finally, the assumption of given capacity within which the price differentials occur, calls for scrutiny. If it is large enough to serve more than market *A*, though a capacity just enough for *A* is possible, or if the plants meant to serve *A* and *B* are separable but come under a single unit of organisation, namely, the enterprise, it is inaccurate to assume that serving *B* at a price below total cost, but above marginal cost, does not prejudice *A*'s price interests. Here is a clear case of *B*'s prices containing subsidy elements at the expense of *A*, assuming that the enterprise aims at break even or a surplus.

Even where the different markets served by an enterprise do not entail losses but produce surpluses, the price–cost relationships may be quite heterogeneous, warranting the inference that the different consumer groups carry diverse burdens of tax elements. In the case of multi-market enterprises making losses, their prices could contain diverse benefits of subsidy.

A special case of heterogeneous price–cost differentials presents itself when an enterprise adopts uniform prices for outputs supplied under conditions of unequal costs. Many public utilities come under this description. Uniform electricity charges for domestic consumers and a uniform fare basis on government road transport services illustrate this feature. The diverse price–cost ratios in the different (separable) markets obviously signify that some consumers bear higher prices than they should by cost criteria and that some others pay lower prices than they should, by cost criteria.[1]

Four different market situations encountered by an enterprise working on uniform prices are illustrated in Figure 10.1. The market (i) graph refers to a market where the price–cost relationship is the most profitable; the market (ii) graph to a market where it is less profitable; the market (iii) graph to a market where the full costs are not recovered; and the market (iv) graph to a market where even the marginal costs are not recovered by the price. Assuming that the enterprise raises an overall surplus or at least reaches a break even, the uniform price contains the highest tax elements in market (i) and less so in market (ii), while it contains elements of subsidy in market (iii), and more so in market (iv). If it sustains an overall loss, a definitive conclusion is difficult. Apparently all the markets enjoy subsidised prices, though some benefit more than the others. It is also possible that the overall loss is traceable to some markets – like (iii) and (iv) – so that while markets (iii) and (iv) do enjoy subsidised prices, other markets like (i) – or even (ii) – bear tax burdens through the uniform price. In other words, the benefits of cost economies which may have been possible in the supply of the output in those markets – (i) and (ii) – have been withheld from them.

It is of interest to note that where a uniform price is imposed as a sequel to public regulation, opportunities of entry do not alter the above situation. For no private enterprise enters markets (iii) and (iv); those that

Figure 10.1 Tax and subsidy elements under uniform pricing

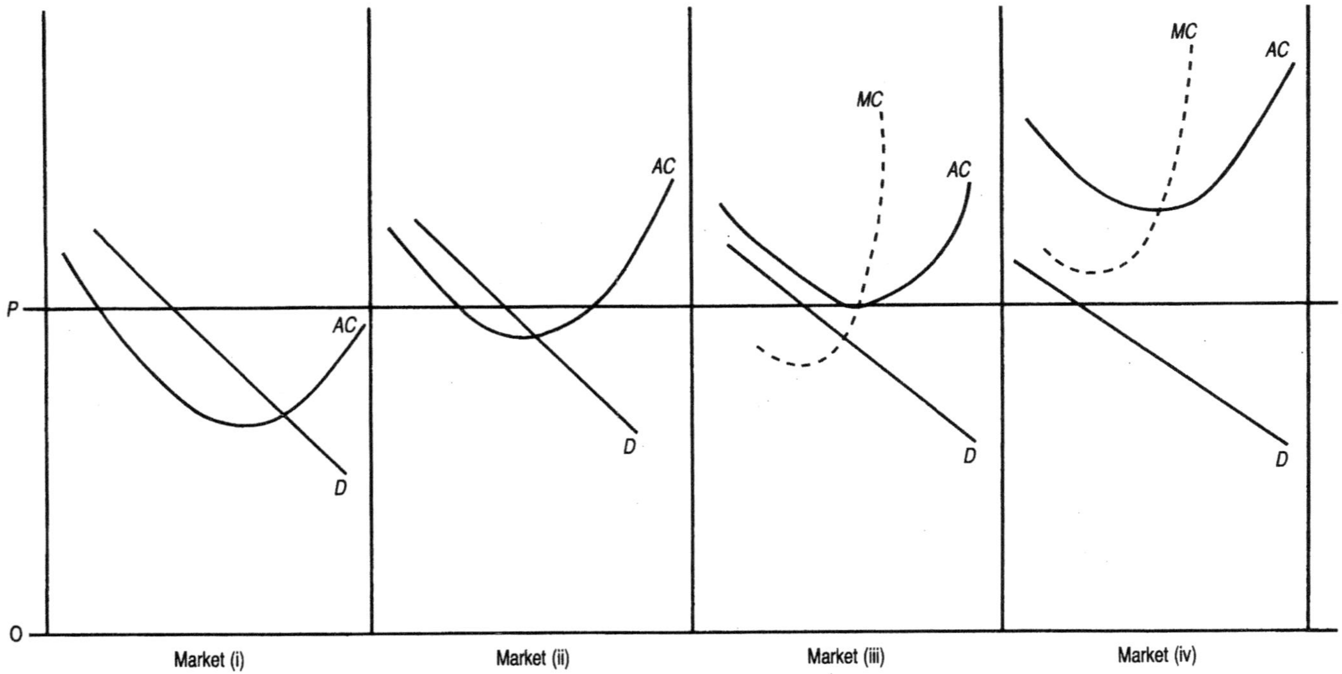

Note D = demand; AC = average cost; MC = marginal cost.

enter markets (i) and (ii) enjoy the high surpluses on the assumption of 'administered' uniform prices; and the tax-burden characteristic of their prices continues to exist.

The phenomenon of prices far exceeding, or falling short of, related costs is not exclusive to public enterprise. It exists in private enterprise too. But there are significant points of asymmetry:

(i) Entry is, on the whole, easier and more likely in a sector served by a private monopoly than in a sector served by a public enterprise monopoly. Hence the limits to the tax elements can be more effective in the former case.
(ii) Monopoly control from a public agency, generally, works more effectively against prices far removed from the related-cost basis in the private sector. In fact, until the early 1980s the Monopolies and Mergers Commission in the UK was excluded from inquiring into public enterprise prices. The Monopolies and Restrictive Practices Commission in India does not yet have jurisdiction over public enterprises.
(iii) Several private enterprise prices contain tax elements, but it is unlikely that, barring temporary circumstances, they contain subsidy elements, whereas public enterprise prices – through both the average level and internal structures – can harbour subsidisations over a long term.
(iv) At least some instances of indirect taxation and subsidisation which public enterprises implement may be at the informal wishes of the government. They are tantamount to disguised budget measures.
(v) There can be a difference in the rationale of price discriminations. While in private enterprise it is essentially motivated by profit maximisation, a public enterprise may charge some markets high prices so as to be able to charge some others prices below full cost or even below marginal cost. The reason may lie in a formal or informal pressure from the government or, occasionally, in an interpretation by the enterprise management itself of what seems to be the 'public interest'.[2]

Finally, the proportion of large and monolithic enterprises is far higher in the public sector than in the private, so much so that the frequency of tax and subsidy elements in prices is relatively extensive in the former case. In fact in several countries – developing and developed, including the UK until recently – the largest monopolies, whose outputs belong to the 'non-transferable' type, are in the public sector. Hence the particular importance of the problem under analysis.[3]

The tax-and-subsidy elements of public enterprise prices have not yet attracted adequate attention, even at the analytical level. For instance, in 1976 the NEDO report, in the UK, observed that the sponsor departments 'have not apparently pursued the implications of extensive cross-subsidisation within some of the nationalised industries'. In 1987 the Comptroller and Auditor-General of India observed that, in spite of the comments of the Committee of Public Undertakings in 1981–2 – on routes operated by Indian Airlines Corporation (IAC) – without covering even the direct costs – it did not conduct a detailed review, even after the government's instruction to it to do so, and IAC continued to operate such routes.[4]

The basic issue is one of the relationship of price to cost, on which emphasis has been growing in recent years (see MMC's observations in several cases, for example, that the British Railways Board should study 'the costs of particular services . . . and their relation to fares' and consider 'whether the relations between fares and costs could be made closer'.[5]

In concluding this section, an interesting qualification may be made to the inference of subsidy elements in loss-making prices. Where the prices relate to a market in which the public enterprise faces competition from other enterprises, the consumer of its outputs does not receive from it any particular benefit of a subsidised price, though the enterprise makes a loss on the sale concerned, whatever the reason. He pays just the ruling price in the market. The loss implies a subsidy to the employees or other factors of production, though on grounds of market economics they should be scaled down or totally dispensed with. (The National Textile Corporation Ltd of India is a classic example in this connection. It has heavy losses and its products, on the whole, are sold in competitive markets.)

THE 'RELATED COST'

Let us examine the concept of 'related cost', which is relevant to conclusions on the tax or subsidy elements in prices.

First, one has to be certain that the costs charged to the revenue account (or profit and loss account) represent all items of cost properly chargeable to that account and stand at their market value. Chapter 5 shows how this principle is not satisfied by most public enterprise accounts and suggests adjustments with the object of estimating 'economic costs'.[6]

The net revenue figures coming out of such adjustments would be lower than the 'net profit' figures indicated in the accounts. The real tax elements in prices would, therefore, be lower than are apparently suggested by the net profit figure. On the same ground, the real subsidy elements would be higher than are suggested by the loss figures in the accounts.

Second, all resources raised for self-financing contain elements of taxation. If targets of self-financing are set and are exceeded, the enterprise, on its own, would be introducing tax elements in its prices.

Third, the related cost has to be arrived at after a careful scrutiny of the 'capacity' of the enterprise. For example, does the capacity meant essentially for market *A* represent the most economical minimum size possible for *A*'s demand, though *A* does not fully use its capacity and, therefore, market *B* can be served as well? Or, is the capacity separable between *A*'s demand and *B*'s, though *A*'s might by far be the larger demand? The related cost for *A* or *B* varies in the two cases.

Fourth, the related cost would be the more useful as a reference point, the greater the cost disaggregations within the enterprise. However, the exercise of cost allocation should not be cumbersome and heavily controversial; the cost of undertaking it should not exceed its usefulness in production planning or marketing; and the pricing refinements that it leads to should be understandable to the consumers and satisfactory to regulatory agencies.

A few examples of cross-subsidisations may be mentioned here. The Port Authority of New York and New Jersey carried 'operating losses' (before general administrative and development expenses and interest expenses) in bus terminal and bus programme and rail operations, while it realised 'operating' profits in the rest of its business – tunnels and bridges, air terminals, marine terminals, and the World Trade Center (in 1980 and 1981).[7]

The PTT in the Netherlands (Posts and Telecommunications enterprise) has long maintained elements of indirect taxation. The prices exceeded the levels permitted by the Prices Act.[8] The Marketing Boards in Nigeria earned considerable profits through high margins between the export prices and lower producer prices. Here the taxes effectively had an incidence on the producers.

The level of enterprise efficiency has a crucial implication for the analysis. When it is extemely low, price proceeds falling below costs cannot at once be interpreted as reflecting subsidy elements. They may in fact be higher than, and can cover, the costs associated with normal efficiency, in which case what they contain might be tax elements. If, in spite of a high cost structure, the enterprise records a surplus, then not only tax elements exist but they are higher than what the accounts suggest.

POLICY IMPLICATIONS

The minimal implication of tax and subsidy elements in public enterprise prices is that the government has to create a system whereby such elements are identified and quantified, taking into account the several qualifications to the concept of related cost. The exercise has to proceed market by market. (For instance, the Secretary of State gave London Regional Transport a direction to show 'separately gross turnover and expenditure by main categories and operating profit or loss for bus operations, rail operations, commercial advertising, London Transport International, LT Museum, Property and Central Departments and Corporate Expense'.)[9]

The next step would consist of examining how far the identified elements of taxation or subsidisation agree with, exceed, or fall short of any policy directions the government may have given the enterprise in respect of pricing or other matters that have an effect on pricing. In specific terms, the extent to which an enterprise raises surpluses far beyond the target set for it by the government has to be identified as a tax element not conceived by the government.

The argument should also be applied to enterprise losses which reflect subsidy elements. Here again it is important to examine how far the actuals are wide of expectations or targets of loss or break even agreed between the government and the enterprise.

The exercise is best carried out by an agency such as a Public Enterprise Commission as suggested in chapter 9. Its independence from the government can ensure impartiality in the computations and in verifying cost allocations. This work agrees with the general thrust of the evaluatory functions proposed for it.

At this point two issues may be raised from the angle of government–enterprise dichotomy. First, the enterprise managers have no right to operate measures of indirect taxation or subsidisation of certain consumers at their discretion or through lack of caution in their pricing function. This argument is exactly the same as in the context of extra-enterprise objectives considered in chapter 3. Second, the government must not undertake indirect taxation or subsidisation through public enterprise prices, defeating parliament's right to examine, and vote on, all finance measures.

Where it can be assumed that a tax-laden price is at the instance of the government, openly or otherwise, the question arises whether the revenues above cost raised through it reach the government or stay with the enterprise itself. It would, ordinarily, be appropriate that they find a way of passing into the exchequer. (Chapter 11 goes into this question in detail.) Likewise it would be correct that the revenue losses occasioned by subsidised prices are reimbursed by the government, so that intra-enterprise cross-subsidisations could be minimised.

There are three alternative methods which the government can pursue when it wishes to raise a revenue for the exchequer from the consumers of a product supplied by a public enterprise:

(i) It can determine a relatively high target of profit, accompanied by the stipulation that a substantial portion of it be transferred to the government under a specified formula.
(ii) It can encourage or stipulate a relatively high price, as compared with costs, at which the enterprise may sell its output, and also stipulate a surplus transfer to the government as in the above case.
(iii) It can levy an excise duty (or in some cases, an export or import duty) on the product in which the enterprise trades.

The first alternative has the advantage of leaving the enterprise free to exercise any possible managerial strategy, including cost reductions. Where the high target is met through cost economies, without prices being raised, the government does not succeed in bringing the consumers of a given product under the impact of an indirect tax, if that were the intention. The prices concerned may remain constant or even fall, though a higher surplus is realised. In fact the whole process could have taken place without reference to the government having set a high target; the latter may have only occasioned it. The interrelationships among prices, costs, and surplus depend on the elasticity of demand and the behaviour of costs, and could be the most profitable when the demand is highly elastic and the enterprise works under conditions of decreasing cost.

The second alternative closes the options of price or marketing strategy to the enterprise, as well as the need for exploring cost economies, except for any other reason. The government's determination that the consumers of a given product be taxed is satisfied. In the process, however, demands characterised by relatively high elasticity in the affected price range may contract. The success of this measure is qualified by two factors. For one thing, the employees can gradually develop ideas of claiming increasing proportions of the surplus towards their own bonus emoluments. For another, the managers could develop a false sense of looking to price increases as a means of maintaining a surplus position. Necessary conditions against either of these dangers creeping in must be built into the price raising instruction of the government.

The third is a straight option and commends itself particularly in a situation where several public and private enterprises operate in the sector concerned. The open tax measure presumably passes through all finance ministry tests and parliamentary attention. There is no reason why the enterprise(s) concerned should not explore all possible marketing (including price) measures and cost-economising techniques, so that while collecting for the government the tax levied, they may also endeavour to minimise any possible adverse effects on their own surpluses.

In brief, the government should treat tax elements in public enterprise prices as an aspect of public finance and deal with them appropriately.

TAX AND SUBSIDY ELEMENTS: AN ILLUSTRATION FROM THE UK

A detailed analysis of the finances of the British Airports Authority, a monolithic organisation prior to privatisation (and a holding company afterwards), illustrates several points of interest concerning the imputation of tax and subsidy elements in prices.

The figures of costs and revenues are disaggregated in its published reports between the two major sources of revenue: traffic operations (aircraft and passenger fees) and commercial activities (concessions, rents, and services); and among the seven airports – Heathrow, Gatwick, Stansted, Glasgow, Edinburgh, Prestwick, and Aberdeen. (Subtotals are also provided, for the South-East airports and the Scottish airports.) All the costs including depreciation are subdivided, by adopting techniques of allocation where necessary; and the 'trading profit' is shown separately for each airport under each major source of revenue.

The figures analysed are not for one year but for five years (1982–7), of which the last two related to the public limited company status of the enterprise in preparation for privatisation. The trading profit, before interest on capital employed, is expressed as a percentage of the revenue from each of the two markets at each of the seven ports, and also in the aggregate (see Appendix 10.2 for details).

The negative figures suggest subsidies and the positive figures tax elements. (Or, the latter markets subsidised the former.) On the whole, and at every airport (except Glasgow), commercial activities subsidised traffic activities. Among the airports, Stansted was subsidised, clearly, while Prestwick and Heathrow were the most subsidising airports with high trading profits in terms of total revenue; Gatwick and Glasgow came next and Aberdeen and Edinburgh last. In other words, the price–cost differentials were quite heterogeneous, implying that the consumers concerned were exposed to varying degrees of indirect taxation, in eventual terms.

There are two qualifications to the conclusion. The costs of remunerating the capital employed are outside the costs considered above in arriving at the trading profit figures. When they are brought in and allocated, the conclusion is likely to undergo a change. The other qualification relates to the correctness of the allocation methodology that has preceded the compilation of the trading profit. It was estimated, in 1984–5, that with reference to commercial activities 33 per cent of the costs were identifiable as 'direct', 43 per cent as 'indirect' and 24 per cent as 'common overheads'. Refining the identification would be a continuous process. MMC recommended that the results of activities at each airport should show:

> first, the contribution made by each activity and airport, after deducting only direct expenditure and indirect expenditure which can be attributed with reasonable accuracy to that activity ('specific expenditure') . . . From that contribution there should then be deducted an appropriate allocation of general overhead expenses ('non-specific expenditure'), made according to the Authority's best judgment and accompanied by a note explaining in some detail the basis used . . . The contribution made by each activity would thus be stated with an acceptable degree of accuracy and the extent to which the published results of activities are dependent on the use of judgment to allocate non-specific expenditure would also be made clear.[10]

AN EMPIRICAL STUDY

The following study is intended to bring out the significance of the tax and subsidy contents in the prices of Indian public enterprises, which are many in number, constitute a large area of economic activity in the country, and belong to almost all sectors of industry, trade, and finance. The data refer to 203 enterprises of the central government, covered by the Bureau of Public

Enterprises (BPE), Government of India. They exclude the departmental enterprises, major port trusts, several financial institutions such as the nationalised banks and insurance enterprises, and the growing numbers of state government enterprises of the autonomous as well as the departmental type. The data are taken from the Public Enterprise Survey of BPE, published annually. The figures for three years 1982–5 are employed, rather than those for a single year, in order to even out any peculiarities of a single year's figures.

The methodology adopted is as follows. For each enterprise the figure of gross profit that should be earned at the notional rate of 10 per cent is computed on the basis of the three-year average figure of total capital employed. The actual gross profit earned, before interest and tax – the three-year average – is compared with it. The excess of the actual over the notional figure is considered as representing tax elements, while the shortfall of the actual below the notional figure is considered as reflecting subsidy elements prevalent in the gross revenues. The difference is expressed as a percentage of the turnover (again, the three-year average). This, briefly, indicates, if it is positive, the extent of tax in the average price paid by the consumers, or, if it is negative, the extent of subsidy contained in the average price.

The limitations of this analysis need to be noted. First, the conclusions can only be regarded as rough and indicative and are subject to the comments on related costs made in the second section of this chapter and in chapter 5. For instance, no adjustments to costs are made for the factor of cost efficiency of each enterprise, or for any excess capacity in certain cases, though in a few obvious cases mention will be made of the implications of these factors.

Artificially low interest rates, paid by several enterprises, do not affect the analysis; for we go by a notional 10 per cent as the cost of capital uniformly in all cases. The varying capital compositions of the enterprises are no hindrance to the analysis, either; for the notional cost of capital applies to total capital employed, irrespective of its composition.

Second, a word about the notional 10 per cent. It is perhaps on the low side, in representing the opportunity cost of capital or the normal profit. If we assume a higher notional cost of capital, it will correspondingly diminish the notional or 'true' surpluses and, therefore, the tax elements in the case of profit-making enterprises; while it will inflate the notional deficits and, therefore, the subsidy elements in the case of the loss-making enterprises.

Third, the tax/subsidy elements indicated here relate to the average price (that is, gross revenues divided by the volume of sales). In many cases, for example, the Heavy Engineering Corporation Ltd, and Hindustan Machine Tools Ltd, there is a whole structure of prices within an enterprise activity. Possible intra-enterprise cross-subsidisations, with implications of taxes and subsidies, are not brought out in the computations that follow.

For these to be established, one needs to calculate, for each enterprise, the 'related costs' of the different markets and compare them with the almost readily available revenue figures for the respective markets – as worked out, for example, by the Comptroller and Auditor-General of India in the case of the Indian Airlines Corporation (see Appendix 10.1) and the State Trading Corporation of India Ltd (see Appendix 10.3).

Fourth, the calculation of notional costs of capital are based on historical cost figures of investment. It is also probable that the gross profit figures, taken from the accounts, are net of historical-cost depreciation. Thus the former are understated and the latter are overstated.[11] In effect, the difference between gross profits and notional costs of capital are doubly understated. The real subsidy elements in prices would be higher than those suggested by the tables in Appendix 10.4, and the real tax elements, lower.

Appendix 10.4 contains the data in detail. Table 10.4 presents for each enterprise the data on capital employed, notional gross profit at 10 per cent on capital employed, actual gross profit, the difference between the gross and notional profit figures, the turnover and the difference between the gross and notional profits, notional and actual, as a percentage of the turnover. It is from the last column that conclusions are derived.

The data are arranged sector-wise so as to facilitate a broad understanding of any sectoral implications. They are classified in Table 10.5 by size of probable tax or subsidy elements. Columns (3), (4), (5) and (6) indicate respectively the number of enterprises carrying tax elements in prices below 25 per cent, 25 to 50 per cent, 50 to 100 per cent, and above 100 per cent respectively. Similar are columns (8) to (11) in respect of subsidy elements in prices.

Table 10.6, referring to subsidy elements only, shows the numbers (and relative proportions) of enterprises, capital employed, and turnover, which are characterised by subsidy elements, sector by sector.

On the whole, there were more enterprises that operated on subsidised prices (122) than those that operated on tax-bearing prices. The 122 accounted for a fifth of the total turnover of the public enterprises covered. The petroleum and the trading enterprises, thanks to their monopoly powers in general, kept the aggregate proportion of subsidised turnover relatively low. If these two sectors were excluded from the calculation, about half of the total turnover was sold at prices that did not cover the costs.

The sectoral diversities are interesting. Almost all prices in steel, coal, textiles, tourist services, and financial services were below cost. The first two are monopoly sectors; textiles represent the nationalisation of 'sick' or ungainful enterprises with the objective of subsidising the wage incomes; and the last two sectors consist of select service markets with a developmental focus. Minerals and metals, chemicals, and contracts and construction services, come next as sectors in which about half of the total turnover carried below-cost prices.

At the other extreme lie the sectors of petroleum, trading, consultancy services, medium and light engineering, transportation equipment, and power generation. Here about 90 per cent or more of the turnover carried higher-than-cost prices.

Sectoral aggregates have limited use for inference except where a whole or almost a whole sector is either tax-oriented (like petroleum) or subsidy-oriented (like coal or textiles). It is figures relating to individual enterprises that are more significant than sectoral averages. For all the enterprises within a broadly designated sector such as 'medium and light engineering' or 'consumer goods' are not similar in their market structures. Even where they produce similar products, for example, in the 'chemicals, fertilisers and pharmaceuticals' sector, the cost efficiencies and degrees of utilisation are heterogeneous; hence enterprisewise analyses are more meaningful.

While one has to refer to the basic Table 10.4 for the data on each enterprise, Table 10.5 helps in intra-sectoral reviews to some extent, through the classification contained in columns (3) to (12). In the aggregate, only 14 per cent of the 81 enterprises with tax-bearing prices had tax elements that exceeded 25 per cent of their (average) prices. In the categories of 'above-50' per cent the number was negligible.

On the other hand, among the 122 enterprises whose prices were below costs, about a third carried subsidy elements above 25 per cent of their (average) prices. Thus the subsidy orientation of public enterprises was more conspicuous than the tax orientation during 1982–5. Column (11) indicates that subsidies exceeded the prices themselves, in the case of 11 enterprises. Their gross losses exceeded the sales revenues, for example, Punjab Maize Products Ltd and Nagaland Pulp and Papers Ltd; or the gross losses together with the imputed costs of capital exceeded the sales revenues, for example, Semi-Conductor Complex Ltd and Cochin Shipyard.

Table 10.6 offers an interesting conclusion when the turnover proportions characterised by subsidised prices in different sectors are compared with the corresponding sectoral proportions of capital employed. For example, enterprises with subsidy elements accounted for 49 per cent of the total turnover of the chemicals sector; but when it came to the capital employed the proportion was 79 per cent. That is, the more capital-intensive units carried relatively high subsidy elements. In six out of the nineteen sectors the two proportions were almost similar – steel, coal, textiles, tourist services, financial services, and contracts; the figures were 100 per cent or very near that in the first five. The proportion of sectoral capital characterised by subsidised prices was higher than that of sectoral turnover in all the other sectors, except for trading and transport services where the alignment of the figures was marginally opposite. This detailed analysis helps in exploring the relationship between deficits and price subsidies on the one hand and underutilisation on the other in different sectors and enterprises. Prima facie one can suspect a direct relationship; enterprises with subsidised prices commanded, in the aggregate, more than half of the capital employed (in the 203 enterprises), while accounting for only a fifth of the total turnover.

The situation was different in respect of the enterprises with tax-bearing prices. In sixteen sectors the turnover proportion of such enterprises out of the aggregate was either higher than or nearly equal to the capital proportion. It is only in minerals and metals that the opposite tendency was prominent. On the whole there was better utilisation of the capital resources.

These conclusions help us in speculating on the effect of an improved utilisation of capacity on tax and subsidy elements in prices. In most cases a reduction in the average cost follows. If the current price level stays, the result will be an increase in net revenue or a reduction in losses. Correspondingly the currently losing enterprises will have smaller shortfalls below the notional costs of capital and those will be spread over a larger turnover than of now. The net elements of subsidy in prices are likely to be lower than of now. The situation will be reversed if the improved utilisation results in an excess of surplus above the notional costs of capital. There is an important qualification. If improved utilisation only results from a reduced average price as the ouput sold increases, the net effect on the subsidy elements in prices cannot be predicted with certainty. It depends on the relative fall in average price and average cost.

Likewise in the case of enterprises with tax-bearing prices, improved utilisation of capacity reduces the unit cost. If the average price does not fall, the elements of taxes contained in its prices increase; whereas if it falls, the net effect will depend on the relative extent of fall in the average cost and average price.

The basic point of the foregoing paragraphs is that an enterprise can wield increases in utilisation as a means of bringing prices nearer to related costs and thereby reducing the tax or subsidy elements in its prices.

One final comment. It may be recalled that the calculations are based on historical costs in most costs. If current cost accounting were adopted instead, the deficits, and therefore the subsidy elements deduced, would turn out to be far higher.

CONCLUSION

While the tax and subsidy elements in public enterprise prices are deducible from the price relationships with related costs, it would be wise to overlook minor differences between prices and costs. Likewise it would be wise not to draw conclusions from a single year's differences.

If the tax and subsidy elements are not appropriately dealt with, the social accountability of public enterprise would be damaged. For the managers might be acting unwittingly or deliberately, without due sanction from the government; and the government might itself escape accountability by either being sanguine in regulating the managers' actions or abusing public enterprise as an instrument of policy without the checks and balances that the parliamentary system of government provides.

The incidence of the subsidy elements, which are not cross-subsidised within the enterprise, is on the government budget, almost immediately in some cases; whereas the budget is not necessarily the beneficiary of the tax elements contained in the prices. The revenues concerned might not be turned over to the government; or what is worse, they might be utilised for conspicuous expenditures and excessive employee remunerations within the enterprise.

Encouragement to competition and permission for easy entry in a given sector of activity can deal with the tax elements in the prices; and uninhibited policies of liquidation can have an effect in minimising the subsidy elements.

APPENDIX 10.1

Table 10.1 Routes operated at prices below direct costs by Indian Air Lines (1983–4) (in Rs.)

Route (1)	*Traffic revenue* (2)	*Direct operating costs* (3)	*Difference between (2) & (3)* (4)	*(4) as % of (2)* (5)
Bombay–Poona	39.34	51.72	12.38	31
Bombay–Keshod–Porbander	86.79	119.36	32.57	38
Bombay–Baroda	40.97	42.07	1.10	3
Bombay–Pune	89.14	95.55	6.41	7
Guwahati–Dibrugarh	34.73	61.74	27.01	78
Calcutta–Gauhati–Tejpur–Jorhat–Lilabari–Dibrugarh	105.95	258.13	152.18	144
Calcutta–Agartala	12.00	16.12	4.12	34
	38.17	60.43	22.26	58
Gauhati–Dimapur	36.98	52.65	15.87	43
Calcutta–Gauhati	57.52	97.56	40.04	70
Delhi–Kanpur–Allahabad–Varanasi–Gorakhpur	130.67	194.07	63.40	49
Delhi–Amritsar–Srinigar	34.33	340.39	306.06	892
Bhopal–Jabalpur–Raipur	87.77	91.70	3.93	4
Madras–Bangalore–Madurai	269.97	282.30	12.33	5

Table 10.1 Continued

Route (1)	*Traffic revenue* (2)	*Direct operating costs* (3)	*Difference between (2) & (3)* (4)	*(4) as % of (2)* (5)
Bangalore–Cochin	39.92	50.45	10.53	26
Trivandrum–Cochin	25.53	55.41	29.88	117
Hyderabad–Nagpur–Delhi	28.21	71.44	43.23	153
Hyderabad–Tirupati	12.03	23.35	11.32	94
Madras–Trichy–Trivandrum	284.71	300.57	15.86	56
Bangalore–Coimbatore	63.53	80.11	16.58	26
Bangalore–Mangalore	94.70	114.62	19.92	21
Calcutta–Kathmandu	186.22	188.30	2.08	1
Patna–Kathmandu	0.61	42.28	41.67	6,831
Gauhati–Agartala	34.76	52.43	17.67	51

No. of routes operated at prices that did not cover direct costs was:
24 in 1983–84
25 in 1982–83
26 in 1981–82
26 in 1980–81
24 in 1979–80

Source: Report of the Comptroller and Auditor-General of India, Union Government (Commercial) 1987, part–II, *Indian Air Lines*, p. 32 (New Delhi, 1987)
Note: The computations in columns (4) and (5) are made by the author.

APPENDIX 10.2

Table 10.2 Cross-subsidisations within the British Airports Authority (1982–87)

	All airports	*Heathrow*	*Gatwick*	*Stansted*	*Glasgow*	*Edinburgh*	*Prestwick*	*Aberdeen*
Trading profit (or loss) as per cent of total revenue:								
A. Traffic	−14.5	−3.5	−46.6	−206.8	2.0	−8.0	−82.1	−8.8
B. Commercial	54.2	51.6	63.3	19.5	62.2	35.4	27.3	40.9
Total revenue	19.4	24.7	17.5	−114.3	16.1	7.2	45.1	7.9

Source: Annual Report and Accounts, British Airports Authority, for the years 1982–87, London. (The computations are made by the author.)

APPENDIX 10.3

Table 10.3 Cross-subsidisations in the State Trading Corporation of India Ltd (profit as percentage of turnover, 1972–73)

Product division	*Imports*	*Exports*	*Domestic trade*
1. Industrial products	4	2	
2. Produce	−3	2	−1
3. Development		−2	
4. Consumer goods		−3	
5. Fruits and vegetables		−6	
6. Films		2	
7. Leatherware		0.4	
8. Chemicals & pharmaceuticals		1.5	
9. Chemicals I	10		
10. Chemicals II	7		
11. Drugs & pharmaceuticals	16		
12. IRMAC	1		
13. Oils & fats	11		
14. Imported cars			44
Total	8	0.2	10

Source: Calculated from the profit and turnover figures found in Report of the Comptroller and Auditor-General in India (1974), Union Government of India (Commercial) 1974, Part II, *The State Trading Corporation of India Ltd*, New Delhi, p. 420.

APPENDIX 10.4

Table 10.4 Tax and subsidy elements in public enterprise prices in India (1982–85)

Enterprise (1)	*Capital employed (Rs lakhs)* (2)	*Notional gross profit at 10% of (2) (Rs lakhs)* (3)	*Actual gross profit (loss) (Rs lakhs)* (4)	*(4)–(3) (Rs lakhs)* (5)	*Turnover (Rs lakhs)* (6)	*(5) as % of (6)* (7)
Steel						
1. Ferro Scrap Nigam Ltd	9,70	97	2,37	1,40	7,24	19
2. The Indian Iron & Steel Co. Ltd	92,95	9,30	–20,20	–29,50	–316,47	–9
3. Isco Stanton Pipe & Foundry Co. Ltd	7,78	78	2,41	1,63	23,32	7
4. Mishra Dhatu Nigam Ltd	8,42	84	–7,12	–7,96	9,10	–87
5. Sponge Iron India Ltd	13,07	1,31	31	–1,00	3,87	–26
6. Steel Authority of India Ltd	31,21,44	3,12,14	47,85	–2,64,29	23,16,82	–21
Total	32,53,36	3,25,34	25,62	–2,99,72	26,76,82	–11
Minerals and Metals						
7. Bharat Aluminium Co. Ltd	2,38,67	23,87	–22,93	–46,80	1,59,73	–29
8. Bharat Gold Mines Ltd	36,37	3,64	–5,48	–9,12	22,20	–41
9. Bharat Refractories Ltd	38,89	3,90	–6,14	–10,13	12,70	–80
10. Hindustan Copper Ltd	2,08,25	20,83	–1,85	–22,68	1,62,30	–14
11. Hindustan Copper Ltd	2,05,25	20,53	–7,02	–27,56	1,14,23	–24
12. India Firebricks & Insulation Co. Ltd	2,66	27	–2,09	–2,36	6,42	–37
13. Indian Rare Earths Ltd	26,68	2,67	3,78	1,11	17,47	6
14. Kudremukh Iron Ore Co. Ltd	2,28,41	22,84	–24,54	–47,38	19,26	–6
15. Manganese Ore (India) Ltd	16,00	1,60	96	–64	17,82	–4
16. National Mineral Dev. Corp. Ltd	1,06,06	10,61	9,97	–64	1,09,00	–0.6
17. Neyveli Lignite Corp. Ltd	4,29,77	42,98	59,59	16,61	1,74,82	10

Table 10.4 Continued

Enterprise (1)	*Capital employed (Rs lakhs)* (2)	*Notional gross profit at 10% of (2) (Rs lakhs)* (3)	*Actual gross profit (loss) (Rs lakhs)* (4)	*(4)–(3) (Rs lakhs)* (5)	*Turnover (Rs lakhs)* (6)	*(5) as % of (6)* (7)
18. Pyrites, Phosphates & Chem. Ltd	17,50	1,75	61	–1,14	8,54	–13
19. Uranium Corp. of India Ltd	15,16	1,52	1,02	–50	12,47	–4
Total	15,70,02	1,57,00	5,88	–1,51,23	8,36,96	–18
Coal						
20. Bharat Cooking Coal Ltd	5,25,70	52,57	–54,14	–1,06,71	4,79,90	–22
21. Central Coalfields Ltd	8,44,99	84,50	77,59	–6,91	6,58,69	–1
22. Coal India Ltd	26,67,77	2,66,78	4,32	–2,62,46	63,68	–412
23. Eastern Coalfields	3,75,42	37,54	–37,93	–75,47	4,49,12	–17
24. Western Coalfields Ltd	5,57,67	55,76	28,16	–27,60	3,72,72	–7
Total	49,71,55	4,97,16	17,00	–4,80,16	20,24,11	–24
Power Generation						
25. National Hydroelectric Power Corp. Ltd	3,00,69	30,07	19,29	–10,78	18,76	–58
26. National Thermal Power Corp. Ltd	8,50,03	85,00	2,15,87	1,30,87	1,71,43	76
27. North Eastern Electric Power Corp. Ltd	1,01,73	10,17	3,22	–6,95	5,06	–137
Total	12,52,45	1,25,24	2,38,38	1,13,14	1,95,16	58
Petroleum						
28. Bharat Petroleum Corp. Ltd	1,64,79	16,48	37,25	20,77	19,07,60	1
29. Bongaigaon Refinery & Petrol-chemicals Ltd	1,06,06	10,61	5,80	–4,81	1,43,14	–3
30. Cochin Refineries Ltd	61,88	6,19	9,55	3,36	4,81,37	0.6

31. Hindustan Petroleum Corp. Ltd	2,69,24	26,92	47,54	20,62	24,15,89	1
32. Hydro Carbons India Ltd	38,85	3,89	2,14	–1,75	6	–1
33. Indian Oil Blending Ltd	2,52	25	62	37	3,50	11
34. Indian Oil Corp. Ltd	11,54,95	1,15,50	2,30,53	1,15,03	1,04,46,25	1
35. IBP Co. Ltd	12,09	1,21	6,03	4,82	5,09,81	1
36. Lubrizol India Ltd	19,66	1,97	5,44	3,47	74,53	5
37. Madras Refineries Ltd	1,65,91	16,59	18,99	2,40	7,42,40	0.3
38. Oil India Ltd	1,79,62	17,96	2,08,30	1,90,34	3,96,94	48
39. Oil & Natural Gas Commission	22,79,87	2,27,99	15,75,83	13,47,84	32,86,56	41
Total	44,55,44	4,45,54	21,48,02	17,02,48	2,04,08,05	8
Chemicals, Fertilisers & Pharmaceuticals						
40. Bengal Chemical & Pharma. Ltd	8,44	84	–1,68	–2,52	11,07	–23
41. Bengal Immunity Ltd	8,80	88	–59	–1,47	6,65	–22
42. Cement Corp. of India Ltd	1,83,39	18,34	17,49	–85	1,71,31	–5
43. Damodar Cement & Slags Co. Ltd	1,98	20	12	–8	–	–
44. The Fertilisers & Chemicals (Travancore) Ltd	1,49,48	14,95	13,34	–1,61	1,83,05	–1
45. The Fertilisers Corp. of India Ltd	4,85,93	48,59	–23,29	–71,88	3,00,53	–24
46. Goa Antibiotics & Pharma. Ltd	1,75	18	–5	–23	41	–56
47. Hindustan Antibiotics Ltd	52,97	5,30	3,30	–2,00	37,07	–5
48. Hindustan Fertilisers Corp. Ltd	5,23	52	–34,22	–34,74	1,60,78	–22
49. Hindustan Insecticides Ltd	39,20	3,92	2,83	–1,09	49,45	–2
50. Hindustan Organic Chemicals Ltd	65,07	6,51	6,60	9	37,99	0.2
51. Hindustan Salts Ltd	3,99	40	10	–30	1,34	–22

Table 10.4 Continued

Enterprise (1)	*Capital employed (Rs lakhs)* (2)	*Notional gross profit at 10% of (2) (Rs lakhs)* (3)	*Actual gross profit (loss) (Rs lakhs)* (4)	*(4)–(3) (Rs lakhs)* (5)	*Turnover (Rs lakhs)* (6)	*(5) as % of (6)* (7)
52. Indian Drugs & Pharma. Ltd	1,01,15	10,12	–5,11	–15,23	1,15,11	–13
53. Indian Medicines Pharma. Corp. Ltd	55	6	–4	–10	10	–100
54. Indian Petro-chemical Corp. Ltd	3,89,09	38,91	59,21	20,30	5,00,45	4
55. Karnataka Antibiotics & Pharma. Corp. Ltd	1,69	17	14	–3	79	–4
56. Madras Fertilisers Ltd	61,74	6,17	14,12	–7,95	1,77,61	–4
57. Maharashtra Antibiotics & Pharma Ltd	2,85	29	–15	–44	1,39	–32
58. National Fertilisers Ltd	4,69,57	46,96	54,14	7,18	3,73,38	2
59. Orissa Drugs & Chemicals Ltd	92	9	–5	–14	45	–31
60. Punjab Maize Products Ltd	4,53	45	–1,20	–1,65	39	–423
61. Rajasthan Drugs & Chemicals Ltd	84	8	–3	–11	1,14	–10
62. Rashtriya Chemicals & Fertilisers Ltd	4,51,36	45,14	53,91	8,77	3,64,80	2
63. Sambhar Salts Ltd	2,46	25	16	–9	1,83	–5
64. Smith Stainstreet Pharma. Ltd	6,21	62	41	–21	5,69	–4
65. Southern Pesticides Corp. Ltd	4,27	43	26	–17	2,36	–7
66. U.P. Drugs & Pharma. Co. Ltd	5,20	32	87	55	7,53	7
Total	65,41,04	6,54,10	1,06,30	–5,47,80	25,12,67	–22
Heavy Engineering						
67. Bharat Heavy Electricals Ltd	8,81,78	88,18	1,68,43	80,25	13,47,93	6
68. Bharat Heavy Plate & Vessels Ltd	26,71	2,67	7,44	4,77	56,90	8
69. Bharat Process & Mechanical Engineers Ltd	4,18	42	–60	–1,02	7,35	–14
70. Bharat Wagon & Engineering Co. Ltd	8,05	81	1,07	26	7,62	3
71. Braithwaite & Co. Ltd	18,47	1,85	–39	–2,24	26,30	–9

72. Bridge and Roof Co. (India) Ltd	11,53	1,15	3,12	1,97	49,55	4
73. Burn Standard Co. Ltd	47,69	4,77	2,92	–1,85	81,26	–23
74. Heavy Engineering Corp. Ltd	1,46,24	14,62	–35,88	–50,50	91,11	–55
75. Jessop & Co. Ltd	55,28	5,53	59	–4,94	56,36	–9
76. The Lagan Jute Machinery Co. Ltd	4,47	45	–	–45	4,54	–10
77. Mining & Allied Machinery Corp. Ltd	41,36	4,14	–4,96	–9,10	50,72	–18
78. Triveni Structural Ltd	7,53	75	–70	–1,45	19,74	–7
79. Tungabhadra Steel Products Ltd	8,11	81	78	–3	6,22	–0.5
80. Weighbird India Ltd	12	1	–29	–30	1,01	–30
Total	12,61,52	1,26,15	1,41,53	15,38	18,06,61	9
Medium and Light Engineering						
81. Andrew Yule & Co. Ltd	28,11	2,81	6,08	3,27	41,01	8
82. Balmer Lawrie & Co. Ltd	22,60	2,26	4,86	2,60	65,20	4
83. Bharat Brakes & Valves Ltd	4,05	41	–48	–89	5,19	–17
84. Bharat Dynamics Ltd	4,53	45	–1,37	–1,81	3,95	–46
85. Bharat Electronics Ltd	1,31,38	13,14	33,40	21,26	1,61,24	13
86. Bharat Pumps & Compressors Ltd	37,82	3,78	3,50	–28	31,22	–1
87. Biecco Lawrie Ltd	1,32	13	–57	–70	6,02	–12
88. Central Electronics Ltd	5,75	58	–4	–62	2,82	–22
89. Electronics Corp. of India Ltd	47,50	4,75	5,69	96	73,69	1
90. Hindustan Cables Ltd	1,02,01	10,20	16,76	6,56	1,25,14	5
91. H.M.T. Ltd	2,81,27	28,13	49,02	20,89	3,18,45	7
92. HMT Bearings Ltd	9,19	92	74	–18	6,77	–3
93. Hindustan Teleprinter Ltd	13,55	1,36	1,05	–31	9,56	–3
94. Indian Telephones Industries Ltd	2,59,67	25,97	42,52	16,55	2,10,36	8
95. Instrumentation Ltd	47,55	4,76	8,67	3,91	66,39	6
96. National Instruments Ltd	4,32	43	–1,00	–1,43	6,06	–24
97. Praga Tools Ltd	15,02	1,50	2,10	60	14,30	4
98. Rajasthan Electronics & Instrumentation Ltd	78	8	17	9	1,85	5
99. Richardson & Cruddas (1972) Ltd	19,76	1,98	–1,08	–3,06	34,38	–9
100. Semi Conductor Complex Ltd	32,25	3,23	–1,37	–4,60	3,55	–130
Total	10,68,23	1,06,82	11,68,65	61,83	11,87,15	5

Table 10.4 Continued

Enterprise (1)	*Capital employed (Rs lakhs)* (2)	*Notional gross profit at 10% of (2) (Rs lakhs)* (3)	*Actual gross profit (loss) (Rs lakhs)* (4)	*(4)–(3) (Rs lakhs)* (5)	*Turnover (Rs lakhs)* (6)	*(5) as % of (6)* (7)
Transportation Equipment						
101. Bharat Earth Movers Ltd	2,86,05	28,61	66,58	37,97	3,81,37	10
102. Central Inland Water Transport Corp. Ltd	–14,01	–1,40	–5,30	–6,70	9,55	–70
103. Cochin Shipyard Ltd	98,42	9,84	–3,54	–13,38	12,38	–108
104. Cycle Corp. of India Ltd	6,19	62	–2,06	–2,68	14,11	–19
105. Garden Reach Shipbuilders and Engineers Ltd	37,62	3,76	4,66	90	61,02	1.4
106. Goa Shipyard Ltd	8,15	82	3,12	2,30	15,80	15
107. Hindustan Aeronautics Ltd	4,90,49	49,05	53,84	4,79	3,45,64	1
108. Hindustan Shipyard Ltd	33,74	3,37	–5,81	–9,18	34,11	–27
109. Maruti Udyog Ltd	74,95	7,50	11,20	3,70	64,20	6
110. Mazagon Dock Ltd	1,83,29	18,33	20,07	1,74	11,43,790	1.1
111. National Bicycle Corp. of India Ltd	3,71	37	–1,58	–1,95	5,20	–38
112. Scooters India Ltd	–5,47	–55	–2,82	–3,37	27,65	–12
Total	12,03,13	1,20,32	1,38,36	18,04	25,30,02	1
Consumer Goods						
113. Bharat Opthalmic Glass Ltd	1,10	11	–76	–87	1,70	–51
114. Brushware Ltd	5	0.5	2	1.5	18	8
115. Hindustan Latex Ltd	3,42	34	78	44	6,91	6
116. Hindustan Newprint Ltd	1,40,10	14,01	77	–13,24	51,01	–26
117. Hindustan Photofilms Mfg Co. Ltd	62,00	6,20	11,13	4,93	91,03	5
118. Hooghly Printing Co. Ltd	30	3	–1	–4	71	–6
119. Hindustan Vegetables Co. Ltd	42,79	4,28	6,66	2,38	2,38,28	1
120. Mandya National Paper Mills Ltd	5,80	58	2,31	1,78	7,36	24

121. Modern Food Industries (India) Ltd	11,05	1,11	2,29	1,18	3,26,64	4
122. Nagaland Pulp & Papers Ltd	57,24	5,72	–10,69	–16,41	1,82	–902
123. National Jute Manufacturers Corp. Ltd	1,55	16	–18,03	–18,19	90,78	–20
124. The National Newsprint & Paper Mills Ltd	20,18	2,02	1,93	–9	35,92	–0.3
125. Rehabilitation Industries Corp. Ltd	–6,74	–67	–1,99	–1,32	5,43	–24
126. Tannery & Footwear Corp. of India Ltd	3,04	30	–2,54	–2,84	5,31	–53
127. Tyre Corp. of India Ltd	8,16	82	–7,48	–8,30	7,39	–112
Total	3,50,04	35,00	–15,61	–50,61	8,70,47	–5
Agro-based Industries						
128. Andaman & Nicobar Islands Fores and Plantations Dev. Corp. Ltd	3,11	31	1,74	1,43	3,67	39
129. Banarhat Tea Co. Ltd	5,50	55	3,72	3,17	15,51	20
130. Basmatia Tea Co. Ltd	71	7	60	53	1,57	34
131. Hoolungooree Tea Co. Ltd	67	7	14	–7	1,05	67
132. The Mim Tea Co. Ltd	4	0.4	–5	–5.4	39	–14
133. Murphulani (Assam) Tea Co. Ltd	49	5	34	29	1,07	27
134. North Eastern Regional Agricultural Marketing Corp. Ltd	1,91	19	6	–13	67	–19
135. National Seeds Corp. Ltd	11,84	1,18	85	–33	22,61	–1.5
136. Rajgarh Tea Co. Ltd	1,30	13	1,08	95	3,44	28
137. State Farms Corp of India Ltd	9,40	94	6	88	9,76	9
Total	34,97	3,50	7,54	6,32	59,74	11
Textiles						
138. The British India Corp. Ltd	19,96	2,00	2,19	19	21,00	1
139. The Elgin Mills Ltd	–1,10	–11	–4,82	–493	23,61	–21
140. National Handlooms Dev. Corp. Ltd	1,24	12	–21	–33	1,49	–22
141. National Textile Corp. Ltd (Holding) Co.)	5,16,46	51,65	16,60	–35,05	17,59	–199

Table 10.4 Continued

Enterprise (1)	*Capital employed (Rs lakhs)* (2)	*Notional gross profit at 10% of (2) (Rs lakhs)* (3)	*Actual gross profit (loss) (Rs lakhs)* (4)	*(4)–(3) (Rs lakhs)* (5)	*Turnover (Rs lakhs)* (6)	*(5) as % of (6)* (7)
142. NTC (AP, Karnataka, Kerala & Mahe) Ltd	55,72	5,57	–9,20	–14,77	83,14	–18
143. NTC (Delhi, Punjab & Rajasthan) Ltd	23,04	2,30	–5,39	–7,69	36,02	–21
144. NTC (Gujarat) Ltd	54,83	5,48	–12,17	–17,65	90,63	–19
145. NTC (MP) Ltd	31,87	3,19	–6,70	–9,89	65,25	–15
146. NTC (Maharastra North) Ltd	40,83	4,08	–9,32	–13,40	70,53	–19
147. NTC (S. Maharastra) Ltd	71,90	7,19	–7,66	–14,85	83,18	–18
148. NTC (Tamil Nadu & Pondicherry) Ltd	60,13	6,01	2,54	–3,47	86,33	–4
149. NTC (UP) Ltd	24,36	2,44	–7,31	–9,75	37,04	–26
150. NTC (East Bengal, Assam, Bihar and Orissa) Ltd	31,87	3,19	–17,66	–20,85	34,29	–61
Total	9,31,11	93,11	–40,43	–1,52,44	6,28,85	–24
Trading & Marketing Services						
151. Bharat Leather Corp. Ltd	2,26	23	–24	–47	2,42	–19
152. Cardamom Trading Corp. Ltd	46	5	0	–5	26	–19
153. The Cashewnut Corp. of India Ltd	6,98	70	97	27	5,18	5
154. Central Cottage Industries Corp. of India Ltd	2,14	21	10	–11	8,61	–1.3
155. Central Warehousing Corp. Ltd	1,03,14	10,31	17,32	7,01	37,66	19
156. C.M.C. Ltd	15,20	1,52	1,55	3	15,50	0.2
157. Cotton Corp. of India Ltd	15,46	1,55	17,75	16,20	2,59,94	6
158. Electronics Trade & Technology Dev. Corp. of India Ltd	13,22	1,32	2,05	73	42,75	2

159. Food Corp. of India Ltd	41,75,31	4,17,53	4,55,63	38,10	46,03,25	1
160. Handcrafts & Handlooms Export Corp. of India Ltd	9,21	92	86	–6	1,15,12	–0.05
161. HMT (International) Ltd	6,62	66	1,29	63	6,44	10
162. Jute Corp of India Ltd	50,42	5,04	97,38	92,34	1,18,15	78
163. Metal Scrap Trade Corp. Ltd	2,81	28	3,38	3,10	1,17,78	3
164. Mica Trading Corp. of India Ltd	6,61	66	73	7	25,08	3
165. Minerals & Metals Trading Corp. of India Ltd	1,91,07	19,11	51,48	32,37	13,70,46	2
166. North Eastern Handicrafts & Handlooms Dev. Corp. Ltd	94	9	–14	–23	87	–26
167. Projects & Equipment Corp. Ltd	18,21	1,82	3,51	1,63	87,29	2
168. State Trading Corp. of India Ltd	2,14,48	21,45	68,88	47,43	23,04,23	2
169. Tea Trading Corp. of India Ltd	12,13	1,21	–1,40	–2,61	29,47	–9
Total	48,46,67	4,84,67	7,21,10	2,36,43	91,50,46	3
Transport Services						
170. Air India	6,45,86	64,59	90,11	25,52	7,71,89	3
171. Air India Charters Ltd	5	0.5	0	–0.5	1,52	–0.3
172. Indian Airlines	5,52,18	55,22	79,57	24,35	5,31,53	5
173. International Airports Authority of India Ltd	1,23,77	12,38	40,48	28,10	78,21	36
174. Vayudoot	3,58	36	–25	–61	3,04	–20
175. Dredging Corp. of India Ltd	65,41	6,54	8,15	1,61	27,91	6
176. Mogul Line Ltd	43,78	4,38	–13,38	–17,76	33,08	–54
177. Shipping Corp. of India Ltd	5,84,77	58,48	18,78	–39,70	5,61,13	–7
178. Delhi Transport Corporation	–68,70	–6,87	–56,51	–63,38	61,45	–103
Total	19,50,70	1,95,07	1,50,65	–44,42	20,69,76	–2
Contracts & Construction Services						
179. Hindustan Prefab Ltd	2,18	22	–74	–96	5,15	–19
180. Hindustan Steelworks Constn Ltd	15,90	1,59	–1,49	–3,08	1,65,97	–2
181. Indian Railway Constn Co. Ltd	72,40	7,24	22,71	15,47	1,60,58	10

Table 10.4 Continued

Enterprise (1)	*Capital employed (Rs lakhs)* (2)	*Notional gross profit at 10% of (2) (Rs lakhs)* (3)	*Actual gross profit (loss) (Rs lakhs)* (4)	*(4)–(3) (Rs lakhs)* (5)	*Turnover (Rs lakhs)* (6)	*(5) as % of (6)* (7)
182. Indian Road Constn Corp. Ltd	51,36	5,14	5,03	–11	58,96	–0.2
183. Mineral Exploration Corp. Ltd	27,72	2,77	2,35	–42	18,71	–2
184. National Building Constn Ltd	1,20,32	12,03	16,99	4,96	1,09,75	5
185. National Projects Constn Corp. Ltd	71,22	7,12	5,77	–1,35	1,00,40	–1
Total	3,61,10	36,11	50,62	14,51	5,19,12	3
Industrial Development & Technical Consultancy Services						
186. Central Mine Planning & Design Institute Ltd	13,65	1,37	1,41	4	24,53	0.2
187. Educational Consultants India Ltd	11	1	–7	–8	14	–57
188. Engineers India Ltd	28,97	2,90	13,17	10,27	44,61	23
189. Engineering Projects (I) Ltd	47,44	4,74	–4,03	–8,77	89,72	–10
190. Hospital Services & Consultancy Corp. (India) Ltd	25	3	–3	–6	7	–86
191. Metallurgical & Engineering Consultants (India) Ltd.	26,21	2,62	8,53	5,91	67,30	9
192. National Industrial Dev. Corp. Ltd	1,56	16	15	–1	1,66	–0.6
193. Projects & Development India Ltd	7,72	77	–2,13	–2,90	21,09	–14
194. Rail India Technical & Economic Services Ltd	17,10	1,71	5,15	3,44	20,52	17
195. Telecommunications & Consultants (India) Ltd	12,96	1,30	5,32	4,02	15,57	26

196. Water & Power Dev. Consultancy Services (India) Ltd	4,37	44	68	24	2,89	8
Total	1,60,34	16,03	28,15	12,12	2,88,10	4
Development of Small Industries						
197. National Small Industries Corp. Ltd	26,57	2,66	3,12	–46	24,94	2
Tourist Services						
198. Hotel Corp. of India Ltd	29,73	2,97	99	–1,98	18,66	–11
199. India Tourism Dev. Corp. Ltd	73,40	7,34	4,01	–3,33	49,08	–7
Total	1,29,70	12,97	8,12	–4,85	92,68	–5
Financial Services						
200. Export Credit & Guarantee Corp. Ltd	12,81	1,28	97	–31	16,24	–2
201. Housing & Urban Dev. Corp. Ltd	5,21,63	52,16	40,83	–11,33	46,53	–24
202. National Film Dev. Corp. Ltd	13,09	1,31	1,35	4	4,66	1
203. Rural Electrification Corp. Ltd	15,06,92	1,50,69	94,50	–56,19	95,80	–59
Total	20,54,45	2,05,45	1,37,65	–67,80	1,63,23	–42
Section 25 Companies						
204. Artificial Limbs Manufacturing Corp. Ltd	4,09	41	–1,14	–1,55	85	–182
205. Indian Dairy Corp.	3,48,64	34,86	19,28	–15,58	1,12,66	–14
206. National Research Dev. Corp. of India	3,20	32	16	–16	1,09	–15
207. Trade Fair Authority of India	14,21	1,42	52	–90	12,80	–7

Source: For basic data (columns (2), (4), and (6): Bureau of Public Enterprises, *Public Enterprises Survey*, Annual Reports, New Delhi. The other computations are made by the author.

Table 10.5 Sectoral analysis of tax and subsidy elements in public enterprise prices in India (1982–85)

Sector		*No. with net (notional) surpluses over 10%* *No. with % of turnover*					*No. with net (notional) deficit below 10%* *No. with % of turnover*				
		Below 25	*25–50*	*50–100*	*100 and above*	*Total no.*	*Below 25*	*25–50*	*50–100*	*100 and over*	*Total no.*
(1)	(2)	(3)	(4)	(5)	(6)	(7)	(8)	(9)	(10)	(11)	(12)
1. Steel	6	2	–	–	–	2	2	1	1	–	4
2. Minerals and metals	13	2	–	–	–	2	7	3	1	–	11
3. Coal	5	–	–	–	–	–	4	–	–	1	5
4. Power generation	3	–	–	–	1	1	–	–	1	1	2
5. Petroleum	12	8	2	–	–	10	2	–	–	–	2
6. Chemicals, fertilisers and pharmaceuticals	27	5	–	–	–	5	16	2	1	3	22
7. Heavy engineering	14	4	–	–	–	4	8	1	1	–	10
8. Medium and light engineering	20	10	–	–	–	10	8	1	–	1	10
9. Transportation equipment	12	6	–	–	–	6	2	2	1	1	6
10. Consumer goods	15	6	–	–	–	6	4	1	2	2	9
11. Agro-based industries	10	2	4	1	–	7	3	–	–	–	3
12. Textiles	13	1	–	1	–	1	9	1	1	1	12
13. Trading and marketing services	19	12	–	–	–	13	5	1	–	–	6
14. Transport services	9	3	1	–	–	4	3	–	1	1	5
15. Contracts & construction services	7	2	–	–	–	2	5	–	–	–	5
16. Industrial development & technical consultancy services	11	5	1	–	–	6	3	–	2	–	5
17. Development of small-scale Industries	1	1	–	–	–	1	–	–	–	–	–
18. Tourist services	2	–	–	–	–	–	2	–	–	–	2
19. Financial services	4	1	–	–	–	1	2	1	–	–	3
Total	203	70	8	2	1	81	85	14	12	11	122

Source of basic data: Bureau of Public Enterprises, *Public Enterprises Survey*, Annual Reports, New Delhi. The other computations are made by the author.

Table 10.6 The relative extent of subsidy-oriented prices in Indian public enterprises (1982–85)

	Aggregate			*Enterprises with notional deficits below 10%*			*Enterprises with notional deficits below 10% (as % of sectoral total)*		
Sector (1)	*No. of enterprises* (2)	*Capital employed (Rs crores)* (3)	*Turnover (Rs crores)* (4)	*No. of enterprises* (5)	*Capital employed (Rs crores)* (6)	*Turnover (Rs crores)* (7)	*No. of enterprises (5) as % of (2)* (8)	*Capital employed (6) as % of (3)* (9)	*Turnover (7) as % of (4)* (10)
1. Steel	6	32,53	26,77	4	32,35	26,46	67	99	99
2. Minerals and metals	13	13,70	8,37	11	9,13	6,45	85	67	77
3. Coal	5	49,72	20,24	5	49,72	20,24	100	100	100
4. Power generation	3	12,52	1,95	2	4,02	24	67	32	12
5. Petroleum	12	44,55	2,04,08	2	1,45	1,43	17	3	0.7
6. Chemicals, fertilisers and pharmaceuticals	27	65,41	25,13	22	51,63	12,29	81	79	49
7. Heavy engineering	14	12,62	18,07	10	3,34	3,44	71	26	19
8. Medium and light engineering	20	10,68	11,87	10	1,33	1,10	50	12	9
9. Transportation and equipment	12	12,03	25,30	6	1,23	1,03	50	10	4
10. Consumer goods	15	3,50	8,70	9	2,25	2,00	60	64	23
11. Agro-based industries	10	35	60	3	18	24	30	51	40
12. Textiles	13	9,31	6,29	12	9,11	6,08	92	98	97
13. Trading and marketing services	19	48,47	91,50	6	25	1,56	32	0.5	2
14. Transport services	9	19,51	20,70	5	5,64	6,60	56	29	32

Table 10.6 Continued

	Aggregate			Enterprises with notional deficits below 10%			Enterprises with notional deficits below 10% (as % of sectoral total)		
Sector (1)	No. of enterprises (2)	Capital employed (Rs crores) (3)	Turnover (Rs crores) (4)	No. of enterprises (5)	Capital employed (Rs crores) (6)	Turnover (Rs crores) (7)	No. of enterprises (5) as % of (2) (8)	Capital employed (6) as % of (3) (9)	Turnover (7) as % of (4) (10)
15. Contracts & construction services	7	3,61	5,19	5	1,69	2,49	71	47	48
16. Industrial development & technical consultancy services	11	1,60	2,88	5	57	23	45	36	8
17. Development of small-scale industries	1	27	25	–	0	0	–	0	0
18. Tourist services	2	1,30	93	2	1,30	93	100	100	100
19. Financial services	4	21	1,63	3	20	1,58	75	95	97
Total	203	3,41,89	4,80,45	122	1,75,39	94,39	55	51	20
Without petroleum and trading	172	2,48,87	1,84,87	94	1,93,90	91,40	55	78	49
Without steel and coal	192	2,59,64	4,33,44	114	1,13,53	47,69	59	44	11

Source: As for Table 10.5.

11 Public enterprise and the public exchequer

The idea that public enterprise is, in many respects, an aspect of public finance, was already hinted at in earlier chapters – 3 and 10 in particular. Here we shall make a comprehensive analysis of the relationships, especially the cash relationships, between public enterprise and the public exchequer.

At the outset mention will be made of certain structural features of developing countries relevant to the budget link with public enterprise. The typology of the cash equation between the two will be outlined next. There will be a discussion on whether the budget receives enough from government investments in enterprises; and a case will be made out for an arrangement of profit transfer from the enterprises to the exchequer in certain circumstances. The implications of the cash relationships for the budget will be examined, and the consequences of the budget processes for the enterprises will be noted. Finally, the budget documentation with reference to public enterprise, which is desirable from the angle of parliament and the public, will be indicated.

The implications of privatisation for the exchequer will be deferred to chapter 14.

SPECIAL CONSIDERATIONS IN THE CASE OF DEVELOPING COUNTRIES

Though the relationships between the budget and public enterprise are fundamentally similar in the case of developed and developing countries, there are several special considerations that merit emphasis in the latter case.

First, there is a structural difference in the budgets of the two sets of countries. Data on their composition over several years reveal the far greater importance of capital expenditures in developing countries. (Though the data used here refer to all capital expenditures, public enterprises have been the main component.) The figures of capital expenditures as percentages of total expenditures (and lending minus repayments) are plotted in Figure 11.1 for thirteen years, 1974–86. The totals for all developing countries have been nearly twice as important as those in the case of developed countries (or 'industrialised countries' – the International Monetary Fund (IMF) term). Among the former the order is Africa, Middle East, Asia, and Latin America. The highest figures are not exclusively associated with economies declared socialist.[1]

Figure 11.1 Central government: capital expenditure as percentage of total expenditure and lending minus repayments

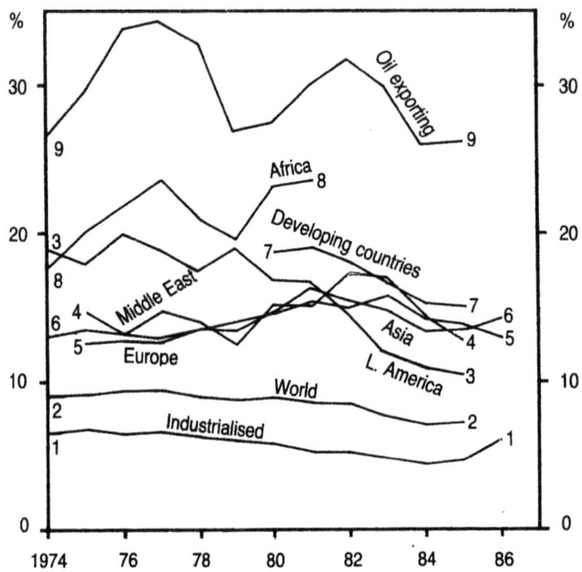

Source: Government Finance Statistics Year Book, vol. VI, 1982 and vol. XI, 1987, IMF.

Corroboratory data can be produced in terms of the government's expenditure on 'economic services', whose major components are agriculture, forestry, fishing and hunting, transport, and communications, as a percentage of total expenditure. Table 11.1 shows the spread of countries over different ranges of the percentage and shows that all but two of the industrialised countries spent less than 20 per cent of their budget expenditures on this 'function', while two-thirds of all countries in Africa and Asia spent more than 20 per cent on economic services.

All these data suggest that finding investment resources for public enterprises has been a major concern of the budget, that the exchequer has shouldered heavy burdens of debt servicing and should be anxious to have commensurate inflows of revenue from the enterprises, and that the exchequer ought to look for prompt inflows of loan repayments from the enterprises.

Table 11.1 Government expenditure on economic services (as a percentage of total expenditure)

Region	*No. of enterprises*						
	Below 10	*10–19*	*20–29*	*30–39*	*40–49*	*Above 50*	*Total*
Industrialised countries	5	11	2	–	–	–	18
Developing countries:							
Europe	–	2	3	–	–	1	6
Africa	1	10	11	8	2	1	33
Asia	–	6	5	1	4	1	17
Middle East	4	–	5	1	–	–	10
Western hemisphere (L. Am.)	4	8	10	2	1	–	25
Total	14	37	36	12	7	3	109

Source: International Monetary Fund (1987) *Government Finance Statistics Year Book, 1987*, Washington, DC, pp. 34–5. The data relate to the most recent year for which figures are available in each case.

Second, a far larger proportion of developing than industrialised countries had budget deficits exceeding 20 per cent of total expenditure. Table 11.2 shows that the countries with deficits in excess of 30 per cent of total expenditure have all belonged to the category of developing countries and that, while half the total number of industrialised countries had deficits below 10 per cent, only a fifth of the total number of developing countries came within that figure.

Table 11.2 Budget deficits/surpluses (as a percentage of total expenditure and lending minus repayments)

Region	*Deficits (no. of countries)*					
	Below 10	*10–19*	*20–29*	*30 and above*	*Total*	*Surplus*
Industrialised countries	10	4	4	–	20	2
Developing countries:						
Europe	3	2	2	–	9	2
Africa	3	13	13	5	41	7
Asia	5	4	4	2	18	3
Middle East	1	3	2	2	10	2
Western hemi-sphere (L. Am.)	9	8	3	5	31	6
Total	31	34	28	14	129	22

Source: As for Table 11.1.

An obvious inference is that developing country budgets are in a state of precarious imbalance and the questions of how far public enterprises cause it and how far they can be induced to remedy it assume importance.

There is another inference with immense significance. It comes from a review of how the budget deficits are financed. As shown by Table 11.3, developing countries have been financing budget deficits through resources from abroad to a far greater extent than industrialised countries. In the case of industrialised countries, with the exception of two, 'financing abroad' was within 5 per cent of total budget expenditures. On the other hand, less than a third of developing countries came within this description, and for another third the percentage exceeded 10. Africa led this list.

Table 11.3 'Financing abroad' of budget deficit (as a percentage of total expenditure and lending minus repayments)

	No. of countries					
Region	*Below 5*	*5–9*	*10–19*	*20–29*	*30 and above*	*Total*
Industrialised countries	11	2	–	–	–	13
Developing countries:						
Europe	3	1	1	–	–	5
Africa	5	10	10	6	1	32
Asia	6	2	3	–	–	11
Middle East	2	2	1	–	1	6
Western hemisphere (L. America)	8	4	4	–	–	16
Total	35	21	19	6	2	83

Source: As for Table 11.1.

The significance of these figures is that foreign debts owed by developing countries have been growing, while their ability to service them has not. For forty least-developed countries alone, the United Nations Conference on Trade and Development (UNCTAD) estimated that the total external debt – about US $41.7 billion by 1985 – was well over 50 per cent of their combined gross domestic product; and debt servicing, including interest, exceeded US $2.2 billion, equal to a little less than a quarter of their combined exports of goods and services.[2] For developing countries as a whole, the total external debt varied between 133 per cent and 168 per cent of their exports of goods and services during 1983–9, as per IMF's estimates. (Latin America had the highest figure, 306 per cent, followed by Africa, 233 per cent.) Debt service payments varied between 17 and 22 per cent during that period (38 per cent for Latin America and 25 per cent for Africa).[3]

Public enterprise is both a (partial) cause of this budget situation and a victim of it. Its responsibility arises partly from the sizeable influx of foreign funds towards its capital expenditures,[4] and its relative inability to contribute to the budget adequately for servicing the debts. It suffers from the consequent constraints on the foreign exchange reserves of the country, which eventually limit the import of equipment and technology needed by it even for full utilisation of capacity.

Third, there are differences in the revenue composition in government budgets as between industrialised and developing countries. One of these is of particular relevance to the present discussion and concerns the relative proportions of direct and indirect tax revenues. Taxes on individuals accounted for more than 20 per cent of all revenues in half the industrialised countries, while only less than a quarter of the developing countries belonged to this category. In about two-thirds of the latter group – as against two in twenty industrialised countries – personal tax incomes were less than 10 per cent of the total revenues (see Table 11.4).

Table 11.4 Individual tax incomes (as a percentage of total revenue)

	No. of countries				
Region	*Less than 10*	*10–19*	*20–29*	*Above 30*	*Total*
Industrialised countries	2	7	5	6	20
Developing countries:					
Europe	2	3	1	–	6
Africa	26	12	2	1	41
Asia	8	3	1	1	13
Middle East	3	–	1	–	4
Western hemisphere (L. America)	12	11	1	–	24
Total	53	36	11	8	108

Source: As for Table 11.1.

Indirect taxes are the more important component of the budget revenues in developing countries. While only two industrialised countries raised more than 40 per cent of the budget revenues from domestic and international taxes, 36 (out of 43) developing countries in Africa, 14 out of 18 in Asia, and 22 out of 32 in Latin America did so. In other words, government budgets in developing countries contain heavy elements of regressive taxation – a point to bear in mind as we examine the cash relationships between the exchequer and public enterprises in the following sections.

Finally, differences exist between industrialised and developing countries in the techniques of implementing the cash relationships between the exchequer and public enterprises, as this chapter shows. These, on the whole, aggravate the problems of the budget link in developing countries.

THE TYPOLOGY OF THE BUDGET LINK

The cash relationships between the exchequer and public enterprise may be presented as shown in Table 11.5.

Table 11.5 Cash relationships between the exchequer and public enterprise

Item (1)	*Inflows* (2)	*Outflows* (3)	*Net* (4)
Capital items:			
Grants		X	
Equity		X	
Loans	(Repayments) X	X	X
Guaranteed loans	(Repayments) X	X	X
Capital injections on write-offs		X	
Net proceeds of asset sales	X		
Deposits	X	X	X
Revenue items:			
Interest on loans	X		
Dividend	X		
Share in profits	X		
Guaranteed interest	(Repayments) X		
Subsidies		X	
Temporary advances	(Repayments) X	X	X

X indicates where the figures occur. The terms grants, equity, and loans do not call for any annotation. The cash injections during write-off refer to those cases where the accumulated deficits far exceed the government capital. They are not additional investments meant for expansion. Guarantees refer to the payments of debts by the government, for example, in the case of Air Lanka, the Ceylon Shipping Corporation and the Cement Corporation of Sri Lanka, or of interest on debts contracted by enterprises under government guarantee. Any repayments received from them are entered in column (2).

Receipts of sale proceeds of assets divested should be recorded, strictly, in column (2) under one of the first three heads of capital items, to the extent they are relatable to them. Only where the incoming amount exceeds the original capital contribution from the exchequer (either as equity or loan or in both forms), is the excess to be entered against the 'net proceeds' line.

The term 'share in profits' refers to any transfer to the exchequer of the profits of an enterprise over and above interest and dividend. Subsidies refer to all kinds of subventions, whatever the name used, offered by the government – towards operating costs or administrative costs, or specific functions, or for meeting deficits. (For example, public enterprises in Hungary receive consumer subsidies, producer price subsidies, agricultural policy supports, tax rebates to exporters, import subsidies, and subsidies to enable enterprises to implement the agreements with CMEA countries.)

Temporary advances from the government – probably to meet a liquidity crisis which bank finance may not relieve – constitute a non-capital item, though in some cases these stay unredeemed for a long time.

Deposits refer to the excess cash resources available to an enterprise, deposited with the government under one method or another, for example, it may buy treasury bills or just turn cash into the consolidated fund.

Excise, customs, and other duties as well as income or corporation taxes are not entered in the format, since they constitute an accrual to the exchequer, not because of its lending or ownership relationships with public enterprises, but because of the general tax levies under the Finance Act, applicable to all enterprises or individuals. These may be variously designated: cess, royalty, stamp duty, excise duty, import duty, export duty, tax on income or corporation tax, tax surcharge, property or wealth tax, capital gains tax, and so on. They do not represent income to the government as a claimant of ownership returns. There has been a tendency in several studies to include such tax incomes as incomes from public enterprises, along with interest and dividends.[5]

There are two qualifications, however. The first is in relation to the corporation tax income. Its size depends on the way in which the capital contribution by the government is designated. In exactly similar circumstances of enterprise performance and net revenue results the income received under the head of corporation tax can be dissimilar. Assume three enterprises: one with all equity capital, one with half equity and half loan capital, and the third with all loan capital, and assume that everyone has the same amount of net revenue before interest and tax. The accounting (and legal) position of interest and tax payments will be different from one to another, as shown in Table 11.6A.

Table 11.6A Profits and tax receipts (in US $)

Item (1)	*Enterprise A* (2)	*Enterprise B* (3)	*Enterprise C* (4)
Government capital			
Equity	100	50	–
Loan	–	50	100
Total	100	100	100
Net revenue before interest and tax	18	18	18
Interest income to government at 10% on loan	–	5	10
Net profit before tax	18	13	8
Corporation tax (say, at 50%)	9	6.5	4

The tax receipts are high in the case of *A*, simply because there was no cost-of-capital deduction from the assessable income, under the income tax law; and *C* presents the opposite situation. The income that may be directly designated as investment income comes from *A* wholly in the form of dividend, from *B* partly as dividend and partly as interest, and from *C* wholly in the form of interest. If we assume that all the enterprises wish to retain a profit of US $4 for reinvestment, *A* will be able to pay a dividend of US $5 (that is, 5 per cent on equity) and *B*, US $2.5 (also at 5 per cent on equity). On the whole the investment incomes received from *A*, *B* and *C* stand at US $5, US $7.5 (5.0 plus 2.5), and US $10 respectively. The differences are a result of the corporation tax law, the capital composition, and also the interest rate.

The role of the interest rate may be seen by assuming a 'soft' rate, say, 6 per cent. The figurework will be as shown in Table 11.6B.

Table 11.6B Interest and tax incomes

Item (1)	*A* (2)	*Tax receipts (in US$)* *B* (3)	*C* (4)
Interest income (at 6%)	–	3	6
Net profit before tax	18	15	12
Corporation tax	9	7.5	6

The higher tax receipts in the case of *B* and *C* are a function of the subsidised interest rate at which loan capital is provided by the government. To that extent they contain elements of investment income.

The investment-income content of the corporation tax receipts may be quantified, approximately, with reference to the equity-loan ratio in the private corporate sector. If, on an average, the ratio is more in favour of equity in public enterprise, the corporation tax receipts would be relatively high and contain elements of investment incomes. An attempt should be made to isolate them (see Appendix 11.1 – similar to Table 11.6A – for an illustration.)

There is a qualification as regards the excise, customs, and other duties, which are levied in relation to a specific product or service, whoever may be the supplier. Where a public enterprise is the only producer in a given case, the government may be indifferent to enhancing the rates of duty from time to time, if it can presume that the enterprise can be induced to adopt a profit-maximising policy within the limits imposed by the market, and that the profits find a way into the exchequer. Where either of these conditions is not satisifed, the government may prefer to use the duty as a budget instrument openly. In this way there is a conceptual overlap between excise, and so on, duty incomes and investment incomes in the case of sectors where public enterprises are the only producers.

It is of interest to refer to the gas levy imposed by the government in the UK in the early 1980s. The purpose was to divert to the exchequer 'rental' profits earned by the British Gas Corporation as a result of its long-term contracts entered into with oil-supplying companies in the early 1960s in respect of its oil inputs. As oil prices sky-rocketed, it realised windfall profits which, in the absence of any device for transferring its profit to the exchequer, were caught through the levy. In one sense this could be construed as an indirect tax or excise duty on the consumer. If it is assumed that gas consumers were entitled to ask for prices that gave the enterprise no higher than normal profits, the gas levy was no different from an excise duty which would not disturb the price–profit relationship. The gas levy could also be interpreted as a device for keeping the price paid by the consumer in tune with the long-term marginal cost of the enterprise. But then the amount collected ought to have stayed with the enterprise for its long-term cost-recovery purposes, though in the immediate context it represented surplus cash.

Where the demand for a product supplied by a public enterprise is so inelastic as to permit it to raise prices for increasing its profits, the government may decide to impose an excise duty if it owns the enterprise less than fully. For minority shareholders have a claim for a share in profits, but not in revenues collected as excise duties. (The minerals tax in Zambia collected through the Zambia Consolidated Copper Mines Ltd, in which the government owns about 60 per cent of the equity shares, illustrates the point.)

The overlap between investment incomes and tax incomes is of a unique kind in centrally-planned economies. Turnover taxes are a major device for drawing public enterprise net revenues into the exchequer. Often the rates are not uniform. They result from discussion with the enterprises. The tax incomes drawn into the exchequer can be relatively high, as in Somalia with a turnover tax, an income tax, and a depreciation tax. Together these exceeded the taxes levied on private enterprises and should be interpreted as a device for drawing budget incomes from public enterprises, considering that the major tax base of the country lies in the public sector.

Before we proceed to discuss the utility of the typology and its policy implications, mention should be made of an important item which is missing in Table 11.1, namely, the debt-servicing outflows from the exchequer, that is, on public borrowings which correspond to the government's investments in the enterprises. They are apparently not direct cash transactions between the government and public enterprises, but they are conducted by the government on behalf (or on grounds) of public enterprises. They have to be computed, exercising discreet judgement at certain points, for example, as regards the actual total that represents the investments, the demarcation of that figure between domestic debt and foreign debt, the way in which foreign exchange losses in debt-servicing are to be apportioned,[6] and the rate of interest to be adopted in the calculation. Some of the judgements involved would be tough, but there is no option.

The utility of the budgetary inflow–outflow equation *vis-à-vis* public enterprise arises from the fact that the government can assess the balance either in terms of aggregate incomings and aggregate outgoings without making a distinction between the capital and revenue characteristics of the flows, or distinctly in terms of capital inflows and outflows, and revenue inflows and outflows. The former is not an uncommon practice. (The British government adopts that method and certain statistical compilations of international agencies[7] go by such aggregate figures.) This may be described as a 'total cash approach'. It has an advantage for the government in that it shows the liquidity position of the budget in so far as all its transactions involving public enterprises are concerned, and arrangements may then be made appropriately to fill the cash gap, if the outflows exceed the inflows. In the generality of countries where the government continues to invest in enterprises on a sizeable scale, for example, under five-year plans, it is likely that the outflows outstrip the inflows, especially if capital redemptions by the enterprises are smaller than current government investments. There is no intrinsic danger in this imbalance, except where the lag represents heavy arrears.

The other method – the 'two-tier balancing' – is perhaps more accurate, in that a balance is struck, first, as between current capital outflows, including the public debt redemptions traceable to public enterprise investments, on the one side, and capital inflows or redemptions (through loan repayments by enterprises and asset sales or enterprise liquidations), on the other; and next as between revenue incomes (on investments) and revenue outflows such as subsidies and interest payments by the government on continuing public debt traceable to public enterprises. (Even 'temporary advances' should strictly be kept out. They rather belong to the non-revenue account, except that they represent short-term loans.) The net income derived by the exchequer as a result of its investments will then be clear, and one can proceed to evaluate if that is adequate, or if it is so high as to contain elements of disquised taxation, or if it is so low as to suggest an inefficient use of investible funds or a disguised subsidisation.

THE SIZE OF EXCHEQUER INCOMES FROM PUBLIC ENTERPRISES

Let us look at the proposition that the exchequer ought to receive enough income from its investments in enterprises, barring an occasional shortfall for reasons of business fluctuations. The question is different from whether public enterprises earn enough – that is part of financial-target fixing, considered in chapter 7. Nor is it the same as how high public enterprise prices should be allowed to earn – considered in chapters 6 and 7.

The two sides to compare are as follows:

Incomes: Interest on loan capital, dividends on equity capital, any share in profits, recoveries of interest met by the government under guarantee commitments, and investment–income elements in corporation taxes.
Expenditures: Payments of interest under guarantee commitments, subsidies, and interest on the amount of public debt traced to public enterprise investments.

Three major adjustments are necessary, before proceeding with the comparison.

First, capital expenditures that can be identified as those occasioned by relatively non-commercial considerations have to be isolated, for example, the township expenditures in the case of several public enterprises in India and portions of the 'endowment fund' in the case of IRI of Italy meant primarily to enable it to undertake capital projects in southern Italy. The debt-servicing costs borne by the budget in respect of such investments should be excluded from 'expenditures' above.

Second, several capital expenditures incurred by public enterprises in pioneering new technologies under difficult conditions belong to the category of national development costs. In many cases they would be too high to be recovered through annual net revenues in the foreseeable future, and in some they are probably infructuous and represent dead capital. Wherever it is possible to identify such expenditures, they should be separated out and the debt servicing costs attributable to them excluded from 'expenditures' above.

Third, an adjustment for gestation of capital expenditures is necessary. Many public enterprises belong to the category of capital-intensive industries characterised by heavy elements of gestation. An attempt should be made to put them together and allow for them while evaluating the budget balance *vis-à -vis* public enterprise. Care should be taken not to be over-generous in giving credit for the impacts of gestation. These should be self-balancing over the long run – or over the span of individual projects. However, it is possible that elements of gestation persist continuously, in the aggregate sense, if the government continuously invests in enterprises. When the gestation introduced by additional investments outstrips that expected to be self-balanced in the case of earlier investments, *ad infinitum*, the question to consider goes beyond the budget balance *vis-à-vis* public enterprise at a given unit of time. The issue is whether the investment strategy of development pursued by the government is in the interest of the national economy, without producing serious disadvantages – inflation, to name one, and underutilisation, to name another. (The National Development Corporation of Tanzania, the major development agency of the government, illustrates the point. It has begun to explore 'short-term and quick-return' investments, having been under the 'negative' impacts of long-gestation projects.)[8]

On the whole, the adjustment for the gestation factor would be time-bound, in that gestation is likely to self-finance itself over time. The other two adjustments are more fundamental.

In one sense, the concept of balance as between the exchequer and all public enterprises in the aggregate has significance. It upholds the theme that the government's investments, which have opportunity costs, must at least earn enough to meet the cash outgoings they involve. Assuming that the adjustments suggested above take care of individual investments whose returns have to be measured further than in terms of financial returns, this theme has justification. Nevertheless, the 'aggregate' concept conceals an important aspect of its composition, namely, that some enterprises might be contributing more than others, in whatever relative terms, and that some might not be contributing at all. The phenomenon is analogous to raising incomes through indirect taxation in some cases and offering indirect subsidies in some others, in different degrees in both respects. Thus the achievement of a budget balance *vis-à-vis* public enterprises on the whole or in the aggregate is not the last word in the area of budget policy, however useful it may be from the budget liquidity point of view.

To revert to the concept of aggregate balance between the costs of the exchequer and the incomes from public enterprise, the question arises whether the comparison of the incomes should be with the costs actually incurred or with the economic costs of the investments. It is well-known that the interest charges on public debt are lower than the market rates for funds; in some cases the government secures from a foreign donor a grant, an interest-free loan, or a low-interest loan, which it onlends to a public enterprise. Subject to the adjustments suggested above, the exchequer should look for incomes from public enterprise that compare with the economic costs of the invesments.

Three inferences can be drawn from examining the structure of exchequer incomes from public enterprises in a large number of countries. The first is that the interest incomes are low for any of the following reasons:

(i) The rates are fixed low, and the loan agreements run for long periods.
(ii) Interest holidays or moratoria are granted in some cases.
(iii) Interest arrears are waived sometimes.
(iv) Interest is provided for in the accounts of the enterprises but not paid to the exchequer.
(v) Interest due may be capitalised; it is added on to the loan.
(vi) Interest is received but at once a like amount is paid out to the enterprise as a subvention under some designation; or the enterprise is offered an exemption under some head of tax. Interest receipts in such cases are mere book entries.

The second inference is that dividend incomes are low because:

(i) Many enterprises have no profit after interest and tax to declare a dividend.
(ii) Those that have profits, declare no dividends or low rates of dividend.[9]
(iii) Some of these that declare dividends do not actually pay them to the exchequer.

The third inference is that there are few other devices through which public enterprise profits are channelled into the exchequer.

The propositions concerning dividends and profits call for further examination. Public enterprises, in general, have transferred to the exchequer relatively small proportions of their net profits after tax as dividends.[10] (The data for India and Pakistan shown in Appendix 11.2 indicate that about three-quarters of the dividend-paying enterprises in India took out less than a third of their net profits after tax for dividends in 1986–7; in fact a third used less than 10 per cent of their net profits for this purpose.) Two questions arise: are the dividends paid adequate and are the profit retentions by enterprises justified?

Empirically, the answer to the first question is in the negative, for many enterprises keep paying below 10 per cent on paid-up capital. The more basic point, however, is different, namely, that the dividends paid do not remunerate the exchequer for its total equity interest in the profit-making enterprises.[11] They have accumulated sizeable reserves which, in several cases, are twice as large as the equity capital.[12] Being neither paid-up capital nor loan capital, reserves fetch the government neither dividend nor interest income.

The point also applies to cases where the capital contributed by the government takes the shape of grants which do not rank for dividends. For example, the National Development Corporation in Tanzania has a capital fund built up through grants only; there are neither loans nor equity shares.[13]

It is interesting to note at this point that several nationalised industries in the UK, which have only loan capital from the government, have, over the years, built up such huge reserves that interest charges – an obligatory payment to the government – amount to a minor fraction of their net profits. Detailed figures are worked out in Appendix 11.3 for the British Airports Authority and British Gas Corporation before privatisation. They reveal that only 4 per cent of the gross profit before interest had to be paid towards interest to the government in the former case in 1986, when reserves accounted for 97 per cent of the total capitalisation and government loans for only 3 per cent. In the case of the British Gas Corporation there was not even an outstanding loan by 1986, and reserves accounted for the entire capitalisation. The government did not receive any income from this enterprise. The positive external financing limit in this case, quite high as a target which was exceeded in practice (in 1984–5 and 1985–6) meant a repayment of its loan capital and not a current income to the exchequer.

No doubt the reserves belong to the government, wholly in the case of enterprises whose equity capital is entirely owned by the government. When the enterprise is sold away or wound up for any reason or when some of its assets are disposed of, the government receives an amount that exceeds its original equity investment. But until such an event takes place, which is unlikely in many cases, a current income receivable by the government is being constantly capitalised. Where the accounts are not required to be kept or evaluated in terms of current costs, and where targets are not determined in terms of current costs or at all, there can be a tendency on the part of certain enterprise managements not to aim at earning adequately for remunerating the capital employed represented by reserves. The shares are probably not quoted on the stock exchange and the net profit after interest is apparently high in terms of the paid-up capital.

A closely allied aspect of the proposition is that reserves represent a plough-back or reinvestment of profits, and that it may be considered that the disadvantage of the exchequer not receiving them is apparent rather than real. Enterprise managers generally resist the idea of parting with a substantial share of the profits in favour of the exchequer. They argue that it would be an unnecessarily circuitous process to transfer the funds, in the first place, to the exchequer, and then to get them back for investment, and that often it would be difficult to get the funds back or receive them quickly enough.

The argument raises macro issues of investment strategy. The basic principle is that a contemplated investment should be justified. The justification has to be established at two levels: first, whether in the context of a given enterprise or sector of activity, it has justification on grounds of adequate returns; and second, whether it is advisable to undertake the investment, given the alternative possibilities of using the funds anywhere else in the economy.

An automatic plough-back in a public enterprise which makes high profits cannot, therefore, be justified on the mere ground that it has been able to make high profits. Other tests are warranted, which bring the government into the picture. (Chapter 4 considers this question.) A reinvestment decision, by and large, is heavily influenced by the enterprise board, whereas a decision to invest, once the funds reach the government, is duly under the additional impact of extra-enterprise and macro considerations. Further, where the funds come back to the same enterprise for an approved investment, the government has the opportunity of deciding on the nature of its capital contribution and, if it is given as a loan, of fixing the rate of interest consistently with market rates.

There is another strong reason why the exchequer is justified in attracting a sizeable share in the profits of a public enterprise. High profits are, in the end, a symptom of monopoly power. As shown in chapter 10, the prices, which bring them, contain elements of indirect taxation.

Further, there might be cases where the minister of finance deliberately prefers to let profits rise at the enterprise level, instead of introducing an excise duty on the product concerned. The proceeds, therefore, rightly belong to the exchequer, in some measure.

High profit retentions sometimes prompt enterprise managers to utilise large amounts for over-generous bonuses or social expenditures. One hears of proposals by managers for the construction of conspicuous office buildings and staff quarters. Are the former essential and the latter consistent with the government's overall policies on the proportion of social and economic or commercial capital expenditures in a given situation of the national economy?

EXCHEQUER DEVICES FOR A SHARE IN PROFITS

In general, institutional arrangements grossly limit the exchequer incomes derived from (profit-making) public enterprises. Let us look at the ways in which the situation can be improved.

The simplest method would be to insist on a dividend being declared and paid, at a high enough rate consistent with the profit of the enterprise. The obvious reasons why a reserve is to be built up – as a matter of commercial prudence – have to be respected. Depending on the nature of business fluctuations to which the enterprise is exposed, the board of directors should agree the most appropriate dividend with the government.

The method by itself does not transfer a large enough amount to the exchequer where the profits earned are very high and the paid-up equity is relatively small. (Trading enterprises are a typical case.) The existence of a relatively large reserve capital is an important version of the situation. Here the technique of converting a major part of the retained profits (or reserves) into share capital through the issue of bonus shares is helpful. This is a normal practice in the private corporate sector. There have been some cases of issue of bonus shares in the public enterprise sector: for example, in Pakistan, India, and Zambia;[14] but these have been few, on the whole. While the funds stay in the enterprise itself and their reinvestment utilisation remains unaffected, the formal modality of financing it changes in favour of share capital. The dividend-claiming equity base is widened; and more of the profits will reach the exchequer through dividends than when the earning assets were represented by high proportions of reserve capital.

There can be an open measure of profit transfer to the exchequer, under which a specified part of the profits, which otherwise could be retained by the enterprise, should be paid into the exchequer. There are not many examples. Among the earliest are the following Italian and Syrian provisions.

Under the Statutory Instrument 51 of 1948, enacted as Law 561 of 1956, IRI's net annual profits were apportioned as follows:

The net annual profits . . . shall be apportioned as follows:

20% towards the ordinary reserve fund;
15% towards the fund described under Section 24;

the remaining 65% shall be allocated to the State Treasury in repayment of the endowment fund and the sums granted to the Institute by the Treasury. When repayment has been completed, the 65% shall be allocated to a special reserve fund. (Section 17)

The 15% share of the profits mentioned [above] shall be put into a special fund to finance industrial management training ventures and vocational training and social welfare schemes.

Laboratories and industrial and management training courses may be set up and subsidized. (Section 24)

The Syrian Decree – Law no. 21 of 1967, required that 'the profits of each enterprise shall be distributed as follows: 25 per cent to the workers; 75 per cent to the State'.[15] The Syrian economy has been so public-enterprise oriented that a regulation like this clearly reflects the integral relationship between public finance and public enterprise.

In Egypt 80 per cent of the surplus goes to the exchequer, 10 per cent to workers' welfare, and 10 per cent to reserves.

Sri Lanka's statutory provisions applying to all sectors of public enterprises have the intention of transferring a part of the profits to the exchequer. For example, the State Industries Corporations Act of 1957 (Section 27) provides that:

out of the profits of the corporation in each year the board of directors shall, with the approval of the Minister, pay to general or specific reserves of the corporation such sums of money as may be determined by such board with such approval, and the balance, if any, of such profits shall, with the approval of the Minister of Finance, be paid to the Deputy Secretary of the Treasury to be credited to the Consolidated Fund of Ceylon.

However, the arrangement does not seem to have worked out in practice.

Some Indian Acts provide for the payment of profits (after all charges and depreciation) to the government (for example, the *International Airports Authority Act 1971*, Section 20).

An example of a statutory intention, which has no automatic force, may be cited from Kenya. Among the very few of the Acts covering this subject the Agricultural Finance Corporation Act (Section 16) distinguishes itself with the following clause:

> As soon as the reserve fund and other funds of the Corporation total such amount as in the Board's opinion is adequate to enable the Corporation fully to carry out its objects, there shall . . . be paid to the Permanent Secretary to the Treasury such amounts as the Board shall direct out of:
>
> (a) the profits of the Corporation and
> (b) the reserve funds of the Corporation.
>
> [The amounts so paid] shall be applied towards the redemption of any loans made by the Government to the Corporation, and interest upon the amount repaid shall cease to be payable as from the date of repayment.

The transfer of profits and reserves to the exchequer is subject to the decision of the board of directors, and is likely to depend on the government's influence on the board. Besides, this regulation does not strictly refer to a revenue transaction; it provides for scheduled or out-of-turn loan redemptions.

In some countries there are statutory provisions which empower the minister of finance to direct a payment to the Treasury, of 'surplus funds' lying with an enterprise, that is, funds in excess of 'existing or anticipated requirements'.[16] This, again, is not necessarily a profit transfer, though it reflects the idea that the government wants to take a total view of all liquid resources available in the public sector.

A clear example of profit transfer provisions comes from Canada. The Canadian National Railway Company is required to pay 'a dividend equal to 20 per cent of net income . . . or such greater percentage as the Governor in Council may direct'.[17]

Enforceable and definitive arrangements for transferring some of the profits of a public enterprise to the exchequer are desirable. Broadly, enough profits should be left with the enterprise to enable it to meet fluctuations associated with its input and output markets; to undertake risks in marketing as well as new production techniques; to meet foreseeable foreign exchange losses, and to maintain steady dividend payments. Such profit retentions protect its share values in the stock exchange, assuming that the shares are quoted. Once the appropriate size of the reserve is agreed on these considerations, a profit-transfer arrangement can be suitably designed. Where the needs of investment are obvious and agreed with the government, it is possible to permit profit retention corresponding to such needs, so as to avoid certain costs of bureaucracy implicit in transferring the funds to the government first and shifting them back again. But there are two important provisos, namely, that such retention does not unduly scale down the current income transfers to the exchequer necessary for meeting the costs of government borrowings corresponding to the capital employed in the enterprise; and that bonus shares are issued in favour of the government, even if once in two or three years; or the reinvestments are treated as loans from the government.

There can be different ways of determining the amount of profit that an enterprise has to turn over to the exchequer. Perhaps a threshold may be provided, beyond which the transfer formula operates. There can be three options. The transfer may be at an increasing percentage of the retainable net profit, that is, profit after tax and dividend, expressed as a percentage of total capital employed; it may be at a constant rate, or it may be at a decreasing rate. The first option is the best from the exchequer standpoint and is justified on the ground that very high profits represent a monopoly situation and contain elements of disguised taxation.

There ought to be provision for deviations from such a general formula in individual cases, from time to time, by mutual agreement between the exchequer and the enterprise; and parliament should be duly informed of them.

Finally, there is the turnover tax method employed in some centrally-planned economies like Ethiopia and Hungary, where profits are drawn into the exchequer by means of either a uniform formula of turnover taxes or a formula that permits of differences in the relative extent of transfers from the enterprises.

In conclusion, the profit-transfer policy need not affect the financial interest or the sense of pride of the employees. Presumably, whatever profit bonus they are entitled to get is linked with the overall net revenues; and the transfer formula suggested above begins to operate after all such profit appropriations are made. The pride of profit, a non-monetary value, is not destroyed either, since there is mention of bonus shares which reflects reinvestments of retained profits. They can be shown as a distinctive category under the caption of capital. Incidentally, it improves 'disclosure' in accounting presentations.

THE IMPACTS OF PUBLIC ENTERPRISE ON THE BUDGET

Let us analyse the problems that the financial flows between public enterprises and the exchequer cause for the latter. (There have been some implicit references to them in the earlier sections.) The situation of a net outflow from the exchequer will be considered first.

The revenue budget

There will be a budgetary stringency, which the exchequer has to resolve in some way. Before we examine this question, some issues of substance and methodology have to be considered.

The entire net outflow cannot be treated as a consequence of public enterprise operations *per se*. As shown in the fifth section of chapter 5, some of their deficits owe to budget policies originating in social preferences. The cash outflows caused by such factors have to be separated while defining the public enterprise impact. Such an adjustment would not be necessary where the government pays specific compensations for the 'social' or extra-enterprise functions, and the enterprise includes them in its gross revenues, the deficit figures do not need any adjustment under the head of policy deficits.

The net cash outflow is not the only figure we have to look at while analysing the impacts of public enterprises on the budget. Several enterprises have no profits after interest and do not therefore pay corporation taxes. In this way the budget sustains a 'constructive' loss, which is real wherever it can be assumed with reasonable certainty that the enterprises concerned would have raised profits enough for tax payments, if they were efficient or if they were located in the private sector. This loss may be computed by estimating the possible figures of net profit after interest in the case of such profitable enterprises in the sector concerned and by calculating corresponding tax receipts, possible but not realised. The possible figures of profit may be estimated by applying a notional rate to the capital employed minus the loan capital on which interest is a prior (cost) charge; or by applying the average rate of net profit after interest associated with the profit-making enterprises in the sector or a similar average rate applicable to the private corporate sector in the sector or in the country as a whole. (One may extend the argument to cover public enterprises which have made very low net profits after interest.) The purpose of this computation is simply to indicate a loss of revenue which the exchequer sustained, not as an investor but as a taxing authority.

The net cash outflows plus the tax losses represent the budgetary problem, which the exchequer faces in many countries, the more seriously, the larger the public enterprise sector in relation to total economic activity or the gross domestic product. (For example, the Ninth Finance Commission of India, in 1989, drew particular attention to this alarming feature of the government's budget.) The consequences would be as follows:

(a) Taxes may be raised. There are three problems:

   (i) The tax base is not wide and the tax burdens are already heavy in many developing countries.
   (ii) The proportion of indirect taxes being relatively heavy, the regressivity of the tax system gets aggravated.
   (iii) Tax enhancements could operate as a disincentive to investment.

(b) The government may increase its borrowings in order to meet even the revenue deficits – a situation pointed out by the Ninth Finance Commission in India. The burdens of debt servicing will increase, and aggravate the budget imbalance. Besides, there can be adverse effects on the interest rates on borrowings.

(c) Deficit financing may increase, leading to inflation.
(d) There can be random directives to public enterprises to deposit their apparently surplus liquid funds with the exchequer at low or no rates interest and with uncertainty of being made available to them on demand and at the precise point of need.

The capital budget

Here the problem relates not so much to an aggregate imbalance between the capital repayments from public enterprises and the current investments by the government, as to the non-receipt of loan repayments due from the enterprises as per schedule.[18] The former is essentially a part of the government's investment strategy, though it has an analytical connection with the pace of repayments in respect of earlier investments. The investment initiative can be continuously maintained by the government if it has the characteristic of being 'rotational', rather than being continuously 'additional', that is, if old investments come back as new ones are launched. This would be possible in one of two ways. Current profit transfers from the enterprises may be far larger than those at market rates of interest; or, the capital structure may be so designed that there is an emphasis on capital 'repayments' – for example, by keeping the loan ratio relatively high, by making the loan terms relatively short, and by offering advance repayment terms.

The more serious problem arises from the inability of public enterprises to repay loans on schedule. Loan arrears mount up. In some cases the instalments are repaid technically, but like amounts are again borrowed from the government; loans are often converted into equity; and there are instances of enterprise managements claiming that what the treasury treats as loans are in fact equity or grants.[19] The impact on the budget is as follows: The exchequer may have to increase its borrowings, probably at short notice, or it may have to curtail certain capital expenditures. In the latter case the impacts may prove to be quite sudden and not always well deliberated.

The budget can be under strain in another way. If public enterprises expected to be self-financing to a specified extent fail to do so, if further investments in them are considered necessary nevertheless, and if their only source of funds is the government, the exchequer has to raise the money for facilitating their investments.

On the whole the deficits of government budgets have tended to make their composition unfavourable in the sense that expenditures on 'personnel', which have a relatively 'fixed' character, become disproportionately large; these are not easy to curtail, while those on operational items, which really contribute to the effectiveness of the personnel, are alarmingly low. For example, the employee costs in the department of agriculture are high, while the tractors and other equipments necessary for their effective work are not adequately provided for, so much so that the productivity of government programmes is seriously affected. All this cannot be wholly attributed to the budgetary imbalance caused by public enterprises, but the latter is a major contributory factor.

So far we have considered the impacts of a net outflow from the exchequer to public enterprise. Where there is a net inflow, the effects would be of the opposite kind. Tax reductions are possible. There can, however, be no generalisation on the nature of benefits that follow. If they apply more to the direct taxes than to commodity taxes (or, among the latter, more to luxury commodities) they can have regressive effects. As regards the direct taxes, the distributional effects depend on how far the reductions benefit the lower-income brackets and on how far they are designed to encourage investment and growth. In fact, the government may implement a disguised tax reduction by revising the financial targets for certain public enterprises and by altering their cash relationships with the exchequer in such a way that the consumers of the (selected) products can enjoy the benefits of reduced prices. In other words, there would be a reduction in the indirect taxation that had prevailed.

Another possibility is that, without attempting to reduce taxes, the government may decide to implement certain new expenditures. These can be revenue expenditures, of which some may be welfare expenditures; or they may represent capital expenditures, of which some may be commercial.

As for the effect of the net inflow on capital account, chapter 14 on privatisation contains extensive discussion.

THE BUDGETARY PROCESS

This section considers briefly the implications of the budgetary process for public enterprises. (The wider aspects of government–enterprise relationships are covered in chapter 13.)

First, government budgets have a relatively short-term focus as compared with enterprise budgets, though there have been significant reforms in most countries to extend the exchequer perspective beyond a year. Some version of forward budgeting is common today. In countries where development plans exist, some minimal long-term planning of exchequer operations is implicit. Enterprises, as a rule, have to frame long-term budgets consistent with the life-span of the projects undertaken, and provide for a continuous availability of the required funds. Further, their financial planning is influenced by the nature of gestation inherent in their operations – not only in respect of capital expenditures, but also in respect of their pricing policies aimed at long-term maximisation (of whatever is sought to be maximised). Hence a full understanding is necessary between the exchequer and a public enterprise on the temporal prospects of mutual cash flows. There may be years when a net inflow into the exchequer is not to be expected, while in other periods a compensatorily high net inflow is to be programmed. If governmental budgeting disregards this aspect of enterprise operations, the enterprise finds itself stifled in its drive for long-term efficiency.

To some extent the corporate plans of public enterprises can provide relief in this respect, provided that they clearly commit the government to the resource flows incorporated in the plan, and that the plan is formulated with technical competence and agreed by the government in full knowledge of its resource implications. If corporate plans end up as formal documents which no one takes seriously, they do not help in bridging the temporal conflicts between the exchequer and the enterprise.

Second, the government budget is, by and large, 'resource-based', as contrasted with an enterprise budget which is 'need-based'.[20] This distinction has qualifications on both sides. The government can estimate the national needs it aims to satisfy through budget expenditures and correspondingly plan to raise the requisite resources through taxation and borrowings; and an enterprise may be able to defer expenditures, other than the most needed ones, consistently with the resources available to it. Broadly, however, the situation has long been one in which the exchequer feels constrained in funds and public enterprises need funds, even towards working capital and for being able to improve the utilisation of capacity already set up. They present demands for funds in the light of their needs, and the exchequer finds it hard to concede them on grounds of resources. The exchequer sets ceilings on enterprise borrowings, for example, under external financial limits in the UK; or may oblige the enterprises to go to commercial banks.

Third, assuming that some method of limiting the government's outflows to public enterprises is inevitable in many countries,[21] the more so under the structural adjustment agreements with the IMF, public enterprises are often inconvenienced by the way in which the mechanism operates. If a proper system of investment appraisal does not exist in effect, even though a sophisticated document of guidelines is expected to be followed, the claims presented by the enterprises are subjected to endless motions of review by the sectoral ministries, the planning agency, a 'co-ordinating' agency in the prime minister's (or president's) office, and the finance ministry. The ceilings fixed for the sectoral ministries – frequently without knowledge of the requirements of their several enterprises – get transmitted to them either in a merely arithmetical manner, that is, a percentage cut in demand, or in an *ad hoc* manner, often dependent on the mutual personal relationships among the parties involved. In this process some enterprises feel forsaken mid-stream; sometimes their chances of getting funds depend on the bargaining relationships of their parent ministries with the finance ministry or the president's (or prime minister's) office. Most enterprises take the exercise of presenting budget demands to the government lightly, on which intensive technical inputs may be proved wasteful in the end. There develops, further, the familiar trick of over-demanding, in the hope that, after the inevitable percentage cut, enough funds may be received.

The situation is aggravated in countries where public enterprises are many in number, the finance ministry cannot by itself effectively go through the process of investment review, and the sectoral ministries themselves are not well equipped to conduct the task of harmonising the enterprise demands with funds available under their respective budget votes.

The restrictive impacts of exchequer ceilings are serious for enterprises which cannot or are not allowed to raise resources from outside the government.

An interesting aspect of budget allotments is the 'token budget vote' in favour of an enterprise, for example, in Kenya. It is understood to imply governmental acceptance of its request for funds; but the amount of allotment and its timing remain uncertain.

The system of annual lapsing of funds is another common aspect of the governmental budget. Unless the necessary qualifications are effectively introduced, enterprises, which do not utilise the allotments in a given year even for justifiable reasons and in the interest of economy of expenditure, tend to forfeit the allotment. This induces them often to draw the funds and use them up, even if spending them later on might be more economical.

Fourth, foreign aid received in respect of a specified project can have unfavourable effects on other enterprises in a subtle way, if there is a condition attached to it that the government has to provide a specified amount of local resources in its turn. Where the aided project is not a priority project for the economy and is undertaken on grounds of political relationships with the donor, the allotment of government funds to it represents an inadequately justified diversion from more eligible demands on the part of other enterprises. (Where, in addition, the donor supplies the technology which is expensive or inefficient, the disadvantage is compounded.) Where the budgetary resources are not plentiful, the constraints on the availability of funds for the cross-section of public enterprises can be severe.

Finally, despite budgetary reforms undertaken with enthusiasm in many countries, there is a general unwillingness on the part of governments to recognise that many a public enterprise is in urgent need of a cash injection. Once they do so, they would be obliged to work towards the remedy, or restructure its finances and plan a budget strategy for coping with the situation over a period in a well-deliberated manner. This is necessary but not done, in general; and the budgetary process encourages *ad hoc* triangular bargaining among the enterprise, the sectoral ministry, and the finance ministry. Often the result could be in the nature of a distribution of patronage.

To conclude: the exchequer has its own problem of illiquidity, which is bound to impact on public enterprises. However, three relieving directions of action can be suggested: (i) to develop a system under which each enterprise knows what it is likely to get from the exchequer over a period; (ii) to rationalise the adjudication among competing demands from the enterprise; and (iii) to allow, if not encourage, capable enterprises to go to the market for funds.

THE BUDGET DOCUMENTATION ON PUBLIC ENTERPRISES

In view of the close interrelationships between public enterprise and the exchequer, it is important that, in countries with an extensive public enterprise sector, the budget documents of the government should be supplemented with adequate information on its financial aspects, as proposed in Appendix 11.4. It helps parliament and the general public take an overall view of the way in which the ministry of finance formulates the budget, taking account of the impacts of public enterprise operations. It offers three advantages, in particular.

First, it incorporates all the cash transactions of the government with public enterprises at one place, under captions that suit economic analysis, as against the ordinary budget format of revenue and expenditure in which the figures of public enterprises are dissipated over different ministries and by vote head (see Tables 11.11, 11.12, 11.13, 11.16, 11.17, 11.18 and 11.19 in Appendix 11.4).

Second, while the budget documents essentially contain cash transactions, several non-cash aspects of public enterprise operations are also relevant for a proper perspective on their budget link (for example, column (5) of Table 11.11 and column (4) of Table 11.15, and Tables 11.22 and 11.25).

Third, the supplementary documentation provides basic facts of public enterprise, which help prompt policy changes in respect of their ownership, organisation, and operations. (For example, it provides a total picture of the extent of public enterprise operations (see Tables 11.14 and 11.20). It reflects their financial efficiency from several angles (see Tables 11.21, 11.23 and 11.24). It shows the government's ownership and lending relationships in relative terms (see Table 11.20). It provides data on certain policy aspects of the government's interface with public enterprises, for example, cross-debts between the government and the enterprises (see Table 11.25); the tax and subsidy elements in public enterprise prices, (see Table 11.21); and divestments (see Tables 11.11 and 11.19). It indicates the nature of public enterprise impacts on the government's budget and on public debt (see Tables 11.26 and 11.27).)

The data sought to be covered by the tables in Appendix 11.4 are different in focus for the most part from those suggested as necessary in the context of evaluation in chapter 9.

The supplementary documentation suggested here facilitates the 'co-ordination' of public enterprise finances with public finance. This term signifies, broadly, that public enterprises operate consistently with the government's policies in different sectors of the economy, and that they do not negate them, unwittingly or deliberately. 'Integration' and 'harmonisation' are some of the other terms used to express the same ideas. There is no way of inserting the budgets or autonomous enterprises in the government's own budget; nor is it of much value to append all their financial statements to the budget. These would be in the nature of raw data and we would miss the wood for the trees; hence the need for processed documentation, as suggested here.

Practice varies among countries as regards the presentation of public enterprise data relevant to the budget. In the UK the government makes some information available in its annual publication 'The Government's Expenditure Plans' (but this is limited to 'capital requirements') and 'financing tables' of the major nationalised industries. And the 'Financial Statement and Budget Report' shows 'interest and dividends within the public sector', 'current grants within the public sector', and 'National Loans Fund receipts and payments', which show the total of loans to nationalised industries and other public corporations.

As per the amendment to the Financial Administration Act in Canada in 1984, the President of the Treasury Board submits a consolidated annual report to parliament, comprised of (a) aggregate financial and employment data (including assets, liabilities and shareholder's equity, net new borrowings, budgetary funding and employment), and (b) audited financial statements of individual corporations. The latter commence with a financial summary of several years' performance, along with some basic information. The report does not bring out the budget link in all its facets as delineated in this chapter.

In India the government provides, through the Bureau of Public Enterprises' annual surveys, not only the individual balance sheets and profit and loss accounts for all the enterprises, but certain 'ratios' and an overview where sectoral and overall aggregates are presented and processed in several ways. The information is plentiful, but does not address the budget link from an analytical angle.

Pakistan's annual volumes, *Government Sponsored Corporations*, issued by the Ministry of Finance, and *Public Sector Industries*, issued by the Experts Advisory Cell of the Ministry of Production, contain information on individual enterprises along with some 'ratios', in the latter volume, limited to manufacturing enterprises, but the budget link as such is not analysed.

In some countries like Nepal, the annual *Economic Survey* (issued at the budget time) contains limited data on the financial results of public enterprises in aggregates and the incomes to the government from them.

In Jamaica the government has evolved the policy of presenting, along with the general government budget, the 'Financing Plan' (comprised of aggregate estimates of revenue, expenditure and cash flow) of twenty-one selected public enterprises. It is informative in so far as the aggregate finances of the twenty-one are concerned, but does not quantify the budget link as argued in this chapter, except for the few lines 24 to 28 in the statement on source and application of funds (see Appendix 11.5).

CONCLUSION

Both economic logic and empirical review suggest that the relationships between the exchequer and public enterprises are in need of fundamental reformulation in all countries. The need is the more urgent in developing countries where the enterprise impacts on the budget are particularly serious. The impacts are often disguised but clearly imply increased tax burdens and public debt servicing costs. Subject to exceptions, the enterprises should be treated as investments; and the exchequer should look for investment incomes in terms of cash every year. Where reinvestments are justified on their own merits, the government should, as far as possible, openly rank as a shareholder or as a lender.

Inadequacy of data on the budget link with public enterprises keeps parliament and the public from realising the (often alarming) nature of the link. Appropriate documentation revealing its various aspects would be a first step in rationalising it.

Most governments have been under external pressures to rationalise their budgets and expenditure plans. Rationalising the exchequer relationships with public enterprises would be an important step in that direction.

APPENDIX 11.1

Table 11.7 Profits and tax receipts (US $)

Item (1)	*Public enterprise* (2)	*Private enterprise* (3)	(4)
Equity	150	100	75
Loan capital	150	200	225
Total	300	300	300
Net revenue before interest and tax	36	36	36
Interest on loan at 10%	15	20	22.5
Net profit after interest	21	16	13.5
Corporation tax (at 50%)	10.5	8	6.75

Note: The assumed equity–loan ratio is 1:1 in column (2), 1:2 in column (3) and 1:3 in column (4).

The corporation tax receipts from public enterprises contain investment incomes of US $ 2.5 on the analogy of 1:1 ratio between equity and loan in the corporate sector, and of US $ 3.75 on the analogy of 1:2 ratio.

APPENDIX 11.2

Table 11.8 Dividends and net profits (after tax): Indian public enterprises (1986–87)

Net profit after tax (Rs lakhs) (1)	*% of net profit declared as dividend* Below 10 (2)	10–19 (3)	20–29 (4)	30–49 (5)	50 and above (6)	*Total* (7)
Below 50	–	1	1	2	1	5
50–99	1	1	–	2	–	4
100–499	4	2	5	4	–	15
500–999	2	2	1	2	–	7
1,000–1,999	2	–	3	–	–	5
2,000–3,999	2	2	3	–	2	9
4,000–9,999	5	1	–	2	–	8
10,000 and above	2	–	–	–	–	2
Total	18	9	13	12	3	55

Source: Bureau of Public Enterprises (1988) *Public Enterprises Survey 1986–87*, vol. 1, New Delhi, pp. 55–7, 64–5.

Table 11.9 Dividends and profit retentions of public enterprises in Pakistan (1986–87)

Sector	*Number of enterprises* *Total*	*With net profit after tax*	*Declaring dividend*	*Total net profit (Rs mill.)*	*Dividend as % of net profits*
Chemicals and ceramics	15	7	0	80.10	0
Fertilisers	7	4	4	586.92	83
Automobiles	13	7	5	156.37	14
Industrial development	10	1	–	2.17	0
Cement	14	11	8	869.83	9
Engineering	12	6	1	27.29	8
Petroleum	4	4	3	142.90	87
Total	75	40	21	1,865.58	39

Source: Ministry of Production (1988), *Annual Report 1986–87*, vol. II, *Public Sector Industries*, Experts Advisory Cell, Islamabad (the data relate to manufacturing enterprises only).

APPENDIX 11.3

Table 11.10 Exchequer incomes from certain nationalised industries in the UK (1985 and 1986) (£ million)

British Airports Authority	*1985*	*1986*
1. Capitalisation:		
Department of Transport loans	43	39
Reserves	924	1,119
Total	967	1,158
2. Profit before interest on government loans	67.6	79
3. Interest on government loans	3.6	3
4. Profit after interest	64.0	76

Item 3 is what the government received; and item 4 represents profit retention by the enterprise.

British Gas Corporation	*1985*	*1986*
1. Capitalisation:		
Reserves	16,629	18,183
2. Operating profit	651	688

The government received little by way of investment income. The positive External Financing Limit really represented a capital receipt which corresponded to the reserve capital; for loan capital had been repaid by the Corporation almost completely.
Source of data: Annual Reports of the enterprises.

APPENDIX 11.4 Supplementary budget documentation on public enterprise

Table 11.11 Government's equity investments: as on —

Enterprise (1)	*At the begin-ning of the year* (2)	*During the year* (3)	*Divestments during the year* (4)	*Write-offs during the year* (5)	*Total to date (2)+(3)−(4)−(5)* (6)

Note: This table presents the net cumulative equity investment of the government in each enterprise at the end of the year, after allowing for any write-offs or divestment during the year. Any tax remissions converted into equity or any issue of bonus shares would figure in column (3), though no cash has passed from the government to the enterprise towards the equity. An explanatory note may be asterisked.

Table 11.12 Government loans: as on —

Enterprise (1)	*At the beginning of the year* (2)	*During the year* (3)	*Repayments* (4)	*Write-offs* (5)	*Total to date (2)+(3)−(4)−(5)* (6)

Note: This likewise shows the government's cumulative capital contributions in the form of loans to each enterprise at the end of the year, after allowing for any reductions during the year reflecting loan repayments by the enterprise and any write-offs affecting the loan figure. Any conversion of loans into equity will figure in column (4), with a corresponding contra entry in column (3) of Table 11.11. An explanatory note may be asterisked.

Table 11.13 Government's capital grants: as on —

Enterprise (1)	*At the beginning of the year* (2)	*During the year* (3)	*Total (2)+(3)* (4)

Note: This reflects the grants of a capital nature, which have the legal status of neither equity nor loans. Any conversion of equity or loan into grants (under a capital restructuring) would figure in column (3), with a corresponding contra entry in column (5) of Table 11.11 or column (5) of Table 11.12. An explanatory note may be asterisked.

Table 11.14 Government's total investments: as on —

Enterprise (1)	*Equity* (2)	*Loans* (3)	*Grants* (4)	*Total* (5)

Note: This reflects the structure of the government's contributions by status of designation – equity, loans, and grants, which have diverse implications of paying-out costs for the enterprise. Inter-enterprise diversities found in the structure can be interesting and can provoke thought on their rationale.

Table 11.15 Loan repayments to government: year —

Enterprise (1)	*Loans due to date* (2)	*Loan repayments during the year* (3)	*Arrears to date* (4)

Note: This indicates the size of loan arrears of each enterprise. A comparison of column (4) with column (2) can prompt the question of whether relatively large arrears are the result of inability or unwillingness of an enterprise to repay loan instalments.

Table 11.16 Loans guaranteed by the government: as on —

Enterprise	*Amount guaranteed*			*Serviced under guarantee*					
	To date			*Interest*		*Principal*		*Total*	
	Domestic	*Foreign*	*Total*	*Domestic*	*Foreign*	*Domestic*	*Foreign*	*Domestic*	*Foreign*
(1)	(2)	(3)	(4)	(5)	(6)	(7)	(8)	(9)	(10)

Note: This highlights the debt-servicing in which the government is involved in respect of loans borrowed by public enterprises directly from non-government sources. The information has a bearing on the appropriateness of the borrowings, if the government is continuously called upon to step in, under the obligations of a guarantor. The 'foreign' columns reflect the particular seriousness of the situation.

Table 11.17 Current incomes from public enterprises: year —

		Dividends received			*Interest received*			*Total current*
Enterprise (1)	*Govern-ment equity* (2)	*Amount* (3)	*As % of (2)* (4)	*Govern-ment loans* (5)	*Amount* (6)	*As % of (5)* (7)	*Share in profits received* (8)	*incomes (3)+(6) −(5)* (9)

Note: This shows, separately under the heads of dividend, interest, and share in profits, the incomes received by the exchequer from each enterprise. Columns (4) and (7) facilitate meaningful comparisons with market rates of remuneration for the use of capital.

Table 11.18 Subsidies: 5-year period

Enterprise (1)	*Amount during the year* (2)	*Total during four prior years* (3)	*For five years to date* (4)

Note: This provides an idea of the subsidies given by the government to each public enterprise, under whatever arrangement, for example, to meet its administrative costs, or to meet its deficits. The 5-year period averages out annual ups and downs in the figures and offers a proper perspective on the transaction. A larger period could be chosen for columns (3) and (4), if desired.

Table 11.19 Public enterprises: financial aggregates

Details (1)	*Amount* (2)
As on — Year	
Grants	
Equity	
Loans	
Arrears of loan repayments	
During — Year	
Write-offs	
Divestments	
Subsidies	
Dividend incomes	
Interest receipts	
Profit receipts	
Others	
Arrears of interest	
Debt servicing on guaranteed	
Loans:	
Interest	
Principal	

Note: This aggregates financial data under several heads for the entire public enterprise sector. The first part refers to cumulative magnitudes of grants, equity, loans and loan repayment arrears; while the second part refers to the year's data. The figures would be drawn from the respective totals recorded in the earlier tables, and refer to the government–enterprise transactions only.

Table 11.20 Total capital outlay: as on —

		Equity		*Loans*			
Enterprise	*Grants*	*Total*	*Govt holding (%)*	*Total*	*Govt loans (%)*	*Reserves*	*Total capital outlay (2)+(3)+(5)*
(1)	(2)	(3)	(4)	(5)	(6)	(7)	(8)

Note: This is similar to Table 11.14 but records the capital structure of each enterprise, inclusive of both government and non-government contributions. Columns (4) and (6) reflect the government's share in equity holding and in loans.

Table 11.21 Return on capital outlay: year —

Enterprise (1)	*Total capital outlay* (2)	*Net revenue before interest and tax* (3)	*(3) as % of (2)* (4)

Note: This refers to all capital, whether derived from the government or from non-government sources, and is composed of grants, equity, loans, and reserves – as in column (8) of Table 11.20. Net revenue before interest and tax indicates the earnings structure of the enterprises irrespective of their capital composition.

Table 11.22 Capital write-offs: as at —

Enterprise (1)	*Capital write-offs to date* (2)	*(2) as % of government investments* (3)

Note: This shows the cumulative figure of capital write-offs for each enterprise and expresses it in relative terms of the government's investments. Such a derivative would be of interest in that it shows the seriousness of the loss of capital (most commonly, the government's investments). Short of such a table as this, it would not be possible to decipher these facts from the current balance sheet of an enterprise.

Table 11.23 Accumulated losses: as on —

Enterprise (1)	*Accumulated losses* (2)	*Accumulated losses as % of total non-loan capital* (3)

Note: This quantifies the accumulated losses up to date and expresses them as a proportion of the total non-loan capital, which, as equity and grants, is commonly the government's contribution.

Table 11.24 Capital expenditure: during year —

		Financed by		
Enterprise (1)	*Total capital expenditure* (2)	*Government contributions* (3)	*Other sources* (4)	*Internal resources* (5)

Note: This records the capital expenditures incurred by each enterprise during a year and indicates the way in which they were financed. The definitions of capital expenditure and internal resources are material. Whatever they are, they ought to be consistently applied to all the enterprises.

Table 11.25 Government – public enterprise dues: as on —

Enterprise (1)	*Enterprise dues to the government* (2)	*Government's dues to the enterprise* (3)	*Net dues to the government* (4)

Note: This refers to a chronic problem, namely, non-payment by the government to a public enterprise, of its dues, and vice versa. Column (4) would have plus or minus entries indicating the dues from the enterprise to the government, or vice versa. In the former case a liquidity problem of the enterprise may be the cause, while in the latter, it may be a result.

Table 11.26 Impacts on the public exchequer: during year —

Enterprise (1)	*Total incomes (dividends + interest + profits)* (2)	*Interest on public debt at x% on total government investment (grants + equity + loans + reserves)* (3)	*Difference + − (2) − 3* (4)

Note: This reflects the equation of the government's revenues from an enterprise and the costs attributable to its investments in the enterprise. The latter, covered by column (3) have to be computed at a rate that is analogous to the average rate of interest paid by the government on its public debt during the year; and the principal to which the rate is applied has to be comprised of grants, equity, loans, and reserves, though interest is not a paying-out cost in every one of these cases, in so far as the enterprise is concerned. In so far as the government is concerned, all these have their relevance for the public debt. The reserves are included here, since they really represent reinvestments, and to that extent have the indirect effect of inflating the public debt correspondingly. Where the enterprise has private capital participation, column (3) refers to the government's proportion in each segment of the capital heads.

Table 11.27 Impacts on public debt: during —

Enterprise (1)	*Government investments in public enterprises (grants + equity + loans + reserve additions)* (2)	*Loan repayments by public enterprises* (3)	*Divestment receipts from public enterprises* (4)	*Net impacts on public debt (2)−(3)−(4)* (5)

Note: This refers to the impacts that the government's investments in a public enterprise during the year had on the public debt. Columns (3) and (4) represent funds paid into the public exchequer as a result of loan repayments and divestments. And it is assumed that these accounts would go towards a reduction in the size of the public debt; for, either a corresponding part of the existing public debt is paid off, or additions to public debt through fresh borrowings by the government would be scaled down to a corresponding extent.

APPENDIX 11.5

Table 11.28 Financing plan for twenty-one selected public sector enterprises: Jamaica

			(J$ millions)		
	1980–81	*1985–86*	*1986–87*	*1987–88*	*1988–89*
(i) Surplus from operations	–37.7	694.3	778.74	755.48	781.00
(ii) *Less* amortisation (excluding GOJ)	105.9	376.8	448.32	448.02	307.92
(iii) Balance of surplus available for capital expenditure	143.6	317.5	330.42	306.46	473.08
(iv) Percentage of capital expenditure financed by surplus	Nil	29.3	35.5	28.5	40.1
(v) Capital expenditure and investment	239.7	807.7	930.44	1,077.18	1,178.74
(vi) Amount financed by surplus as at (iii) above	Nil	317.5	330.42	306.46	473.08
(vii) Balance of capital expenditure deficit	383.3	490.2	600.02	770.72	705.63
Financed by:					
Foreign loans	116.6	357.5	233,83	308.63	422.04
Domestic loans	32.9	2.6	132.14	100.04	60.82
GOJ loans	91.3	55.9	293.50	102.52	134.87
Grants	–	–	85.54	157.32	38.38
Equity	19.8	99.7	118.94	79.30	12.22
Capital Revenue	127.5	138.3	246.95	531.61	699.18
Total	388.1	654.0	1,110.90	1,279.42	1,367.51
Balance	4.8	163.8	510.88	508.70	661.88
Used for:					
(i) GOJ repayment	12.9	11.7	108.72	31.03	139.92
(ii) Working capital	–8.1	172.1	402.16	476.60	521.78

Note: (a) Equity includes conversion of debts to GOJ and local bodies.
(b) GOJ loans include external funds.

Excerpt from consolidated statement of source and application of funds: items 24–28

GOJ Transfers				
24. Loans	293.50	200.38	102.52	134.87
24A Proceeds – NHP divestment (to GOJ)	–	–	–	–63.18
25. Equity	118.94	154.62	79.30	12.04
26. Grants	85.54	–	157.32	38.38
27. Principal repayments	108.72	30.07	32.03	77.73
28. Net	389.26	324.93	307.11	44.38

Source: Public Sector Enterprises (Selected), Estimates of Revenue and Expenditure for the Year ended 31 March 1989, Kingston, 1988.

12 The distributional effects of public enterprise

The first chapter refers to the distributional motivations of public enterprise derived from the development plan strategies in most countries. Here we shall analyse its distributional effects in some detail.[1] The relationship between the size and structure of public enterprise with income distribution will be discussed first. Then follow analyses of effects through wage and other input policies, pricing and the net revenue situation and policies of regional development.

OVERALL RELATIONSHIPS

As the size of public enterprise expands, the profit opportunities of private entrepreneurs are narrowed. And there will be effects of primary income distribution through changes in property ownership in the long run. The investments in public enterprises, most certainly in their initial stages, are made possible mainly through government borrowings. Such borrowings are likely to be at lower than market rates of interest. Assuming that they are invested in such a way that profits accrue, profit opportunities are shifted to the public sector from private persons who become lenders; and their claims are limited to the relatively low interest rates on public borrowings. Even where public enterprises themselves borrow funds from the market, whether under government guarantee or otherwise, their interest payments to private persons would probably be less than the profits they could realise by using those funds themselves.

Figure 12.1 illustrates the point.

P represents the profits earned by the enterprises; *B* represents interest payments on the borrowings by the enterprises; and *A* represents interest payments if the borrowings are by the government. The surpluses diverted from private entrepreneurs for the use of the public sector – either public enterprise or the exchequer – equal the difference between the curves *P* and *B*, if the enterprises borrow directly from the market, or between *P* and *A*, if the funds are borrowed by the government. On the assumption that the diversion is from the relatively rich sections of the community, who subscribe to the government bonds, it has a favourable distributional

Figure 12.1 Profits and interest payments

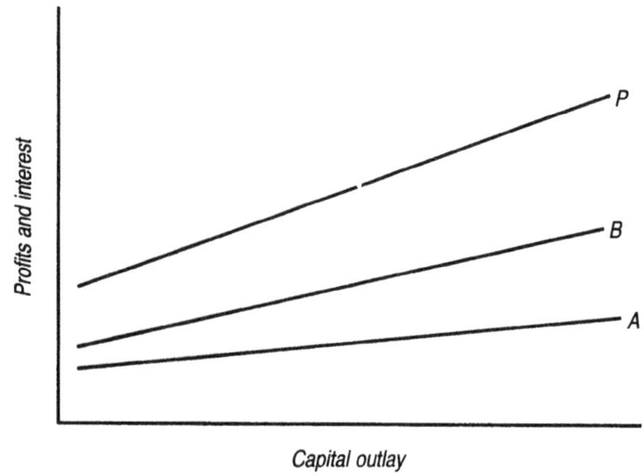

implication. The favourable implication is reinforced if, additionally, the benefits of the diversion go to the relatively low income brackets of the population in some way. (The argument that the private lenders significantly include institutions such as pension funds will be considered in chapter 14. It does not totally refute the point.)

This is the theory. In practice, neither assumption seems to have been sufficiently true. For one thing, the general financial performance of public enterprise has been poor in many countries as shown in chapter 5, so much so that the graph takes a different shape – as in Figure 12.2; and the public exchequer sector tends to finance the interest claims of the lenders from its tax and other incomes. Diversions of the latter to private lenders have an anti-distributional implication; it is true, however, that the private claimants' benefits are limited to the interest rates. If public enterprise makes losses (*L*), the diversion of funds from the public sector to private lenders is represented by the gap between the curves *L* and *A* or *B*. If public enterprises earn a small profit before interest, for example, *P*, the diversion is equal to the gap between the curves *P* and *A* or *B*.

The other assumption, namely, that the distributional benefits reach the lowest income brackets is not invariably valid in practice, as later sections of this chapter show.

Let us look at the nature of investments in public enterprise. Most of these have been slow-yielding in nature. They may be consistent with the development strategy of the country, as argued in chapter 1, but they have two unfavourable distributional consequences in practice. First, the gestation has been for longer than planned in a majority of cases, so much so that profit accrual has been delayed. Thus for a long time the situation has resembled the presentation in Figure 12.2. Second, the elongated gestation has implied a relatively high lock-up of capital; outputs have been slow in

Figure 12.2 Profits/losses and interest payments

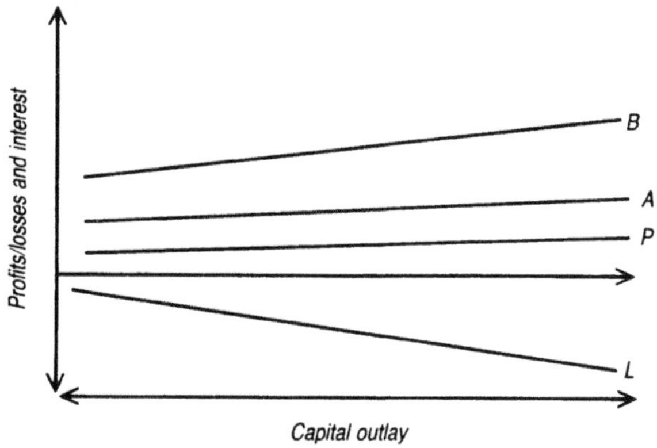

coming, and trends of inflation have been aggravated. The disadvantages of inflation have been particularly serious for the low income brackets, the fixed income groups, and those without incomes, of whom there are many in developing countries, namely, the unemployed.

Further, a significant proportion of public enterprise investments have been in capital intensive sectors. Two consequences relevant to distribution followed. For one thing, employment opportunities have not been high under such investment decisions; in some cases there was no option in respect of the production function. For another, the output–capital ratios have been rather low, so much so that the disadvantage, mentioned earlier, of relatively low output sizes for large capital applications presented itself.

An illustrative calculation of the investment proportions in different sectors of central government enterprises in India, covered by BPE surveys, is presented in Appendix 12.1. The proportion of investments in capital-intensive sectors such as steel, power, petroleum, and heavy chemicals is high; and that in 'consumer goods' industries and 'agro-based' industries very low. To cite another example, Brazil has extensive investments in basic industry and public utilities which have focused on industrial growth rather than on the objective of employment creation.[2]

There is one public sector activity that has a fairly direct effect on employment and, therefore, on the distributional pattern, namely, financial intermediation aimed at small-scale establishments. It enables labour-intensive units to come into being. The less urban they are in location, the more commendable would the income effects be. (Kenya Industrial Estates Ltd is an example of such enterprises.) However, the proportion of such activities in the totality of the public enterprise is very small, even with agricultural corporations included.

Governments have been realising the need for public sector initiative in areas that are very relevant to distributional policies. Whether it can be pursued through public enterprises is, however, debatable, on three grounds:

(a) Many of the activities, for example, those in areas of agriculture and informal activities, are likely to be undertaken by government departments, partly because of their close connection with administrative procedures, and partly because of the deep social and political interests involved.
(b) The scale of activity in most cases may be so small that it may be considered advantageous to promote independent local units, probably as co-operative societies, though certain kinds of overall organisational assistance may be made available either directly from the government or through a contract with specialist agencies.
(c) Recent thinking has raised serious questions about the usefulness of public enterprises in areas where their comparative advantage is nominal or negative. Public sector may be limited to channels of financing and promoting organisational efficiency, instead of being extended to direct operations, in which its comparative advantage is doubtful.

Moreover, the government will find it advantageous to encourage a public enterprise, wherever possible, to contract out some of its operations to small units. The underlying justification is that wage incomes would be higher than if the operations continued to be undertaken by the large enterprise itself. While in some cases the volume of employment may be the same whether within the enterprise or in the small contractee units, it is generally likely that more labour is employed in the latter for doing the work. If it is assumed that the wage rate is lower than in the contracting enterprise, there may be no input disadvantage on balance. If this assumption does not prove correct, or if the quality of work – in any sense – is poor, the inputs would be expensive; and the financial impacts have to be borne by someone – the government, the consumers, or the employees of the enterprise.

WAGE INCOMES

Public enterprises can be, and have been, a vehicle of enhancing wage incomes. If such a result is favoured on distributional grounds, they can be considered an instrument of public policy.

There are many reasons why the wage incomes may be 'high', as compared with the wage benefits accruing from similar enterprise in the private sector:

(a) The wage rates may be high, the more so in a monopoly enterprise[3] (see Appendix 12.2 for an illustration).

(b) Excess labour may be on the pay roll – a common feature of most public enterprises in developing as well as developed countries (for example, in the UK till recently and in France).[4]
(c) Labour productivity may be low, so much so that, even where the wage rates appear to be similar to those prevailing in comparable segments of the economy, the aggregate wage payments made by the enterprise are relatively high for the output produced.
(d) A special version of (a) consists of incentive payments related to a low base of output per person.[5]
(e) Expenditures on 'social welfare' may be high. These include housing and other amenities offered to the employees at rents and charges that meet a small part of the expenses incurred. Increases in such expenditures are claimed by governmental agencies as an indication of the 'significant role of the public enterprises in meeting their social obligations as model employers'.[6]

The benefits of wage incomes in public enterprise appear to be distributionally commendable at first sight. There are two problems, however.

First, there can be serious impacts on the other sections of society which yield the benefits. They include the consumers whose prices bear the burdens of the high wages,[7] the shareholders whose opportunities of dividends are reduced – they may also lose from certain incidental decisions of the enterprise such as reduced provisions of depreciation resulting in poor maintenance of capital, and the national economy in several senses, for example, through a scaling-down of the R & D activities. Where the enterprise is a monopoly and therefore a price-maker not adequately exposed to monopoly control, these disadvantages can persist without remedy for a long time.

Second, conditions of dualism in the economy develop. The employees of public enterprises are not the lowest-income section of society in developing countries. Those in the informal sector, rural labour, and the large numbers of unemployed persons, constitute the lowest income brackets. (For example, between 35 and 40 per cent of the population live below 'the poverty line' in India and Nepal; and the average urban household incomes are twice those in rural areas in Botswana.)[8] Public enterprises tend to divert benefits to a relatively small proportion of the population employed in public enterprise, from the consumer and the taxpayer. In the words of Julius K. Nyerere of Tanzania, it would be 'very unfair . . . if the few people who happened to be lucky enough to get jobs in a place like Williamsons Diamond Mines . . . were to have all the profits of that place paid out to them in wages'.[9]

The sectoral characteristics of public enterprise investments, mentioned earlier, limit similar benefits reaching the lowest income brackets.

Appendix 12.3A illustrates the conditions of dualism in twelve developing countries, and Appendix 12.3B has a similar purport in emphasising that in Peru the employee incomes in public enterprises as a proportion of total wages in the country far exceeded their employment as a proportion of all non-independent employment.

PRICES

Several aspects of pricing relevant to distributional motivations are covered in chapter 6. Here we shall confine ourselves to a few overall comments.

First, a public enterprise which offers some or all its consumers 'low' prices (in relation to costs) with a distributional motivation may not necessarily be conferring on them distributional benefits, if

(a) its cost structure is high through inefficiency;
(b) another enterprise or form of organisation is likely to be in a position to offer better (that is, lower) prices on grounds of greater efficiency and a lower cost structure.

This is an important question which has to be raised from the standpoint of the consumer, who may be neutral to the nature of organisation that provides him with a product. There are examples of operations in some sectors (like road passenger transport in the UK) being offered, on privatisation, at lower prices than those that prevailed when they remained in the public sector. There are severe qualifications to such a conclusion, no doubt. However, one should be circumspect in assuming that apparently low prices on the part of a public enterprise effectively have invariably a distributional effect in every case.

Second, there is an asymmetry in the effects of high wages and low prices, employed as distributional tools. High wages could have the effect of pushing prices upward, but low prices do not push the wages downward, in practice. In some cases losses result or certain expenditures, for example, maintenance, replacements, and R and D, are continuously postponed.

Third, prices kept low when a given consumer group was deemed to be in need of a special benefit through low prices are difficult to raise when it ceases to deserve the low prices. This applies, in particular, to products like electricity and fertilisers. Some of the initially favoured consumers may, in the course of time, be able to pay higher prices; but they may enjoy political support in favour of the prices remaining unenhanced. In other words, their low prices cease to have a distributional justification as time goes by.

Fourth, there is a somewhat unnoticed channel of benefit accrual to preferred sections of the clientele. Financial public enterprises offer loans, without rigorous criteria, to small-scale industrialists and those engaged in the informal sector. The loans might be irrecoverable over time, partly because the lending enterprises, in practice, are not strict in pressing for recoveries, and partly because the borrowers are too 'sick' to repay.[10] Whether the social benefits in this process are real is a debatable question. In any case, the burden of the benefits is borne by the other customers of the lending enterprises or by the taxpayer in the event of their losses.

NET REVENUES

Where a public enterprise ends up with a deficit (and this continues year after year), certain distributional consequences follow. Whether the deficits are the result of distributional motivation or not is immaterial at this point of the discussion. In fact they are often due to a variety of factors not connected with such motivations, as Figure 5.1 in chapter 5 shows. Out of the eleven causes of deficits identified there, only *A*1 and 10(i) to 10(iv) could contain an eventual distributional impact on the community.

First, they have an impact on the government's budget, as shown in chapter 11. Where the consequence is a reduction in capital or revenue expenditures on the part of the exchequer, an increase in taxation, or increased net borrowing, there is damage to certain groups of people affected by the policies of the government. To the extent that it falls on the poorer sections, the distributional effects would be unfavourable.

Second, where the deficits of the enterprises are met from bank credit instead of from the exchequer, for example, in Mauritius, Benin, and Peru in several years, the above consequences unfold themselves over time, since the government has to bail out the banks, probably public sector institutions. In the short run, the customers of the banks suffer, in the sense that their interest payments might increase and/or the funds available for their borrowings decline. These consequences have corresponding distributional effects.

Third, enterprises recording deficits might find it difficult to secure funds for expansions even from the government, though such investments are intrinsically justified on distributional grounds. The real loss devolves on regions or consumers who would have benefited from the expansions or modernisations that have a cost-reduction potential.

Fourth, preserving the distributional benefits of the employees of an enterprise in deficits should not be an overriding consideration. It is possible that not closing it may imply loss to other groups of people – taxpayers and certain groups of consumers. What we need to look for is a trade-off between the two sides. Besides, it is not to be forgotten that, once the enterprise is closed or restructured, the resources can be used in an allocationally more efficient way, so that the initially displaced workers may find employment again. The community might be better off in the long run.

Finally, turning to an enterprise which makes profits, we have to adjudicate the alternative distributional merits of the consumers of the enterprise, whose incomes suffer because of high prices, and the taxpayers, whose incomes might be favourably influenced by corresponding reliefs in tax burdens through the budget. Gains might also accrue to the employees of the enterprise through devices of enhanced wage incomes.

REGIONAL DEVELOPMENT

In several countries, especially the large-sized ones, considerable differences exist in per capita incomes among different regions. Public enterprise is often intended to serve as a means of reducing the disparities.[11] Different methods can be adopted in this regard:

(a) A nation-wide enterprise may offer products at relatively low prices in the underdeveloped regions. The benefits accrue exclusively to those regions if the products are such as cannot be transported to other regions by the initial buyers. Some public utility services like electricity and transport are among the few that satisfy this condition. In other cases administrative restrictions on interregional movement of the products concerned – for example, cement, foodgrains, and fertilisers – may be devised. They may or may not be fully effective.

   Within the region the benefits are spread indiscriminately among all income brackets, unless the sale conditions are so formulated as to restrict the lowest prices to the most deserving among the income brackets.

   Uniform pricing on the part of the nation-wide enterprise has elements of cross-subsidisation, as shown in chapter 10, and conveys income benefits to the underdeveloped regions on the assumption that the costs of supply are relatively high in such regions.

(b) The government may undertake investments in an underdeveloped region, which private entrepreneurs do not consider to be viable. Several results follow:

   (i) They create employment; hence wage incomes in the region increase.

   (ii) They stimulate secondary employment by promoting activities dependent on the major public investments, first, in the servicing sectors and then in allied production sectors. The consumer expenditures which the wage incomes make possible would have a multiplier effect in the course of time.

   (iii) If most of the inputs, other than unskilled labour – for example, equipment and technology – are derived from outside the region, and maintenance expenditures might, for a long time, end up in remittances outside the region, the benefits to the region as supplier of inputs are correspondingly limited.

   North-East Brazil – an underdeveloped region sought to be developed through SUDENE and other means – illustrates the above points.

(iv) If the goods produced are such as are mostly consumed in outside regions, and if they belong to the category of intermediate goods, the multiplier effects of their production in the region are limited.

(v) If the public investments belong to the labour-intensive category and produce goods of direct use in promoting further production activity, possibly through local initiative, the good effects of public enterprise in regional development would be real. However, a serious limitation is experienced in many countries in this respect. The informal sector to which these investments refer, or which these investments seek to promote, have been unviable in a majority of cases, the main reasons being poor marketing or no markets. These have to be remedied before income benefits can be expected to flow from such investments.

The question as to whether an underdeveloped region is to be developed is one of national development strategy; and whether it should be through public enterprise is partly a technical question. Once a decision is made in favour of it, the government has the option of setting up a nation-wide enterprise to subsidise the development of selected regions, or of establishing enterprises specific to the regions. The former method might be more economical on grounds of economies of scale, but it raises the problem of regional cross-subsidisations. The latter method generally calls for a direct subsidy to the region from the federal or regional budget.

There is another difficult question. This concerns the wage rates in the underdeveloped region. The opportunity cost of labour may be lower than in the other regions. If an enterprise is allowed to benefit from this favourable cost factor, the chances of its viability would be greater and quicker than otherwise. But if union pressures or political interests make this difficult and raise the wage rates to levels obtaining in the more developed regions, the enterprise has one prospect less in its favour. And the chances of its competitiveness with other enterprises in the country are correspondingly reduced. Perhaps it is possible for the government to work out an agreement with the workers for wage enhancements to the national levels over a period, under a linkage with the viability of the enterprise.

CONCLUSION

Experience suggests that the distributional results of public enterprises have been essentially in favour of the employees and less so in favour of consumers, and that their operating results have implied a general disadvantage to the taxpayer.

Three types of distributional elements in enterprise operations may be distinguished: (a) those transmitted by the government, (b) those operated by the enterprises themselves, and (c) those that follow the net-revenue position which may not have been due to specific distributional motivations. As suggested in chapters 3 and 13, government preferences should be communicated to the enterprises transparently and be subject to parliamentary accountability. Preferences implemented on enterprise volition should generally be disfavoured; and an attempt should be made, through public control and evaluation, to bring out, adjudicate, and control the distributional implications of enterprise policies, whether deliberate or otherwise.

Except for overriding reasons and reasons of proven economy, income distribution measures should flow from the government budget rather than the enterprise medium.

APPENDIX 12.1

Table 12.1 Investment structure of Indian public enterprises as on 31 March 1989

Sector	*% of total investment*
Enterprises under construction	6.0
Steel	8.7
Minerals and metals	7.3
Coal	11.8
Power	16.5
Petroleum	9.8
Chemicals, fertilisers and pharmaceuticals	8.6
Heavy engineering	2.2
Medium and light engineering	2.3
Transportation equipment	2.8
Consumer goods	2.1
Agro-based	0.07
Textiles	2.3
Trading and marketing	3.2
Transportation services	4.5
Contract and construction	0.5
Industrial development and technical consultancy	0.5
Tourist services	0.2
Financial services	8.4
Telecommunications services	2.5
Cos under Section 25	0.2
Total	100

Source: Bureau of Public Enterprises (1988) *Public Enterprises Survey 1986–87,* vol. 1, New Delhi, pp. 120–1.

APPENDIX 12.2

Table 12.2 Average annual earnings in public and private enterprises in Kenya (£)

Year	*Public enterprise*[1]	*Private enterprise*[2]
1980	753	611
1981	971	689
1982	912	733
1983	1,059	786
1984	1,276	780

Source: Statistical Abstract 1985, Nairobi, p. 242.
Notes:
[1] Parastatal bodies and majority control by the public sector.
[2] Incorporated companies, co-operatives and minority shareholding by the public sector.

APPENDIX 12.3A Dualism in income distribution in twelve developing countries

Figure 12.3 Employment and incomes in the agricultural sector in twelve countries

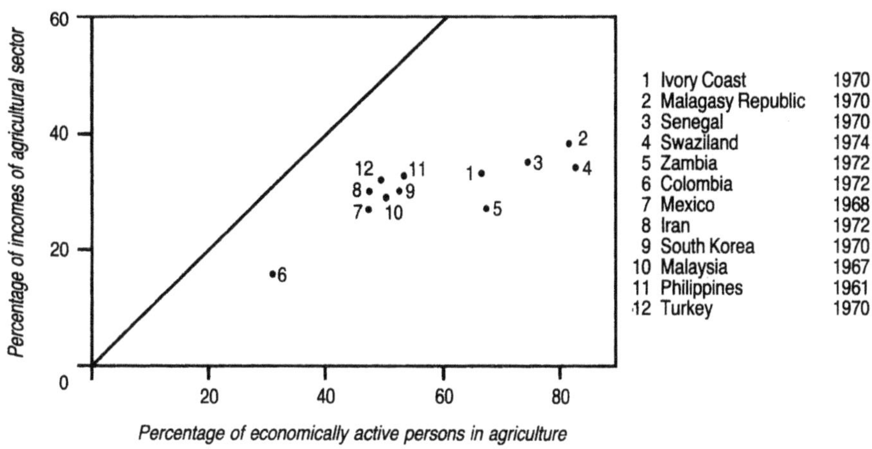

Source: Lecaillon, J. *et al.* (1984) *Income Distribution and Economic Development*, Geneva, ILO, p. 55.

APPENDIX 12.3B Dualism in income distribution in Peru

Figure 12.4 Public enterprise (PE) proportions in employment and wage earnings in Peru (1974–79)

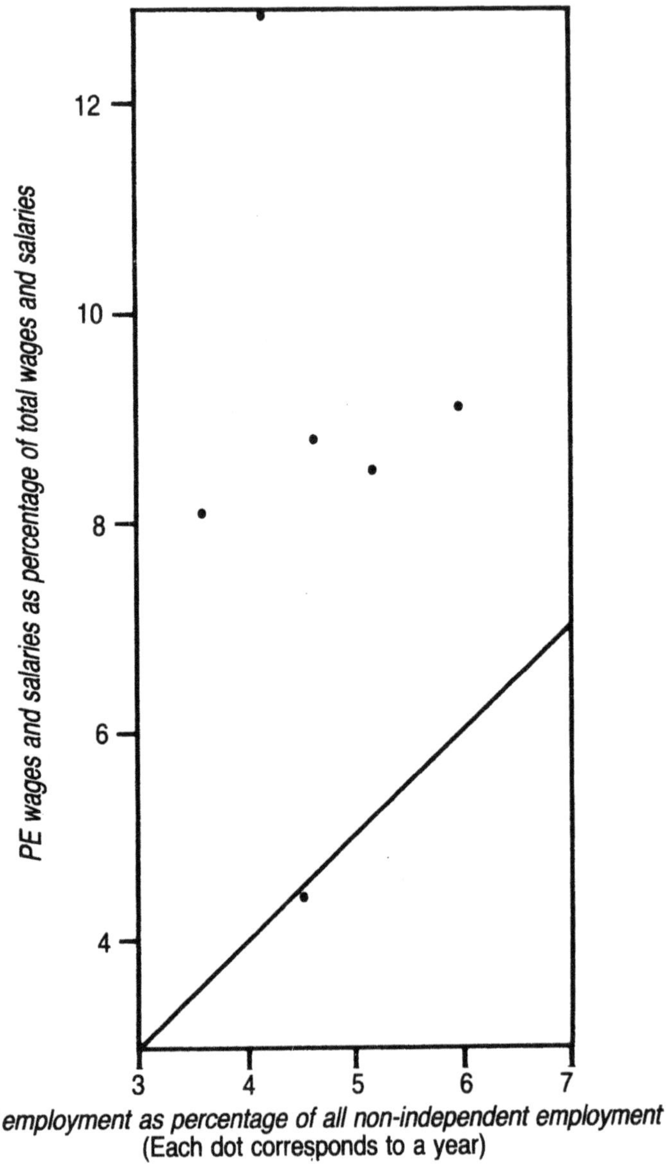

Source: Saulniers, A. H. (1988). *Public Enterprises in Peru: Public Sector Growth and Reform.*

13 Government relationships with public enterprise

The broad theme of this chapter is that public enterprise is, in some senses, a part of public administration. Many previous chapters were concerned with specific issues in the relationships between the government and public enterprises. Here we shall analyse the fundamental aspects of the relationships.[1]

We shall first examine the concept of government relationships and argue for evolving a proper 'system' of relationships. These will be considered in detail next with reference to the substance, the means, and the agencies. An argument will be advanced in the end for some decentralisation of government relationships to other public agencies.

THE CONCEPT OF GOVERNMENT RELATIONSHIPS WITH PUBLIC ENTERPRISES

The government's relationships with public enterprises broadly take the following forms: decision to invest, expand, or divest; directoral and operational involvement; dialogue; monitoring; control, and evaluation.

Decision to invest, expand, or divest

The decision to invest in an activity and set up an enterprise signals the beginning of all further relationships. The substantive aspects of initial investment as well as expansions are covered in chapters 1 and 4, and to some extent in the third section of chapter 11. Divestment is considered in chapter 14.

Directoral and operational involvement

The appointment of directors, the chief executive, and other top personnel, is an important power in the hands of the government, which, together with its interventions in operational matters, heavily impacts on the working of the enterprise. The fourth section of this chapter examines this aspect. Chapter 2 contains some comments on government entrepreneurship.

Dialogue

This signifies that the government undertakes constant consultation with the enterprise management, so that its understanding of the working of the enterprise improves and ensures proper monitoring, control, and evaluation. The dialogue differs from a monologue from the side of the government or from a 'crisis probe'.

Monitoring

This represents a running appraisal of operations, considered in chapter 8.

Control

It ought to signify an attempt by the government to institute an appropriate framework of control over an enterprise or all enterprises, which gives effect to the substantive desiderata under various heads from investment, through operations, to evaluation. In practice, however, mere control instruments (or attitudes) take the place of dialogue, monitoring, evaluation, and substantive judgement. There is extensive evidence of this phenomenon.[2]

Evaluation

This represents a distinctive approach with systemic validity as to content and process, as chapter 9 shows.

Of all the relationships cited above, control assumes a dominant position; and it permeates many others, for example, directoral and managerial involvement.

THE RATIONALE OF GOVERNMENT CONTROL

The simplest argument is that the government is the owner of the enterprise; hence it has the right to control it. This is an institutional and legalistic argument. Unlike in the private sector, there is no clarity of income interest on the part of the government as owner. Besides, the identity of the shareholder is not clear; it is sometimes the ministry of finance, sometimes the sectoral ministry, sometimes an inter-ministerial committee, and sometimes a holding company, on the government's behalf.

The more important arguments rest elsewhere. First, public enterprise lacks several of the market disciplines that ordinarily compel an enterprise to strive for maximum 'efficiency', by whatever definition. Ordinarily it derives its capital from government sources, it can get subsidies and periodic 'gifts' of write-offs of capital; it may enjoy tax exemptions[3] and certain advantages in acquiring inputs or in marketing its outputs; it has little fear of liquidation, exceptions apart; the managers have meagre hopes of personal, not illegal, gain from the profits of the enterprise; and so on. It can be argued, therefore, that public control can be devised as a substitute for market discipline. This proposition is valid to the extent that the substance of control reproduces elements of market discipline, instead of introducing imperfections, without due cause, as discussed in chapter 3.

Among the market insulations enjoyed by a public enterprise there is one that is unique, namely, that inefficient managers stay on.[4] Paradoxically, this is exactly what the disciplines of managerial markets ought to remedy.

Third, public enterprise has to uphold certain basic characteristics of public administration. These include concepts of 'fairness in the administration of funds' – a term used in legislating on what the Auditor-General of Sri Lanka should ensure with reference to every public corporation[5] – uniformity, openness, precedent, amenability to further scrutiny, and parliamentary answerability for moneys spent from public funds. (For example, Canadian public enterprises have to adopt principles of 'equity employment'.) These are good moral values which a variety of control instruments seek to uphold; sometimes they may be adapted specially to the requirements of particular enterprises. Even where the enterprises formulate their own regulations, those are expected to be compatible with the 'public' ethos of their organisation, though it adversely impacts on the requirements of enterprise operations, such as an enterprise-specific bonus system, an undelayed change in prices, rapid recruitment of direly-needed skills, merit-oriented promotions, redeployment of work-force, productivity improvements, changes in the organisational structure, and effective techniques of market promotion.

Fourth, some instruments of public control originate in the fact that effective internal control systems do not exist in several public enterprises.[6] The government steps in to fill the gaps. It would be an uphill task for the better-managed enterprises, which have developed good systems of internal control over time, to earn relief from standardised external controls. In this way many internal controls are externalised into public controls routinely applicable to all or most enterprises. A classic example of this process may be drawn from Nigeria where the management practices in major public enterprises (such as the Nigerian Railways Corporations, Nigeria Airways Corporation, Nigerian Ports Authority, and Electricity Corporation of Nigeria) were so defective and unsystematic (in the 1960s) that the government was prompted to introduce public control over personnel and purchase matters by establishing the Statutory Corporations Service Commission and the Statutory Corporations Tenders Board, respectively. (These bodies were abolished by the mid-1970s.)

Finally, controls are exercised so as to ensure that the enterprises operate consistently with macro policies. The argument has relevance to developed countries also. In the UK, for example, different governments have visualised the role of public enterprises as 'an instrument for curbing inflation', 'the maintenance of jobs at all costs', 'to improve or modernise an industry', 'to achieve co-ordination among competing services', 'to ensure public safety', 'to stimulate economic planning', 'to protect the public against exploitation by private monopolies', and 'to rescue industries in danger of collapse';[7] and corresponding controls on investments, prices, rate of growth or contraction, and input policies have been designed from time to time. The NEDO Report in 1976 indicates how the 'large and politically sensitive issues of policy raised by the nationalised industries' have made the government 'more interventionist' during the 1970s.[8] The heavily subsidised passenger operations of VIA Rail Canada Inc. are another illustration. In France and Ireland public enterprises have been used as tools of government policy.[9]

To conclude: While the arguments for government control are individually valid, they conflict with one another in respect of their impact on enterprise efficiency. Where the impact of a control instrument is unfavourable to the enterprise, the suggestions of chapter 3 should be carefully followed.

THE SUBSTANCE OF THE RELATIONSHIPS

The efficacy of the government's relationships with public enterprises depends fundamentally on their substance. Means are best when there is clarity on what they seek to achieve; and agencies for implementing the relationships can appropriately follow.[10] Experience suggests that the sequence has been in the reverse order and that governments have been unduly concerned with 'who' controls, and by what means, rather than with the criteria of relationships. Substance is linked most with economic issues (macro and micro); means with the logistics of effective implementation, and agencies with institutional issues in achieving the best results.

Figure 13.1 provides a total perspective of the substantive issues implicit in the relationships. A control structure which pays little regard to them or to their mutual impacts represents a poor version of the relationships.

The debate on whether 'major policy' can be distinguished from 'operations' or 'means' is a familiar one. The purpose of the distinction here is limited to suggesting that items I and III are nearer to the 'publicness' of the enterprises, and item II to their enterprise characteristics. However, problems of control arise because the government may find it necessary to extend control to item II in order that its aims under item I are realised.

As most of the items in the figure have been discussed in other chapters in detail, comments at this point will be limited to indicating, briefly, the substance of the control context under each head.

Figure 13.1 The substance of government relationships with public enterprises

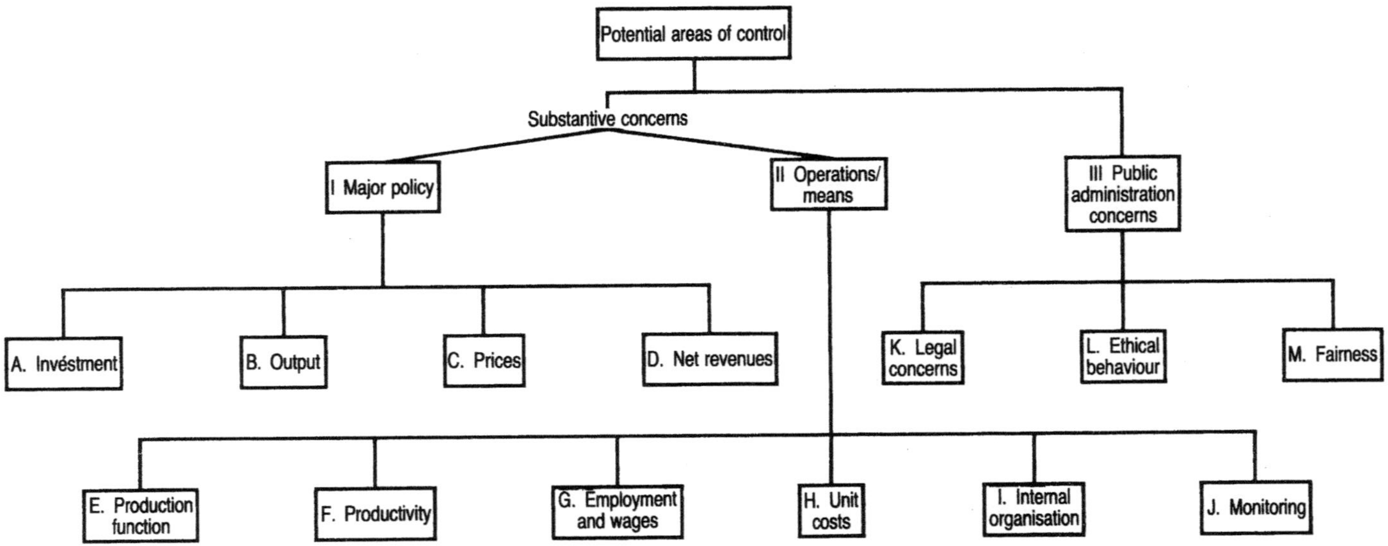

I Major policy

A Investment

Control should be so designed (in terms of instruments and agencies) as to ensure the following:

(a) that the investment criteria considered appropriate in a given case are strictly followed in practice and are not defeated by faulty procedures between the investment decision and the commissioning of the plant;
(b) that the government communicates to all enterprises uniform test discount rates, shadow prices for foreign exchange resources, and estimates of inflationary price changes anticipated over a long enough period, for use in preparing project feasibility studies;
(c) that every investment proceeds in full recognition of its opportunity costs;
(d) that plough-backs of profit attract the same attention of the government as other channels of financing capital expenditures;
(e) that the timing of borrowings from the capital markets is proper on macro considerations;
(f) that direct foreign borrowings by an enterprise are agreed with the ministry of finance; and
(g) that contingency plans are worked out to take care of any shortfall in the availability of needed funds.

Practice varies widely from these postulates.[11]

Many countries have made attempts to tighten public investment procedures (for example, the UK, India, and Kenya) without much success. There have been 'considerable variations' in the practices of different ministries in the UK;[12] and doubts are expressed as to whether the control arrangements are effective enough to avoid misallocation of resources.[13] Appendix 13.2 shows the elaborate technical focus of investment approval in India; yet many reports of the (Parliamentary) Committee on Public Undertakings and the Comptroller and Auditor-General bring out the serious weaknesses in government interface that persist in this area.[14] In countries like Kenya the data demanded are good, in theory, but difficult to produce.[15]

B Output

The following are the important aspects of output which the control system should cover:

(a) where the government determines that the output of an enterprise ought not to fall below a specified size, or its major segments are distinguished and their sizes quantified, or where the size of output is set in terms of the location of activity in the case of non-transportable products;

(b) where intra-sectoral considerations dictate the need for stipulating the size, mix, and location of its output, for example, in the case of coal or gas or electricity;

(c) where adequate provision should be made for ensuring the quality of output as per specified technical and other consumer-oriented standards, particularly in the case of public utilities and from the angle of environmental requirements.

C Prices

Controls in this area have to ensure:

(a) that they do not unduly restrict enterprise autonomy in determining its price structures;

(b) that any preferred basis of pricing – for example, average cost or marginal cost (long run) or any preferred pattern of cross-subsidisations, for example, as between domestic and industrial consumers of electricity, or low fertiliser prices for farmers owning two acres of land or less – is strictly given effect to;

(c) that the pricing policies of an enterprise are the best in reaching agreed targets; and

(d) that the pricing policies do not represent an abuse of monopoly power, where the enterprise enjoys it.

D Net revenues

The approach of control should be to ensure that:

(a) no less or more than a desired amount should be earned over a period of years; and

(b) that transfer of some profit to the exchequer takes place.

II Operations/means

Broadly, the areas of operations mentioned in the chart should be left to the autonomous managerial initiative of individual enterprises, and any macro constraints should be transparently communicated to them.

E Production function

Investment controls already influence the production function. If any additional impacts are desired from time to time, the full sequence of their consequences have to be worked out and controls in the affected area suitably formulated; for example, the effects on productivity and unit cost.

F Productivity

The aim should be to ensure improvements in productivity. For instance, external controls may be necessary to prevent an enterprise from working on a low productivity base in introducing incentives and to insist on linking wage determinations with productivity.

G Employment and wages

Controls which prevent enterprises from pursuing economical employees and wage policies must be minimised. Where they prove necessary, the government should own its interventions and provide for the necessary compensations. On the other hand, where a monopolistic enterprise indifferently adopts policies which prove disadvantageous to the consumer, the government should introduce appropriate preventive controls.

H Unit costs

Controls insisting on a reduction in unit costs from year to year have to depend on the individual circumstances of the enterprises, for example, opportunities of improved utilisation of capacity, scope for reduction in the consumption of energy, better deployment of manpower, and a thoroughly market-oriented product mix. Further, they should be consistent with the fact that the costs concerned are within managerial control.

Controls in this area have to address a basic question: how real is the concept of unit cost in practice? Where the output is homogeneous, it is. Where it is heterogeneous, it can only be meaningful in terms of the unit cost, product by product. Only then can cost-related pricing be insisted upon; and opportunities of cost reduction, identified product by product can be fully explored.

I Internal organisation

In theory, matters of internal management should be outside the purview of external control. But there are several circumstances in which the latter is necessary.

First, where an enterprise is large in size or is monopolistic, organisation below the apex level tends to be a matter of concern to the government. For instance, should it be a monolith (like GIHOC of Ghana till recently or Bharat Heavy Electricals in India) or broken into separate units (as illustrated by periodic hiving-off of activities from INDECO in Zambia), or given the form of a holding company with many subsidiary companies (for example, Renault of France and IRI of Italy)? (See chapter 2 for comments on this question.)

Second, controls have to ensure that a large enterprise conducts inter-divisional transfers of inputs and outputs on the basis of economic costing, instead of practising disguised cross-subsidisations.

Third, control may be necessary for promoting managerial decentralisation to the utmost extent, consistent with economy and efficiency.[16] This would be the best source of managerial growth in the long run – a point of particular interest to developing countries.

Government interventions in internal management structures should, by and large, be limited to questions of top organisation and size and to insistence on efficient methods of internal organisation. British Steel Corporation provides an interesting illustration. The nationalising Act (1967) required the Corporation to present a scheme of organisation for the minister's approval; the minister could at any time ask it to review the organisation, and it could not revise its organisation without obtaining the minister's consent and consulting the trade unions.[17] An important reason for these provisions is that its organisational structure was 'capable of having regional and political implications, impinging on Scottish and Welsh Devolution, for example'.[18]

J Monitoring

The limited role of government intervention in monitoring an individual enterprise, as explained in chapter 8, should not be overextended with a plethora of unnecessary controls.[19]

III Public administration concerns

This term is in the nature of a shorthand expression relating to the code of conduct in public service. Chapter 9 refers to this from the evaluation standpoint.

K Legal concerns

These relate to laws enacted to give effect to substantive intentions: for example, the content of financial statements, their submission for audit, and consultation with the government before closing down a major plant.

L Ethical behaviour

Corruption and nepotism call for control. Objectionable in themselves, they attract the glare of publicity when they refer to the public sector. It is not managers alone but civil servants and ministers as well, that deserve a probe on occasion, as with Air Zimbabwe (in 1986).[20]

M Fairness

It is argued that, since public enterprises are a part of the public sector, the conventions applying to the latter should also apply to them. Purchases and staff procedures are usually brought under the patterns of control that are associated with departmental activities, for example, in Nigeria, and Trinidad and Tobago, and the Auditor-General is usually empowered to audit the enterprises. (The UK is a notable exception.) An extreme version of the concept of public-sector uniformities is found in India where the highest Court has declared that employees in public enterprises have the same fundamental rights of job security as government employees. Such a view overemphasises the 'public' aspect at the cost of the 'enterprise' aspect.[21]

Two concluding observations may be made. First, this section delineates the substance of external control. It does not suggest that the control should be exercised wholly by the ministries. The fifth and sixth sections look at this question. Second, the fact that many substantive issues tend to be covered by external control makes *B*-level evaluation important. The substance of evaluation suggested in chapter 9 hints at the close connection between it and the areas of external control outlined in this section.

THE MEANS OF IMPLEMENTING THE RELATIONSHIPS

The substantive concerns of control outlined in the previous section apply to all public enterprises irrespective of the organisational form (departmental enterprise, public corporations, and government companies). The means of implementing government relationships may be classified under the following heads:

Legislation
Departmental interventions:
  (a) Structured
  (b) Unstructured
Appointment of boards of directors and top managers

Legislation

There can be an overall Act governing all public enterprises. But it can only cover broad organisational matters such as organisation, board of directors, minister's powers in a general way, presentation of accounts and audit arrangements. It would have the value of establishing some uniformity in the government's interface with all public enterprises. Or else, wide differences might exist, without reason. These may be illustrated with reference to the reporting requirements of public enterprises in Australia, some of them having no obligation at all to report to parliament or to the minister, since 1979.[22]

We may draw an illustration from another country. According to the Tanzania Audit Corporation, companies under the Companies Ordinance, unlike public corporations, do not have their account and reports tabled in parliament (Report for 1980).

An overall Act exists in a few countries only. Tanzania has the Public Corporations Act of 1969, the Presidential Circular no. 1 of 1970, and the Parastatal Organisations (Modification of Management Provisions) Act of 1976. Kenya passed the State Corporations Act in 1986. Sri Lanka has three overall Acts respectively for industrial, trading, and agricultural corporations (1957, 1970 and 1972), besides the important provisions of Part II of the Finance Act of 1971 applicable to all public enterprises. India has overall sectoral Acts with reference to the state-level corporations in road transport, warehousing, and industrial finance. Somalia issued Law no. 16 and Decree 74 in 1970 specifying the managerial structures including the formation of a management committee and a labour committee. Other Laws (58 of 1972 and 17 of 1974) dealt with the finances of non-financial enterprises and the minister's powers. Canada's Financial Administration Act, amended in 1984, applies to all Crown Corporations as regards budgets, corporate plans, audit, and minister's powers.

The law on democratisation passed in France in 1983 is another example of an overall Act (with many enterprise exceptions). It deals mainly with matters of organisation, including board formation.

With such exceptions, there has been no attempt in most countries to enact comprehensive legislation governing all public enterprises. Two disadvantages followed – departmental organisations, public corporations, and government companies have come under different patterns of governmental interface, for no other reason than their legal form; and even among the enterprises within one of these categories, significant differences exist in the government's interface with them.

All nationalised industries in the UK, and some of the earliest in many other countries, were established under individual Acts. In theory, there is a merit in this method. The specific features of the industry concerned and the circumstances of the markets encountered by the enterprise can be given due attention while drafting the legislation. Where the enterprise is a public utility or has monopoly potential, extra-enterprise objectives may be important, and can be suitably provided for in somewhat tailored terms – especially as regarding cross-subsidisations and 'duties' towards consumers.

However, most of the enterprise-specific Acts have fallen short of providing proper enterprise-specific answers in major matters such as pricing and net revenues. Many of them have turned out to be replicas of one another. From a close review of the enterprise-specific Acts in a broad regional spectrum, for example, the UK, India, Kenya, Tanzania, Malaysia, Pakistan, Sri Lanka, Papua New Guinea, Trinidad and Tobago, and Barbados, we can draw the following conclusions:

The Acts have not given adequate attention to several of the substantive concerns of control mentioned in the previous section. Appendix 13.3 provides a selective illustration. The best coverage is found in the UK Acts; even these are not definitive on issues like investment criteria, pricing, unit cost, and net revenues. Many such issues had to be addressed – and were – in the course of time through governmental stipulations outside the Acts themselves. (The 'not-less-than' provision is among the few emulations of the UK Acts in many other countries,[23] though not all Acts invariably contain even this clause.)

Some improvements in legislative coverage could be found in the recent Acts in the UK, as compared with the 1945-era Acts. For example, the Airports Authority Act passed in 1965 empowered the minister to 'require the whole or any part' of the surplus to be paid to the exchequer (section 3(7) and (8)). The 1972 Gas Act made such a power of the minister conditional on the Corporation's reserves exceeding 10 per cent of the value of its net assets at the beginning of the year (section 16). The Act governing the Aircraft and Shipbuilding Industries clearly provided for the minister's powers to set financial duties 'from time to time ... with the approval of the Treasury and after consultation with the Corporation concerned' (section 10 (1)). The 1981 Act on British Telecommunications empowered the minister to make 'different determinations' 'for different periods' 'in relation to different assets and activities' (section 24). Section 25 regarding his powers in the area of reserve allocation is similarly of interest from the standpoint of economic logic.

Sri Lanka, among developing countries, illustrates some improvements in legislation over time. Part II of the Finance Act no. 38 of 1971 introduced financial control in such areas as net revenues, surplus disposal, capital expenditure, budgets, aggregate borrowings, foreign exchange liabilities, and subsidies for non-commercial pricing policies. The provisions have significant omissions, though (for example, they do not prevent cross-subsidisations).

On the whole, changes in legislation in most countries referred mainly to broad financial matters. Output, cost, productivity, employment, internal organisation, and monitoring generally remain unsatisfactorily dealt with. Even the 'financial' changes referred mainly to the minister's powers regarding budgets and capital expenditures but left the more difficult issues of pricing, self-financing, and budget-enterprise link inadequately touched.

The statutes are particularly unsatisfactory in defining the duties of the enterprise. (This has to be the trump card of an enterprise-specific Act!) Size, product mix, location of activity, conditions of supply and questions like 'When must an enterprise provide a supply and when can it refuse?' and 'What are the relationships between a physical duty and pricing or net revenues?', require statutory guidelines, where an enterprise-specific Act exists. It is said with reference to the UK Acts that not only these are, broadly, absent, but 'some nationalised industry legislation specifically excludes the power of juridical review in respect of their duties'. Besides, many duties are expressed in such vague terms as to approximate 'duties of imperfect obligation' and are thus 'unenforceable at law'. For instance, the

Post Office Act 1969 'provides little guidance on the definition and extent of public service obligations'.[24]

'Duties' inadequately touched by the Acts may be illustrated from Kenya. The Kenya Meat Commission Act makes the Commission a buyer of last resort of cattle, but does not indicate what this means precisely. Its buying obligations during the drought of 1985 aggravated its already precarious financial condition. The Kenya Tea Development Authority does not define the limits to its leaf-buying activity in terms of intake at a buying centre.

The statutory requirements involving the minister and other government agencies are variously worded in the Acts (see Appendix 13.4 relating to the 1981 British Telecommunications Act, the State Industrial Corporation Act of 1957 of Sri Lanka, and the State Corporations Act of Kenya, for illustration):

(i) The minister 'shall' take a specified action, for example, he shall determine the financial duty of the enterprise (section 10 of the Aircraft and Shipbuilding Industries Act 1977, in the UK).

(ii) The minister 'may' take a specified action, for example, he may 'from time to time determine' the financial duty of the enterprise (section 24 (1) of the Kenya Railways Corporation Act).

(iii) The minister's power has to be exercised under a statutory guideline, for example, his determination of the financial duty of the enterprise should take the form of 'a percentage annual return on the value of assets' (the Kenya Posts and Telecommunications Act).

(iv) The minister 'has to consult' the board before taking an action, for example, giving directions against undue preference (section 6 (5) of the British Telecommunications Act 1981). There is a vivid provision on the nature and process of dialogue between the minister and the board, in the Commonwealth Banks Act 1965 of Australia (see Appendix 13.5). On the other hand, the Kenyan Acts, with a rare exception in the Kenya Tourist Development Corporation Act, do not require the minister to consult the board before issuing a general or specific direction.

(v) The minister has to 'approve' the board's proposals, for example, a general programme of substantial outlay on capital account (section 6 (10) of the British Telecommunications Act).

(vi) The sectoral minister can act 'with' the Treasury's approval. Several financial provisions belong to this category.

(vii) The finance minister has 'direct' powers in some cases, for example, he may 'require' that his recommendation be obtained before the corporate plan or amendment to it is submitted to the Governor in Council (the Financial Administration Act (1985) in Canada; also under the State Corporations Act 1986 in Kenya).

(viii) The minister should 'lay' the annual report of the enterprise before

> parliament. A few Acts (for example, Electricity and Gas in the UK) require him to lay before parliament an annual report on the performance of his functions.

In general, the UK Acts do not confer direct powers on the Treasury, though it has substantial control in many ways. In several African countries there is a clear dichotomy of powers between the president and the minister.

It is important that the Acts provide for the accountability of the minister to parliament. They should insist on the inclusion of all information on government interventions in the annual report of the enterprise on the understanding that the managers would be held responsible for all results that are not attributable to the published interventions. Likewise, there should be a general law requiring ministers to present to parliament annual reports on the actions they have taken under the Acts. These would enable parliament to adjudge their role in impacting on the performance of public enterprises. A fairly uniform format would be desirable for all ministries, covering the following issues: appointment of boards, top managers, and auditors; corporate plans; budgets: capital and revenue; pricing; borrowings; financial and other targets; disposal of net profit and self-financing; foreign exchange transactions; formation of subsidiaries; major organisational changes; major changes in work-force; incentive schemes; technology development and R & D; directives; pension schemes; and consumer affairs.

Such an annual report by each minister who has public enterprises under his jurisdiction should cover not only enterprises governed by specific Acts but all enterprises, including government companies.

At this point we shall look at certain problems of control specific to government companies. These are governed, along with private sector companies, by the Companies Act. The focus of this Act is on the organisation and management of an enterprise as a corporate entity, protecting the shareholders and the creditors, providing for adequate disclosure, preventing malpractices and mismanagement, orderly expansion or contraction of capital under well-defined legal procedures, winding up, and so on. It is not intended to deal with the substantive issues of any particular industry or enterprise, nor with questions of special interest to public enterprises, though special provisions applicable to them can be inserted, like section 619 of the Indian Company Act, covering the audit of government companies. The government company is governed by its memorandum and articles of association which are 'internal' documents and do not attract the notice of parliament,[25] and the power to change them belongs to the shareholders, that is, the government. It escapes parliamentary accountability far more easily than a public corporation with a specific Act does. The disadvantage could be so serious that the Estimates Committee of Indian Parliament observed many years ago that:

> all wholly state-owned public undertakings should generally be in the form of statutory corporations or, when required for special reasons, in the form of departmental undertakings; and the company form should be an exception resorted to only for organisations of a specified nature.[26]

(India has hundreds of government companies.)

More recently the Administrative Reforms Committee in Sri Lanka emphasised the desirability of the corporation form under a specific Act for each 'infrastructural' activity (Report no. 10, Colombo, 1988, p. 20).

It is doubtful if public corporations or their parent ministries have been more accountable to parliament and the public than government companies and their parent ministries. The desirable solution in this regard consists of an overall legal requirement, as suggested earlier in this section, that the minister shall lay before parliament an annual statement of all his interventions in public enterprises attached to his ministry – public corporations or companies. And the accountability of the enterprises can only be ensured through a proper stipulation of criteria they are expected to satisfy, whether they are public corporations or companies.

Departmental interventions

This section refers to interventions from ministers and/or departments, of which some have direct sanction in the Acts or articles of association and some might not. These can be of two kinds: structured interventions and unstructured interventions. The former are systematic and transparent, while the latter are *ad hoc* and/or informal.

Structured interventions

Issue of directives:

It would be ideal to limit these to broad issues of national interest.[27] Specific directives should be an exception – a principle not universally followed.[28] Some Australian Acts specify the areas in which directions cannot be issued, for example, directions on rates of postage or fees (section 8 of the Postal Services act 1975), and directions on rentals or charges (section 7 of the Telecommunications Act 1975). The broad principle is that where an extra-enterprise objective is sought to be realised, which the enterprise by itself does not undertake, a directive may be given, after consulting the board, and it should be published in its annual report and presented to parliament. The more specific the directive, the more necessary to demonstrate that it is not based on questionable grounds, political or personal.

Control of the annual budget:

Legal requirements vary in this respect from country to country or from enterprise to enterprise within the same country. In practice the annual budget is presented to the government in most cases for its approval.[29] Whatever the legal phraseology in this respect, the 'budget link' discussed in chapter 11 confers on the government *de facto* powers of approval, the more so in the case of losing enterprises. Strictly, what needs government approval is the net revenue estimate, especially when it is negative, and the cash transfer between the enterprise and the exchequer has to be agreed *ex ante,* if it is already not governed by any set formula. Subject to such a bottom line, it is desirable to give the enterprise adequate autonomy to formulate its own budget, vary it as conditions require, and constantly exercise initiative in the direction of improving the financial results. The more rigorous the budget control, the greater the responsibility of the government itself for the results.

Target determination:

As may be seen from chapter 7, this comes at the end of extensive substantive preparation concerning the objectives, markets, investment criteria, and pricing principles.

Programme contracts or memoranda of understanding:

These have the same significance as 'target determination', above, in the control context.

Corporate planning:

The corporate plan of a public enterprise is a document that reflects its operating and investment plans over a period, longer than that for the two items above; and it must be agreed with the government. It presupposes continuous dialogue between the two sides, the parent and the finance ministries playing their due role in the delineation of the content of the plan. The planning ministry's attention may also be necessary on certain items involving investments and inter-industry relationships.

The corporate plan should cover the following aspects: the objectives of the enterprise – commercial as well as extra-enterprise; the output: size, mix, regional spread, and quality; cost economies and pricing: any deviations from the cost basis, cross-subsidisations, limits to price enhancements; net revenues, self-financing, and payments to the exchequer; expansion plan, in the aggregate and in regional and productwise breakdown – or contractions; sources of finance for expansions; major organisational matters, including retrenchments, employee participation in management and training; prominent questions of inter-industry relationships; consumer orientation; technology and R & D; and foreign capital and managerial skills. The corporate plan should be in the nature of a roving plan; but the changes from year to year should not be so great either quantitatively or qualitatively as to make it an ineffective document.

The corporate plan can have 'a central place in the relationships' between a public enterprise and the government, as stated in the White Paper (Cmnd 7131) in the UK in 1978, thirty years after the first nationalisation Acts took effect. It is an exacting document, which is of value not only to the enterprise in respect of its operations but to the economy in postulating its role in the totality of business activity in the country. It can also have a political value *vis-à-vis* particular interests.[30] Its utility and effectiveness depend on conditions that are not easy to satisfy, namely, technical expertise in preparing it, reasonable clarity on 'exogenous' factors, definiteness within the government as to the objectives of a given enterprise, and commitment on its part to honour the plan. Where economic and political factors seriously affect these conditions, the corporate plan ends up as a decorative piece yielding to conflicting instruments of control which pay little regard to its contents. This is a real problem in many developing countries.

Unstructured interventions

These refer to interventions or interferences for which there is no formal provision in the instruments of government business applicable to public enterprises. They include pressures which are not owned by the minister before parliament,[31] nor published in the annual reports of the enterprise. They can stem from either political preferences or personal interests and reasons of patronage. Top officials may also be the source of such interventions.

The extent of such interventions depends on the political system, though, independently of it, individual ministers and officials may also be able to practise them as long as they are not found out. Enterprise managers may collude, even if passively, in the hope of favours or under fear of losing the job itself – a real risk in many developing countries.

Unstructured interventions can be exploited by the managers themselves for personal ends. A union of illegitimate interests can develop between the managers and their masters.

Appointment of boards of directors and top managers

The powers of the government to appoint the directors of a public enterprise board are an important means of exercising control, the more so when the selection is in favour of persons who are likely to be receptive to the government's wishes.[32] Their term – during 'pleasure' – and remuneration can be so determined as to strengthen this possibility.

Where politicians are included in the boards, either as members or as chairmen, political influence gets internalised at the level of board decisions.[23] The desirability of keeping extra-enterprise considerations strictly external in source and transparent is likely to be compromised.

A general conclusion from empirical studies is that board appointments represent 'patronage rather than expertise'.[34] For example, the appointment process is alleged to be 'intensely political', even in developed countries like Canada[35] and Japan.[36]

Where a minister is on the board, probably as chairman, the potential for external impacts is obvious. Besides, the scope for his informal influence would be immense.

The appointment of civil servants as directors is sought to be justified on the following grounds:

(i) They help in co-ordinating the activities of a public enterprise with government policies and national criteria, since they are supposed to have knowledge of them.
(ii) They eliminate delays in government response to, or approval of, a board decision which needs it.
(iii) Being bound by public service codes, they act 'fairly' and without self-interest.
(iv) In many developing countries which lack directoral skills, civil servants are considered a ready source, and a relatively inexpensive one.

There are unfavourable consequences, however:

(i) It is not certain that they carry to the boardroom clear policies or responses of the government in a transparent manner or at all. Their participation in board discussions does not necessarily represent the kind of enterprise-government dialogue which is desirable. It is possible that they refrain from committing themselves clearly; instead, they play safe by deferring an issue for further consideration or by recommending too frequently that an issue under discussion be referred to the government before a final decision is taken.
(ii) While a civil servant finds himself placed on a board by virtue of his ex-officio position, it is not certain that he has inherent capability for the directorship concerned. Further, his impact on the board is likely to be out of proportion to his competence.
(iii) He can be an easy medium of transmitting a minister's interest, which the minister himself is not prepared to issue as a directive.
(iv) He can ultimately prove restrictive of the initiative of top managers of the enterprise and condition its efficiency which it ought to be an important objective of government interface to promote.

Appointees from the private sector can be useful, if the selection is made on considerations of merit and not patronage, and if the talents and experience of an appointee are relevant to the enterprise concerned. The criteria of selection mentioned in most Acts are vague and permit of almost any person; for example,

> from amongst persons appearing to be qualified as having wide experience of and shown capacity in matters relating to banking, manufacturing, housing, commerce, finance, professional or administration, or to be otherwise suitable ... by virtue of their special knowledge and experience. (National Paddy and Rice Authority Act 1971, Malaysia)

Even such a description does not apply to government companies which have no individual governing Acts. It is possible to fit in political patronage or include politicians whom the government wishes to accommodate for some reason extraneous to the interests of the enterprise.

The last category is that of functional or executive directors, drawn from within the enterprise itself. Their technical utility to the board would be at a maximum, once the objectives and targets of the enterprise are set by the government in a transparent manner. It is interesting to note that India has a Public Enterprise Selection Board, set up by the government, for empanelling functional directors.

A board composed exclusively of insiders can have the disadvantage of excessive inbreeding. Hence it is in the interests of efficiency to include in it a sizeable number of non-executive directors so that they can bring into the boardroom considerations and questions that knowledgeable outsiders assume to be important. They can be associated with the audit committee as well. (The Financial Administration Act of Canada places a ceiling – 50 per cent of board – for insiders. In practice, non-executive directors are the dominant proportion.)

Practice varies greatly among countries in respect of board composition. Except for short-lived experiments, the UK has excluded civil servants and representatives of sectional interests as such (like labour) from the boards; and a significant number of executive directors has been the rule with a full-time chairman, for example, 20 out of 20 on the Electricity Council (1987–8), 7 out of 11 in British Coal (1985–6), 10 out of 13 in British Telecom, and 7 out of 11 in the Post Office (1987–8). Tripartite boards are the French method, composed of civil servants, insiders, and consumer interests. In most countries, especially in developing countries, officials constitute a prominent proportion of the boards. Even the chief executives are often drawn from civil service.[37] And the tenures are short in many cases.

It is difficult to standardise the circumstances of an enterprise warranting a high proportion of executive directors, for example, that it is loss-making and hence there is need for a considerable role of the functionals in decision-making. This might precisely be the government's reason for introducing a high proportion of official and other non-executive directors. That the enterprise is on the technological and expansion march is another circumstance which can be used for as well as against a high executive proportion. There is one factor, however, which weighs heavily in favour of executive directors, namely, that many public enterprises have been poor in performance during non-executive dominance on the boards for a long time – not necessarily for that reason alone. A change is likely to improve their performance; and there has gradually been an acute awareness of the need for it in most countries.

Representational boards have a subtle consequence. Whenever they give rise to conflicts of interest and complicate decision-making, the government directors or the ministry itself steps in, overplaying a conflict-resolving role.

In view of the crucial relevance of boards for enterprise efficiency, it would be interesting to look at some evidence on board composition which prejudices the concept of good government interface with public enterprises.

Sixty per cent of the total number of directors of public enterprises of Nepal were government servants (in 1978–9); 18 per cent were drawn from the public enterprise sector; and 22 per cent were from the private sector. Executive directors have been exceptional. In 1988–9 sixteen enterprises out of fifty-three had a chairman-cum-general manager, and six of them were civil servants. The part-time chairman was a civil servant, generally a secretary or additional secretary, in thirty-one enterprises. Boards generally had official majorities, irrespective of the sectoral nature of the enterprises.[38]

In Pakistan twenty-five out of fifty-seven enterprises had civil servants as chairmen in 1981–2, three were retired civil servants, and nine were military personnel.

The state government enterprises in India are dominated by civil servants. In Andhra Pradesh thirty-one out of fifty-five enterprises had for the managing director an Indian Administrative (IAS) or Police Service Officer in 1987; eighteen had an IAS as chairman, and thirteen, a politician. In some cases both the chairman and the managing director were IAS personnel. In Bihar, in 1984–5 twelve out of forty-eight chairmen were members of the state legislature of parliament; six were ministers; eight others were 'active politicians'; nine were civil servants; and three were full-time chairmen-cum-managing directors. In the State of Karnataka,

Table 13.1 Average term of chairman/managing director (State of Karnataka, India)

Average term (1)	*Chairman or managing director* (2)	*Managing director* (3)
Less than 1 year	7	1
1 to 2 years	24	21
2 to 3 years	11	10
3 years and over	4	6

the average term held by a chairman or managing director was as shown in Table 13.1.

In Kenya there is no provision for an executive chairman or chairman-cum-managing director; or for functional directors except for the managing director. Up to five in a board of eleven can be civil servants. The chairman is appointed by the president and the rest by the minister concerned. This has a potential for power clash in the board.

The purpose of the above evidence is to suggest that board appointments have been a vehicle of government influence. Their utility in establishing commendable co-ordination between the government and the enterprises, or in orientating the enterprise towards efficiency, remains unproven. While it would be unrealistic to expect many governments – even in developed countries – to keep civil servants from the boards, some improvements can be effected:

(i) The number of official members should be kept to a bare minimum.
(ii) Official members of the boards should be sent to board meetings with clear instructions on major issues, reflecting the government's views.
(iii) The regulations or articles of association governing the board should indicate the nature of issues on which prior consultation or approval of the government is deemed necessary; and (ii) can take care of this aspect substantially.
(iv) In the course of an inquiry or evaluation of the enterprise, the responsibility of the official members, along with the others, for any composite errors of the board should be presumed as a rule, unless there is specific evidence to the contrary.

There are helpful requirements of a second order too, for example, a different official should not be sent to the board meetings from a ministry every time; official directors should be given some training or orientation in the discharge of their responsibility with knowledge; more than one official should not be appointed to a board from the same department; one should not be nominated to a large number of boards;[39] and after every board meeting the official members should be asked to submit brief reports to their respective superiors on matters of major interest. Further, it is doubtful if the secretary of a ministry should be a member of the board or its (part-time) chairman;[40] at the minimum he would inhibit the autonomy of the managers (see Appendix 13.6 for recent trends in board constitution in some countries).

To conclude:

(a) The appointing prerogative of the government has been so used, in general, as to prejudice enterprise efficiency. It introduces imperfections in the managerial markets.
(b) It is difficult to establish the precise responsibility of the civil servants on the boards for lapses in enterprise efficiency and there seems to be little interest on the part of governments in doing so, either.

(c) In developing countries where the supply of competent directors is limited and the directoral skills of civil servants, overburdened with other and heavier responsibilities, are not plentiful, a 'directoral core', consisting of functional directors, should be created.
(d) The powers of appointment seem to be too heavily concentrated in the highest level of government in *de facto* terms in many developing countries, whatever the written word in this respect.
(e) Board (and top manager) appointments ought not to be used as a device for internalising external control.

THE AGENCIES

This section deals with where control powers and other media of government interface should be located, with the twin objectives of maximising the efficiency of public enterprises and ensuring their public accountability. The first step in the analysis concerns the identity of 'government', a term which we have been using all along. Keeping aside parliament and the Auditor-General, the parent ministry, the finance ministry, some other sectoral ministries like labour, planning and environment, and the president or prime minister, participate in the control process. Three questions arise:

1. What are the areas in which each of them has an interest?
2. Do conflicts arise among them and how can they be resolved?
3. Should a focal or nodal point be set up, in which the government's concerns for public enterprise vest?

With regard to the first question, the parent ministry (the 'sponsoring' ministry, to use the UK term) possesses, by definition, the utmost sectoral knowledge concerning a given enterprise, and can develop specialist competence in monitoring its working. It can co-ordinate between the public and private enterprises in the sector. It can take a good view of the inter-industry relationships relevant to the enterprise in question. It can formulate the patterns of extra-enterprise objectives to be realised from each enterprise in its jurisdiction.

The finance ministry has a major role in the control process, though indirectly in *de jure* terms. The reason rests mainly on the budget link of public enterprises. (In Canada there exists a Treasury Board which is distinct from the ministry of finance, and both have control powers.) Technically, in many countries the government's investments are vested in its name.

Among the other ministries, planning (if one exists separately from finance) has a significant interest in public enterprise operations, partly on financial and physical grounds, since their investments, outputs, employment, and returns have a bearing on development planning.

The president or prime minister may have reason for intervention on grounds of political stability, interregional balance of interests, international relations and, not unimportantly, his personal interests of survival. It is possible that many of his interventions belong to the unstructured category.

With regard to the second question, problems arise from the multiplicity of control interests within the government. Each agency has its own angle. For example, the finance ministry's insistence on a net revenue target and its focus on the 'public expenditure implications' of enterprise operations may be incompatible with the output preferences of the parent ministry. Its efficiency aim may have a different definition from that of the finance ministry (or the Ministry of Labour).

Many parent ministries are inadequately equipped to cope with the requirements of monitoring and control.[41] They let the control initiative pass into the hands of the finance ministry.[42] The initiatives can also pass to the presidency or the prime minister's office, in the name of co-ordination and monitoring. The angle of that office may override the techno-financial criteria relevant to a situation.

With regard to the third question, these problems can be met in several ways:

Inter-ministerial committees

CIPE for economic planning and CIPI for industrial policy in Italy illustrate this method. The former consists of seven ministers, with the prime minister as chairman, and the latter has eight ministers. CIPE expresses an opinion on a public enterprise's proposals of capital expenditure and formulates the criteria for evaluating 'the extra-cost of political origin'.[43] After considering CIPI's recommendations as well as those of the Ministry of State Holdings and the State Court of Accounts, parliament makes allocations, by law, to the 'endowment fund' of enterprises like IRI.

Investment control arrangements in India may be cited as another illustration. Investment proposals are examined by the Public Investment Board (which includes the Secretary (Expenditure) in the Ministry of Finance as chairman, the secretaries of Economic Affairs, Industrial Development, the administrative ministry concerned, the prime minister's office, the Planning Commission, and the Bureau of Public Enterprises) as to their relevance from the angles of finance, technical, economic, and management viability, overall plan objectives, availability of resources and social costs and benefits. Then they go for government approval 'at the highest level'.[44]

Such committees reflect the bargaining strengths of the different parties and run the risk of being considered as too routine in the course of time, the more so if ultimate decisions are seen to be emerging from the president, or prime minister, or the finance minister, without reference to, or flouting, their findings.

A focal agency may be set up at some point in the government

In this case all a government's public enterprise concerns may be concentrated in the agency. This may be of three kinds.

First, a central bureau, whatever its exact name, may be set up, probably in the Ministry of Finance. The Bureau of Public Enterprises in India is a clear example. (It was shifted to the Ministry of Industry in 1986.) Appendix 13.7 shows its functions. Sri Lanka has a Public Enterprise Division, and a powerful Investment Commission was set up in 1989; Nepal has a Corporations Co-ordination Division; Indonesia has a Directorate of State Enterprises; Kenya has a Government Investments Division; and Israel has a Government Companies Authority. Most of these are located in the Ministry of Finance. Such an agency has the merit of looking at public enterprise matters, though from the financial angle on the whole, and advising the parent ministries. It can be a data bank, process facts and figures, and help parent ministries and the Ministry of Finance by making comparable data available for decisional purposes. It can act as a consultant to individual enterprises, if necessary. However, it does not have executive powers; parent ministries tend to keep them and rightly so. Unless the lines of communication are properly evolved and advice is clearly distinguished from approval, enterprise managements would be unclear as to where their allegiance should lie and whom they should look to for a decision. The serious problem that remains is that such a focal point is not automatically in a position to determine the trade-off between the conflicting forces impacting on a public enterprise.

Second, a high-powered body with executive powers may be set up to cover a specified range of functions. The best example is the Standing Committee on Parastatal Organisations (SCOPO) of Tanzania. Its functions include:

(i) the formulation of a training programme for the employees of public enterprises (parastatal organisations);
(ii) the review of salaries and fringe benefits of public enterprise employees, 'to ensure that they are consistent with the salaries and allowances paid to employees in the public service requiring the same skills and qualifications';
(iii) the review and approval of the conditions of secondment from public service to public enterprises;
(iv) the approval of staff transfers between the Central Government and public enterprises; and
(v) review of localisation or indigenisation arrangements.

The effectiveness of such an agency depends on how narrow and homogeneous its functions are. SCOPO's focus on personnel matters illustrates the point. There is a disadvantage, however; an excessive standardisation develops in the control approach; individual managements can have reason to feel frustrated in initiative.[45]

Other examples of this method are the Parastatal Commission in Malawi, to which all public enterprises report, the Public Enterprise Commission in Uganda without executive authority, and the Department of Public Enterprise Administration in the Ministry of Finance in Ethiopia, the Inspectorate of State Corporations and the State Corporations Advisory Committee, both in the president's office in Kenya, and the State Enterprises Commission (SEC) set up in 1987 in Ghana. The SEC has the following wide-ranging functions:

(*a*) to promote within the framework of Government policy, the efficient and profitable operation of the prescribed body;
(*b*) to review the objectives, programmes and plans of the prescribed body and to monitor as well as evaluate their performance in relation to agreed targets;
(*c*) to undertake operational and management audit where necessary with a view to improving the performance of the prescribed body;
(*d*) to transmit Government policies with appropriate guidelines for implementation by the prescribed body;
(*e*) to review the organisational structure and personnel policies and practices of prescribed bodies and advise the Government on the remuneration and other conditions of service of the staff of the prescribed bodies, including incentives and bonuses.
(*f*) to advise Government on the criteria for the establishment of new state enterprises and where necessary advise the sector ministries on state enterprises rationalisation and rehabilitation programmes;
(*g*) to advise Government on the appointment and removal of chief executives or members of Boards or other governing bodies of the prescribed bodies;
(*h*) to examine financial structures and major investment proposals of the prescribed bodies and make appropriate recommendations to Government;
(*i*) to ensure that appropriate dividends are paid to Government by prescribed bodies;
(*j*) to ensure that the prescribed bodies establish internal audit units, corporate planning and management information systems and also to ensure the institution and implementation of managerial and professional training programmes for their staff;
(*k*) to make recommendations on application to the Ministry of Finance and Economic Planning for additional credit, government guarantees, financing of capital expenditure and investment plans, for the prescribed bodies;
(*l*) to provide consultancy services to a prescribed body for an agreed fee which shall be paid into the Consolidated Fund.

(*m*) to perform any other functions which are incidental to the objects of the Commission.

Source: Section 2, State Enterprises' Commission Law, 1987, Accra.

The citation has been purposefully elaborate. It allows us to make comments of general value. The Commission, by itself, is not meant to evolve the 'framework of government policy' (see (a) and (b)). It is essentially a recommendatory body (see (e), (f) (g), (h), and (k)). Its purpose is over-ambitious for a single body (see (b), (c), (h) and (k)). It combines involvement in managerial detail (see (e)), management audit, monitoring, and evaluation, of which most part is best left to other agencies. Monitoring calls for the skills of the sectoral ministries and the Ministry of Finance, and evaluation calls for full-fledged non-governmental attention. Finally, it is doubtful if it can command the necessary technical skills for all its functions so that it can talk on equal terms with major enterprises like the Ghana Industrial Holding Corporation. Apparently it is a non-governmental body set up under a specific law, but its chairman is a minister. (For these reasons, it cannot be considered as a close version of the Public Enterprise Commission suggested in chapter 9.)

Third, a Ministry of Public Enterprise may be set up, bringing together the responsibilities exercised by all the sectoral ministries having public enterprises in their jurisdiction and aimed at ensuring their efficiency. The functions of the minister may be as follows:[46]

(i) appointment (and dismissal) of the members of all the Boards;
(ii) laying down the adopted pricing and investment policies for the industry;
(iii) agreeing on the financial objective that follows from (ii) above;
(iv) reviewing investment programmes and approving investment projects;
(v) approving capital structures and borrowing;
(vi) furthering co-ordination and co-operation between industries in the interest of their commercial efficiency;
(vii) general oversight of the structure and organization of the industries with regard to their efficiency;
(viii) undertaking or making arrangements for efficiency studies;
(ix) approving research programmes, training and education programmes and so on;
(x) approving the forms of the accounts;
(xi) laying annual reports and accounts before parliament; and
(xii) accounting to parliament for all their own activities and answering on the adjournment debates and so on, on the activities of the industries as commercial bodies.

It is argued that the ministry can evolve more consistent relationships with public enterprises than those that emanate from different ministries and implement common techniques of control; that it helps in harmonising the use of expert staff resources in government devoted to public enterprise matters; and that it can present a strong stand to the Treasury and the cabinet on behalf of all public enterprise.

The problems that such a ministry can create may be excerpted from the following observations of the Treasury in the UK before the Select Committee on Nationalised Industries in 1967–8:[47]

> (i) It is not possible 'to separate the responsibility for securing public interests from the responsibility of seeing that the industries are efficiently run'; (ii) ministers should continue to be responsible for sectors, whether they are in public or private ownership; (iii) the new ministry 'would withdraw from the policy-making departments the experience and overall view of their industries which they must have in order to have full regard for the sector of the economy for which they are responsible'; (iv) it would enter into management to an undue extent; and (v) it would have 'such a variety of functions ... that it would be difficult for one ministry to embrace them.

Developing countries present two additional problems: (i) they have such a large number of public enterprises, unlike the few (more or less) public utilities in the UK, that a Ministry of Public Enterprises would be too complex and tend to be in the nature of a Ministry of the National Economy; (ii) the extra-enterprise objectives of public enterprises are quite significant, unlike in the UK, so much so that the major problems of finding a trade-off in objectives remains the role of the sectoral ministries; and the Ministry of Finance remains unrelieved by the advent of the new ministry.

The idea of a separate Ministry of Public Enterprises has not been implemented except in a few countries like Italy, Mexico, Malaysia, Mali, Ivory Coast, and Togo. Its coverage is not total in many cases.[48] The Select Committee's recommendation in favour of such a ministry was rejected by the government in the UK.

To conclude: The question is not one of identifying a single agency of control, but of setting the totality of government relationships on a logical footing.

The relative roles of the finance ministry, the parent ministry, and a 'focal' point, merit particular analysis. The finance ministry's major concern is with the cash flows between the exchequer and a public enterprise, in the short run and in the long run, or with the arithmetic of annual surpluses, investments, and mutual cash transfers. It looks at the enterprise budget from that angle. Its competence is also limited to this task and to the scrutiny of the budget format. It does not extend to a scrutiny of how the surpluses are earned or should be earned, what outputs the enterprise produces or should produce, and what extra-enterprise objectives it is, or should be, assigned. These are enterprise-specific questions within the competence of the parent ministry; and the factors that determine them ought to come within its technical review. The finance ministry is, no doubt, interested in them; but the answers to the above questions should be derived from a dialogue among the parent ministry, the finance ministry, the planning ministry (and any other concerned ministry like labour), and the enterprise, in the shape of agreed objectives, targets, and investment ceilings. It is in this sense of arriving at a focus that the concept of a focal point is valid, but not in the sense of creating a single executive agency for all public enterprises.

Reforms which are triggered by dismay at the financial losses of public enterprises tend to overemphasise budget control by the Ministry of Finance, overlooking the logic of the situation. They are likely to end up as strict financial controls rather than represent proper government relationships with public enterprises. These comments apply in particular to countries which have a large number of public enterprises spread over almost all sectors, carrying heavy extra-enterprise objectives.

Before we proceed to analyse non-government agencies of control, a few observations may be made on two important non-executive wings of the government, namely, the Auditor-General and parliament. Neither is, strictly, a direct control agency.

The Auditor-General

In most countries the Auditor-General (AG) is empowered to audit the accounts of public enterprises. The relevance of the AG to the control system is as follows:

(i) At the minimum he brings out irregularities in the activities of the enterprise and has the healthy effect, in the long run, of controlling their recurrence.
(ii) He produces reliable data, and suggests the necessary adjustments to the net revenue data (see Appendix 5.3).
(iii) He is an arm of parliament and substantially helps the Public Accounts Committee and other committees in their functions *vis-à-vis* public enterprises.
(iv) He can conduct his inquiries in such a way as to bring out, though not deliberately, the responsibility of the ministries for certain results of the enterprise. In this way he helps in adjudicating ministerial accountability.
(v) He has an intangible impact on the managers, for example through his 'ratio analyses'. They develop cost-consciousness and profit-orientation.

Parliament

Parliament can have a control impact, not only through legislation, but through the question hour, debates, receipt of annual and other reports, and committee inquiries (for example, Estimates, Public Accounts, Public Investment and Public Enterprises).[49]

Parliamentary (Committee) criticism generally proves effective, though the Committee's observations are recommendatory. The Committee reports often bring out rich material otherwise not available to the public, and can be an important substantive base for control instruments. Occasionally they bring out the responsibility of the ministries for certain enterprise results. In this way they can help in ensuring ministerial responsibility, though they seem to be doing less yet than they can in this direction. An important area they can usefully explore is the relationship between government policy and ministerial interventions, especially in cases of poor results. Parliament's control impacts would be unfavourable if its attitudes to public enterprises were political and partisan.

DECENTRALISATION OF THE RELATIONSHIPS

We have so far looked at the agencies which are within the government. It would be desirable to decentralise certain aspects of the government's interface to other institutions so that:

(a) the technical work relating to an area of control can be undertaken with expertise free from political pressures;
(b) the government would be obliged to express itself in reasonably clear terms on what is sought to be realised from a non-departmental agency acting on its behalf;
(c) there can be some uniformity in the government's approach through different departments, towards public enterprises; and
(d) the government's energies can be concentrated on strategic decisions of control, instead of being dissipated over activities that can be entrusted to others with advantage.

There are several possibilities of decentralising government control, some obvious and some subtle.

Independent commissions

The government may set up a public agency like CONADE in Peru, MMC in the UK, the Public Utilities Commission in Trinidad and Tobago, the State Corporations Advisory Committee in Kenya, or semi-autonomous agencies like the Experts Advisory Cell in Pakistan, and SCOPO in Tanzania, with statutory powers in specified areas of enterprise operations. They offer the following benefits:

(a) They can develop cross-sectional expertise in specified areas and enrich the control system with institutional memory. They can promote inter-enterprise uniformity, wherever desirable.

(b) They can dispassionately interpret for the government the implications of an extra-enterprise objective and evaluate the factual responses of the enterprises concerned.
(c) They can minimise inappropriate government interventions in enterprise matters which are statutorily within their remit.
(d) They can play a role in improving ministerial accountability to parliament and the public by giving them an 'informed' opportunity to review government actions as against enterprise criteria and the requirements of the markets.

The usefulness of the commissions depends, first, on their composition. If they are dominated by officials, as with SCOPO or the Central Tenders Board of Trinidad and Tobago, their scope for autonomous action tends to be limited.

Second, their utility depends on the nature of functions sought to be covered. When they touch on the public interest or extra-enterprise objectives, the government should give them the necessary guidelines; and they may be constituted as recommendatory rather than mandatory bodies. The MMC in the UK is an apt illustration.

Third, either an agency specific to public enterprise may be created with a set coverage, like the Parastatal Service Commission in Zambia, or the Statutory Corporations Service Commissions and the Central Tenders Board in Nigeria; or public enterprises may be brought within the jurisdiction of a bisectoral agency covering both public and private enterprises. The (former) Price Commission and the MMC in the UK are examples. This method has particular justification where it is important to maintain parity of public interface in the two sectors; and also where the public enterprises are too few to justify an exclusive body for them. Where a problem is specific to public enterprises, it is desirable to set up an exclusive agency for the purpose. For example, pricing as between public enterprises or as between them and government departments, 'which cannot be settled by mutual discussion', may be entrusted to a non-departmental agency set up exclusively for public enterprise. In India such pricing is referred, instead, to '*ad hoc* Pricing Committees' normally chaired by the Director-General of the Bureau of Public Enterprises.[50]

Finally, should all decentralised (control and allied) functions be entrusted to a single agency or to different agencies? The answer depends, broadly, on the homogeneity of the functions to be decentralised. When more than one agency is created, care should be taken to minimise conflicts of jurisdiction among them; or else multiple agencies would create new problems.

Consumer councils

Organised consumer interests can play a part in controlling public enterprises, essentially in second-order matters concerning the availability and quality of the product and the terms of supply. They can fill the gap in legislation regarding the 'duties' of the enterprises, to some extent. They can help in setting 'consumer standards'.[51] Broader issues, which are certainly of interest to them, are, however, more difficult than can be tackled at their level, for example, the price level, cross-subsidisations, and net revenues. Even here their views and complaints supported by facts can be of use to other agencies dealing with such questions.

The UK is about the only country where consumer councils have been set up statutorily for most nationalised industries with functions such as the following: 'considering any matter affecting the interests of consumers of gas generally or any class or description of consumers of gas', 'notifying their conclusions to the Corporation', 'considering any matter referred to them by the Corporation' and 'reporting' to it, and 'considering, and reporting to the Secretary of State on any such matter which may be referred to them' by him (Gas Act 1972, section 10 regarding the National Gas Consumers' Council).

They are funded by the enterprise (for example, see Schedule 3 of the Gas Act 1972) and their annual reports are published. The managements are required to consult them on specified issues including their 'general plans' (for example, the Gas Act 1972, section 10).

The effectiveness of such bodies depends partly on the factual material and analytical expertise they can gather and on the unanimity they can command among the many submarkets into which consumers are divided. There can be different councils for consumers in major markets, for example, industrial consumers and residential consumers of electricity. They can establish good links with the management in the solution of local or specific problems. Where they step into areas in which the enterprise is constrained by overall finance or managerial requirements, or into areas that are the legitimate preserve of the management, clashes arise.

Consumer councils have statutory access to the minister;[52] and this can be a source of strength for them. Their reports can be a sounding board for the government while formulating instruments of control which are of immediate interest to the consumers.

Organisational innovations

The holding company structure can be used, within limits, as a means of decentralising government control. Subject to the earlier comments on holding companies (in chapter 2), we can visualise a holding apex taking over controls which have a management orientation, and which, strictly, ought not to be the aim of the government to assume but are assumed by it because of the serious managerial shortcomings of the operating companies in some cases. The powers of the Guyana State Corporation illustrate the point:

> 'to exercise supervision and control' over the public enterprises; to issue 'general or specific directions' (a) for securing co-ordination of the functions of some or all of the public enterprises; and (b) 'in respect of matters relating to the personnel, including conditions of service, finance, management and organisation of any such public enterprise'.
> (*Public Corporations Act*, Section 5, Georgetown, 1975)

But there is the danger of the holding apex overplaying the role of the government, with two consequences, namely, that it affects the autonomy and long-run efficiency of the operating companies, and that there can be problems in the precise demarcation of the respective roles of the government and the holding apex. The problems may even relate to the power structure *vis-à-vis* the companies. Where the government steps into areas delegated to the holding apex, the situation would be worse than without the holding apex device.

Reference may be made to a change in the interface of the Ministry of Industry with its (more than 150) enterprises in Egypt. Under legislation introduced in 1983, six 'public sector corporations' were set up for the enterprises grouped under food, textiles, metallurgy, engineering, and mining. They act on behalf of the ministry in respect of certain important relationships between the government and the enterprises.

A holding apex may operate as if it were the government where it is composed of ministers. ZIMCO of Zambia is an excellent example. The top board includes ministers, with the president of the country as chairman.

A holding company which serves in effect as a surrogate for the government can have the disadvantage that ministers take decisions at the level of an autonomous organisation, without being directly accountable to parliament, unless suitable devices are formulated for the parliamentary discussion of such events.

Another organisational arrangement with some potential for control decentralisation is the 'policy council', recommended by the NEDO study in 1976 in the UK. This would be above the board of directors, with the following functions: to agree corporate aims and objectives, agree strategic policies necessary for achieving them, endorse corporate plans including annual budgets, and so on, and monitor performance against predetermined policies and criteria.[53] The board will act as the 'executive authority'.

The policy council would be too close to the board and identified with the enterprise to discharge control functions as a delegatee of the government. It might, on the other hand, affect efficiency by interference with management in practice. The nationalised industries in the UK objected to the idea and the government did not accept it.[54]

CONCLUSION

The interface of the government with public enterprise has to be understood in terms of relationships rather than control. Control is one aspect of the relationships, and it can be decentralised, to some extent, in favour of non-departmental public agencies. What is needed is public control as against exclusive control by government departments.

Government relationships have to be implemented on the basis of relevant substantive knowledge of the goals to be realised. Control instruments which are *ad hoc* in nature and affect enterprise inefficiency ought to give way to a properly structured system, in which the determination of objectives and targets and monitoring have an important place.

Since the ministries have extensive powers of controlling public enterprises and influencing their operations, it is essential to devise an effective system of making them accountable to society (parliament). Decentralisation of the control exercise and preserving enterprise autonomy as far as possible are some of the steps that parliament and the public may find useful in this regard. The most potent guarantor of autonomy is, of course, market discipline, provided its lessons are duly taken by the government. Reference may be made to the 'operational measures' indicated as one of the three options under privatisation in chapter 14.

APPENDIX 13.1 Internal/managerial inadequacies of public enterprises

This is an illustrative compilation of the internal/managerial inadequacies of public enterprises, quoted from high-level sources, in Kenya, Pakistan, and India.

A. *Kenya*

The internal management problems include:

(i) a number of parastatals have extended their activities beyond their primary mandates, spreading their management talent too thinly over too many activities;
(ii) second level staff are often poorly selected and inadequately trained;
(iii) responsibilities are often not delegated to qualified staff, resulting in an overworked senior staff and frustration among more junior people;
(iv) discipline in planning, financial and implementation functions is lax, leading to corruption, low morale, and inefficiency;
(v) delays in compiling internal financial data and producing audited financial statements reduce management efficiency and Government ability to evaluate performances; and,
(vi) inadequate planning and control of management services and consultancies.

Source: Report of the Working Party on Government Expenditures, Nairobi, 1982, p. 45.

B. *Pakistan*

Sind Engineering Ltd

Redundant and surplus machines not disposed of. Heavy losses of man hours.
Large inventories, including those of locally-manufactured parts
Defective stores management
Weak marketing organisation; 'non-commercial approach in marketing'
Highly-centralised organisations; managing director had sixteen line managers reporting to him
Excessive personnel
Average employee costs on the high side
Liberal overtime payments
No manager level budgetary control
Poor overall standard of internal audit; internal audit cell not an independent unit

National Fibres Ltd

No proper records of process wastes
Excessive raw material stock levels
Purchase of stores in excess of consumption needs
Dead stock of finished goods not promptly disposed of
Excessive personnel strength

Source: Performance Evaluation of Public Enterprises, Reports of the Auditor-General of Pakistan, vol. I, 1986, Lahore.

Kohat Cement Co. Ltd

Excessive consumption of raw materials, fuel, etc.
Below-capacity operations
Excessive breakdowns
Employees 34 per cent in excess of the provision

Maple Leaf Cement Factory Ltd

A sizeable quantity of obsolete spares
Persistent decrease in capacity utilisation
Rapidly increasing overtime bill, while production per employee declined
Internal audit entrusted to a deputy manager who had no staff
Reports prescribed in the accounting manual not being prepared

Source: Ibid., vol. II (1986).

Kakakhel Industries Ltd

Low capacity utilisation (in soap production)
Heavy stock balances
Production per worker on the decline, though total overtime payments increased

Source: Ibid., vol. III (1986).

C. *India*

1. 'There was no manual laying down the detailed procedure for compilation and maintenance of accounts in 46 companies' (p. 1).

   'In the Delhi State Industries Development Corporation the financial powers were heavily centralised.'

   In the Bharat Leather Corp. Ltd, 'there was no proper laid-down procedure for allowing discounts' (p. 5).

   In Coal India Ltd there was 'lack of uniformity in book keeping in the Regional Sales Offices' (p. 14).

   In the Western Coalfields Ltd, 'proper records for materials issued to contractors were neither maintained nor financial entries therefore passed' (p. 17). 'There was lack of control over payment of wages and accounting thereof' in Kanhan area (p. 17).

   In the Electronics Trade and Technology Development Corp. Ltd, the 'procedure for write-off was not adequate' (p. 22).

   In the Hindustani Steel Works Construction Ltd, 'records relating to hire charges recoverable at the end of the year had not been maintained' (p. 23).

   In the India Tourism Development Corp., 'detailed records of breakages and shortages of crockery, cutlery, pillow-linen, blankets and empties had not been kept' (p. 25).

   In the National Textile Corp. (S. Maharashta) Ltd, 'there was no specific procedure for write-off of non-recoverable debts and advances' (p. 25).

   In the National Textile Corp. (Gujarat) Ltd, 'adequate records for consumption of stores and spare parts' were not maintained (p. 26).
2. 'Property, plant/assets registers were not maintained' in eight enterprises; 'were not reconciled with financial books' in eleven enterprises; 'were not maintained properly' in ten enterprises (pp. 34–40).
3. Stores accounting records had 'various deficiencies' in 23 enterprises (pp. 40–9).
4. 'There was no manual outlining the scope and programme of work for Internal Audit' in forty-five enterprises (p. 51); 'there was no system of internal audit' in two enterprises (p. 52); 'internal audit was not conducted' in ten enterprises (p. 52); 'the existing system of internal audit was not considered to be comprehensive and adequate' in seventeen enterprises (p. 54); in the India Tourism and Development Corp. Ltd, 'there was no system of pricing of stores issued', 'in the cost of raw materials, cost of food consumed by operational staff of catering establishment had been included' (p. 59); in the Fertiliser Corp. of India Ltd, 'internal audit was confined to routine checking of cash transactions, checking of invoices etc.' (p. 61); 'the programme drawn up for internal audit was not fully implemented' in nine enterprises (p. 63); 'follow-up action on points thrown up in internal audit was not adequate' in nine enterprises (p. 65).

5. 'There were large variations between budget estimates and actuals' in twenty-nine enterprises (p. 68); 'there was no system of preparing capital, revenue, production and sales budgets' in ten enterprises (p. 69).
6. 'Targets of production/rated/installed capacity were not achieved' in seventeen enterprises (p. 70).
7. 'No costing system was in operation' in eight enterprises (p. 75). In Coal India Ltd, 'no separate set of cost records to ascertain the cost of production of coal and bricks had been kept' (p. 76). In Braithwaite and Co. Ltd, 'proper accounts indicating cost of each unit of principal products had not been maintained' (p. 77). In forty-six enterprises a 'system of standard costing had not been introduced/standard costs had not been fixed' (p. 79).
8. 'Selling price was less than the cost of production' in thirty-one enterprises (p. 91).
9. 'There was no system of ascertaining idle time for labour and machinery, specifying the reasons therefore' in forty-one enterprises (p. 95).
10. 'Certain equipment, plant and machinery remained idle/uninstalled' in nineteen enterprises (p. 97).
11. 'Norms for manpower were not fixed' in twenty enterprises (p. 102); 'actual strength of manpower was more than sanctioned strength/ norms fixed by the management' in fifteen enterprises (p. 103); 'maximum and minimum limits, re-ordering levels of stores/spare-parts etc. had not been fixed' in fifty-one enterprises (p. 104); 'there was no system of determining periodically surplus/unserviceable/ obsolete stores' in fourteen enterprises (p. 110); 'Stores and spares . . . had not moved for two to three years' in forty-five enterprises (p. 113); 'the surplus/obsolete stores . . . were awaiting disposal' in twenty-nine enterprises (p. 119); there was no 'physical verification' of stores, etc. in many cases (p. 123).
12. 'The system of obtaining confirmation of balances from sundry debtors was not in vogue and/or confirmation of balances had not been obtained from all parties' in sixty enterprises (p. 130). 'A uniform system of allowing credits' did not exist in the Central Inland Water Transport Corp. Ltd (p. 133); 'there was no proper system of allowing credits' in the Delhi State Industries Development Corp. Ltd' (p. 134). Large debts were 'outstanding for three years and above' in seventy-two enterprises (p. 135); 'vigorous efforts were not being made for realisation of debts resulting in increase of doubtful debts . . . there was neither any recovery nor any procedure for write-off was adopted . . . realisations were not effected promptly . . .' in certain enterprises (p. 144).

Source: Report of the Comptroller and Auditor-General of India, Union Government (Commercial) 1983, Part V, New Delhi, 1984.

APPENDIX 13.2 Modalities of approval of investments in public enterprises in India

2.1 Investment proposals for establishment of new projects or for expansion of existing units emanate either from the Ministries/Departments of the Government or from the enterprises desiring expansion and growth. The broad nature of investment is determined by the priorities indicated in the National Plan. Individual investment proposals are required to be in keeping with the overall programme outlined in the plan document. Govt. exercises a measure of control over the size and pattern of investments in the public enterprises by reserving to itself the power to approve capital outlays exceeding certain financial limits. Government also exercises control over such investments through the mechanism of scrutiny and approval of the annual capital budgets of the concerned enterprises.

2.2 The investment proposals are examined by various agencies of the Govt. including the Project Appraisal Division of the Planning Commission, the Plan Finance Division and the Bureau of Public Enterprises from financial, technical, economic and management viability angles. Their relevance to the overall plan objectives, availability of resources, social cost-benefit, etc. are also assessed. All investment proposals exceeding Rs 10 crores require approval of the Govt. at the highest level after these are cleared by the Public Investment Board. The Public Investment Board is constituted with the Secretary (Expenditure) in the Ministry of Finance as Chairman. Its other members include Secretary, Dept. of Economic Affairs, Secretary, Planning Commission, Secretary, Industrial Development, Secretary to the Prime Minister and Secretary of the Administrative Ministry concerned bringing up the investment proposal before the Board. Besides the above, Bureau of Public Enterprises is also represented by Secretary, Dept. of Public Enterprises. The investment proposals ranging between Rs 2 crores to Rs 10 crores are examined and approved by the Expenditure Finance Committee chaired by the

(Rs in crores)

Public enterprise with gross block of	*Power to sanction capital expenditure without prior approval of Government*
Less than Rs 100 crores	Rs 2 crores
Between Rs 100 crores and Rs 200 crores	Rs 4 crores
Above Rs 200 crores	Rs 10 crores

Secretary (Expenditure) where the enterprise concerned does not have the power to incur capital expenditure of the size proposed. In September 1982 the powers of the Board of Directors of public enterprises to sanction capital expenditure were enhanced. At present the powers of the Board of Directors are as indicated above.

2.3 With a view to achieving a greater element of selectivity with emphasis on cost effectiveness and the need for introducing increased disipline in project formulation and appraisal so as to avoid subsequent cost escalations without justifiable reasons, the Public Investment Board Procedure has been modified in August, 1984. As per the modified procedure, it has been decided that only those projects with a financial rate of return and an economic internal rate of return both exceeding 12% should be posed to the Public Investment Board for their consideration. The economic internal rate of return shall be computed as per the existing guide lines, i.e, excluding taxes and duties, adopting a premium of 25% on foreign exchange and shadow pricing for energy costs, transport charges, etc. where necessary.

2.4 In those cases where either the financial rate of return or the economic internal rate of return is over 12%, but the other one falls short of the norm, and the administrative ministry still considers it essential that the project should be taken up for implementation, the reasons therefore should be gone into in detail at the pre-PIB meetings and also set out in the memorandum for the PIB. The PIB shall consider such cases only in exceptional circumstances and that too only if the projects are in the core sector.

2.5 Under no circumstances shall projects with both the financial and economic internal rates of return falling below 12% be considered by the PIB.

2.6 Where the proposals put up to PIB have very high costs in terms of rupees in relation to the amount of foreign exchange saved, in a situation where rupee resources are also scarce, it is important to ensure that the rupee cost of saving foreign exchange is not unduly high. In order to focus attention on this problem, it was stressed that all proposals for consideration of the PIB should contain a calculation of 'Domestic Resource Cost' of saving foreign exchange.

2.7 A number of projects which at the time of approval were found justified on the basis of time and cost schedules as set out in the feasibility reports presented to the PIB, were subsequently seen to have become totally unviable because of inordinate delays in implementation and cost over-runs. In order to bring out impact of such over-runs on the viability of the proposed projects, the Project Appraisal Division of the Planning Commission shall in its appraisal carry out a sensitivity analysis on the internal rates of return for different levels of time and cost over-runs. In respect of undertakings, which have implemented and/or are implementing projects, one of the points in the sensitivity analysis shall be the 'average' delay noticed in the implementation of projects by the undertakings.

2.8 Some of the guidelines already in force were amplified/modified in August, 1984 as indicated below.

2.9 All proposals whether new projects or Revised Cost Estimates to be brought before PIB should first be examined at a pre-PIB meeting taken by the Financial Advisor. Representatives of the concerned division of the Planning Commission and the Ministries/Departments of the Govt. of India like Railways, Dept. of Electronics, Environment etc. concerned with the project should also be associated at the meeting. The minutes of the pre-PIB meeting should be appended to the PIB memorandum. The PIB memo should set out clearly the project cost as well as the phasing, the approved plan outlay and if there is a gap, how it is proposed to bridge the gap. It is necessary to ensure that investment decisions are taken only on the basis of well prepared feasibility reports.

2.10 Where initial investment clearance is given on the basis of feasibility report and not a Detailed Project Report, the administrative ministry should bring to the PIB the firmed up cost estimates along with the detailed project report within a period of one year. In those cases where it is expected that the preparation of the DPR would take more time, the reasons for this should be brought to the notice of the PIB within the stipulated one year period along with the latest cost estimates, the details of scope changes etc. and the PIB will set a fresh date by which the firmed up cost estimates and DPR are to be brought before it for consideration. In respect of all projects approved for implementation on the basis of PIB clearance, the administrative ministry shall send to the BPE and to the PIB Secretariat, a report every quarter reviewing in detail the progress made in their implementation of the project till it is completed.

2.11 Taking into account the need for better preparation of project reports with a greater degree of reliability in regard to cost estimates and time schedules and also the need for adequate funding for pre-investment activities necessary for the preparation of good feasibility reports, in March, 1985, it was decided that project approvals should in future be given in two stages; proposals for preparation of feasibility report being cleared in the first stage and investment decisions being taken at the second stage.

2.12 Proposals for preparation of feasibility reports will be considered by a Committee of the PIB consisting of the Secretary (Expenditure) as the Chairman and the Secretary (Planning Commission) and the Secretary of the administrative ministry concerned as members. The Committee, while clearing such proposals would also authorise the incurring of necessary expenditure for the preliminary activities. When major policy decisions are seen to be involved or where the Committee anticipates that implementation of the project would call for very large investments or where there are major linkages, the Committee may recommend consideration of the proposal by the PIB or seeking approval of the Cabinet Committee of Economic Affairs.

2.13 It was also decided that the administrative ministries themselves can sanction preparation of feasibility reports costing up to 20 lakhs where the project cost is less than Rs 20 crores subject to availability of necessary budget and Plan Provision. All other cases where the cost of FR exceeds 20 lakhs or where the cost of the Project is more than as 20 crores would be placed before the Committee for consideration. This procedure is expected to help expditious preparation of feasibility reports.

Source: Bureau of Public Enterprises (1985), *Public Enterprises Survey 1984–5,* vol. 1, New Delhi, pp. 161–2.

APPENDIX 13.3

Table 13.2 Substantive coverage of public enterprise Acts in the UK, Kenya, and Pakistan

	UK			
Aspect	*Gas Act 1972*	*Br. Shipbuilders Aircraft and Building Industries Act*	*Airports Authority Act*	*Br. Airways Board Act*
A. Investment	Section 5, 17, 18	7(1), 11(7), 13, 15(1)	3(2) (6), 5(1), 7(1)	5, 9, 10(4), 12, 14(b)
B. Output	7(2)(a), 26(1), Schedule 4, 2(1), 3(1), 4(1), 10(1)(4)	2(5)(1), 2(1)(2)	–	–
C. Prices	14, 23(4), 25(5)(3), 4, 12(1)	–	–	–
D. Net revenues	14, 16, 38	10(1)(5)	2(1), 3(5), 15(1)	13(1)(3)(5)
E. Production function	3(3)	–	–	–
F. Productivity	–	–	–	–
G. Employment	3(1), 35	2(8), 5(4), 6(2), 50(1)	Schedule 1(10)(1)	Schedule 1(14)(1)
H. Unit costs	–	–	–	–
I. Internal Organisation	4(1)(3)(4)	5(2)	–	3(1)(3)
J. Monitoring	–	9(1)	–	–

Table 13.2 Continued

	Kenya							Pakistan		
	State Corps Act	*K. Railways Corp Act*	*National Construction Corp Act*	*Kerio Dev. Auth. Act*	*Agr. Dev. Corp Act*	*Agr. Fin. Corp Act*	*Kenya Meat Comm. Act*	*Pakistan Water and Power Dev. Auth. Act*	*Pakistan International Airlines Corp Act*	*House Building Fin. Corp Act*
A.	–	12(d)	21	11(b)	–	14(2)	24(a)	15	15, 25(2) (3)(4)	24, 25, 21
B.	–	88(i)(a)	–	–	–	37(2)	7, 9	–	–	–
C.	–	38(i)(b), 11(a), 12(b)	–	–	–	–	8	25(2), 26	–	32(1)
D.	11(1), 12	24(i)	19	–	12(2)	16(4)(6), 4(5)	12(2), 13(1)	–	–	15
E.	–	–	–	–	12(3)	–	–	–	–	–
F.	–	–	–	–	19(3)	–	–	–	–	–
G.	–	10(e)(f)	–	–	–	–	–	–	–	–
H.	–	–	–	–	–	–	–	–	–	–
I.	–	10(a)(f)	16	–	–	–	–	–	9(2)	7, 15
J.	18(1)(2), 27	–	–	–	–	–	–	–	–	–

Note: Numbers in columns refer to sections of the particular Acts.

APPENDIX 13.4 Ministers' powers under the Acts

Table 13.3 UK: Minister's powers under the British Telecommunications Act, 1981

Powers	*Section*	*Qualifications*
1. To appoint the chairman and members of the board	1	Members; after consulting the chairman
2. To consent to the Corporation promoting Bills in Parliament	2 (5)	
3. To approve schemes of reorganisation of properties etc. among wholly-owned subsidiaries	4 (5)	
4. To consent to transfer of Corporation's interest in a wholly-owned subsidiary to some other person	5 (3)	
5. To give general directions	6 (2)	After consultation with the Corporation
6. To give directions for remedying any defect in the general plans of the Corporation	6 (2)	After consultation with the Corporation
7. To give directions regarding things to be done or not to be done, on certain national grounds	6 (4)	
8. To give directions against undue preference	6 (5)	After consultations with the Corporation
9. To give directions regarding schemes of reorganisation among wholly-owned subsidiaries	6 (6) 6 (6)	
10. To give directions to dispose of any part of the undertakings or assets	6 (6)(b)	After consultation with the Corporation, and without affecting the duties under section 3(1)
11. To lay before each House of Parliament a copy of every direction given under section 6 (6)	6 (7)	Except on grounds of national security or commercial interests of any person
12. To give opinion against disclosure of any direction, by the Corporation	6 (8)	On similar grounds as above
13. To consult the Corporation on settling a general programme of technological research	6 (9)	
14. To approve a general programme of substantive outlay on capital account	6 (10)	
15. To specify the information he wants from the Corporation	6 (11)	
16. To receive an annual report on the Corporation's performance and lay it before each House of Parliament	6 (12)	After consultations with the Corporation
17. To be consulted on the Corporation 'group' undertaking substantially greater work or different work 'than during the relevant period'/during the three preceding years	7 (1)(2)	

Table 13.3 Continued

Powers	*Section*	*Qualifications*
18. To approve the Corporation constructing . . . 'things of any kind to a substantial extent'; and to publish particulars of any such approval	8 (1)(3)	
19. To determine from time to time the financial duties of the Corporation, having regard to 'the not-less-than' subsection 24 (1); different determinations for different periods, assets and activities	24 (2)	With the approval of the Treasury and after consultations with the Corporation
20. To direct allocations to reserves	25	With the approval of the Treasury and after consulting the Corporation
21. To lend or consent to borrowings	26 28	With the approval of the Treasury
22. To specify from time to time limits of indebtedness within £6,500 million	27 (2)	To be approved by the House of Commons
28. To send to the CAG accounts of funds received and disposed of by him during the financial year	30	CAG to lay a report before each House of Parliament
29. To specify the Group coverage in annual accounts for audit; to notify the information etc. to be contained in them	31	With the consent of the Treasury and after consultations with the Corporation
30. To appoint auditors	31 (6)	After consulting the Corporation
31. To receive and lay before each House of Parliament audited accounts	31 (8)	
32. To make orders about pensions	33	
33. To appoint the Post Office Users' National Council and County Councils To refer to the National and County Council any matter for report To receive their reports and lay them before each House of Parliament To pay allowances and remunerations to the Council members etc. To decide whether any proposal is major enough to be referred by the Corporation to the National Council	14 and 15 of Post Office Act, 1969	
Treasury's powers of guarantee etc; to lay statement before each House of Parliament	29	

Note: This analysis excludes the sections on transfers of property, statutory rights and liabilities as to telegraphs, exclusive privileges of the Corporation, savings for things done under a licence, approval of apparatus, offences due to default of third person, schemes for charges, deemed contracts and limitation of liability, rating, land offences and miscellaneous matters.

Table 13.4 Sri Lanka: Minister's powers under the State Industrial Corporation Act No. 49 of 1957 (1966)

Powers	*Section*	*Qualifications*
1. The Minister, with the approval of the Government, may by Order (hereinafter referred to as the incorporation Order) published in the Gazette – (i) specify the industrial undertaking referred to as the 'specified industrial undertaking' to which the Order relates; (ii) declare that a corporation shall be established for the purpose of setting up and carrying on, or taking over and carrying on, as the case may be, the specified industrial undertaking; (iii) assign a corporate name to the corporation; (iv) specify the initial capital of the corporation which shall not exceed such amounts as shall have been approved by the House of Representatives; (v) state the principal place of business of the corporation; (vi) fix the number of members of the Board of directors of the corporation, the number so fixed being not less than three and not more than seven; (vii) appoint as the first members of such board any persons who, under this Act, are qualified for being such members; and (viii) appoint one of the members of such board as the chairman of such board	2 (1)	
2. To alter the objects of the Corporation by Order published in the Gazette	3 (2)	With government approval
3. To determine the limits to borrowings from time to time	5 (2)	With the concurrence of the Minister for Finance
4. To appoint directors . . . with experience and capacity in industrial, administrative, commercial, financial or legal matters, applied sciences, or the organisation of workers; to appoint one of the directors as Chairman; to appoint one of the directors as Managing Director and determine his terms; to remove a director other than the managing director	12 13 14 (1)(3) 18	
5. To determine the directors' remuneration	20	With the concurrence of the Minister for Finance
6. To transfer to the Corporation any Crown property, contracts and liabilities	25 (1)	By Order published in the Gazette; with the

Table 13.4 Continued

Powers	*Section*	*Qualifications*
		concurrence of the Minister for Finance/ Minister for Commerce
7. To determine certain terms of public officers appointed in the Corporation	26 (1)	
8. To approve payments of profits to general or specific reserves; the balance to be paid into the Consolidated Fund	27	With the approval of the Minister for Finance
9. To appoint the auditor; to determine his remuneration	29 (1)	On the advice of the Auditor-General with the concurrence of the Minister for Finance
10. To receive the annual report and accounts together with the AG's comments; and lay them before the House of Representatives for approval	30 (1) (2)	
11. To give, from time to time, general directions or special directions	31 (1)	Special directions after consultation with the board
12. To direct enquiries	31 (2)	
13. To provide, by regulation, for the application of any provision of the Companies Ordinance with or without modification	34 (1)	
14. To make regulations	39(1) (2)	The regulations take effect only with Senate and House Representatives approval

Notes: Specific references to Parliament:
1. Increase of initial capital (section 23 [2]).
2. Annual accounts and report (section 30 [2]).
3. Regulations made by the Minister (section 39 [2]).

No provision for the publication of Minister's directions in annual report of Corporation.

Table 13.5 Kenya: Government's powers under the State Corporation Act, 1986

The President's powers	*Section*	*Qualifications*
1. To declare any body corporate not to be a state corporation	2 (b) (vii)	
2. By order, to establish a state corporation	3 (1)	
3. To assign ministerial responsibility for any state corporation	4	
4. To appoint the chairman	6 (1)	
5. To give directions of a general or specific nature	7 (1)	
6. To revoke the appointment of a board member and nominate a new member	7 (3)	
7. To constitute a new board	7 (3)	In consultation with SCAC
8. To appoint the chairman of the State Corporations Appeal Tribunal (SCAT)	22 (3)	
9. To appoint eight members to the State Corporations Advisory Committee (SCAC) and its secretary	26 (1)(e), (3)	
10. To give any directions regarding the SCAC's procedures	26 (4)	
11. To approve SCAC's remunerations etc.	26 (5)	
12. To make regulations generally for the better carrying into effect of the provisions of this Act	30	
Parent Minister's powers	*Section*	*Qualifications*
1. Consent needed for borrowings of a state corporation	5 (2)	Subject to limitations imposed by the Treasury
2. To approve terms and conditions of employees	5 (4)	In consultation with the Treasury and SCAC
3. To appoint not more than seven board members	(6)(1)(e)	
4. To appoint alternate directors	6 (4)	In consultation with SCAC
5. To approve annual budget	11 (1)(2)	Along with the Treasury
6. Approval in writing, needed for any expenditure not included in the annual estimate	12	Along with the Treasury
7. To approve sale of assets	13 (2)	Along with the Treasury
8. To direct, in writing, the disposal of surplus	16 (2)	In consultation with the Board
Powers of the Minister for Finance	*Section*	*Qualifications*
1. To make rules for acquisition and disposal of assets	13 (2)	In consultation with SCAC
2. To prescribe the forms of Accounts	14 (2)	
3. To require the whole or part of the surplus moneys to be paid into the Consolidated Fund	16 (3)	
4. To approve regulations regarding the credit facilities to directors	17	

Table 13.5 Continued

Powers of the Minister for Finance	*Section*	*Qualifications*
5. To appoint two members to the SCAT	22 (3)	As nominated by Council of Law Society and Council of the Institute of Certified Public Accountants

State Corporations Advisory Committee's powers	*Section*	*Qualifications*
1. To approve a board meeting at any place other than the registered or principal office	8 (c)	
2. To be informed of the appointment of a board committee	9	
3. To specify the scales of remuneration of board members and travelling and other expenses	10 (1)(2)	
4. To approve terms and conditions of credit to director	17	
5. To approve SCAT's allowances etc.	22 (14)	In consultation with the Treasury
6. To review and investigate a state corporation and make recommendations to the President	27 (1)(a)	
7. To advise the President on the establishment, reorganisation or dissolution of a state corporation	27 (1)(b)	In consultation with the Attorney-General and the Treasury
8. To advise on staff matters	27 (1)(c)	
9. To examine any management or consultancy agreement made by a state corporation	27 (1)(d)	
10. To examine a state corporation's proposals to acquire interests in any business or enter into a joint venture	27 (1)(e)	

APPENDIX 13.5 Provisions regarding differences between the Board and the Government

Section 11

1. The Board shall, from time to time, inform the Government for:
   (a) any policy of the Corporation which, in the opinion of the Board, should be made known to the Government; and
   (b) the banking policy of the Trading Bank, the Savings Bank and the Development Bank.
2. In the event of a difference of opinion between the Government and the Board whether any policy referred to in the last preceding subsection is

directed to the greatest advantage of the people of Australia and has due regard to the stability and balanced development of the Australian economy, the Treasurer and the Board shall endeavour to reach agreement.

3. If the Treasurer and the Board are unable to reach agreement, the Board shall forthwith furnish to the Treasurer a statement in relation to the matter in respect of which the difference of opinion has arisen.
4. The Treasurer may then submit a recommendation to the Governor-General, and the Governor-General, acting with the advice of the Federal Executive Council, may, by order, determine the policy to be adopted by the Corporation, the Trading Bank, the Savings Bank or the Development Bank, as the case may be, but so that the policy so determined is not inconsistent with the *Banking Act* 1959, with the regulations under that Act or with the monetary and banking policy of the Reserve Bank.
5. The Treasurer shall inform the Board of the policy so determined and shall at the same time inform the Board that the Government accepts responsibility for the adoption by the Corporation, the Trading Bank, the Savings Bank or the Development Bank, as the case may be, of that policy and will take such action (if any) within its powers as the Government considers to be necessary by reason of the adoption of that policy.
6. The Board shall thereupon ensure that effect is given to the policy determined by the order and shall, if the order so requires, continue to ensure that effect is given to that policy while the order remains in operation.
7. The Treasurer shall cause to be laid before each *House* of the Parliament, within fifteen sitting days of that House after the Treasurer has informed the Board of the policy determined under subsection (4) –
   (a) a copy of the order determining the policy;
   (b) a statement by the Government in relation to the matter in respect of which the difference of opinion arose; and
   (c) a copy of the statement furnished to the Treasurer by the Board under subsection (3).

Source: Commonwealth Banks Act 1959, Canberra.

APPENDIX 13.6 Some recent trends in board constitution

The State Corporations Act 1986 of Kenya standardises it as follows: the Chairman (to be appointed by the President), the Permanent Secretary of the Treasury, the Chief Executive of the enterprise, and not more than seven others, of whom no more than three can be public officers (to be appointed by the parent minister); there is no provision for an executive chairman; and there are no functional directors, except for the managing director.

The Administrative Reforms Committee in Sri Lanka recommended in 1988 that the board of an infrastructural corporation should consist of a full-time Chairman (to be appointed by the Cabinet upon the joint recommendation of the sectoral ministry and the Ministry of Finance), a part-timer, who is not a staff member of the sectoral ministry or of any department under it (to be designated by the sectoral ministry), another similarly to be designated by the Ministry of Finance, another to represent the interests of the consumers (to be appointed by the Cabinet from a panel recommended by the sectoral ministry), and three functional directors (Finance, Operations and Personnel). (A crucial point concerns the variety of appointing authorities.) In the case of the Public Investment Corporation proposed by the Committee, the board is to consist of the deputy secretary to the Treasury as chairman, the secretaries of the ministries of industry and agriculture and two others to be designated by the Cabinet on the recommendation of the Minister of Finance. The board of each enterprise under this holding company will be appointed by it: a full-time managing director and four other part-timers; there is no mention of functional directors of any kind.

ZIMCO, the 'ultimate holding company' for all public enterprises in Zambia, has the President of the country as chairman, the Prime Minister as vice-chairman, nine other ministers, five from Zambia Congress of Trade Unions, chief of the economic sub-committee of the Party, director general of National Commission for Development Planning, economic adviser to President, permanent secretary, finance, managing director, National Housing Corporation, Director-General of ZIMCO, one from the Central Committee of the Party, and one from the private sector. ZIMCO, it may be noted, is in the nature of an all-economy organisation. (*ZIMCO: Zambia's Force for Growth,* Lusaka, p. 8).

APPENDIX 13.7 Functions of the Bureau of Public Enterprises (India)

(i) *Monitoring performance*

1. To consolidate and prepare quarterly analytical reports on the performance of public sector as a whole.
2. To identify the enterprises facing serious problems such as fall in production, continuous losses, heavy inventories, surplus labour on a large scale etc., and give timely signals to Government.
3. To analyse and monitor the annual performance of each Government company against the pre-determined benchmarks of

physical, commercial, financial and other performance indicators and submit to the Government a combined annual performance appraisal of the public sector.

4. To collect and act as a repository of the accumulated knowledge and experience on the results of investigations and research to determine ways and means of improving the performance of public enterprises as a whole.
5. To undertake jointly with the administrative Ministries continuous indepth studies of individual public enterprises as also groups of enterprises so as to make useful contribution towards the better functioning of public enterprises.
6. To compile and analyse statistical data with regard to public enterprises as, for instance, data on project cost per unit of capacity, unit operating or production cost trends, accounting ratios, etc. between different enterprises in the same field of activities leading to interfirm comparisons.

(ii) *Management Development in Public Enterprises*

1. To assist the Public Enterprises Selection Board in the Selection Board level appointments and determining their terms and conditions of employment.
2. To maintain a computerised data bank of senior management personnel below the Board level in respect of all the public enterprises and to classify persons with reference to their qualifications, service background, experience and potential for planning their training needs and career development.
3. To organise in-service training programme for managerial personnel at all levels utilising the services of the existing organisations engaged in the field of training.
4. To interact with the efficient public and private enterprises abroad, as also with advanced management training organisations overseas with a view to taking advantage of such good managements practices as can be introduced in the Indian Companies.
5. To assist the Government in the formation of new Government Companies. The capital structure, Articles and Memorandum of Association of different companies would be examined by BPE as also the organisational structure at the top level of each company.
6. To maintain a panel of consultants for different areas for reference to public sector undertakings, also to provide management consultancy services, especially to smaller public enterprises, in specified areas where such assistance is sought for.

(iii) *Investment and Performance Appraisal*

1. To appraise project reports/investment proposals for Public Investment Board/Expenditure Finance Committee, avoiding duplication of work of the Project, Appraisal Division in Planning Commission

but paying greater attention to project management aspects and systems highlighting strength and weakness of the public enterprises Managements for taking up the projects.

2. To assist the administrative Ministries concerned in the periodical monitoring of the implementation of new projects and conducting Post-completion studies on new projects – BPE would also act as a repository of information on such completed projects.

(iv) *Parliamentary Work and Public Relations*

1. To assist COPU to the extent required, as and when BPE's assistance is sought for, in close consultation with the administrative Ministries.
2. To discharge the role of an efficient public relations agency for the public sector as a whole.

(v) *General*

1. To assist any special Committee which Government may appoint to examine the operations of public enterprises. While the implementation of the decision of any Committee is to be left to the concerned administrative Ministry, BPE may, however, monitor the action taken on such recommendations.
2. With a view to ensuring coordination in respect of employees' remuneration in the Public Sector, to issue guidelines in the areas of salaries and wages in the public enterprises keeping in view overall economic considerations and the relativities between the Government employees and employees in the public sector, and having regard to long term industrial relations.
3. To issue guidelines to public enterprises for implementation of Government policy in special areas like reservations for Scheduled Castes/Scheduled Tribes etc.

Source: Bureau of Public Enterprises (1986) *Public Enterprises Survey 1984–85*, vol. 1, New Delhi, pp. 363–4.

Part IV

Conclusion

14 Privatisation

The term privatisation essentially denotes marketisation or bringing the enterprise under the disciplines of the market. There can be three options of policy: ownership changes, organisational changes, and operational changes. The first by itself – divestiture – does not necessarily guarantee full marketisation, nor does a desired degree of marketisation necessarily call for it in every case.

The three options are set out in detail in Figure 14.1. The second and third often go under the name of public enterprise reform or performance improvement and may be considered as a second-order version of privatisation. They are covered in the earlier chapters, except for leasing and contracting-out. Apart from a few comments on these two measures, this chapter focuses on privatisation in the sense of divestiture.

THE CONCEPT OF PRIVATISATION

The concept of privatisation is in the nature of a continuum, ranging between I (1) which represents total denationalisation and III (15) which little implies even changes internal to the enterprise as such.

This chapter commences with an analysis of the reasons for privatisation (through divestiture). We then look at the substantive implications of privatisation, especially the distributional, regulatory, and exchequer concerns. The unique problems of developing, as against developed, countries are kept in mind right through.[1]

This chapter does not seek to cover the mechanics of privatisation, except for brief references to matters of implicit relevance to substantive issues and to complications arising from the labour context.

Three conclusions follow from the figure. First, operational and organisational changes may alone be adequate to realise the objective of efficiency in the case of certain public enterprises and in certain situations.[2] Second, such changes may be an appropriate – in some cases, necessary – step in eventual divestiture. Third, the government should keep in mind the total package of options before deciding on any one of them, the more so on divestiture, for compared to the other two, it is somewhat irreversible.

Figure 14.1 Privatisation: the policy options

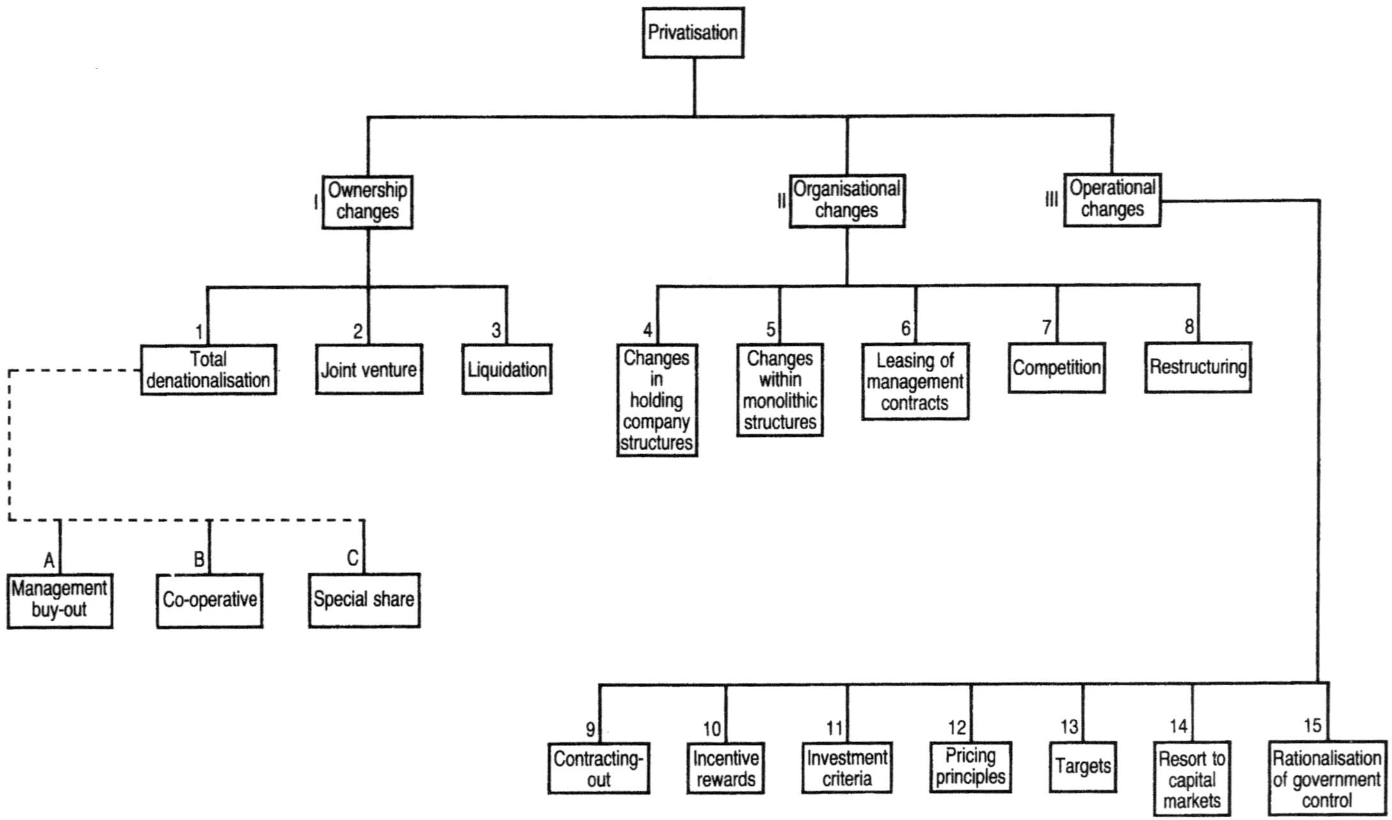

Figure 14.2 Privatisation: the content

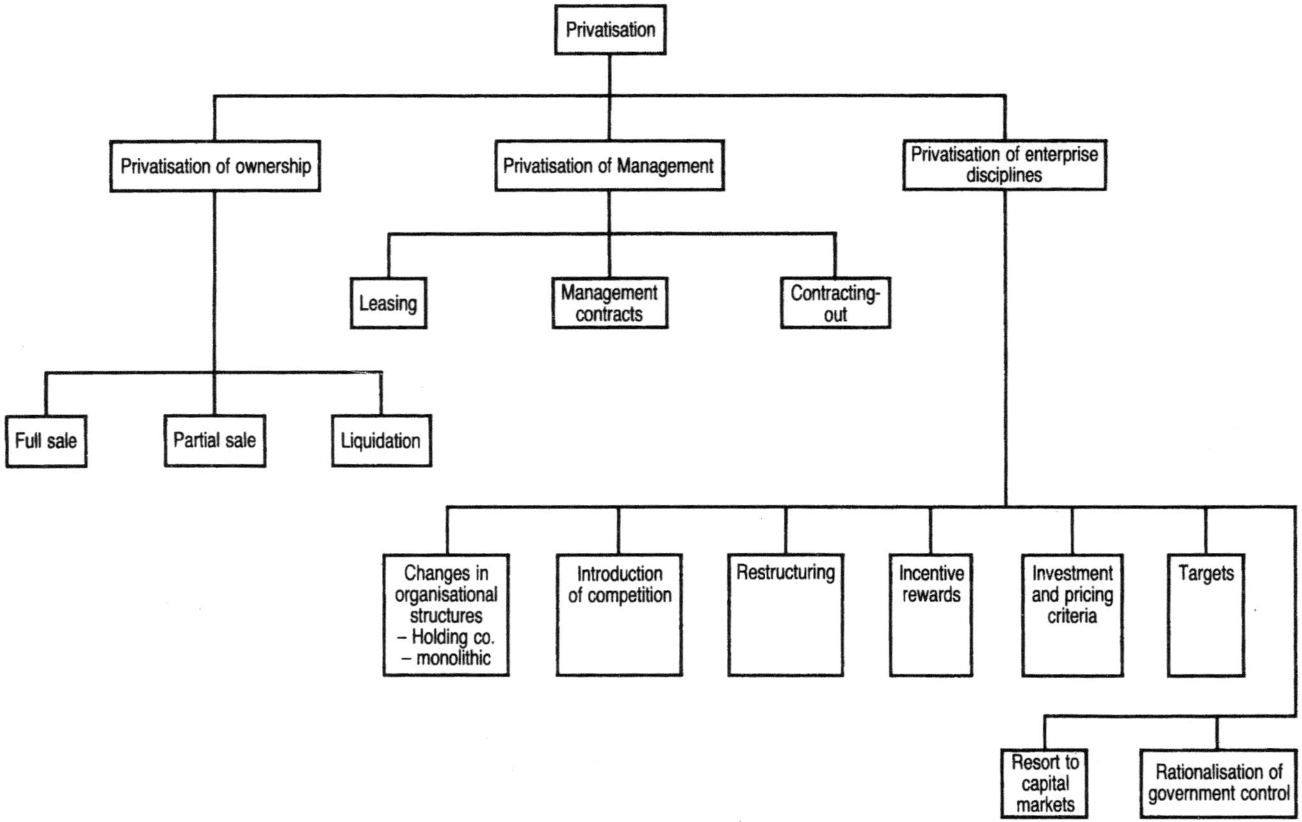

For instance, Nigeria categorises its total public enterprise sector into candidates for divestiture, for 'full commercialisation' or 'partial commercialisation', the latter two terms signifying the organisational and operational options.

The emphasis on the organisational and operational options is clearly discernible from the way joint ventures are developing, with private capital coming in for rationalising a public enterprise, for example, in Jamaica.[3]

The concept of privatisation may be expressed in another way, highlighting the precise nature of what is privatised: namely, privatisation of ownership, privatisation of management and privatisation of enterprise disciplines. It may be noted that the content of the earlier chart is rearranged from this angle.

THE RATIONALE OF PRIVATISATION

The reasons for privatising an enterprise have been mentioned variously in official documents in different countries. (A strange elaboration is found in the White Paper on water privatisation in the UK Cmnd 9734, HMSO, London, 1986.)

Let us confine ourselves to the basics of the argument.

It is argued that privatisation improves the efficiency of the enterprise. This is in the nature of an umbrella argument and needs to be broken into several parts.

The enterprise begins to be exposed to market forces, with all the resultant benefits for the economy

The argument is valid if privatisation does in fact produce effective competition in the sector concerned, not on paper but in reality, and if disguised cartels do not develop underneath the apparently competitive structure of the sector. The argument is not conclusive if it is possible, without divestiture, to promote competition in the sector through policies of liberalisation or effective 'yardstick competition' within the public enterprise concerned, or to formulate and effectively monitor its pricing and investment criteria in such a way that the consumers are protected from the evils of monopoly and a misallocation of resources does not take place.

It is doubtful if in developing countries effective competition can prevail subsequent to the privatisation in certain sectors. The markets are too small to prevent the emergence of a monopoly situation of some kind. In fact chapter 1 mentions this as a major factor that induced governments to nationalise or establish enterprises in several sectors. As long as the smallness of markets remains – and it will be for a long time in many cases, assuming the international non-competitiveness of their industries which confines them to domestic markets – the perceived benefits of efficiency through competition and the play of market forces are to be viewed with circumspection.

In many cases the very mechanics of divestiture tends to be promotive of cartelisation. Where a private placement is undertaken, as against a public share allotment, and where the buyer is an enterprise already incumbent in the sector, less rather than more competition will ensue from the privatisation. It is estimated in a World Bank study that about three-fifths of private sales in developing countries and about three-quarters in developed countries have been to investors 'known to be in the same industry'.[4] There might be justifiable reasons for a private sale in a given case, the more so when technological restructuring of the enterprise is essential, but in terms of the competition argument it can have a negative effect.

In theory, regulation helps where elements of monopoly persist after privatisation. The UK experience raises doubts about its efficacy, and developing countries have less experience in regulation.

The enterprise managers will have an incentive for maximal performance, for two reasons

They can gain in emoluments, through salary increases,[5] bonuses, and stock options. It is well known that managers' salaries in public enterprise compare badly with those of their counterparts in the private sector, and that only in a few countries – like Pakistan and Korea – have they recently been made eligible for performance incentive payments. The other reason – a strong one – is that they will be relieved of government controls and interferences; and this spurs autonomous behaviour on their part.[6]

A privatised enterprise will be under constant shareholder control directed towards profit and under threats of take-over

These induce the managers and other employees to be on the alert all the time and aim at attaining high efficiency. Where the workers hold shares in the enterprise, the shareholder interest might be distinctly direct.

Before we proceed further, the very concept of 'efficiency', which privatisation is expected to enhance, needs a probe. In so far as it is understood to represent financial profit, the claim is positive. But in so far as social returns or net social benefits are concerned, it is debatable; and unless special arrangements are devised – see the section on regulation – it is likely that losses occur in terms of social efficiency, subject to the comments, in chapter 12, on distributional equity resulting from low prices and losses. In other words, some social benefits which a public enterprise might be yielding are likely to be lost on its privatisation.

The same kind of circumspection is necessary in respect of the claim that privatisation puts an end to the misallocation of resources.

In considering the argument of efficiency, we have to distinguish between developed and developing countries. The element of social returns is, on the whole, of limited significance in the former, while many of the latter have needed, and perhaps still need, to seek them through enterprise policies that produce low profits (see chapters 1 and 3). The anatomy of public enterprise losses presented in Figure 5.1 merits reference at this point. The major benefits of privatisation accrue, in a developed country, from the removal of the causes of losses *A* (investment factors), *D* (government interventions) and *E* (managerial inefficiency); and a privatised enterprise will have full autonomy to deal with *C* (structural factors) and *B* (exogenous factors) to the best of its ability. In a developing country, on the other hand, the only cause of losses, which probably can disappear, is *E* (managerial inefficiency), whereas the rest are still likely to persist in some way and in varying degrees, under the hypothesis of social returns. In brief, a major privatised enterprise is unlikely to be fully equated with a private enterprise for a long time.

There is another efficiency-oriented argument, namely, that a privatised enterprise undertakes 'innovation'[7] eagerly and successfully

Here again it is difficult to bundle up all countries together for a conclusion. It is doubtful if it applies to the cross-section of private enterprises other than multinationals and their branches, in many developing countries (see chapter 1). There is another related issue. Where the risks of an investment, whether in R & D or in expansions, are significant, there is no reason why a privatised enterprise should go after them, as long as other channels of investment – even if in real estate – are open to it. Government pressure, coupled with some price incentive, capital grant or subsidy, may be necessary to ensure that the economy does not suffer from a possible under-supply of outputs or technological progress in a given sector. (Water and nuclear power privatisations in the UK illustrate the point.)

A powerful claim for privatisation is that it has favourable impacts on the government budget, in that it relieves it of the need to subsidise the losses of public enterprises and of the obligation to find resources for capital expenditures.[8] Structural adjustment agreements with the World Bank and the IMF place particular emphasis on these benefits – in Ghana, for example, where a time-bound programme of privatisation is a part of the conditions of World Bank assistance.

Three questions beg themselves. First, do these benefits necessarily accrue in every case? Wherever the government wishes to maintain a loss-making output, whatever the reasons, it pays the privatised enterprise a price (or subsidy) that takes care of the element of loss on the supply concerned. It might be lower than the subsidy offered to the enterprise, when in the public sector. But this burden on the exchequer continues; and the scope for it is greater in a developing country than in a developed country, for example, in providing rural transport, rural electrification, fertiliser, seeds, and housing finance.

As regards the capital expenditures, it is not certain that in developing countries domestic investors are able or willing to take the place of the government by investing in sectors considered important in the development strategy adopted by the government. They may show a preference for 'light' industries. One of two results follows. Foreign capital comes in the shape of equity or under government guarantee; or certain 'desired investments' do not take place.

Second, assuming that the budget burdens are lightened, what would be the effects on distributional benefits? This question, however, seems to be more significant in theory than in practice (see chapters 6 and 12); for barring exceptions, the spread of benefits derived from budget subsidies to public enterprises has been indiscriminate and often anti-distributional in natüre. In the generality of cases privatisation will have the effect of eliminating 'blanket' subsidies in the name of distributional equity, while limiting the budgetary subsidies to the most needed cases, implemented through privatised enterprises or in other ways reaching the target group.

Third, is privatisation through divestiture the only means of eliminating or reducing the budget burdens imposed by public enterprises? Not necessarily. Public enterprises themselves can bring about a similar result if the lessons of chapters 3, 6, 7, 8, 12 and 13 are learnt; that is, if distributional and other extra-enterprise objectives are rigorously evaluated before being assigned to the enterprises, if the pricing basis is enunciated and distributional prices are kept under public scrutiny, if surplus and other targets are suitably determined, if there is effective monitoring of investments, and if, above all, the government exorcises its instinct for intervention. While this argument is valid in theory, it is empirically inconclusive; for there are too many 'ifs' to be satisfied. However, several non-divestiture versions of privatisation can be of help, for example, leasing, management contracts, contracting-out, and creating genuine competition.

Contracting-out can result in the enterprise acquiring an input at a lower price than it would cost it to produce 'in-house'. The more extensive the decisions to contract out, the better the financial results of the enterprise, and correspondingly the lower the burden that the enterprise places on the exchequer.

Leasing a part or whole of the enterprise brings in a stable income to the enterprise and passes the risks of operations to the lessee. Where leasing is feasible and has no long-term disadvantages to the enterprise, it can be an option from which the exchequer eventually derives a benefit.

Privatisation eliminates the phenomenon of excessive benefits being enjoyed by public enterprise employees relative to, or at the expense of, the interests of the consumers, the labour force elsewhere in the economy, and the taxpayer.[9]

The two reasons for the bargaining strength of the employees are that they attract political support and that many public enterprises are monopolies. Where neither of these conditions is affected by privatisation, their bargaining strength is not necessarily weakened. In many developing countries that seems to be the situation; and labour emoluments and compensations tend to be high, both under law and through strikes. In fact, the workers could bring about a situation in which renationalisation of a privatised enterprise might seem necessary.

A good argument, which has not been sufficiently emphasised in the literature, is that public enterprises involve government officials so heavily (yet inefficiently) in their affairs, in the name of controlling and monitoring, that the energies of the civil service are excessively distracted into matters outside their regular domain of responsibility. Expanding the civil service is no answer, since most matters in any case move up to the top echelons, and the demands on their time, energy, and capacity will still be there.

The argument can be extended to cover parliament. The larger the public enterprise sector, the wider parliament's responsibility to ensure its public accountability, as well as the accountability of civil servants for their actions and inactions. Given the constraints on their time and approach, it is doubtful that it can fulfil its responsibility efficaciously.

On this ground there is a case for contracting the public enterprise sector to the 'core'.

Ideology apart, the fundamental reason why a public enterprise deserves to be privatised is that it has lost its comparative advantage, as against an incumbent or prospective private (or co-operative) enterprise. Chapter 1 presents the various facets of the concept, while chapter 2 shows how the perceived comparative advantage of many a public enterprise has been seriously affected even as it came into being, and later on. Since the national objective is to maximise the net social returns from a given set of operations or transactions, they should be shifted into the private sector wherever the comparative advantage of a private enterprise is superior. Beesley and Littlechild's condition – 'if the net benefits to consumers are positive' – has a similar purport;[10] but we should go by 'all' benefits or 'social benefits', a concept with great practical significance in a developing country.

In terms of this principle, that a public enterprise has made losses, is no reason why it should necessarily be privatised, for the losses may have been the result of extra-enterprise objectives pursued through its operations, and/or they might not be there if certain organisational and operational changes were effected, as suggested by Figure 14.1

Likewise, that an enterprise making profits need not be privatised is not a valid proposition, either. Its comparative advantage may have declined, though it makes profits; and the net benefit to the national economy may be higher if it is privatised.

Thus the debate, commonly noticed in many developing countries, as to whether losing public enterprises or the profitable ones should be the first to be privatised, evades the basic criterion for divestiture, namely, comparative advantage. Both can be fit candidates.

Public policy ought to rest on establishing the precise objective of privatisation in an enterprise-specific manner. It is possible that a decision is taken in some cases, independently of, or contrary to, the comparative advantage principle, if the government attaches paramount value to realising revenues through the sale of an enterprise or if the desire is just to 'roll back the state'. Water and electricity privatisations in the UK are probably an example of the latter.

The 'widening' of share ownership, often claimed as an objective of privatisation programmes,[11] is not an *objective* in fact. It may be an aspect of the *modus operandi* or a result in some cases, and is not relevant to certain others like private placements. The next section goes into this question at length from the angles of distribution and efficiency.

So far we were concerned with privatisation at the micro level, that is, at the level of an individual enterprise. Let us turn to privatisation at the macro level. This may be analysed under two heads: liberalisation and investment strategy.

Liberalisation, if effective, introduces competition and induces the enterprise to strive for maximum efficiency. An enterprise may remain public; yet the benefits of competition ensue, without the need for transforming it into a private enterprise. In some countries like India there is an emphasis on liberalisation.[12] It is, however, doubtful if there is effective liberalisation or marketisation in respect of financial intermediation of which a major part happens to be the prerogative of the public sector.

As regards investment strategy as a means of privatising the economy, three lines of approach may be highlighted:

(a) The government stops investing in commercial ventures, while private investments take place.
(b) The government continues to invest, but at a lower pace than private investment. This is a more realistic case than (a), for there might be continuing needs of public investment in some sectors, for example, in Zimbabwe[13] and Jamaica.[14] Pakistan's development plans have begun to allot a far higher role to the private sector than to the government in the industrial sector. The latter essentially looks after balancing and modernisation investments. In centrally-planned economies, while public investments continue to be predominant, a beginning is made in letting in private investments, for example, in Hungary, where the permissible limit of employment in a private unit is raised from 35 to 500, in Poland where such limits are scrapped altogether,[15] and in Egypt where 38.6 per cent of new industrial investment under the 1987–92 plan is directed to the private sector, as against the 23 per cent in the preceding plan.[16]

(c) The government inducts private capital in a public enterprise in respect of its expansions. A joint venture results, but it differs from that arising out of partial divestiture (modality I 2 of Figure 14.1).

THE DISTRIBUTIONAL IMPLICATIONS

The distributional implications of divestiture may be analysed, broadly, under three heads: divestiture *per se*; processes and techniques of divestiture; and use of divestiture proceeds.

Divestiture *per se*

Large-scale divestitures can have unfavourable distributional effects in the following circumstances:

(a) Where the enterprises concerned are profit-making, transferring them to the private sector will have the effect of transferring the profit incomes minus the corresponding interest charges to the private investors, as argued in chapter 12. The public sector would lose them and, correspondingly, the taxpayer has a disadvantage, as against the buyers of the privatised enterprises.

(b) Where the enterprises concerned offer significant extra-enterprise benefits, privatisation might eliminate or contract them, subject to any continuing arrangements of subsidy from the government, to the private owners. If such arrangements do not exist or are nominal, the taxpayer no doubt will enjoy the benefit of a saving in the budget; but the recipients of benefits which the extra-enterprise objectives of the enterprises offered will lose them.

(c) When a privatised enterprise retrenches labour, as is likely in the majority of cases, there will be employment losses and, correspondingly, losses of wage incomes for certain groups of people. If the situation is met by high redundancy payments drawn (eventually) from the exchequer, the workers concerned may not be at a loss, but the taxpayer sustains a disadvantage. If using the same amount for restructuring the enterprise were a plausible alternative, there is a chance that the taxpayer's initial disadvantage will be offset by the viability of the enterprise.

(d) Where the programme of privatisation involves the divestiture of profit-making enterprises, by and large, while the losing enterprises remain in the public sector (like the nuclear power-plants in the UK), the taxpayer will sustain the disadvantage of a loss of profit incomes for the exchequer, coupled with continuing losses to be fed from the budget.

(e) Where a privatised enterprise retains its monopoly power and effective competition in the sector concerned is doubtful, it can perpetuate imperfections in pricing and in the distribution of revenues among the factors. Both the workers and the shareholders are likely to be the gainers.

On the other hand privatisation will have favourable distributional effects in the following cases:

(a) Where the enterprises concerned are loss-making, and there are no redeeming extra-enterprise circumstances, the taxpayer will benefit from the divestitures.
(b) Where the employees extract high benefits at the expense of the consumers and the shareholder (that is, the government) – independently of whether the enterprise concerned makes profits or losses – privatisation will benefit both the consumers and the taxpayers. Here the assumption is that the privatised enterprise does not continue to possess the same degree of monopoly as it did while in the public sector.
(c) Where consumers who do not deserve low prices enjoy them, privatisation can erase them. This in itself will be a favourable development; it will be doubly valuable in that it eases the burdens on workers or the shareholder (that is, the exchequer) and/or eliminates the cross-subsidies among consumers, which may have existed.

One cannot be certain that the second and third effects will be realised immediately on privatisation; for political pressures can delay them.

Processes and techniques of divestiture

The processes and techniques of divestiture have distributional implications.

Where the organisational structure of a public enterprise enjoying monopoly is not disturbed through privatisation, the distributional implications of a monopoly continue to prevail. The scope for high profits, high employee remunerations, high prices, and cross-subsidies in pricing, will be directly proportional to the ineffectiveness of regulation applied to a privatised enterprise. Where the conditions for regulatory capture are strong, these results are most certain.

Where an enterprise is privatised through a private sale, totally or substantially, two distributional consequences follow. First, the 'block' buyer comes from the wealthy section of the community. Second, if the buyer is an enterprise in the same line, the degree of concentration in the supply of the outputs concerned increases. This disadvantage is most probable in an economy 'dominated by just a handful of big private groups', as in Italy,[17] where they are nicknamed as 'private sector dynasties' (such as the Agnelli family, Orlando family, and Edizione family),[18] or in the Asian region in general.[19]

There is considerable evidence on private placements. In Italy and New Zealand there have been more private sales than market flotations.[20] Of the ten enterprises privatised so far in Turkey, only one (Teletas) was floated on the stock exchange;[21] the rest went to a 'core block'.[22]

The proneness to concentrated ownership may be subdued by following techniques of 'wide' share ownership. The UK has taken a significant lead in adopting them.[23]

Wide ownership has distributional and managerial implications.

A large number of shareholders does not indicate that there is no concentration in ownership. It is not their proportion in the total number of shareholders in an enterprise that matters, but the proportion of their capital holding out of its total equity. Where this is not high – as in the UK itself – the effect of privatisation in diluting ownership is not significant.[24]

Would these shareholders, each owning lss than a specified number of shares in a given flotation, belong to the relatively low income categories? Not necessarily. The OECD Survey on the UK observes that 'share ownership is concentrated in the higher age and income groups'.[25] The situation is more clearly one of heavy skewness in share ownership and wealth in developing countries, for example, in some 200 families in Pakistan.[26] Given the lack of investing interest and knowledge of share availability through privatisations, the vast majority of the population, non-urban in location, agricultural in occupation, or unemployed, is unlikely to invest in the privatised shares.

Restrictions on share allotment, which aim at keeping an individual's holding low, will lose force if, in the course of time, share transfers are permitted, which add to the equity holding of large shareholders. This can be met by introducing a clause in the articles of association – or in the company law itself – that no individual can own more than a specified (low) percentage of the share capital with voting rights. It is difficult to say how effective that would be as an anti-concentration measure in a developing country; for shares can be owned in the names of different family members or of individuals that constitute a business group. The point that matters is that all such shares vote as a 'block', and derive the power to influence directoral decisions in their favour.

It is a feature of most privatisations (in the UK included) that the proportion of equity capital held by the small shareholders declines as their number declines, that is, as they begin to sell their shares away,[27] and that of institutions increases. This cannot invariably be claimed as a favourable development from the angle of distribution. Apparently the major share of the profits of the enterprise reaches, not (rich) individual shareholders, but financial institutions and pension funds. But they eventually get distributed, in one form or another, among their shareholders or clients, *not equally*, but in the ratio of their claims on the institutions. For instance, a unit trust which receives dividends from a privatised enterprise eventually passes them on to its share- or unit-holders; and the larger (that is, richer) holders derive higher incomes from the units held by them than the smaller ones would.

At this point we may refer to a likely managerial disadvantage of too wide a share ownership. The small owners are unlikely to get on to the board. It is improbable that the institutional shareholders take an active interest in the management of the enterprise, as long as they receive good dividends. A few relatively large equity holders, who collect proxies, begin to enjoy directoral powers disproportionately with their own equity stake. Besides, the managers can exploit the situation, partly by getting on the board with relative ease. Without affecting the prospect of a reasonable rate of dividend, which keeps the average shareholder happy, they can manipulate the use of resources in their favour through high salaries, bonuses and stock options; and collusion can develop between them and a few major equity holders in favour of operations that offer them both excessive benefits at the expense of the other, particularly the small, shareholders.[28] Limits to effective competition in the sector concerned can intensify such a possibility. It is assumed that the managers and the dominant shareholders act in such a way as not to provoke the 'golden' shareholder, if there is one in a given case, into countervailing action.

Statistics indicate that in several countries, including the UK and Japan, the proportion of share ownership by individuals has been on the decline in recent years, while that of institutions has been on the increase.[29] The above scenario is, therefore, a real possibility.

Where a public enterprise is sold at a relatively low price, there is a transfer of wealth from the taxpayer to the buyer. Assuming that the average buyer is richer than the average taxpayer, this has been an unfavourable distributional effect.

There is considerable evidence of 'low' sale price in many countries. In the UK the main motive of the government was 'to achieve a successful flotation';[30] 'the maximization of the proceeds of a sale, while extremely important, was a secondary consideration'.[31] The Committee of Public Accounts referred, as reasons for its inference of low prices in the early flotations in the UK, 'to considerable oversubscriptions' (for example, nine times the shares available in the case of British Telecom)[32] and the far higher prices which were recorded on the first day of trading.[33]

The underpricing can take place in many ways.

The price itself may be low in relation to the assets transferred. (It is estimated that there was an underpricing of £300 million on the sale of British Airways shares at £900 million;[34] and that at 125 p. – 'an insider deal of the century' – there was an undervaluation of £200 million in the case of British Steel.)[35]

There may be a write-off of debts owed by an enterprise on the verge of privatisation – for example, write-offs proposed in the case of British Water, British Coal, and the Scottish Electricity Boards, of some £4.4 bn, £1 bn, and £2.6 bn respectively.

A cash 'dowry' may be offered for certain capital expenditures – as with British Water (£1 bn) for some urgent capital expenditures.

Certain accumulated obligations of the enterprise owed to the government may be waived, for example, a £55 million dividend obligation on the part of British Aerospace, in the interest of its 'attractiveness to the market'.[36] Another instance, in the UK, is the government's payment of about £47 million towards the National Freight Corporation (NFC) pension funds at the time of the management buy-out.

Shareholders who held on to their shares in a privatised enterprise may be offered a 'loyalty bonus', for example, one free share for every ten shares held by individuals continuously until 31 July 1990, subject to a maximum of 200 shares, in the case of British Airports Authority plc (1987); and one free share for every ten held for eighteen months by French citizens up to a maximum of fifty in the case of Cle de Saint Gobain (1986).

A price discount may be offered to 'small' shareholders; for example, to buyers of up to 200 shares in the case of Unicer in Portugal, provided they held on to them for two years. This is another version of a loyalty bonus. The privatisation of British Water has introduced a discount on the offer price of the second and third instalments of the issue.

A variety of concessions may be offered to the employees of the enterprise. Appendix 14.1 shows the details with reference to the UK. Broadly, they include preferential treatment in allotment, a specified number of free shares at government expense, and matching shares for shares purchased by an employee within a specified period.

The concessions offered to the employees raise questions on grounds of distribution, for, as argued in chapter 12, they are far from being in the lowest income brackets. A part of the nation's property gets transferred to them at the expense of the taxpayer. This is a point of asymmetry with concessional share offers to employees in private enterprises where the property belongs to the shareholders, who are not obliged to examine the distributional considerations of the measure on a macro scale. The distributional inequity of the plethora of concessions offered to employees during privatisation is a matter of serious interest in developing countries, though they may be designed to assuage the opposition of labour to privatisation. For their conditions of dualism are far more considerable than those in developed countries.

Under-pricing of privatised enterprises is found, not only in the UK, but in several other countries, for example, in France,[37] Italy,[38] Turkey,[39] and Togo.[40] It is likely to be ubiquitous in developing countries which have no capital markets and are anxious to attract buyers. Further, the general state of poor performance of public enterprises stands in the background as a point that strengthens the bargaining power of the buyer.

Unless regulatory provisions are scrupulously formulated, the purchase of an enterprise by an ethnic or regional group, even if domestic, could cause serious social tensions and be considered as opposed to the distributional aims underlying national policies – stated as in Malaysia or unstated as in Nigeria and Kenya. It is said that the Muslims in the less-developed northern regions of Nigeria are averse to the likely purchase of public enterprise located in those areas by the moneyed southern Christians, 'for a song, condemning the north to a permanently inferior status'.[41] In Kenya, for example, privatisation would favour the Kikuyu, 'the most privileged ethnic group in the country'.[42] In Malaysia the New Economic Policy (NEP) has been to transfer wealth, as per a time schedule, from the non-Malays, particularly the Chinese, to the Malays; but this may be difficult to accomplish if the success of divestitures depends on allowing the non-Malay nationals also to buy. (The time schedule of NEP has recently been relaxed.) In several African countries like Kenya, Tanzania, and Uganda, there is an ethnic resentment to non-indigenous nationals purchasing the divested shares. They might be the more likely buyers, at least initially, if programmes of divestiture should succeed. But distributional tensions are certain to arise.

Another serious aspect of divestiture transactions is the influx of foreign capital, partly because there may not be enough of investor capability in the country, and partly because the technological restructuring which some of the candidates for privatisation require might call for a foreign input. There is plentiful empirical evidence, for example, from Togo, Guinea, and Malaysia.

Other things being equal, the influx of capital from abroad should be welcome to developing countries whose investment needs are high and domestic resources are scarce. But other things are not equal, especially in the context of privatisation.

First, the foreign investor succeeds in extracting very generous terms while buying an enterprise; and the government might be unable to discover this or remedy it, particularly when it is under the advice of foreign merchant bankers assisting the privatisation transaction. The government's anxiety to make a success of privatisation induces it to accept the terms.

Second, the equity-debt swaps can be too favourable to the foreign investor in a situation of heavy external debt burdens on the exchequer.

Third, where foreign capital comes into a joint venture with the government (still holding some shares), the familiar process, in which it continually extracts concessions of various kinds 'in the interest of government investment', can repeat itself.

Fourth, the more profitable segments of the public enterprise sector, which are easy to sell, might go to the foreign investor, while the rest remains for the local investor or probably with the government for a long time.

Fifth, the restructuring transactions, technology, and costs would hardly be subject to effective global tending, once a foreign buyer comes in; and he can enjoy monopoly in the supply of all the inputs concerned. On paper the government may have powers of inquiring into them; but history unfolds their ineffectiveness.

Every one of these disadvantages may not ensue in every case. But there is clear scope for them in a situation in which too many governments have too many enterprises which they are anxious to privatise too soon under internal stress and external pressures. The foreign investor has a buyer's market before him.

It is difficult to trace the distributional implications of foreign capital in the context of privatisation. On the one hand it helps improve the financial results of the enterprises and correspondingly relieves the taxpayer's burdens. It helps improvise the rate of growth and correspondingly benefits the low-income brackets to the extent that the country's development strategy provides for it. On the other hand, to the extent it enjoys monopoly power, it unleashes the same distributional effects as any other monopoly in the country does. If its repatriations, through high profits (and malpractices, if any) are heavy, the benefits that reinvestment of profits could offer the country will be lost, and along with them any benefits that might have flowed in favour of the poorer sections of the community.

It is interesting to note that, in several UK privatisations, restrictions are placed on the extent of foreign ownership.[43] (In some cases like British Petroleum for example, – the foreigner (indirectly) the Government of Kuwait – was persuaded to sell away some of its shares so as to reduce its percentage ownership.)[44] But in developing countries heavy block ownership by foreigners is not only permitted but sought.[45]

Use of divestiture proceeds

The way in which the government utilises the sales proceeds following divestiture has distinctive distributional implications.

The sale proceeds may be utilised for filling the budget deficits. Where the latter refer to revenue deficits, divestiture helps in keeping down additional taxation and in preventing curtailments in current expenditures. The distributional effects would be positive if the taxes referred to were regressive taxes, and if the expenditures referred to those that benefited the low-income brackets, or else they would be unfavourable.

The incomes may be used to finance new budget expenditures (current or capital). Here the distributional effects depend on which income groups derive the benefits of the expenditures. For instance, if the expenditures refer to elementary schools and public health, the low-income brackets are likely to benefit.

The incomes may be used to repay public debt – as had to be done in France, to some extent statutorily. Or government borrowings may be scaled down – as in the UK.[46] There would be no change in the benefits received by different income groups from government expenditures, particularly capital expenditures, since these remain unaffected by such public debt transactions. Incidentally, the economy experiences a reduction in the segment of fixed-interest 'gilt' securities, generally sought by certain institutions including pension funds, and an increase in 'risk' paper or private (non-government) debentures.

THE EXCHEQUER IMPLICATIONS

Let us examine how privatisation directly benefits the exchequer. We shall first take the case of a losing enterprise.

A losing enterprise

Assume that the enterprise makes losses which are fed by government subsidy. Privatisation or liquidation gives relief to the exchequer, first, to the extent of the recurring loss. If the sale proceeds are not less than the government's investment in the enterprise, the government is enabled to liquidate that part of the public debt which corresponds to that investment and gets relief from the recurring interest charges on that amount. This is the second benefit. (If the sale proceeds are used, not for debt repayment, but for some other purpose, the financial implications of the budget policy are independent of the privatisation transaction, except only that privatisation has occasioned an income.)

If the sale proceeds are less than the investment – as is likely in many cases – the relief from interest on public debt will be less than in the previous case. For public debt, corresponding to the shortfall of sale proceeds, will remain. The net effect will consist of relief from recurring losses minus continuing debt charges.

A losing enterprise which has accumulated losses represents one version of the above situation. The government has to raise funds for wiping them out, that is, for paying the creditors of the enterprise who were financing them. The net annual benefit to the government will be the difference between the annual losses not subsidised and the continuing interest charges on a larger amount of public debt than in the previous case.

If, instead of selling the enterprise, the government borrows funds for restructuring it rather than paying redundancies, and the enterprise turns around and makes profits, the exchequer will be at an advantage compared with the above situation. While its debt servicing costs will be the same as in the above situation, there will be no losses to subsidise; and probably profits accrue which help it meet the increased debt costs, partly or wholly.

A profit-making enterprise

Divestiture in the case of a profit-making enterprise has the obvious effect of loss of income to the exchequer or the public sector. (Here we treat together the profits actually transferred to the exchequer and the profits retained by the enterprise.) There will be a saving, however, of the costs of the public debt corresponding to the enterprise, assuming that the debt is repaid. The net loss to the exchequer is equal to the difference between the profits lost and the costs of debt saved, from year to year. This appears to be large if we consider as the 'corresponding debt' the government's investment that appears in the books of the enterprise under the heads of equity and loans only. In fact we have to add to it the reserves as well; for they notionally represent government investments, assuming that the retained profits were first turned over to the government and then came back as an investment. The amounts notionally returned to the enterprise or not actually received by the exchequer have to be treated as having impacted on the public debt, in the same way as an equity contribution would.

The higher the sale proceeds, the greater the public debt that could be repaid, and hence the smaller the unfavourable impact of divestiture on the exchequer. Under-pricing has the opposite effect.

Divestiture of profitable enterprises earns the accusation of 'selling family silver', partly because of the recurring net disadvantage to the exchequer, and partly because of the probable use of the sale proceeds for current purposes such as tax cuts.

Qualifications to the analysis

While estimating the effects of divestiture on the exchequer, we need to note several qualifications.

The net sale proceeds have to be computed after adjusting for the following: (i) the free 'gifts' which the government offers the enterprise before privatisation in order to make it an attractive flotation; (ii) the costs of privatisation such as underwriting commissions and publicity; and (iii) the costs of any 'matching' shares or 'loyalty bonus' offers which will have to be met at the end of a specified period after privatisation.

In estimating the continuing impacts on the budget, an adjustment has to be made for the costs of the regulatory framework set up for a privatised industry. An opposite adjustment is necessary in respect of the savings effected by the ministries because of the elimination (or absolute minimisation) of supervisory attention to the enterprise.

Assuming that a privatised enterprise is likely to make higher profits than it did while in the public sector, the exchequer gains from an increase in tax revenues. Wherever the assumption proves correct, subject to possible tax evasions, there is an indirect benefit to the exchequer. This is obvious in the case of a losing enterprise privatised, and probable in the case of a profitable enterprise privatised.

THE REGULATORY IMPLICATIONS

One of the main arguments for privatisation has been that it relieves the enterprise from the unproductive intervention of the government – 'from the dead hand of Whitehall'.[47] Paradoxically, privatisation introduces the involvement of the government or of agencies external to the privatised enterprise in regulating it in many areas of organisation and operation in direct or indirect ways. The purposes of the regulation are twofold: to ensure that the major objective of privatisation is realised, namely, efficiency through competition and the full play of market forces; and to prevent certain unfavourable consequences of monopoly and ownership concentration and minimise the social costs of private enterprise in a given sector.

There are two interesting points concerning regulation that goes with privatisation. First, it is fundamentally of the same kind that most private enterprises warrant, though privatisation has highlighted it in the case of certain enterprises. Hence the question can be raised as to why the regulatory interest on the part of the government should not be extended to the generality of private enterprise, subject to sectoral characteristics.

Second, several aspects of the regulation sought to be introduced over a privatised enterprise were relevant to that enterprise when it was in the public sector, for example, the introduction of a penalty clause or a 'compensation-to-consumer' clause in respect of interruption of supply of, say, gas or electricity. To take another example, there is no reason why 'yardstick competition' cannot be promoted within a public enterprise, to realise, to a significant extent, the same good results that competition encouraged through regulation is expected to produce in the case of a privatised enterprise.

Privatisation regulation is divisible into two categories – during privatisation, and post-privatisation.

During privatisation

The most important step that could be taken *while* privatising a monolithic enterprise is to reorganise it into several units without sacrificing technical efficiency. After being privatised, the units work as a different enterprise, with inter-enterprise contractual relationships prompted by market forces or, where necessary, under public regulation. In this respect, the UK experience is an opportunity missed in transferring public monopolies (like British Gas) to the private sector. The short-term motive of high sale proceeds for the exchequer, the political motive of making a success of the flotations, and the top managers' interest is heading an unbroken empire, were all responsible for less having been done than could be, in providing a competitive basis for the efficient operations of the privatised enterprises.

While private placements or 'core' sales lead to (some) concentration, public share offers can be so designed as to reserve a specified part of the equity for 'individual' applicants and restrict the extent of an individual's eligibility to share allotment. For instance, the Nigerian law on privatisation stipulates that 'in the case of oversubscription, no individual shall be allowed to hold more than 1 per cent equity in any one enterprise'.[48] In the UK, most privatisations restricted an individual's ownership to 15 per cent of the voting shares. The limit can be ensured as long as the Articles of Association cannot be altered with a view to relaxing it. The 'golden share', where it exists, can take care of this. There is one snag, namely, that investors can act in concert to beat the law, as in Jamaica's second tranche of sale of National Commercial Bank shares, where a 7.5 per cent limit was imposed.[49]

The government may hold a 'special share' known as the 'golden share' in the UK (or the 'Kiwi share' in New Zealand). The special share has no voting rights but is activated in circumstances of violation of the limits applicable to shareholding (for example, 15 per cent) and to the issue of any shares 'with voting rights not identical to those of the ordinary shares', of restrictions on foreign ownership or foreign directorships (for example, British Aerospace), of disposal of a major part of the assets, and of voluntary winding up of the company.[50] The special share, if limited to these areas, does not have any direct relevance for competition or efficiency on the part of the privatised enterprise. (Nor does the special share exist in every case in the UK.) There is no reason, however, why it cannot be used as an 'inside' tool of regulating managerial behaviour towards efficiency, except that the more it is active the less the investor's interest in a privatised enterprise; and the defects of government control characteristic of public enterprises may repeat themselves.

Post-privatisation

Where the privatised enterprise faces competition, the stress on regulation would be limited. The question, however, is how effective the competition is in reality. If the privatised enterprise has a high degree of monopoly power (like British Telecom plc), encouragement for the entry of relatively small units (such as Mercury) will have limited effect in producing competition in the short run which may indeed be quite long. The situation can be worse if the new entrants have to depend on the privatised giant for certain infrastructural inputs (like a network of cables).

Besides, entry into an apparently contestable market may be discouraged by innocent or passive barriers, as well as strategic or active barriers. The former arise from the very fact that the incumbent enterprise – a large-sized one – is there, possessing established advantages in the supply of products or services and in attracting customers; and it conveys an automatic feeling of fear in potential entrants. The strategic barriers refer to the active, 'predatory' measures which it can adopt to drive away an entrant. Being large in size and possessing sufficient 'reserve' resources, it can harm an entrant to the point of exit, even if its actions cause it some loss.

Regulation post-privatisation is expected to remedy the situation in which monopoly continues, with little or no effective contest from any existing firms or new entrants. It has to deal also with practices of duopoly or oligopoly on the part of the units in the sector concerned. The higher the elements of monopoly, duopoly,[51] or oligopoly are, which survive the modalities of privatisation, the greater would be the burdens on regulation. The evergrowing areas under the jurisdiction of the regulators in the UK – for example OFTEL and OFGAS – illustrate the proposition.

One of the basic tasks of regulation should be to bring about an effective division of the operations of the privatised enterprise into monopoly segments and competitive segments, so that the pressures of competition can work in the latter case. As regards the former, however, techniques of monopoly control have to be implemented. Where a division between the two categories of operations is not established, questions of cross-subsidisation stand out for regulatory evaluation all the time.

Attempts to break a monopoly would not be purposeful in the case of natural monopolies like electricity distribution or water-supply. Even as regards the activities which do not belong to the category of natural monopolies, the size of the market in many a developing country may be so small as to render the creation of several units, in the place of one, a heroic rather than an economical attempt, for the multitude of enterprises in a given sector operate as infra-optimal units. Wasteful competition results, as well as an erosion of capital, assuming that attempts on their part to amalgamate are resisted on grounds of monopoly policy. Thus privatisation cannot be assumed to guarantee economical competition in 'small-market' economies in many sectors, even if they do not belong to the category of public utilities or natural monopolies.

Developing countries face several other problems as regards regulation post-privatisation. Unlike in the UK, they have a large number of public enterprises to be privatised. For instance, Nigeria has listed sixty-seven for full privatisation – these refer to the Federal Government enterprises only; they include many light industries, for example, fruit, wood, textiles, films, and shrimps; in fact, public utilities like railways, airports, and electricity, are outside the divestiture list. Many on the privatisation list do not, strictly, call for regulation post-privatisation; but the mantle of former public enterprise status persists, and regulation may be forced on them against closures, retrenchment of labour, and even price enhancements. The needs of regulation would vary from one category of enterprise to another, and yet interest groups can see it standardised. It is doubtful if, as in the UK, enterprise-specific agencies of regulation will be, or should be, set up in a case like this. They may be considered wasteful and unnecessary, and all the 'regulatory eggs' may be placed 'in one basket', leading to 'serious mistakes which would not necessarily come to light'.[52] A balance has to be struck, considering the pros and cons of a single regulatory agency as against as many agencies as the enterprises privatised. Sectoral agencies are a possibility, but it might be better to constitute a single agency, with sectoral subdivisions. Regulatory inexperience is also an argument against the creation of multiple agencies. The overall aim should be to regulate well while the need lasts, but to dispense with regulation as a privatised enterprise tends to be synonymous with private enterprise in general. Industrywise, technical regulations are a different matter, and should be provided for independently of regulation considered necessary as a sequel to privatisation.

The above approach should not rule out the establishment of a specific regulatory agency for a major public utility like electricity or railways. Few developing countries, however, are likely to fully privatise such enterprises in the near future.

There is a common constraint on regulatory approach in developing countries, namely, that many a public enterprise is not likely to be fully privatised at one stretch. In the Nigerian case, forty-three enterprises are listed under partial divestiture, leaving the government's equity holding above 50 per cent in some cases and reducing it to not more than 40 per cent in the majority of cases. With so much holding resting with the government, the notion remains that it is directly involved in the conduct of the enterprise operations; and the emphasis on regulation from an external agency might be limited.

There is another point of particular relevance to developing countries. It is doubtful how far the notion of social returns associated with a public enterprise changes on its privatisation. This not only complicates the task of regulation, but dampens the investor's incentives and suppresses the full play of market forces.

A privatised monopoly calls for controls over prices in the interest of the consumers and, additionally, over profits in the interest of distributional equity.

The US experience of public utility control in terms of a 'fair rate of return' brings out the disadvantage that the enterprise over-invests since a return is secure under the control method. It is also possible that it tends to be more capital-intensive than is necessary for technical reasons. Further, the managers would have no incentive to economise costs, since a fair return on investment is guaranteed under the control mechanism.

All that is correct under certain assumptions, namely, that the investors are anxious to over-invest, as if they do not have other options of investmnt on a guarantee of at least the rate of return that the control mechanism offers, that the enterprise is indifferent to rigorous project evaluation, and that the regulator is neutral to, or ineffective in establishing, the reasonableness of capital expenditures and the efficiency of the cost structures.

There is a different method of control, namely, price control, which the

UK has adopted. The privatised enterprises are price-controlled under the formula 'RPI minus *X*'. In brief, this signifies that over, say, a five-year period, they cannot raise prices beyond the rate of increase in the retail index minus *X*. *X* is a number which varies among the enterprises and represents the extent to which a given enterprise is expected to absorb inflationary cost increases through internal economies. It represents efficiency gains. Once in five years the formula is reviewed and desirable changes in *X* are effected.

In some cases a 'plus *Y*' factor is introduced, to relieve the enterprise of cost disadvantages flowing from exogenous circumstances over which it has no control, for example, the offshore operations of British Gas.

Then there is the *K* factor, conceived in connection with the privatisation of water in the UK. It is a system of 'cost pass through' which provides for price enhancements owing to specific investment obligations like environmental improvements, or for correcting predictive errors in estimating the investment requirements of a privatised enterprise.

The RPI minus *X* formula starts on the implicit assumption that the prices prevailing at the time of privatisation are 'correct' or 'acceptable', and regulates changes during a five-year period in terms of the retail price index. The reason why an *X* is devised is two-fold: it forces the enterprise to strive for cost economies and absorb a part of the inflationary cost increases through efficiency gains; and price changes reflected in the retail price index do not affect every enterprise in the same manner. (Indices of input prices, specific to each enterprise, would provide a more reliable base with which to link its price changes.) Hence, different numbers are set for *X* for different enterprises, for example, 2 for British Gas and 3 for British Telecommunications. The scope for cost economies as demand expands – through improved utilisation of fixed capital works – is an important factor considered in determining *X*.

It would be a mistake to claim that the RPI minus *X* formula is only a price control formula and has no reference to profits. The very concept of *X* signifies that in its absence the enterprise can earn, through price increases, even if limited to the RPI changes, a level of profits which the government determines it ought not to. *X* prompts cost economies, no doubt, without which the RPI minus *X* formula affects its profits. If, in spite of genuine efforts, it cannot realise cost economies or efficiency gains, its profit level declines, and when the formula comes up for review (in five years) *X* has to be set lower than before, unless new circumstances have arisen which ensure an acceptable profit level with the same *X* as before.[53]

We can bring out the implicit relationship between the RPI minus *X* formula and profit control by another route. The investment needs of the enterprise, which might imply long periods of gestation, have to be taken into account while determining *X*, from time to time. It may have to be lowered during the periods of gestation, so that the profit earned is not unduly low in relation to the total capital outlay; and on the same ground it may have to be raised in subsequent periods when economies of scale begin to be realised.

The *K* factor, apparently specific to water privatisation in the UK, openly brings out the connection between the RPI minus *X* formula and profit regulation. To quote from *The Financial Times*, 'the Government has been forced by the peculiarities of the industry to move close to the US system of setting prices to yield a "fair" rate of return on capital employed', through 'the mysterious *K* factor set by the regulator'.[54] The regulator's task would be no less complex and no less subject to regulatory capture than under the rate-of-return control system, for he would have to adjudicate on the investments, cost structures, efficiency attained, and efficiency possible.[55]

It might be necessary in developing countries to extend the coverage of control or regulation beyond prices and profits.

There may be need in some cases to stipulate that within a specified period after privatisation there will be no lay-off of labour.[56] Such a condition dampens investor interest in the first place. Assuming, however, that agreed labour redundancies at the point of privatisation are already dealt with, this condition dissuades the enterprise from going in for labour-substituting technologies, even if they are economical. These may be permitted if the production expands such that no part of the existing labour has to be retrenched. Regulations of this kind amount to the injection of an extra-enterprise objective, for which the enterprise deserves a compensation. Permission to price high is no solution, for it amounts to a clear cross-subsidy from consumers to workers.

Another version of the previous situation is the closure of parts of the enterprise on grounds of loss of demand. It should not be seen as a responsibility of the government to guarantee against demand losses. The sale price must have been a function of all available knowledge on demand. Labour redundancies on closure have to be dealt with under the general laws dealing with the subject.

However, where a closure results from the investors' intention to cannibalise the factory and make highly lucrative real estate business out of the site, there ought to be a preventive rule – not for all time, but for a reasonable, agreed period after privatisation. In fact the sale price should take such a possibility or likelihood into account on a 'contingent basis', in the sense that, if the closure occurs for reasons of real estate business within a specified period, a substantial part of the profits resulting from it should be deemed to be a 'deferred' part of the privatisation price and turned over to the government. Capital gains taxes, if applicable to such a transaction, might not fully take care of the situation in which public wealth is virtually available for private benefit on a silver platter.

Regulation post-privatisation has to include provisions regarding the extent of foreign control over the enterprise.[57] This can vary from sector to sector. Such regulation is necessary, not only in developing countries, but in developed countries as well. For instance, it is stipulated that the chief executive of British Telecommunications plc shall be a British citizen.

Developing countries may wish to go further in providing broad regulatory guidelines for board constitution in the case of major privatisations, for example, not less than – and not more than – a specified proportion of the board should be executive directors, or drawn from worker-shareholders, or shareholders holding less than a specified number of shares each.

It is debatable if there should be a government director in a fully privatised enterprise. A case can be made in terms of the 'golden share', if any, so as to ensure that the various regulatory provisions are complied with. But it would be far better to leave regulatory assurances to other machinery than a government director. The latter would reintroduce the defects of government directorships on public enterprise boards.

Finally, the need for regulation varies from case to case; so do the nature of it and the period over which it has to be applied. For example, privatised electricity or water stands at one extreme in all these respects, while a privatised laundry or flour mill stands at the other. It would be a mistake to over-extend regulation, keeping a privatised enterprise needlessly different from an ordinary private enterprise, permanently.

Further, certain parts of the regulatory framework would be equally applicable to other private enterprises. For example, the RPI minus *X* formula can be applied to major steel or chemical works in the private sector enjoying monopoly power; likewise provisions concerning foreign directorships would be equally good in the case of major private enterprises.

CONCLUSION

Ideology apart, the decision to privatise should be enterprise-specific, and depend on the comparative advantage of the enterprise remaining in the public sector. Neither losses invariably reflect loss of comparative advantage, nor profits necessarily imply its continued enjoyment of comparative advantage.

In countries with large public enterprise sectors, complete privatisation can take many years, for example, twenty-five years in Senegal.[58] To hasten it might achieve the transfer of enterprises to the private sector but at the cost of the long-term interests of the economy, as with the twenty-two textile mills privatised in 1982–3 in Bangladesh.[59]

Distributional consequences of privatisation, along with the long-term effects of the influx of foreign equity in controlling proportions call for careful deliberation. This should not be blurred by an anxiety for quick flotation.

In several cases divestiture is not the only modality that brings about efficiency gains in the operations of an enterprise. Non-ownership measures can be an equally, if not more, powerful means. However, they have to be introduced with a genuine intention of improving efficiency and not merely to avoid divestiture. In so far as the centrally-planned economies are concerned, non-divestiture options would constitute the option in the immediate future, apart from joint ventures with foreign capital.

Divestiture is a means to an end, not an end in itself. Efficiency is the end either in a given sector of operations or in the economy as a whole.

Finally, there are serious differences of scenario – economic and political – between developed and developing countries, which are relevant to the policy and implementation of divestiture.[60] It is unrealistic to expect that the results recorded in a Thatcherite model will fully unfold themselves in most developing countries.

The privatisation scenario of centrally-planned economies trying to transform themselves into market economies is unique. The forthcoming document of the United Nations Development Programme, *Guidelines on Privatisation* (Part V) illustrates this.

APPENDIX 14.1 Some instances of special terms of share offers to employees

1. Amersham International plc

(i) 35 shares free, at the Government's expense.
(ii) The Government matched, one for one, purchases by employees up to 350 shares per employee (with a maximum of 217,700 shares): these shares are held in the Amersham Share Participation Scheme.
(iii) Preferential consideration in allotment (up to 2.5 million shares).

2. Associated British Ports Holdings plc
First issue 1983
(i) 53 free shares for each eligible employee, at the Government's expense.
(ii) Matching shares up to 225 per employee: held by the Trustees of Associated British Ports Employee Share Ownership scheme.
(iii) Preferential consideration up to 3 per cent of the issued capital, less (ii).
Second issue 1984
Preferential consideration up to 1,000 shares per employee.

3. BAA plc 1987
(i) 41 free shares per employee.
(ii) Matching shares up to 111 per employee.
(iii) Preferential consideration up to 4,082 shares per employee/pensioner.

4. British Aerospace plc
First issue 1981
(i) 33 free shares per eligible employee.
(ii) Matching shares up to 600 per employee.
(iii) Preferential consideration up to 2.5 per cent of the issue capital.
Second issue 1985

Preferential consideration up to 10,000 shares per employee, within 2 per cent of the issued share capital.

5. British Airways plc 1987
(i) 76 free shares per employee.
(ii) Matching shares (two for one) up to 120 per employee.
(iii) Up to 1600 shares by each employee under the priority offer were offered at a discount of 10 per cent.

6. British Gas plc 1986
(i) 52 free shares per employee (56 for a pensioner).
(ii) Matching shares (two for one) up to 111 per employee.
(iii) 10 per cent discount on 1,481 shares per employee purchased under the priority arrangements.

7. British Petroleum Co Ltd
First issue 1977:
Preferential consideration
Second issue 1978:
(i) Preferential consideration up to 137 shares per employee.
(ii) Matching shares, one for one.
Third issue 1983:
Preferential consideration up to 250 shares per employee.

8. British Telecommunications plc 1984
(i) 54 free shares per employee.
(ii) Matching shares, two for one, up to 77 per employee.
(iii) 10 per cent discount up to 1,600 shares per employee purchased under the priority arrangements.

9. Britoil plc
First issue 1982
(i) Free shares of the value of £60 per each eligible employee.
(ii) Matching shares, one for one.
(iii) Preferential consideration up to 11,500 shares per employee.
Second issue 1985
Preferential consideration up to 10,000 shares per employee within 3 per cent of the issued share capital.

10. Cable and Wireless plc
First issue 1981
(i) Preferential consideration within 5 per cent of issued share capital.
(ii) 285,833 free shares to Cable and Wireless Employee Share Schemes.
Second issue 1983
Preferential consideration up to 1,000 shares per employee.
Third issue 1985
Preferential consideration up to 5,000 shares per employee (2,500 per pensioner) within 15 per cent of issued share capital.

11. Enterprise Oil plc 1984
Preferential consideration up to 13,500 shares per employee.

12. Jaguar plc 1984
15 per cent of issued share capital reserved for employees.

13. Rolls-Royce 1987
- (i) 41 free shares per eligible employee.
- (ii) Matching shares, two for one, up to 88 per employee.
- (iii) Priority reservations of 5,882 shares per employee (pensioner) up to 5 per cent of the issued share capital; 10 per cent discount on 1,176 shares out of this.
- (iv) A total of 10 per cent issued share capital reserved under the above arrangements.

Source: *Privatisation: The Facts*, London, Price Waterhouse, 1987.

15 The future of public enterprise

If the future of public enterprise lies merely in its disappearance, our conclusions will be limited to the implications of divestiture. But while some public enterprises will be transferred to the private sector 100 per cent or liquidated, several will operate as joint ventures with minority or majority participation by private investors, and many are likely to continue as public enterprises. The precise numbers in each of these categories depend on such factors as (i) the absorbing capacity of private investors, (ii) government policies towards the influx of foreign capital, (iii) development strategy in terms of investment priorities, regional development, and distributional equity, (iv) exchequer strains, (v) external pressures and, above all, (vi) political environment. The numbers are bound to change constantly and the proportions of the categories would be different from developed to developing countries and among developing countries themselves. What is of greater significance is that governments have become flexible in their attitude towards holding on to (or establishing) a public enterprise. The initial era of bias for it has ended.[1] There is a clear awareness of the proposition that public enterprise is a means to an end, the end being national well-being, and not an end in itself, that the end is more important than the means and that the means should be suitably revised in the interest of accomplishing the end.

This chapter provides a concluding overview of the three possible scenarios of what may be termed the second era or policy mix, namely, divestitures, joint ventures, and continuing public enterprises. The earlier chapters contain the supporting detail.

DIVESTITURE

The success of divestiture has to be evaluated in terms of its long-term effects. A major determinant is the very efficiency of private enterprise in the country. Here we refer to the domestic entrepreneurs and managers and not the multinationals. Making a profit is not invariably an index of their efficiency, for many developing countries present the phenomena of sellers' markets and dubious relationships between the entrepreneurs and government officials. While profits accrue, the interests of consumers and, perhaps, workers suffer, and the distributional implications of divestiture considered in chapter 14 unfold themselves.

There is a more basic question. How 'private' is private enterprise in developing countries? An unduly large part of the capital comes from financial institutions and as loan capital, as, for example, in India or Pakistan. Financial intermediation is predominantly in the public sector. Two consequences follow. First, the decisions of the financing agency are under government control, openly or informally. Often the central bank sets quotas of investment in selected fields, and the controller of capital issues – a government agency – takes into account, among other things, the need for investment in a given sector. There might also be controls, in effect, on investments by 'groups'. Second, the real stake of the 'core' investor in an enterprise is a minor fraction of its total capital outlay, yet he is in control of its use. While he has ample scope to profit from the situation, his risk of loss is relatively small.

Add to this certain alleged malpractices, namely, that several entrepreneurs 'somehow' get back their investment while commissioning the plant, and in the early years of operations, and that some, in fact, might make the enterprise 'sick'.[2] The losers are the creditors, public financial institutions in the main,[3] and the workers who lose employment. An agitation arises for the (re-)nationalisation of the enterprise, in the interest of protecting employment.

The scenario described above would not apply to every privatised enterprise. But the possibility cannot be ruled out in several cases. There would be heavy pressures for regulation – against entrepreneurial and managerial malpractices, high profits and high dividend declarations. Whether capital expenditures have been 'regular' and whether transactions with other parties, which are apparently a business practice, contain elements of illegitimate gains to the entrepreneurs and the managers, would be among the questions to be considered by the regulator.

In these circumstances, how private would privatised enterprise be in developing countries? The question might not be important in the case of small units and units in competitive sectors. Elsewhere it would be significant.

Let us look at the claim that divestiture involving wide share ownership cannot be reversed. Whether a privatised enterprise can be re-nationalised depends on two factors: the adequacy and effectiveness of the regulatory framework; and the political strength of the party in power.

The first is a basic technical consideration. If the expected benefits of privatisation through regulation are not realised, there would be a case for re-nationalisation. But the second factor is the determinant of action. Where the government has clear strength in parliament and where it is not afraid of losing the vote in an election looming round the corner, it can go ahead with a re-nationalising measure. Contrary to the popular contention, wide share ownership does not prevent such action either on the first ground or on the second.

Wide share ownership would not be an obstacle in the mechanics of re-nationalisation, either. For once the government's political strength is undoubted, there can be several ways of dealing with the problem. The UK experience suggests that the initial large numbers of shareholders have been dwindling; the trend might be intensified after the 'loyalty bonus' period expires; and unless the enterprise in question maintains a high profit rate there is no reason why any shareholder should faithfully stick to his shares for ever. In any case, the small shareholders account for a small proportion of the capital. If the government decides on re-nationalisation, it can pass a law, not very different from the 1945 Nationalisation Acts, in so far as the purchase of shares from private shareholders is concerned, and adopt a procedure as follows.

A shareholder may turn in his shares at specified places, including banks and building societies, and will receive compensation at the same places within a specified period. This may be in cash or in bonds. It may be in cash for small shareholders (holding less than a specified number of shares) and in bonds for the others. Some variation can be designed; for example, shareholders choosing to receive bonds may be offered a higher compensation than those taking cash.

Small shareholders may be offered a slightly higher compensation than the others. Worker-shareholders may, additionally, be offered a 'bonus bond' with a loyalty clause at the rate of one for every ten or twenty shares held. These measures can assuage any feeling of discomfort or opposition on their part.

The exchequer and the merchant bankers who invented several inducing devices during privatisation can equally cleverly work out the mechanics of the reverse gear.

In fact nationalisation (or re-nationalisation) is far less difficult than de-nationalisation, given the favourable political conditions. In the latter case the government has the difficult problem of finding an appropriate buyer, whereas in the former the buyer is ready and has the legal power to get the seller to sell. The technical problems of fixing the sale price are equally complex in both cases.

Governments have a wide range of concerns. Divestiture is but one of them. More important is the need to ensure that social tensions do not arise. Where divestiture runs the risk of creating such tensions, the priorities of the government understandably place social harmony above divestiture.

Where a privatised enterprise makes conspicuous profits, it attracts questions regarding its ownership. For example, are the owners rich families, foreigners, or certain openly or implicitly resented ethnic groups? A paradox will develop: the efficiency of the enterprise may depend on the incumbent owners, but their ownership may be resented by large sections of the population.

JOINT VENTURES

In the near future we are most likely to witness a steep increase in the number of joint ventures between the government and private capital. This will be due to:

(a) partial divestitures;
(b) the induction of private capital in public enterprises; and/or
(c) the formation of new joint venture companies.

The most important reasons for the first possibility are as follows:

(i) The government is not prepared to give up ownership and the control that goes with it in certain cases, in particular the basic, heavy or public utility industries and banking.
(ii) The absorbing capacity of the buyers is not large enough to permit total divestitures; and whatever exists can be spread over a larger number of enterprises under a scheme of partial divestiture than when total divestiture is undertaken.
(iii) The government intends to go slow in divestiture and in tranches, to take advantage of experience in the pricing of shares, underwriting arrangements, and the regulatory framework.
(iv) Private investors may wish the government to be an equity partner, so that they can be fairly certain in deriving its support for the successful operations of the enterprise.
(v) National policies governing foreign capital may limit it to less than 100 per cent ownership in many sectors. Hence, where foreign private capital *must* come in, there has to be a joint venture, in some cases with the government.

Except in the first case one may consider that the joint venture or partial divestiture sets the stage for total divestiture over time, subject to two constraints, apart from political attitudes. For one thing, the enterprise may be so profitable that the exchequer feels reluctant to part with its equity holding. For another, civil servants and their political masters may be averse to giving up whatever privileges of patronage the enterprise vests in them.

The circumstances in which private capital may be introduced in a public enterprise are as follows:

(i) The enterprise needs to expand but the government does not have funds enough to finance the expansions. Nor does it want to borrow because of limits on public debt, either self-imposed or enforced by external pressures (for example, the structural adjustment agreements with the IMF and the World Bank).

(ii) The enterprise is in need of technological restructuring or the introduction of a new technology, which the collaborator offers only on condition that he is given an equity share which entitles him to a share in management and in the recurring profits arising out of his efforts. Or, the government wants to bind him with an equity stake which induces him to offer satisfactory technical assistance.

Another way in which a joint venture involving the government comes into being is when a company is floated in which the government and some private investors jointly invest, whatever the proportions. The latter may consist of a few 'block' investors only, or a few such and a number of small shareholders. While this technique can be adopted with reference to any industry, whether chocolates or electricity, in an era when the purpose of government ownership is under severe review, it is most likely to be applied to sectors which have the characteristics of a public utility or of monopoly and capital intensity. The government's ownership involvement may be considered as purposeful in such cases. A sector which offers itself as an easy candidate for this method is electricity. For example, some bulk consumers of industrial power have been forming joint ventures with the state electricity boards in India.[4] The alternative might be power scarcity for them and, indirectly, for others.

On the whole, joint ventures will assume great prominence in the near future. However, their success depends on evolving a relationship between the government's ownership and the government's involvement in the management of the enterprise. The principle of proportional involvement will limit the expected benefits of private managerial skills, not only in the case of joint venture in which the government has a majority holding, but also in cases where its minority holding is substantial, or provides government directors with disproportionate power. It would be ideal if the government limits its interest to gaining a good dividend income and to ensuring that managerial malpractices, ownership concentration, take-over bids, and so on, do not occur. Broadly, government ownership should be in the spirit of the 'golden share'. The regulation that the enterprise calls for by virtue of its sectoral characteristics or of macro considerations like labour redundancies should be left to outside regulatory agencies and laws. It would be preferable, by and large, not to internalise them *on the ground* that the government is part owner of the enterprise.

Joint ventures with foreign capital introduce all the familiar problems of drawing up the contract. While many governments today have the benefit of experience and advice from the UN Centre on Transnationals, there are two factors which weaken their position in arriving at a satisfactory contract without loopholes:

(i) the urgency of the transaction, owing to exchequer difficulties and international pressures; and

(ii) the poor financial condition of public enterprises into which foreign capital is invited.

Thus the joint ventures will be far from a bed of roses.

CONTINUING PUBLIC ENTERPRISES

Under this head we consider enterprises which remain under government ownership. These belong to several categories:

(a) Enterprises selected, but waiting, for divestiture.
(b) Enterprises which deserve to be transferred to the private sector but are not, for political or other reasons, for example, the privatisations recently stopped in France.
(c) Enterprises whose monopoly and public utility characteristics are such that making them private monopolies is not a superior option, for example, electricity or water.
(d) Enterprises which the government decides not to transfer to the private sector on grounds of national development strategy, for example, the 'core' industries.
(e) Enterprises which will remain in the public sector as a matter of national policy, for example, in economies choosing to remain centrally planned.

It would be desirable for the government to arrive at a rough classification of public enterprises on the above lines, not because privatisation is the 'buzz' word today, but because the case for public enterprise in a given sector may have declined over time, even in terms of the argument in chapter 1. The classification should not be static over time.

The operations of enterprises belonging to the first category call for a clearly private sector model. This implies that the managers are given autonomy in taking input and output decisions, for example, in laying off labour that is unproductive. The emphasis of the operations should be on profit as if the enterprises are privately owned, and an attempt should be made to limit their extra-enterprise objectives (and design the mechanics of any continuing obligations). The government has to ensure that they operate in such a way that their appeal to potential buyers improves rather than deteriorates over time. In particular, labour surplus, if any, should be amicably dealt with, through redundancy payments or transfers to other enterprises or retraining or absorption in expansions. It may be advantageous in some cases to place the enterprises under a management contract or a lease agreement with private parties, so that they work virtually like private enterprises except for the profits (or losses) accruing to the exchequer. Most importantly, the government should suitably prepare the flotation of the enterprises at the right time, so that the exchequer raises the maximum proceeds of sale possible and the taxpayer does not sustain a disadvantage.

The enterprises in the second category signify that their comparative advantage of staying in the public sector is little, but their transfer to the private sector is obstructed by reasons not related to efficiency considerations. As long as those reasons continue, the policy should be one of injecting the private sector model into their operations, subject to any extra-enterprise obligations. Here again, techniques of contracting-out, leasing and management contracts can be liberally adopted.

The third category calls for all the regulations necessary in the case of monopolies, irrespective of the fact that the enterprises remain in the public sector.

The fourth and fifth categories, along with the third, simply call for reforms in investment decision, in the assignment of extra-enterprise obligations, in the rules of operations, in monitoring, in evaluation, and in the exercise of government relationships, as indicated in the earlier chapters. There is the danger that far less attention than necessary might be paid to the introduction and genuine implementation of the reforms, in the expectation that one day these enterprises will also be denationalised.

There are some fundamental problems to be addressed. First, public enterprise entails certain intrinsic costs spread over all stages of its working – from investment decision at one end to evaluation at the other. These cannot be totally eliminated, but they can and must be minimised; for experience suggests that the benefits associated with certain sources of such costs are far less substantial than are imagined. To the extent of success in this direction, the comparative advantage of public enterprise improves.

Second, does the national development strategy adopted by the government necessarily require the size and composition of public enterprise that exists? If it is uncritically assumed that it does, many basic questions on its propriety tend to be pushed under the carpet. Countries where the concept of 'core' industries is emphasised in defence of a large public enterprise sector would benefit from an unbiased review of this question.

Third, where public enterprise can be an acceptable tool of an extra-enterprise objective, for example, of a certain pattern of growth or income distribution, are its conditions of investment and operations such as can render it a tool capable of the maximum possible results expected by the community? Very often acceptable objectives are defeated by government interface with the enterprises; and being obsessed with the objectives, one does not attach enough attention to this problem.

A study on public enterprise cannot be concluded without reference to development strategy. In many countries the latter has aimed at higher goals than could be achieved and public enterprise has been created as the main agency to realise the goals. In some cases the development strategy might be within reach, but the government translates it to public enterprise in a manner that leads to financial losses. Nor is it certain that offsetting social returns are realised in the process.

Thus inefficient plan strategies and inefficient government administrations have resulted in the inefficiency of public enterprises to a substantial extent. To deal with the latter only would amount to dealing with symptoms rather than root causes.

If development strategies and government directives begin to emphasise the earning of large surpluses from public enterprises, there is no reason why they should not be able to show profits. However, there can be the danger of a total swing of policy towards profits; for public enterprise has justification, conceptually, on grounds of its 'publicness'. This has to be synthesised with the goal of financial profit. The synthesis may never be equally perfect in the view of every one; but it should be agreed by parliament and made transparent to the public, enterprise by enterprise.

Notes

CHAPTER 1 THE CONCEPT AND RATIONALE OF PUBLIC ENTERPRISE

1 For a full discussion see Ramanadham, V. V. (1984) *The Nature of Public Enterprise*, part I, London.
2 Musolf, L. D. (1959) *Public Ownership and Accountability*, Harvard, p. 102.
3 An opposite situation is possible, though very rarely, as illustrated by Israel whose company law provides that 'a government company shall act in accordance with the business considerations by which a non-government company is normally guided, unless the government with the approval of the (Finance) Committee (of Parliament), prescribes other considerations for acting' (cited by Yair Aharoni in 'The State-owned Enterprise: An Agent without a Principal', Second BAPEG Conference on *Public Enterprise in Mixed Economy LDCs*, Boston, April 1980).
4 For purposes of National Income and Expenditure statistics in the UK, public corporations are defined 'as public trading bodies which have a substantial degree of financial independence of the public authority – generally the central government – which created them'. (*National Accounts Statistics – Sources and Methods,* Central Statistical Office, London, 1968).
5 Some definitions of public enterprise are shown below:

L. D. Musolf: 'Public Enterprise is used here to refer to governmental activities operated exclusively or primarily on the economic model', *Organisation and Administration of Public Enterprises*, p. 111.

United Nations (1968): 'Publicly-owned and/or controlled enterprises ... incorporated public corporations, i.e. by virtue of company acts or other public acts ... or large unincorporated units (government enterprises) that sell most of the goods ... they produce to the public', *A System of National Accounts*, United Nations E. 69, XVII 3, p. 78.

V. V. Ramanadham (1977): 'The term "public enterprise" may be understood to signify an economic activity of which the majority ownership or managerial control vests in the government and/or other public agencies ... we shall limit the term "enterprise" to signify an activity whose costs, primarily, are expected to be financed from the sale proceeds – generally and in the long run', Commonwealth Secretariat, *The Role and Management of Public Enterprises*, London, p. 29

L. P. Jones (1975): 'A public enterprise is a productive activity which is owned and/or controlled by public authorities and whose output is marketed', *Public Enterprise and Economic Development: The Korean Case*, Seoul, p. 23.

W. Keyser and R. Windle (eds) (1977): 'Public enterprise will be taken to mean "all corporate entities (with or without legal personality) which pursue a wholly or largely economic purpose and whose capital is for an "important" part owned by public authorities . . . or which have been granted special or exclusive rights by the public authorities, or whose operations are to a large extent determined by them', *Public Enterprise in the EEC*, p. 2, Brussels.

6 Ullman, F. (1979) 'The Austrian Model of its Nationalised Industrial Sector', Expert Group Meeting on the Role of the Public Sector in the Industrialisation of the Developing Countries, UN Industrial Development Organisation (UNIDO), Vienna, p. 4. See also Lauterbach, A. L. (1978), *The Austrian Public Sector in International Perspective: A Socio-historical Evaluation*, Austin, Texas. Austria inherited 'a set of ownerless enterprises', none untarnished by a Nazi past to take over (p. 1).

7 Marsan, V. A., (1986) 'Istituto per la Recostruzione Industriale', in Ramanadham V. V. (ed.) *Public Enterprise: Studies in Organisational Structure*, London, pp. 82–3.

8 'Private industry is generally concerned with short-term profit maximisation, while nationalised industries and the Government have to take a longer view or, to put it in another way, to take account of the "social time preference"' Jones, T. P. (1984) *What Should We Expect From Our Nationalised Industries?*, London.

9 UN Industrial Development Organisation (1979) *The Public Sector and Industrial Development*, Vienna, p. 16.

10 Short, P. P., (1984) 'The Role of Public Enterprises: An International Statistical Comparison' in *Public Enterprise in Mixed Economies: Some Macroeconomic Aspects*, Washington DC: International Monetary Fund. The data are no doubt subject to several qualifications of coverage and accuracy. Further, in some cases, for example, Chile, Peru and Jamaica, the figures for certain earlier years were widely different, reflecting rather sudden changes in policies.

11 The calculations are derived from Table 8 of E/5690/Add. 1 of *The Role of the Public Sector in Promoting the Economic Development of Developing Countries*, New York: Report of the Secretary-General, United Nations, 1975.

12 Ibid., Table 9.

13 A Nigerian study reported by J. Olutimeyin in 1986 concluded that public enterprises and joint ventures at government level led to technical development, while private enterprises and subsidiaries of foreign companies did not. ('Factors Affecting Utilisation of Foreign Technologies for Technological Development in Developing Countries: A Nigerian Case Study', *Nigerian Management Review*, Lagos.

Jeffrey James observed in his 'Introduction' to several studies on technological development that 'in practice direct intervention through public enterprises has played an important part in the indigenous efforts of several large countries' (*The Technological Behaviour of Public Enterprises in Developing Countries*, London, 1989 p. 3).

In India there has been a great effort at research and development (R & D) and adaptation by SOEs (state-owned enterprises) relative to POEs (privately-owned enterprises.) Anil B. Deolalikr and Anant K. Sundaram, ibid., p. 115).

Jeffrey James concludes in his 'Introduction' that 'more specifically both the absolute and relative size of the R & D and technology adaptation efforts appear to be greater in publicly than in privately-owned firms' (ibid., p. 14).

14 K. D. Kaunda observed that 'five banks in Zambia are too many' (*Take up the Challenge,* Lusaka, 1970, p. 65; UN Industrial Development Organisation (1977) *Industrialisation of the Least Developed Countries*, ID/WG 234/13,

Vienna, refers repeatedly to the 'smallness' of markets in Afghanistan, Chad, Ethiopia, Niger, Somalia, Gabon, Mauritania, and so on.

15 Lakshman, W. D. (ed.) (1979) *Public Enterprises in the Economic Development of Sri Lanka*, Colombo, p. 159.

16 *Performance of Public Enterprises in Nepal* (Macro Study), Kathmandu, 1977, p. 155.

17 Ahmad, M. (1980) *Public Sector in a Developing Economy: A Politico-economic Study of Bangladesh*, Dacca, pp. 7, 115.

18 See pp. 31–4.

19 Baklanoff, E. N. (1986) 'The State and Economy in Portugal: Perspectives on Corporation Revolution and Incipient Privatisation', in Glade, W. P. (1986) *State Shrinking: A Comparative Inquiry into Privatization*, Austin, Texas, p. 274.

20 Nelson, H. P. (1980) *Promotion of Ghanaian Enterprises and Ghanaian Participation in Foreign Enterprises*, Ljubljana, International Centre for Public Enterprises (ICPE).

21 Other agencies in Malaysia with similar, among other, functions are Majlis Amanah Rakyat, Perbadanan Nasional, Bank Bumiputra, and Bank Pembangunam and State Economic Development Corporations.

In Ghana the Development National Finance Holding Ltd held shares not taken up by Ghanaians 'for the time being', to be sold to them at a subsequent date when they were in a position to pay for them. Besides, the government itself had to buy certain indigenised shares 'to bring up Ghanaian participation . . . to the level prescribed by the Indigenisation Decree' (H. P. Nelson, ibid.).

22 Julius K. Nyerere, (1968) *Economic Nationalism*, Dar es Salaam, p. 264.

23 *White Paper on Public Participation in Industrial and Commercial Activities*, Port-of-Spain, 1972, pp. 3–4.

24 Kaunda, K. D. (1968) *Zambia's Economic Revolution*, Lusaka, pp. iv, v, 50.

25 UN Industrial Development Organisation (1983) *Role of the Public Industrial Enterprise Sector in Mexico,* Vienna.

26 *Permanent Sovereignty over Natural Resources*, Report of the Secretary-General of the United Nations, A. 1971b, New York, 20 September 1974.

27 Ibid., Report in March 1979, p. 5.

28 Ramanadham, V. V. (1984) op. cit., p. 167.

29 Reid, G. L. and Allen, K. (1973) *Nationalized Industries*, London, p. 17.

30 Kelf-Cohen (1969) *Twenty Years of Nationalisation*, London, p. 52.

31 Syed, R. E. (ed.) *Role and Performance of Public Enterprises in the Economic Growth of Pakistan*, pp. 34–5.

32 The Finance Minister said in his budget speech in 1970 that 'a developing country cannot leave development at the mercy of the inter-play of forces which are motivated by the profit instinct' Lakshman, W. D. (1979) op. cit., pp. 15–29.

33 Ahmad, M. (1980) op. cit.

34 Sauliniers, A. H. (1985) *Beyond Management Control: A System Approach to Public Enterprises*, Austin, Texas, p. 1.

35 Baklanoff, E. N. (1986) in Glade, W. E. (ed.) op. cit., p. 264.

36 Kennedy, P. J. Jr (1986) 'State Shrinkage: The Jamaican Experience', in Glade, W. P. (ed.) op. cit., p. 179.

37 *Deuxième Plan Quadriennal, 1974–1977*, Rapport General, p. 29.

38 Gracey, D. (1979) 'Public Enterprise and the Public Interest', Proceedings of an International Seminar, *Commonwealth Seminar Report on National Policies and Programmes for Public Enterprise Management Training*, London, p. 103.

Also, 'public enterprise in Canada has been and continues . . . to be of major importance in the pursuit of broad economic, social and other goals in the public interest' (p. 104).

CHAPTER 2 THE EMERGENCE OF PUBLIC ENTERPRISE

1 The term 'sponsoring' is used in the UK literature to signify the department of the government within which a nationalised industry comes.

2 Lakshman, W. D. (ed.) (1979) *Public Enterprises in the Economic Development of Sri Lanka*, Colombo, p. 38.

3 *Measures for Improving the Performance of Public Enterprises in Developing Countries*, vol. I, New York: United Nations, 1970, p. 7.

4 'On the day following the nationalisation, there were in fact no top executives . . . to assume immediate responsibility.' Hence *ad hoc* arrangements had to be made, Sobhan R. and Ahmad, M. (1980) *Public Enterprise in an Intermediate Regime: A Study in the Political Economy of Bangladesh,* Dacca, pp. 150–2.

5 International Symposium on Economic Performance of Public Enterprises, Beg, H. U. (1981) 'Project Cost Overruns, Nature and Impact of Delays in Project Implementation'. Islamabad, pp. 1–2.

6 Jeffrey James (ed.) (1989) *The Technological Behaviour of Public Enterprises in Developing Countries*, London.

7 For example, as between spinning and weaving equipments in Somaltex in Somalia (see *A Casebook of Public Enterprise Studies*, introduced by Praxy Fernandes and Vladimir Keacic, Ljubljana: International Center For Public Enterprises 1982, p. 14).

8 For a full discussion on development corporations see Carey-Jones, N. S., Patankar, S. M. and Boodhoo, M. J. (1974) *Politics, Public Enterprise and the Industrial Development Agency*, London; Ramanadham, V. V. (1974) *Organisation, Management and Supervision of Public Enterprises in Developing Countries*, chs 2 and 3, New York: United Nations; and Hanson, A. H. (1959) *Public Enterprise and Economic Development*, London.

9 For illustrative evidence, see Ayub, M. A. and Hegstad, S. O. (1986) *Public Industrial Enterprises: Determinants of Performance*, Washington, DC: World Bank, Industry and Finance Series, vol. 17, Table 6.

10 For example, in Nigeria, 'the dividing line between the Governing Boards of the parastatals and the supervisory ministries is not clear' Fadahausi, O. (1984) 'Institutional Arrangements for Monitoring the Performance of Nigerian Public Enterprises', in *Performance Evaluation of Public Enterprises in Developing Countries: Criteria and Institutions*, New York: United Nations.

11 The Industry and Trade Committee of the British Parliament observed,

> We are left with the impression that since the separation of the Post Office and British Telecommunications there has been a return to the form of financial and managerial control in the Post Office similar to that exercised when the Corporation was a Government Department.

(Fifth Report from the Industry and Trade Committee (Session 1981–82), *The Post Office,* London, 1982, p. ix)

12 Roman, Z. (1981) *Government Control and Performance Evaluation of Public Enterprises in the Hungarian Industry*, Ljubljana: International Center for Public Enterprises.

13 The Economist Intelligence Unit, *Hungary: Country Profile 1986–87*, London, p. 24.

14 Delgado, J. H. (1961) *The Contribution of Nacional Financiera to the Industrialisation of Mexico*, Mexico, p. 14.

15 Roseveare, R. W. (1986) 'British Steel Corporation', in Ramanadham, V. V. (ed.) *Public Enterprise: Studies in Organisational Structure*, London.
16 Vela, E. (1979) 'Public Enterprises in Spain', Regional Meeting on the Role of the Public Sector in Developing Countries, Ljubljana.
17 Aubrey Jones's evidence in favour of 'a large state holding company rather like those that operate in Italy', before the Select Committee on Nationalised Industries, (Session 1967–68) (1968) *Ministerial Control of the Nationalised Industries*, vol. I, London: HMSO 371–1, pp. 202–3. Also Holland, S. (ed.) (1972) *The State as Entrepreneur*, London, p. 261 ('The only government within the communities by the mid-1970s without its own IRI or IRC type agency would be Britain'.)
18 Ramlogan, V. (1970s) 'Organisation and Control of Public Enterprises in Trinidad and Tobago' Port-of-Spain.
19 Report of the Committee to Review the Policy for Public Enterprises, (1984), New Delhi, ch. III.
20 Robinson, E. A. G. (1931) *The Structure of Competitive Industry,* Cambridge; Coase, R. H. (1937) 'The Nature of the Firm', *Economica*, November; Florence, S. (1972) *The Logic of British and American Industry,* London.
21 Ramanadham, V. V. (1954) *The Structure of the British Electricity Supply Industry*, Mangalore; and Pryke, R. (1970) 'Public Enterprise and the Economies of Large Scale Production', *Annals of Public and Co-operative Economy*, vol. 41, no. 1, Brussels.
22. Wadehra, B. L. (1954) 'Coal India Ltd.', in Ramanadham V. V., (ed.), ibid.
23 An illuminating illustration of the size-and-unification issue is provided by the Report of the Committee of Inquiry into Civil Air Transport, chaired by Sir Ronald Edwards, *British Air Transport in the Seventies* (London, 1960s). They identified the following only as activities in which scale economies could be expected: project engineering; computers; bulk purchasing; fleet standardisation; product standardisation; traffic handling and passenger service costs; ability to ride out bad times; and economies of sub-contracting.

The Committee observed: 'There is no case for making airlines artificially larger than they need to be to secure the major advantages of size.'
24 For example the objectives of the Steel Authority of India Ltd, created in 1973 were:

(i) to, plan, promote and organise an integrated and efficient development of the iron and steel and associated input industries such as iron ore, coking coal, manganese, limestone and refractories in accordance with national economic policy and objectives laid down by government from time to time;
(ii) to co-ordinate the activities of its subsidiaries, to determine their economic and financial objectives/targets and to review, control, guide and direct their performance with a view to securing optimal utilisation of all resource placed at their disposal;
(iii) to act as an entrepreneur on behalf of the State, to identify new areas of economic investments, and to undertake, or help in undertaking, such investments; and
(iv) to formulate and recommend to government a National Policy for the development of iron and steel and related input industries and to advise it on all policy and technical matters.

Iyer, R. R. (1985) 'Sectoral Corporations: Some Organisational Experiments in Public Sector in India', *Economic and Political Weekly,* vol. XX, no. 8, New Delhi.
25 First Report from the Select Committee on Nationalised Industries (Session

1967–68) (1968) *Ministerial Control of the Nationalised Industries*, vol. I, London: HMSO 371–1, p. 203.

26 Bianchi, P. (1987) 'The "Relazione programmatica della partecipazioni statali per il 1987"', The Privatization of Italian Public Industry, Conference on Privatisation Policy in Europe, Oxford.

27 'The Iraqi system of management is quite centralised . . . Decisions tend to be referred to one level higher than necessary for approval . . . and confirmation . . . even though they are within the jurisdiction of lower management levels.' Higher levels 'unduly overrule' lower level decisions, in 'Review and Appraisal of the Process of Decision-Making and Management in the Public Industrial Enterprises in Iraq', Expert Group Meeting on Review and Appraisal of Progress in the Implementation of the International Development Strategy for the Second Development Decade, Beirut, 1973.

28 The Post Office strike originated in the introduction of pay supplements of £7.50 to £20 a week at fifty-five post offices in the south-east where problems of retaining employees were experienced. (Turnover rates in some offices were as high as 55 per cent a year.) The union demanded that the supplements be paid everywhere or not at all (*The Financial Times*, London, 25 August and 31 August 1988).

29 Ahlstrand, B. and Purcell, J. (1988) 'Employee Relations Strategy in the Multi-divisional Company', *Personnel Review,* vol. 17, no. 3, London.

30 Edwards, P. K. (1980) 'Size of Plant and Strike Proneness', *Oxford Bulletin of Economics and Statistics*, vol. 42, no. 2; Prais, S. J. (1978) 'The Strike Proneness of Large Plants in Britain', *Journal of the Royal Statistical Society*, vol. 141, no. 3.

31 Stephenson, G. *et al.* (1983) 'Size of Organisation and Attitudes at Work', *Industrial Relations Journal*, vol. 14, no. 2, and 'Inter-Group Understanding and Size of Organisation', *British Journal of Industrial Relations,* November.

32 For instance, an important consideration in making the major steel plants 'divisions', rather than independent subsidiaries of the Steel Authority of India Ltd, was that the losses made by one unit could be set off against the profits made by others. Iyer, R. R. op. cit.).

33 For instance, the *Report on the Administration and Operation of State Enterprises under the Work Schedule of the State Enterprise Secretariat*, for the period 1964–5, Ghana, recognised that 'some of our state enterprises are so small in size and of no strategic importance and so simple to operate that they are considered more suitable for small private entrepreneurs', (p. 10). And many of them were sold away, for example, the bakery, laundries, and tyre services.

34 This is illustrated by the study of Sebastian Morris and G. R. G. Raman with reference to India, *The Process of Investment Decisions in the Public Sector: A Study of the Delays and Cost Overruns*, Hyderabad, 1988.

35 The following observation of H. R. Zayyad (1986) on Nigeria applies to many countries: 'The ministry usurps the powers of the board of directors; the latter tramples on the rights of management. The management in its turn centralise all powers themselves', *Nigerian Management Review*, June, Lagos, p. 156.

In the UK, the Committee of Public Accounts referred to the 'present level of departmental intervention in matters which are properly the responsibility of the industries . . . leading to a blurring of responsibilities and possible resentment', Seventh Report, Department of Industry, Transport and Energy (1983) *The Monitoring and Control Activities of Sponsor Departments of Nationalised Industries*, London: HMSO, p. xvii.

In the 'India Survey' of *The Financial Times* the observation was made that 'under the present system public company chiefs . . . are often simply door mats for heads of departments' of the government, London, 25 November 1987, p. xiv.

36 Barlow, Sir W. (1981) *The Problems of Managing Nationalised Industries*, London.
37 For an extensive discussion on parliamentary accountability of public enterprise, see Robson, W. A. (1960) *Nationalised Industries and Public Ownership*, London; and Ramanadham, V. V. (1964) *Control of Public Enterprises in India*, New York.
38 Report of the Select Committee on Nationalised Industries, London, 1953.
39 Garner, M. R. (1982) 'Auditing the Efficiency of Nationalised Industries: Enter the Monopolies and Mergers Commission', *Public Administration*, London, Winter.
40 It is interesting to refer to a comment made by a public enterprise executive at a seminar on targets, held at Naivasha in Kenya in 1987, that public enterprise is 'born with a potential for inefficiency', a somewhat sweeping statement.
41 *The Zambia National Report on the Role of the Public Sector in Developing Countries,* International Center for Public Enterprise, Ljubljana, 1982, pp. 40–42. Also, *The Promise of Privatization*, 'The nonfinancial performance of Zambia's state-owned enterprises had always been even worse than their financial performance', Washington DC, 1988, p. 209.
42 This was wound up in 1988.
43 *Report and Recommendations of the Working party on Government Expenditures*, Nairobi, 1982, pp. 40–1.
44 Twenty-second Report of the Committee on Public Undertakings, on *Bharat Heavy Plate and Vessels Ltd*, New Delhi, 1987, p. 14.
45 *Report of the Auditor-General*, Accra, 1980.
46 MacKay, D. 'Down in the forest, It's time something stirred', *The Financial Times*, 27 April 1988, London. 'Even where it creates jobs, the cost of job creation is far higher than in other activities'. He refutes the arguments of 'import saving, downstream processing, employment creation in rural areas and recreational and environmental benefit'.
47 *Annual Report 1986–87*, vol. I, *Public Sector Industries*, Ministry of Production, Experts Advisory Cell, Islamabad, 1988.
48 The sports stadium at Volta has too few spectators.
49 The glass factory was set up to create employment when a mine was closed in the early 1950s, hoping that suitable sand was available within a few miles. Actually good raw materials come from nearly 120 miles away, involving enormous truck transport.
50 For instance, it is observed with reference to Ghana that 'too many industries were created in too short a time with too little or no proper planning'. Quarshire, R. A. *Ghana's Industrial Complex*, Accra.
51 An interesting reference may be made to the heavy public sector investments in transportation in Nicaragua during the 1965–9 plan. The Organisation of American States (OAS) observed in its Evaluation of the National Economic and Social Development Plan of Nicaragua that, 'whatever is being made to improve the transportation network seems justified so far; however, later investments in roads should be judged in the light of other investment goods with more careful criteria on priorities and opportunity costs'. Washington, DC, 1966, p. 267.
52 It is interesting to cite G. E. Mills' observation that the Jamaican experience, even after the pro-private sector PNP Government came in, 'seems to validate the hypothesis that in developing countries a degree of public enterprise is an imperative irrespective of the ideological orientation of the governing party', (Ramanadham. V. V. (ed.) (1989) *Privatisation in Developing Countries*, London, ch. 19.)

CHAPTER 3 EXTRA-ENTERPRISE OBJECTIVES

1 With reference to the Secretary of State's decision not to close the Ravenscraig plant but retain all the five integrated steel making sites, the Industry and Trade Committee (session 1982–3) took the view that 'the decision . . . was essentially a political rather than an economic decision'. The closure would have saved £100 million a year under certain assumptions of demand. The non-closure decision affected the operating costs of the other four plants:

> Plants which might have been viable with the closure of one of the major sites will now suffer the penalty of having to bear higher costs per tonne of steel produced, as a result of lower plant-loading. This aspect of the enhanced operating costs resulting from the Secretary of State's policy will have a direct impact on jobs in plants other than, say, Ravenscraig.
>
> (Second Report from the Industry and Trade Committee (Session 1982–3) (1983) *The British Steel Corporation's Prospects*, London, pp. xi, xiii)

2 *Performance Evaluation of Public Enterprises in Developing Countries: Criteria and Institutions,* New York: United Nations, TCD/SEM, 84/5, 1984.

3 First Report from the Select Committee on Nationalised Industries, Session 1967–68 (1968) *Ministerial Control of the Nationalised Industries*, London: HMSO 371–1, p. 150.

4 Some examples from the UK, cited by the Select Committee on Nationalised Industries, are: 'some of the less profitable air services provided . . . by both B.O.A.C. and B.E.A', because the Corporations 'appeared to consider them to be in the public interest'; the Central Electricity Generating Board 'voluntarily accepted the coal preference policy'; and the Post Office '. . . have chosen to handle mail to and from remote rural areas, at considerable loss, for no extra charge' (ibid., p. 151).

5 Yoshitake, K. (1973) *An Introduction to Public Enterprise in Japan*, London, p. 139.

6 Rural Development Corporation of Zambia, *Annual Report 1976*, Lusaka, p. 27.

7 For instance, the Finance Minister of India observed at the Conference of Public Enterprise Chief Executives in Delhi in 1983 that 'to avoid delay, in our haste to get the project-approval, we bring half-baked projects'. *Lok Udyog*, New Delhi, April 1983, p. 121.

8 For instance, the proportion of foreign funds in development expenditures is about 65–70 per cent of the total during the Seventh Plan period (1985–90) in Nepal.

9 Central Electricity Generating Board, *Annual Report, 1977–78*, London, p. 6.

10 National Coal Board, *Report and Accounts, 1977–78*, London, p. 7.

11 For instance, the British Railways Board has been under some pressure sometimes to buy 'British' high speed engines, though those from other countries such as the USA might have been better.

12 Shortage of foreign exchange was a major factor responsible for the operation of all but three of the companies under the National Development Corporation in Tanzania in 1986 'at less than 50%' of capacity, *Annual Report of NDC, 1988*, Dar es Salaam, p. 1.

13 *Gas Act 1972*, section 3 (3); *Coal Industry Nationalisation Act 1946*, section 3; *Electricity Act* 1957, section 7.

14 The water privatisation legislation proposed in the UK in 1988 illustrates the stringent measures of environmental regulation on the water companies in the private sector.

15 National Economic Development Office (1976) *A Study of UK Nationalised Industries: their role and control in the future*, London, p. 40.

16 The British Steel Corporation had six trade unionists 'who are full-time active employees of the Corporation' on the Board since 1978 (*Hansard*, London, 2 August 1978, columns 357–8). This arrangement was later given up.
17 It is interesting to note the recent statutory concession offered in Egypt to enterprises with private foreign capital, by not applying to them the requirement of compulsory worker membership on the board (Article 10 of Law No. 43 of 1974).
18 Pozen, R. C. (1976) *Legal Choices for State Enterprises in the Third World*, New York, pp. 39, 42, 43, 46.
19 Republic of Korea (1962) *Summary of the First Five–Year Economic Plan, 1962–1966*, Seoul, p. 10.
20 Yoshitake, K., op. cit., p. 136.
21 For instance, John Murray Brown observes that in Indonesia 'public policy is often little more than the private interest of a few powerful individuals', (*The Financial Times*, 24 November 1988).
22 For example, a government inquiry showed that Nkrumah 'had pursued the covert objective of increasing his personal wealth through kickback schemes involving public corporations' (Pozen, R. C., op.cit., p. 159).
23 For instance, the minister's letter to the new chairman of the British Railways Board in 1982 envisaged that the Board should 'go faster' so as to reduce the Public Service Obligation payment by the Government to £635 million from the original figure of £700 million in 1986; it mentioned the desirability of 'introducing some guaranteed and subsidised substitution of bus services' in some routes; it stressed the need to avoid wasteful duplication of services in the London area; it said that 'the railway must not use its market position to raise fares unreasonably'; it emphasised the importance of securing 'improvements to the railways' present industrial relations machinery, which have hampered good communications and slowed down the necessary pace of change'; it observed that 'Sealink must be ready for privatisation as soon as possible' and that 'rationalisation of British Rail Engineering Limited's excess capacity should be completed as soon as possible'; and on the whole, the theme was that 'your investment programme should relate directly to the financial and business objectives'. This statement was acclaimed by the chairman as 'the first significant move in the direction of sensible objectives'.
24 The Committee on Public Undertakings (of the Indian Parliament) makes the interesting observation that most ministries seemed to be under the impression that if objectives have been laid down in the Memorandum of Association, no further action was called for on their part (Forty-ninth Report (1982) *Public Undertakings: Management and Control Systems*, New Delhi, p. 5).
25 For example, in the case of the Kenya Tea Development Authority.
26 For instance, the *Air Corporations Act 1953* (of India) provides governmental compensation for 'directed' services, which make losses, only 'if the Corporation has suffered an overall loss in respect of the operation of all its air transport services' (section 34). The Postal Services Act 1975 of Australia has a similar approach. Where the minister refuses a pricing 'determination' proposed by the Postal Commission, the government is to pay it the difference between the actual revenue earned during the year and the revenue necessary for meeting all revenue and defined capital expenditures, or the difference between the actual revenue and the revenue estimated by the Commission under the (rejected) pricing proposal, or the difference between the actual revenue and the revenue which, in the opinion of the minister, the Commission would have received had its proposal been approved by the minister, 'whichever is the least' (section 19).
27 See Appendix 3.3 for purpose-specific compensations to the National Coal Board.

28 The Working Party on Government Expenditures, Nairobi, 1982, 'If parastatals are expected to implement public policies at a loss, such losses should be explicitly subsided by Government through a clearly earmarked subvention in the budget', (p. 44).

29 For example, in Seychelles the Ministry of Finance may 'remit or exempt in whole or in part any specified liability to tax' on the part of the National Investment Corporation or any of the subsidiaries or associated enterprises (the National Investment Corporation Decree 1979, section 19).

30 These are referred to as 'improper burdens' which represent 'the additional costs which, unlike any privately controlled enterprise operating in the same sector, an enterprise in which the State is a shareholder, incurs in consequence of determined choices imposed on the "esti di gestione" by the political authorities', (Professor C. M. Guerci (1978) *Public Enterprise in the EEC*).

CHAPTER 4 INVESTMENT AND CAPITAL STRUCTURE

1 For instance, in a recent study relating to Pakistan the basic level of income is defined as a subsistence level or poverty line. In other words, a rupee of consumption going to someone having an income above the subsistence level is given a weight of less than 1.0, while a rupee of consumption going to an individual whose income is below the subsistence level has a weight of more than 1.0 (Weiss, J. (1980) *Practical Appraisal of Industrial Projects: Application of Social Cost-Benefit Analysis in Pakistan*, New York: UNIDO, p. 35.

2 Weiss, J. (1980), ibid., pp. 3–4.

3 Weiss, J. (1980) ibid., p. 158.

4 For example, 'there has been a phenomenal cost-escalation of the order of 116 per cent and an abnormal delay of over 6 years in the completion of the Centaur Hotel Juhh Beach Project' (Tenth Report from the Committee on Public Undertakings (1986) *Hotel Corporation of India Ltd*, New Delhi, p. 34.)

5 *The Daily Nation*, 1 March 1985 (Nairobi).

6 For instance H. R. Zayyad observes that in Nigeria

> there are countless still-born public enterprises where operating equipments have been acquired and paid for but remained stored up in crates because the factory buildings are yet to be completed or because the project was wrongly conceived and/or inadequately funded
>
> (*Nigerian Management Review*, June 1986, Lagos, p. 156.)

7 While giving evidence to the Treasury and Civil Service Committee (in the UK), the Accepting Houses Committee and the Issuing Houses Association observed in their Memorandum: 'It is true that nationalised industries would not in general be able to borrow in the market in their own names without a government guarantee on as fine terms as the Government.' (HMSO, 348–11, p. 201). On a thorough examination of the issue, the Treasury and Civil Service Committee (in the UK) came to the conclusion, in 1981, that 'allowing the nationalised industries to borrow on their own account rather than through the National Loans Fund would appear ... to increase the cost of their borrowing without bringing any offsetting advantages' (vol. I, p. xxvii).

8 The recommendations of Lord Radcliffe's Committee were in favour of such a policy (*Report on the Working of the Monetary System*, London: Cmnd 827, para. 595, 1960).

9 *The Nationalised Industries*, London: HMSO, Cmnd 7131, 1978, p. 29.

10 See *Annual Reports of National Bus Company* (London).

11 Observations of the Chairman of the British Coal Corporation, *Report and Accounts 1987/8,* London.

CHAPTER 5 FINANCIAL PERFORMANCE

1 (1961) Cmnd 1337, London: HMSO, p. 4.
2 Bokhari, R. (1989) 'Privatisation in Pakistan', in Ramanadham, V. V. (ed.) *Privatisation in Developing Countries*, London.
3 Ministry of Public Enterprises (1989) 'Privatisation in Malaysia', in Ramanadham, ibid.
4 Prasad, S. S. (1988) Privatisation in Nepal: Public Exchequer Aspects', Corporation Co-ordination Division, Government of Nepal, High level workshop on privatisation in Nepal, Kathmandu, August.
5 *Report and Recommendations of the Working Party on Government Expenditures*, Nairobi, 1982, p. 40.
6 Karanja, R. W. (1989) Privatisation in Kenya', in Ramanadham, op. cit.
7 *Structural Adjustment Programme for Nigeria, July 1986 – June 1988*, Lagos, 1986, p. 13.
8 Adda, W. (1989) 'Privatisation in Ghana', in Ramanadham, op. cit.
9 Callaghy, M. and Wilson, E. J. (eds) (1988) vol. III, 'Africa: Policy Reality or Ritual', in Vernon, R. (ed.) *The Promise of Privatisation*, Washington, DC, p. 209.
10 Ibid., p. 219.
11 Nellis, R. J. (1986) *Public Enterprises in Sub-Saharan Africa*, Washington, DC. World Bank.
12 Park, Y. C. (1986) *A System of Evaluating the Performance of Government Invested Enterprises in the Republic of Korea*, Washington, DC: World Bank.
13 Haggard, S. (1988) 'The Philippines: picking up after Marcos', in Callaghy, T. M. and Wilson, E. J., op. cit., p. 96.
14 Mills, G. E. (1989) 'Privatisation in Jamaica, Trinidad and Tobago', in Ramanadham, op. cit.
15 Felipe Ortiz de Zavillos, M. (1989) in Ramanadham, op. cit.
16 For further evidence, relating to Bangladesh, Somalia, Algeria, Thailand, Tunisia, and Indonesia, see Ahmed, Z. U. (1982) (ed.) *Financial Profitability and Losses in Public Enterprises of Developing Countries*, Ljubljana.
17 Bureau of Public Enterprises (1988) *Public Enterprises Survey 1986–87*, New Delhi.
18 For a full discussion on economic costs, see *Accounting for Economic Costs and Changing Prices*, vols I and II, A Report to HM Treasury by an Advisory Group, London: HMSO 1986.
19 For example, the Meat Marketing Board of Ghana has only grants and no other capital from the government *Report of the Auditor-General on the Accounts of State Enterprises*, Accra, 1980, p. 19.
20 For example, the Industrial and Commercial Development Corporation Ltd of Kenya did so for many years.
21 For example, the State Printing Corporation (of Sri Lanka) was provided with machinery 'free of charge' by the government (Ninth Report from the Committee on Public Enterprises, Parliamentary Series no. 88, Colombo, 1986, p. 48).
22 The Auditor-General of Sri Lanka referred to adjustments for unrealised profits on 'internal transfers' of materials in the case of Ceylon Plywoods Corporation; and 'several other accounting deficiencies' resulting in converting the actual operating deficit of Rs 9 million to a surplus of Rs 2.6 million in the case of the National Apprenticeship Board (ibid., pp. 43, 45).
23 *Report and Accounts of British Airways for the years 1983–87*, London.
24 Referring to the Salem Steel Plant of the Steel Authority of India Ltd, the Committee on Public Undertakings (in India) observed: 'Salem's product cost

reportedly bears an element of Rs 4,501 per tonne on account of the interest burden arising out of the dormant investment in the infrastructure', of about Rs 750 millions (*Thirtieth Report*, New Delhi, 1987, pp. 41–2).

Further, the observation of the Committee on Public Enterprises in Sri Lanka on 'idle capacities, surplus assets, etc. leading to over-capitalisation . . . without due regard to considerations of feasibility', is interesting in this context (Seventh Report, Colombo, 1985, p.32).

Likewise, uneconomical location characterised the cement factory at Kankesanthurai, the paper factory at Valaichenai, the chemicals factory at Parauthan, textiles at Veyanguda, and wood works at Avissawala, in Sri Lanka.

There were many non-viable investment decisions and locations in Pakistan through the Pakistan Industrial Development Corporation (*Annual Report, 1982–83*, Experts Advisory Cell, Islamabad, 1984).

CHAPTER 6 PRICING

1 (1961) *The Financial and Economic Obligations of the Nationalised Industries*, Cmnd 1337, London: HMSO, p. 10.
2 *Administered Prices: A Discussion Paper*, Ministry of Finance, New Delhi.
3 For example, 'the Committee of Public Undertakings are shocked to observe that the feasibility reports prepared by Indian Petro-Chemicals Corporation Ltd for the revised Acrylcities Project were not based on detailed technical and equipment data', (Committee on Public Undertakings (1988) Forty-eighth Report, *Indian Petro-Chemicals Corporation Ltd: Project Implementation*, New Delhi, p. 5).
4 (1978) *The Nationalised Industries*, Cmnd 7131, London: HMSO. p. 25.
5 There has been an extensive controversy on this topic ever since the early article by Hotelling, H. (1938) 'The General Welfare in Relation to Problems of Taxation and of Railway and Utility Rates', *Econometrica*, vol. 6, pp. 242–69; Coase, R. H. (1945) 'Price and Output Policy of State Enterprise: A Comment', *Economic Journal*, vol. 55, pp. 112–13; (1946) 'The Marginal Cost Controversy,' *Economica* (NS) vol. 13, pp. 169–82; and (1947) 'The Marginal Cost Controversy: Some Further Comments', *Economica* (NS) vol. 14, pp. 150–53; Rugles, N. (1949–50) 'Recent Developments in the Theory of Marginal Cost Pricing', *Review of Economic Studies*, vol. 17, pp. 107–26; and Slater, M. (1989) 'The Rationale for Marginal Cost Pricing', in *The Market for Energy*, Oxford.
6 Though not a precise analogy, reference may be made to the allegation that tapering prices on gas announced by British Gas plc in 1989, under which large consumers gain, price-wise, by jumping in to a higher slab of consumption, have encouraged wasteful consumption in several cases.
7 For a discussion of the impacts of marginal-cost pricing on the exchequer, see Meade, J. E. (1944) 'Price and Output Policy of State Enterprise', *Economic Journal*, vol. 54, pp. 321–8.
8 Self-financing was 100 per cent in the case of the British Gas Corporation and British Airports Authority in many years in the 1980s.
9 For example, price rises were implemented by the British Gas Corporation from time to time: 'to enable the Corporation to achieve its financial objective for the year' (*Annual Report for 1979–80*, p. 8). (In 1977–8 the increase in gas prices was described as the main reason for the increase in profits compared with 1976–7 (*Annual Report for 1977–8*, p. 8)).
10 Economist Intelligence Unit (1969), Report no. 2 on Indonesia, London, p. 12.
11 National Economic Development Office (NEDO) (1976), Appendix volume, Appendix D, London, p. 99.

12 Committee on Public Undertakings (1987–8), Forty-seventh Report on Indian Airlines – Fare and Cost Aspects, New Delhi, pp. 5–6.
13 Beesely, M. and Littlechild, S. (1983) 'One of the prime aims of nationalisations was to facilitate cross-subsidies from the more profitable services', *Lloyds Bank Review*, July, p. 8.
14 For instance, the Electricity Council (in the UK) argued before the Select Committee on Nationalised Industries (SCNI):

> We are not qualified to look into social matters. We have no powers to enquire about people's income. It would be distasteful to us to start trying to apply means tests, and frankly our staff are not recruited for social purposes.
>
> *Fourth Report from SCNI*, London: HMSO, pp. xli–xlii

15 Glade, W. P. (1979) *Entrepreneurship in the State Sector: CONAPSU of Mexico*, no. 203, off-print series, Austin, Texas.
16 For a discussion on 'fuel poverty' and the limits to the enterprises' own finances dealing with it, see *In the Absence of Competition: A Consumer View of Public Utilities Regulation*, National Consumer Council, Appendix I, 'Low Income Consumers and the Fuel Industries: the Obligation to Supply' (London: HMSO, 1989).
17 (1983) *Government Sponsored Corporations 1981–82*, Islamabad, p. 195.
18 Forty-ninth Report from the Committee on Public Undertakings (1982) *Public Undertakings: Management and Control Systems*, New Delhi, p. 25.
19 Eighth Report from the Committee on Public Undertakings (1986) *Oil and Natural Gas Commission: Organisational Structure and Project Clearance*, New Delhi.

CHAPTER 7 TARGETS

1 The White Paper of 1961 – the first on the subject of targets in the UK – was entitled 'The Financial and Economic Obligations of the Nationalised Industries', but went on to use the term 'financial objectives' (on p. 7, for example). By 1967 the title phrase used in the White Paper (Cmnd 3437) shifted to 'objectives', and yet another word clearly crept in – 'targets' (p. 3). The 1978 White Paper (Cmnd 7131) conspicuously emphasised the term 'performance aims' (p. 20). This term has gained currency besides 'targets' in recent years.

In India the Bureau of Public Enterprise (Ministry of Finance) and the Comptroller and Auditor-General (CAG) have been using the terms 'obligations and objectives' together (see the Bureau's Office Memorandum of 3 November 1970 and the CAG's report on Scooters of India Ltd, 1981).

2 Even a more recent Act (The British Telecommunications Act 1981) contains equally general sections on duties, for example, 'so to exercise its powers as to provide throughout the British Islands . . . such telephone services as satisfy all reasonable demands for them . . .' (Section 3).
3 First Report from the Select Committee on Nationalised Industries (SCNI), Session 1971–72 (1972) *British Transport Docks Board*, London: HMSO, 312, p. x.
4 *Hansard*, Written Answers, 18 March 1983, London.
5 Ibid.
6 For example, The Airports Authority Act; the Iron and Steel Act 1967, Section 16 (1); the Civil Aviation Act 1971, Section 5 (1); and the Post Office Act 1969, Section 31 (1).
7 British Telecommunications Act 1981, Section 24; Gas Act 1972, Section 14.
8 Aircraft and Shipbuilding Industries Act 1977, Section 10 (1), and Petroleum and Submarine Pipelines Act 1975, Section 5 (1).

9 In the earlier cited instance of the British Transport Docks Board, the SCNI discovered certain elements of social preferences in the management's own formulation of objectives and observed:

> it might with advantage limit its objectives to discharging the duties laid down upon it and for which its skills are pertinent and rely on the sponsoring department to direct it when, in the Government's view, national, regional or local interests call for it to act otherwise than in the long-term interests of its port undertakings.
>
> (First Report from the Select Committee on Nationalised Industries, Session 1971–72 (1972) *British Transport Docks Board*, op. cit.)

10 For example, the Secretary of State's stipulation to the National Coal Board in 1983 of 'a satisfactory return on capital while competing in the market place' is in the nature of an *objective*. He added that it 'will be quantified in due course'. This will be a *target*.

Likewise, the British Railways Board was given an *objective* in December 1974 – 'to provide a public service which is comparable generally with that provided by the Board at present' (Direction by the Secretary of State (19 December 1974) as cited in British Railways Board, *Annual Report and Accounts 1981*, p. 19). But targets on output mix needed formulation. Later directions from him were aimed at filling the gap.

11 The (UK) Electricity Council's Annual report for 1981–82 spoke of discussions with the government 'with the object of establishing a number of performance aims in respect of various key aspects of the Industry's operations over which it has substantial control' (p. 13).

In reverse, certain internally set aims regarding quality of service were termed by the (UK) Post Office as 'targets' in its Annual Report for 1982–83 (p. 16).

12 For instance, the National Bus Company was set by the Secretary of State for Transport 'a performance aim for 1982 of 1.5% reduction in real terms in operating cost per vehicle mile' (Annual Report, 1982, p. 3).

13 The 1978 White Paper *The Nationalised Industries* insisted on 'suitable aims in terms of performance and service', *besides* 'the financial targets' and 'the cash limit' (p. 20).

14 For instance, the memorandum of British Shipbuilders, submitted to the Treasury and Civil Service Committee (Session 1980–81) in the UK in 1981, referred to the absence of private sector disciplines and observed that 'individual management's incentive for ensuring a viable trading operation disappears since, in the last resort, it is assumed that the Treasury will always have to underwrite any losses made' (*Report on Financing of the Nationalised Industries*, vol. III, London: HMSO, 348–III, 1981, p. 18).

15 (1979) *Review of Statutory Boards* (Chairman: Philip Ndegwa), Nairobi, p. 3.

16 For instance, *The Report of the Elias Commission of Inquiry into the Administration, Economies and Industrial Relations of the Nigerian Railway Corporation* (Lagos, 1960) observed that 'it has been clearly established before us that . . . (the Chairman) abused his office of Chairman and that he derived financial advantages as a result of it' (p. 277).

17 Mbanefe, A. C. I. (1973) 'The Management of Public Enterprises, Control, Autonomy – External and Internal Problems', Twelfth Inter-African Public Administration Seminar held in Ibadan, Nigeria.

18 First Report from the Select Committee on Nationalised Industries, Session 1973–74 (1973) *Capital Investment Procedures*, London: HMSO, 65, p. xxvii.

The British Transport Docks Board, in order to achieve by 1975 a return of not less than 9 per cent on average net assets, had to improve upon its 1971 budgeted figure of 5.5 per cent by approximately 1 per cent per annum. First

Report from the Select Committee on Nationalised Industries, Session 1971–72 (1972) *British Transport Docks Board*, (op. cit.).

19 For example, the board of directors of the Kenya Tea Development Authority includes a large number of tea growers' representatives, by law.

20 'Clear financial targets . . . would remove some of the difficulties of members representing particular "interests" when participating in corporate consideration of proposals affecting the Board's finances' (Memorandum by South Wales Electricity Board to the Select Committee on Nationalised Industries, Session 1977–78 (1978) *Comments by Nationalised Industries and others on the Government White Paper on the Nationalised Industries*, London: HMSO, 638, p. 54).

21 For instance, the Government of France undertakes not to oppose moderate increases in tariffs necessary to balance the revenue account and concedes managerial autonomy necessary for achieving the financial equilibrium – of a minimum real return of 13 per cent on investments, envisaged under the 'contrat de programme' with Société Nationale des Chemins de Français (see Maurice Garner (1976) *Aspects of the French, West German and Swedish Experience of Government Relationships with Public Enterprises*, Background Paper 2, London: National Economic Development Office, pp. 61–3.

22 Competition Act 1980, Section 11 (8).

23 (1967) *Nationalised Industries: A Review of Economic and Financial Objectives*, Cmnd 3437, London: HMSO, p. 7.

24 National Ports Council (1975) *Financial Objectives for the Port Industry*, London, p. 4.

25 Pryke, R. (1971) *Public Enterprise in Practice*, London, p. 352.

26 The RRR was fixed at 5 per cent 'in real terms before tax' to be earned on new investments 'over their working life'. This quantification was influenced by 'the pre-tax real returns which have been achieved by private companies and the likely trend in the return on private investment' (*The Nationalised Industries*, Cmnd 7131, London: HMSO, 1978, p. 24).

27 This factor has been important in the determination of net revenue targets in the UK. Several explanatory pieces of evidence are available, for example:

The Post Office submitted to the Select Committee on Nationalised Industries in 1967 that a 'break-even' would be 'inadequate for a growth industry' (First Report from the Select Committee on Nationalised Industries (1967) *The Post Office*, vol. I, London: HMSO, p. 174).

The North of Scotland Hydro Electric Board viewed that 'the financial target should be based on capital requirements over a defined future period, and considered the extent to which these should be financed internally' (Second Special Report from the Select Committee on Nationalised Industries, Session 1976–77 (1977) *Comments by Nationalised Industries on the Nationalised Economic Development Office Report*, London: HMSO, 345, p. xlvii).

28 First Report from the Select Committee on Nationalised Industries, Session 1973–74 (1973) *Capital Investment Procedures*, op. cit.
Some further evidence from the UK:

National Freight Corporation: 'To break even is not an acceptable target' because of needs of 'business development' (*Annual Report 1977*, p. 9).

National Coal Board's objective in 1976–77 was 'to achieve a sufficient overall surplus to enable internal sources of funds to provide 50 per cent of fixed capital formation' (*Report and Accounts 1976–77*, p. 17).

29 For instance, the target could have been 0.5 per cent higher in the case of British European Airways in the early years of financial targeting, 'but for their intention of maintaining certain unprofitable domestic services which fulfil a

social need' (First Report from the Select Committee on Nationalised Industries, Session 1967–68 (1968) *Ministerial Control of the Nationalised Industries* vol. I, London: HMSO, 371–I, p. 107).

30 See references to British European Airways and the Post Office in the First Report from the Select Committee on Nationalised Industries, Session 1967–68 (1968) *Ministerial Control of Nationalised Industries*, ibid.

31 Eighth Report from the Treasury and Civil Service Committee, Session 1980–81 (1981) *Financing of the Nationalised Industries*, vol. II, London: HMSO, 348–II, p. 47.

32 *The Nationalised Industries*, op. cit., p. 24.

33 *British Steel Corporation*: 'to reduce loss before interest to £225 million in 1981–82'.
British Railways Board: Inter-city services: 'to achieve' by 1982 '£28 million improvement (at 1979 prices) in 1978 level of contributions to total indirect costs of the railway . . .'
British Shipbuilders: '1981–82 maximum trading loss of £75 million'.
(Eighth Report from the Treasury and Civil Service Committee, Session 1980–81 (1981) *Financing of the Nationalised Industries*, vol. II, op. cit., pp. 47–8.)

34 For the British Airports Authority.

35 British Steel Corporation (1983) *Annual Report and Accounts 1982–83*, London, p. 9.

36 Eighth Report from the Treasury and Civil Service Committee, Session 1980–81 (1981) *Financing of the Nationalised Industries*, vol. II, op. cit.

37 See Appendix 7.2.

38 For instance, Wessex Water Authority, while commenting on the NEDO Report, observed 'Current thinking on return of assets and self-financing ratios are not relevant in a monopoly or near monopoly situation' (Second Special Report from the Select Committee on Nationalised Industries, Session 1976–77 (1977) *Comments by Nationalised Industries on the National Economic Development Office Report*, London: HMSO, 345, p. xii).
The rise in postal tariffs in 1979 and 1980 was due to the (UK) Post Office's need to attain the financial target and to cover high costs of wage settlement (The Monopolies and Mergers Commission (1980) *The Inner London Post*, London: HMSO, HC 515, p. 99).

39 For instance, the Telecommunications Department of Sri Lanka makes profits; but there has been a decline in service standards over 1975–84: 'Trunk call failures rose from 9 per cent in 1975 to 30 per cent in 1984, while a high proportion of telegrams are in fact posted (Reference to the Auditor-General's criticism in Economist Intelligence Unit, Country Report no. 2, 1989, on Sri Lanka, London, p. 21).

40 First Report from the Select Committee on Nationalised Industries, Session 1967–68 (1968) *Ministerial Control of the Nationalised Industries*, op. cit., p. 53.

41 First Report from the Select Committee on Nationalised Industries, Session 1973–74 (1973) *Capital Investment Procedures*, op. cit., p. xxiv.

42 Ibid., The Treasury's evidence, p. 53.

43 Ibid.

44 'The prime target should be the financial rate of return under-pinned by suitable performance objectives and decisions taken annually, with Government approval, on levels of investment' – The Post Office (UK) (Treasury and Civil Service Committee, Session 1980–81 (1981) *Financing of the Nationalised Industries*, vol. III, op. cit., p. 8).

'Within any framework of economic and financial control, a clearly defined financial target is of prime importance' – The Post Office (UK) (Second Special

Report from the Select Committee on Nationalised Industries, Session 1976–77 (1977) *Comments by Nationalised Industries on the National Economic Development Office Report*, op. cit., p. lv).

'The main financial policy determinant of prices is the financial target' – Electricity Council, ibid., p. 14.

'A rate of return target is a reasonably basic one (target) if the measurement is over a cycle of years' – British Airways, ibid., p. 22.

'Your Committee agree with the N.F.C. (National Freight Corporation) and the Department of Environment that the rate of return earned on capital employed appears to be the best single measure of success that is available' – Select Committee on Nationalised Industries (Second Report, Session 1972–73 (1973) *National Freight Corporation*, London: HMSO, 461, p. xix).

'The rule of maximising output subject to a profit constraint can be our working principle' – Michael Posner *Public Enterprise in the Market Place*, Nationalised Industries Chairman's Group NIC Occassional Papers no. 1, London, 1979, p. 3.

'Financial targets are seen by the Treasury as the primary instruments of control in the medium term' – Treasury and Civil Service Commission (UK) (Eighth Report, Session 1980–81 (1981) *Financing of the Nationalised Industries*, vol. 1, London: HMSO, 348–I, p. xii).

45 The British Gas Corporation's memorandum to the Second Special Report from the Select Committee on Nationalised Industries, Session 1976–77 (1977) observes: 'A guidelines package ... could well encourage more – rather than less – Government interference in the day-to-day affairs of the Corporation', op. cit., p. xiv.

46 For example, through the 'contrat de programme' technique.

47 For example, under the Memorandum of Understanding signed by the Government of India and individual public enterprises.

48 As reflected in the agreements between the Experts Advisory Cell and the public enterprises in Pakistan.

49 For example, the 'lettre de mission' with the Senegal River and Delta Development Authority for 1981–4.

50 Eighth Report from the Treasury and Civil Service Committee, Session 1980–81 (1981) *Financing of the Nationalised Industries*, vol. I, op. cit., p. xiii.

51 See *The Post Office: Report and Accounts 1982–83*, p. 6; and the British Railways Board's *Annual Report for 1982* (London).

52 For example, the British Airports Authority (see Treasury and Civil Service Committee, Session 1980–81 (1981) *Financing of the Nationalised Industries*, vol. II, op. cit., p. 24. According to the evidence of the Nationalised Industries Chairman's Group, six corporations had a 'total of £470 million shortfall in their investment programmes in the current year or over the medium term due to the restrictive effect of EFLs' (Eighth Report from the Treasury and Civil Service Committee, 1980–81 (1981) *Financing of the Nationalised Industries*, vol. I, op. cit., p. xxi).

53 'No experienced industrialist would seriously envisage controlling the development of (such) capital-intensive, basic industries, with their long "lead times", by reference to short-run, cash-control considerations alone.' (Evidence of Nationalised Industries Chairman's Group, ibid., vol. II, p. 5.)

54 The British Airport Authority increased its charges 'by at least 10 per cent over inflation at 1 April 1980 ... as a result of EFL constraints ... in order' to

maintain its investment programme, op. cit., *Financing of the Nationalised Industries*, p. 31.

55 British Airways was set a net repayment obligation of £58 million for 1983–84, representing advance repayments of loans owing to government (*Annual Report 1983–84*, London, 1984, p. 43).

56 See the Memorandum by the British Railways Board to the Treasury and Civil Service Committee, 1980–81 (1981) *Financing of the Nationalised Industries*, vol. II, op. cit., p. 152.

57 Ibid., vol. III, p. 3, referring to the National Coal Board.

58 *Financing of the Nationalised Industries*, vol. II, p. xxiv.

59 Ibid., vol. II, p. 154.

60 Ibid., vol. III, p. 19, referring to British Shipbuilders.

61 Ibid.

62 The Treasury's observation on this point was as follows (in the UK):

'In cases of conflict the commercial interests of a particular corporation would not necessarily outweigh the Government's overall economic objectives and constraints', ibid., vol. I, p. xiii.

On the supremacy of financial controls as against economic controls that ensued from the EFL technique, see Heald, D. 'The economic and financial control of U.K. nationalised industries', *The Economic Journal*, June 1980, pp. 243–65.

63 For example, an increase of Coal India's capacity from 114 million tonnes in 1981–2 to 358 million tonnes by the year 2000 (Wadehra, B. L. (1986) 'Coal India Ltd.', in Ramanadham, V. V. (ed.) *Public Enterprise: Studies in Organisational Structure*, London.

64 British Airports Authority, *Annual Report and Accounts 1985/6*, London, p. 2; another example is 6 per cent improvement per annum in terms of ATKs per employee in the case of British Airways, for 1982–4.

65 For instance, the NEDO Report observed, 'nearly all boards see themselves performing a primarily commercial role within the constraint of maintaining security of supply and standards of service which satisfy "reasonable demand". The White Papers of 1961 and 1967 are seen as endorsing this approach' (*A Study of UK Nationalised Industries: Their Role in the Economy and Control in the Future*, London, 1976, p. 23).

'The DEN said that public corporations should act "commercially"' (Fourth Report from the Select Committee on Nationalised Industries, Session 1975–76 (1976) *Gas and Electricity Prices*, London: HMSO, 353, p. xxxviii).

66 A recent illustration comes from Mexico. Emphasis was placed, in 1983, on 'the financial organisation of public enterprises, leading to their self-financing . . . to avoid their deficits putting pressure on the Treasury'. But the 'Executive Agreement' of May 1984:

> also established . . . as policies for the public enterprises, their contributions to the raising of the employment level and to the structural transformation of the economy, including, e.g., the integration of industrial production, the mass production of basic consumption goods, and finally, maintenance of productive plant.

(Baranstein, J. (1984) 'Evaluation and Control of Public Enterprises in Mexico', *Performance Evaluation of Public Enterprises in Developing Countries: Criteria and Institutions*, TCD/SEM, 84/5, New York, pp. 214–16.)

67 For example, British Airways earned an average real rate of return of 10.4 per cent on net assets during the two years 1982–3, against the target of 5.25 per cent (British Airways, *Annual Report for 1983–84*, London, p. 28).

68 Green, D. (1982) 'Government and Industry in France: A Contractual Approach', *Public Money*, September, London, pp. 29–30.
69 *Memorandum of Understanding between the Public Sector Undertakings and Government of India for 1988–89*, New Delhi, 1989.

CHAPTER 8 MONITORING

1 British Steel Corporation (1987) *Report and Accounts 1986–87* London, p. 22.
2 The Electricity Council (1987) *Annual Report and Accounts 1986/87*, London, p. 7.
3 British Airports Authority (1986) *Annual Report and Accounts 1985/86*, London, p. 13.
4 British Railways Board (1988) *Annual Report and Accounts 1987/88*, London, pp. 32–6.
5 Bureau of Public Enterprises (1988) *Public Enterprises Survey 1986–87*, vol. 1, New Delhi, p. 12.
6 For example, the *Government's Expenditure Plans 1988–89, vol. I,* indicated that '98 per cent of new investment is expected to be financed internally, that is, by commercially generated funds . . . The industries are expected to be broadly self-financing overall in 1989–90 and to generate a positive cash inflow, in aggregate, in 1990–91', London: HM Treasury, p. 81.

CHAPTER 9 EVALUATION

1 Ramanadham, V. V. (1959) *Public Enterprise in Britain*, London, p. 113.
2 Report on the National Economic Development Office, London, 1976, p. 39.
3 For instance, the cost impacts of government interventions may be inferred from the following observation relating to the Central Electricity Generating Board in the UK: 'The Board could have had lower costs in recent years if it had been free to pursue the objective of cost reduction by every means possible.' (The Monopolies and Mergers Commission (1981) *Central Electricity Generating Board*, London, pp. 291–2.)
4 For example, the Workshop on Performance Evaluation of Public Enterprises in Developing Countries: Criteria and Institutions, held by the United Nations at ICPE, Ljubljana, in November 1983, concluded: 'A total evaluation of public enterprise performance could not exclude an evaluation of the validity and efficiency of decisions taken externally to the enterprise's board of directors' (New York: UN, TCD/SEM, 84/85, p. 8).
5 Some public enterprises in Sri Lanka provide vehicles and other facilities – 'all free of charge' – to government officials (1984) *Sixth Report from the Committee on Public Enterprises*, Colombo, Sri Lanka, p. 64.
6 For example, the Acts governing railways, ports and posts in Kenya, empower the minister to fix the net revenue targets; but he has hardly exercised the power.
7 For instance, with reference to the British Railway Board: London and South East Commuter Services:

> whether, in supplying the . . . services, the Board could improve its efficiency and thereby reduce its costs without affecting the quality of service provided or improve the quality of service provided without any increase in its costs, with particular reference to: (a) the extent to which any deficiency in the quality of service provided is the result of inefficiency; (b) the scope for improvements in efficiency and manpower productivity, having regard to the extent and effect of manpower-savings already made; and (c) the efficiency of

the Board in adjusting services to match demand, and whether greater efficiency in this matter would increase net revenue.

(Cmnd 8046, London, HMSO, 1980)

8 'Clear financial objectives . . . serve as one of the standards by which success or failure over a perod of years may be judged' (*Nationalised Industries: A Review of Economic and Financial Objectives*, Cmnd 3434, London, 1967, p. 12.
9 For comments on the limitations of 'aggregate' indices, see Woodward, N. (1986) 'Performance indicators and management performance in nationalised industries', *Public Administration*, vol. 64, no. 3, London, p. 303.
10 For example, the inquiries into Nigerian railways, ports, electricity, and airways in the 1960s.
11 For example, the First Report from the Select Committee on Nationalised Industries in the UK (1974) Session 1974–75, on '*the purchasing of powered roof supports and spares by the National Coal Board*' (London: HMSO, 129); the report by the Bureau of Public Enterprises (in India) on the flight of technical personnel and managerial morale in public enterprises (New Delhi, 1972); and the inquiry into irregularities and malpractices in the grant of import licences in Ghana (Accra, 1967).
12 See *Government Policy for the Management of Public Enterprises*, vols 1 and 2, for the innumerable circulars, New Delhi, 1979. By 1979 they totalled 516 – financial: 110, general management: 201; construction management: 83, production and materials management: 121, and general information: 1.
13 Informe Final de la Comision Multisectoral de Empresas del Estado (Lima, 1976), cited in Felipe Ortiz de Zevallos's paper 'The case of Peru: an insider view', in Glade, W. (ed.) (1986) *State Shrinking: A Comparative Enquiry into Privatisation*, Austin, Texas.
14 An interesting illustration is provided by the CAG's highly critical report in India in 1989 on certain defence transactions (popularly entitled the Bofors case), which the government rejected and which was an apparent cause for resignations *en masse* by the Opposition members in parliament.
15 Resolution setting up the Committee on Public Undertakings in India on 18 November, 1963.
16 The Committee on Public Undertakings (of the Sixth Lok Sabha, that is, Parliament, in India) presented reports with heavily tendentious titles, for example, 'Extravagant and Infructuous Expenditure on Entertainment by Public Undertakings', 'Galloping Rise in Foreign Tours and Costs thereof', 'Unusually High Expenditures on Head Offices', and 'Extravagant Expenditures on Guest Houses'. In fact, the first of these reports opened with the following statement:

> It is a matter of common knowledge that many of the public sector undertakings are managed by disinterested, unscrupulous, inconsiderate mercenaries who are busy fulfilling their own self-interests rather than the service of the public sector undertakings which they are expected to serve. (First Report of Sixth Lok Sabha, New Delhi, 1978)

17 Felipe Ortiz de Zevallos, M. (1984) 'The case of Peru: an insider view', Conference on *State Shrinking: A Comparative Inquiry into Privatisation*, Austin, Texas. Also see Branch, B. (1982) *Public Enterprises in Peru: The Perspectives for Reform*, Institute of Latin America Studies, Austin, Texas.
18 For full discussion of SIGEP, see Boneo, H. (1984) 'Evaluation of economic performance in public enterprises: the case of Argentina', in *Performance Evaluation of Public Enterprises in Developing Countries: Criteria and Institutions*, New York: United Nations, TCD/SEM. 84/5.
19 Chambers, D. (1984) 'Plans as promises: what does corporate planning mean in

a publicly owned corporation?' *Public Administration*, vol. 62, no. 1, London, p. 48.
20 Committee of Public Accounts (1983) Session 1982–83, Minutes of Evidence, Department of Industry, London, p. 1.
21 W. A. Robson suggested the establishment of an Efficiency Audit Commission (see First Report of the Select Committee on Nationalised Industries (1968), Session 1967–68, on *Ministerial Control of the Nationalised Industries*, vol. II, London, p. 534).
22 *Annual Report 1986–87,* vol. 1, *Public Sector Industries*, on Harnai Woollen Mills Ltd, Ministry of Production, Experts Advisory Cell, Islamabad, 1988, p. 316.
23 For a full discussion see Ramanadham, V. V. (1986) *Studies in Public Enterprise: From Evaluation to Privatisation*, Part I, London.
24 Ghosh, A. (1986) *Public Sector Undertakings in India – Recommendations, Actions and Remedies*, New Delhi, p. 42.
25 The facts relating to the system are taken from Park, Y. C. (1986), *A System for Evaluating the Performance of Government-Invested Enterprises in the Republic of Korea*, Washington, DC: World Bank.
26 The facts relating to Argentina are taken from Boneo, H. (1984) *Performance Evaluation of Public Enterprise in Developing Countries: Criteria and Institutions*, New York: United Nations, TCD/SEM. 84/5.

CHAPTER 10 TAX AND SUBSIDY ELEMENTS IN PUBLIC ENTERPRISE PRICES

1 Ramanadham, V. V., (1988) *Public Enterprise and Income Distribution*, Appendix 3.1 'Cross-subsidisations in a monolithic enterprise: a case study', London.
2 The Indian Drugs and Pharmaceuticals Ltd observed before the Committee on Public Undertakings that it interpreted its objective to consist of 'medicines for millions rather than millions from the medicines' (Twenty-ninth Report of the Committee on Public Undertakings, 1987, New Delhi).
3 National Economic Development Office (1976) *A Study of the UK Nationalised Industries: Their Role in the Economy and Control in the Future*, London, p. 31.
4 *Report of the CAG of India, Union Government (Commercial) 1987, Part II, Indian Airlines*, New Delhi, 1987, pp. 6–7; also the Forty-second Report of the Committee on Public Undertakings, 1981–82, Part II, para. 2; and the Fifty-seventh Report, 1982–83, New Delhi, p. 11.
5 MMC (1987) *British Railways Board: Network South East*, Cm. 204, London: HMSO, p. 119; also (1980) *British Railways Board: London and South East Commuter Services*, Cmnd 8046, London: HMSO, p. 148; (1980) *Domestic Gas Appliances*, London: HMSO, 703, p. 107; (1983) *London Electricity Board*, Cmnd 8812, London: HMSO, p. 35; (1984) *South Wales Electricity Board*, Cmnd 9165, London: HMSO, pp. 126–7; (1988) *Post Office Counters Services* Cmnd 398, London: HMSO; and (1988) *Gas*, Cmnd 500, London: HMSO.
6 Economic costs may be defined as 'the costs of resources used at the price they would be traded at in a highly competitive market, where entry to and exit from the market was easy', in (1986) *Accounting for Economic Costs and Changing Prices*, A Report to HM Treasury by an Advisory Group, vol. I, London: HMSO, p. 5.
7 'The Port Authority of New York and New Jersey', in Ramanadham, V. V. (ed.) (1986) *Public Enterprise: Studies in Organisational Structure*, London.
8 Parris, H., Pesstieau, P., and Saynor, P. (1987) *Public Enterprise in Western Europe*, London, p. 128.

9 *London Regional Transport, Report and Accounts 15 months ended 31st March 1985*, London, 1985, p. 20.
10 Monopolies and Mergers Commission, *British Airports Authority*, Cmnd 9644, London: HMSO, p. 74.
11 For example, the difference between the net return as a percentage of net assets on the historical and current cost bases may be illustrated with reference to the British Gas Corporation's figures. For 1985–6 it was 13.6 on historical cost basis but only 3.9 on current cost basis (British Gas Corporation (1986) *Annual Report and Accounts 1985–6*, London, p. 46).

CHAPTER 11 PUBLIC ENTERPRISE AND THE PUBLIC EXCHEQUER

1 For example, Cameroon, Gabon, Guinea-Bissau, Indonesia, and Rumania devoted more than 40 per cent of total expenditure and lending minus repayments on capital expenditure; and the Cameroons, Swaziland, Malawi, Maldives, Sri Lanka, Western Samoa, and Bahrain, between 30 and 40 per cent in the mid-1980s.
2 UNCTAD (1988) *The Least Developed Countries: 1987 Report*, New York.
3 International Monetary Fund (1988) *World Economic Outlook*, Washington, DC, p. 174.
4 To cite an example, public enterprises account for about two-thirds of Portugal's total foreign debt.
5 The studies on public enterprise performance promoted by the International Development Research Council of Canada in the late 1970s almost uniformly emphasised the tax payments by public enterprises, apart from their payments of dividends and profit transfers to the government. For example, the composition of the payments by public enterprises in Nepal in 1974–5 was shown as follows:

Dividends	1.3%
Interest	2.5%
Direct tax	10.4%
Indirect tax	82.9%
Royalty	2.9%
	100.0%

(*Source: Performance of Public Enterprises in Nepal (Macro Study)*, HMG Office of Corporation Co-ordination Council and Industrial Services Centre, Kathmandu, 1977, p. 225.)

The study on Sri Lanka presented data under 'direct revenues' and 'indirect revenues' of the exchequer from public enterprises. The former included incomes for the consolidated fund, analogous to interest income, dividends and profits, and constituted 43 per cent of the total in 1974, while the latter covered business turnover tax, import duties, and FEECs on imported inputs. (Lakshman, W. D. (ed.) (1979) *Public Enterprise in the Economic Development of Sri Lanka*, Colombo, pp. 87–102.)

The *Public Enterprise Survey* of the Bureau of Public Enterprises, Government of India, presents a statement entitled 'contribution to Central Exchequer', which includes dividends declared, corporate tax provisions, excise duty, customs duty and other duties. The first was only 2.1 per cent of the aggregate contribution for the seven years 1980–87. (Bureau of Public Enterprises (1988) *Public Enterprises Survey, 1986–87*, vol. 1, New Delhi, p. 11.)

6 For instance, most of Egypt's foreign debt owes to public enterprises. Portugal was cited earlier.
7 For example, *Public Enterprise in Mixed Economies: Some Macroeconomic Aspects*, International Monetary Fund, Washington, DC, 1984, pp. 146–9.
8 National Development Corporation (1987) *22nd Annual Report 1986*, Dar es Salaam, p. 7.
9 It is interesting to note at this point that, of the sixty Indian public enterprises which declared dividends in 1981–2, six declared below 6 per cent on paid-up capital, and eighteen between 5 and 10 per cent.
10 Using the data of Indian public enterprises, only 109 out of 214 had profits during 1986–87; of these only 61 declared dividends (Bureau of Public Enterprises (1988) op. cit., pp. 24, 32).
11 For instance, in Nigeria 'surplus, unlike profits in the private sector, is hardly ever applied to the payment of dividends' (Falae, S. O. (1985) 'Co-ordination between Government Budget and Public Enterprise Budget in Public Enterprise Financing', *Nigerian Management Review*, December, Lagos, p. 108).

To take an example from the developed world: dividends received by the government from nationalised industries in France totalled only FFr. 1.7 billion over 1982–9, while the government 'poured in' some FFr. 103 billion of capital over those years (*The Economist*, 8 April 1989).
12 See Appendix 7A and 7B in Ramanadham, V. V. (1983) *Capital Structures of Public Enterprises*, The Fifth Shoaib Memorial Lecture, Karachi.
13 National Development Corporation (1987) op. cit.
14 For example, Trading Corporation of Pakistan Ltd issued bonus shares out of profits, to the extent of Rs 92.50 million, making the very small original figure of share capital much larger (*Government Sponsored Corporations 1980–81*, Islamabad, 1982). ZIMCO, the all-public enterprise conglomerate, has pursued 'an aggressive dividend policy', in the words of Zambia's president, since 1986. In 1988 it declared a cash dividend of K 40 million and bonus shares of K 110 million. However, reserves still stood high – at K 9,708 million, as against the share capital of K 1,616 million on 31 March 1988 (*ZIMCO, Annual Report 1988*, Lusaka).
15 Chadarevian, T. (1968) 'The Financing of Industrial Enterprises in the Public Sector in Syria', Interregional Seminar on Financial Aspects of Manufacturing Enterprises in the Public Sector, Rome, December.
16 *The Industrial Development Ordinance, 1962*, governing the Industrial and Commercial Development Corporation of Kenya, Nairobi.
17 Public Accounts of Canada, vol. III, The President of the Treasury Board, *Annual Report to Parliament on Crown Corporations and other Corporate Interests of Canada, 1987–88*, Ottawa, p. 151.
18 For instance, thirty-three government companies failed to repay loan instalments on time in India, during 1986–87. The dues amounted to Rs 577.65 crores (*Report of the Comptroller and Auditor-General (1988)*, Union Government, Commercial, vol. 1, New Delhi, p. x).
19 Kenya provides extensive evidence – see *The Appropriation Accounts, Other Public Accounts, and the Accounts of the Funds*, together with the reports thereon by the Controller and Auditor-General. Kenya Railways accounts show as subventions funds received as loan (1980–81 Report, Nairobi, p. viii). Funds were passed on to the Kenya Tourist Development Corporation in 1984–5, 'but it is not clear whether the payment represents loans or equity investment' (1984–5 Report, p. 91). Other cases include the Industrial and Commercial Development Corporation Ltd, Kenya Industrial Estates Ltd, and the Tana River Development Authority.
20 Premchand, A. (1983) 'Government and Public Enterprise: The Budget Link',

in Reddy, G. R. (ed.) *Government and Public Enterprise*, London, p. 33.

21 Budgets have had to develop a 'reverse capability to reduce expenditures and manage cut-backs without excessive distortions' (Premchand, A. (1989) 'Management of Public Money: Issues in Government Financial Management', New York: United Nations, (ST/SG/AC.G/1989/L.2)).

12 THE DISTRIBUTIONAL EFFECTS OF PUBLIC ENTERPRISE

1 For a full discussion see Ramanadham, V. V. (1988) *Public Enterprise and Income Distribution*, London.

2 Trebat, T. J. (1980) *An Evaluation of the Economic Performance of Large Public Enterprises in Brazil 1965–75,* Austin, Texas, pp. 11–12; also *Brazil's State-owned Enterprises: A Case Study of the State as Entrepreneur,* Austin, Texas, p. 199.

3 The Financial Secretary to the Treasury in the UK observed in 1983 that 'public sector trade unions have been extraordinarily successful in gaining advantages for themselves in the pay hierarchy by exploiting their monopoly collective bargaining position' (Treasury Press Release 190/83, London).

4 With reference to the British Steel Corporation: 'The Select Committee, while fully accepting the need for the Corporation to maintain a competitive position and to install the most efficient plant, is able to countenance closures only where alternative work is available for those displaced' (First Report from the Select Committee on Nationalised Industries, Session 1972–73 (1973) *British Steel Corporation,* London: HMSO, p. 14).

In the French steel industry the government announced job losses of 20,000, 'representing one-fifth of the total work force by 1987 . . . whereas it has been established that at least 30,000 jobs had to be shed over the next couple of years if the industry was to balance its books by the end of 1985 under EEC conditions' (*The Times,* London, 30 March 1984).

5 For example, while introducing an incentive scheme, the Mineral Exploration Corporation Ltd (of India) 'revised further to the lower side' the base line output, 'without any valid justification' (Fourth Report from the Committee on Public Undertakings (1985) *Mineral Exploration Corporation Ltd,* New Delhi).

6 *Public Enterprises Survey 1981–2,* vol. 1, New Delhi, p. 291.

7 Sir William Barlow observed that 'The unions do not put the needs of the customer first despite their public statements of customer care . . . The wage settlements in 1980 showed that to be the case' (1981) *The Problems of Managing Nationalised Industries,* London, p. 10.

8 *National Development Plan 1976–81,* Gaborone, p. 19.

9 (1967) *After the Arusha Declaration,* Dar es Salaam, p. 13.

10 It is said that about 90 per cent of the sick units in the small-scale sector in India cannot be revived and 'the prospects of recovery of the large sums of bank finance locked up in those units was very bleak' in the view of some commercial banks in India (*The Economic Times,* New Delhi, 15 January 1989).

To cite another example, the bad debts of Kenya Industrial Estates Ltd are relatively large for similar reasons.

11 Some examples of public enterprises intended for the special benefit of underdeveloped or 'development' areas in the country are the Dutch Restructuring Company, Northern Development Company, Development Company for Overijssel and Limburg Institute for Development and Finance in the Netherlands, the Sudene in Brazil, the Corporacion Venezolana de Guayana in Venezuela, and the Tana River Valley Authority in Kenya.

13 GOVERNMENT RELATIONSHIPS WITH PUBLIC ENTERPRISE

1 Reference may be made to some detailed studies from out of the extensive literature available on the subject: Ramanadham, V. V. (1964) *Control of Public Enterprises in India* – one of the earliest works on the subject; Robson, W. A. (1960) *Nationalised Industries and Public Ownership;* Select Committee on Nationalised Industries (1968) *Ministerial Control of the Nationalised Industries,* vols I, II and III – a monumental report; Ramanadham, V. V. (1974) *Organisation, Supervision and Management of Public Enterprises in Development Countries,* United Nations; National Economic Development Office (1976) *Study of UK Nationalised Industries: Their Role in the Economy and Control in the Future* – a critical survey of the subject; *Control Systems for Public Enterprises in Developing Countries,* containing empirical material from several countries, published by the International Center for Public Enterprises in 1979; and Reddy, G. R. (1984) *Government and Public Enterprise* – consisting of topic-oriented as well as country-oriented studies.

2 For example, in Brazil: 'Procedural controls have proliferated . . . Objective control has been less emphasized than formal control by rules and patterns of public administration' Motta, P. R. (1979) in *Control Systems for Public Enterprises in Developing Countries,* Ljubljana, p. 195.
In Tunisia: 'When looking at the systems of internal and external control of the public enterprises in Tunisia the dominant trait which emerges is the inconsistency, the multiplicity, and the dispersal of the methods of control' (Sòntini, K. (1979), ibid., p. 412).

3 For example, several public enterprises in Australia have no tax liability: the Australian National Railways Commission, Australian Telecommunications Commission, Australian Postal Commission, and Australian Wheat Board. The Kenya Tea Development Corporation is exempt from income tax. A number of public enterprises in Barbados are exempt from income tax, trade tax or customs duty, for example, the National Housing Corporation, Barbados Port Authority, and Barbados Industrial Development Corporation.

4 This may be best illustrated from Kenyan experience:

> Other than in extremely few cases, chief executives continued to be appointed from among those civil servants who had reached such top positions as Permanent Secretary or Provincial Commissioner and had not necessarily excelled themselves in their performance at the top position in the Civil Service. In some cases their appointment to head a statutory board, corporation or authority was done not to place a person of proven ability at the top of the organisation concerned but rather to remove a not-so-good performer from the Civil Service. By and large, the results of these practices . . . were disastrous to the organisations concerned.
>
> Indeed the poor selection of civil servants who have been appointed to head parastatal organisations has been the root cause of poor management in most of these organisations.
>
> The managing directorships should not be seen 'as retiring points for top civil servants'.
>
> (*Report of the Civil Service Committee 1979–80,* Nairobi, 1980, pp. 195–6, 204, 205).

5 *Finance Act* no. 38 of 1971 (Section 13 (3)), Colombo.

6 For instance, the Committee, which reviewed statutory boards in Kenya in 1979, observed that 'in the case of a number of parastatals, no budgets are prepared' (*Report of the Civil Service Committee 1979–80,* op. cit., p. 8). Also see Appendix 13.1 for a compilation of observations on the internal managerial

inadequacies of public enterprises in a number of countries. No wonder they invited external controls.

7 Robson, W. A. (1977) 'The Control of Nationalised Industries', *National Westminster Bank Quarterly Review,* November.

8 National Economic Development Office (1976) op. cit., pp. 10, 22.

9 *Public Enterprise in the European Economic Community, CEEP Review 1984,* Centre European de l'Entreprise Publique, p. 104. In some countries like West Germany, Austria, and the Netherlands the use of public enterprises as tools of government policy has not been conspicuous, except for price controls (see Parris, H., Parris, P., Pestieau, P., and Saynor, P. (1987) *Public Enterprise in Western Europe,* London, Chapters 6 and 7.

10 The Select Committee on Nationalised Industries in the UK (1973) observed that 'the Government has been far from successful in its self-imposed role . . . of exercising its control publicly and according to well-defined ground rules, without interfering with the management functions of the industries themselves', *Capital Investment Procedures,* London: HMSO.

11 The National Fibres Ltd project was approved in January 1975 at a capital cost of Rs 290.21 million. There was a delay of about 73 months in the execution of the project, due mainly to inexperience, inefficiency of the consultants, and problems of finance. The project selection itself did not satisfy technical or commercial considerations. Cost escalations occurred on grounds of original omissions of certain essential items and underestimation of costs. The final cost of the project came to Rs 670 million (Auditor-General of Pakistan (1986) *Performance Evaluation of Public Enterprises,* vol. I, Lahore).

12 Fifth Report from the Committee of Public Accounts, Session 1985–86 (1985) *Monitoring and Control of Investment by the Nationalised Industries in Fixed Assets,* Departments of Transport, Trade and Industry and Energy, London: HMSO, p. xviii.

13 Select Committee on Nationalised Industries, Session 1967–68 (1968) *Ministerial Control of the Nationalised Industries,* vol. I, London: HMSO, 371–I, p. 25.

14 *Report of the Comptroller and Auditor-General of India,* Union Government (Commercial) 1983, Part VII, *Hindustan Petroleum Corporation Ltd,* New Delhi, 1983, pp. 19–20; Twenty-seventh Report of the Committee on Public Undertakings 1972–73 (1983) *National Newsprint and Paper Mills Ltd,* New Delhi, p. 13; and *Fifteenth Report on Indian Petrochemicals Corporation Ltd,* New Delhi, 1987.

15 The Treasury's circulars issued in 1986–7, calling for elaborate data of a sophisticated nature.

16 For instance, 'Sind Engineering Ltd's organisation was highly centralised at the level of Managing Director who had sixteen line managers reporting to him directly. The Managing Director also headed the production and marketing division directly' (Reports of the Auditor-General of Pakistan (1986) *Performance Evaluation of Public Enterprises,* vol. I, Lahore, p. 15).

Ifeyori, I. Ipimodu observed, from a study of some public commercial enterprises in Nigeria, that 'despite lack of experience of some members of the Boards, several of them are alleged to have attempted to take over management functions by being involved in the day-to-day administration of the enterprises' ('Managing Public Commercial Enterprises in Nigeria: the Case of Kwara State Commercial Parastatals', *Public Administration and Development,* vol. 6, London, 1986, p. 234).

17 Iron and Steel Act 1967, London, 1967.

18 Roseveare, R. W. (1986) 'British Steel Corporation', in Ramanadham, V. V. (ed.) *Public Enterprise: Studies in Organisational Structure,* London, pp. 25–6.

19 For example, in India, 'in general it would be true to say that public enterprises suffer from an excess of reporting requirements' (Iyer, R. R. (1986) in Ramanadham, ibid., p. 239).

20 The Committee which inquired into Air Zimbabwe in 1986 observed that 'a number of appointments were made on the direction or at the suggestion of the Minister. In one case, the person concerned is related to the Minister'. 'Appointments allegedly ordered by the Minister ranged from those of security guards and labourers to divisional heads' (*Daily Nation,* Nairobi, 14 November 1986).

21 The Supreme Court decided that public corporations and government companies are to be treated as 'State' as defined in Article 12 of the Constitution of India and are thus subject to writ jurisdiction of the courts for enforcement of fundamental rights against them (Narain, L. and Murty, B. S. (1984) *Public Enterprises and Fundamental Rights,* Bombay).

22 To report to the Minister as soon as practicable after the end of the financial year, with the Minister to table in the Parliament within 15 sitting days of receipt. This is the 'standard' or most common requirement.

To report to the Minister as soon as practicable after the end of the financial year, but with no time limit on tabling by the Minister, or no provision for tabling at all.

To report annually, but with no time provision for either presentation or tabling.

In addition to these, there is a wide range of other time limits on presentation and tabling of reports on individual authorities, e.g. there are those who report direct to the Parliament rather than to a Minister.

In fact, twenty-nine bodies were under no obligation to report to the minister or to parliament, from 1979: 'This situation is a direct abrogation of a fundamental principle of parliamentary government in a democracy.'
Senate Standing Committee on Finance and Government Operations (1979) *Statutory Authorities of the Commonwealth,* Canberra, pp. 63–4.

23 For example, section 26 of the Zimbabwe Mining Development Corporation Act 1982 adopts the phrase: 'to ensure that its income, taking one year with another, is not less than sufficient to enable the Corporation to meet the expenditure of the Corporation and other matters properly chargeable to revenue account'.

24 Heath, J. B. in NEDO (1976) *A Study of the UK Nationalised Industries,* Appendix vol., pp. 140–1, and p. 24.

25 For a detailed discussion of the articles of association of government companies in India, see Ramanadham, V. V. (1964) *The Control of Public Enterprises in India,* New York, pp. 65–77.

26 Estimates Committee, 1959–60, Eighteenth Report, New Delhi, p. 5.

27 For example, section 4 of the Air Corporations Act and section 5 of the British Telecommunications Act of the UK.

28 For example, there is provision for 'directions of a general or specific nature' under the State Corporations Act 1986 of Kenya (section 7 (1)), section 9 of the Sri Lanka State Trading Corporation Act no. 33 of 1970, and section 31 (1) of the State Industrial Corporation Act no. 49 of 1957 (of Sri Lanka).

29 For example, section 7 of the National Railways Act 1917 of Australia, and section 15 of the State Enterprises Commission Law 1987 of Ghana.

30 Prosser, T. (1986) *Nationalised Industries and Public Control,* Oxford, p. 112.

31 In the UK 'in practice there is a great deal of interference and much of it stops short of issuing definite instructions to nationalised industries' (Sir William Barlow (1981) *The Problems of Managing Nationalised Industries,* London, p. 6).

32 An analysis of the background of 510 board members of 75 public enterprises in Thailand revealed that 12 per cent of them were politicians, 29 per cent military, 53 per cent civil servants, and 6 per cent others (National Economic and Social Development Board, Division of Public Enterprise, A Summary of Public Enterprise Data, Bangkok, 1973, as cited in *Management and Performance of Public Enterprises in Thailand,* National Institute of Development Administration, Bangkok).

The appointment system implied 'control by patronage'. 'The appointees gain both power and wealth while the ones who appoint them gain loyalty' (Sowanabul, I. (1980) 'Management Manpower Planning in Public Enterprises in Thailand', ICPE paper, Ljubljana, p. 9).

In the Seychelles general managers are appointed by the boards 'only after my approval'; and general managers may appoint staff 'but again only after my approval' (Presidential Circular relating to parastatals, 15 December 1982).

In France, departmental interventions are reinforced through the powers assigned to government commissioners, state controllers, and other officials who can attend and speak at board meetings and in some cases, suspend or veto decisions (Parris, H. *et al.* (1987) op. cit., p. 105).

33 For instance, 'most members' of boards in Nigeria in the 1960s were politicians. A one-time chairman of the board of directors did not know 'the difference between the offices of the Nigerian Airways and those of the NCNC political party' (Report of the Inquiry into Nigerian Airways, 1967, p. 14; also Reports of Inquiry into Nigerian Ports Authority (p. 194) and Nigerian Railways Corporation (p. 154)).

See also Zayyad, H. R. (1986) 'Organisational Problems in Nigerian Public Enterprises', *Nigerian Management Review,* June, Lagos, p. 156.

34 Borfins, S. F. and Brown, L. (1986) *Investments in Failure,* Toronto, p. 153.

35 'There is considerable agreement that the appointment process is too subject to political patronage. [It is] in reality intensely political, with significant input from the minister concerned, his or her political staff, senior advisers in the Prime Minister's Office (PMO), and the Prime Minister. The use of directorships as political (and economic) reward for the party faithful is endemic to the process.' (Tuppa, A. and Doern, G. B. (1981) *Public Corporations and Public Policy in Canada,* Montreal, pp. 37–8.)

'It is widely acknowledged in departments and corporations [in the UK that] the power of appointment and reappointment is sometimes used by the government as an inducement to individual members when the government is seeking to implement its policies' (NEDO, op. cit., p. 35).

36 'It has become clear that boards of Japan are monopolised by bureaucracy of the central government' (Yoshitake, K. (1973) *An Introduction to Public Enterprise in Japan,* London, p. 247).

37 For example, in Kenya

> many of the chairmen and chief executives ... have been drawn from the civil service and have had little experience in economic management, tending – as top civil servants do – towards issuing directives even before they have acquainted themselves with the problems they are setting out to solve.
>
> *(Daily Nation,* Nairobi, 5 March 1987)

38 For example, National Industrial Development Bank, Hetaudi Cement, Rastriya Banijya Bank, Dairy Development Corporation, Nepal Oil Corporation, and Royal Drugs Ltd.

39 In Singapore 'about twenty top civil servants appear repeatedly on the boards of directors of public enterprises' (Lee Sheng Yi (1976) 'Public Enterprise and

Economic Development in Singapore', *Malayan Economic Review*, vol. XXI, no. 2, October, p. 56).

40 For example, the Committee on Public Undertakings (in India) emphasised this point 'in a number of reports' (Twenty-fourth Report, *Air India*, p. 58. New Delhi, 1987).

41 National Economic Development Office (1976) op. cit., p. 40.

42 For instance, M. H. Mkulo (1985) observes, with reference to Tanzania, that 'despite the role of the parent industry, the Treasury Registrar with enhanced status, shall be the focal point for the overall control of the parastatal sector', in *Essays on Relations between Governments and Public Enterprises,* International Center for Public Enterprises (ICPE), Ljubljana.

43 For details, see Marsan, V. A. (1986) 'Istituto per la Recostruzione Industriale', in Ramanadham, V. V. (ed.) *Public Enterprise: Studies in Organisational Structure,* London, pp. 99–102.

44 Bureau of Public Enterprises (1985) *Public Enterprises Survey 1984–85,* vol. 1, New Delhi, pp. 161–2.

45 Mkulo, M. H. (1985) 'The Search for a Focal Point: Tanzania's Experience', in *Essays on Relations between Government and Public Enterprises,* ICPE, Ljubljana, p. 179.

46 First Report from the Select Committee on Nationalised Industries, Session 1967–68, *Ministerial Control of the Nationalised Industries,* vol. I, London, p. 193.

47 Ibid., pp. 200–2.

48 For example, the Ministry of Public Enterprises in Malaysia covers mainly the state economic development corporations, and a few others.

In Italy the Report on Government Participation presented to Parliament in 1981 suggested limiting the attention of the Ministry of State Holdings essentially to the determination of objectives and the verification of results (*CEEP Review,* 1984, p. 192).

49 For a full empirical survey see Narain, L. 'Parliament and Public Enterprise in India', in Reddy, G. R. (ed.) (1983) *Government and Public Enterprise,* London, pp. 264–84.

50 Bureau of Public Enterprises, *Annual Report on the Working of Industrial and Commercial Undertakings of the Central Government, 1975–76,* New Delhi, p. 155.

51 Consumer Councils (1968) *Consumer Consultative Machinery in the Nationalised Industries,* London: HMSO.

52 For instance, the Post Office Users National Council in the UK is empowered to consider any aspect of Post Office policy and advise the minister on the action to be taken (Post Office Act 1969, section 14(8)(a), London: HMSO).

53 NEDO (1976) 'A Study of the UK nationalised industries: their role in the economy and control in the future', London, p. 46.

54 Second Special Report from the Select Committee on Nationalised Industries (1977) Session 1976–7, *Comments by Nationalised Industries on the National Economic Development Office Report,* London: HMSO.

CHAPTER 14 PRIVATISATION

1 From the emerging literature on privatisation, some titles may be highlighted: Vickers, J. and Yarrow, G. (1989) *Privatisation in the UK: An Economic Analysis*, Massachusetts Institute of Technology; Ramanadham, V. V. (ed.) (1988) *Privatisation in the UK*, London and (1989) *Privatisation in Developing Countries*, London; Cook, P. and Kirkpatrick, C. (eds) (1989) *Privatisation in the LDCs*, London; Vernon, R. (ed.) (1988) *The Promise of Privatisation*, New

York; Kay, J. Mayer, C., and Thompson, D. (eds) (1984) *Privatisation and Regulation: The UK Experience*, London.

2 For example, substantial organisational restructuring has been initiated in Austria in respect of the huge OIAG. Seven sectorwise holding companies were created in 1985. Losses have been cut since (*The Economist*, 25 February 1989).

3 *The Guidelines for the Divestment Committee* (in Jamaica) state that 'if viability can be established from reorganisation, re-financing, restructuring, or any other measure, Government will seek private sector participation to fund and operate such enterprises in the event that an outright sale is not affected'.

4 Candoy-Sekse, R. (1988) *Inventory of Country Experience and Reference*, vol. 3, World Bank Technical Paper no. 98, Washington, DC.

5 The salary increases in privatised enterprises in the UK have been considerable.

6 For instance, the Conservative Manifesto claims that 'their companies have been released from the detailed controls of Whitehall and given more freedom to manage their own affairs' (*The Next Moves Forward* (1987) London, pp. 35–7).

7 Rees, R. (1986) 'Privatisation', *Public Money*, March, London.

8 For instance, the list of seventeen companies for privatisation in Zaire has 'in common their urgent need for investment funds, which the government cannot meet in the foreseeable future because of its budgetary restraints and priorities' (Economist Intelligence Unit (1989) Country Report no. 1, London, p. 12).

9 'Public sector trade unions have been extraordinarily successful in gaining advantages for themselves in the pay hierarchy by exploiting their monopoly collective bargaining position' (Moore J. (1983) *Why Privatise?*, London).

10 *Lloyds Bank Review*, July 1983, London.

11 H. M. Treasury (1986) *Privatization in the United Kingdom: Background Briefing*, London; Grimstone, G. (1988) 'The Financial Processes of Privatisation', in Ramanadham V. V. (ed.) *Privatisation in the UK*, London, p. 106.

12 Sankar, T. L. and Reddy, Y. V. (eds) (1989) *Privatisation and Diversification of Ownership*, Hyderabad.

13 *The Economist*, 22 April 1989, London.

14 There has been an increase in public investments in the bauxite refinery owned by the Aluminium Co. of America, though the government has adopted an overall policy of privatisation (*The Financial Times*, 29 June 1988, London).

15 *The Economist*, 11 February 1989, London.

16 *The Financial Times*, 27 June 1988, London.

17 Prodi, R. (1989) Chairman of IRI, *The Financial Times, Italy Supplement*, London.

18 'The Network of Power: Italy's Private Sector Dynasties', *The Financial Times*, 21 June 1989, London.

19 'The domination of the private corporate sector by a few families is a curiously Asian phenomena', *The Financial Times*, 11 September 1989, London.

20 It is said of Italy that 'in some cases the only available Italian buyers are to be found among the half dozen leading private sector groups. Thus privatisation could lead to a further concentration of economic power in the hands of a few families' ('Privatisation, Italian Style', *The Financial Times*, 28 September 1987, London).

21 This has been a 'disappointment to the buyers' (Economist Intelligence Unit (1989) Turkey, no. 1, London).

22 *The Financial Times*, 13 February 1989, London.

23 It is estimated that the number of shareholders in the UK, France, and Japan increased by 55 per cent 'probably because of newly privatised companies' (Seth, R. (1988) *Federal Reserve Bank of New York, Quarterly Review*, Summer, vol. 14, no. 2, New York, p. 30).

24 For example, 2.15 million shareholders in British Gas plc, each holding below 500 shares, accounted for only 15.3 per cent of the total number of shares in 1988 (British Gas plc, *Financial and Operating Statistics 1988*, London, p. 4.
25 *OECD Economic Surveys: U.K.* (1986/87), p. 55.
26 Overseas Development Institute (1986) *Briefing Paper*, September , London.
27 For example, in the UK the initial 150,000 shareholders in Cable and Wireless slumped to 26,000 within a year; in British Aerospace the number fell in the first year from 44,000 to 3,300 (TUC Submission to the House of Commons Energy Select Committee, *The £13 Billion Gas Bill*, London). In Amersham International the number fell from 65,000 in 1982 to 8,600 that very year and to 5,800 by 1989. In Associated British Ports the number was 48,000 in 1983 but by the end of that year it fell to 7,500 (*The Independent*, 29 July 1989, London). Whether such a decline takes place in every privatised enterprise has to be watched *after* the loyalty bonus period expires.
28 Defects analogous to those of the 'managing agency system' – abolished under the company law in India in the 1930s – can repeat themselves.
29 *Federal Reserve Bank of New York, Quarterly Review*, op. cit., p. 32.
30 The Tenth Report from the Committee of Public Accounts, Session 1981–82, *Sale of Shares in British Aerospace: Sale of Government Shareholdings in other Publicly-owned Companies and in British Petroleum Ltd; Postponement of Payments*, London: HMSO, 189, p. viii.
31 Seventeenth Report from the Committee of Public Accounts, Session 1983–84, *Sale of Government Shareholdings in Publicly-Owned Companies*, p. viii.
32 Third Report from the Committee of Public Accounts, Session 1985–86, *Sale of Government Shareholding in British Telecommunications plc*, London: HMSO, 35, pp. ix–x.

The following figures relating to the privatisation of British Telecommunications are interesting in this context:

Share price after issue:

one day	93.0 pence (50p paid)
one week	92.5
one month	106.5
one year	202.0 (90p paid)
two years	195.0 (130p paid)

Source: Privatisation: The Facts, London: Price Waterhouse, 1987, p. 42.
33 Tenth Report from the Committee of Public Accounts, op. cit., p. x.
34 Observation to this effect by the National Audit Office was described as a 'nice piece of understatement' by Tomkins, R. (1987) *Financial Times, Privatisation Survey*, 16 September, London, p. III.
35 *The Financial Times*, 24 November 1988, London.
36 Second Report from the Committee of Public Accounts, Session 1981–82, *Sale of Subsidiary Companies and other Assets*, London: HMSO, 34, p. vi.
37 See the table relating to St Gobain, Paribas, Commercial de France, Compagnie Generale d'Électricité, Navas, Société Generale, and TFI, in *The Financial Times*, 2 December 1987, London.
38 There is an accusation that the private sector is buying potential profit-makers 'cheaply'.
39 E.G., Airline Bogazici Hava Tasimicilligi, and five cement factories (*The Financial Times*, 14 February 1989, London).
40 UNCTAD refers to the 'generous terms to set the process in motion' (*The Least Developed Countries 1987 Report*, New York, p. 45).

41 Vernon, R. (ed.) (1988) op. cit., p. 196.
42 Ibid., p. 193.
43 For example, 25 per cent in the case of British Airways plc.
44 For a criticism of the British Government's action, see Ian Seymour, 'Britain's free market credibility at risk', *The Financial Times*, 1 September 1988, p. 15, London.
45 In Malaysia, constraints on foreign investment are relaxed; it can even be 100 per cent in some cases.

In Chile 'the foreign investment regime became one of the most liberal in the world ... foreign investors were placed on the same footing as nationals' (Economist Intelligence Unit, *Country Profile on Chile 1989–90*, London, p. 10).

In Senegal an enterprise may be 100 per cent foreign-owned (Nicholas Woodworth, *The Financial Times*, 3 November 1987, London).
46 For example, New Zealand intends to limit its external debt to NZ $14 billion by 1993 'chiefly through asset sales' (Richard Evans, *The Financial Times*, 27 July 1988, London).
47 Hatch, J. (1988) 'Privatisation and the Consumer', in Ramanadham, V. V. (ed.) *Privatisation in the UK*, London, p. 60.
48 *Privatisation and Commercialisation Decree 1988*, Section 7 (6), Lagos.
49 Canute James, *The Financial Times*, 29 June 1988, London.
50 *Privatisation: The Facts*, London: Price Waterhouse, 1987.
51 The fear is expressed, in the case of electricity privatisation in the UK, that 'the two very large companies might well exercise their market power to cream off profits and exclude new entrants' (*The Financial Times* (editorial), 26 June 1989, London).
52 These terms are taken from the National Consumer Council (1989) *In the Absence of Competition*, London, p. 4.
53 For a survey of the RPI minus *X* formula, see Helm D. (1987) 'RPI minus X and the Newly-Privatised Industries: A Deceptively Simple Regulatory Rule', *Public Money*, June, London.
54 *The Financial Times* (editorial), 6 July 1989, London; see also *The Financial Times* (editorial), 7 February 1989: 'Sooner or later ... the industry must settle down in a highly controlled regime in which the return on capital is regulated and price rises largely reflect needed investments.'
55 It is interesting to note that OFTEL, the regulating authority in respect of British Telecom, did enquire into its high profits, though the RPI minus *X* formula is claimed to be a price formula; and OFGAS has gone into an analysis of British Gas's financial figures with a view to insisting on a division of the costs and profits among its three sectors, namely, domestic consumers, contracts with commercial and industrial consumers, and pipeline business. The observation of the Director-General of OFGAS that 'the reward in the tariff sector should be closer to that on a gilt-edged stock than on a high-risk investment' smacks of a profit control approach (*The Financial Times*, 22 February 1989, London).
56 The emphasis on the labour dimension may be illustrated by the Finance Minister's categorical observation in his budget speech in Pakistan in 1985: 'We have no intention to either close down a factory or to sell it unless appropriate arrangements have been made for the labour of such factories.'
57 The Workshop of Directors of Public Enterprises in Africa, held by CAFRAD, CFTC, and BADEA at Freetown in April 1987, observed: 'To privatise in the developing countries ... may imply the handing over of key sectors of the economy back to foreign hands.'
58 In the view of the minister concerned, as cited in *The Financial Times*, 2 November 1989, London.

59 Lorch, K. *Privatisation of Textile Mills in Bangladesh*, a case study sponsored by UNDP: 'The objectives of a privatisation policy are sacrificed for the effectiveness of its implementation; the means prevail over the ends.'
60 Cook, P. and Kirkpatrick, C. (eds) (Brighton, 1988) op. cit., Chapter 3.

CHAPTER 15 THE FUTURE OF PUBLIC ENTERPRISE

1 For instance, the Socialist International which met in Stockholm in June 1989 and consisted of more than 80 left-wing and social-democratic parties from around the world, rejected nationalisation as a remedy for social ills. Willy Brandt, the president of the organisation, observed that 'broad experience' convinced the socialist parties that they were mistaken in having a strong confidence in the role of the state in the economic process. The new socialist manifesto asserted that 'markets can and must function as a dynamic way of promoting innovation and signalling the desires of consumers through the economy' (as reported in *The Financial Times*, 23 June 1989, London).
2 For a description of how the project is made sick from the time it is born, see *The Nation*, 25 December 1987 (Lahore, Pakistan).
3 For example, the outstanding bank credit to units identified as 'sick' in India in 1986 was about 15 per cent of the total bank credit to industry. There were several large units in the 'sick' category (Reserve Bank of India (1987) *Annual Report 1986–87*, Bombay, p. 82).
4 For a brief description of such a venture in India, see *Interregional Network on Privatisation*, Bulletin no. 4, 1 October 1989, Oxford.

Index

For Product Safety Concerns and Information please contact our EU
representative GPSR@taylorandfrancis.com
Taylor & Francis Verlag GmbH, Kaufingerstraße 24, 80331 München, Germany

www.ingramcontent.com/pod-product-compliance
Ingram Content Group UK Ltd.
Pitfield, Milton Keynes, MK11 3LW, UK
UKHW022212190926
475702UK00003B/325
* 9 7 8 0 3 6 7 1 9 0 4 5 3 *